T0212026

Lecture Notes in Artificial Intelligence   12816

Subseries of Lecture Notes in Computer Science

Han Qiu · Cheng Zhang ·
Zongming Fei · Meikang Qiu ·
Sun-Yuan Kung (Eds.)

Knowledge Science, Engineering and Management

14th International Conference, KSEM 2021
Tokyo, Japan, August 14–16, 2021
Proceedings, Part II

 Springer

Editors
Han Qiu
Tsinghua University
Beijing, China

Cheng Zhang
Ibaraki University
Hitachi, Japan

Zongming Fei
University of Kentucky
Lexington, KY, USA

Meikang Qiu ⓘ
Texas A&M University – Commerce
Commerce, TX, USA

Sun-Yuan Kung
Princeton University
Princeton, NJ, USA

ISSN 0302-9743   ISSN 1611-3349   (electronic)
Lecture Notes in Artificial Intelligence
ISBN 978-3-030-82146-3   ISBN 978-3-030-82147-0   (eBook)
https://doi.org/10.1007/978-3-030-82147-0

LNCS Sublibrary: SL7 – Artificial Intelligence

This Springer imprint is published by the registered company Springer Nature Switzerland AG
The registered company address is: Gewerbestrasse 11, 6330 Cham, Switzerland

Han Qiu · Cheng Zhang ·
Zongming Fei · Meikang Qiu ·
Sun-Yuan Kung (Eds.)

Knowledge Science, Engineering and Management

14th International Conference, KSEM 2021
Tokyo, Japan, August 14–16, 2021
Proceedings, Part II

 Springer

Editors
Han Qiu
Tsinghua University
Beijing, China

Cheng Zhang
Ibaraki University
Hitachi, Japan

Zongming Fei
University of Kentucky
Lexington, KY, USA

Meikang Qiu 🆔
Texas A&M University – Commerce
Commerce, TX, USA

Sun-Yuan Kung
Princeton University
Princeton, NJ, USA

ISSN 0302-9743   ISSN 1611-3349   (electronic)
Lecture Notes in Artificial Intelligence
ISBN 978-3-030-82146-3   ISBN 978-3-030-82147-0   (eBook)
https://doi.org/10.1007/978-3-030-82147-0

LNCS Sublibrary: SL7 – Artificial Intelligence

This Springer imprint is published by the registered company Springer Nature Switzerland AG
The registered company address is: Gewerbestrasse 11, 6330 Cham, Switzerland

Preface

The three-volume set contains the papers presented at the 14th International Conference on Knowledge Science, Engineering, and Management (KSEM 2021), held during August 14–16, 2021, in Tokyo, Japan.

There were 492 submissions. Each submission was reviewed by at least 3 reviewers, and on average 3.5 Program Committee members. The committee decided to accept 164 full papers, resulting in an acceptance rate of 33%. We have separated the proceedings into three volumes: LNCS 12815, 12816, and 12817.

KSEM 2021 was the 14th edition in this conference series which started in 2006. The aim of this interdisciplinary conference is to provide a forum for researchers in the broad areas of knowledge science, knowledge engineering, and knowledge management to exchange ideas and to report state-of-the-art research results. KSEM is in the list of CCF (China Computer Federation) recommended conferences (C series, Artificial Intelligence).

KSEM 2021 was held in Tokyo, Japan, following the traditions of the 13 previous successful KSEM events in Guilin, China (KSEM 2006); Melbourne, Australia (KSEM 2007); Vienna, Austria (KSEM 2009); Belfast, UK (KSEM 2010); Irvine, USA (KSEM 2011); Dalian, China (KSEM 2013); Sibiu, Romania (KSEM 2014); Chongqing, China (KSEM 2015), Passau, Germany (KSEM 2016), Melbourne, Australia (KSEM 2017), Changchun, China (KSEM 2018); Athens, Greece (KSEM 2019), and Hangzhou, China (KSEM 2020).

We would like to express our gratitude to the honorary general and Steering Committee chairs, Ruqian Lu (Chinese Academy of Sciences, China), and Dimitris Karagiannis (University of Vienna, Austria), and the members of the Steering Committee, who provided insight and guidance at all stages. The KSEM 2021 general co-chairs, Meikang Qiu (Texas A&M University-Commerce, USA), and Sun-Yuan Kung (Princeton University, USA) were extremely supportive in the conference organizing, call for papers, and paper review process, and played an important role in the general success of the conference.

The objective of KSEM 2021 was to bring together researchers and practitioners from academia, industry, and government to advance the theories and technologies in knowledge science, engineering, and management. KSEM 2021 focused on three broad areas: Knowledge Science with Learning and AI (KSLA), Knowledge Engineering Research and Applications (KERA), and Knowledge Management with Optimization and Security (KMOS).

We would like to thank the conference sponsors: Springer LNCS, Waseda University, the North America Chinese Talents Association, and the Longxiang High Tech Group Inc.

August 2021

Han Qiu
Cheng Zhang
Zongming Fei
Meikang Qiu
Sun-Yuan Kung

Bo Ma   Chinese Academy of Sciences, China
Zili Zhang   Deakin University, Australia
Long Yuan   Nanjing University of Science and Technology, China
Shuiqiao Yang   UTS, Australia
Robert Andrei Buchmann   Babeş-Bolyai University of Cluj Napoca, Romania
Yong Deng   Southwest University, China
Dawei Cheng   Tongji University, China
Jun-Jie Peng   Shanghai University, China
Oleg Okun   Cognizant Technology Solutions GmbH, USA
Jianxin   Deakin University, Australia
Jiaojiao Jiang   RMIT University, Australia
Guangyan Huang   Deakin University, Australia
Li Li   Southwest University, China
Ge Li   Peking University, China
Ximing Li   Jilin University, China
Daniel Volovici   Lucian Blaga University of Sibiu, Romania
Zhenguang Liu   Zhejiang Gongshang University, China
Yi Zhuang   Zhejiang Gongshang University, China
Bo Yang   Jilin University, China
Maheswari N.   VIT University, India
Min Yu   Chinese Academy of Sciences, China
Krzysztof Kluza   AGH University of Science and Technology, Poland
Jia Xu   Guangxi University, China
Jihe Wang   Northwestern Polytechnical University, China
Shaowu Liu   University of Technology, Sydney, Australia
Wei Luo   Deakin University, Australia
Yong Lai   Jilin University, China
Ulrich Reimer   University of Applied Sciences St. Gallen, Switzerland
Klaus-Dieter Althoff   DFKI/University of Hildesheim, Germany
Jiali Zuo   Jiangxi Normal University, China
Hongtao Wang   North China Electric Power University, China
Salem Benferhat   University d'Artois, France
Xiaofei Zhou   Hangzhou Dianzi University, China
Shiyu Yang   East China Normal University, China
Zhisheng Huang   Vrije Universiteit Amsterdam, the Netherlands
Guilin Qi   Southeast University, China
Qingtian Zeng   Shandong University of Science and Technology,
                               China
Jing Wang   The University of Tokyo, Japan
Jun Zheng   New Mexico Institute of Mining and Technology, USA
Paolo Trunfio   University of Calabria, Italy
Kewei Sha   University of Houston-Clear Lake, USA
David Dampier   University of Texas at San Antonio, USA
Richard Hill   University of Huddersfield, UK
William Glisson   University of South Alabama, USA
Petr Matousek   Brno University of Technology, Czech Republic

Preface

The three-volume set contains the papers presented at the 14th International Conference on Knowledge Science, Engineering, and Management (KSEM 2021), held during August 14–16, 2021, in Tokyo, Japan.

There were 492 submissions. Each submission was reviewed by at least 3 reviewers, and on average 3.5 Program Committee members. The committee decided to accept 164 full papers, resulting in an acceptance rate of 33%. We have separated the proceedings into three volumes: LNCS 12815, 12816, and 12817.

KSEM 2021 was the 14th edition in this conference series which started in 2006. The aim of this interdisciplinary conference is to provide a forum for researchers in the broad areas of knowledge science, knowledge engineering, and knowledge management to exchange ideas and to report state-of-the-art research results. KSEM is in the list of CCF (China Computer Federation) recommended conferences (C series, Artificial Intelligence).

KSEM 2021 was held in Tokyo, Japan, following the traditions of the 13 previous successful KSEM events in Guilin, China (KSEM 2006); Melbourne, Australia (KSEM 2007); Vienna, Austria (KSEM 2009); Belfast, UK (KSEM 2010); Irvine, USA (KSEM 2011); Dalian, China (KSEM 2013); Sibiu, Romania (KSEM 2014); Chongqing, China (KSEM 2015), Passau, Germany (KSEM 2016), Melbourne, Australia (KSEM 2017), Changchun, China (KSEM 2018); Athens, Greece (KSEM 2019), and Hangzhou, China (KSEM 2020).

We would like to express our gratitude to the honorary general and Steering Committee chairs, Ruqian Lu (Chinese Academy of Sciences, China), and Dimitris Karagiannis (University of Vienna, Austria), and the members of the Steering Committee, who provided insight and guidance at all stages. The KSEM 2021 general co-chairs, Meikang Qiu (Texas A&M University-Commerce, USA), and Sun-Yuan Kung (Princeton University, USA) were extremely supportive in the conference organizing, call for papers, and paper review process, and played an important role in the general success of the conference.

The objective of KSEM 2021 was to bring together researchers and practitioners from academia, industry, and government to advance the theories and technologies in knowledge science, engineering, and management. KSEM 2021 focused on three broad areas: Knowledge Science with Learning and AI (KSLA), Knowledge Engineering Research and Applications (KERA), and Knowledge Management with Optimization and Security (KMOS).

We would like to thank the conference sponsors: Springer LNCS, Waseda University, the North America Chinese Talents Association, and the Longxiang High Tech Group Inc.

August 2021

Han Qiu
Cheng Zhang
Zongming Fei
Meikang Qiu
Sun-Yuan Kung

Organization

Honorary General Chairs

Ruqian Lu — Chinese Academy of Sciences, China
Dimitris Karagiannis (Chair) — University of Vienna, Austria

General Chairs

Meikang Qiu — Texas A&M University-Commerce, USA
Sun-Yuan Kung — Princeton University, USA

Program Chairs

Han Qiu — Tsinghua University, China
Cheng Zhang — Waseda University, Japan
Zongming Fei — University of Kentucky, USA

Steering Committee

Ruqian Lu (Honorary Chair) — Chinese Academy of Sciences, China
Dimitris Karagiannis (Chair) — University of Vienna, Austria
Hui Xiong — The State University of New Jersey, USA
Yaxin Bi — Ulster University, UK
Zhi Jin — Peking University, China
Claudiu Kifor — Sibiu University, Romania
Gang Li — Deakin University, Australia
Yoshiteru Nakamori — Japan Advanced Institute of Science and Technology, Japan
Jorg Siekmann — German Research Centre of Artificial Intelligence, Germany
Martin Wirsing — Ludwig-Maximilians-Universität München, Germany
Bo Yang — Jilin University, China
Chengqi Zhang — University of Technology Sydney, Australia
Zili Zhang — Southwest University, China
Christos Douligeris — University of Piraeus, Greece
Xiaoyang Wang — Zhejiang Gongshang University, China

Publicity Chair

Peng Zhang   Stony Brook University, USA

Finance Chair

Hui Zhao   Henan University, China

Technical Committee

Chao Feng   National University of Defense Technology, China
Zhong Ming   Shenzhen University, China
Hiroyuki Sato   The University of Tokyo, Japan
Shuangyin Ren   Chinese Academy of Military Science, China
Thomas Austin   San Jose State University, USA
Zehua Guo   Beijing Institute of Technology, China
Wei Yu   Towson University, USA
Keke Gai   Beijing Institute of Technology, China
Chunxia Zhang   Beijing Institute of Technology, China
Hansi Jiang   SAS Institute Inc., USA
Weiying Zhao   University College London, UK
Shangwei Guo   Chongqing University, China
Jianlong Tan   Chinese Academy of Sciences, China
Songmao Zhang   Chinese Academy of Sciences, China
Bo Ning   Dalian Maritime University, China
Leilei Sun   Beihang University, China
Tong Xu   University of Science and Technology of China, China
Ye Zhu   Monash University, Australia
Jianye Yang   Hunan University, China
Lifei Chen   Fujian Normal University, China
Fan Zhang   Guangzhou University, China
Xiang Zhao   National University of Defense Technology, China
Massimo Benerecetti   University di Napoli "Federico II", Italy
Knut Hinkelmann   FHNW University of Applied Sciences
                                 and Arts Northwestern Switzerland, Switzerland
Shuang Li   Beijing Institute of Technology, China
Yuliang Ma   Northeastern University, China
Xin Bi   Northeastern University, China
Cheng Li   National University of Singapore, Singapore
Hechang Chen   Jilin University, China
Chen Chen   Zhejiang Gongshang University, China
Mouna Kamel   IRIT, Paul Sabatier University, France
Yuan Li   North China University of Technology, China
Shu Li   Chinese Academy of Sciences, China
Serge Autexier   DFKI, Germany
Huawen Liu   Zhejiang Normal University, China

Contents – Part II

Knowledge Engineering Research and Applications (KERA)

A Semantic Textual Similarity Calculation Model Based on Pre-training Model

Zhaoyun Ding, Kai Liu$^{(\boxtimes)}$(ID), Wenhao Wang, and Bin Liu

Science and Technology on Information Systems Engineering Laboratory,
National University of Defense Technology, Changsha, China
{zyding,liukai18}@nudt.edu.cn

Abstract. As a basic research topic in natural language processing, the calculation of text similarity is widely used in the fields of plagiarism checker and sentence search. The traditional calculation of text similarity constructed text vectors only based on TF-IDF, and used the cosine of the angle between vectors to measure the similarity between two texts. However, this method cannot solve the similar text detection task with different text representation but similar semantic representation. In response to the above-mentioned problems, we proposed the pre-training of text based on the ERNIE semantic model of Paddle-Hub, and constructed similar text detection into a classification problem; in view of the problem that most of the similar texts in the data set led to the imbalance of categories in the training set, an oversampling method for confusion sampling, OSConfusion, was proposed. The experimental results showed that the method proposed in this paper was able to solve the problem of paper comparison well, and could identify the repetitive paragraphs with different text representations. And the ERNIE-SIM with OSConfusion was better than the ERNIE-SIM without OSConfusion in the prediction process of similar document pairs in terms of precision and recall.

Keywords: Text similarity · Pre-training · Classification · Natural language processing · Deep learning

1 Introduction

In the process of NLP (natural language processing), how to calculate the similarity between two texts was often involved. From a mathematical point of view, text could be represented as a high-dimensional semantic space, and the cosine of the angle between vectors was used to measure the similarity between two texts. With the measurement method of text similarity, we could use a partitioning

Supported by organization Research and Innovation Project for Postgraduate of Hunan Province (Grant No. CX2018B023, No. CX20190038).

H. Qiu et al. (Eds.): KSEM 2021, LNAI 12816, pp. 3–15, 2021.
https://doi.org/10.1007/978-3-030-82147-0_1

method, K-means, the DBSCAN (Density-Based Spatial Clustering of Applications with Noise), or the model-based probability method to perform cluster analysis on the text; on the other hand, we could also use the similarity between texts to pre-delete the duplication of large corpora or to detect the repeat-ability of academic papers. With the popularity of neural networks, especially deep learning in NLP, scholars converted text similarity into a classification problem on the basis of BERT pre-training model, improving the calculation effect of text similarity to a certain extent, especially improving the detection effect of similar texts with different text representation but similar semantic representation. For the two documents shown in the Table 1, although their similarity of TF-IDF text vector was not very high, their semantic representation similarity was high.

Table 1. Example of document pair with similar semantic representation.

Document 1	Document 2
The SQL language used by MySQL is the most commonly used standardized language for accessing relational databases	The SQL (Structured Query Language) of MySQL is the most commonly used standardized language for accessing databases

In this paper, for texts with different text representation but similar semantic representation, we utilized the ERNIE model of PaddleHub to pre-train the text, then constructed similar text detection into a classification problem to evaluate the similarity between texts. In the process of constructing the training set, to deal with the unbalanced {0,1} classes in the training set caused by most of the similar texts in the data set, an oversampling method for confusion sampling called OSConfusion was proposed. The real data set of 10,000 similar sentence pairs in the repetitive papers on the duplicate search website of an academic journal was used as the experimental data set. The results showed that the method proposed in this paper was able to solve the problem of paper comparison well, and could identify the re-petitive paragraphs with different text representations. The results also showed that the ERNIE-SIM with OSConfusion was better than the ERNIE-SIM without OSCon-fusion in the prediction process of similar document pairs in terms of precision and recall.

The rest of this paper is organized as follows: Sect. 2 gives the related work of this mission from aspects of language model and text similarity calculation. Section 3 is the detailed descriptions of proposed model and approaches. Experimental results and its analysis on our task are shown in Sect. 4. Finally, we conclude the paper in Sect. 5.

2   Related Work

2.1   Language Model

Vector Space Model (VSM) was proposed by salton [1] in 1970s; it transformed texts into vectors in vector space, and then used the similarity between space vectors to represent sentence similarity. Hinton proposed a way to represent words named distributed representation, which was usually called word vector. The combination of neural network and language model originated from the idea of using neural networks to build binary language models proposed by Xu et al. [2]; while the efforts of using three-layer neutral networks to build n-gram models by Bengio et al. [3] pushed the combination of neural network and language model training to a new level. As a milestone of deep learning in the field of NLP, the Word2vec was simple and effective. The Word2vec proposed by Mikolov et al. included two models: CBOW [4] and Skip-gram, and its basic idea was to predict by determining the head word and the size of context window.

2.2   Calculation of Text Similarity

With difference of computing granularity, the text similarity calculation approaches were usually subdivided into character-based ones and term-based ones. Character-based approaches covered Levenshtein Distance (LD) [5], longest common sequence (LCS) [6], Hamming distance [7], N-gram [8], etc. and there were many variations on the LD algorithm, such as Weighted-Levenshtein, Damerau-Levenshtein [9], Optimal String Alignment, Jaro Winkler [10], etc. that were widely used in the field of spelling error correction and linking; while the Needleman-Wunsch [11] algorithm and Smith-Waterman [12] algorithm (belonging to LSC) carried out global optimal alignment and local optimal alignment respectively for two sequences based on the idea of dynamic programming, and they were mainly used in DNA sequence alignment.

According to different representation methods during calculation, the term-based approaches might be categorized as Surface Term/word-based, Vector Space Model (VSM)-based [13] and Hash-based ones. Among them, N-Gram, Jaccard Sim-ilarity [14], Dice Coefficient [15], and Overlap Coefficient were used to calculate the matching degree of terms directly, and their core idea was to convert the text similarity problem into a set problem. VSM-based approaches contained Matching Coefficient, Cosine, Euclidean Distance, Manhattan Distance [16], Chebyshev Dis-tance, Bray-Curtis Dissimilarity [17], etc., among which Manhattan Distance, Eu-clidean Distance and Chebyshev Distance could be uniformly expressed as Minkow-ski Distance. Hash-based approaches covered Locality Sensitive Hashing (LSH) algorithm and Locality Preserving Hashing (LPH) algorithm, and these two types of algorithms dealt with the Nearest Neighbor Search problems. Simhash and Minhash were two LSH algorithms widely used in large-scale data processing [18]. The text similarity calculation would be more important in future NLP task [19–21].

3   Approachs

3.1   Construction of Training Set

Each piece of data in the original data set D_n contained two documents D_1 and D_2, and the similarity between them ($Sim_{1,2}$). To convert the text similarity problem into classification problem, the data set needed to be converted into a training set $\{0, 1\}$, where class $\{1\}$ indicated that two documents were similar, while class $\{0\}$ indicated that two documents were dissimilar. We set the similarity threshold ε, and constructed the following mapping relationship:

$$class = \begin{cases} 1 \ , Sim_{1,2} \geq \varepsilon, \\ 0 \ , Sim_{1,2} < \varepsilon, \end{cases} \quad (1)$$

Based on the above mapping function, the original text similarity data could be converted into training set $t = \{(D_{11}, D_{12}, \{0, 1\}), (D_{21}, D_{22}, \{0, 1\}), \cdots, (D_{n1}, D_{n2}, \{0, 1\})\}$ of two texts $(D_1, D_2, \{0, 1\})$ and $\{0, 1\}$ class labels, where n was the size of the training set. Since the similarity (Sim) of most documents in the original data set D_n was relatively high, the $\{0, 1\}$ class data of the training set t obtained by the above approach would encounter imbalance problem. To solve the problem of low model efficiency caused by unbalanced binary classification, based on the construction of training set, we further proposed OSConfusion, an oversampling algorithm for confusion sampling, as shown below.

(1) For all data in $t = \{(D_{11}, D_{12}, \{0, 1\}), (D_{21}, D_{22}, \{0, 1\}), \cdots, (D_{n1}, D_{n2}, \{0, 1\})\}$
(2) Random sampling a training data $(D_{i1}, D_{i2}, 1)$ where the label is $\{1\}$
(3) Given reference of document D_{i1}, random sampling a document $D_j \neq D_{i1}$
(4) Constructing a dissimilarity training data $(D_{i1}, D_j, 0)$
(5) Repeat until the balance of the training $\{0, 1\}$

On the basis of the original training set t, a class label of $\{1\}$ was randomly sampled as the training set $(D_{i1}, D_{i2}, 1)$, then a document $D_j \neq D_{i1}$ was randomly sampled from the original data set D_n as the comparison document based on the first document D_{i1} to construct the training set of dissimilar documents $(D_{i1}, D_j, 0)$; repeated the above steps until the training set data with class labels of 0 and 1 in the training set were roughly the same. In this way, the original data set D_n was converted into a balanced training set $T = \{(D_{11}, D_{12}, \{0, 1\}), (D_{21}, D_{22}, \{0, 1\}), \cdots, (D_{m1}, D_{m2}, \{0, 1\})\}$, where m was the scale of the final balanced training set, and $m > n$.

3.2 Sentence Pair Classification Model Based on ERNIE Semantic Model

Based on the balanced training set $T = \{(D_{11}, D_{12}, \{0, 1\}), (D_{21}, D_{22}, \{0, 1\}), \cdots, (D_{m1}, D_{m2}, \{0, 1\})\}$, each pair of documents (D_{i1}, D_{i2}) was taken as the input of ERNIE semantic model. After coding by ERNIE semantic model, the coding was further pooled, and the document pair (D_{i1}, D_{i2}) was converted into vector(u, v). On the basis of the pre-training of ERNIE semantic model, the vector(u, v) not only contained the information of each word itself, but also implied its contextual semantic information, which contained more information;

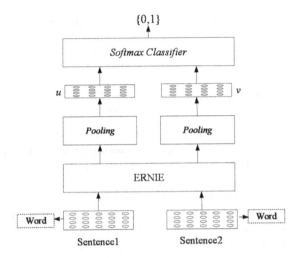

Fig. 1. Sentence pair classification model based on ERNIE semantic model.

On this basis, the encoded and pooled vector was used as the input of the classifier, and the class label {0,1} of each document pair (D_{i1}, D_{i2}) was used as the output of the classifier to train the classification model. The specific model framework was shown in the Fig. 1

On the basis of model training, for any pair of test documents (TD_{i1}, TD_{i2}), we only need the prediction by the classifier based on ERNIE semantic model coding and pooling, and used its output {0, 1} to determine whether the test document pair (TD_{i1}, TD_{i2}) was similar. If the classifier outputs 1, the document pair was similar; if the classifier outputs 0, the document pair was dissimilar. Vectorized representation of input text formed by the implementation of algorithm model:

Step 1: The input text was vectorized, and the input sentence was vectorized, that is, the embedding process. After word segmentation, a sentence could be divided into several tokens. Based on word2vector method, each token was converted into a fixed-length dense vector representation, and then combined into a matrix representation of the sentence to form the bottommost sentence vectorized representation. For example, the vector length of each word was L_v, and the matrix dimension of each sentence was defined as $L_s \times L_v$ according to the longest sentence length L_s, if the length of the sentence was less than the maximum sentence length, the word vector with all elements of 0 was used to complement. Finally, the matrix dimensions of all sentences were the same. Meanwhile, in order to express the word order in the input sequence, an additional position vector: Positional Encoding, was added; and when the input was a sentence pair, the vector segment embedding of the sentence to which a token belongs was expressed. Three vectors with the same dimensions were merged into a token input vector as the input of the subsequent pre-training model.

Positional Encoding was calculated using the following formula:

$$PE(pos, 2i) = sin(\frac{pos}{10000 \times \frac{2i}{d_{model}}}) \qquad (2)$$

$$PE(pos, 2i + 1) = cos(\frac{pos}{10000 \times \frac{2i}{d_{model}}}) \qquad (3)$$

Where, pos denoted the position of current word in the sentence, i denoted the subscript of each value in the vector. It showed that the sine coding was used in even positions while the cosine coding was used in odd positions.

However, such traditional static vectorized representation could reflect the similarity between words, but the vector corresponding to each token after training would be fixed, as for later use, no matter what the context word of the new sentence was, the Word Embedding of the token would not change with the change of the context, so it was difficult to solve polysemy problem. Therefore, the researchers proposed the ELMO model based on the dynamic adjustment of context, and proposed a large-scale pre-training fine-tuning model BERT that fused lexical and syntactic information by combining with the bidirectional transformer model. The ERNIE model used in this paper combined the knowledge graph to embed knowledge into the underlying text representation process.

Step 2: In the ERNIE model, there were two core modules: T-Encoder and K-Encoder. T-Encoder was responsible for capturing basic lexical and grammatical information from the text, which was mainly composed of a multi-headed bidirectional transformer structure. Transformer was composed of self-attention and feed-forward neural network. The main strategy of self-attention is to initialize a set of matrices, including 3 matrices W^Q, W^K, W^V, which were multiplied by the token-input vector X above to form three new matrices Q, K, V:

$$(W^Q, W^K, W^V) \times X = (Q, K, V) \qquad (4)$$

Then, self-attention was input to calculate the similarity of Q, K by dot product, and then the weight distribution of V was determined:

$$Z = softmax(\frac{Q \times K}{\sqrt{d_k}}) \times V \qquad (5)$$

The multi-headed attention mechanism was to initialize multiple sets of matrices, and each set of matrices would output a self-attention matrix Z_i. Then, through the normalization function:

$$LN(x_i) = \alpha * \frac{x_i - \mu_L}{\sqrt{\sigma_L^2 + \varepsilon}} + \beta \qquad (6)$$

The input was converted into data with a mean of 0 and a variance of 1. Because the feed-forward neural network layer received a matrix (where the vector in each row represented a word), it was necessary to integrate multiple matrices into one matrix, so we chose the following transformation: first, integrating Z_i generated by self-attention into one matrix, and then multiplying it with the weight matrix W^O to form a matrix Z, which had the same size as the input sentence matrix.

$$Z = (z_1 z_2 \cdots z_i) \times W^O \qquad (7)$$

Words at each position went through the Self-Attention layer, and all resulting output vectors went through the same feed-forward neural network separately. Finally, the vectorized representation $\{w_1, \cdots, w_n\}$ of each token containing lexical and grammatical information was obtained, and this process was T-Encoder:

$$\{w_1, \cdots, w_n\} = T - Encoder(\{w_1, \cdots, w_n\}) \qquad (8)$$

Step 3: ERNIE model also contained information from knowledge graphs, i.e. K-Encoder, which was also based on the multi-headed attention mechanism. Firstly, the existing entities $\{e_1, ..., e_m\}$ of the text were obtained, such entities were transformed into corresponding vector representations $\{e_1, ..., e_m\}$ through the knowledge graph embedding method (TransE), and then the vector representation of the entity and the vectorized representation $\{w_1, ..., w_n\}$ of the token were sent into the multi-headed self-attention mechanism (MA-ATTS) respectively:

$$\{\widetilde{W}_1^{(i)}, \cdots, \widetilde{W}_n^{(i)}\} = MH - ATT(\{w_1^{(i-1)}, \cdots, w_n^{(i-1)}\}) \qquad (9)$$

$$\{\widetilde{e}_1^{(i)}, \cdots, \widetilde{e}_m^{(i)}\} = MH - ATT(\{e_1^{(i-1)}, \cdots, e_m^{(i-1)}\}) \qquad (10)$$

Then, after passing through an aggregator, the two were aggregated:

$$h_j = \sigma(\widetilde{W}_t^{(i)} \widetilde{w}_j^{(i)} + \widetilde{W}_e^{(i)} \widetilde{e}_k^{(i)} + \widetilde{b}^{(i)}) \qquad (11)$$

$$w_j^{(i)} = \sigma(W_t^{(i)} h_j + b_t^{(i)}) \qquad (12)$$

$$e_k^{(i)} = \sigma(W_e^{(i)} h_j + b_e^{(i)}) \qquad (13)$$

where h_j represented the internal hidden state that integrated vocabulary and entity information, and $\sigma(\cdot)$ was the GELU function.
So that was the K-Encoder:

$$\{w_1^o, \cdots, w_n^o\}, \{e_1^o, \cdots, e_m^o\} = K-Encoder(\{w_1, \cdots, w_n\}, \{e_1, \cdots, e_m\}) \quad (14)$$

Such a vector formed after being processed by T-Encoder and K-Encoder not only contained the vocabulary and syntactic information of the text itself, and the knowledge information in the knowledge graph, but also organically integrated such information into a unified vector space. Then the dimensionality of ERNIE's output vector was reduced by the pooling layer.

Step 4: We took the pooled vector as the input, and used the SoftMax function for classification. When the output was 0, the texts were dissimilar; when the output was 1, the two texts were similar.

4   Experimental Analysis

The experimental data sourced from similar sentence pairs in the repetitive papers on the duplicate search website of an academic journal, including a total of 10,000 sentence pairs with high similarity, and each sentence pair containing two documents, as well as the similarity between the documents. The training stage of experiments is conducted on a Linux platform with GeForce-RTX-2080Ti GPUs.

Firstly, the histogram distribution of similarity of 10,000 document pairs was calculated, as shown in the Fig. 2. We learned from the figure that the similarity distribution interval of document pairs laid in [55%, 95%], and the similarity of most documents was higher than 72%. Through the above histogram analysis, the similarity threshold ε was set in the experimental process, that is, when the similarity was higher than the threshold ε, the class label of the document pair was set to 1, and when the similarity was less than the threshold ε, the class label of the document pair was set to 0.

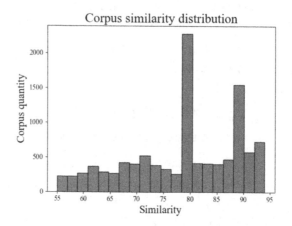

Fig. 2. Document pair similarity distribution.

Based on the setting of similarity threshold $\varepsilon = 68\%, 70\%, 72\%, 74\%, 76\%$, the oversampling algorithm for confusion sampling OSConfusion was used to construct a balanced training set. The scale of the training set $T = \{(D_{11}, D_{12}, \{0,1\})\ , (D_{21}, D_{22}, \{0,1\}), \cdots, (D_{m1}, D_{m2}, \{0,1\})\}$ included 8741, 8337, 7816, 7431, and 7100 positive samples, 8741, 8337, 7816, 7431, and 7100 negative samples, respectively. The positive samples indicated similar document pairs while the negative samples represented dissimilar document pairs. Based on the balanced training set construction, 70% of the training set was sampled, and the document pair similarity measurement model was built by using the sentence pair classification model ERNIE-SIM based on ERNIE semantic model. In the process of model building, the relevant parameters were set. In the training process of the model, the entire training set was repeatedly trained for 10 epochs, the batch_size was set to 64, and the maximum sequence length was 128; the stochastic gradient descent strategy Adam was selected for optimization, and its parameters were: learning rate 5×10^{-5}, warm-up ratio 0.1 and decay weight 0.01, the linear decay strategy was selected for the update of learning rate. The remaining 30% of the data in the training set was used as the test set. Based on such test set, the precision, recall and F1 value of the model were evaluated.

On the other hand, in order to compare the role of OSConfusion in constructing a balanced training set, we also conducted performance evaluation experiments on the initial training set $t = \{(D_{11}, D_{12}, \{0, 1\}), (D_{21}, D_{22}, \{0, 1\}), \cdots, (D_{n1}, D_{n2}, \{0, 1\})\}$. We also set the threshold $\varepsilon = 68\%, 70\%, 72\%, 74\%, 76\%$, including a total of 8741, 8337, 7816, 7431, 7100 positive samples, and 2061, 2465, 2986, 3371, 3702 negative samples. The number of positive samples in the initial training set t was significantly higher than the number of negative samples. The relevant parameters of model were set. In the training process, the entire training set was repeatedly trained for 10 epochs, the batch_size was set to 64, and the maximum sequence length was 128; the stochastic gradient descent strategy Adam was selected for optimization, and its parameters were: learning rate 5×10^{-5}, warm-up ratio 0.1 and decay weight 0.01, the linear decay strategy was selected for the update of learning rate. Similarly, in the initial training set, 70% of the data was used for training and 30% of the data was used for testing to evaluate the precision, recall and F1 value of the model.

It needed about 6 min and 19 s for training the model. And the predict processing just costs around 10 s. The specific experimental results were shown in Table 2, where the ERNIE-SIM with OSConfusion represented the performance evaluation of the model considering the OSConfusion, while the ERNIE-SIM without OSConfusion represented the performance evaluation of the model without considering the OSConfusion. The comparison of the results was shown in the Fig. 3 and Fig. 4.

Table 2. Table captions should be placed above the tables.

	ERNIE-SIM with OSConfusion					ERNIE-SIM without OSConfusion				
	68%	70%	72%	74%	76%	68%	70%	72%	74%	76%
Precision	88.40	89.21	**89.99**	88.87	86.91	81.57	82.43	83.08	**84.47**	83.87
Recall	88.22	88.75	**89.19**	86.81	83.42	**86.85**	84.49	84.16	84.40	82.77

The results showed that in terms of the precision of document pair similarity prediction, ERNIE-SIM with OSConfusion performed better than ERNIE-SIM without OSConfusion in training sets with different similarity thresholds ε. ERNIE-SIM with OSConfusion had the highest precision when $\varepsilon = 72\%$, while ERNIE-SIM without OSConfusion had the highest precision when $\varepsilon = 74\%$, because if the similarity threshold ε was set too low, the quality of the training set would be reduced, and the precision of the model would decrease. On the

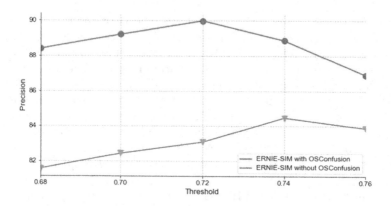

Fig. 3. Comparison of precision.

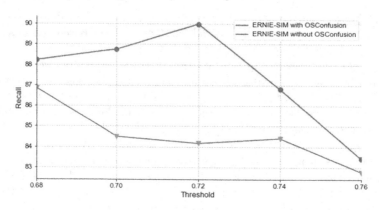

Fig. 4. Comparison of recall.

contrary, if the similarity threshold ε was set too high, the scale of the training set would be reduced, and the precision of the model would decrease.

In terms of the recall of document pair similarity prediction, ERNIE-SIM with OSConfusion performed better than ERNIE-SIM without OSConfusion in training sets with different similarity thresholds ε. ERNIE-SIM with OSConfusion had the highest recall when $\varepsilon = 72\%$, because if the similarity threshold ε was set too low, the quality of the training set would be reduced, and the recall of the model would decrease. ERNIE-SIM without OSConfusion had the highest recall when $\varepsilon = 68\%$, because without considering the OSConfusion, the lower the similarity threshold ε, the model could predict more document pairs as similar documents, which would increase the recall at the expense of precision.

Based on the performance evaluation of the model, we further predicted the model randomly sampled from 30% of the balanced training set T as 1, i.e. as similar document pair. The results of sampling 10 similar document pairs were shown in Table 3.

Table 3. The results of sampling 10 similar document pairs.

No.	Document 1	Document 2
1	Whether teachers can properly employ classroom questioning is related to whether they can stimulate students' interest in learning	Therefore, whether teachers can properly employ classroom questioning is related to whether they can stimulate students' interest in learning mathematics
2	Logic pen: the logic pen can test the level state and the existence or absence of pulse signal of the test point in the digital circuit	Logic pen: the logic pen can test the level state (high or low) and the existence or absence of pulse signal of the test point in the digital circuit
3	Specific matters are completely resolved by the public institution independently, and the institution's human rights, property rights, financial rights and other self-management rights are gradually expanded	Specific matters are completely resolved by the public institution independently, focusing on the separation of responsibilities, management methods and means between the government and the public institution
4	The navigation device of the missile, the control of various instruments on the aircraft, the network communication and data transmission of the computer, the real-time control of the industrial automation process and	At present, the SCM has penetrated into all areas of our lives, the navigation device of the missile, the control of various instruments on the aircraft, the network communication and data transmission of the computer...
5	The existing cross-border e-commerce models can be divided into B2B (business to business) and B2C (business to customer) and C2C (customer to	Cross-border e-commerce is divided into three models: B2B, B2C, and C2C
6	Then it will automatically jump to the personal login information page.	After successful registration, it will automatically jump to the login page.
7	In the system, the "travel route" entity and the "complaint message" entity are connected through an "add" relationship, and at the same time, a one-to-many relationship	In the system, the "administrator" entity and the "order information" entity are connected through an "add" relationship, and at the same time, a one-to-many relationship...
8	The SQL language used by MySQL is the most commonly used language for accessing databases	SQL (Structured Query Language) of MySQL is the most commonly used language for accessing databases
9	The more cash flow it brings, the stronger the company's solvency will be	At the same time, the stronger the profitability, the more cash flow it brings, and the stronger the company's solvency will be
10	For hardware, the LM1812N chip is used and the ultrasonic signal is processed in an analog way	In terms of hardware, the LM1812N chip was used and the ultrasonic signal was processed in an analog way

The experimental results showed that although the predicted similarity documents had some differences in text representation, their semantic representations were basically consistent, indicating that the proposed method could not only detect similar texts with consistent representations, but also further detect similar texts with consistent semantics.

5   Conclusion

For similar text detection task with different text representation but similar semantic representation, we proposed the pre-training of text based on the ERNIE semantic model of PaddleHub, and converted similar text detection into a classification problem to evaluate the similarity between texts. The experimental results showed that the method proposed in this paper was able to solve the problem of paper comparison well, and could identify the repetitive paragraphs with different text representations, and the ERNIE-SIM with OSConfusion was better than the ERNIE-SIM without OSConfusion in the prediction process of similar document pairs in terms of precision and recall. The next step is to expand the semantic textual model and improve the language adaptability in similarity detection. Meanwhile, on the basis of the application of the paper duplication check, we will further develop paper writing assistants based on the semantic textual model, which can automatically recommend writing expression languages according to research topics.

References

1. Salton, G.: Automatic processing of foreign language documents. J. Am. Soc. Inf. Sci. **21**, 1–28 (1970)
2. Xu, W., Rudnicky, A.: Can artificial neural networks learn language models?. In: Proceedings of the 6th International Conference on Spoken Language Processing, pp. 202–205. ICSLP, Beijing (2000)
3. Bengio, Y., Ducharme, R., et al.: A neural probabilistic language model. J. Mach. Learn. Res. **3**, 1137–1155 (2003)
4. Mikolov, T., Chen, K., Corrado, G., et al.: Efficient estimation of word representations in vector space. Computer Science (2013)
5. Levenshtein, V.I.: Binary codes capable of correcting deletions, insertions, and reversals. Soviet Phys. Doklady **10**(8), 707–710 (1966)
6. Melamed, I.: Automatic evaluation and uniform filter cascades for inducing n-best translation lexicons. In: Proceedings of the 3rd Workshop on Very Large Corpora, pp. 184–198. arXiv, Engish (1995)
7. Kondrak, G.: N-gram similarity and distance. In: Consens, M., Navarro, G. (eds.) SPIRE 2005. LNCS, vol. 3772, pp. 115–126. Springer, Heidelberg (2005). https://doi.org/10.1007/11575832_13
8. Bard, Gregory, V.: Spelling-error tolerant, order-independent pass-phrases via the Damerau-Levenshtein string-edit distance metric. In: Proceedings of the Fifth Australasian Symposium on ACSW Frontiers, Ballarat, pp. 117–124 (2007)

9. Winkler, W.: String comparator metrics and enhanced decision rules in the fellegi-sunter model of record linkage. In: Proceedings of the Section on Survey Research Methods, ASA, Alexandria, pp. 354–359 (1990)
10. Needleman, B., Wunsch, D.: A general method applicable to the search for similarities in the amino acid sequence two proteins. J. Molec. Biol. **48**(3), 443–53 (1970)
11. Smith, F., Waterman, S.: Identification of common molecular subsequences. J. Molec. Biol. **1**(147), 195–197 (1981)
12. Salton, G., Wong, A., Yang, C.: A vector space model for automatic indexing. Commun. ACM **18**(11), 613–620 (1975)
13. Jaccard, P.: Étude comparative de la distribution florale dansune portion des Alpes et des Jura. Bull. de la Société Vaudoise des Sci. Naturelles **1**(37), 547–579 (1975)
14. Dice, L.: Measures of the amount of ecologic association between species. Ecology **26**(3), 297–302 (1945)
15. Eugene, F.: Taxicab Geometry. Dover Publications, Dover (1987)
16. Bray, J., Curtis, J.: An ordination of upland forest communities of southern Wisconsin. Ecol. Monogr. **1**(27), 325–349 (1957)
17. Zhao, J., Zhu, T., Lan, M.: ECNU: one stone two birds: ensemble of heterogeneous measures for semantic relatedness and textual entailment. In: Proceedings of the 8th International Workshop on Semantic Evaluation, Dublin, pp. 271–277 (2014)
18. Shrivastava, A., Li, P.: In defense of minhash over simhash. Eprint Arxiv **7**(3), 886–894 (2014)
19. Chen, M., Zhang, Y., et al.: SPHA: smart personal health advisor based on deep analytics. IEEE Commun. Mag. **56**(3), 164–169 (2018)
20. Tao, L., Golikov, S., et al.: A reusable software component for integrated syntax and semantic validation for services computing. In: IEEE Symposium on Service-Oriented System Engineering, pp. 127–132. IEEE, San Francisco Bay (2015)
21. Gai, K., Qiu, M.: Reinforcement learning-based content-centric services in mobile sensing. IEEE Netw. **32**(4), 34–39 (2018)

Representation Learning of Knowledge Graph with Semantic Vectors

Tianyu Gao, Yuanming Zhang$^{(\boxtimes)}$, Mengni Li, Jiawei Lu, Zhenbo Cheng, and Gang Xiao$^{(\boxtimes)}$

College of Computer Science and Technology, Zhejiang University of Technology, Hangzhou, China
{2111812095,zym,2111712339,viivan,czb,xg}@zjut.edu.cn

Abstract. Knowledge graph (*KG*) is a structured semantic knowledge base, which is widely used in the fields of semantic search, such as intelligent Q&A and intelligent recommendation. Representation learning, as a key issue of *KG*, aims to vectorize entities and relations in *KG* to reduce data sparseness and improve computational efficiency. Translation-based representation learning model shows great knowledge representation ability, but there also are limitations in complex relations modeling and representation accuracy. To address these problems, this paper proposes a novel representation learning model with semantic vectors, called TransV, which makes full use of external text corpus and *KG*'s context to accurately represent entities and complex relations. Entity semantic vectors and relation semantic vectors are constructed, which can not only deeply extend semantic structure of *KG*, but also transform complex relations into precise simple relations from a semantic perspective. Link prediction and triple classification tasks are performed on TransV with public datasets. Experimental results show that TransV can outperform other translation-based models. *Mean Rank* is reduced by 66 and *Hits@10* is increased by 20% on average for link prediction task on FB15K.

Keywords: Knowledge graph · Representation learning · Semantic vectors · Complex relation · Accurate representation

1 Introduction

Knowledge graph (*KG*) was officially proposed by Google in 2012, and its original intention was to enhance search efficiency. *KG* is essentially a large-scale semantic network, which is intended to describe various entities, concepts and relations existing in the real world. As an important knowledge representation approach in the era of big data, *KG* has become one of key technologies of artificial intelligence (*AI*). It is widely used in the fields of semantic search, such as intelligent Q&A and intelligent recommendation. The basic organization of *KG* is (*entity, relation, entity*) or (*entity, attribute, attribute value*). A large-scale structured network is constructed by related links between entities or between attribute values. WordNet [1] and FreeBase [2] are representative *KG*s. The former is a commonly used language knowledge base of NLP, which contains synonymy, antisense, upper and lower relations between words. The latter

© Springer Nature Switzerland AG 2021
H. Qiu et al. (Eds.): KSEM 2021, LNAI 12816, pp. 16–29, 2021.
https://doi.org/10.1007/978-3-030-82147-0_2

describes real-world entities such as people, places, institutions, and their relationships. For example, Jobs is the founder of Apple.

Knowledge representation is a key issue of knowledge acquisition and application. The most direct method of knowledge representation is to use graph database, but this representation method would lead to data sparseness and high computational complexity. Therefore, representation learning has been proposed and becomes a hotspot in *KG*. It aims to construct a continuous low-dimensional vector representation space, and map entities and relations to the space and retain their original attributes. After that, a large number of efficient numerical calculation and reasoning approaches can be applied to better solve data sparseness. Representation learning also has great significance for completion and inference of *KG*.

Some representation learning models of *KG*, such as translation-based models [3–15], distance model [16], energy model [17] have been proposed. Since the translation-based model is simpler, more accurate and easier to implement, it has become a popular representation learning model. **TransE** [3] is a classical translation-based model. Its basic idea is to treat relation r as a translation from head entity h to tail entity t for a given triple (h, r, t), that is, $h + r \approx t$. However, the model is too simple to represent complex relations of 1-to-N, N-to-1 and N-to-N in *KG*. For example, assume two triples: (*US, President, Obama*) and (*US, President, Trump*). They have the same head entity and the same relation. With TransE, the tail entities *Obama* and *Trump* will have the same embedding representations. However, that doesn't make sense. The reason of that is the relation *President* is complex relation of 1-to-N.

To handle this problem, some improved models based on **TransE** have been proposed in recent years. **TransH** [4] projects entities into relational hyperplanes, and maps entities and relations in the same semantic space. It simply makes relation r and normal vector w_r approximately orthogonal when selecting hyperplanes. **TransR** [5] maps entities to relation space, so that head entity and tail entity share a common projection matrix. However, this model has too many parameters. **DKRL** [6] introduces entity descriptions. It explores two encoders, including continuous bag-of-word model and deep convolutional neural model to encode entity descriptions. The limitation is that the semantics of *KG* cannot be well structured, and there still exists data sparseness.

Since existing models mostly focus on local structure information of *KG*, they have inherent limitations. To handle complex relations modeling and improve representation accuracy, this paper proposes a novel representation learning model with semantic vectors. The semantic vectors enrich semantics of *KG* by combining external corpus semantics and context semantics, and are great helpful to improve representation accuracy.

The main contributions of this paper include:

- This paper firstly introduces entity text description information and entity context into representation learning and models them with semantic vectors to enrich entity semantic information and extend semantic structure of *KG*.
- This paper proposes a novel representation learning with semantic vectors named TransV that can accurately transform complex relations into multiple simple relations by semantic vectors, and also designs a new score function to model complex relations.

- The TransV model has been evaluated on public datasets, and experimental results show that this model has higher accuracy and better performance than some existing translation-based models.

The rest of this paper is organized as follows. In Sect. 2 we introduce some related works on knowledge graph embedding. In Sect. 3 we present the principle, semantic vectors construction, semantic matrices construction and new score function in detail. In Sect. 4 we give the evaluation results of link prediction and triple classification. Finally, we conclude this paper in Sect. 5.

2 Related Work

Representation learning aims to embed entities and relations of *KG* into continuous vector spaces, and generates low-dimensional dense vectors representation by automatic learning. Currently, translation-based representation learning model is a hotspot in *KG* area and shows great advantages. Therefore, this paper mainly analyzes related work on translation-based representation learning models.

General Translation-Based Models. For a given triple *(h, r, t)*, the classical **TransE** [3] regards relation *r* as a translation vector from head entity *h* to tail entity *t*. It makes $h + r \approx t$. **TransH** [4] uses both translation vector r' and hyperplane with w_r as normal vector for each relation *r*. **TransR** [5] embeds entities and relations into different spaces. **TransC** [7] encodes each concept in *KG* as a sphere and each instance as a vector in the same semantic space. It uses relative positions to model relations between concepts and instances (i.e., instanceOf), and relations between concepts and sub-concepts (i.e., subClassOf). **KG2E** [8] believes entities and relations are uncertain. It uses Gaussian distribution to represent entities and relations. The mean denotes the position of entities and relations in semantic space, and the variance denotes their uncertainty. It can effectively model uncertainty of entities and relations. However, it does not consider the type and granularity of entities. **CrossE** [9] considers crossover interactions–bi-directional effects between entities and relations, and learns general embedding and multiple triple specific embeddings named interaction embeddings, for each entity and relation. And an explanation for a triple is regarded as a reliable closed-path between head entity and tail entity. It only considers *KG* itself, and does not introduce additional information.

Translation-Based Models with External Information. **DKRL** [6] is the first model that introduces text descriptions in representation learning of *KG*. It associates each entity *e* with two vector representations, a structure-based e_s and a description-based e_d. The former represents structural information of *KG*, while the latter represents textual information represented in entity descriptions. The description-based representation is constructed by constituent word embeddings, via either a continuous bag-of-words encoder or a convolutional neural network encoder. However, this model does not capture semantic knowledge well, and the sparseness of *KG* has not been solved. **TEKE** [10] constructs a co-occurrence network composed of words and entities with text corpus to obtain entity description information. Description information of relation is intersection of its head entity and tail entity, and thus, relations in different triples have different representations. This helps to deal with representation of complex relation (1-to-N, N-to-1 and N-to-N) in KG. However, this model involves large amount of words. **TKRL** [11] believes that entities should have multiple representations in different types. It considers hierarchical types as projection matrices for entities, with two type encoders designed to model hierarchical structures. Meanwhile, type information is also utilized as relation-specific type constraints. However, it has a relatively high space complexity since it associates each category with a specific projection matrix. **PTransE** [12] considers that multi-step relation path contains rich inference information among entities. It searches relation path between head entity and tail entity, and embeds relation path into semantic space. It represents KG by using semantic relation path information. **AATE** [13] enhances representations by exploiting entity descriptions and triple-specific relation mention. And a mutual attention mechanism between relation mention and entity description is proposed to learn more accurate textual representations for further improving knowledge graph representation. It can effectively deal with ambiguity of entities and relations. **CKGE** [14] generates neighborhood context with a flexible sampling strategy, and analogizes entity neighborhood context with word context. It learns vector representation of KG structure by Skip-gram, which ignores the relational information in the KG. **KEC** [15] embeds entities and concepts of entities jointly into a semantic space with common-sense concepts information of entities from a concept graph. Fact triples from a KG are adjusted by common-sense concept information of entities from a concept graph. It projects loss vector into concept subspace to measure possibility of triples.

Other Models. In addition to above translation models, distance model and energy model are two other classical representation learning models. **Structured Embedding (SE)** [16] is a distance model that uses two separate matrices M_{rh} and M_{rt} to project head entities and tail entities for each relation r. The score function is $f_{r(h,t)} = \|M_{rh}h - M_{rt}t\|$. This model uses two independent matrices for optimization, and cannot accurately capture relation between entity and relation. **Semantic Matching Energy (SME-linear)** [17] is an energy model that uses neural network architecture for semantic matching. It maps entities and relations into vectors at input layer, and performs linear algebra operations on hidden layers and head/tail entities to abstain $g_u(h, r)/g_v(t, r)$ respectively. The final score function is $f_r(h, t) = (M_1 l_h + M_2 l_r + b_1)^T (M_3 l_t + M_4 l_r + b_2)$. This method simply represents each relation with a single vector and makes all relations have the same parameters in algebraic operations. In the experiments, we also compare our approach with these two typical models.

In order to deal with low representation accuracy [3–5] and data sparseness [6, 8], this paper proposes a representation learning model based on semantic vectors. This model introduces text corpus and KG's context in the embedding, and constructs semantic vectors to model them. It also builds a semantic matrix for each relation to represent relation semantics more accurately and designs a new score function to model entities and relations. This can deeply extend semantic structure of KG. It provides a novel approach to transform complex relations in KG into several precise simple relations from a semantic perspective by combing semantics of KG itself and external semantics.

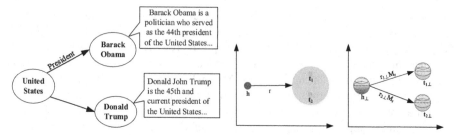

Fig. 1. A KG with semantic information   **Fig. 2.** Comparison of TransE and TransV

3 Representation Learning Model with Semantic Vectors

3.1 TransV Principle

Generally, *KG* contains large amount of entities and relations. Each entity and relation have their own rich semantics, which are helpful to accurately represent entities and relations.

Figure 1 shows a simple *KG* example. There are three entities and two relations. The relation between entity *United States* and entity *Obama* is the same to the relation between entity *United States* and entity *Trump*. This figure shows some semantics of entity *Obama* and entity *Trump*. By using semantics, it will be possible to accurately represent entity *Obama*, entity *Trump* and relation *President*. For example, the relation *President* can be further refined, that is, *the 44th President* and *the 45th President*. However, current translation-based representation learning models, such as TransE [3], don't utilize these semantics, and therefore the entities *Obama* and *Trump* are represented as the same.

To use semantics for more accurate representation, this paper proposes a translation-based representation learning model with semantic vectors, called TransV. This model constructs entity and relation semantic vectors by using external text corpus and *KG*'s context. It also constructs a semantic matrix to acquire main semantic dimensions and make different vector representations of the same relation have high similarity by clustering all semantic vectors of one relation. These semantic vectors are used to embed entities and relations into vectors.

Figure 2 further compares the principles of TransE and TransV. For two given triples (h, r, t_1) and (h, r, t_2) in TransE, when head entity h and relation r both are the same, the two different tail entities t_1 and t_2 are equal to $h + r$, so they will have identical embedding vectors. That means two tail entities fall into the same set. In TransV, entities and relations are transformed into semantic vectors, shown as $h_\perp, r_{1\perp}, r_{2\perp}, t_{1\perp}, t_{2\perp}$. The semantic vectors $r_{1\perp}, r_{2\perp}$ combine semantics of head entities and tail entities and are further semantically transformed into different representations. The vectors of $t_{1\perp}$ and $t_{2\perp}$ are not the same any more. Not only different entities in *KG* have different representation vectors, but also similar relations also have different representation vectors with semantics (more accurate representations). That means TransV can better model complex relations. For example, the 1-to-N relation is translated into multiple 1-to-1 relation. Therefore, TransV can accurately represent head entities and tail entities by fully utilizing low-dimensional and dense semantic vectors.

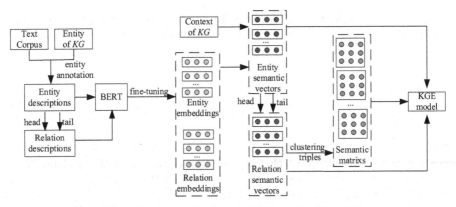

Fig. 3. Representation learning framework of TransV

Semantic vectors, which are low-dimensional semantic representations, combine external text corpus and context of entities and relations in *KG*. Figure 3 gives the representation learning framework of TransV. For a given *KG* and text corpus, we first annotate entities in the corpus to get descriptions of entities, and then also get descriptions of relations. We use BERT [20] to vectorize these text descriptions respectively, and then fine-tune to get semantic vectors of entities and relations that fuse text descriptions. After that, we use structure information of *KG* to get context of entities and relations. Besides, we also utilize the above semantic vectors as inputs to vectorize context, and then get semantic vectors of entities and relations that fuse text descriptions and context. Moreover, we construct a corresponding semantic matrix for each relation, and propose a new score function to model the semantic vectors. After training with the new score function, final vector representations of the entities and relations can be obtained automatically.

For ease of latter description, we define symbols of some proper nouns. Q represents external text corpus related to KG, $E = \{e_1, e_2, e_i, ..., e_n\}$ represents a set of entities in KG, $R = \{r_1, r_2, r_i, ..., r_n\}$ represents a set of relations in KG, and T represents a set of triples in KG. V_{e_i} and V_{r_i} are representation vectors of an entity and a relation.

3.2 Semantic Vectors Construction

First, semantic vectors of entities and relations with external text corpus are constructed. For a given KG, appropriate external text corpus Q are selected, such as Wikipedia corpus. Then, for each entity e_i, its corresponding text description in Q, referred to as Q_E, is extracted through physical link tools, such as Tagme [18] and Wikify [19]. Text preprocessing is performed on Q_E including stemming, normalizing case, deleting stop words and high frequency words. Then, we further get text descriptions of relations, specifically the weighted sum of words intersection in text descriptions of head entities and tail entities.

Second, the preprocessed text descriptions are encoded to generate semantic vector of entity e_i and relation r_i, referred to as V_{e_i} and V_{r_i} by utilizing a pre-trained BERT of Google. It should be noted that the text descriptions should be grouped according to the word length before encoding. Since BERT contains too much semantics and prior knowledge, the above original semantic vectors need to be fine-tuned, including dimensionality reduction operation. The specific fine-tuning methods are as follows:

$$V'_{e_i} = V_{e_i}X + b, \tag{1}$$

$$V'_{r_i} = V_{r_i}X + b, \tag{2}$$

where V_{e_i} is a vector representation of an entity, V_{r_i} is a vector representation of a relation, X is a vector matrix of 768 * n; n is vector dimension of entity/relation, b is n-dimensional offset vector, V'_{e_i} is a vector representation of the fine-tuned entity, V'_{r_i} is a vector representation of the fine-tuned relation.

Taking V'_{e_i} and V'_{r_i} as inputs and V'_{e_i}(head) $+ V'_{r_i} = V'_{e_i}$(tail) as score function, the final V'_{e_i} and V'_{r_i} are trained by using stochastic gradient descent method, which are the final semantic vectors of entities and relations with external text corpus.

Third, semantic vectors of entities and relations with *KG*'s context are constructed. The *KG*'s context of an entity refers to a set in which each entity has a path with specified entity. This set shows some necessary semantics of an entity. The context of an entity is obtained by traversing path, and then the context of relations, which is the weighted sum of context intersection of head entities and tail entities, can be obtained.

$$Context(e_i) = \{t_i | (e_i, r, t_i) \in T \vee (t_i, r, e_i) \in T\} \vee$$

$$\{t_i | ((e_i, r_i, t_j) \in T \wedge (t_j, r_j, t_i) \in T) \vee ((t_i, r_i, e_j) \in T \wedge (e_j, r_j, e_i) \in T)\} \tag{3}$$

Finally, final semantic vectors of entities are obtained by merging text corpus-based semantic vectors and context-based semantic vectors. That is

$$V''_{e_i} = \sum_{e_j \in C(e_i)} nV'_{e_j}, \tag{4}$$

where V''_{e_i} is the final semantic vector of entity e_i.

The semantic vector of relation is constructed by merging all semantic vectors of its head entity and its tail entity. That is

$$V''_{r_i} = \sum_{w_j \in C(e_h) \cap C(e_t)} nV'_{w_j}, \tag{5}$$

where $C(e_h)$ is the head entity context; $C(e_t)$ is the tail entity context; w_j is the context intersection of $C(e_h)$ and $C(e_t)$; n is the weight of w_j being set according to the number of occurrences of w_j in the context; and V''_{r_i} is the semantic vector of relation.

3.3   Semantic Matrices Construction

In practice, the dimension of relation semantic vectors is very high and not every dimension contains semantic information, and the same relation has different representations in different triples, resulting in low semantic similarity of the vectors corresponding to the relation. To select desired dimensions from semantic vector that can accurately express semantics of current relation and make different vector representations of the same relation have higher similarity, a corresponding semantic matrix for each relation is further built.

The matrix should contain all the semantics of the relation, so the original matrix is composed of semantic vectors corresponding to the relation, specifically: each column is a semantic vector of the relation. However, since the dimension of semantic matrix is determined by the number of relation semantic vectors, the matrix dimension of different relations may be different. In order to unify the dimension of all matrices, it is necessary to cluster each column of the matrix to compress the matrix. The distance between vectors can be calculated by Euclidean distance.

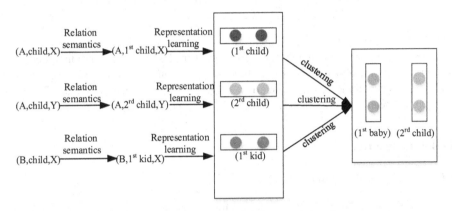

Fig. 4. Construction process of semantic matrix

The specific method is: assuming that the number of elements in the set of triples corresponding to the relation r is N, then the relation r has N semantic vectors. Since the dimension of semantic vector of relation r is n, it is necessary to select n expected semantic vectors from N semantic vectors. For example, the relation child in Fig. 4 corresponds to three triples, namely (A, child, X), (A, child, Y), (B, child, X). First, fuse semantic information of the relation, then the triples are represented as (A, 1st child, X), (A, 2rd child, Y), (B, 1st kid, X), and the three relations are expressed in vectors to get three different semantic vectors, but vector dimension is two, so the dimension of the matrix should be unified into two, and it is necessary to select two vectors that can represent all semantics of the relation from original three semantic vectors to compress the matrix. The idea of this operation is similar to clustering algorithm, therefore, the k-means [21] can be used to complete this step. After selecting two semantic vectors and using them as each column vector of semantic matrix, the final semantic matrix corresponding to the relation can be obtained.

3.4   Representing Learning Model and Training

A new score function of TransV is designed as:

$$f_r(h, t) = ||h_\perp + rM_r - t_\perp||_{1/2}, \tag{6}$$

where $h_\perp$, $r_\perp$ and $t_\perp$ are semantic vectors of head entity, relation and tail entity respectively rather than ordinary vectors in TransE, and M_r is semantic matrix of a relation. In practice, there are some constraints to normal form of embeddings $h_\perp$, $r_\perp$, $t_\perp$, and make $||r_\perp M_r||_2 \leq 1$, $||h_\perp||_2 \leq 1$, $||t_\perp||_2 \leq 1$, $||r_\perp||_2 \leq 1$.

The TransV uses error function based on the maximum interval classification as optimization function of training model:

$$L = \sum_{(h,r,t)\in S} \sum_{(h',r,t')\in S'} [\gamma + f_r(h, t) - f_r'(h', t')]_+, \tag{7}$$

where $[x]_+$ denotes $\max\{0, x\}$; γ denotes a margin hyperparameter; S denotes a set of correct triples; and S' denotes a set of incorrect triples. Stochastic gradient descent is used to optimize above optimization function. Generally, since KG only has correct triples, it is necessary to construct incorrect triples. The approach, as adopted in TransE, is to replace head/tail entity in correct triples with equal probability.

4   Experiments

4.1   Experimental Datasets

We employ two public KGs, WordNet [1] and FreeBase [2], to evaluate the proposed TransV. The WordNet provides semantics of words, in which each entity is a collection of words corresponding to different meaning. The FreeBase provides entities and their relations about people, locations, institutions, and other things in the real world. Two benchmark datasets, WN18 and WN11, are generated by WordNet. The other two benchmarks, FB15K and FB13, are generated by FreeBase.

External text corpus is generated from English Wikipedia dump archived in 2016. We link titles in text corpus to entities in FreeBase and WordNet, and then preprocess text corpus including stemming, capitalization, deletion of stop words and low-frequency words.

We compare our TransV with some typical representation learning models, such as SE, SME, LFM, TransE, TransH, TransR and CKGE through link prediction and triple classification tasks.

4.2   Link Prediction

Link prediction aims to predict missing head/tail entity for a fact triple. For each missing head/tail entity, link prediction gives a ranking list of candidate entities from KG, rather than just gives a best answer. The benchmark datasets are FB15K and WN18.

Evaluation Criteria. In testing stage, we replace head/tail entity for each test triple (h, r, t) with all entities in *KG*, and then compute scores of these new constructed triples according to the score function f_r shown in Sect. 3.4. We sort these scores in ascending order, and obtain possible correct triples. Two indicators are used as evaluation criteria. The first indicator is the average ranking of correct entities denoted as *Mean Rank*. The second indicator is the proportion of correct entities ranked in top 10 denoted as *Hits@10*. That means a better link prediction approach will produce lower *Mean Rank* and higher *Hits@10*.

It is worth noting that if constructed negative triple exists in *KG*, this kind of triple is an actual positive triple. The link prediction result should be considered correct for actual positive triple. In the experiments, negative triples in training, testing and validation sets are filtered to eliminate effects of this situation. This kind of experimental results are *Filter*. If the negative triples are not filtered, the experimental results are *Raw*.

Implementation. We compare our TransV with SE, SME, LFM, TransE, TransH, TransR and CKGE on FB15K and WN18. We select learning rate α for stochastic gradient descent among {0.1, 0.01, 0.001}, margin γ among {1, 2, 4, 6}, embedding dimension of entity and relation k among {50, 100} and batch size B among {20, 120, 480, 1440, 4800}. The optimal parameters are determined by validation set. For FB15K, the optimal configurations are as follows: {$\lambda = 0.001$, $\gamma = 2$, $k = 100$, $B = 100$}. For WN18, the optimal configurations are as follows: {$\lambda = 0.001$, $\gamma = 4$, $k = 100$, $B = 100$}. In training stage, we traverse all training triples 1,000 times.

Table 1. Experimental results on link prediction

DataSets	FB15K				WN18			
Metric	Mean Rank		Hits@10(%)		Mean Rank		Hits@10(%)	
	Raw	Filter	Raw	Filter	Raw	Filter	Raw	Filter
SE (Bordes et al. 2011)	273	162	28.8	39.8	1011	985	68.5	80.5
SME (linear) (Bordes et al. 2012)	274	154	30.7	40.8	545	533	65.1	74.1
LFM (Jenatton et al. 2012)	283	164	26.0	33.1	469	456	71.4	81.6
TransE (Bordes et al. 2013)(unif)	243	125	34.9	47.1	263	251	75.4	89.2
TransH(Wang et al. 2014)(unif)	211	84	42.5	58.5	318	303	75.4	86.7
TransR(Lin et al. 2015)(unif)	226	78	43.8	65.5	232	219	78.3	91.7
CKGE(Nie et al. 2018)(unif)	226	88	48.7	68.5	---	---	---	---
TransV(unif)	·191	**48**	**51.1**	**75.6**	**230**	**216**	**78.7**	**92.2**

Result Analysis. Table 1 shows the experimental results. It can be seen that the accuracy of TransV is significantly higher than other models on FB15K. *Mean Rank* of TransV is reduced 66 on average compared with that of TransE, and *Hits@10* of TransV is increased by 20% on average compared with that of TranE. *Mean Rank* and *Hits@10* of TransV both are superior to other models on WN18.

Table 2 shows individual experiments results on link prediction for four relation types: 1-to-1, 1-to-N, N-to-1, N-to-N on FB15K. It shows that TransV has the highest *Hits@10* for both simple relation and complex relation. Compared with TransE, the accuracy of TransV is improved to 26%–40%. This proves that TransV is also suitable for complex relations of *KG*. Furthermore, it can also be found that *Hits@10* for head entities is 94.3% and *Hits@10* for tail entities is only 52.1% for 1-to-N relation. The reason is that head entities appear frequently, and their number is small, and therefore their semantic vectors are fully trained. In contrast, tail entities appear infrequently, and their number is large, and therefore their semantic vectors are not well trained.

Table 2. Experimental results on FB15K by mapping properties of relations (%)

Tasks	Predicting Head(Hits@10)				Predicting Tail(Hits@10)			
Relation Category	1-to-1	1-to-N	N-to-1	N-to-N	1-to-1	1-to-N	N-to-1	N-to-N
SE (Bordes et al. 2011)	35.6	62.6	17.2	37.5	34.9	14.6	68.3	41.3
SME (linear) (Bordes et al. 2012)	35.1	53.7	19.0	40.3	32.7	14.9	61.6	43.3
TransE (Bordes et al. 2013)	43.7	65.7	18.2	47.2	43.7	19.7	66.7	50.0
TransH(Wang et al. 2014)	66.7	81.7	30.2	57.4	63.7	30.1	83.2	60.8
TransR(Lin et al. 2015)	76.9	77.9	38.1	66.9	76.2	38.4	76.2	69.1
CKGE(Nie et al. 2018)	75.2	91.7	18.6	43.9	76.4	26.8	91.0	47.5
TransV	**81.8**	**94.3**	**52.1**	**74.8**	**81.4**	**56.8**	**92.7**	**77.5**

4.3   Triple Classification

Triple classification aims to judge whether a given triple *(h, r, t)* is correct or not in *KG*. We use FB13 and WN11 to evaluate our TransV. The two datasets themselves already contain negative triples.

Evaluation Criteria. A score for each triple *(h, r, t)* is also computed according to the score function f_r shown in Sect. 3.4. If its score is below a threshold σ_r of a specific relation, the triple is positive, otherwise it is negative. The threshold σ_r is optimized by maximizing classification accuracies of validation set.

Implementation. Parameters of this experiments are set as follows: learning rate α is among {0.001, 0.002, 0.004}; margin γ is among {4, 5, 6, 8}; vector embedding dimension k is among {50, 100, 150}; batch size B is among {100, 480, 1000} and threshold C is among {0.001, 0.002, 0.005, 0.25}. The optimal parameters on WN11 are as follows: {$\alpha = 0.002, \lambda = 6, k = 50, B = 100, C = 0.25$}, and the optimal parameters on FB13 are as follows: {$\alpha = 0.002, \lambda = 4, k = 100, B = 100, C = 0.005$}.

Result Analysis. FB13 and WN11 have more entities and fewer relations. This means that the entities are very dense and closely linked. Table 3 shows the experimental results

Table 3. Evaluation results of triple classification (%)

DataSets	FB13	WN11
SE	75.2	53.0
SME (bilinear)	63.7	70.0
LFM	**84.3**	73.8
TransE(unif)	70.9	75.9
TransH(unif)	76.5	77.7
TransR(unif)	74.7	**85.5**
CKGE(unif)	75.9	----
TransV(unif)	83.8	82.0

of triple classification. It can be seen that the classification accuracy of TransV is 0.5% lower than that of LFM on FB13 and 3.5% lower than that of TransR on WN11. However, combining the two datasets, TransV is the most accurate and stable. This demonstrates that TransV is effective and applicable.

5 Conclusions

Translation-based representation learning models have shown great promising to embed entities and relations of *KG* into a continuous low-dimensional vector space. However, it is limited by general complex relation and low representation accuracy. To address these problems, this paper proposed TransV that is a novel representation learning model with semantic vectors. Text descriptions and *KG*'s context were combined to generate semantic vectors of entities and relations. A semantic matrix was further constructed to more accurately represent semantic information of a relation. A new score function was designed to calculate triple score. Experiments results of link prediction and triple classification showed that TransV was more accurate and applicable than existing translation-based representation models. Our future work will focus on extending the semantics of entities and relations in *KG* for more accurate embeddings, and then studying possible applications, such as *KG* reasoning and completion.

Acknowledgements. The work was supported by the National Natural Science Foundation of China (NO. 61976193), the Science and Technology Key Research Planning Project of Zhejiang Province (NO. 2021C03136), and the Natural Science Foundation of Zhejiang Province (No. LY19F020034).

References

1. Miller, G.A.: WordNet: a lexical database for English. Commun. ACM **38**, 39–41 (1995)
2. Bollacker, K., Evans, C., Paritosh, P., Sturge, T., Taylor, J.: Freebase: a collaboratively created graph database for structuring human knowledge. In: Proceedings of the ACM SIGMOD International Conference on Management of Data, pp. 1247–1250 (2008)

3. Bordes, A., Usunier, N., Garcia-Duran, A., Weston, J., Yakhnenko, O.: Translating embeddings for modeling multi-relational data. In: Advances in Neural Information Processing Systems, pp. 2787–2795 (2013)
4. Wang, Z., Zhang, J., Feng, J., Chen, Z.: Knowledge graph embedding by translating on hyperplanes. In: Proceedings of the 28th AAAI Conference on Artificial Intelligence, pp. 1112–1119 (2014)
5. Lin, Y., Liu, Z., Sun, M., Liu, Y., Zhu, X.: Learning entity and relation embeddings for knowledge graph completion. In: Proceedings of the 29th AAAI Conference on Artificial Intelligence, pp. 2181–2187 (2015)
6. Xie, R., Liu, Z., Jia, J., Luan, H., Sun, M.: Representation learning of knowledge graphs with entity descriptions. In: Proceedings of the 30th AAAI Conference on Artificial Intelligence, pp. 2659–2665 (2016)
7. Lv, X., Hou, L., Li, J., Liu, Z.: Differentiating concepts and instances for knowledge graph embedding. In: Proceedings of the Empirical Methods in Natural Language Processing, pp. 1971–1979 (2018)
8. He, S., Liu, K., Ji, G., Zhao, J.: Learning to represent knowledge graphs with gaussian embedding. In: Proceedings of the 24th ACM International on Conference on Information and Knowledge Management, pp. 623–632 (2015)
9. Zhang, W., Paudel, B., Zhang, W., Bernstein, A., Chen, H.: Interaction embeddings for prediction and explanation in knowledge graphs. In: Proceedings of the ACM International Conference on Web Search and Data Mining, pp. 96–104 (2019)
10. Wang, Z., Li, J., Liu, Z., Tang, J.: Text-enhanced representation learning for knowledge graph. In: Proceedings of the 25th International Joint Conference on Artificial Intelligence, pp. 1293–1299 (2016)
11. Xie, R., Liu, Z., Sun, M.: Representation learning of knowledge graphs with hierarchical types. In: Proceedings of the 25th International Joint Conference on Artificial Intelligence, pp. 2965–2971 (2016)
12. Lin, Y., Liu, Z., Luan, H., Sun, M., Rao, S., Liu, S.: Modeling relation paths for representation learning of knowledge bases. In: Proceedings of Empirical Methods Natural Language Process, pp. 705–714 (2015)
13. An, B., Chen, B., Han, X., Sun, L.: Accurate text-enhanced knowledge graph representation learning. In: Proceedings of the 2018 Conference of the North American Chapter of the Association for Computational Linguistics: Human Language Technologies, pp. 745–755 (2018)
14. Nie, B., Sun, S.: Joint knowledge base embedding with neighborhood context. In: Proceedings of the 24th International Conference on Pattern Recognition, pp. 379–384 (2018)
15. Guan, N., Song, D., Liao, L.: Knowledge graph embedding with concepts. Knowl.-Based Syst. **164**, 38–44 (2019)
16. Bordes, A., Weston, J., Collobert, R., Bengio, Y.: Learning structured embeddings of knowledge bases. In: Proceedings of the 25th AAAI Conference on Artificial Intelligence, pp. 301–306 (2011)
17. Socher, R., Chen, D., Manning, C.D., Ng, A.: Reasoning with neural tensor networks for knowledge base completion. In: Proceedings of Advances in Neural Information Processing Systems, pp. 926–934 (2013)
18. Ferragina, P., Scaiella, U.: Tagme: on-the-fly annotation of short text fragments. In: Proceedings of the 19th ACM Conference on Information and Knowledge Management, pp. 1625–1628 (2010)
19. Mihalcea, R., Csomai, A.: Wikify!: linking documents to encyclopedic knowledge. In: Proceedings of the 6th ACM Conference on Conference on Information & Knowledge Management (2007)

20. Devlin, J., Chang, M.W., Lee, K., Toutanova, K.: BERT: pre-training of deep bidirectional transformers for language understanding. In: The North American Chapter of the Association for Computational Linguistics, pp. 4171–4186 (2018)
21. MacQueen, J.: Some methods for classification and analysis of multivariate observations. In: Proceedings of the 5th Berkeley Symposium on Mathematical Statistics and Probability, pp. 281–297 (1967)

Chinese Relation Extraction with Flat-Lattice Encoding and Pretrain-Transfer Strategy

Xiuyue Zeng[✉], Jiang Zhong, Chen Wang, and Cong Hu

College of Computer Science, Chongqing University,
Chongqing 400030, People's Republic of China
{zxyh,zhongjiang,chenwang,hucong}@cqu.edu.cn

Abstract. Relation Extraction (RE) aims to assign a correct relation class holding between entity pairs in context. However, many existing methods suffer from segmentation errors, especially for Chinese RE. In this paper, an improved lattice encoding is introduced. Our structure is a variant of the flat-lattice Transformer. The lattice framework can combine character-level and word-level information to avoid segmentation errors. We optimize the position encoding scheme to embrace the relative distance between spans and target entities. Moreover, to reduce the classification errors between positive instances and negative instances in our model, we propose a pretrain-transfer strategy. Specifically, the main idea is to migrate the classification ability of the binary classifier to multi-class identification. Experiments on SanWen, FinRE, and ACE-2005 corpora demonstrate that our methods are effective and outperform other relation extraction models in performance.

Keywords: Chinese relation extraction · Flat-lattice encoding · Transformer · Pretrain-transfer strategy · Classification errors

1 Introduction

Relation Extraction (RE) is an important subtask in Natural Language Processing (NLP). Semantic relations between entity pairs can be used for many NLP tasks including question answering, knowledge graph construction, etc. Recently, many studies have focused on relation extraction. However, this task faces massive challenges such as the propagation of segmentation errors in Chinese text [8].

The existing Chinese RE methods can be summarized into three types: word-based [16,23], character-based [25], and character-word approaches [7,8,17]. For the character-based methods, they map each character in the sentence to a low-dimensional vector. These methods can capture sentence features, but rarely consider the word-level information in context. The word-based methods overcome this shortcoming by feeding word sequences into the model. These word-based approaches can obtain more features than character-based ones, but extra word

H. Qiu et al. (Eds.): KSEM 2021, LNAI 12816, pp. 30–40, 2021.
https://doi.org/10.1007/978-3-030-82147-0_3

segmentation on sentences is needed. Besides, the quality of segmentation will seriously affect the accuracy of the word-based models. To avoid segmentation errors, methods based on a hybrid of characters and words are widely used. Currently, the character-word lattice effectively leverages the word information over the raw character sequences. The lattice structure converts the input information to a directed acyclic graph, where each node denotes a character or word [7]. However, due to the complexity of lattice architecture, it suffers from difficulties in parallel computation.

In applications, we notice the classification errors of training data. Previous works have demonstrated that in the Chinese corpus of ACE-2005, 62.8% of classification errors come from predicting a negative instance into a positive one [19]. Besides, we analyze the prediction results of the Chinese SanWen corpus. We observe that 45.1% of negative instances are wrongly predicted as positive instances. Meanwhile, 28.5% of positive instances are misclassified. Classification errors between negative instances and positive instances seriously affect the overall accuracy of our model.

To address these issues, inspired by the Flat-Lattice Transformer (FLAT) [7], we propose an improved flat-lattice encoding and a pretrain-transfer strategy. The FLAT reconstructs the character-word lattice and enhances the parallelization ability. Our structure is a variant of the FLAT framework. In our methods, a span denotes a word or a character and its position in the raw lattice structure. We optimize the position encoding scheme by embracing the relative distance between spans and target entities. In our pretrain-transfer strategy, we first pretrain a binary classifier, which can distinguish the negative instances and positive instances effectively. And then, to further enhance the recognition ability of negative instances in multi-class identification, the performance of the pre-trained model is transferred to the multi-classifier.

To summarize, our contributions are as follows:

- We introduce an improved flat-lattice encoding based on the FLAT. Our key addition is the relative position encoding scheme, which embraces the relative distance between spans and target entities.
- We analyze the significant impact of negative instances misclassification in Chinese RE and propose a pretrain-transfer strategy to better distinguish between positive instances and negative instances.
- The performance of Chinese relation extraction in three different fields corpora is significantly improved. Experimental results prove that our methods are effective and achieve state-of-the-art results.

2   Related Work

Extracting entity-relation triples from text plays an indispensable part in natural language processing. Previous relation extraction methods mostly were based on feature engineering. For example, Mintz et al. [12] combined syntactic, lexical, and entity-tag features of the sentence to enhance the performance of relation extraction. With the development of deep learning, relation extraction models employed the neural network to learn features automatically. For example, Liu et al. [9] introduced the Convolutional Neural Network (CNN) to realize relation extraction innovatively. On this basis, Zeng et al. [21] proposed a novel CNN network using max-pooling and entity position features to enrich sentence representation. Considering the different effects between each word and relation type, Zhu et al. [27] calculated the similarity between words and target relations. Besides, some researchers introduced technologies such as reinforcement learning and generative adversarial network to better the performance [6,13].

On the other hand, Zhang et al. [22] introduced the Recurrent Neural Network (RNN), which achieved the same effect as the CNN structure [21]. Zhou et al. [26] proposed the Attention-Based Bidirectional Long Short-Term Memory Networks (AttBLSTM) model to capture the most important sentence features. Current Chinese relation extraction models are mostly based on the RNN family. Considering the influence of Chinese word segmentation errors, Zhang et al. [24] utilized the character-word lattice LSTM to obtain sentence representation. Then, Li et al. [8] further solved the polysemy problem of Chinese words, proposing the MG Lattice model.

Recently, researchers have demonstrated that deep language representation learned by the Transformer capture rich contextual features [5,14,15]. In the relation extraction task, the pre-trained language representation is used to reduce the dependence on explicit linguistic features [1,2]. The self-attention mechanism in Transformer can obtain long-distance dependencies effectively. The Transformer structure and its variants are widely used in many tasks, such as text generation and machine translation [10,15].

3   Methodology

In this section, we describe our proposed methods in detail. As illustrated in Fig. 1, the architecture of our model mainly consists of three parts: Input Layer, Transformer Encoder, and Relation Prediction. These components will be introduced below.

3.1   Input Layer

Our model can be defined as a set of spans. After matching the input sequence with a lexicon to get the words in it, a lattice structure can be acquired [7]. Note that the acquired word sequences may split the target entity up. In our model, each span corresponds to a token (character or word) and its position index in the original lattice. Given an input sequence $S = \{t_1, t_2, t_3, ..., t_n\}$ with two target entities $e1$ and $e2$, where t_i denotes a character or a word. The input sequence is first transformed into a matrix E, which contains word embedding based on the word2vec model and position embedding [8,11]. The dimension of word embedding and position embedding is d_t and d_p respectively.

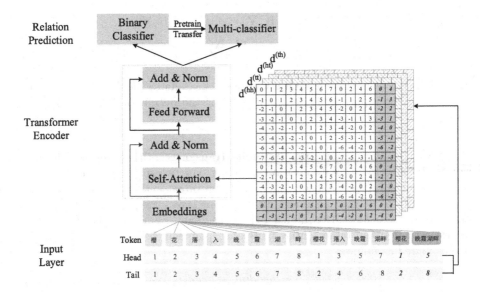

Fig. 1. The architecture of our model. There are three portions depicted in detail: (a) One is the acquisition of flat-lattice structure and the corresponding encoding in the input layer; (b) Another is the Transformer encoder with revised self-attention layer; (c) The third one is the pretrain-transfer strategy in the relation prediction layer, where contains a binary classifier and a multi-classifier.

Flat-Lattice Encoding. As depicted in Fig. 1, for each span, the head and tail represent the position index of the token's first and last character in the raw sentence respectively. We take x_i^t to denote the vector representation of the i-th token. After getting the original lattice structure, we convert it into the flat-lattice counterpart. To capture the relevance of different words relative to the target entities, we add the position indices of two target entities behind the span sequences. The representation of two target entities is x^{e1} and x^{e2}, and the input embedding matrix is defined as $E = \{x_1^t, x_2^t, ..., x_n^t, x^{e1}, x^{e2}\}$, where $x_i^t, x^{e1}, x^{e2} \in \mathbb{R}^d$, $d = d_t + 2d_p$. Then, the span sequences are fed into the Transformer encoder and used in the calculation of the self-attention layer.

3.2   Transformer Encoder

In this section, the basic Transformer structure is introduced first. In our model, we only utilize the Transformer encoder, which contains the self-attention and fully connected feed-forward network sublayer. Residual connection and layer normalization are applied around each sublayer. The Transformer structure performs self-attention on the sentence by N heads of attention separately and then concatenates the result of N heads. For per head, the calculating formulas are as below.

$$\mathbf{Q}, \mathbf{K}, \mathbf{V} = E_x' \mathbf{W}_q, E_x' \mathbf{W}_k, E_x' \mathbf{W}_v \tag{1}$$

$$Attention(\mathbf{Q}, \mathbf{K}, \mathbf{V}) = softmax(\mathbf{R})\mathbf{V} \tag{2}$$

$$\mathbf{R}_{mj} = (\frac{\mathbf{Q}_m \mathbf{K}_j^T}{\sqrt{d_k}}) \tag{3}$$

where $\mathbf{W}_q, \mathbf{W}_k, \mathbf{W}_v \in \mathbb{R}^{d \times d_k}$, and $d = N \times d_k$, d_k denotes the dimension of each head. E' is the input embedding matrix E or the output of last Transformer layer.

Relative Distance Encoding. In vanilla Transformer, the sequential information is obtained by absolute position encoding. For two spans x_m and x_j in the flat-lattice, the relation between them and two target entities can be indicated by four types of relative distances. In the input layer, the position information of target entities have been added behind the span sequences. Therefore, the interactions between target entity pairs and spans will be contained. They can be calculated as follows:

$$d_{mj}^{(hh)} = head[m] - head[j] \tag{4}$$

$$d_{mj}^{(tt)} = tail[m] - tail[j] \tag{5}$$

$$d_{mj}^{(ht)} = head[m] - tail[j] \tag{6}$$

$$d_{mj}^{(th)} = tail[m] - head[j] \tag{7}$$

where $d_{mj}^{(th)}$ indicates the distance between tail of x_m and head of x_j. The x_m and x_j can be a token or a target entity. Similarly, the $d_{mj}^{(hh)}$, $d_{mj}^{(tt)}$, $d_{mj}^{(ht)}$ have corresponding definitions. After that, a non-linear transformation of four distances is utilized to encode the relative position. The equations can be written as:

$$R_{m,j} = ReLU(W(\mathbf{P}_{d_{mj}^{(hh)}} \oplus \mathbf{P}_{d_{mj}^{(tt)}} \oplus \mathbf{P}_{d_{mj}^{(ht)}} \oplus \mathbf{P}_{d_{mj}^{(th)}})) \tag{8}$$

$$\mathbf{P}_{s,2r} = sin(s/10000^{2r/d}) \tag{9}$$

$$\mathbf{P}_{s,2r+1} = cos(s/10000^{2r/d}) \tag{10}$$

where W is a hyper-parameter, $\oplus$ is the concatenation operation. As in the FLAT, the position embedding $\mathbf{p}_d$ can be obtained by Eq. (9) and Eq. (10),where s denotes $d_{mj}^{(hh)}, d_{mj}^{(tt)}, d_{mj}^{(ht)}$ or $d_{mj}^{(th)}$ and $r \in [0, \frac{d}{2}]$. Then, an adapted self-attention mechanism [4] is adopted to leverage the relative position encoding.

$$\begin{aligned} \mathbf{R'}_{m,j} = & \mathbf{W}_q^T \mathbf{E}_{x_m}^T \mathbf{E}_{x_j} \mathbf{W}_{k,E} + \mathbf{W}_q^T \mathbf{E}_{x_m}^T \mathbf{R}_{mj} \mathbf{W}_{k,R} \\ & + \mathbf{u}^T \mathbf{E}_{x_j} \mathbf{W}_{k,E} + \mathbf{v}^T \mathbf{R}_{mj} \mathbf{W}_{k,R} \end{aligned} \tag{11}$$

where $\mathbf{v}, \mathbf{u} \in \mathbb{R}^{d_k}$ and $\mathbf{W}_q, \mathbf{W}_{k,E}, \mathbf{W}_{k,R} \in \mathbb{R}^{d \times d_k}$. Similar to Li et al. [7], the $\mathbf{R}$ in Eq. (2) is replaced by $\mathbf{R'}$ and the after computations follow the vanilla Transformer. Next, the last state $\mathbf{h}$ of the final state representation is sent to the relation prediction layer.

3.3   Relation Prediction

Pre-training. In this part, the output after the Transformer encoder layer is first fed into the sigmoid function for binary classification. The binary classifier is utilized to distinguish the positive instances and negative instances.

$$\hat{p}\,(y|s) = sigmoid(\mathbf{W}_0\mathbf{h} + \mathbf{b}_0) \tag{12}$$

where $\mathbf{W}_0$ is the transformation matrix, $\mathbf{b}_0$ is the bias vector, and $\hat{p}\,(y|s)$ is the predicted results. Next, we use cross-entropy as the objective function. For the training data $\{(s_i, y_i)\}\,|_{i=1}^{T}$, p_i is the ground truth, and θ_0 denotes all parameters in our model.

$$L(\theta_0) = -\sum_{i=1}^{T} p_i log\hat{p}(y_i|s_i, \theta_0) + (1 - p_i)log(1 - \hat{p}(y_i|s_i, \theta_0)) \tag{13}$$

Empirical Transfer. Through the pre-trained binary classifier, positive instances and negative instances can be better distinguished. In our multi-class classifier, we pay more attention to reducing classification errors within positive samples and avoiding adverse effects from negative instances. Based on the pre-trained weights, the empirical transfer is conducted. Parameters with the same dimension are shared between the multi-classifier and binary classifier. Meanwhile, we select cross-entropy as the loss function.

$$\hat{o}(y|s) = softmax(\mathbf{W}_1\mathbf{h} + \mathbf{b}_1) \tag{14}$$

$$L(\theta_1) = -\sum_{i=1}^{T} o_i log\hat{o}(y_i|s_i, \theta_1) \tag{15}$$

where $\mathbf{W}_1$ and $\mathbf{b}_1$ have identical meanings with $\mathbf{W}_0$ and $\mathbf{b}_0$. o_i is the ground truth and θ_1 denotes all parameters in multi-class classifier. To better distinguish the negative instances, the given θ_0 is transferred to initialize the specific parameters of θ_1.

4   Experiments

4.1   Datasets and Experimental Settings

Our experiments are conducted on three datasets which include FinRE [8], SanWen [18], and ACE-2005 Chinese corpus. The FinRE dataset is a financial news corpus. It contains 44 relation types including the special relation NA which denotes there is no relation between entity pairs. There are 13486, 3727, 1489 samples for training, testing, validation respectively in the FinRE. The SanWen dataset includes 9 relation types and is obtained by manually labeling literary articles. For the SanWen, it contains 17227, 1793, 2220 instances for training, validating, testing respectively. The ACE-2005 Chinese corpus covers three areas:

Table 1. Detailed parameter settings.

Hyper-parameter	Value
Word embeddings size	100
Postion embedding size	10
Head	8
-momentum	0.9
Dropout	0.5
Learning rate	0.001

broadcast, weblogs, and newswires [3]. For this dataset, we randomly choose 75% of it to train our model and the rest is used for evaluation [19].

In our experiments, the grid search is utilized to tune the parameters of our model. We adopt dropout with a rate of 0.5. The optimizer is stochastic gradient descent, and the learning rate is 0.001. The detailed parameter settings are displayed in Table 1. Following the previous studies, the area under the curve (**AUC**) and F1-score (**F1**) are reported to evaluate our methods.

4.2 Comparison with SOTA Methods

In our experiment, we choose the following models for comparison:

PCNN [20]: Zeng et al. combine multi-instance learning with the piecewise convolutional neural network.

BLSTM [22]: Zhang et al. propose to utilize a bidirectional LSTM networks to perform relation extraction.

MG Lattice [8]: Li et al. introduce the lattice structure and combine multi-grained information for Chinese relation extraction.

The final results are shown in Table 2, where the best results are bold. The baseline models include PCNN, BLSTM, MG Lattice, which achieved state-of-the-art performance on SanWen, FinRE, and ACE-2005 datasets. From Table 2, we can observe that the MG Lattice performs better than other baselines. This is because that the MG Lattice adopts the character-word lattice and multi-grained information to capture deep semantic information of the raw text [8]. However, we notice that these baseline models don't perform as well as ours. Our methods yield the best F1-score on three corpora, which are 68.35%, 50.60%, and 79.81% respectively. Besides, compared to the MG Lattice, the AUC value of our model increases 1.81%, 1.29%, 2.03% on three datasets respectively. The results indicate that our proposed flat-lattice encoding and transfer strategy are effective. Meanwhile, it also demonstrates the Transformer structure can better model the long-term dependencies between lattice input and final output. Overall, our methods achieve new state-of-the-art performance on three distinct datasets.

Table 2. AUC and F1-score of different models on three corpora.

Models	SanWen		FinRE		ACE-2005	
	AUC	F1	AUC	F1	AUC	F1
PCNN	48.26	61.00	30.49	45.51	66.10	74.33
BLSTM	50.21	61.04	28.80	42.87	60.40	70.03
MG Lattice	57.33	65.61	38.74	49.26	72.28	78.17
Our model	**59.14**	**68.35**	**40.03**	**50.60**	**74.31**	**79.81**

4.3   Ablation Study

To further evaluate the effectiveness of our proposed pretrain-transfer strategy, ablation experiments are conducted. The comparative experiment results are shown in Table 3.

Table 3. F1-score on distinct models: Pr-Tr: pretrain-transfer strategy.

Models	SanWen	FinRE	ACE-2005
PCNN	61.00	45.51	74.33
BLSTM	61.04	42.87	70.03
MG Lattice	65.61	49.26	78.17
PCNN+Pr-Tr	61.79	46.05	74.82
BLSTM+Pr-Tr	61.85	43.31	70.54
MG Lattice+Pr-Tr	66.37	49.78	78.64
Our model w/o Pr-Tr	67.55	50.03	78.81
Our model	**68.35**	**50.60**	**79.81**

The results indicate that the F1-score of our model using pretrain-transfer strategy increases from 67.55% to 68.35%, 50.03% to 50.60%, 78.81% to 79.81% on three datasets respectively. Meanwhile, we incorporate our strategy into PCNN, BLSTM, MG Lattice to form three new methods: PCNN+pretrain-transfer, BLSTM+pretrain-transfer, and MG Lattice+pretrain-transfer. From Table 3, we note that thanks to our pretrain-transfer, the F1-score of these models has been improved. For example, for the Sanwen dataset, the F1-score of PCNN increases from 61.00% to 61.79%, the F1-score of BLSTM increases from 61.04% to 61.85%, while the F1-score of MG Lattice increases from 65.61% to 66.37%. Such improvements verify the effectiveness of our pretrain-transfer strategy.

From the above results, we observe that the model with pretrain-transfer strategy obtains better performance, which means that our strategy contributes to performance improvement. To figure out the reasons, we further show the confusion matrix of our model based on the SanWen corpus, which can visualize

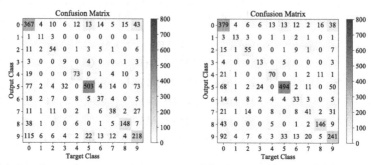

(a) Results without pretrain-transfer   (b) Results with pretrain-transfer

Fig. 2. Impacts of pretrain-transfer module. 0 to 9 on the coordinate axis denote NA, *Create*, *Use*, *Near*, *Social*, *Located*, *Ownership*, *General-Special*, *Family*, *Part-Whole* relation respectively. In (a), after training our model on SanWen corpus, it shows the confusion matrix for all relation classes without pretrain-transfer strategy. In contrast, the confusion matrix of the model with pretrain-transfer is reported in (b).

the performance of our pretrain-transfer strategy. As listed in Fig. 2, for class NA, when we apply the pretrain-transfer strategy on our model, the number of correctly identified instances increases from 367 to 379. In addition, for other factual relation types, the total number of wrongly identified instances decreases from 293 to 281. This shows that after exploiting our strategy, more negative instances are correctly classified, and less positive instances are predicted as negative ones. Besides, the classification accuracy between positive instances has also improved. For example, the number of instances where relation *Part-Whole* is misclassified as relation *Located* reduces from 73 to 50. This suggests that our pre-trained binary classifier does mitigate the misclassification problem. Our pretrain-transfer strategy can enhance the ability of our model to recognize negative instances and improve overall performance.

5   Conclusion

In this paper, we first introduced the improved flat-lattice encoding, which optimized the position encoding scheme in the FLAT framework. We innovatively included the distance encoding between target entities and spans. And then, based on the analysis of training data, we proposed a pretrain-transfer strategy to reduce the classification errors between positive and negative instances. Compared to various baselines, experimental results showed that our model achieved better performance on three distinct datasets. In the future, we plan to study the effect of other factors to further enhance the performance of relation extraction.

Acknowledgments. This research was partially supported by the National Key Research and Development Program of China (2017YFB1402400 and 2017YFB1402401), the Key Research Program of Chongqing Science and Technology Bureau (cstc2020jscx-msxmX0149, cstc2019jscx-mbdxX0012, and cstc2019jscx-fxyd0142).

References

1. Alt, C., Hübner, M., Hennig, L.: Fine-tuning pre-trained transformer language models to distantly supervised relation extraction. arXiv preprint arXiv:1906.08646 (2019)
2. Alt, C., Hübner, M., Hennig, L.: Improving relation extraction by pre-trained language representations. arXiv preprint arXiv:1906.03088 (2019)
3. Chen, Y., Zheng, Q., Chen, P.: Feature assembly method for extracting relations in Chinese. Artif. Intell. **228**, 179–194 (2015)
4. Dai, Z., Yang, Z., Yang, Y., Carbonell, J., Le, Q.V., Salakhutdinov, R.: Transformer-xl: attentive language models beyond a fixed-length context. arXiv preprint arXiv:1901.02860 (2019)
5. Devlin, J., Chang, M.W., Lee, K., Toutanova, K.: Bert: Pre-training of deep bidirectional transformers for language understanding. arXiv preprint arXiv:1810.04805 (2018)
6. Feng, J., Huang, M., Zhao, L., Yang, Y., Zhu, X.: Reinforcement learning for relation classification from noisy data. In: Proceedings of the AAAI Conference on Artificial Intelligence, vol. 32 (2018)
7. Li, X., Yan, H., Qiu, X., Huang, X.: Flat: Chinese ner using flat-lattice transformer. arXiv preprint arXiv:2004.11795 (2020)
8. Li, Z., Ding, N., Liu, Z., Zheng, H., Shen, Y.: Chinese relation extraction with multi-grained information and external linguistic knowledge. In: Proceedings of the 57th Annual Meeting of the Association for Computational Linguistics, pp. 4377–4386 (2019)
9. Liu, C.Y., Sun, W.B., Chao, W.H., Che, W.X.: Convolution neural network for relation extraction. In: Motoda, H., Wu, Z., Cao, L., Zaiane, O., Yao, M., Wang, W. (eds.) ADMA 2013. LNCS (LNAI), vol. 8347, pp. 231–242. Springer, Heidelberg (2013). https://doi.org/10.1007/978-3-642-53917-6_21
10. Liu, P.J., et al.: Generating wikipedia by summarizing long sequences. arXiv preprint arXiv:1801.10198 (2018)
11. Mikolov, T., Sutskever, I., Chen, K., Corrado, G.S., Dean, J.: Distributed representations of words and phrases and their compositionality. Adv. Neural Inf. Process. Syst. **26**, 3111–3119 (2013)
12. Mintz, M., Bills, S., Snow, R., Jurafsky, D.: Distant supervision for relation extraction without labeled data. In: Proceedings of the Joint Conference of the 47th Annual Meeting of the ACL and the 4th International Joint Conference on Natural Language Processing of the AFNLP, pp. 1003–1011 (2009)
13. Qin, P., Xu, W., Wang, W.Y.: Dsgan: Generative adversarial training for distant supervision relation extraction. arXiv preprint arXiv:1805.09929 (2018)
14. Radford, A., Narasimhan, K., Salimans, T., Sutskever, I.: Improving language understanding by generative pre-training (2018)
15. Vaswani, A., et al.: Attention is all you need. In: Advances in Neural Information Processing Systems, pp. 5998–6008 (2017)
16. Wu, W., Chen, Y., Xu, J., Zhang, Y.: Attention-based convolutional neural networks for Chinese relation extraction. In: Sun, M., Liu, T., Wang, X., Liu, Z., Liu, Y. (eds.) CCL/NLP-NABD -2018. LNCS (LNAI), vol. 11221, pp. 147–158. Springer, Cham (2018). https://doi.org/10.1007/978-3-030-01716-3_13
17. Xu, C., Yuan, L., Zhong, Y.: Chinese relation extraction using lattice GRU. In: 2020 IEEE 4th Information Technology, Networking, Electronic and Automation Control Conference (ITNEC), vol. 1, pp. 1188–1192. IEEE (2020)

18. Xu, J., Wen, J., Sun, X., Su, Q.: A discourse-level named entity recognition and relation extraction dataset for chinese literature text. arXiv preprint arXiv:1711.07010 (2017)
19. Ye, W., Li, B., Xie, R., Sheng, Z., Chen, L., Zhang, S.: Exploiting entity bio tag embeddings and multi-task learning for relation extraction with imbalanced data. arXiv preprint arXiv:1906.08931 (2019)
20. Zeng, D., Liu, K., Chen, Y., Zhao, J.: Distant supervision for relation extraction via piecewise convolutional neural networks. In: Proceedings of the 2015 Conference on Empirical Methods in Natural Language Processing, pp. 1753–1762 (2015)
21. Zeng, D., Liu, K., Lai, S., Zhou, G., Zhao, J.: Relation classification via convolutional deep neural network. In: Proceedings of COLING 2014, the 25th International Conference on Computational Linguistics: Technical Papers, pp. 2335–2344 (2014)
22. Zhang, D., Wang, D.: Relation classification via recurrent neural network. arXiv preprint arXiv:1508.01006 (2015)
23. Zhang, Q.Q., Chen, M.D., Liu, L.Z.: An effective gated recurrent unit network model for Chinese relation extraction. DEStech Transactions on Computer Science and Engineering (wcne) (2017)
24. Zhang, Y., Yang, J.: Chinese ner using lattice lstm. arXiv preprint arXiv:1805.02023 (2018)
25. Zhang, Z., Zhou, T., Zhang, Y., Pang, Y.: Attention-based deep residual learning network for entity relation extraction in Chinese EMRS. BMC Med. Inf. Decis. Mak. **19**(2), 55 (2019)
26. Zhou, P., et al.: Attention-based bidirectional long short-term memory networks for relation classification. In: Proceedings of the 54th Annual Meeting of the Association for Computational Linguistics, vol. 2: Short Papers, pp. 207–212 (2016)
27. Zhu, J., Qiao, J., Dai, X., Cheng, X.: Relation classification via target-concentrated attention cnns. In: International Conference on Neural Information Processing, pp. 137–146. Springer, Heidelberg (2017). https://doi.org/10.1007/978-3-319-70096-0_15

English Cloze Test Based on BERT

Minjie Ding⬤, Mingang Chen$^{(\boxtimes)}$⬤, Wenjie Chen, and Lizhi Cai

Shanghai Key Laboratory of Computer Software Testing and Evaluating,
Shanghai Development Center of Computer Software Technology,
Shanghai, China
{dmj,cmg,cwj,clz}@sscenter.sh.cn

Abstract. Cloze test is a common test in language examinations. It is also a research direction of natural language processing, which is an important field of artificial intelligence. In general, some words in a complete article are hidden, and several candidates are given to let the student choose the correct hidden word. To explore whether machine can do cloze test, we have done some research to build down-stream tasks of BERT for cloze test. In this paper, we consider the compound words in articles and make an improvement to help the model handling these kind of words. The experimental results show that our model performs well on questions of compound words and has better accuracy on CLOTH dataset.

Keywords: Cloze test · BERT · Compound word · Deep learning

1 Introduction

Natural language processing is an important branch of artificial intelligence. With the development of neural networks and deep learning, through feedforward neural network [1] or recurrent neural network [2], we can solve the long-distance dependence problem of sentences which can not be solved by statistical probability based models such as N-gram. Some neural network language models can even capture sentence structure. Since 2018, with the proposal of Attention [18] and Transformer [3], there have been many pre-training language models with large amount of parameters, such as BERT [4], GPT [5], etc. The performance of NLP can be greatly improved in multiple tasks. Cloze is a kind of language test which often appears in English test [11]. It can accurately evaluate the language ability of the students [12]. The teacher hide several words in an article, and give the hidden words and several wrong candidates to let the students to choose the right words. Some cloze datasets are used to measure the reading comprehension ability of machines, such as CNN/Daily Mail [13], Children's Book Test [14], and CLOTH [7]. Cloze requires the testee to infer from the context, which is very difficult for machines. Although some models perform well in cloze, the characteristic of the candidate words are not fully considered.

Supported by National Key R&D Program of China (No. 2018YFB 1403400).

H. Qiu et al. (Eds.): KSEM 2021, LNAI 12816, pp. 41–51, 2021.
https://doi.org/10.1007/978-3-030-82147-0_4

In this paper, we analyse the characteristic of compound words and build down-stream task of pre-trained BERT to handle with those words in cloze articles. Our model performs better on the questions contain compound words and has better accuracy on CLOTH dataset than other models.

The first part is the introduction. We will discuss related work in the second part. Then in the third part, we introduce our approach, and in the fourth part, we show the experimental results of our approach and do some analysis. Finally, in the fifth part, we will draw our conclusions and explain the future direction of our work.

2 Related Work

Cloze test is a kind of language test. There are many such type of questions in the English test papers of junior and senior high schools in China, which are like Fig. 1. In the past, the cloze question type was obtained by the way of automatic generation, that is, some words were randomly hidden from the whole article, and several options were given. However, the quality of data obtained in this way will not be high, and most of them are hardly difficult for human beings, so the research value is relatively low.

```
When someone asks me what business I am in. My face feels (1)_____. I envy people who can say
that they are writers, bookkeepers and doctors. All these jobs speak for themselves.
    I really do make a living by (2)_____ , and a good one, too. I can laugh like a king or like
a schoolboy. It is a skill that I have learned, (3)_____ the skill of mending shoes. Whenever
and however laugher is needed — I am asked t o do (4)_____. I laugh like a bus driver or a
shopkeeper. I laugh (5)_____, kindly and happily.
    I need (6)_____ point out that a job of this kind is tiring. I spend most evenings in
nightclubs. My job is to laugh during the (7)_____ part of the show. My loud, hearty laugher
must be timed carefully. It must not come too soon, (8)_____neither must be too late.
    I go through life quietly. I can (9)_____ the laugher of others. I can laugh in many
different ways. But I'm not sure that I have ever heard the sound of (10)_____ own laugher.
( )1. A. warm B. cool C. her D. cold
( )2. A. laughing B. writing C. speaking D. working
( )3. A. at B. to C. by D. like
( )4. A. one B. it C. those D. these
( )5. A. gladly B. sadly C. truly D. suddenly
( )6. A. clearly B. easily C. badly D. hardly
( )7. A. weaker B. stronger C. more terrible D. more wonderful
( )8. A. for B. so C. but D. and
( )9. A. get B. make C. copy D. have
( )10.A. their B. my C. her D. his
```

Fig. 1. Cloze test.

RACE (2017) [6] is a large-scale reading comprehension dataset containing more than 28,000 articles and 100,000 questions, which comes from junior high school and senior high school English tests in China. The questions are mainly composed of several problems and corresponding options.

CLOTH (2017) [7] is a large-scale cloze dataset with 7,131 articles and 99,433 questions. Questions in CLOTH are like Fig. 1. It also comes from junior high school and senior high school English tests in China. The difference between RACE and CLOTH is that RACE is a question and answer dataset, while CLOTH is a cloze dataset.

In addition, there are some other datasets and works close to CLOTH, such as LAMBADA [18], NTCIR QA Lab [16] and AI2 reasoning challenge [17].

MPNet(2017) [19] is a model consists of an input layer, a multi-perspective aggregation layer and an output layer. The input layer applied BiGRU [20] to get contextualized word representations of the article. The aggregation layer directly input the entire context and used attention to model long-range dependence. And the output layer computed the probability of the candidates with a sigmoid function.

BERT (2018) is a large-scale pre-training language model, which is composed of multi-layer transformer models. First, pre-training of masked language model and next sentence prediction is carried out in massive corpus. This process requires a lot of computing power, and it often takes several days to train on dozens of GPUs or TPUs. After pre-training, the model can be used for fine-tuning in different down-stream tasks. Compared with pre-training, fine-tuning only needs to train a small part of parameters. Due to the characteristics of the pre-training model, we can build the down-stream task model according to our own needs to achieve the required functions.

3 Our Approach

In this paper, we use pre-trained BERT, and build the down-stream task model for cloze. Using the pre-trained parameters, we train the down-stream task model on the CLOTH dataset. Because the pre-training process of BERT includes masked language model, that is, to replace a small part of words in the text with [MASK], and let the model predict the words replaced by [MASK]. This task is very similar to cloze, so we can use cloze to test BERT's masked language model capability in longer and more [MASK] texts.

First, all the blanks that need to be filled in the dataset will be replaced with [MASK] tags, and then all the articles and candidate words will be converted into tokens in the BERT vocabulary for subsequent work.

In the pre-training task of BERT, 15% of the words are replaced with [MASK], which is a relatively small proportion, and the sentences entered at one time are often short, such as: my dog is hairy - > my dog is [MASK]. In the down-stream task of this paper, because each [MASK] of cloze needs to fully consider the context information of the whole article, not just the text information near the [MASK], it is necessary to input the whole article into BERT for calculation and prediction at one time.

The original article is noted as $article$, and its dimension is $[batch, max\_article\_len]$, where $batch$ is the training batch size, $max\_article\_len$ is the longest text length in the batch. Article is directly input into the BERT model to get the output $bert(article)$, and its dimension is $[batch, max\_article\_len, hidden\_size]$, $hidden\_size$ is the hidden layer cell size of BERT. Take BERT-base as an example, $hidden\_size$ is 768. That is to say, the BERT model transforms every token ID into a 768 dimensional vector output after bidirectional semantic calculation.

We record all the positions of [MASK] first. After getting the output of BERT, we find the vector of the corresponding position, which is the prediction of [MASK] by the model. We use the function of BERT to transform it into the vector who has the length of the vocabulary size, which represents the prediction probability of each word in the vocabulary.

The next step is to improve the performance of the model. In English, a word often has many forms, such as past tense, present continuous tense, singular and plural. If the different forms of each word are recorded in the model vocabulary, the vocabulary will become very large. The vocabulary size of BERT is 30522. When it converts some compound words into tokens, it will separate the root and prefix, suffix, such as: refusals - > ['refusal', '##s']. In other words, the plural 's' is treated as a suffix, which effectively reduces the vocabulary size and the number of parameters. In the prediction stage, after outputting the prediction probabilities of all 30522 tokens, we find the tokens corresponding to the four options. For the above compound words, there will be multiple tokens. On the leaderboard of the CLOTH dataset, the best model(we call it BERT-base(average) in this paper) adds these tokens and takes the average value as the final probability output of the option, like function:

$$p_i = \frac{\sum_j token_{ij}}{len(\sum_j token_{ij})},$$

where $token_{ij}$ is the probability of occurrence of the j-th token of the i-th option. After analysis, we think that the average value of this step is actually unnecessary. In the example of 'refusals' above, we think that the model will have a higher probability output for the root 'refusal' while the probability output for the suffix 's' is very small, which can be ignored. If the average value is taken after adding the probabilities, the correct answer output will be affected. Therefore, we simplify the formula for calculating the accuracy of each option as follows:

$$p_i = \sum_j token_{ij}.$$

We will also analyze the experimental results in the experimental part to illustrate the effectiveness of this method.

Our final loss function is the cross entropy loss function of multi-classification:

$$L = \frac{1}{N} \sum_i (-\sum_{c=1}^{M} y_{ic} log(p_{ic})),$$

Where M is the number of categories. In our cloze test, we usually take 4. y_{ic} is the indicator variable. If the correct answer of question i is the same as c, it is 1, otherwise it is 0. p_{ic} is the probability that the model predicts the correct answer of question i to be c. The algorithm is shown in Algorithm 1, and the structure of the model is shown in Fig. 2.

Algorithm 1. BERT for cloze test

Input: Training articles Δ, Mask positions **POS**, Option tokens **O**, True Answers **A**
Output: Probabilities **P**

> **loop**
>> $\Delta \leftarrow bert(\Delta)$ //input the article in the train set into BERT
>> $Questions \leftarrow \Delta[\textbf{POS}]$ //find the position of [MASK] indicated by **P**
>> $token \leftarrow Questions[\textbf{O}]$ //find the probability represented by each token from questions
>> $p_i \leftarrow \sum_j token_{ij}$ //calculate the probability of each option
>> update loss: $L = \frac{1}{N} \sum_i (-\sum_{c=1}^{M} y_{ic} log(p_{ic}))$
> **end loop**

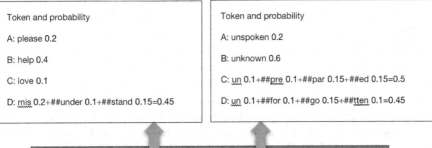

Fig. 2. BERT for cloze test.

4   Experiments and Analysis

The dataset used in this paper is CLOTH, which is an English cloze dataset collected by teachers. It contains more than 7,000 cloze questions in junior high school and senior high school. The types of questions are shown in Fig. 1. Some statistical information of the CLOTH dataset is shown in Table 1.

Table 1. CLOTH dataset.

Dataset	CLOTH-M			CLOTH-H			CLOTH(Total)		
	Train	Dev	Test	Train	Dev	Test	Train	Dev	Test
# passages	2,341	355	335	3,172	450	478	5,513	805	813
# questions	2,2056	3,273	3,198	54,794	7,794	8,318	76,850	11,067	11,516
Vocab. size	15,096			32,212			37,235		
Avg. # sentence	16.26			18.92			17.79		
Avg. # words	242.88			365.1			313.16		

In this paper, we use the PyTorch version BERT-base by HuggingFace. The parameters of its pre-training model are the same as TensorFlow version. The vocabulary size is 30,522, the number of attention head is 12, the number of hidden layer is 12, the size of hidden layer unit is 768, and the maximum input length is 512. Therefore, we divide the articles that exceed this length into several paragraphs according to the length of 512. The experimental environment is shown in Table 2.

Table 2. Experimental environment.

CPU	Intel Xeon Silver 4114 2.2 GHz
GPU	NVIDIA Tesla P100 16 GB
RAM	500 GB
Framework	PyTorch 1.6

We make a statistic on the experimental results of the test set to prove the effectiveness of our strategy. First, we run BERT-base(average) on our computer, find out the wrong results of it whose token length is different from true answers, and then find out the output of our model of the same question. Then we count the number of the wrong output of the average version converted into the correct output by our model. The results are shown in Table 3.

It can be seen from Table 3 that our strategy can correct 16.97% of the wrong output of the BERT-base(average) caused by the token length, which indicates that our strategy is effective and can correct a considerable part of the wrong output. CLOTH-M represents the junior high school part in CLOTH

Table 3. Statistic results.

	CLOTH-M	CLOTH-H	CLOTH	CLOTH-TL
Total question number (T)	3,198	8,318	11,516	2280
Wrong output(W)	500	1678	2178	604
Wrong output caused by token length (WT)	28	137	165	165
Wrong output corrected by our model (C)	4	24	28	28
Wrong output ratio (WT/W)	5.6%	8.16%	7.58%	27.32%
Correction error ratio (C/WT)	14.29%	17.52%	16.97%	16.97%

dataset, CLOTH-H represents the senior high school part in CLOTH dataset, CLOTH-TL represents the articles contain the fault caused by different token length. However, questions of different token length accounts for a very small proportion of the total number of questions in the test set. In addition, the size of CLOTH is not very large in contrast with other NLP datasets. Therefore, in the final experimental results in Table 4, the improvement of our model compared with the average version is limited. In addition, some other useful information can be obtained from the statistical results. For example, most of the wrong outputs caused by token length are from the senior high school part of CLOTH (137/165). This is because junior high school does not teach too many complex words, and their token length is usually 1. The experimental results on the CLOTH dataset are shown in Table 4. BERT-base(average) is the experimental result of the BERT-base model on the leaderboard of CLOTH running on the computer used in this paper, and BERT-base(ours) is the experimental result introduced in the previous chapter after removing the operation of averaging the sum of token probabilities in the prediction part of the model.

Table 4. Experimental result.

Model	CLOTH-M(%)	CLOTH-H(%)	CLOTH(%)	CLOTH-TL(%)
LSTM	51.8	47.1	48.4	–
Stanford Attentive Reader	52.9	47.1	48.7	–
MPNet-ngram	53.2	49.0	50.1	–
SemiMPNet-ngram	67.6	58.3	60.9	–
BERT-base(average)	79.8	**84.3**	81.0	73.5
BERT-base(ours)	**80.1**	84.0	**81.2**	**74.8**

It can be seen from Table 4 that the experimental results of our BERT-base model on the CLOTH-M and CLOTH-TL are the best, and the average accuracy of our model on the whole CLOTH is also better than BERT-base(average).

For a more detailed explanation, we select several examples from the experimental results, as shown in Fig. 3. The left and right represent the output of our model and the BERT-base(average) respectively. The number below each token represents the probability of the token. The sentence containing the question is '[MASK] the farmer interviewed applicants for the job, he received many [MASK]'. The second [MASK] is the blank need to be filled. We can see that the affected option is A: refusals, because it will be transformed to 'refusal ##s'. Therefore, the length of its answer vector is 2. When dealing with it, the BERT-base(average) will divide the probability by 2, which greatly reduces the occurrence probability of option A. Therefore, we can see on the right that the output answer of the model is B, and the correct answer is A. In the output result of our model on the left side of the figure, the probability of A is 9.90, which is slightly higher than that of B. In fact, both A and B are smooth in this sentence, but A is more appropriate than B when combined with the context. The output probability of the average model on the right side of the figure is 17.46(before averaged), which is much higher than that of B. This should be due to the influence of the loss function and the ground truth 'A', which makes the model expect a higher probability of output to A. However, because the sum of its token probability will be divided by 2, the final probability is still less than B, which leads to the wrong choice of B as the correct answer. In addition, we can see that in our model, the probability of '##s' is much smaller than in average model, which is more intuitive.

```
[                                  [
    Ours                               Average
    A "refusal    ##s    [PAD]",       A "refusal    ##s    [PAD]",
      "8.61       1.29   0.0",           "8.74       8.72   0.0",
    B "suggestions [PAD] [PAD]",        B "suggestions [PAD] [PAD]",
      "9.78       0.0    0.0",           "9.08       0.0    0.0",
    C "rewards    [PAD]  [PAD]",        C "rewards    [PAD]  [PAD]",
      "9.18       0.0    0.0",           "8.91       0.0    0.0",
    D "desires    [PAD]  [PAD]",        D "desires    [PAD]  [PAD]",
      "0.76       0.0    0.0",           "-0.33      0.0    0.0",
    Output:              "A",           Output:              "B",
    Ground truth:        "A"            Ground truth:        "A"
],                                 ],
```

Fig. 3. Sample of cloze test 1.

Figure 4 is another example, similar to Fig. 3. On the left is the output of our model and on the right is the output of BERT-base(average). The relevant context is 'a lot of people [MASK] homeless people.' Correct answer D: misunderstand consists of three tokens, the average model will divide the sum of the token probabilities at the end of each line by 3, which is less than the probability of B by 6.00. Therefore, the average model wrongly outputs B as the correct answer, while our model removes the average strategy, which does not affect the output of answer D. In this case, we can see that in our model, the probabilities of tokens of 'understand' are similar to each other (3.27, 4.76 and 5.23 in Fig. 4). This is because the token '##under' and '##stand' contain more semantic information than simple token '##s' (the case of 'refusal ##s' in Fig. 3).

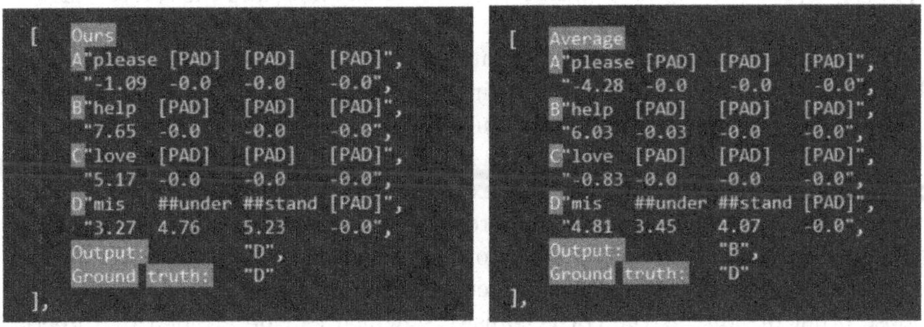

Fig. 4. Sample of cloze test 2.

From the analysis above, we can see that our model can better deal with compound words (words composed of multiple tokens in the vocabulary), and when dealing with cloze questions with compound words as the correct answer, it can avoid the probability reduction problem caused by taking the average value, so as to choose the correct answer.

In addition, we selected some other wrong outputs of our model for analysis, as shown in Fig. 5.

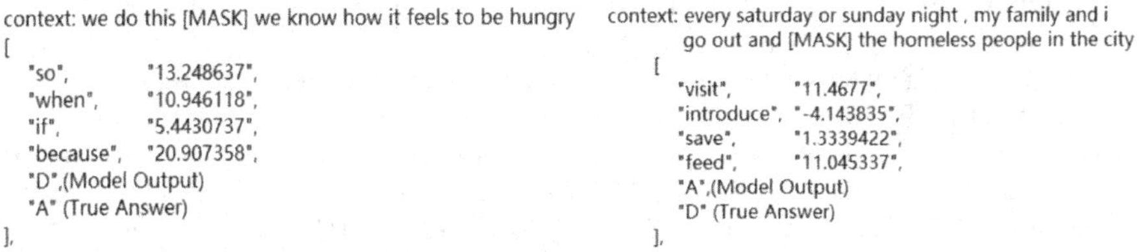

Fig. 5. Sample of cloze test 3.

As can be seen from Fig. 5, most of these wrong options are consistent in part of speech with correct options, but there is a slight difference in semantics. If we only look at the context provided in the figure, almost all options can be correct. If we want to make an accurate judgment, we need to extract information from more context. This also shows that although the current language models are very powerful, their ability to extract information from long-distance context is still limited, and sometimes the prediction may be based on the part of speech, not really understand its semantics (of course, sometimes the part of speech is also a common cloze skill for students). There is still a large research space for models to really understand natural language.

5   Conclusion

In this paper, we built a BERT down-stream task model for cloze, which can input a long text and multiple [MASK] at one time, and found the correct answer of cloze according to its context. The accuracy of our model on CLOTH-M, CLOTH-TL and CLOTH is better than that of all other models. Compared with BERT-base(average), after fully analyzing the compound words and tokenization of BERT, we adopted the strategy of not taking the average of the sum of the token probabilities. Our model performs the best on CLOTH dataset, especially on CLOTH-M and CLOTH-TL. The experimental results show that it is more reasonable to deal with compound words without average value. For questions whose correct answers are compound words, taking the average value will greatly reduce the final probability of the correct options, and lead the model to wrongly choose other options as the correct answers, which can be avoided by directly taking the sum of the token probabilities as the final probability. In addition, the proportion of compound words in the total number of questions is small, so although our model has improved compared with the BERT-base(average) on part of CLOTH, the improvement is not significant on entire CLOTH. There are still many research directions of machine cloze. In the future, a possible improvement direction is to let the machine consider more word characteristics, such as part-of-speech, when doing cloze test. This will help promoting the interpretability of AI.

References

1. LeCun, Y., Bottou, L., Bengio, Y., Haffner, P.: Gradient-based learning applied to document recognition. Proc. IEEE **86**(11), 2278–2324 (1998)
2. Zaremba, W.; Sutskever, I., Vinyals, O.: Recurrent Neural Network Regularization. arxiv:1409.2329 (2014)
3. Vaswani, A.: Attention is all you need, In: Guyon, I. (ed.) Advances in Neural Information Processing Systems 30, Curran Associates Inc, pp. 5998–6008 (2017)
4. Devlin, J., Chang, M.-W., Lee, K., Toutanova, K.: BERT: Pre-training of Deep Bidirectional Transformers for Language Understanding. arxiv:1810.04805 (2018)
5. Radford, A., Narasimhan, K., Salimans, T., Sutskever, I.: Improving language understanding by generative pre-training (2018)
6. Lai, G., Xie, Q., Liu, H., Yang, Y., Hovy, E.H.: RACE: Large-scale ReAding comprehension dataset from examinations. In: Martha, P., Rebecca, H., Sebastian, R. (eds.) EMNLP, Association for Computational Linguistics, pp. 785–794 (2017)
7. Xie, Q., Lai, G., Dai, Z., Hovy, E.H.: Large-scale Cloze Test Dataset Designed by Teachers, CoRR arXiv:1711.03225 (2017)
8. Hochreiter, S., Schmidhuber, J.: Long short-term memory. Neural Comput. **9**(8), 1735–1780 (1997)
9. Cho, K.: Learning Phrase Representations using RNN Encoder-Decoder for Statistical Machine Translation (2014)
10. Chen, D., Bolton, J., Manning, C.D.: A Thorough Examination of the CNN/Daily Mail Reading Comprehension Task. In: ACL (1), The Association for Computer Linguistics (2016)

11. Taylor, W.L.: cloze procedure: a new tool for measuring readability. Journalism Bull. **30**(4), 415–433 (1953)
12. Fotos, S.S.: The cloze test as an integrative measure of efl proficiency: a substitute for essays on college entrance examinations? Lang. Learn. **41**(3), 313–336 (1991)
13. Hermann, K.M.: Teaching machines to read and comprehend. In: NIPS (2015)
14. Hill, F., Bordes, A., Chopra, S., Weston, J.: The goldilocks principle: reading children's books with explicit memory representations. In: Bengio, Y., LeCun, Y. (ed.) ICLR (2016)
15. Paperno, D.: The LAMBADA dataset: word prediction requiring a broad discourse context. In: ACL (1), The Association for Computer Linguistics (2016)
16. Shibuki, H.: Overview of the NTCIR-11 QA-Lab Task. In: Kando, N., Joho, H., Kishida, K. (ed.) NTCIR, National Institute of Informatics (NII) (2014)
17. Clark, P.: Think you have Solved Question Answering? Try ARC, the AI2 Reasoning Challenge, CoRR arXiv:1803.05457 (2018)
18. Bahdanau, D., Cho, K., Bengio, Y.: Neural Machine Translation by Jointly Learning to Align and Translate, arxiv:1409.0473Comment (2014) Accepted at ICLR 2015 as oral presentation
19. Wang, L., et al.: Multi-Perspective Context Aggregation for Semi-supervised Cloze-style Reading Comprehension, CoRR arXiv:1808.06289 (2018)
20. McCann, B., Bradbury, J., Xiong, C., Socher, R.: Learned in translation: contextualized word vectors. In: Guyon, I. et al. (eds.) NIPS, pp. 6297–6308 (2017)

An Automatic Method for Understanding Political Polarization Through Social Media

Yihong Zhang$^{(\boxtimes)}$, Masumi Shirakawa, and Takahiro Hara

Graduate School of Information Science and Technology,
Osaka University, Osaka, Japan
shirakawa@hapicom.jp, hara@ist.osaka-u.ac.jp

Abstract. Understanding political polarization is an important problem when one studies the culture of a democratic country. As a platform for discussing social issues, social media such as Twitter contains rich information about political polarization. In this paper, we propose an automatic method for discovering information from social media that can help people understand political polarization of the country. Previous researches have answered the "who" question, as they proposed methods for identifying ideal points of social media users. In our work, we make a step forward by answering the "what" question. Our method consists of two main techniques, namely, ideal point estimation and discriminative natural language processing. The inputs of our method are raw social media data, and the outputs are representative phrases for different political sides. Using real-world data from Twitter, we also verify that the representative phrases our method generates are consistent with our general knowledge of political polarization in Japan.

Keywords: Political polarization · Bayesian method · User profiling · Social media

1 Introduction

Political polarization is a significant yet sometimes puzzling phenomenon when one studies the culture of a democratic country [6]. It occurs when one finds information or people being associated with one political extreme or the other, bounded by certain ideology. Political polarization can be difficult to understand in several scenarios. For example, a young university graduate, who has been limiting his intake of political information from certain sources with similar ideologies, for the first time comes into contact with information sources of different stand points. Another example scenario can be that a foreigner, who has moved into the country recently, tries to figure out the ideologies and standing points of news and people in order to avoid unnecessary arguments. In both scenarios, we assume that the information consumer does not have prior knowledge

© Springer Nature Switzerland AG 2021
H. Qiu et al. (Eds.): KSEM 2021, LNAI 12816, pp. 52–63, 2021.
https://doi.org/10.1007/978-3-030-82147-0_5

of the political polarization situation of the country, and wishes to grasp such knowledge in a most efficient way.

We set Japan as our country for study. Political polarization in Japan is particularly interesting for a few reasons. First, there is no clear cut of two opposing parties like Democrat and Republican in the US. Second, the main party (Jimintou) holds on to majority for a long period of time, while lesser parties form and dissolve frequently. Third, individual in a party can sometimes have an ideology that is different from their party. These situations make political polarization in Japan especially hard to understand [7].

Social media platforms such as Twitter is known to have a *echo chamber* behavior [3]. It has been shown that political discussion has a strong presence in social media platforms [13]. At the same time, social media users tend to associate themselves with people of the same political orientation, through actions such as *following* and *retweeting* [14]. By following, a user can see realtime updates of what the followed person posts. By retweeting, a user repeats someone else's message to be seen by their own followers. Both actions contribute to the segmentation of user groups with different political ideologies. While many consider it as a undesirable behavior, we would like to leverage this behavior to help us understand political polarization.

In this paper we propose a solution for understanding political polarization through social media. The aim of our solution is to allow information consumer to grasp key ideologies and concepts associated with different sides in the polarization without any prior knowledge. The technique for estimating user ideal points is similar to previous works. More specifically, we use an unsupervised Markov chain Monte Carlo (MCMC) [1] that learns the separation among the retweeter of a number of political tweets. But unlike previous works, we go a step further by analyzing text contents after identifying polarization through a natural language processing (NLP) technique. The combination of NLP and ideal point estimation makes it possible to generate understandable descriptions of the polarization from raw social media data. One thing to note is that, although we choose Japanese social media as the data platform, our approach can be applied easily to analyzing political polarization in other democratic countries, since none of our techniques is language dependent. In the reminder of this paper, we will first discuss related work in Sect. 2. Then we will present our method in full details, and discuss our experimental results, in Sect. 3 and 4 respectively.

2 Related Work

Given the importance of understanding political polarization, in recent years a number of researches have proposed methods to tackle this problem, especially since large scale social media data became available. One type of approach is through supervised machine learning, in which a number of information units are manually labeled by their ideal points for the training purpose, and then the trained model is applied to predict the ideal point of new information. For example, Pennacchiotti and Popescu proposed such a method to classify Twitter user political affiliation, with features including behavior and linguistic features generated from user activities and messages they post affiliation [9]. Another example is by Rao et al., who proposed a similar method to classify Twitter user political orientations, with a different set of features including social-linguistic features [10]. In some other works, the polarization labels are not provided manually, but obtained from a reference source. For example, Marozzo and Bessi used voting preference to calculate the polarization label, when studying user polarization during Italian constitutional referendum in 2016, while new labels were again predicted using supervised learning models [8]. Another work worth mentioning is by Imai et al., who proposed an interesting Markov chain Monte Carlo method for ideal point estimation that runs not on social media, but on questionnaire [5]. Using important politician as examples, they found their estimation highly correlated with expert analysis. The supervised methods, however, are not desirable in our scenarios, as they require input of expert knowledge or special source, which we assume not available.

Another type of approach is through unsupervised learning, usually based on user connection network. For example, Conover et al. studied political polarization through retweeting and mentioning user network [4]. They found that users who agree politically would retweet each other, while users who mention each other can have different ideologies. Takikawa and Nagayoshi proposed another method that used cluster analysis for splitting communities and Latent Dirichlet Allocation for tweet content analysis [12]. While they had a similar goal to our work, we are unable to obtain meaningful understanding of political polarization from their results, most because they divided users into many communities instead of two extremes. Finally, another more prominent example of unsupervised method was proposed by Barbera [2]. In his work, he modeled user ideal points as latent variables, and proposed that a user will follow another user if their ideal points are similar. Based on the data of follower network and a Markov chain Monte Carlo method, he was able to learn the ideal point of both followers and followees. His work inspired us to use a similar approach to discovering ideal points. However, his model was entirely built on users, and not on the message contents, which are also important for understanding ideologies. Furthermore, his method required selecting popular followees, which in his work were important politicians, while in Japan not all important politicians have social media accounts. Our work therefore deals with such drawbacks by modeling on retweeter-message data.

3   Methodology

Our goal is to provide a fully computational method for understanding political polarization through social media. The input of this method is social media data, and the output of this method is some representative phrases of political polarization that human can easily understand. The process from the input to output should be fully automatic, that is, without the help of human expert knowledge. Two techniques that make this process possible are automatic ideal point estimation and discriminative NLP. The framework of our method is demonstrated in Fig. 1. The first step is to collect and prepare political tweets, clustering them into retweet clusters and collecting descriptive texts. The next step is ideal point estimation based on retweet clusters, followed by extraction of representative phrases using discriminative NLP techniques, which have been used previously in other tasks such as ontology generation [15]. In this section, we will describe each step in the framework in detail.

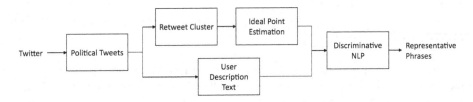

Fig. 1. Framework for extracting representative phrases of political polarization from social media

3.1 Dataset Preparation

We collected a dataset from Twitter for the purpose of studying the political polarization that can be seen in users and messages. The collection was performed in several steps. First, we monitored Twitter and collected all tweets mentioned a politician. We obtained a list of 400 Japanese politician accounts from a website called *meyou*, which lists Japanese Twitter accounts in different categories, including news, talent, and politicians[1]. The website only lists more popular accounts, and that is sufficient for the study because at this stage we are not after completeness but representativeness. All tweets mentioning these politicians can be considered to some degree as political. We monitored Twitter through its Filter API[2] for a period of one month (in January and February, 2020) and collected about 2 million tweets.

Second, we clustered these tweets into clusters of retweets. Twitter has two ways for a user to retweet a message, retweet manually, or through the retweet button. In manual retweets, the retweeter can comment or criticize the original tweet, expressing a different view, while retweeting through the button will only repeat the message without additional comments. In this study, to have a more orderly view, we only consider the second way of retweeting, and users who retweet this way are considered as agreed to the ideology of the message. The button-type retweets also have an identifier indicating the id of original message, making them convenient for clustering. The clusters of retweets were formed simply by grouping the retweets with the same original message id. After clustering, we removed clusters with fewer than 100 retweets. As the result, we obtained 1,010 clusters with a median number of retweets of 192.

---

[1] The list of Japanese politician: https://meyou.jp/group/category/politician/.

[2] https://developer.twitter.com/en/docs/tweets/filter-realtime/api-reference/post-statuses-filter.

Third, we collected user information for a subset of more frequent retweeters. We selected users who retweet at least 30 messages among the 1,010 obtained messages, and this results in 1,169 users, with a median number of retweets of 41. We then collected profile description of these users using Twitter User API[3]. Furthermore, we removed messages that have been retweeted less than 5 times by the selected users, reducing the number of messages to 926. Finally, this dataset of 926 messages and 1,169 users with a total of 54,392 retweets will be main subject of this study.

3.2 Ideal Point Estimation

We challenge the problem of estimating user ideal point through their retweeting behavior. The intuition is that, users will only retweet messages that have similar ideal point to express agreement and support. This is especially true when a user uses the retweet button to simply repeat the message without additional comments, as we mentioned previously. In this way we assume each user has an ideal point, denoted as θ_i, and each message also has an ideal point, denoted as ϕ_i. Our task is to learn the likely value for these parameters through a computational method automatically, in other words, without any guidance of human experts. We consider this to be possible because the retweeting behaviors already contain sufficient information for splitting users and messages by their ideal points.

The computational technique we deploy for this task is Markov chain Monte Carlo (MCMC) [1]. It is a computational technique that approximates a likely distribution for one or many random variables by repeatedly sampling from a proposal distribution and evaluating them. The whole process can be seen as moving the value of a parameter randomly in the search space, and the desire distribution is then taken as the aggregation of the points in the path. It is computationally efficient because due to the Markov chain property, only the value of the previous point is required for calculating the next move. This technique is especially useful when the desired distribution cannot be derived analytically. Indeed, MCMC has made many unconventional probabilistic models usable, and caused Bayesian modeling to become popular since about twenty years ago.

To apply MCMC for learning our parameter, we model retweeting behavior as the following. First we denote the probability of user i to retweet message j as $p(y_{ij} = 1)$. We calculate the probability as:

$$p(y_{ij} = 1|\theta_i, \phi_j) = \text{logit}^{-1}(\theta_i - \phi_j)^2 \tag{1}$$

In this way, the closer the ideal point between the user and the message, the more likely the user will retweet the message. Assuming independence of each retweeting behavior, we have the likelihood of the retweet data as:

---

[3] https://developer.twitter.com/en/docs/accounts-and-users/follow-search-get-users/api-reference/get-users-lookup.

$$p(Y|\theta,\phi) = \prod_i \prod_j [f(\theta_i,\phi_i)]^{y_{ij}} [1 - f(\theta_i,\phi_i)]^{1-y_{ij}} \qquad (2)$$

where $f(\theta_i,\phi_i) = \text{logit}^{-1}(\theta_i - \phi_j)^2$.

Since parameter distributions are very difficult to derive analytically from this likelihood function, we use MCMC to approximate. Particularly, we will use a modified version of Metropolis algorithm [1]. This algorithm is a variation of MCMC techniques. In Metropolis algorithm, a new move from a previous position takes three steps. First, a new value of the parameter is drawn from a proposal distribution. Second, the probability of a jump is calculated based on the posterior probability given the new parameter value. More specifically, the jump probability $p_{jump} = p(\theta_{old})/p(\theta_{new})$. Third, a random value is drawn to determine whether to jump or stay at the old value.

We provide our implementation in Algorithm 1. The algorithm iterates through each θ_i and ϕ_j, performing the Metropolis jump at each instance. The three steps of the Metropolis jump are derived as the following. The proposal distribution is taken as the normal distribution with previous parameter value as the mean, and 1 as the variance (Line 4, 12). Since we assume parameter independence, when getting a new value for a parameter, we only calculate the posterior using the data involving the parameter. This can greatly reduce the computational cost. The posterior in turn is calculated using Eq. (2) (Line 5–6, 13–14). Finally a random real number between 0 and 1 is drawn for deciding the jump (line 7–9, 15–17).

One consideration we especially take is that, given any user i, the messages he retweets are much fewer than the message he does not retweet, regardless of his ideal point. The same for the messages with regard to users. This causes the number of negatives to be much larger than the positives, and as a result, the algorithm would be confused and unable learn the proper parameter value. Therefore in our implementation, instead of using all negatives, we randomly sample the negatives with the same number of positives (Line 5, 13). Practically, we find that this modification can lead the algorithm to much more proper behaviors.

3.3   Extracting Representative Phrases

After completing previous steps, we now have ideal point estimations for the selected messages and users. Representative phrases extraction can be done directly on the description of these 1,169 users, but it is desirable to have a larger description corpus. Therefore we generate another user dataset from the retweeters of the messages that have most extreme ideal points. More specifically, we select 100 messages that have lowest ideal points, and generate a text corpus consists of all the profile descriptions of users who retweet these messages. This corpus is denoted as D_A. Similarly we generated corpus of the other extreme, denoted as D_B.

We apply discriminative NLP on these two corpora to generate representative phrases. The phrases generated will have extremeness scores to indicate their

---

Algorithm 1. Metropolis algorithm with negative sampling

1: flat initialization
2: **for** *iter* in n iterations **do**
3:      **for** each θ_i **do**
4:          draw θ_i' from $N(\theta_i, 1)$
5:          $Y' \leftarrow$ positives of user i and randomly picked equal number of negatives
6:          $p \leftarrow p(Y'|\theta_i', \phi)p(\theta_i', \phi)/p(Y'|\theta_i, \phi)p(\theta_i, \phi)$
7:          **if** $a \sim$ Uniform$(0, 1) < min(1, p)$ **then**
8:              $\theta_i \leftarrow \theta_i'$
9:          **end if**
10:     **end for**
11:     **for** each ϕ_i **do**
12:         draw ϕ_i' from $N(\phi_i, 1)$
13:         $Y' \leftarrow$ positives of message j and randomly picked equal number of negatives
14:         $p \leftarrow p(Y'|\theta, \phi_j')p(\theta, \phi_j')/p(Y'|\theta, \phi_j)p(\theta, \phi_j)$
15:         **if** $a \sim$ Uniform$(0, 1) < min(1, p)$ **then**
16:             $\phi_j \leftarrow \phi_j'$
17:         **end if**
18:     **end for**
19:     **if** *iter* > *burninIter* **then**
20:         store θ and ϕ
21:     **end if**
22: **end for**

---

position in the polarization. Intuitively, the phrases appear much more frequent in the left corpus than in the right corpus should have a higher extremeness score towards the left. There are several existing NLP techniques that can be used to achieve this result. The technique we use in this paper was proposed by Shirakawa et al., which is based on N-gram and the set cover problem [11]. This is a discriminative NLP technique as it is applied to a target corpus by comparing it to a reference corpus. Originally it is designed to detect bursty phrases, with a target corpus D_T of current time and a reference corpus D_R of a previous time. The degree of difference or burstiness of a phrases g is measured as the z-score using the formula:

$$zscore(g) = \frac{df(g) - \mu(g)}{\sigma(g)}$$

where $df(g)$ is the frequency of g in D_T, and $\mu(g)$ and $\sigma(g)$ are respectively the mean and standard deviation for the frequency of g estimated from D_R. We can easily substitute D_T and D_R with D_A and D_B and apply this technique to our dataset to extract polarized representative phrases, and the z-score calculated can be seen as the extremeness score of the extracted phrases.

One advantage of Shirakawa's technique is that it can detect all frequent phrases based on the set cover problem where the smallest number of phrases overlap all frequent N-grams. For example, given frequent phrase "catch me if you can", sub phrases such as "catch me", "catch me if" and "if you can" are also frequent, but a single phrase "catch me if you can" is finally detected to cover all of them. Another advantage is that it does not require language-dependent techniques. Thus our proposed method keeps language independent nevertheless of incorporating text content analysis.

4   Experimental Result Analysis

We verify our approach through experiments with two questions. First, whether our ideal point estimation correctly divides the users and messages based on their ideal points. Second, whether we can extract meaningful representative phrases that show the polarization, based on the estimated ideal points. The dataset used in the experiment is already described in Data Preparation section. In this section, we will present and discuss our experimental results.

4.1   Convergence of Polarization

We first test whether our method corrected divides users and messages based on their ideal points. Since our Metropolis algorithm is an iterative method, we record the parameter changes in each iteration. We let our algorithm run 300 iterations, which we will show to be more than enough for achieving convergence. The ideal point parameters θ and ϕ in each iteration are shown in Fig. 2, where each line shows changes of an individual θ_i and ϕ_i. The parameters are initialized by drawing from a normal distribution of 0 mean and 1 variance. As the algorithm runs, the discrimination takes effect, and at the end of 50 iteration users and messages start to split. At 100 iterations, we see that there is a clear separation of two groups, especially for the messages. At this point we can consider that the parameters have converged, and the trend continues for the remaining iterations. The split can more clearly seen in Fig. 3, which shows the distribution of θ and ϕ, produced using the expected values of each parameter. Clearly the distributions of both θ and ϕ have two modes. This shows that our algorithm has divided the users and messages into two groups based on the retweeting behavior.

However, does this separation correspond to the political polarization that, as we understand it, has a left wing and a right wing? To verify, we manually check a number of users and message from both groups, labeling them as left and right based on our understanding of left and right wing ideologies. The result is shown in Table 1.

Based on the result, it is clear that user group A and message group A are associated with the left wing ideology, and user group B and message group B are associated with the right wing ideology[4]. We thus conclude from these experimental results that our method has successfully divide the users and messages into left and right wing groups based on their ideal points.

---

[4] Please note that when it is unclear for a user, it does not mean the user has no political standing point. It may only mean that the user did not express his political standing point in his profile description.

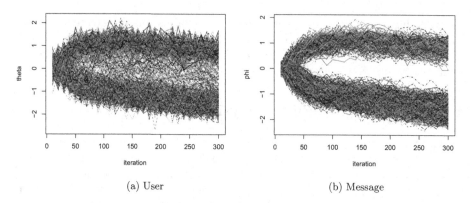

(a) User   (b) Message

Fig. 2. Convergence of user and message ideal points. They show that after some iterations, users and messages are divided into two clearly separated groups.

Table 1. Statistics of left and right manually-assigned labels in the separated groups.

	Total	Left	Right	Unclear	Left ratio	Right ratio
User group A	25	14	0	11	0.56	0.00
Message group A	25	20	0	5	0.80	0.00
User group B	25	0	12	13	0.00	0.48
Message group B	25	0	13	12	0.00	0.52

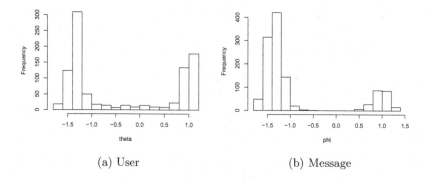

(a) User   (b) Message

Fig. 3. Distribution of user and message ideal points

4.2 Representative Phrases Extraction

Our next goal is to verify whether our method can effectively help human readers understand political polarization. This is done by analyzing outputs of the method and comparing them with our general understanding of political polarization in Japan. The outputs are representative phrases, each of which is associated with an extremeness score indicating its position in polarization.

We visualize this result using word clouds[5], shown in Fig. 4. The font size corresponds to the extremeness score of each phrase. To make the figure legible we only show top 25 words in terms of extremeness score.

(a) Left

(b) Right

Fig. 4. Top phrases extracted from left and right corpora

Based on the result, the most prominent phrases for the left wing ideology include れいわ新選組 (Reiwa Shinsengumi), 肉球新党 (Meatball New Party), 原発 (Nuclear power), 山本太郎 (Yamamoto Taro). Investigation shows that Reiwa Shinsengumi is a left-wing political party founded recently in 2019. Meatball New Party is not a political party but a group of people commonly identify themselves for liking cats. This group supports the ideology of anti-war, anti-nuclear power, and living peacefully with animals. Nuclear power has been an issue that appears often in the attacks of left wing activists. Yamamoto Taro is the leader of Reiwa Shinsengumi. The most prominent phrases for the right wing ideology include 反日 (anti-Japanese), 偏向報道 (biased news report), 日本が大好き (I love Japan), 特亜 (Specific-Asia). Investigation shows that anti-Japanese is a term used by right wing activists as an attack towards left wing activists. While the phrase describes a left-wing characteristic, and may appear confusing as a right wing phrase, we can quickly understand the reference if we look at other prominent terms that include "I love Japan", "I am Japanese", "pride". Biased news report is an issue often brought up by right wing activists who generally consider Japanese news media to be unfair with the current government. Specific-Asia is a reference to China and Korea, often used by right wing activists in discriminative contexts. Other phrases in Fig. 4 are also found to be important issues in their respective ideology.

---

[5] An example package that provides word cloud visualization: https://cran.r-project. org/web/packages/wordcloud/index.html.

Furthermore, we can search representative phrases that contain the word 支持 (supporting), 賛成 (agreement), 反 (anti-), to get a quick grasp on the important policies in left and right wing ideologies. Table 2 lists top-5 phrases found in this way (with 反日 (anti-Japanese) removed, given the reason explained in the previous paragraph). According to the table, the most important policies left wing activists support are overthrow of Abe government, stopping war and discrimination, and stopping nuclear power, while for the right wing activists are supporting Abe government, constitutional amendment, and stopping immigration. These policies are consistent with our knowledge of left and right wing ideologies in Japan. We thus conclude that these representative phrases automatically generated with our method do convey meaningful information for understanding political polarization.

Table 2. Top extracted policy phrases

left	right
反安倍 (Anti-Abe)	安倍政権支持 (Supporting Abe government)
反戦 (Anti-war)	憲法改正賛成 (Supporting constitutional amendment)
反差別 (Anti-discrimination)	外国人参政権反対 (Anti-voting rights for foreigners)
反ファシズム (Anti-fascism)	移民反対 (Anti-immigration)
反核 (Anti-Nuclear power)	改憲賛成 (Agreeing to constitutional amendment)

5   Conclusion

In this paper we propose a solution to automatically generate representative phrases from social media data, which can lead to the understanding of political polarization. Our method is a combination of ideal point estimation and discriminative NLP. Experimental result analysis shows that the generated phrases do help us understand the said phenomenon. Here we would like to briefly address some issues that have not yet taken into consideration. First, in this work we assume a one-axis polarization that provides left-right split. Some have claimed this system is too simple and have proposed multi-axis spectrum, such as a two-axis system that provides liberty–control and irrationalism–rationalism splits. How to handle multi-axis system in ideal point estimation remains an unsolved question. Second, in this paper we address the what and who questions in political polarization, but have yet to address the why question. Without knowing the reason behind individual's split in polarization, we cannot claim we have gained full understanding of the phenomenon. In future works, we plan to investigate political polarization in social media further with the aim to reveal the reasons behind it.

Acknowledgement. This research is partially supported by JST CREST Grant Number JPMJCR21F2.

References

1. Andrieu, C., De Freitas, N., Doucet, A., Jordan, M.I.: An introduction to mcmc for machine learning. Mach. Learn. **50**(1–2), 5–43 (2003)
2. Barberá, P.: Birds of the same feather tweet together: Bayesian ideal point estimation using Twitter data. Polit. Anal. **23**(1), 76–91 (2015)
3. Boutyline, A., Willer, R.: The social structure of political echo chambers: variation in ideological homophily in online networks. Polit. Psychol. **38**(3), 551–569 (2017)
4. Conover, M.D., Ratkiewicz, J., Francisco, M., Gonçalves, B., Menczer, F., Flammini, A.: Political polarization on twitter. In: Fifth International AAAI Conference on Weblogs and Social Media (2011)
5. Imai, K., Lo, J., Olmsted, J.: Fast estimation of ideal points with massive data. Am. Polit. Sci. Rev. **110**(4), 631–656 (2016)
6. Körösényi, A., et al.: Political polarization and its consequences on democratic accountability. Corvinus J. Sociol. Soc. Policy **4**(2), 3–30 (2013)
7. Leiserson, M.: Factions and coalitions in one-party Japan: an interpretation based on the theory of games. Am. Polit. Sci. Rev. **62**(3), 770–787 (1968)
8. Marozzo, F., Bessi, A.: Analyzing polarization of social media users and news sites during political campaigns. Soc. Netw. Anal. Min. **8**(1), 1–13 (2017). https://doi.org/10.1007/s13278-017-0479-5
9. Pennacchiotti, M., Popescu, A.-M.: A machine learning approach to twitter user classification. In: Proceedings of the Fifth International Conference on Weblogs and Social Media, pp. 281–288 (2011)
10. Rao, D., Yarowsky, D., Shreevats, A., Gupta, M.: Classifying latent user attributes in Twitter. In: Proceedings of the 2nd International Workshop on Search and Mining User-generated Contents, pp. 37–44 (2010)
11. Shirakawa, M., Hara, T., Maekawa, T.: Never abandon minorities: Exhaustive extraction of bursty phrases on microblogs using set cover problem. In: Proceedings of the 2017 Conference on Empirical Methods in Natural Language Processing, pp. 2358–2367 (2017)
12. Takikawa, H., Nagayoshi, K.: Political polarization in social media: Analysis of the "twitter political field" in Japan. In: 2017 IEEE International Conference on Big Data (Big Data), pp. 3143–3150. IEEE (2017)
13. Tumasjan, A., Sprenger, T.O., Sandner, P.G., Welpe, I.M.: Predicting elections with Twitter: What 140 characters reveal about political sentiment. In: Proceedings of the Fourth International Conference on Weblogs and Social Media, pp. 178–185 (2010)
14. Wu, S., Hofman, J.M., Mason, W.A., Watts, D.J.: Who says what to whom on Twitter. In: Proceedings of the 20th International World Wide Web Conference, pp. 705–714 (2011)
15. Zhang, Y., Szabo, C., Sheng, Q.Z., Zhang, W.E., Qin, Y.: Identifying domains and concepts in short texts via partial taxonomy and unlabeled data. In: Proceedings of the 29th International Conference on Advanced Information Systems Engineering, pp. 127–143 (2017)

An Improved Convolutional Neural Network Based on Noise Layer

Zhaoyang Wang⬤ and Shaowei Pan$^{(\boxtimes)}$ ⬤

School of Computer Science, Xi'an Shiyou University, Shaanxi 710065, China

Abstract. In order to solve the over-fitting problem in Convolutional Neural Networks (CNN), a new method to improve the performance of CNN with noise layer on the basis of the previous studies has been proposed. This method improves the generalization performance of the CNN model by adding corresponding noise to the feature image obtained after convolution operation. The constructed noise layer can be flexibly embedded in a certain position of the CNN structure, and with each iteration of training, the added noise is also constantly changing, which makes the interference to the CNN model more profound, thus the more essential features of the input image are obtained. The experimental results show that the improved CNN model based on the noise layer has better recognition effect on some test images than the CNN model without any improvement; for different CNN models, the position of the noise layer which can improve the recognition accuracy is different; as the number of layers deepens, to improve the generalization performance of the CNN model, the position of the noise layer needs to be moved back. The improved CNN model based on the noise layer proposed in this paper solves the overfitting problem to a certain extent, and it has a certain reference significance for studying how to improve the generalization performance of CNN.

Keywords: CNN · Noise layer · Feature image · Recognition effect · Generalization performance

1 Introduction

In the current field of computer vision, image classification with CNN is a hot topic [1, 2]. However, CNN has serious over-fitting problems in image classification [3]. In order to solve such problems, many scholars have carried out a lot of exploration, and some people have proposed Dropout and Batch Normalization [4, 5]. Dropout is a regularization method, which zeroes the output of a node in CNN with a certain probability, and the weight of this node will not be updated when the weight is updated in the back propagation. Batch Normalization can normalize the input value of each layer to a normal distribution with a mean of 0 and a variance of 1. These two methods can improve the generalization performance of CNN to a certain extent, but there are still shortcomings.

H. Qiu et al. (Eds.): KSEM 2021, LNAI 12816, pp. 64–74, 2021.
https://doi.org/10.1007/978-3-030-82147-0_6

Therefore, in order to further improve the generalization performance of CNN, this paper proposes a new method to solve the problem of over-fitting based on the previous studies. This method is to add an adaptive noise layer to CNN that can add noises to the characteristic images, so that the CNN model can learn more essential characteristics of the images under interferences of the noise layer. Different from the traditional method of adding noises to the images to be learned, this method will add corresponding noises to the characteristic images obtained from the convolution operation. The noise layer can be added at any position between the convolutional layer and the pooling layer, and it can be used with Dropout and Batch Normalization.

The specific method of adding an adaptive noise layer is to first initialize a tensor and ensure that its dimension is consistent with the dimension of the characteristic image tensor before the convolution operation; Then perform the same convolution operation on the initialized tensor and the characteristic image respectively; Finally, add results of the above two convolution operations together as the input value of the next network layer. Since the convolution kernel is constantly updated with the training of the CNN model, different noise tensors will be get from convolution operation on the tensor obtained by initialization and each updated convolution kernel. Then the purpose of adding noises to the feature images is achieved randomly by adding different noise tensors to the original feature images. In this way, random noises can be added to the input characteristic images and the noise added to the training of each time is different. Hence the CNN model can be trained with more noise interferences, and it can learn more essential characteristics from the input images, achieving the purpose of improving its generalization performance.

Our contributions are as follows:

(1) We design a noise layer which can improve the generalization performance of CNN.
(2) We propose an improved CNN model based on the noise layer.
(3) For the designed noise layer, we give the test results of applying it to different CNNs and different locations in the same CNN.

2   Related Works

It is a common method to improve the robustness of machine learning model by adding noise, many researchers have done a lot of work in this area. A well-known example is Dropout, which randomly turns off a subset of hidden units of neural networks by multiplying noise sampled from a Bernoulli distribution [4, 6]. Since then, some researchers have made improvements to Dropout to improve the generalization performance of the CNN model [7–9].

To improve the generalization performance of the CNN model, a method of injecting noise into the input data has been proposed [10]. Some methods of adding noise to the weights of neural networks have also been applied [11, 12]. A low-overhead and easy-to-implement technique of adding gradient noise has been discussed, and the experimental results show that this technology achieves the surprising effect when training these very deep architectures [13].

In this paper, it is believed that the previous methods of adding noise to the CNN model improve its generalization performance to a certain extent, but ignore the method that can also add noise interference to the feature images obtained by convolution operation. Therefore, this paper proposes a method to add noise to the feature images obtained by convolution operation. The purpose is to increase the interference of noise to the training of the CNN model, so that it can learn more essential features of the input images.

3 Methodology

3.1 CNN

The basic concepts, principles and specific applications of CNN can be found in the references at the end of this paper [1, 14–17], which are not repeated here. And some other excellent papers also provide important references for the proposed method of this paper [18, 19].

3.2 Noise Layer

The purpose of improving the generalization performance of machine learning model can be achieved by adding noises to expand the existing dataset. The method of adding noise layer proposed in this paper is to place a noise layer into CNN, and the position of the noise layer will change with the change of the convolution kernel.

Assuming that the output result of the i-th layer is H_i, the output result of H_i entering the noise layer after convolution operation is H_{i+1}. The working principle of the noise layer proposed in this paper can be expressed by the following formulas:

$$H_{i+1} = H_i \otimes W_{i-1} \tag{1}$$

$$H'_{i+1} = H'_i \otimes W'_{i-1} \tag{2}$$

$$O_{i+1} = H_{i+1} + H'_{i+1} \tag{3}$$

Formula (1) indicates the case that the output of the previous network layer enters the noise layer for convolution operation, where W_{i-1} is the convolution kernel for convolution operation of the input tensor in the noise layer. Formula (2) indicates that a tensor H'_i with the same dimension as H_i is initialized inside the noise layer, and the same convolution operation as (1) is performed on H'_i. W'_{i-1} is the convolution kernel for convolution operation of H'_i, and the dimension of its convolution kernel is the same as W_{i-1}. Formula (3) indicates that the output result O_{i+1} of the noise layer can be obtained by adding H_{i+1} and H'_{i+1}.

3.3   The Improved CNN Model Based on Noise Layer

CNN with the added noise layer has very good compatibility, so it can be used in conjunction with Dropout and Batch Normalization. The improved CNN based on the noise layer is denoted as N-CNN. Figure 1 shows the basic flow of the noise layer processing the input image. As can be seen from Fig. 1, the N-CNN processing flow of the input image is as follows:

(1)   After the input images enter the Layer (Layer refers to the various network layers except the noise layer in N-CNN), it will be calculated and output according to the rules.

(2)   After step (1), the input image enters the noise layer, and its operation in the noise layer is divided into two steps. The first step is shown on the left side of the dotted box in Fig. 1, the corresponding tensor of the input image is obtained according to the conventional convolution operation. In the second step, as shown on the right side of the dotted box in Fig. 1, the noise tensor whose dimension is consistent with the input dimension of the convolution layer is initialized, and then its convolution operation is performed according to the same rules as on the left of the dotted box in Fig. 1.

(3)   The result tensor of the input image on the left side of the dotted box and the result tensor of the noise tensor on the right side of the dotted box obtained by convolution operation are added, and the result is activated by the Relu function, which is the output of the noise layer.

(4)   After the tensor output by the noise layer enters the Layer, the same operations as (1), (2) and (3) above is performed.

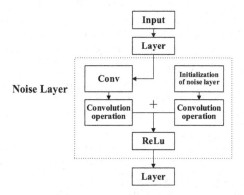

Fig. 1. Processing flow of the noise layer on the input image.

It should be pointed out that there can be multiple layers before and after the noise layer in Fig. 1, and Fig. 1 only shows how the noise layer is connected to other network layers.

4   Experiment and Discussion

4.1   Data Description

The cifar-10 dataset is used in this experiment. The cifar-10 dataset is a classic dataset in the field of image classification, it has a total of 50,000 pictures as the training dataset and 10,000 pictures as the test dataset. The cifar-10 dataset is divided into 10 types of RGB images, each of which contains 6000 images. The 10 types of RGB images are airplanes, cars, birds, cats, deer, dogs, frogs, horses, boats and trucks. Part of the cifar-10 dataset is shown below (Fig. 2).

Fig. 2.   Part of the cifar-10 dataset.

4.2   Implementation Details

In this experiment, the typical CNN VGG-13, VGG-16 and VGG-19 are adopted. They are improved by adding the noise layer mentioned in the previous section, and then their performance is tested with the cifar-10 dataset. After adding the noise layer, the specific network structures of VGG-13, VGG-16 and VGG-19 are shown in Fig. 3. In Fig. 3, the left part is the VGG-13 network structure improved by the noise layer; the middle part is the VGG-16 network structure improved by the noise layer; the right part is the VGG-19 network structure improved by the noise layer. The Dropout and Batch Normalization in Fig. 3 indicate that the layer uses Dropout and Batch Normalization respectively. The processing flow of VGG13 in Fig. 3 for the input images is as follows:

(1)   A 96 * 96 pixel RGB image is input into the VGG-13 network structure.
(2)   After passing through the Con3-64 convolution layer, the input image enters the Noise Layer 1, which is designed in this experiment.
(3)   In the same way, the output image will pass through the Con3-64 convolution layer, Noise Layer 2 and other network layers. Finally, it will enter the fully connected layer of FC-4096 and FC-10 and Softmax function.

The work flow of VGG-16 and VGG-19 improved by the noise layers is the same as that of VGG-13, which will not be repeated here.

It should be pointed out that the noise layers in Fig. 3 are not added to the CNN structure all at once in the experiment, but only added to a certain network layer or several network layers at a time. In order to show the specific positions of the noise layers in the three different network structures of VGG-13, VGG-16 and VGG-19 more clearly, all the noise layers are shown in Fig. 3. In the following experiment, if a noise layer is used, it will be marked; the unused noise layer will not appear in Fig. 3. Then, the cifar-10 dataset is to train and test VGG-13, VGG-16 and VGG-19 with different noise layers in the Python language environment.

VGG-13

- Input(96*96)RGB
- Conv3-64 + Noise Layer1
- Conv3-64
- BatchNormaliaztion + Noise Layer2
- Maxpooling
- Conv3-128 + Noise Layer3
- Conv3-128
- BatchNormaliaztion + Noise Layer4
- Maxpooling
- Conv3-256 + Noise Layer5
- Conv3-256
- Dropout(0.3)
- BatchNormaliaztion
- Maxpooling
- Conv3-512 + Noise Layer9
- Conv3-512 + Noise Layer10
- Dropout(0.5)
- BatchNormaliaztion
- Maxpooling
- Conv3-512 + Noise Layer13
- Conv3-512
- Dropout(0.5)
- BatchNormaliaztion
- Maxpooling
- FC-4096
- Dropout(0.5)
- FC-4096
- FC-10
- softmax

VGG-16

- Input(96*96)RGB
- Conv3-64 + Noise Layer1
- Conv3-64
- BatchNormaliaztion + Noise Layer2
- Maxpooling
- Conv3-128 + Noise Layer3
- Conv3-128
- BatchNormaliaztion + Noise Layer4
- Maxpooling
- Conv3-256 + Noise Layer5
- Conv3-256 + Noise Layer6
- Conv3-256
- Dropout(0.3)
- BatchNormaliaztion + Noise Layer7
- Maxpooling
- Conv3-512 + Noise Layer9
- Conv3-512 + Noise Layer10
- Conv3-512
- Dropout(0.5)
- BatchNormaliaztion + Noise Layer11
- Maxpooling
- Conv3-512 + Noise Layer13
- Conv3-512 + Noise Layer14
- Conv3-512
- Dropout(0.5)
- BatchNormaliaztion
- Maxpooling
- FC-4096
- Dropout(0.5)
- FC-4096
- FC-10
- softmax

VGG-19

- Input(96*96)RGB
- Conv3-64 + Noise Layer1
- Conv3-64
- BatchNormaliaztion + Noise Layer2
- Maxpooling
- Conv3-128 + Noise Layer3
- Conv3-128
- BatchNormaliaztion + Noise Layer4
- Maxpooling
- Conv3-256 + Noise Layer5
- Conv3-256 + Noise Layer6
- Conv3-256 + Noise Layer7
- Conv3-256
- Dropout(0.3)
- BatchNormaliaztion + Noise Layer8
- Maxpooling
- Conv3-512 + Noise Layer9
- Conv3-512 + Noise Layer10
- Conv3-512 + Noise Layer11
- Conv3-512 + Noise Layer12
- Dropout(0.5)
- BatchNormaliaztion
- Maxpooling
- Conv3-512 + Noise Layer13
- Conv3-512 + Noise Layer14
- Conv3-512 + Noise Layer15
- Conv3-512
- Dropout(0.5)
- BatchNormaliaztion
- Maxpooling
- FC-4096
- Dropout(0.5)
- FC-4096
- FC-10
- softmax

VGG-13   **VGG-16**   **VGG-19**

Fig. 3. Structure diagram of different CNNs based on the improved noise layers.

4.3 Results and Discussion

The experiment only verifies the influence of adding one noise layer to VGG-13, VGG-16 and VGG-19 each time and the noise layer position in the network structure on the recognition accuracy of images in the test dataset. The final experimental results are shown in Table 1, 2 and 3. Table 1 shows the experimental results of the improved VGG-13 based on a single noise layer. In Table 1, the first row is the different CNN structures, and the second row is the recognition accuracy on the test dataset of the corresponding CNN structures. In the first row of Table 1, VGG-13 represents the VGG-13 structure without adding any noise layer; NL1 represents VGG-13 with the first noise layer added, and the specific position of the noise layer is shown in Fig. 3. NL2, NL3 and NL13 represent the VGG-13 structure with the second, third and thirteenth noise layers added, respectively. The meaning of each row in Table 2 and Table 3 is the same as that in Table 1, which will not be repeated here.

Table 1. Experimental results of the improved VGG-13 based on a single noise layer.

Network structure	VGG-13	NL1	NL2	NL3	NL4	NL5	NL6	NL9	NL10	NL13
Acuuracy	0.8625	0.8748	0.8739	0.8754	0.8611	0.8509	0.8525	0.8365	0.8576	0.8373

Table 2. Experimental results of the improved VGG-16 based on a single noise layer.

Network structure	VGG-16	NL1	NL2	NL3	NL4	NL5	NL6	NL7	NL9	NL10	NL11	NL13	NL14
Acuuracy	0.8507	0.8579	0.8682	0.8757	0.8516	0.8382	0.8713	0.8299	0.8146	0.8606	0.8620	0.8498	0.8775

Table 3. Experimental results of the improved VGG-19 based on a single noise layer.

Network structure	VGG-19	NL1	NL2	NL3	NL4	NL5	NL6	NL7	NL9	NL10	NL11	NL12	NL13	NL14	NL15
Acuuracy	0.8477	0.8395	0.8520	0.8323	0.8548	0.8475	0.8307	0.8493	0.8123	0.8062	0.8456	0.8530	0.8550	0.8560	0.8629

It can be seen from Table 1 that the recognition accuracy of VGG-13 with Noise Layer 1, Noise Layer 2 or Noise Layer 3 is higher than that of VGG-13 without adding any noise layer. Among them, the VGG-13 with Noise Layer 3 shows the highest recognition accuracy, which is 0.8754. As can be seen from Table 2, after adding any noise layer in Noise Layer 1, Noise Layer 2, Noise Layer 3, Noise Layer 4, Noise Layer 6, Noise Layer 10, Noise Layer 11 and Noise Layer 14, the recognition accuracy of VGG-16 is higher than that of VGG-16 without any noise layer, and the recognition accuracy of VGG-16 with Noise Layer 14 is the highest, which is 0.8775. As can be seen from Table 3, after adding any noise layer in Noise Layer 2, Noise Layer 4, Noise Layer 7, Noise Layer 12, Noise Layer 13, Noise Layer 14 and Noise Layer 15, the recognition accuracy of VGG-19 is higher than that of VGG-19 without any noise layer added, and the recognition accuracy of VGG-19 with Noise Layer 15 is the highest, which is 0.8629.

The Fig. 4, Fig. 5 and Fig. 6 show the variation curves of the recognition accuracy of VGG-13, VGG-16 and VGG-19 with a single noise layer added respectively. In Fig. 4, Fig. 5 and Fig. 6, the abscissa is the different CNN structures, and the ordinate is the recognition accuracy of the corresponding CNN structures. As can be seen from Fig. 4, the recognition accuracy of some VGG-13 network structures with a single noise layer added is indeed improved, and the added noise layers are located in the front of VGG-13 network structure. In Fig. 5, for VGG-16, the recognition accuracy is improved after the addition of a single noise layer. Most of these added noise layers are located in the front of VGG-16 network structure, and a few are located in the middle and back of VGG-16 network structure. In Fig. 6, for VGG-19, most of the noise layers that can improve the recognition accuracy are located in the back, but there are few noise layers in the front and middle of VGG-19 network structure.

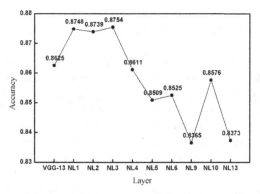

Fig. 4. Variation curve of the recognition accuracy of VGG-13 network structure with a single noise layer.

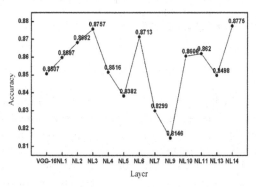

Fig. 5. Variation curve of the recognition accuracy of VGG-16 network structure with a single noise layer.

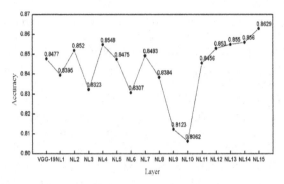

Fig. 6. Variation curve of the recognition accuracy of VGG-19 network structure with a single noise layer.

From the above analysis of the experimental results, we can conclude that adding a single noise layer to CNN can indeed improve its recognition accuracy to a certain extent. To improve the recognition accuracy of the different CNN models, a single noise layer needs to be added at different positions, and with the deepening of the number of the CNN layers, the position of a single noise layer to improve the recognition accuracy gradually moves back. VGG-13, VGG-16 and VGG-19 improved by single noise layer in this paper are all processed by Dropout and Batch Normalization, and achieve higher recognition accuracy. We can also conclude that the method of adding a single noise layer proposed in this paper can be used together with Dropout and Batch Normalization to improve the recognition accuracy of CNN.

When the noise layer is only one layer, the CNN model proposed in this paper is only one more convolutional layer than the traditional CNN model, so compared to the traditional CNN model, its time complexity does not increase significantly. When the number of noise layers increases, the time complexity of the CNN model will gradually increase with the increase of noise layers. Therefore, it is suggested to add a small number of noise layers to the CNN model.

5 Conclusions

(1) Aiming at the insufficient generalization performance of the traditional CNN, an improved CNN model based on noise layer has been proposed in this paper.
(2) From the experiments in this paper, we can conclude that compared with the CNN network structure without adding any noise layer, the recognition accuracy of the CNN network structure with a certain noise layer will indeed be improved; for the different CNN network structures, the position of the noise layer that can improve their recognition accuracy are different, and as the number of layers deepens, the effect of adding noise layer interferences in the shallow area of the CNN network structure is not obvious enough. Therefore, the position of a single noise layer needs to be moved back to improve the generalization performance of the CNN network structure.

(3) The experiment in this paper only verifies the influence on the recognition accuracy of adding a single noise layer to the different CNN structures. However, the influence on the recognition accuracy of adding multiple noise layers to CNN is not given, which needs to be explored in the future research.

Acknowledgement. The research was supported by the National Natural Science Foundation Projects of Shaanxi Provincial (No. 2019JM-174 and 2020JM-534) and the Scientific Research Program Funded by Shaanxi Provincial Education Department (18JS086).

Author Contributions. Shaowei Pan contributed to the writing of the manuscript and the evaluation of the algorithms. Zhaoyang Wang contributed to the formulation of the research question and the design of the experiments and the implementation of the algorithms.

References

1. Lecun, Y., Bottou, L.: Gradient-based learning applied to document recognition. Proc. IEEE **86**(11), 2278–2324 (1998)
2. Krizhevsky, A., Sutskever, I., Hinton, G.E.: ImageNet classification with deep convolutional neural networks. Adv. Neural Inf. Process. Syst. **25**, 1097–1105 (2012)
3. Xu, Q., Zhang, M., Gu, Z., Pan, G.: Overfitting remedy by sparsifying regularization on fully-connected layers of CNNs. Neurocomputing **328**, 69–74 (2019)
4. Srivastava, N., Hinton, G., Krizhevsky, A., Sutskever, I., Salakhutdionv, R.: Dropout: a simple way to prevent neural networks from overfitting. J. Mach. Learn. Res. **15**(1), 1929–1958 (2014)
5. Ioffe, S., Szegedy, C.: Batch normalization: accelerating deep network training by reducing internal covariate shift. In: International Conference on Machine Learning, pp. 448–456. PMLR (2015)
6. Noh, H., You, T., Mun, J., Han, B.: Regularizing deep neural networks by noise: its interpretation and optimization. arXiv preprint arXiv:1710.05179 (2017)
7. Gal, Y., Hron, J., Kendall, A.: Concrete dropout. arXiv preprint arXiv:1705.07832 (2017)
8. Li, Z., Gong, B., Yang, T.: Improved dropout for shallow and deep learning. arXiv preprint arXiv:1602.02220 (2016)
9. Bulò, S.R., Porzi, L., Kontschieder, P.: Dropout distillation. In: International Conference on Machine Learning, pp. 99–107. PMLR (2016)
10. Jin, J., Dundar, A., Culurciello, E.: Robust convolutional neural networks under adversarial noise. arXiv preprint arXiv:1511.06807 (2015)
11. Kingma, D.P., Salimans, T., Welling, M.: Variational dropout and the local reparameterization trick. arXiv preprint arXiv:1506.02557 (2015)
12. Wan, L., Zeiler, M., Zhang, S., Lecun, Y., Fergus, R.: Regularization of neural networks using dropconnect. In: International Conference on Machine Learning, pp. 1058–1066. PMLR (2013)
13. Neelakantan, A., et al.: Adding gradient noise improves learning for very deep networks. arXiv preprint arXiv:1511.06807 (2015)
14. Karahan, S., Yildirum, M.K., Kirtac, K., Rende, F.S.: How image degradations affect deep CNN-based face recognition? In: International Conference of the Biometrics Special Interest Group (BIOSIG), pp. 1–5. IEEE (2016)

15. Zhang, M., Li, W., Du, Q.: Diverse region-based CNN for hyperspectral image classification. IEEE Trans. Image Process. **27**(6), 2623–2624 (2018). A Publication of the IEEE Signal Processing Society

16. Kang, M., Leng, X., Lin, Z., Ji, K.: A modified faster R-CNN based on CFAR algorithm for SAR ship detection. In: International Workshop on Remote Sensing with Intelligent Processing (RSIP), pp. 1–4. IEEE (2017)

17. Dolz, J., Gopinath, K., Yuan, J., Lombaert, H., Desrosiers, C., Ayed, I.B.: HyperDense-Net: a hyper-densely connected CNN for multi-modal image segmentation. IEEE Trans. Med. Imaging **38**(5), 1116–1126 (2018)

18. Chen, M., Zhang, Y., Qiu, M., Guizani, N., Hao, Y.: SPHA: smart personal health advisor based on deep analytics. IEEE Commun. Mag. **56**(3), 164–169 (2018)

19. Gai, K., Qiu, M.: Optimal resource allocation using reinforcement learning for IoT content-centric services. Appl. Soft Comput. **70**, 12–21 (2018)

Syntactic Enhanced Projection Network for Few-Shot Chinese Event Extraction

Linhui Feng, Linbo Qiao$^{(\boxtimes)}$, Yi Han, Zhigang Kan, Yifu Gao, and Dongsheng Li$^{(\boxtimes)}$

National Key Laboratory of Parallel and Distributed Processing, National University of Defense Technology, Changsha, China
{linhuifeng,qiao.linbo,hanyi12,kanzhigang13,gaoyifu,dsli}@nudt.edu.cn

Abstract. Few-shot learning event extraction methods gain more and more attention due to their ability to handle new event types. Current few-shot learning studies mainly focus on English event detection, which suffering from error propagation due to the identify-then-classify paradigm. And these methods could not be applied to Chinese event extraction directly, because they suffer from the Chinese word-trigger mismatch problem. In this work, we explore the Chinese event extraction with limited labeled data and reformulate it as a few-shot sequence tagging task. To this end, we propose a novel and practical few-shot syntactic enhanced projection network (SEPN), which exploits a syntactic learner to not only integrate the semantics of the characters and the words by Graph Convolution Networks, but also make the extracted feature more discriminative through a cross attention mechanism. Differing from prototypical networks which may lead to poor performance due to the prototype of each class could be closely distributed in the embedding space, SEPN learns to project embedding to space where different labels are well-separated. Furthermore, we deliberately construct an adaptive max-margin loss to obtain efficient and robust prototype representation. Numerical experiments conducted on the ACE-2005 dataset demonstrate the efficacy of the proposed few-shot Chinese event extraction.

Keywords: Few-shot learning · Chinese event extraction · Syntactic embedding · Conditional Random Field · Robust loss

1 Introduction

Event extraction (EE) is a task aimed at extracting structural event information from unstructured texts. And it can be decomposed into two sub-tasks, event detection and argument extraction. Event detection (ED) refers to the task of identifying event triggers, which are the words or phrases that express event occurrences. The argument extraction aims to find the attributes and participants of the event trigger. As illustrated in Fig. 1, EE needs to identify the word "受了伤 (injured)" as the event trigger for *Injured* event and classify word "士兵 (soldier)" as it's *Victim* participants. Current works in EE employ traditional

© Springer Nature Switzerland AG 2021
H. Qiu et al. (Eds.): KSEM 2021, LNAI 12816, pp. 75–87, 2021.
https://doi.org/10.1007/978-3-030-82147-0_7

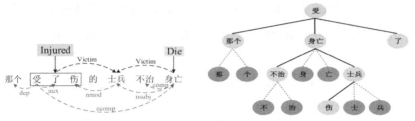

(a) Chinese event extraction example. (b) Dependency tree in the event mention.

Fig. 1. An example of Chinese event extraction, in which "受" and "了" may be ignored in existing English event extraction system, and the dependency tree is used to help the event extraction.

supervised learning based on feature engineering [13] and neural networks [17]. However, the performances of these works heavily depend on a large number of human-annotated training data, which is time-consuming and labor-intensive. When there is no adequate training data, they are inevitably struggling on the EE task and can not quickly generalize to unseen classes.

Intuitively, people can quickly absorb new knowledge and derive a new class by learning from a few examples. This is because the human brain can synthesize and transfer knowledge from different learned classes. The process of learning new types from a small number of samples is usually called few-shot learning (FSL) [18]. The FSL has only been explored in English event detection (FSED) [5,11,12], but not in Chinese event extraction. And it may has the word-trigger mismatch challenges when applied in the Chinese field: 1) A trigger might be composed of multiple words. In Fig. 1 (a) where three words trigger an *Injure* event together. 2) Due to the characteristics of Chinese, a single character or some consequent characters inside a word can be a trigger. For example, the word "击毙 (shoot and kill)" respectively triggers *Attack* and *Die* event. So, it is important to integrate the semantic information between characters and words for Chinese, especially for learning with a small number of samples.

In this work, we explore the Chinese event extraction with limited labeled data and reformulate it as a few-shot sequence tagging task to avoid the error propagation problem caused by the identify-then-classify paradigm. And we propose a few-shot syntactic enhanced projection network (SEPN). Specifically, we use a syntactic learner to get better embedding. It mainly contains two parts, the first part is to learn the dependence between words within a sentence by Graph Convolution Networks (GCNs). The second part is to highlight semantic information of the target class, making the extracted feature more discriminative by a cross attention mechanism. Differing from prototypical networks averaging feature embedding, which may be closely distributed in the embedding space, SEPN learns to project embedding to space where different classes are well-separated.

The main contributions of this paper are as follows:

- We reformulate the Chinese event extraction (CEE) task with limited labeled data as a Few-Shot sequence labeling problem. To our best knowledge, this is a novel research task that has not been explored on CEE.
- A few-shot syntactic enhanced projection network for CEE is proposed, which exploits a syntactic learner to not only integrate the semantics of the characters and the words, but also make the extracted feature more discriminative.
- Considering performance perturbation always hurts learning efficacy, we construct an adaptive max-margin loss to obtain a robust representation.
- Several numerical experiments are conducted on a real-world dataset. The experimental results demonstrate the effectiveness of the proposed method.

The rest of this paper is organized as follows. Section 2 is the related work. In Sect. 3, we presents the problem definition of few-shot Chinese event extraction. Section 4 is the detailed descriptions of our proposed model. Finally, we report experimental results in Sect. 5 before concluding remarks in Sect. 6.

2   Related Work

Traditional event extraction task relies on elaborately-designed features and complicated processing tools [13,14], and these methods are limited to the quality of the designed features. Recently, models based on deep learning have been widely used. To improve the transmission of event information between neural network layers, Chen et al. [3] improved the traditional CNN model and added a dynamic multi-pool mechanism. In response to the problem of error propagation, Nguyen et al. [17] combine BiLSTM and RNN models to simultaneously extract event trigger and event arguments. Considering the deep learning models require a large amount of training data, Chen et al. [2] proposed a method to automatically label large-scale event extraction tasks using external knowledge. And Yang et al. [21] also generate labeled data by BERT pre-training model, and improve the performance of event extraction. In real applications, new event types tend to appear frequently. It is difficult for most traditional models to correctly classify unknown event types with few samples.

In recent years, there have been some researches on the combination of event extraction tasks and few-shot learning. To extract new event types without additional annotations, Huang et al. [8] designed a transfer neural structure to map event mentions and types into the same shared semantic space. But they used extra data generated from abstract meaning representation. Deng et al. [5] regard the event detection task with limited labeled data as a few-shot learning problem. A prototype network based on dynamic memory (DMB-PN) is proposed to learn better event prototypes. However, the identify-then-classify paradigm will cause cascading errors, especially in the few-shot setting. Lai et al. [11,12] focused on the few-shot trigger classification, which split the part of the support set to act as the auxiliary query set to training the model. However, these models treat triggers provided by human annotators which is unrealistic.

3 Problem Definition

FSL decomposes the data set into different meta-tasks, and each task has a support-set S and a query-set Q. In the training stage, N categories are randomly selected from the training set and each category has K samples. Then, a batch of samples from the remaining data of these N categories are extracted as the query set. The goal of the model is to predict the tags of the query set based on the categories that appear in the support set. In the testing stage, the classification can be completed without changing the learning model.

In this paper, we formulate these problems with the K-shot sequence tagging task. Each character is assigned a label, and we utilize the BIO tagging scheme. An event sentence $x = (x_1, x_2, \ldots, x_n)$ is defined as a sequence of characters and a label sequence of the sentence is given as $y = (y_1, y_2, \ldots, y_n)$. For the convenience of building word-character representation, we set $w_i = x_{i:j}$ to indicate the i-th word respectively, which starts with x_i and ends with x_j. $S = \left\{ \left(x^{(i)}, y^{(i)} \right) \right\}_{i=1}^{N \times K}$ is a support set of (x, y) pair which contains N classes and has the BIO label set $L_S = \{l_i\}_{i=1}^{2N+1}$, $2N+1$ means one none type O and N event types with *B-EventType* and *I-EventType*. In particular, considering that the random selection of N types of arguments is of little significance, we select the arguments with the same event type. To simplify the description, we assume N is the same for few-shot argument extraction.

In addition to the support set, the query set Q are remaining samples except for S and subject to prediction based only on the observation in S. Formally, a $\{S, Q\}$ pair forms one few-shot episode and is called an N-way K-shot task.

The sequence labeling task is defined as follows: given a support set S and an input query sequence $x = (x_1, x_2, \ldots, x_n)$, find x's best label sequence y^*:

$$y^* = (y_1^*, y_2^*, \ldots, y_n^*) = \arg\max_y p(y \mid x, S). \tag{1}$$

4 Methodology

Generally, we divide few-shot Chinese event extraction (FSCEE) into two subtasks: few-shot Chinese trigger detection and few-shot Chinese argument classification. Following the widely used CRF framework [7], we propose our SEPN-CRF framework, which includes two parts: the transition module and the emission module (SEPN). Figure 2 gives an illustration of our model. First, we briefly introduce the basic framework of the model.

In order to find the globally optimal label sequence for each input, we use Linear chain Conditional Random Fields (Linear-CRF) which considers both the transition score and the emission score. We apply the SEPN-CRF based on the few-shot setting by modelling the label probability of label y given query sentence x and a K-shot support set S:

$$p(y \mid x, S) = \frac{1}{Z} \exp(\text{TRANS}(y) + \lambda \cdot \text{EMIT}(y, x, S)), \tag{2}$$

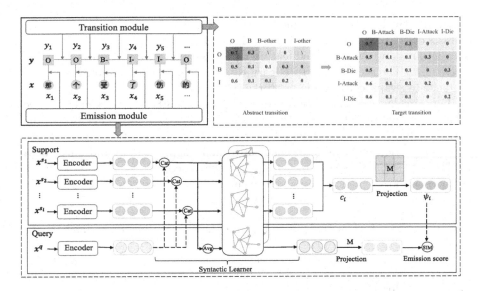

Fig. 2. Overall framework. The key idea is to use the syntactic learner to integrate the semantics of the characters and the words by GCNs, and make the extracted feature more discriminative by a cross attention mechanism.

where Z is a normalizing factor,

$$Z = \sum_{y' \in Y} \exp \left(\text{TRANS} \left(y' \right) + \lambda \cdot \text{EMIT} \left(y', x, S \right) \right), \qquad (3)$$

where Y is the set of all possible sequences. $\text{TRANS}(y)$ gets the Transition score to capture the dependencies between labels and $\text{EMIT}(y, x, S)$ is the Emission score to compute the similarity. Compared to the latest CRF framework in a few-shot setting [7], SEPN-CRF can obtain a more robust sequence representation and a better prototype on the FSCEE task. Next, we will detail each component.

4.1   Syntactic Enhanced Projection Network

SEPN calculates the emission score according to the character's similarity to representations of each label:

$$\text{EMIT}(y, x, S) = \sum_{i=0}^{n} f_e \left(y_i, x, S \right), \qquad (4)$$

and

$$f_e \left(y_i, x, S \right) = \text{SIM}(E(x), \psi_i), \qquad (5)$$

where $f_e \left(y_i, x, S \right)$ mainly contains two parts: feature embedding function E and the prototype reference ψ_i for label y_i. SIM is a similarity function.

Syntactic learner is designed to get better feature embedding. It mainly consists of two parts, the first part is to highlight semantic information of the target class, making the extracted feature more discriminative by a cross attention mechanism. The second part is to learn the dependence between words within a sentence by graph convolution networks (GCNs).

In particular, due to the lack of support data in an FSL scenario, one instance with a representation far from other instances will cause a huge deviation of the corresponding prototype. To get a better character representation $e^c(x_i)$, we use a cross-attention embedding mechanism to make support data and query data in the same semantic space. In detail, we make $|S|$ copies of each sample in the query set. And we retrieve the sentence embedding that combines the semantics of the support sentence x^s and query sentence x^q:

$$[e^c(x_0^s),\dots,e^c(x_i^s),e^c(x_0^q),\dots,e^c(x_i^q)] = \text{BERT}([x^s;x^q]), \qquad (6)$$

where $[;]$ denotes the concatenation operation. Finally, we update the character embedding $[e^c(x_0^s),\dots,e^c(x_i^s)]$ for x^s and average the second half of embedding of $|S|$ copies for x^q.

Then, we fuse character and word information to obtain a sentence representation based on a dependency tree. Given an undirected graph $\mathcal{G} = (\mathcal{V},\mathcal{E})$ as the syntactic parsing tree for word-level sentence, where $\mathcal{V} = \{v_1,v_2,\dots,v_n\}$ is a set of words, and $\mathcal{E} = \{e_1,e_2,\dots,e_m\}$ is a set of syntactic relations. n is the number of words in the sentence and m is the number of dependency relations between words. Following [16], we add all the self-loops to get word itself information. Initially, each node contains distributional information about the word w_i, including word embeddings $e^w(w_i)$ and part-of-speech information (POS) $e^p(w_i)$:

$$h_i^{(0)} = [e^w(w_i);e^p(w_i)]. \qquad (7)$$

In the k-th layer of syntactic graph convolution network module, we can calculate the graph convolution vector $h_i^{(k+1)}$ for word v_i by:

$$h_i^{(k+1)} = \sigma\left(\sum_{u\in\mathcal{N}(i)}\left(W_{K(u,i)}^{(k)}h_u^{(k)} + b_{K(u,i)}^{(k)}\right)\right), \qquad (8)$$

where $K(u,i)$ indicates the type label of the edge (u,i); $W_{K(u,i)}^{(k)}$ and $b_{K(u,i)}^{(k)}$ are the weight matrix and the bias for the certain type label $K(u,i)$, respectively; $\mathcal{N}(i)$ is the set of neighbors of x_i including x_i; σ is the activation function. In this work, we use Stanford Parser [10] to generate the arcs in dependency parsing trees for sentences and the POS for words.

The current representation contains approximately 50 different grammatical relations, which is too high for the parameter number of a single layer of GCN and not compatible with the existing few-shot training data scale. We simplify $K(w_i,w_j)$ as follows:

$$K\left(w_i, w_j\right) = \begin{cases} 2, & (v_i, v_j) \in \mathcal{E}, \\ 0, & i \neq j \ \text{and} \ (v_i, v_j) \notin \mathcal{E}, \\ 1, & i == j. \end{cases} \tag{9}$$

Finally, the feature embedding of the i th character in the sentence x is:

$$E(x_i) = [e^c\left(x_i\right); h_i^{(k+1)}], \tag{10}$$

$h_i^{(k+1)}$ is the GCNs output of the word corresponding to the i-th character.

Projection Network. The prototype of label i can be calculated by averaging the feature embedding of characters corresponding to the label:

$$c_i = \frac{1}{K} \sum_{(x^j, y^j) \in S} E\left(x_i^j\right). \tag{11}$$

In event extraction, the label name has a certain indicating effect on the category representation. Specifically, for the trigger type like *Attack* or the arguments type like *Attack-Time-Arg*, we use BERT to get their label embedding, e.g., the label definition of *Attack-Time-Arg* is *when the attack takes place* which is defined in the DEFT annotation guidelines [15]. We further define the reference vector ψ_i:

$$\psi_i = (1 - \alpha)c_i + \alpha s_i, \tag{12}$$

where α is a balance factor and s_i is the label semantics embedding for each class. We use the projection network (PN) which designs a task-dependent adaptive projector M to embed features to a new classification space. The purpose of the matrix M is to map the feature vector $E(x)$ and reference vector $\psi = [\psi_1, \psi_2, \ldots, \psi_i]$ (each class has a reference vector ψ_i) to a classification space, in which the distance between the feature vector and the reference vector of the corresponding category is as small as possible. M is obtained by calculating the matrix solution of the *linear error nulling* process [22]. Then, the character's emission score can be calculated as:

$$f_e\left(y_i, x, S\right) = \text{SIM}\left(M(E(x)), M\left(\psi_i\right)\right). \tag{13}$$

4.2   Transition Module

Because there is no intersection between the test class and the training class, the class label dependency in the training process cannot be directly transferred to the test class. To transfer the label dependency to the new label, we can learn an abstract label dependency matrix from training category labels like Hou et al. [7]. We set five abstract event tags: *O, B, B-other, I, I-other*. For example, $p(O|B)$ and $p(B|O)$ represent the transition probabilities between a trigger/role tag and O tag. The same, $p(B|B)$ and $p(B\text{-}other|B)$ correspond to the probabilities of transitioning from a trigger/role tag to itself and to a different trigger/role tag respectively. These abstract transitions can be extended to an arbitrary target event/role tag set by evenly distributing the abstract transition probabilities into corresponding target transitions. Finally, given a label sequence y, the transition score of the whole label sequence is approximated by:

$$\text{TRANS}(y) = \sum_{i=1}^{n} f_t (y_{i-1}, y_i) = \sum_{i=1}^{n} p(y_i \mid y_{i-1}). \tag{14}$$

4.3 Training Objectives

In a typical sequential tagging network, the loss function is

$$L_{\text{CRF}} = -\log(p(y \mid x, S)). \tag{15}$$

Due to the corpus is relatively small, task-specific performance is limited and unstable if we adopt the CRF loss objective alone. Considering this, in this work, we deliberately proposed a unified training objective function for FSCEE to make better use of small annotated corpus in the support set.

Max-margin Loss: It is considered that the prototypes should distribute far away from each other. So, we can learn a better representation by maximizing the distance between classes. To alleviate misclassification issues, we design the max-margin loss term:

$$L_{\text{margin}} = \frac{1}{1 + \min\limits_{1 \leq i < j \leq N} \{1 - \cos(\psi_i, \psi_j)\}}. \tag{16}$$

Adaptive Robust Loss: One of the most troublesome issues is that the unstable and performance perturbation in few-shot Chinese event extraction. To achieve stable performance, We adopt adaptive robust loss L_{AR} [1] function.

The final loss is as follows:

$$L = L_{\text{CRF}} + \gamma_1 L_{\text{margin}} + \gamma_2 L_{\text{AR}}, \tag{17}$$

where γ_1 and γ_2 are balance parameters to control the contribution of max-margin regularized term and adaptive robust regularized term, respectively.

5   Experiments

5.1 Datasets and Hyper-Parameters

We use the ACE-2005 Chinese dataset to evaluate all of the models in this study. ACE-2005 is a benchmark dataset in event extraction with 33 positive event subtypes, which are grouped into 8 event types: *Business, Contact, Conflict, Justice, Life, Movement, Personnel, and Transaction.* Although the dataset is divided into training, development, and testing sets by previous work [20], we cannot use these splits directly. Because there is no intersection during training and testing in FSL. In our experiment, the event types used for training data in ACE 2005 involve *Business, Contact, Conflict, Justice*, while the event types for testing and development data are *Life, Movement, Personnel, Transaction*. Notably, when splitting the dataset, the following conditions need to be met: 1) For l_i in the label set L_T, it is guaranteed to appear K times in each episode and we set the number of query sets equal to K. 2) To get enough training data for the 5-shot query setting, we delete the class which contains less than 10 samples.

Table 1. Trigger extraction results on ACE-2005 Chinese dataset.

Model	5-way 5-shot			5-way 1-shot		
	P	R	F1	P	R	F1
Proto	73.74	51.10	58.11	44.33	25.29	30.67
MNet	37.38	23.10	27.57	16.39	11.0	12.21
PHATT	**77.64**	53.55	61.48	43.58	24.79	30.16
CCRF	71.51	56.34	61.69	55.21	35.79	40.78
SEPN (ours)	65.52	**68.63**	**66.38**	**59.08**	**41.79**	**45.89**
-GCN	71.19	61.28	64.77	52.70	35.58	40.08
-Cross	64.05	64.69	63.43	56.55	36.71	41.91
-Loss	71.78	61.16	65.00	57.59	40.24	44.45

* Classification results (e.g. Precision, Recall, F1) are averaged scores (%) from all 100 episodes to counter the randomness from the support set.

We use 5-shot and 1-shot FSL settings to evaluate trigger extraction and arguments extraction, respectively. And we adopt the episode training mechanism. For all models, character embeddings are initialized with Chinese-roberta-wwm-ext [4]. The word embeddings are the average of its constituent character embeddings. Besides, we train the model by ADAM [9] optimizer, and the learning rate in initial is set to 3e-5. We learn the scaling parameter λ during training and set α as 0.3. For the GCNs model, the hidden vector size is 256 with 2 layers. The GCNs dropout is set to 0.2. To find the best combination of γ_1, γ_2, we use $\{0, 0.1, 0.2\}$ for grid search. And we employ dot product as the similarity metric. Besides, we follow the traditional event extraction work [3] to judge the correctness of the predicted event mentions.

5.2 Baselines

Because we are the first to solve this task, there is no previous model that can be compared. But for the comprehensive evaluation of our proposed SEPN-CRF model, we re-implement a range of baselines and state-of-the-art methods and compare our model with them.

– **Proto**: Prototypical network [18] uses dot product as the similarity metric.

- **PHATT**: Hybrid Attention-Based Prototypical Networks [6] utilize dot product as the similarity metric.
- **MNet**: Matching network [19] uses cosine function to measure the similarity.
- **CCRF**: Collapsed CRF model [7] which is the state-of-the-art of the few-shot NER task. We re-implement it in our FSCEE task.

5.3 Results

In this section, we perform our experiments in two steps: 1) compare the different FSL models. 2) evaluate the proposed additional training factors. And the overall quantitative results are shown in Table 1, Table 2 and Table 3.

Table 2. Arguments extraction results on ACE-2005 Chinese dataset.

Model	5-shot			1-shot		
	P	R	F1	P	R	F1
Proto	20.16	22.75	21.24	3.41	**11.70**	5.17
MNet	11.16	2.63	4.17	4.78	2.16	2.86
PHATT	20.71	23.19	21.72	9.18	3.20	4.41
CCRF	27.31	39.60	32.33	3.64	8.90	5.02
SEPN (ours)	**39.38**	39.51	**39.32**	18.41	7.82	**10.31**
-GCN	33.37	**42.00**	35.64	3.74	10.57	5.35
-Cross	34.06	40.80	34.66	4.18	11.08	5.94
-Loss	39.05	38.70	37.99	**18.64**	7.36	9.98

Table 3. The trigger extraction results with different noise rates.

Nose rate	Model	5-way 5-shot			5-way 1-shot		
		P	R	F1	P	R	F1
10%	Proto	65.30	51.13	55.32	**36.71**	21.42	25.58
	Proto+ALL	**77.24**	**51.86**	**60.05**	36.12	**26.50**	**28.83**
	CCRF	**77.41**	51.92	59.99	48.04	32.79	36.25
	CCRF+ALL	72.18	**59.41**	**63.72**	50.9	**34.83**	**38.22**
20%	Proto	70.22	43.29	51.05	32.51	19.14	23.87
	Proto+ALL	**77.82**	47.41	**56.32**	**36.83**	20.12	**24.70**
	CCRF	**74.41**	47.05	55.51	43.49	30.96	33.55
	CCRF+ALL	70.32	**53.09**	**58.93**	46.23	**32.08**	**35.38**

Effectiveness of Event Extraction. There are several observations from Table 1 and Table 2. First, we analyze the results of several baseline models: 1) The prototypical network significantly outperform the matching network with a large performance gap across all the settings, which proves the prototype is very effective to a certain extent; 2) Among the baseline models, we observed that CCRF performed best. Next, we compare our proposed model SEPN-CRF with the baseline models: 1) In trigger extraction, SEPN-CRF outperforms CCRF (4.69% and 5.11% respectively) with absolute gaps. We consider that it is because SEPN integrates the semantic information between characters and words, which is important for Chinese event extraction. 2) Comparing the results of 5-shot and 1-shot, it can be found that the performance of models is almost better when using a larger K, which is consistent with our common sense. 3) Although all models do not perform well in argument extraction, SEPN-CRF still improved the predicted F1 score. Specifically, the result of arguments extraction in the SEPN-CRF model is 7.01% (5-shot) and 5.29% (1-shot) higher than the result of the best model among baseline.

Ablation Study. We also do some experiments to examine the contributions of each component in SEPN model. Each component of our method is removed respectively, including dependency tree (GCN), cross attention (cross), and adaptive max-margin loss (loss). From these ablations (see Table 1 and Table 2), we find that: 1) Without the GCN layer, the F1 score result drop dramatically by 1.61% (5-shot), 5.81% (1-shot) in trigger extraction, and 3.68% (5-shot), 4.96% (1-shot) in arguments extraction, respectively. 2) Without the cross attention mechanism, the F1 score result drop by 2.95% (5-shot), 3.98% (1-shot) in trigger extraction, and 4.66% (5-shot), 4.37% (1-shot) in arguments extraction. We attribute these gaps to our proposed syntactic learner which better captures the semantic information of Chinese. The effect is more obvious in the argument extraction of structured information. 3) To prove the effectiveness of the adaptive max-margin method, we remove the extra loss. The performance of the model drops by 1.38% (5-shot), 1.44% (1-shot) in trigger extraction, and 1.33% (5-shot), 0.33% (1-shot) in arguments extraction.

Robustness Against Noise. In fact, there are some errors in manually marking events. Due to the semantic diversity and the granularity of division in Chinese, this problem will turn more prominent. Hence, we conduct robustness experiments with noisy data. We randomly select a portion of the examples in Q and modify the correct labels in the selection to other arbitrary labels to regenerate the query set. Finally, we perform this verification on the trigger extraction task. According to set the percentage of modified labels, the experimental results are shown in Table 3. It can be seen that the models are greatly affected by noise. Besides, We select the prototype network (Proto) and the Collapsed CRF model (CCRF) to add our syntactic learner and loss function (+ALL). The performance can be improved by about 5% in 5-shot settings after adding our method

(+ALL) with 10% noise. Such evidence further confirms the effectiveness and robustness against noisy data of our methods for few-shot learning.

6   Conclusion

In this work, we explore the Chinese event extraction with limited labeled data and reformulate it as a few-shot sequence tagging task. To this end, we propose a novel and practical few-shot syntactic enhanced projection network (SEPN), which exploits a syntactic learner to not only integrate the semantics of the sentence, but also make the extracted feature more discriminative by a cross attention mechanism. Considering the corpus in this task is limited and the performance perturbation, we propose an adaptive max-margin loss. In future work, we will further improve the transition module under the few-shot setting to better capture the dependency between tags.

Acknowledgment. We would like to thank all reviewers for their insightful comments and suggestions. This work is sponsored in part by the National Key Research & Development Program of China under Grant No. 2018YFB0204300, the Open Fund of Science and Technology on Parallel and Distributed Processing Laboratory (PDL), and the National Natural Science Foundation of China under Grant No. 62025208, 61932001, and 61806216.

References

1. Barron, J.T.: A general and adaptive robust loss function. In: Proceedings of CVPR, pp. 4331–4339 (2019)
2. Chen, Y., Liu, S., Zhang, X., Liu, K., Zhao, J.: Automatically labeled data generation for large scale event extraction. In: Proceedings of ACL, pp. 409–419 (2017)
3. Chen, Y., Xu, L., Liu, K., Zeng, D., Zhao, J.: Event extraction via dynamic multipooling convolutional neural networks. In: Proceedings of ACL, pp. 167–176 (2015)
4. Cui, Y., Che, W., Liu, T., Qin, B., Wang, S., Hu, G.: Revisiting pre-trained models for Chinese natural language processing. In: Proceedings of EMNLP, pp. 657–668 (2020)
5. Deng, S., Zhang, N., Kang, J., Zhang, Y., Zhang, W., Chen, H.: Meta-learning with dynamic-memory-based prototypical network for few-shot event detection. In: Proceedings of WSDM (2019)
6. Gao, T., Han, X., Liu, Z., Sun, M.: Hybrid attention-based prototypical networks for noisy few-shot relation classification. In: Proceedings of the AAAI, vol. 33, pp. 6407–6414 (2019)
7. Hou, Y., et al.: Few-shot slot tagging with collapsed dependency transfer and label-enhanced task-adaptive projection network. In: Proceedings of ACL, pp. 1381–1393 (2020)
8. Huang, L., Ji, H., Cho, K., Dagan, I., Riedel, S., Voss, C.: Zero-shot transfer learning for event extraction. In: Proceedings of ACL, pp. 2160–2170 (2018)
9. Kingma, D., Ba, J.: Adam: A method for stochastic optimization. Computer Science (2014)
10. Klein, D., Manning, C.D.: Accurate unlexicalized parsing. In: Proceedings of ACL, pp. 423–430 (2003)

11. Lai, V.D., Dernoncourt, F., Nguyen, T.H.: Exploiting the matching information in the support set for few shot event classification. In: Lauw, H.W., Wong, R.C.-W., Ntoulas, A., Lim, E.-P., Ng, S.-K., Pan, S.J. (eds.) PAKDD 2020, Part II. LNCS (LNAI), vol. 12085, pp. 233–245. Springer, Cham (2020). https://doi.org/10.1007/978-3-030-47436-2_18
12. Lai, V.D., Nguyen, T.H., Dernoncourt, F.: Extensively matching for few-shot learning event detection. In: Proceedings of the First Joint Workshop on Narrative Understanding, Storylines, and Events, pp. 38–45 (2020)
13. Li, Q., Ji, H., Hong, Y., Li, S.: Constructing information networks using one single model. In: Proceedings of EMNLP, pp. 1846–1851 (2014)
14. Li, Q., Ji, H., Huang, L.: Joint event extraction via structured prediction with global features. In: Proceedings of ACL, pp. 73–82 (2013)
15. Linguistic Data Consortium: DEFT rich ERE annotation guidelines: Events v2.9. Technical report (2015)
16. Liu, X., Luo, Z., Huang, H.: Jointly multiple events extraction via attention-based graph information aggregation. In: Proceedings of EMNLP, pp. 1247–1256 (2018)
17. Nguyen, T.H., Cho, K., Grishman, R.: Joint event extraction via recurrent neural networks. In: Proceedings of NAACL, pp. 300–309 (2016)
18. Snell, J., Swersky, K., Zemel, R.: Prototypical networks for few-shot learning. In: Proceedings of NIPS, pp. 4077–4087 (2017)
19. Vinyals, O., Blundell, C., Lillicrap, T., Wierstra, D., et al.: Matching networks for one shot learning. In: Proceedings of NIPS, pp. 3630–3638 (2016)
20. Xiangyu, X., Tong, Z., Wei, Y., Jinglei, Z., Rui, X., Shikun, Z.: A hybrid character representation for Chinese event detection. In: Proceedings of IJCNN, pp. 1–8. IEEE (2019)
21. Yang, S., Feng, D., Qiao, L., Kan, Z., Li, D.: Exploring pre-trained language models for event extraction and generation. In: Proceedings of ACL, pp. 5284–5294 (2019)
22. Yoon, S.W., Seo, J., Moon, J.: Tapnet: neural network augmented with task-adaptive projection for few-shot learning. In: Proceedings of ICML, pp. 7115–7123. PMLR (2019)

A Framework of Data Augmentation While Active Learning for Chinese Named Entity Recognition

Qingqing Li, Zhen Huang$^{(\boxtimes)}$, Yong Dou, and Ziwen Zhang

National Key Laboratory of Parallel and Distributed Processing,
National University of Defense Technology, Changsha, China
{qingqingli,huangzhen,yongdou,ziwen}@nudt.edu.cn

Abstract. Named entity recognition (NER) is a basic task to construct knowledge graph. The training performance is limited with few labelled data. One solution is active learning, which can achieve ideal results by multi-round sampling strategy to augment unlabelled data. However, there is very few labelled data in the early rounds, which leads to slow improvement on training performance. We thus propose a framework of data augmentation while active learning. To validate our claims, we focus on Chinese NER task and carry out extensive experiments on two public datasets. Experimental results show that our framework is effective for a series of classical query strategy. We can achieve 99% of the best deep model trained on full data using only 22% of the data on Resume, 63% labelled data is reduced as compared to pure active learning (PAL).

Keywords: Active learning · Data augmentation · Chinese NER · Deep learning · Query strategy

1 Introduction

NER has been widely studied because of its potential assistance [11] of many tasks, such as knowledge graph, recommendation system and machine translation. In the past few years, deep neural networks are applied to NER, they have achieved remarkable success [19]. However, the advantage of deep learning will diminish when dealing with small datasets. It is difficult to obtain an effective model while labelled samples involved in training are limited. In the meantime, a large number of manually labelled training corpora requires tedious and expensive work by domain experts. Therefore, to make deep learning easier to adapt to various fields, the number of labelled samples should be reduced while the model's performance is ensured.

Data augmentation is a useful method to achieve good results while labelled data is limited. The application of data augmentation to NER has been proven effective [4,5].

Active learning provides better results under the premise of a small amount of labelled data. It uses some effective strategies to select samples for training.

© Springer Nature Switzerland AG 2021
H. Qiu et al. (Eds.): KSEM 2021, LNAI 12816, pp. 88–100, 2021.
https://doi.org/10.1007/978-3-030-82147-0_8

Unlike the supervised learning setting, in which samples are selected at random, active learning aims to select the most informative samples. The main challenge of active learning is to determine which sample is more informative. The most common method is uncertainty sampling, in which the model preferentially selects the sample with the lowest confidence in its current prediction. There have been some effective works for NER through active learning [12,17]. However, some problems still exist. (1). Active learning relies on multi-round sampling strategy. The labelled samples involved in the early rounds is usually few, which causes the model to improve slowly. (2). A specific query strategy is not very universal. The query strategy needs to be booked in advance and cannot be adjusted during training. Therefore, the selected query strategy may not be useful for every dataset.

Thus, we propose a framework consisting of active learning, data augmentation, and the NER model. Our experiments show that our framework is useful for six common query strategies that we adopt. We can achieve the highest level of performance with fewer labelled samples.

Our contributions are as follows: (1). We propose a framework of data augmentation while active learning for Chinese NER. We use multiple sets of experiments to verify the effectiveness of the framework. (2). We prove the universality of our framework by adopting two typical NER models: CNN-BiLSTM-CRF [2] and Lexicon-lstm [13]. It turns out that the framework is effective on both models. (3). We compare and analyse the effects of different data augmentation methods on a variety of commonly used active learning strategies. The results show that different data augmentation methods have different degrees of improvement compared to PAL. Besides, our framework is effective for a series of classical query strategy.

The remainder of this paper is organized as follows. In Sect. 2 we summarize the related works in Chinese NER, active learning for NER and Data augmentation for NER. Section 3 introduces three parts of our framework in details. Section 4 describes the experimental setting and discusses the empirical results.

2   Related Work

2.1   Chinese Named Entity Recognition

The NER models using deep neural networks can be regarded as a combination of encoder and decoder. They can be roughly divided into two categories according to encoders.

The first category relies on context encoding. Due to the long sequence dependence of CNN, a group of studies [8,10] uses BiLSTM. Chiu et al. [2] have successfully employed CNN to extract character features on CoNLL 2003 datasets.

The second category introduces prior knowledge to the encoder. Zhang et al. [20] proposed a Lattice-lstm structure for Chinese NER, which incorporates lexicon information into character-level lstm. Based on Lattice-lstm, Peng et al. [13] proposed Lexicon-lstm, which simplifies the integration of lexicon information. As for decoders, most competitive approaches relied on CRF.

To verify the universality of the framework, we select two typical models in both categories: CNN-BiLSTM-CRF [2] and Lexicon-lstm [13]. The former model is a classic model, from which many variant models come [6,10]. The latter model is a new model coming from the classical model Lattice-lstm [20]. Besides, NER model with BERT [18] is not considered because of the huge computational overhead.

2.2 Active Learning for NER

As with most tasks, labelling data for NER usually requires manual annotations by human experts, which are costly to acquire at scale. Active learning seeks to ameliorate this problem by strategically choosing which examples to annotate. Three broad criteria [16] is defined to construct query strategy: uncertainty, diversity, and representativeness. We explore the uncertainty sampling strategy, which ranks unlabelled samples in terms of the current model's uncertainty on them, due to its simplicity and popularity. Active learning applied to NER has achieved good results. Shen et al. [17] confirmed that the result of large amounts of data can be achieved by relatively little data in active learning. Unfortunately, the performance on the Chinese datasets has not been further improved. Liu et al. [12] propose a new query strategy Lowest Token Probability (LTP), it has a better performance compared with the traditional query strategies, especially on complex datasets, but they still only focus on some English datasets.

Therefore, we focus on Chinese NER and try to find a suitable method for commonly used query strategies.

2.3 Data Augmentation for NER

Many data augmentation methods have been proposed for NLP tasks. For NER, Kumar et al. [9] relies on large pre-trained models, which is not convenient to train. Dai et al. [4] analyses and compares the effects of some traditional data augmentation methods on NER. Experiments show that simple data augmentation can improve performance even over strong baselines. However, the method in this article only verifies the effect on the English dataset. Besides, some of the methods use external resources, such as synonyms retrieved from WordNet. Ding et al. [5] mainly focus on label linearization. It generates new data through language model autoregression. After that, the NER model is trained with all data. This method performs better without using external resources, but it is much more complex because of the extra language model.

Inspired by these efforts, we believe that data augmentation for NER under active learning is necessary. Because of the fact that there are very little labelled samples involved in the training in the early stage of active learning, the model can only achieve limited results. We adopt two simple but effective data augmentation methods for the framework. The effects of data augmentation methods on multiple active learning strategies are analysed and compared.

3 Framework

The entire framework is shown in Fig. 1. There are three main parts, including data augmentation, active learning and the NER model. The framework is a process of multiple rounds. In each round, the following four steps are executed.

①. In the active learning part, the query strategy $\phi(\mathbf{x}; \theta)$ uses the model generated in the previous round to select samples $\mathbf{x}$, which is a small amount of data from the unlabelled pool U.

②. The labelled samples $\langle \mathbf{x}, label(\mathbf{x}) \rangle$ is passed into the labelled pool L.

③. In the data augmentation part, newly labelled samples are generated. Then data from the labelled pool L and newly generated labelled samples $\mathbf{x}^*$ from every previous generation are combined together.

④. In the NER model part, all labelled data $L \bigcup \langle \mathbf{x}^*, label(\mathbf{x}^*) \rangle$ is used to generate model of this round.

In addition, in the first round of training, the query strategy randomly selects part of the data $\mathbf{x}$ from the unlabelled pool U. Through multiple rounds of active learning, we can get the ideal results with a quite low annotation cost. To describe our framework more clearly, Algorithm 1 illustrates the entire training process. In general, data augmentation is cleverly integrated into our framework. Since query strategy selects the most informative instance, the performance of the model can be further improved after augmenting this part of the data.

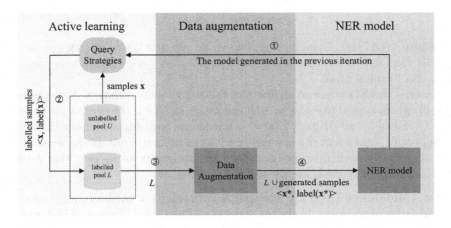

Fig. 1. The overall framework. The framework is made of three parts: data augmentation, active learning and the NER model.

3.1 Active Learning

The main challenge of active learning is to find a query strategy, which is used to select the most valuable samples. We experiment with six common strategies for

Algorithm 1. Data augmentation based active learning framework. It illustrates the entire training process.

Require: L: labelled dataset;
 1: U: unlabelled dataset;
 2: $\phi(\mathbf{x}; \theta)$: query strategy;
 3: B: query batch size;
 4: **while** not reach stop condition **do**
 5:     // Train the model using labelled dataset L
 6:     train $(L \bigcup \langle \mathbf{x}^*, label(\mathbf{x}^*) \rangle))$;
 7:     **for** b=1 to B do **do**
 8:         //select the most informative instance
 9:         $\mathbf{x} = argmax_{\mathbf{x}_i \in U} \phi(\mathbf{x}_i; \theta)$
10:         $\mathbf{x}^* = \mathbf{x}^* + Aug(\mathbf{x})$
11:         $L = L \bigcup \langle \mathbf{x}, label(\mathbf{x}) \rangle$
12:         $U = U - \mathbf{x}$
13:     **end for**
14: **end while**

---

the selection of training samples. We adopt the general pool-based application scenario, where the dataset is divided into unlabelled pool U and labelled pool L. Suppose $\mathbf{x}$ is a representation of an input sequence and n represents the number of tokens in an instance $\mathbf{x}$. Let y^* be the most likely label sequence.

$$y^* = [y_1, \cdots, y_n] \tag{1}$$

Random (RAND). Random sampling is the simplest query strategy possible: we just randomly select samples from the unlabelled pool. In this case, there is no active learning at all.

Besides RAND, we can define the following query strategy formulation: $\phi(\mathbf{x}; \theta)$, which is used to evaluate each instance $\mathbf{x}$ in U, θ is the current parameter set. An useful query strategy $\phi(\mathbf{x}; \theta)$ can evaluate each instance from the unlabelled pool U and select the instance $\mathbf{x}$ with the highest score. In the remainder of this section, we will describe commonly used query strategies $\phi(\mathbf{x}; \theta)$ in detail. The meanings of symbols are the same as above.

Least Confidence (LC) [3]. The samples are sorted in the ascending order of probabilities of the most likely tag sequence. Then the LC score of instance $\mathbf{x}$ can be formulated as follows:

$$\phi(\mathbf{x})^{LC} = 1 - P(y^* \mid \mathbf{x}; \theta) \tag{2}$$

Bayesian Active Learning by Disagreement (BALD) [7]. This strategy combines the ideas of voting with uncertainty of data. It uses Monte Carlo dropout to generate multiple similar models as voting members. Denote $P^1, \cdots, P^m, \cdots, P^M$ as models sampled from the posterior. P^m represents the m-th model. Then, one measure of our uncertainty on the i-th word is $BALD_i$, the fraction of models which disagreed with the most popular choice:

$$BALD_i = 1 - \frac{max_y \mid \{m : argmax_{y'} \, P^m[y^i = y'] = y\} \mid}{M} \tag{3}$$

where $|\cdot|$ denotes cardinality of a set. Then the BALD score can be formulated as follows:

$$\phi(\mathbf{x})^{BALD} = \frac{1}{n}\sum_{j=1}^{n} BALD_j \tag{4}$$

We use $\frac{1}{n}\sum_{j=1}^{n}$ to normalize, which helps to reduce the advantage of long instance.

Maximum Token Entropy (MTE) [1]. The MTE strategy evaluates the uncertainty of a token by entropy. The closer the distribution of marginal probability to uniform, the larger the entropy:

$$\phi(\mathbf{x})^{MTE} = -\sum_{i=1}^{N} p(y^* \mid \mathbf{x}; \theta) \cdot logp(y^* \mid \mathbf{x}; \theta) \tag{5}$$

where N represents the number of classes.

Minimum Token Probability (MTP) [14]. This strategy selects the most informative tokens, regardless of the assignment performed by CRF. This strategy greedily samples the tokens whose highest probability among the labels is lowest.

$$\phi(\mathbf{x})^{MTP} = 1 - min_i max_j h^i(y_i = j \mid \mathbf{x}; \theta) \tag{6}$$

$h^i(y_i = j \mid \mathbf{x}; \theta)$ is the probability that j is the label at position i in the sequences.

Least Token Probability (LTP) [12]. This strategy believes that the sequence selected by the CRF decoder is valuable. It is hoped that each token in the sequence has a high predicted label probability.

$$\phi(\mathbf{x})^{LTP} = 1 - min_{y_i^* \in y^*} h^i(y_i^* \mid \mathbf{x}; \theta) \tag{7}$$

This strategy selects the tokens whose probability under y^* are lowest.

3.2 Data Augmentation

We believe that more augmentation methods can be effective in this framework. But in order to be as simple and effective as possible, we use ERA and TRA [4] . Some adjustments have been made to fit our scene. Here is an example of instances generated by the two methods in Table 1. B, M and E represent the head, middle and end positions of an entity.

ERA (Entity Replacement Augmentation). For the most informative instance $\mathbf{x}$, we enumerate each type of entity. Then we randomly replace entities in the same category. Instances containing labelled entities will generate new instances. We merge the new instances with $\mathbf{x}$ into $\mathbf{x}^*$, which will participate in the next round of training.

Table 1. An example of original instance and augmented instances generated by different augmentation methods. Different colour represents a different entity category.

	instance
original	我 最 近 又 买 了 一 个 富 立 康 的 健 康 有 氧 健 康 机 ， 花 三 千 八 。 O O O O O O O O B M E O O O B M M M E O O B M E O
ERA	我 最 近 又 买 了 一 个 格 力 　 的 健 康 洗 碗 机 　 ， 花 二 千 一 。 O O O O O O O O B E 　 O O O B M E 　 O O B M E O
TRA	我 最 近 又 买 了 一 个 富 立 扬 的 健 康 太 南 健 康 车 ， 花 十 百 盘 。 O O O O O O O O B M E O O O B M M M E O O B M E O

TRA (Token Replacement Augmentation). This method is very similar to ERA, except that it considers replacing tokens instead of entities when generating new instances. In this case, tokens in the same category will swap places to create new entities. This method has more randomness.

3.3   NER Model

We use two different models as the NER model in the experiment.

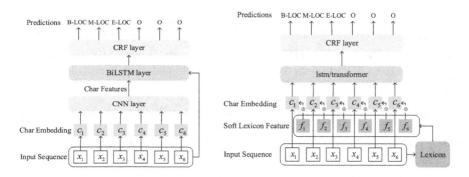

Fig. 2. CNN-BiLSTM-CRF   **Fig. 3.** Lexicon-lstm

CNN-BiLSTM-CRF. As shown in Fig. 2, CNN-BiLSTM-CRF [2] is a simple model that incorporates CNN to extract features of characters, and uses BiLSTM to extract features of sequence.

Lexicon-lstm. The architecture of Lexicon-lstm [13] comprises of an input layer, a character representation layer, an lstm or transformer layer and finally a conditional random field (CRF) layer, which simulates label dependencies in the output. As shown in Fig. 3, lexicon information is integrated into char embedding.

4 Experiments

4.1 Experiment Setting

Evaluation Metric and Datasets. To give an overall evaluation of models, we apply micro-F1 (F1) as our evaluation metrics in the experiments. We evaluated the framework on two general Chinese datasets. Weibo was built based on text in Chinese social media Sina Weibo [15]. Resume was annotated by Zhang et al. [20]. Their statistics are listed in Table 2. All corpora are formatted as "BMESO" sequence representation.

Table 2. Details of datasets

Dataset	Type	Train	Dev	Test
Weibo	Sentence	1.4k	0.3k	0.3k
	Token	73.5k	14.4k	14.8k
Resume	Sentence	3.8k	0.5k	0.5k
	Token	124.1k	13.9k	15.1k

Baseline. To show the overall performance of our framework. We compare with six effective query strategies. Each query strategy under PAL is our baseline.

Implementation Details. To make this work self-completed, we concisely illustrate some primary settings of this work. We combined the training set and the evaluation set as data pool, and we randomly selected 1% of the whole data as the initial training set L_0. Because the model's performance does not improve significantly after 4 epochs, we fixed the number of epochs in each round of active learning to 4. For two different models, we explain the main settings separately.

For CNN-BiLSTM-CRF, the batch size is set to 16, the hidden size is set to 200, and the learning rate is 0.015. We set the dropout to 0.5 to prevent overmatching.

For Lexicon-lstm, we followed most implementation protocols of Lexicon-lstm [13] , including character and word embedding sizes, dropout, embedding initialization, and the number of LSTM layer. We did not use bert and bichar. The hidden size was set to 100 for Weibo and 300 for Resume. The learning rate was set to 0.005 for Weibo and 0.0015 for Resume. We set dropout to 0.1 for Weibo and 0.5 for Resume. When adopting our framework, we set the number of rounds with augmentation to 30.

We empirically compare six common selection strategies, including the uniformly random baseline (Random). We evaluate each selection strategy by constructing learning curves that plot the overall F1. To prevent the contingency of the experiment, we have done 10 experiments for each selection strategy using different random seeds. All results are averaged across these experiments.

4.2 Results

Overall Performance. The performance of the proposed framework is shown in Table 3. We compare with six different strategies under PAL. Almost all results of both models with the framework are better than PAL. Impressively, our framework can achieve 99% of the best deep model trained on full data with only 22% of the data on Resume, 63% labelled data is reduced compared to PAL. In general, our framework can perform better with less label effort.

Table 3. Overall performance of the proposed framework. Here list the percentages of annotations when 99% of the best original model trained on full data are achieved. (CBC denotes CNN-BiLSTM-CRF, LL denotes Lexicon-lstm, CCL denotes CNN-CNN-LSTM.)

Query strategy	Model	Resume		Weibo	
		Percents(%)	F1	Percents(%)	F1
RAND	CBC	44.0	92.60	60.0	47.06
	CBC (+ERA)	**26.0**	92.60	**55.0**	47.06
	LL	**79.0**	94.17	-	58.60
	LL (+ERA)	80.0	94.17	**79.0**	58.60
LC	CBC	48.0	92.60	59.0	47.06
	CBC (+ERA)	**30.0**	92.60	**51.0**	47.06
	LL	84.0	94.17	-	58.60
	LL (+ERA)	**49.0**	94.17	-	58.60
MTE	CBC	46.0	92.60	56.0	47.06
	CBC (+ERA)	**27.0**	92.60	**55.0**	47.06
	LL	77.0	94.17	-	58.60
	LL (+ERA)	**28.0**	94.17	**87.0**	58.60
MTP	CBC	48.0	92.60	56.0	47.06
	CBC (+ERA)	**24.0**	92.60	**49.0**	47.06
	LL	76.0	94.17	-	58.60
	LL (+ERA)	**25.0**	94.17	-	58.60
LTP	CBC	46.0	92.60	57.0	47.06
	CBC (+ERA)	**33.0**	92.60	**52.0**	47.06
	LL	83.0	94.17	-	58.60
	LL (+ERA)	**48.0**	94.17	**90.0**	58.60
BALD	CBC	46.0	92.60	54.0	47.06
	CBC (+ERA)	**29.0**	92.60	**43.0**	47.06
	LL	85.0	94.17	-	58.60
	LL (+ERA)	**22.0**	94.17	**90.0**	58.60

Compare Data Augmentation Methods. Figure 4 shows the results on two datasets, including the result under PAL and our framework. The query strategy shown here is LTP. This strategy has been proven to be very effective recently. We have reproduced this work [12] on two models. We use two different augmentation methods: TRA and ERA. On Resume, both of the methods are effective. On Weibo, TRA is only valid in the early stage. Overall, The ERA method has greater advantages than TRA. We believe that the former produces higher quality samples than the latter.

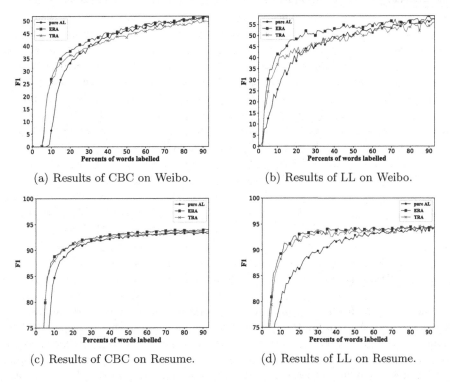

(a) Results of CBC on Weibo.

(b) Results of LL on Weibo.

(c) Results of CBC on Resume.

(d) Results of LL on Resume.

Fig. 4. Results of using different data augmentation methods. The query strategy is LTP.

Compare Different Query Strategies. Table 4 lists the results of using different query strategies on Resume. From the overview, our proposed framework with ERA method achieves better performance for all strategies when comparing to PAL, especially in the early stage. We believe that a certain amount of noise is introduced to the model so that the augmentation effect of the ERA method is not obvious in the later stage of training. For CNN-BiLSTM-CRF, RAND becomes the best strategy with ERA. For Lexicon-lstm, MTE has advantages over other query strategies, but with the help of ERA, MTP catches up.

Table 4. Results of using different query strategies on Resume. (% denotes the percent of labelled data involved in training. PAL denotes the result under pure active learning.)

Resume									
Model	Query strategy	%	PAL	+ERA	Model	Query strategy	%	PAL	+ERA
CBC	RAND	10	83.03	**89.40**	LL	RAND	10	78.07	83.16
		50	92.63	**93.65**			50	92.22	93.39
		90	93.52	**94.05**			90	93.91	94.24
	LC	10	81.64	88.14		LC	10	78.76	88.74
		50	**92.66**	93.43			50	92.02	94.21
		90	93.36	94.00			90	94.06	94.33
	MTE	10	82.23	88.76		MTE	10	79.36	88.79
		50	92.62	93.64			50	**92.36**	94.23
		90	**93.64**	93.95			90	**94.28**	94.95
	MTP	10	82.16	88.33		MTP	10	78.87	**89.60**
		50	92.53	93.37			50	91.85	94.18
		90	93.43	93.82			90	94.04	**95.24**
	BALD	10	80.73	88.83		BALD	10	**80.00**	87.12
		50	92.51	93.18			50	91.87	94.16
		90	93.47	93.80			90	93.78	94.07
	LTP	10	**83.26**	87.95		LTP	10	78.75	88.68
		50	92.60	93.24			50	92.01	93.71
		90	93.40	93.83			90	94.35	94.20

5   Conclusion

In this study, our framework improve the performance of active learning on Chinese datasets. We extend PAL with data augmentation on two typical NER models. Then we explore a variety of different query strategies. Experiments show that our framework is effective in a series of classical query strategy. The results of experiments prove that our framework can use existing labelled data more effectively. Unfortunately, in this article, we only use two simple data augmentation methods to verify the effectiveness of the framework. In addition, since each round of active learning requires query process and data augmentation, the training period takes too long. In future work, we will optimize this framework by introducing augmentation methods with external knowledge and improving the speed of training.

Acknowledgment. This work is supported by the National Key R&D Program of China under Grants (No. 2018YFB0204300).

References

1. Cai, T., Ma, Z., Zheng, H., Zhou, Y.: NE–LP: normalized entropy- and loss prediction-based sampling for active learning in Chinese word segmentation on EHRs. Neural Comput. Appl., 1–15 (2021). https://doi.org/10.1007/s00521-021-05896-w

2. Chiu, J.P., Nichols, E.: Named entity recognition with bidirectional LSTM-CNNS. Trans. Assoc. Comput. Linguist. **4**, 357–370 (2016)

3. Culotta, A., McCallum, A.: Reducing labeling effort for structured prediction tasks, AAAI, vol. 5, pp. 746–751 (2005)

4. Dai, X., Adel, H.: An analysis of simple data augmentation for named entity recognition. In: Proceedings of the 28th International Conference on Computational Linguistics, pp. 3861–3867 (2020)

5. Ding, B., et al.: Daga: data augmentation with a generation approach for low-resource tagging tasks (2020)

6. Dong, C., Zhang, J., Zong, C., Hattori, M., Di, H.: Character-based LSTM-CRF with radical-level features for Chinese named entity recognition. In: Lin, C.-Y., Xue, N., Zhao, D., Huang, X., Feng, Y. (eds.) ICCPOL/NLPCC -2016. LNCS (LNAI), vol. 10102, pp. 239–250. Springer, Cham (2016). https://doi.org/10.1007/978-3-319-50496-4_20

7. Gal, Y., Islam, R., Ghahramani, Z.: Deep Bayesian active learning with image data. In: International Conference on Machine Learning, pp. 1183–1192. PMLR (2017)

8. Huang, Z., Xu, W., Yu, K.: Bidirectional LSTM-CRF models for sequence tagging

9. Kumar, V., Choudhary, A., Cho, E.: Data augmentation using pre-trained transformer models. In: Proceedings of the 2nd Workshop on Life-long Learning for Spoken Language Systems, pp. 18–26 (2020)

10. Lample, G., Ballesteros, M., Subramanian, S., Kawakami, K., Dyer, C.: Neural architectures for named entity recognition. In: Proceedings of NAACL-HLT, pp. 260–270 (2016)

11. Lin, Y., Liu, Z., Sun, M., Liu, Y., Zhu, X.: Learning entity and relation embeddings for knowledge graph completion. In: Proceedings of the AAAI Conference on Artificial Intelligence, vol. 29 (2015)

12. Liu, M., Tu, Z., Wang, Z., Xu, X.: LTP: A new active learning strategy for BERT-CRF based named entity recognition. arXiv preprint arXiv:2001.02524 (2020)

13. Ma, R., Peng, M., Zhang, Q., Wei, Z., Huang, X.J.: Simplify the usage of lexicon in Chinese NER. In: Proceedings of the 58th Annual Meeting of the Association for Computational Linguistics, pp. 5951–5960 (2020)

14. Marcheggiani, D., Artieres, T.: An experimental comparison of active learning strategies for partially labeled sequences. In: Proceedings of the 2014 Conference on Empirical Methods in Natural Language Processing (EMNLP), pp. 898–906 (2014)

15. Peng, N., Dredze, M.: Named entity recognition for Chinese social media with jointly trained embeddings. In: Proceedings of the 2015 Conference on Empirical Methods in Natural Language Processing, pp. 548–554 (2015)

16. Shen, D., Zhang, J., Su, J., Zhou, G., Tan, C.L.: Multi-criteria-based active learning for named entity recognition. In: Proceedings of the 42nd Annual Meeting of the Association for Computational Linguistics (ACL-2004), pp. 589–596 (2004)

17. Shen, Y., Yun, H., Lipton, Z.C., Kronrod, Y., Anandkumar, A.: Deep active learning for named entity recognition. In: Proceedings of the 2nd Workshop on Representation Learning for NLP, pp. 252–256 (2017)

18. Tenney, I., Das, D., Pavlick, E.: BERT rediscovers the classical NLP pipeline. In: Proceedings of the 57th Annual Meeting of the Association for Computational Linguistics, pp. 4593–4601 (2019)
19. Yang, Z., Salakhutdinov, R., Cohen, W.: Multi-task cross-lingual sequence tagging from scratch. arXiv preprint arXiv:1603.06270 (2016)
20. Zhang, Y., Yang, J.: Chinese NER using lattice LSTM. In: Proceedings of the 56th Annual Meeting of the Association for Computational Linguistics (Volume 1: Long Papers), pp. 1554–1564 (2018)

Traffic Route Planning in Partially Observable Environment Using Actions Group Representation

Minzhong Luo[1,2]([⊠]) and Shan Yu[3]

[1] State Key Laboratory of Information Security, Institute of Information Engineering, Chinese Academy of Sciences, Guangzhou, China
luominzhong@iie.ac.cn
[2] School of Cyber Security, University of Chinese Academy of Sciences, Beijing, China
[3] Brainnetome Center and National Laboratory of Pattern Recognition, Institute of Automation, Chinese Academy of Sciences, Beijing, China
shan.yu@nlpr.ia.ac.cn

Abstract. We investigate the problem of optimal route planning formulized as Partially Observable Markov Decision Process (POMDP) [1]: Given a partially traffic-aware road network, we aim to find a route for agent vehicle such that the global travel time cost is minimized. In this paper, we show that the theory of group representation with its ability to make mechanism of $\mathcal{A} \times \mathcal{S}$ (actions acting on states) computable efficiently, which is able to provide significant advantages in multi-step planning with information partially observable. Using the action group Representation, we build a more "visionary" system. Extensive experiments offer insight into the efficiency of proposed algorithms.

Keywords: POMDP · Group representation · Multi-step reasoning

1 Introduction

With the continued development of GPS-enabled devices and online map-based services, route planning has becomes an increasing challenge in recent years (e.g., [30,31,41]), because of many potential benefits: reducing traffic accidents, congestion and violation problems. However, automatic route planning also presents new challenges [2,37]. Traffic route planning is a problem contained the environment unpredictability with uncertainty of traffic lights at remote intersections and other road users behavior. A fascinating question is whether efficient algorithm can plan a route based on given limited knowledge to deduce situation after multiple steps.

There are a variety of diverse methods proposed in literature for route planning to perform a driving scheme with minimized travel cost by treating the problem as a Markov Decision Process (MDP) model [4,28]. Incremental reinforcement learning based algorithms and sampling based route planning methods such as Monte-Carlo Policy Gradient (MCPG) [16] have been proposed for

© Springer Nature Switzerland AG 2021
H. Qiu et al. (Eds.): KSEM 2021, LNAI 12816, pp. 101–113, 2021.
https://doi.org/10.1007/978-3-030-82147-0_9

planning minimized time consuming routes. Even though algorithms incorporating deep reinforcement learning have been proposed [40], system employed environment-overfitted policy $\pi(a^t|s^t)$ can give locally optimal decision. In addition, excessive space complexity of the model and dependence on large-scale training data are common problems of the previous methods [27] (Fig. 1).

In many existing methods [17,18], deep neural networks are utilized by the policy $\pi(a^t|s^t)$ or the interpretation $T(s^{t+1}|a^t, s^t)$ (the transition: action a^t made under state s^t [33]) to fit the probability distribution of environment. A natural idea is whether we can perform simulation to the mechanisms of environment by a homomorphic linear space(which means perform $a^t \otimes s^t \mapsto s^{t+1}$ by a homomorphic map [9] $\rho(\cdot)$ with $\rho(a^t \otimes s^t) = \rho(a^t)\rho(s^t) = \rho(s^{t+1})$).

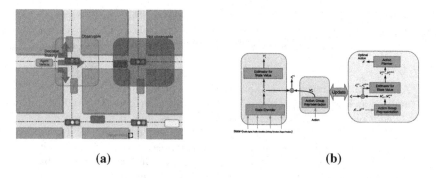

(a)   **(b)**

Fig. 1. (a) The traffic optimal route planning problem formulized as POMDP [1]; (b) The architecture of the planning framework;

In this paper, inspired by the idea above, the **group representation** are employed to learn the homomorphism of the transition mechanisms $\mathcal{A} \times \mathcal{S}$(the actions set act on the states set) of environment. Then the actions $\mathcal{A}$ can be considered as a group and the mechanism $\mathcal{A} \times \mathcal{S} \to \mathcal{S}$ can be considered as "Group Acts on Set" [9]. The actions group $\mathcal{A}$ and states set $\mathcal{S}$ are encoded by homomorphic maps respectively with representation map $\rho : \mathcal{A} \to \mathbb{R}^{N \times N}$ and encoded map $e : \mathcal{S} \to \mathbb{R}^N$.

The main advantage of this method is combining group representation into estimating the state of the environment affected by different decision-making actions with uncertain knowledge. The representations $\{\rho(a) = M_a \in \mathbb{R}^{N \times N}\}$ for actions and encoded linear space $\{e(s) = x_s \in \mathbb{R}^N\}$ for states are generated in the interaction between agent vehicle and environment. Generated representations in linear space is applicated to choose the best vehicle steering to execute based on Partially Observable Markov Decision Process (POMDP) [1] evaluating environment state $x_s^{t+k+1} = M_a^{t+k} \odot \cdots \odot M_a^t \odot x_s^t$ after several steps.

Consequently, given environment actions and states queries (a^t, s^t, s^{t+1}) simultaneously, the system can learn the homomorphic map $\rho(\cdot)$ and $e(\cdot)$ with $a^t \otimes s^t \mapsto \rho(a^t) \odot e(s^t) = e(s^{t+1})$ and use the learned representations to find the optimal $\hat{a}^t = \arg\max_{a^t} \mathbb{E}_\pi [\sum_t^{t+k} \gamma^k r(s^t, a^t)]$ by evaluating environment state representation $x_s^{t+1} \cdots x_s^{t+k+1}$.

The challenges of extending the group representation to solve POMDP problems are: (i) How to sample the states in a trial to find homomorphic map $\rho(\cdot)$ by given the imprecise probabilities from partially observable environment? (ii) How to ensure the convergence of the homomorphic map $\rho(\cdot)$ working for POMDP? These can be addressed by making the following innovative contributions:

- An asynchronous learning algorithm for POMDP problems based on learning homomorphic map $\rho(\cdot)$ employing neural network optimization in terms of states transition constraints is proposed.
- A model $\hat{T}(s^{t+1}|a^t, s^t)$ of the transition dynamics [26] is constructed by homomorphic map $\rho(\cdot)$ learned, which makes multi-step reasoning ability enhanced from an algebraic perspective.
- We empirically compare the proposed methods choosing different hyperparameters in route planning experiments. Which shows there's significant difference between methods with different hyperparameters, theoretical analysis is also given.

2   Related Works

Most important related works mainly involves following three aspects:

- **POMDP-based Reinforcement Learning:** A recent line of work augments POMDP problems using reinforcement learning [14,20], and specified in different forms: function approximator to environment like Gaussian process [10], policies searching with back-propagation by deep learning [24,34], building embodied agents learn control from additional information like linguistic commands or vision [42], etc. In contrast, our focus is on learning an algebraic homomorphic model.
- **Group Representation Learning:** A line of work has extended equivariance to continuous symmetry groups representation learning, most focus on the architectures for SE(2) [39], SE(3) [15], and noncommutative Lie groups [35]. Some have applied group representation to knowledge graph embedding [5,25]. However, the actions group in this work is a noncommutative finite generated group.
- **Traffic Route Planning:** Existing studies of traffic-based global optimization problems can be regarded as the flow assignment problem rather than real-time planning [6,11], where the routes are pre-defined and they search for optimal route to current local traffic conditions [3,13,36].

3   Prelimilaries and Problem Statement

3.1   Generated Group and Group Representation

We describe some group-theoretic definitions used, for more details please see [12] (Table 1).

Table 1. Our method compared to existing available methods for POMDP problem.

Methods	Advantages	Disadvantages	Model features
Q-Learning [38]	Offline learning	Local optimum	Q-table
DQN [32]	Fitting Q-table	Overfitting	Q-Network
MCPG [16]	Efficient in high dimensional space	Local optimum	Monte-Carlo tree
Ours	Efficient in multi-step reasoning	Asynchronous training	Group representation

Definition 1 (Group Homomorphism). *A group homomorphism from $(G, \cdot)$ to $(H, \times)$ is a function $\rho : G \longrightarrow H$ such that for all $g_1, g_2 \in G, \rho(g_1 \cdot g_2) = \rho(g_1) \times \rho(g_2)$. A bijective homomorphism is called an isomorphism.*

Definition 2 (Finite Generated Group). *Let G be a group. A sequence $(g_1, \ldots, g_k)$ of k group elements is said to be cube finite generating set of G if $k < \infty$ and:*

$$G = \{g_1^{\epsilon_1} g_2^{\epsilon_2} \cdots g_k^{\epsilon_k} \mid \epsilon_i \in \mathbb{N}^+\} \tag{1}$$

Definition 3 (Group Representation). *For a group G, an $n-$dimensional (real) group representation $\rho : G \rightarrow \mathbb{R}^{n \times n}$ is a mapping from each element $\alpha \in G$ to an $n \times n$-dimensional matrix $\rho(\alpha)$, such that for any two elements $\alpha, \beta \in G$, we have $\rho(\alpha)\rho(\beta) = \rho(\alpha\beta)$.*

Let G be a group and $\rho : G \rightarrow \mathbb{R}^{n \times n}$ be a representation of G. Then ρ defines a group action on $\mathbb{R}^n$: given a vector $\boldsymbol{u} \in \mathbb{R}^n$ and a group element $\alpha \in G$, then $\alpha \odot_\rho \boldsymbol{u} := \rho(\alpha)\boldsymbol{u}$ (used in computing how actions act on states).

3.2   Reinforcement Learning on POMDP

MDP is defined by tuple $(\mathcal{S}, \mathcal{A}, T, r, \gamma)$, where $\mathcal{S}$ and $\mathcal{A}$ are the state and action spaces. The POMDP focuses on choosing optimal actions in partially observable stochastic domains, where MDPs with uncertain states and limited knowledge is considered.

At each step t, the agent only has a partial observation s^t. Let $\gamma \in (0, 1)$ be a discount factor. $T(s^{t+1} | a^t, s^t)$ is the transition of state, and the reward function is $r(s^t, a^t)$. The goal of reinforcement learning is optimal policy π^* maximizes the expected return (sum of discounted rewards): $\pi^* = \arg\max_\pi \mathbb{E}_\pi [\sum_{t=0}^\infty \gamma^t r(s^t, a^t)]$, where the $s^{t+1} \sim T(s^{t+1} | s^t, a^t)$ and $a^t \sim \pi(a^t | s^t)$.

3.3   The Formulized Traffic Route Planning Problem

The traffic route planning is based on a simplified model. Given a partially traffic-aware road network $G(V, E, \mathcal{S})$, where V denotes traffic intersections, E denotes road sections without traffic lights, and $\mathcal{S}$ denotes global traffic details. Let (v_x, v_y) denote current intersection nearest to agent vehicle and d_a represents driving direction, let (t_x, t_y) denote the intersection nearest to target.

Then agent only has a partial observation s^t of the nearest intersection: status of traffic light l^t, the status $v_l, v_r, v_u \in 0, 1$ about if there are vehicles from all directions, then agent makes an optimal decision from actions set $\mathcal{A} = \{\text{Stop}, \text{Left}, \text{Right}, \text{Straight}\}$ to ensure destination is reached with minimum time.

4 Planning Framework with Group Representation

This section introduces the planning framework with group representation for POMDP.

4.1 State Estimation Learning

let $R : \mathcal{S} \times \mathcal{A} \to \mathbb{R}$ be the reward to agent on its current state and action taken. We define a different reward according to several criteria mentioned as follows, to define a reward regarding the cost to destination, we process state with weighted rules:

$$\text{Reward}_{\text{Observed State}} = a_1 m_1(l^t) + a_2 m_2(v_x, v_y, t_x, t_y) + a_3 m_3(d_a) + a_4 m_\cap(v_l, v_r, v_u) \tag{2}$$

where m_1 measures the effect by traffic light, m_2 and m_3 measures the cost to target and driving direction respectively, $m_\cap(\cdot) = \cap_{i=1}^{3} m_{\text{road}_i}(\cdot)$ measures the effect by other vehicles. For example, running a red light or deviating from the target will be punished with $R < 0$.

To utilize the state transition $T : \mathcal{S} \times \mathcal{A} \to \mathcal{S}$ by linear transformation $\alpha \odot_\rho \boldsymbol{u} := \rho(\alpha)\boldsymbol{u}$, we need to first encode the state observed into $\mathbb{R}^N$, and for the sake of estimating reward R on the encoded linear space $\mathbb{R}^N$, learning a map $\mathbb{R}^N \to \mathbb{R}$ is essential, then state estimation learning can be constructed as neural network as $\mathbf{r}^t = f_{\theta_2}(e_{\theta_1}(s^t))$.

4.2 Actions Group and Representation

Recall **finite generated group** above, actions group based on $\mathcal{A}$ by $G_\mathcal{A} =<\mathcal{A}>$ is defined, for instance, "Turn Right" $\otimes$ "Go Straight" is an element $\in G_\mathcal{A}$.

Learning Actions Group Representation. For a matrix $M \in \mathbb{R}^{N \times N}$ we denote its Frobenius and L_1 norms by $|M|_F^2 = \sum_{1 \leq i,j \leq N} |M_{ij}|^2$ and $|M|_1 = \sum_{1 \leq i,j \leq N} |M_{ij}|$. The approach of learning representation is to first learn group representation on $G_\mathcal{A}$, let the matrices $M_1, \ldots, M_N$ be optimization variables, and define the following target loss to learn state transition $T : \mathcal{S} \times \mathcal{A} \to \mathcal{S}$:

$$\mathcal{L}[M_1 \ldots M_t] = \max_{1 \leq i \leq t} \frac{1}{|M_i|_F^2} \underbrace{\sum_{1 \leq i \leq j \leq k} |M_i \odot x_s^t - x_s^{t+1}|_1}_{\text{Fit the transition}} \tag{3}$$

then the optimization problem for learning $\rho : G_\mathcal{A} \to \mathbb{R}^{N \times N}$ with constraint $\min_{M_1, \ldots, M_k} \mathcal{L}[M_1, \ldots, M_k]$ can be performed with gradient descent in Keras [8].

4.3   Planning Algorithm Based on Multi-step Reasoning

In ideal traffic conditions, agent is expected to implement an action from $\mathcal{A}$ at each intersection. The challenge is local optimum maybe not the global optimum(see Fig. 2), but the state s^{t+1} cannot be reasoning from s^t cause s^{t+1} could be the state of next intersection, and agent only has partial observation s^t at current intersection, so the feasible way to estimate the state transition is fuzzy reasoning with linear transformation $x_s^{t+1} = \rho(a^t) \odot x_s^t$ learned above.

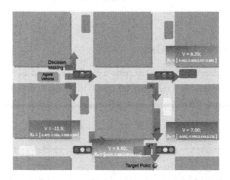

Fig. 2. The local optimum may lead the agent to take a route with more cost.

To address the challenge above, a k-step planning algorithm is proposed, which can plan a route approximates to global optimum better efficiently (see Algorithm 1). The inputed query includes a partially traffic-aware road network $G(V, E, \mathcal{S})$ and the last results of s^{t-1}, s^t, a^{t-1}, the optimal action a^t is executed and the representation map $\tilde{\rho}$ is refined. Initially, we compute updated $M_a = \tilde{\rho}(a)$ by refined map $\tilde{\rho}$. Then, the depth-first search strategy is adopted to mine optimal actions sequence with maximized reward efficiently. Finally, the executed a^t is optimal based on current state x_s^t.

Complexity Analysis. Let t_ρ be the upper time of representation computing, let t_e be the upper time of state encoding, and $t_\odot$ denotes the upper time of state transition reasoning with inner product operation $M_{a^t} \odot x_s^t$. Thus, the time complexity of the k-step planning algorithm is $O(ko_\mathcal{A}t_\odot + o_\mathcal{A}t_\rho + 2t_e)$ where the $o_\mathcal{A}$ is the size of the actions set $\mathcal{A}$.

5   Experimental Study

This section empirically evaluates the proposed planning framework on a traffic simulation environment and presents scalability results on PODMP problems. All experiments are run on a computer with 3.6 GHz Intel Core i7 and 128 GB RAM and Keras [8] is used to setup the optimization problems with method Adam [23] as the stochastic optimizer.

Algorithm 1. Planning algorithm with actions group representation

1: **Input:**Partially traffic-aware road network $G(V, E, S); s^{t-1}, s^t, a^{t-1}, \mathcal{A}$;
2: **Output:**Optimal action a^t;A refined actions group representation $\tilde{\rho}$;
3: Compute $x^{t-1} = e(s^{t-1}), x^t = e(s^t)$;
4: Refine the representation map $\tilde{\rho} = min|\rho(a^{t-1}) \odot x_s^{t-1} - x_s^t|$;
5: **for** each $a \in \mathcal{A}$ **do**
6:     Compute $M_a = \tilde{\rho}(a)$;
7: **end for**
8: // k-step reasoning for planning;
9: **for** $i = 1$ to k **do**
10:     **for** each $a \in \mathcal{A}$ **do**
11:         Compute $R_{i,a^{t+i}} = R_{i,a^{t+i-1}} + \gamma^i r(M_{a^{t+i}} \odot x_s^{t+i-1})$;
12:         Update $x_s^{t+i} = M_{a^{t+i}} \odot x_s^{t+i-1}$;
13:     **end for**
14: **end for**
15: Execute $a^t = max_{a^t} R_{k,a^{t+k}}$;
16: **return** $a^t, \tilde{\rho}$;

5.1 Expiriment Settings

Environment and Evaluation Metrics. The experiments are conducted on a simplified formal traffic simulation environment developed in Python with PyGame library [22], containing 42 vertices and 82 edges. In the task, agent vehicle is desired to choose an optimal action at each vertice from the actions set $\mathcal{A} = \{\text{Stop}, \text{Turn Left}, \text{Turn Right}, \text{Go Straight}\}$, to make time costed to get to the target vertice minimized. At each time step t, the agent vehicle only has a partial observation s^t for the current vertice. The total number of time steps costed to reach target vertice is used to evaluate the performance of the planning method.

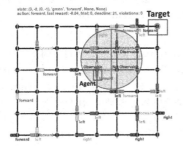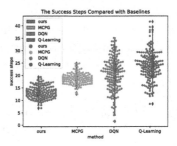

Fig. 3. The traffic simulation environment and the experiment results.

Compared Baselines. We mainly compare proposed method with some top-performing reinforcement learning baseline models for traffic planning task, including Q-Learning [38], DQN [32], MCPG [16]. These baselines have been proved to be excellent in many planning and continuous control tasks in terms of sample efficiency and asymptotic performance [19]. The sources and destinations in the planning tasks are selected randomly, and unless stated otherwise, the experimental results are averaged over 10 independent trials with different source and destination settings. Note that to ensure fairness, the parameters scale of all methods is set to approximate(see Table 2 for details).

Table 2. Compared baselines and our method implementation details.

Methods	Parameters	Steps limit	Training episodes	Evaluation episodes
Q-Learning [38]	<3K	150	1200	200
DQN [32]	2.7K	150	900	200
MCPG [16]	3K	150	900	200
Ours	2.5K	100	600	200

5.2   Experiment Results

Planning Performance Compared to Baselines. Compared with baselines, due to the high abstraction and simplification of the planning task, all the models show high performance. However, our approach still achieves better performance in tasks, which verifies the value of multi-step reasoning with group representation. This also indicates that even in the situation with reduced information mismatch, multi-step reasoning still helps (see details in Fig. 3).

Effect of Steps Number k. Figure 4 shows the efficiency as we vary k. Notice a larger k means the reasoning is more unreliable and inaccurate due to the limited information. While a smaller k means the actions chosen by agents are more likely to fall into local optimum due to the lack of long-term consideration. In addition, a larger k means a larger time complexity, which is $O(ko_\mathcal{A}t_\odot + o_\mathcal{A}t_\rho + 2t_e)$.

Effect of the Dimension N of Representation. To study the effect of N, we apply three groups of contrast experiments and vary N. Intuitively, a larger value of N will significantly slow down the convergence and increase the time complexity. In details, $N = 3$ makes the convergence effect on the reward estimation $v(\cdot)$ and actions group representation map $\rho(\cdot)$ best, notice a larger N also means a larger time complexity in k-step palnning algorithm cause which makes $t_\odot$ larger.

5.3   Theory Analysis

In this section, theoretical discussion and analysis of the experimental results are given, more detailed background information on group representation can be found in [9,21].

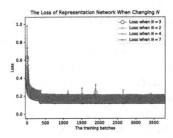

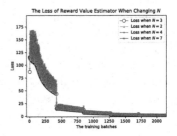

(a) Effect of the dimension N on actions group representation.

(b) Effect of the dimension N on reward estimation.

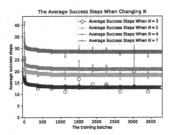

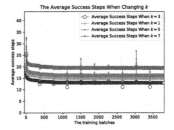

(c) Effect of the dimension N on planning.

(d) Effect of steps number k on planning.

Fig. 4. Experimental study on effect of the dimension N and steps number k.

Definition 4. (ρ, V) *is a K-representation of group G and it's called irreducible, if V has no trival G-invariant subspace; Otherwise it's called reducible.*

Let's rephrase the concept above: if the K-representation (ρ, V) of G is reducible, thus V has at least one non-trivial G-invariant subspace U. Then representation Φ based on ρ has the form:

$$\begin{pmatrix} A(g) & C(g) \\ 0 & B(g) \end{pmatrix}, \quad \forall g \in G \tag{4}$$

where the submatrix on the principal diagonal is a square matrix.

Lemma 1 (Maschke) [21]. *If V is a finite linear space on field K, (V, ρ) is the representation of group G, and U_0 is the G-invariant subspace of V, the character of K cannot divide the order of G. Thus exists G-invariant subspace W of V, such that $V = W \oplus U$, and (V, ρ) is completely reducible.*

Theorem 1. *Actions group G_A acts on the n-elements states set $S = \{s_1, s_2, \cdots, s_n\}$ with the transfer effect: $a \circ s_i = s_a, i = 1, 2, \cdots, n$. This action can induce the n-th permutation representation G_A on field K, denoted by (ρ, V), where*

$$V = \{\sum_{i=1}^{n} c_i s_i \mid c_i \in K, \quad i = 1, 2, \cdots, n\} \tag{5}$$

let $V_1 = \langle \sum s_i \rangle, V_2 = \{\sum c_i s_i \mid \sum c_i = 0\}$. Then ρ_{V_2} is irreducible.

Proof. V_1 and V_2 both are invariant subspaces of ρ [21]; And if the character of feild K cannot divide n, then $V = V_1 \oplus V_2$, thus $\rho \approx \rho_{v_1} \oplus \rho_{v_2}$.

Due to $\dim V_1 = 1$, ρ_V has order of 1. In addition, $\rho_{V_1}(a)(\sum s_i) = \sum s_{a(i)} = \sum s_i$, so $\rho_{V_1}(a)$ is identity transformation of V_1, $\forall a \in G_A$. Thus $\mathrm{Ker}\,\rho_{v_1} = G_A$, which means ρ_{v_1} is the principal representation of G_A.

Now prove ρ_{v_2} is K-representation of G_A and is $n-1$-irreducible: obviously, $\deg \rho_{v_2} = n-1$. Suppose U is Non-zero invariant subspace of ρ_{v_2}, take a nonzero vector $u = \sum c_i s_i$ in U. Due to $u \notin V_1$, at least two components of u the coordinate vector of u are not equal, we may assume $c_1 \neq c_2$, we get:

$$\rho_{V_2}((12))u - u = (c_1 s_2 + c_2 s_1) - (c_1 s_1 + c_2 s_2) = (c_2 - c_1)(s_1 - s_2) \quad (6)$$

where (12) means replacing state 1 with state 2, due to the invariance of U, we have $\rho_{V_2}((12))u - u \in U$, thus $s_1 - s_2 \in U$. Recall the invariance of U, we have $\rho_{v_2}(\sigma)(s_1 - s_2) = s_{\sigma(1)} - s_{o(2)} \in U$. Let σ traverses the elements of S_n we get $s_i - s_j \in U$, and V_2 can be generated by $s_1 - s_2, s_1 - s_3, \cdots, s_1 - s_n$, thus $U = V_2$. Which means ρ_{v_2} only has trival invariant subspace, so ρ_{v_2} is irreducible.

The above theorem theoretically proves that under such condition $V_2 = \{\sum c_i s_i \mid \sum c_i = 0\}$, we can construct irreducible representation of actions group. The following theorem will explain why the planning algorithm corresponding to group representation with dimension $N = 3$ achieved best performance in all experimental segments(Under such conditions, we can prove the representation ρ of with dimension $N = 3$ is irreducible, so we also explain the help of irreducibility to planning tasks).

Theorem 2. *A faithful representation ρ of non-abelian actions group G_A with dimension $N = 3$ on the feild whose character cannot divide group order $|G_A|$ is irreducible.*

Proof. Let (ρ, V) is a faithful representation of non-abelian group G_A with dimension $N = 3$ on the feild whose character cannot divide group order $|G_A|$. Suppose ρ is reducible, then V has G-invariant subspace U with dimension $N = 1$ or $N = 2$. Recall Maschke's lemma above, ρ is completely reducible, so V has G-invariant subspace W $N = 1$ or $N = 2$ such that $V = U \oplus W$. Let $U = \langle \alpha \rangle, W = \langle \beta \rangle$, then α, β forms a basis of V. The matrix representation Φ of ρ under this basis has form as follows:

$$\Phi(g) = \begin{pmatrix} a(g) & 0 \\ 0 & b(g) \end{pmatrix}, \quad \forall g \in G \quad (7)$$

where $a(g), b(g) \in K$. Take any $g, h \in G$, we can get $\Phi(g)\Phi(h) = \Phi(h)\Phi(g)$, so $\Phi(gh) = \Phi(hg)$. Recall ρ is a faithful representation, thus $gh = hg$. Which is in contradiction with G is a non-abelian group, so ρ is irreducible.

6   Conclusion and Perspectives

We use POMDP [1] to characterize the planning problem and "actions group representation" approach is proposed to address multi-step reasoning under partially observable environment. We plan to continue the study with other scenarios and optimize the accuracy of the algorithm to test the other complex environments, and to test our approach on a robotized agent [7,29].

References

1. Kaelbling, L.P., Littman, M.L., Cassandra, A.R.: Planning and acting in partially observable stochastic domains. Artif. Intell. **101**, 99–134 (1998)
2. Aklam, F., Osborn, W.: Dynamic group trip planning queries in spatial databases (2020)
3. Bazzan, A.L.C., Grunitzki, R.: A multiagent reinforcement learning approach to en-route trip building. In: 2016 International Joint Conference on Neural Networks (IJCNN) (2016)
4. Brechtel, S., Gindele, T., Dillmann, R.: Probabilistic decision-making under uncertainty for autonomous driving using continuous POMDPs. In: IEEE International Conference on Intelligent Transportation Systems (2014)
5. Cai, C.: Group representation theory for knowledge graph embedding (2019)
6. Cao, X., Chen, L., Cong, G., Xiao, X.: Keyword-aware optimal route search. Proc. VLDB Endowment **5**, 1136–1147 (2012)
7. Chen, M., Zhang, Y., Qiu, M., Guizani, N., Hao, Y.: SPHA: smart personal health advisor based on deep analytics. IEEE Commun. Mag. **56**, 164–169 (2018)
8. Chollet, F., et al.: Keras (2015). https://keras.io
9. Collins, M.J.: Representations and Characters of Finite Groups. Cambridge University Press, Cambridge (1990)
10. Deisenroth, M.P., Rasmussen, C.E.: PILCO: a model-based and data-efficient approach to policy search (2011)
11. Dotoli, M., Hammadi, S., Jeribi, K.: A multi-agent decision support system for optimization of co-modal transportation route planning services. In: Decision and Control (2014)
12. Dummit, D.S., Foote, R.M.: Abstract Algebra (2004)
13. Fridman, L., Terwilliger, J., Jenik, B.: DeepTraffic: crowdsourced hyperparameter tuning of deep reinforcement learning systems for multi-agent dense traffic navigation. In: Neural Information Processing Systems (NIPS 2018) Deep Reinforcement Learning Workshop (2018)
14. Gai, K., Qiu, M.: Reinforcement learning-based content-centric services in mobile sensing. IEEE Netw. **32**, 34–39 (2018)
15. Gao, L., Du, Y., Li, H., Lin, G.: RotEqNet: rotation-equivariant network for fluid systems with symmetric high-order tensors (2020)
16. Graf, T., Platzner, M.: Adaptive playouts in Monte-Carlo tree search with policy-gradient reinforcement learning. In: Plaat, A., van den Herik, J., Kosters, W. (eds.) ACG 2015. LNCS, vol. 9525, pp. 1–11. Springer, Cham (2015). https://doi.org/10.1007/978-3-319-27992-3_1
17. Gu, S., Holly, E., Lillicrap, T., Levine, S.: Deep reinforcement learning for robotic manipulation with asynchronous off-policy updates. In: IEEE International Conference on Robotics and Automation (2017)

18. Gu, S., Lillicrap, T., Sutskever, I., Levine, S.: Continuous deep q-learning with model-based acceleration (2016)
19. Haarnoja, T., Zhou, A., Abbeel, P., Levine, S.: Soft actor-critic: off-policy maximum entropy deep reinforcement learning with a stochastic actor (2018)
20. Hu, Z., Zhu, M., Liu, P.: Adaptive cyber defense against multi-stage attacks using learning-based POMDP. ACM Trans. Privacy Secur. **24**, 1–25 (2020)
21. Pierre, J.: Linear Representations of Finite Groups. Springer, Heidelberg (2008)
22. Kelly, S.: Basic Introduction to PyGame. Apress, New York (2016)
23. Kingma, D., Ba, J.: Adam: a method for stochastic optimization. Computer science (2014)
24. Levine, S., Finn, C., Darrell, T., Abbeel, P.: End-to-end training of deep visuomotor policies. J. Mach. Learn. Res. **17**, 1334–1373 (2015)
25. Lu, H., Hu, H.: DensE: an enhanced non-abelian group representation for knowledge graph embedding (2020)
26. Luo, Y., Xu, H., Li, Y., Tian, Y., Darrell, T., Ma, T.: Algorithmic framework for model-based deep reinforcement learning with theoretical guarantees (2019)
27. Luong, N.C., Hoang, D.T., Gong, S., Niyato, D., Kim, D.I.: Applications of deep reinforcement learning in communications and networking: a survey. IEEE Commun. Surv. Tutor. **21**, 3133–3174 (2019)
28. Paden, B., Cap, M., Yong, S.Z., Yershov, D., Frazzoli, E.: A survey of motion planning and control techniques for self-driving urban vehicles. IEEE Trans. Intell. Veh. **1**, 33–55 (2016)
29. Rane, K.P.: Design and development of IoT, web-server and ML-AVPR based intelligent humanoid robot for traffic assistance. Int. J. Adv. Trends Comput. Sci. Eng. **9**, 1922–1929 (2020)
30. Shang, S., Liu, J., Zheng, K., Lu, H., Pedersen, T.B., Wen, J.-R.: Planning unobstructed paths in traffic-aware spatial networks. GeoInformatica **19**(4), 723–746 (2015). https://doi.org/10.1007/s10707-015-0227-9
31. Sharifzadeh, M., Kolahdouzan, M., Shahabi, C.: The optimal sequenced route query. VLDB J. **17**, 765–787 (2008)
32. Sharifzadeh, S., Chiotellis, I., Triebel, R., Cremers, D.: Learning to drive using inverse reinforcement learning and deep q-networks (2016)
33. Shen, J., Zhao, H., Zhang, W., Yu, Y.: Model-based policy optimization with unsupervised model adaptation (2020)
34. Shridhar, M., Thomason, J., Gordon, D., Bisk, Y., Han, W.: ALFRED: a benchmark for interpreting grounded instructions for everyday tasks (2020)
35. Shutty, N., Wierzynski, C.: Learning irreducible representations of noncommutative lie groups (2020)
36. Alemzadeh, S., Moslemi, R., Sharma, R.: Adaptive traffic control with deep reinforcement learning: towards state-of-the-art and beyond (2020)
37. Soma, S.C., Hashem, T., Cheema, M.A., Samrose, S.: Trip planning queries with location privacy in spatial databases. World Wide Web **20**(2), 205–236 (2016). https://doi.org/10.1007/s11280-016-0384-2
38. Watkins, C.J.C.H., Dayan, P.: Q-learning. Mach. Learn. **8**, 279–292 (1992). https://doi.org/10.1007/BF00992698
39. Weiler, M., Cesa, G.: General E(2)-equivariant steerable CNNs. arXiv (2019)
40. Xu, T., Wang, N., Lin, H., Sun, Z.: UAV autonomous reconnaissance route planning based on deep reinforcement learning. In: 2019 IEEE International Conference on Unmanned Systems (ICUS) (2019)

41. Xu, Y., et al.: Location-based top-k term querying over sliding window. In: Bouguettaya, A., et al. (eds.) WISE 2017. LNCS, vol. 10569, pp. 299–314. Springer, Cham (2017). https://doi.org/10.1007/978-3-319-68783-4_21
42. Yu, H., Lian, X., Zhang, H., Xu, W.: Guided feature transformation (GFT): a neural language grounding module for embodied agents (2018)

Bayesian Belief Network Model Using Sematic Concept for Expert Finding

Wei Zheng[1,2], Hongxu Hou[1(✉)], Nier Wu[1], and Shuo Sun[1]

[1] College of Compter Science, Inner Mongolia University, Hohhot, China
`cshhx@imu.edu.cn`
[2] College of Science of Science, Hebei North University, Zhangjiakou, China

Abstract. The Expert finding is a research hotspot in the area of entity retrieval. However, due to the small number of search terms, the retrieval effect will be poor due to the mechanical text matching. In view of the above shortcomings, we use Bayesian belief network as a model frame, and two expert finding models are proposed. One is a basic semantic belief network retrieval model, in which BERT and LDA models are used, and the other is a compound semantic belief network model. The compound model uses an effective data fusion technique to integrate the retrieval results of the two sub-models in this paper. The paper presents the topology and retrieval algorithm of two models proposed. The experiments verify the validity of the research content on Amine platform. Experimental results show that the semantic model can improve the MAP value, and the compound semantic model is better than the existing expert finding model on multiple evaluation indicators such as P@N, MAP and MRR, and it can improve the performance of expert retrieval.

Keywords: Expert finding · Semantic · Bayesian belief network · Model · Retrieval

1 Introduction

In recent years, with the rapid development of Internet technology, people's information needs are more diversified, and retrieval technology has a unique application in various fields. Entity Retrieval (ER) is an important branch of information Retrieval technology [1–3].

Expert finding, also known as expert Retrieval, is a special case of ER. The problem it studies is how to find experts with certain prestige and expertise in the relevant field based on a given query, and sort relevant personnel according to their professional level [3–5]. Expert finding has been widely used in the business and in the area of scientific and technological knowledge. In recent years, expert finding has become a research hotspot in the area of information retrieval and knowledge discovery. Many approaches have been proposed to determine the experts in a topic. In the existing approaches, experts were identified heavily depending on the traditional text features, profile information, topic model, relations based citation graph and combination of a few of features.

© Springer Nature Switzerland AG 2021
H. Qiu et al. (Eds.): KSEM 2021, LNAI 12816, pp. 114–125, 2021.
https://doi.org/10.1007/978-3-030-82147-0_10

In this paper, we construct a model framework for expert finding task based on Bayesian belief network. Furthermore, we propose two semantic models to expert finding based on the above framework in order to solve the shortcoming of text matching. Finally, we provide experiment results computed with baseline methods and our methods, meanwhile, the experimental results were analyzed.

Our contributions are the following:

- We construct a model framework of Bayesian belief network, which has four layers, to finish expert finding task.
- We propose a novel models based on semantic concept computation on the frame, in which a semantic expansion model using BERT and LDA models are used to capture the concept information.
- A compound model with two Bayesian belief networks is proposed.
- We propose new data fusion technique for compound model.

The rest of the paper is organized as follows. Section 2 discuss about the related work. Section 3 describes the expert finding model using Bayesian belief network proposed. Section 4 describes the topology and algorithm of the semantic network models. Section 5 shows the experimental result and the analysis of experimental data. Finally Section shows the concluding remarks and future research direction.

2   Related Work

Expert finding system aims to determine The enterprise expert retrieval task organized by the international text retrieval conference, promoted the development of expert retrieval technology [6, 7]. Balog K et al. [6] proposed the language model framework, and realized the expert candidate model and document model for the expert finding task. Jian Liu [8] proposed a method of expert finding based on topic model, which considered the relationships among document and topics, and obtained a better retrieval effect. Chuang, Chen [9] proposes two methods for solving the expert finding problem. In order to enhance the correctness, a Cvalue method is applied to these methods for query expansion. Cifariello et al. [10] proposed a semantic method based on entity links for expert finding, which used the language model and the knowledge semantic map formed by entity links in wikipedia for expert retrieval. Solunke et al. [11] proposed the expert finding algorithm based on the combination social network and ontology learning, constructed the social network among the candidate experts through the ontology calculation between domain concepts, and analyzed the social network of expert according to the concept distance between experts.

Jing Zhang et al. [12] used social network computing to obtain the personal information of experts and the academic cooperation between experts, and proposed a two-stage expert finding approach. Zheng yiping et al. [13] proposed an expert retrieval method based on the correlation propagation using query words to solve the low performance problem of expert retrieval, and fully considered the mutual relations between experts, documents and experts. Sharad chandra et al. [14] used the social network computing method to realize the correlation analysis between authors, and also used the ontology to calculate the similarity of the research field between authors, integrated the content and network dual analysis and used it for expert retrieval tasks.

At present, the research achievements are mainly focused on the direction of expert retrieval representation model and entity relationship mining. The improvement of expert retrieval performance largely depends on concept matching and entity network calculation. Among them, the correlation propagation model in the literature [12, 13] belongs to the two-stage model, and certain effects have been achieved in the expert retrieval task. However, when the data scale is large, the time complexity of iteration calculation in the second stage is high. How to use a framework to integrate the various features of experts and how to achieve semantic reasoning is an important problem.

In recent years, with the rapid development of information technology and the improvement of computing power, some artificial intelligence algorithms have been well applied in solving practical problems. Because Bayesian belief network model has a power ability of modeling, it are applied widely in the area of information retrieval [15–17]. Now, some researchers use the Bayesian belief network model as a basic model to finish a few apply modeling, such as topic detection [18], Microblog retrieval [19]. Bayesian belief network model has good generalization ability in application. However, due to its simple structure, the model needs to be enriched to achieve a better application effect.

Because of the advantages of Bayesian belief network model, our work considers use Bayesian belief network as a frame to finish the expert finding task. In order to overcome the shortcomings of the model, we propose two novel models based on semantic concept computation on the frame, in which a semantic expansion model with BERT and LDA models are used to capture the concept information, and anther compound model is constructed using data fusion technique. The models take advantage of network calculation and reasoning to realize the general retrieval and query reformulation.

3   Basic Bayesian Belief Network Model for Expert Finding

In TREC2005, researchers introduced two language models for expert retrieval tasks, named candidate expert model and document model, which are denoted as Model1 and Model2 in this paper. They are currently more commonly used expert retrieval model frameworks [6], on which many extension methods and new theories are based. Both the candidate expert model and the document model assume that the candidate expert and the query are independent. The problem of expert finding can also be considered as a voting process. The RR data fusion technique is used for evaluating rankings in voting model [20]. The above models are classical and can be used as baseline models in expert finding studies.

Bayesian network is the main method to deal with uncertainty in the field of artificial intelligence. Based on the knowledge of Bayesian belief network and expert retrieval, a basic Bayesian belief network model BBBN (basic Bayesian belief network) is constructed. This model is based on the theory of information retrieval [15]. The topology of BBBN is illustrated in Fig. 1.The topology of the model combines belief network and reasoning network, including four node layers, which are query lay, term lay, document lay and expert lay, namely query layer q, term layer k, document layer d and expert layer c. According to the knowledge of Bayesian probability, conditional independence hypothesis and inference network, the probability formula of expert finding is given.

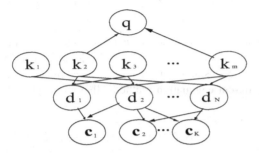

Fig. 1. The topology of the BBBN model

The set U is a knowledge domain about concept in the model, $U = \{k_1, k_2, k_3, \ldots k_m\}$. A subset u of the set U can be used for concept, and each u is associated with a vector k, and $g_i(k) = 1 \Leftrightarrow k_i \in u$. If c is a subset of U, it is used to represent the query or document, then the following formula [18]:

$$P(c) = P(c|u) \times P(u) \tag{1}$$

$$P(u) = \left(\frac{1}{2}\right)^m \tag{2}$$

In the belief network model, $P(d_j|q)$ is used to calculate the ranking of literature about the query.

$$P(d_j|q) = P(d_j \wedge q)/P(u) \tag{3}$$

$$P(d_j|q) = \sum_{\forall u} P(d_j \wedge q|u) \times P(u) \tag{4}$$

Since the term node logically separates the query from the literature, making them independent from each other, Eq. (4) can be changed into:

$$P(d_j|q) = \sum_{\forall u} P(d_j|u) \times P(q|u) \times P(u) \tag{5}$$

The concept u is denoted by k, and Eq. (16) can also be written as.

$$P(d_j|q) = \sum_{\forall k} P(d_j|k) \times P(q|k) \times P(k) \tag{6}$$

Since the term node logically separates the query from the expert, making them independent of each other, the formula for expert retrieval is defined as:

$$P(c_k|q) = \mu \sum_{\forall k,d} P(c_k|k, d) \times P(q|k, d) \times P(k, d) \tag{7}$$

The symbol μ stands for a constant. According to the network topology, it is known that $\forall k, d$ is a kind of concept, and the formula (7) also can be written as:

$$P(c_k|q) = \tau \sum_{\forall k,d} P(c_k|d) \times P(q|k) \times P(d|k) \qquad (8)$$

The symbol τ stands for a constant. The correlation strength of candidate expert c_k and literature d can be represented by $P(c_k|d)$ and $P(q|k)$ represents the semantic matching degree of q and k. $P(q|k)$ stands for a certain retrieval model. When $P(c_k|d)$, $P(q|k)$ and $P(d|k)$ adopt different calculation methods, they correspond to different sorting strategies.

The advantage of BBBN model is that the model is simple and the reasoning is intuitive, while the disadvantage of BBBN is that a simple mechanical matching strategy is used in the model.

4   A Bayesian Belief Network Model Using Semantic Concept

A retrieval model using semantic concept based on Bayesian belief retrieval model is proposed to solve the problem of term mechanical matching in BBBN model. In order to prevent semantic drift in retrieval, two semantic models are proposed.

4.1   A Model Using Sematic Concept Based on BBBN

For a given query q, the Sorting of related documents is considered a matching relationship of concepts, and expert retrieval can also be considered as a process of querying q to match the expert's profile. To do this, we build a conceptual query layer q, and a topic layerTT, which consists of several topics. The set T is a knowledge topic domain about concept in the model. $T = \{t_1, t_2, t_3, \ldots .t_l\}$. A subset t of the set T can be used for present of topic concept, and each t is associated with a vector. The model network topology is shown in Fig. 2.

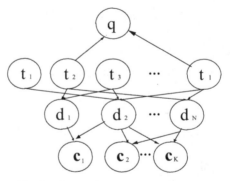

Fig. 2. The topology of the SBBN model

The model showed in Fig. 2 is named SBBN (Semantic Bayesian belief network). Assume that a few topics in topic layer T are associated with the query, which is the only difference from the network topology of the BBBN model. The calculation of $P(c_k|q)$ is an inference process similarly with BBN, so we can get the mathematical reasoning as follow.

$$P(c_k|q) = \ddot{e} \sum_{\forall t,d} P(c_k|d) \times P(d|t) \times P(q|t) \tag{9}$$

For using a vector model, the probabilities of $P(c_k|d)$, $P(d|t)$, $P(q|t)$ expressed as follows

$$P(q|t) = \frac{\sum w_{qi} \times w_{ti}}{\sqrt{\sum w_{qi}^2} \times \sqrt{\sum w_{ti}^2}} \tag{10}$$

$$P(d_j|k) = \frac{\sum w_{qi} \times w_{ti}}{\sqrt{\sum w_{qi}^2} \times \sqrt{\sum w_{ti}^2}} \tag{11}$$

$$P(c_k|d_j) = \begin{cases} 1, & \text{if } d_j \in c_k \\ 0, & \text{else} \end{cases} \tag{12}$$

Since Google announced BERT's outstanding performance in 11 NLP tasks at the end of October 2018, BERT model has become a key technology used in NLP areas [21]. In this paper, Bert model is used construct q vector. LDA model is a generative model widely used in theme modeling and feature extraction [22]. Topic set T can be generated by LDA in SBBN. In order to reduce the complexity of model computation, we used the batch text obtained by the query for LDA model training.

4.2 A Compound Semantic Bayesian Belief Network Model for Expert Finding

The SBBN model has an intuitive network reasoning topology, and "concept" as an intermediate factor of node similarity calculation can realize semantic extension calculation. The matching calculation of semantic concepts can increase the accuracy of query results to a great extent, but there will also be subject drift in the representation of query concepts.

Based on the above shortcoming, a compound semantic network model is proposed, which can consider both the term matching and semantic matching. The model is named CSBBN (compound semantic Bayesian belief network). The network topology of CSBBN is shown in Fig. 3.

In Fig. 3, the network on the left is the basic expert retrieval model BBBN, and the model in the dotted box on the right is the semantic expert retrieval model CSBBN. Query q is equal to q_K and q_T is a term vector constructed in term of q using Bert model. The SBBN model on the right is to use the information retrieval method to obtain the top N documents by querying q to generate LDA model.

A harmonic data fusion technique is used for expert search ranking of two sub networks. $Sort(c_k|q)$ is a grade for expert rank.

$$Sort(c_k|q) = \frac{2 * Score(c_k|q_K) * Score(c_k|q_T)}{Score(c_k|q_K) + Score(c_k|q_T)} \tag{13}$$

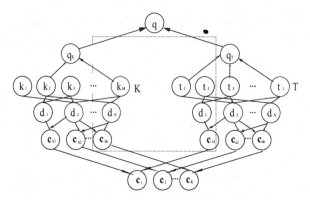

Fig. 3. The topology of the CSBBN model

In this paper, the computation formulas $Score(c_k|q)$ for $Score(c_k|q_K)$ and $Score(c_k|q_K)$ as follow

$$Score(c_k|q) = 1/rank(c_k, q) \qquad (14)$$

The expression $rank(c_k, q)$ is used to represent the rank of experts c_k in the retrieval results.

The retrieval process of CSBBN is shown in Fig. 4.

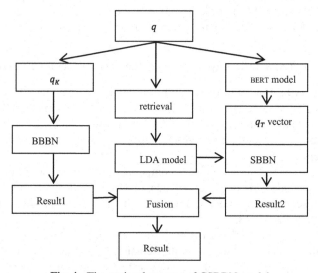

Fig. 4. The retrieval process of CSBBN model

Process is as follows, the firstly, query vector q_T is built to using Bert model for query q_v and LDA model is build using top N documents from retrieval, using these documents for the LDA model, and set result1 sorted can get by BBBN model. Secondly, result2 set sorted can get by using SBBN model, finally, result set can get as a final result by using the fusion formula (23). CSBBB model can integrate the advantages of each model to obtain the optimal effect.

5 Experiment

The purpose of this experiment is to verify the effectiveness of SBBN model and CSBBN model in expert retrieval task. Experiments were carried out by using basic query and semantic query.

Experimental data were obtained from the academic data set of Aminer [23], which is a scientific research data platform in the field of computer science. The social network data set of academic resources was composed of 2092356 articles, 1712433 authors, 8024869 citations, and 4248615 collaborative relationships. Before the experiment, the data set was cleaned to remove the papers and authors with incomplete information, and the corresponding papers and authors with low hi factor were removed. Finally, the number of retained literatures was 129,617, and the number of authors was 33,828. Table 1 shows the query subjects used in the experiment and the number of corresponding experts.

Table 1. List of experts in the field of computer science

Query topics	Authors	Query topics	Authors
Datum mining	180	Ontology alignment	21
Machine learning	17	Semantic web	162
Information extraction	41	Neural networks	43
Intelligent agent	13	Cryptography	78

5.1 Experimental Results and Analysis

The experiments are divided into two parts:

The expert finding experiments are carried out on the compound semantic query in Table 1 using SBBN and CSBBN, in order to determine the optimal number of topics.

Using Model1, Model2, RR, the propagation model mentioned in [13], named the RP and BBBN in this paper as the baseline system, experiments are carried out to verify the effectiveness of BBBN, SBBN and CSBBN models in expert retrieval.

In this experiment, p@5, p@10, p@20, p@30, MAP and MRR were used for evaluating experiment result [10].

In the basic query experiment of BBBN, $P(d_j|k)$ is calculated using the vector space model. When seven different models are used into experiment, Table 2 lists p@ value, MAP and MRR value.

This paper firstly get top 200 documents related to the query topic using document retrieval technology [17], second, the "query concept" vector is build using Bert model. Figure 5 and Fig. 6 show the impact of using different topics on the expert retrieval when query concept vector is build.

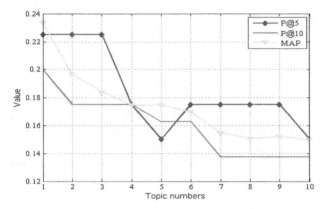

Fig. 5. The influence of topic numbers to SBBN

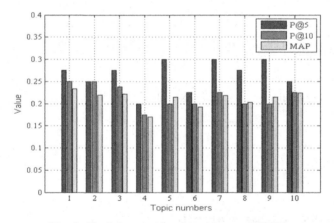

Fig. 6. The influence of topic numbers to CSBBN

Three index curve in Fig. 4 were analyzed, and found that the P@5, P@10 and MAP curve of SBBN approach showed a trend of descend, when the amount of topic amount equals 1 to 10.The data in Fig. 6 shows that when the number of subjects in the CSBBN model is 5, 7 and 9, the maximum value of P@5 value is 0.3, but the corresponding values of P@10 and MAP are not high. When the number of topics equal 1, the values of the three indexes are very high, which are 0.275, 0.25 and 0.2334 respectively. According to Fig. 5 and Fig. 6, the optimal number of topics we selected equal 1. Because of the LDA model is built based on document feedback, the number of subjects selected is reasonable and in line with the original intention.

The data in Table 2 are the experimental results of baseline and semantic Bayesian belief network models proposed.

Table 2. Indicators contrast table of models

Models	Evaluation indicators					
	P@5	P@10	P@20	P@30	MAP	MRR
RP	0.2	0.163	0.138	0.113	0.151	0.3983
RR	0.1	0.1125	0.1	0.0875	0.1531	0.2555
Model1	0.15	0.2125	0.1688	0.125	0.1804	0.3777
Model2	0.250	0.200	0.1688	0.1292	0.2315	0.4753
BBBN	0.250	0.200	0.1563	0.1292	0.2118	0.4106
SBBN	0.225	0.200	0.1438	0.1209	0.2335	0.3627
CSBBN	0.275	0.250	0.1688	0.2251	0.2334	0.4765

By comparing the retrieval performance of the baseline model, the experimental dates show that Model2 has the optimal value on P@5 and MAP, which are 0.25 and 0.2315,and Model1 has the optimal value on the indicators of p@10 and p@30 in the baseline model, which are 0.2625 and 0.175. The retrieval performance of BBBN has little difference with that of Model2 on the P@20, MAP and MRR, but it's P@5, P@30, MAP and MRR values are higher than other three baseline models. Because BBBN uses the vector space model to calculate the correlation between query and documents of candidate expert, the experiment result can get a good score. It can be proved that the application of Bayesian network to expert retrieval task is feasible.

Because SBBN uses the "query concept" vector, it gets good performance than BBBN on MAP, which MAP value can be 10.2% higher than the original MAP. But MRR value can be decrease by 11.7% than the BBBN. Compared with BBBN model, P@20 and P@30 value decrease less in SBBN model. The reason for the above problems is that the SBBN model uses semantic computation to bring topic drift and some uncertainty.

The CSBBN model is a compound model, whose those values of P@5, P@10, P@20 P@30 and MRR are better than all the other models. In particular, compared with BBBN, p@5 value increased by 20%, p@10 value increased by 25%, p@30 value increased by 74%, and MRR value increased by 16. Compared with SBBN model, CSBBN model has a slightly lower MAP value, and it's other indicators are significantly higher than SBBN model.

Overall, Because of using semantic computation, SBBN model has good performance. It has the maximum value among seven models on MAP value, which is 80% higher than the MAP value of BBBN model. The retrieve effect of CSBBN model on the indicators were better than the baseline model. It can be seen that the retrieval CSBBN in this paper are very effective. In the process of compound BBBN and SBBN, the model fusion method proposed in this paper plays an important role.

This models based on Bayesian belief network in paper effectively implement the expert retrieval task, which improve the performance of expert retrieval. There is still space for improvement in the retrieval performance of the compound model. In the future, we will consider introducing the author's social network into the compound model, and at the same time, we will study reliable data fusion methods for model data fusion.

6 Conclusion

The Bayesian belief network model is based on the theory of probability theory and an important contribution is the introduction of concept space. Each index word is regarded as a basic concept and queries and documents are a subset of concept space. Two semantic models based on the Bayesian belief network are proposed. One use vector strategy, and it is found that constructing concept vector can get the better retrieval performance than original query, and another is a compound semantic model using technique of data fusion. Two models get a better retrieval performance, especially, performance of CSBBN model is good.

The follow-up research will focus on the analysis and calculation of the strength of the relationship between the experts and the literature, and improve the experimental results. In the meantime, when the text, content is mined, the strategies of reinforcement learning [24] may be considered.

Acknowledgment. This work is supported by the Natural Science Research Program of Hebei North University (YB2020003), Inner Mongolia Natural Science Foundation of China (2018MS06005) and Inner Mongolia autonomous region science and technology achievements transformation special (2019CG028).

References

1. Balog, K.: People search in the enterprise. In: 30th International Proceedings on ACM SIGIR Conference on Research and Development in Information Retrieval, p. 103. ACM, Amsterdam (2008)
2. Delbru, R., Toupikov, N., Catasta, M., Tummarello, G.: A node indexing scheme for web entity retrieval. In: Aroyo, L., et al. (eds.) ESWC 2010. LNCS, vol. 6089, pp. 240–256. Springer, Heidelberg (2010). https://doi.org/10.1007/978-3-642-13489-0_17
3. Ensan, F., Du, W.: Ad hoc retrieval via entity linking and semantic similarity. J. Knowl. Inf. Syst. **58**(3), 551–583 (2018). https://doi.org/10.1007/s10115-018-1190-1
4. Zhou, G., Zhao, J., He, T., Wu, W.: An empirical study of topic-sensitive probabilistic model for expert finding in question answer communities. J. Knowl.-Based Syst. **66**, 136–145 (2014)
5. Wang, S., Di, J., Lei, S., Fan, Z., Xi, L.: Expert finding in CQA based on topic professional level model. In: Tan, Y., Shi, Y., Tang, Q. (eds.) Data Mining and Big Data. DMBD 2018. LNCS, vol. 10943, pp. 495–465. Springer, Heidelberg (2016). https://doi.org/10.1007/978-3-319-93803-5_43
6. Balog, K., Azzopardi, L., Rijke, M.D.: A language modeling framework for expert finding. J. Inf. Process. Manag. **45**(1), 1–19 (2019)
7. Fang, Y., Si, L., Mathur, A.P.: Discriminative models of integrating document evidence and document-candidate associations for expert search. In: 33rd International Proceedings of ACM SIGIR Conference on Research & Development in Information Retrieval, pp.683–690. ACM, New York (2010)

8. Liu, J., Jia, B., Xu, H., Liu, B., Gao, D., Li, B.: A TopicRank based document priors model for expert finding. In: Fei, M., Ma, S., Li, X., Sun, X., Jia, L., Su, Z. (eds.) LSMS/ICSEE -2017. CCIS, vol. 761, pp. 334–341. Springer, Singapore (2017). https://doi.org/10.1007/978-981-10-6370-1_33

9. Chen, T.C., Yang, K.H., Yu, L.L., Wang, H.H.: Combining query terms extension and weight correlative for expert finding. In: IEEE/WIC/ACM International Joint Conferences on Web Intelligence, pp. 323–326. ACM, New York (2014)

10. Cifariello, P., Ferragina, P., Ponza, M.: Wiser: a semantic approach for expert finding in academia based on entity linking. J. Inf. Syst. **82**, 1–16 (2019)

11. Sharad, S., Nitin, K., Govinda, C.: Expert finder on social networks based on ontological learning. Int. J. Adv. Res. Innov. Ideas Educ. **3**(2), 1924–1927 (2017)

12. Zhang, J., Tang, J., Li, J.: Expert finding in a social network. In: Kotagiri, R., Krishna, P.R., Mohania, M., Nantajeewarawat, E. (eds.) DASFAA 2007. LNCS, vol. 4443, pp. 1066–1069. Springer, Heidelberg (2007). https://doi.org/10.1007/978-3-540-71703-4_106

13. Zheng, Y.P., Wang, Y., Li, J.: Expert retrieval method based on query word correlation propagation. J. Comput. Eng. Des. **35**(6), 2165–2168 (2014)

14. Solunke, S., Khatate, N.B., Chaudhari, G.S.: Expert finder on social networks based on ontological learning. Int. J. Adv. Res. Innov. Ideas Educ. **3**(2), 2395–4396 (2017)

15. Ribeiro-Neto, B.A., Muntz, R.R.: A belief network model for IR. In: 19th Proceedings of ACM SIGIR Conference on Research and Development in Information Retrieval, pp. 253–260. ACM, New York (1996)

16. Zheng, W., Hou, H.X., Wu, J.: Application of Bayesian network in information retrieval. J. Inf. Sci. **36**(6), 136–139 (2018)

17. Xu, J.M., He, D.D., Wu, S.F.: An extended belief network retrieval model based on document relationship. J. China Soc. Sci. Tech. Inf. **38**(1), 1160–1165 (2019)

18. Wu, S.F., Xu, J.M., Sun, X.L.: Topic detection model based on Bayesian belief network. J. Appl. Res. Comput. **3**, 158–161 (2014)

19. Jabeur, L.B., Tamine, L., Boughanem, M.: Featured tweet search: modeling time and social influence for microblog retrieval. In: IEEE/WIC/ACM International Conferences on Web Intelligence and Intelligent Agent Technology, pp. 166–173. ACM, China (2012)

20. Lin, S., Hong, W., Wang, D., Li, T.: A survey on expert finding techniques. J. Intell. Inf. Syst. **49**(2), 255–279 (2017). https://doi.org/10.1007/s10844-016-0440-5

21. BERT: pre-training of deep bidirectional transformers for language understanding (2018). https://arxiv.org/pdf/1810.04805.pdf. Accessed 21 Feb 2021

22. Zhang, T., Wang, Y., Yuan, C., Sun, K.: Analysis of food safety public opinion based on LDA theme model. In: 7th International Conference on Social science and Education Research. Online publication (2018)

23. Tang, J., Zhang, J., Yao, L.: ArnetMiner: extraction and mining of academic social networks. In: 15th International Proceeding on Knowledge Discovery & Data Mining, pp. 990–998. ACM, New York (2008)

24. Gai, K., Qiu, M.: Reinforcement learning-based content-centric services in mobile sensing. J. IEEE Netw. **32**(4), 34–39 (2018)

Towards Solving the Winograd Schema Challenge: Model-Free, Model-Based and a Spectrum in Between

Weinan He and Zhanhao Xiao[✉]

Department of Computer Science, Sun Yat-sen University, Guangzhou 510006, China
heweinan@mail2.sysu.edu.cn, xiaozhh9@mail.sysu.edu.cn

Abstract. The Winograd Schema Challenge (WSC) has attracted much attention recently as *common sense* is recognized to be not only the key to human-level intelligence but also a bottleneck faced by recent progress. Although neural language models (LMs) have achieved state-of-the-art (SOTA) performance on WSC, they fall short on interpretability and robustness against adversarial attacks. Contrarily, methods with structured representation and explicit reasoning suffer from the difficulty of knowledge acquisition and the rigidness of representation. In this paper, we look back on the current model-free and model-based approaches, pointing out the missing ingredients towards solving the WSC. We report our preliminary exploration of formalizing the WSC problems using a variant of first-order language and our first-hand findings of indispensable capabilities of human-level commonsense reasoning. The issues we encounter suggest that a full spectrum of representation tools and reasoning abilities are called for.

Keywords: Commonsense · Knowledge representation and reasoning · WSC · Situation calculus · Natural language understanding

1 Introduction

Common sense has long been regarded as a critical and yet challenging component of human-level intelligence. Recently, Winograd Schema Challenge (WSC), a multiple-choice question-answering problem, was proposed to test whether algorithms understand natural language and are capable of reasoning with commonsense [10]. Systems need to resolve an ambiguous pronoun in a sentence, e.g. *"the man couldn't lift his son because **he** was too heavy. Who was too heavy?"* These problems involve hypothetical daily situations, while the commonsense knowledge required to solve them is unstated.

Although commonsense knowledge and reasoning have long been studied in the area of knowledge representation and reasoning (KR&R), recent progress has been made by end-to-end neural approaches [7,20,21,25]. These approaches typically employ neural language models (LMs) that have learned to predict missing

© Springer Nature Switzerland AG 2021
H. Qiu et al. (Eds.): KSEM 2021, LNAI 12816, pp. 126–138, 2021.
https://doi.org/10.1007/978-3-030-82147-0_11

words in sentences, where implicit common sense is mined from large corpora. State-of-the-art (SOTA) models from these approaches achieved near 90% of accuracy, demonstrating the effectiveness in answering commonsense questions in terms of accuracy [20]. In contrast, model-based approaches characterize the sentences and knowledge using structured representations such as logical formulae or relational triples [5,22]. Typically a separate reasoner is used to provide an answer. The results so far are less impressive.

While both approaches have their merits, we believe it is their shortcomings that could tell us what is missing for a systematic solution. While achieving impressive accuracies, neural approaches are criticized to lack commonsense [2, 8], not being human-comprehensible and being brittle when a minor disturbance is introduced [24]. Further diagnostic evidence suggests such performance might not be achieved by a true understanding of commonsense [28].

The model-based approaches, on the other hand, do not cope well with natural language problems such as the WSC. The obstacle of formalizing natural language sentences into logical representation has hindered progress to study WSC from the perspective of KR&R. In light of this, we set out to investigate potential issues of formalizing WSC problems, which could potentially shed light on future solutions to WSC.

Specifically, we formalize the WSC problems one by one using a variant of first-order logic (FOL) and manually provide the commonsense knowledge. Although our experiments show that the existing theorem prover is able to obtain correct answers with our formalization, we have discovered, or *re-discovered*, many issues concerning commonsense and language understanding. We feel obligated to share our reflections on current approaches and especially the obstacles we encounter. Much of them might not be novel in KR&R, and yet current literature, especially the model-free approaches, seems to overlook these invaluable issues. Based on our preliminary logical exploration and our reflections on current approaches, we propose the essential ingredients for a systematic approach to address the deficiencies from both strands.

In this paper, we first introduce the WSC problems with current approaches and analysis. Then we offer critical reflections on both model-free and model-based approaches. In the end, we discuss what would be needed for a systematic solution, not just to the WSC, but to the quest of common sense.

2 The Winograd Schema Challenge

In this section, we briefly introduce the WSC, current progress, and analysis.

2.1 Conception, Format and Features

The Turing Test, as an early attempt to test machine intelligence, was criticized as being vulnerable to intentional deception without desirable intelligence [10, 19]. To construct a better evaluation scheme, Levesque et al. [10] conceptualized the WSC, as an alternative to the Turing Test, that targets three aspects: 1)

Commonsense knowledge and reasoning; 2) Natural language understanding; 3) Automatic evaluation. A typical WSC problem is a multiple-choice question-answering pair involving coreference resolution as follows:

Example 1. The trophy doesn't fit into the brown suitcase because <u>it</u> is too *large.* What is too *large?*
A. the trophy (correct answer) B. the suitcase

The sentence depicts a daily situation, including two parties (e.g., "the trophy" and "the suitcase") and an ambiguous pronoun (e.g., "<u>it</u>") or a possessive adjective (such as "its"). The following question then asks the subject to resolve the ambiguous pronoun to one of the two options.

WSC employs a special feature to test agents' ability to understand commonsense and reasoning are indeed required. A WSC problem contains a *special* word (e.g., "*large*") that always comes with an *alternate.* Substituting the special word with the alternative will flip the correct choice. For example, when changing "*large*" into "*small*", the pronoun would refer to "the suitcase" instead. WSC problems are designed to come in pairs, in which the two only differ in the special word and answer. By design, WSC problems would not be easy by using mere statistical features mined from a large corpus of text [10]. Instead, possessing the commonsense knowledge absent in the problem and reasoning should be necessary, which relies on a good collection to meet these demands.

2.2   Competition, Dataset, and Analyses

Researchers collected a total of 300 WSC problems available online [3]. Trinh and Le [25] tested their methods on the first 273 of them, named WSC273, which became a popular dataset for the WSC. The NLP benchmark SuperGLUE incorporates a binary classification task based on WSC, referred to as SuperGLUE-WSC [27]. Sakaguchi et al. [20] provided a large-scale problem set similar to WSC, using crowd-sourcing. Bender [1] established the first human baseline evaluation for the WSC, which reported a 92% of accuracy for 400 native English speakers. Answering the questions turns out to require significant mental effort. There was also quality concern about the examples, e.g. the *one-way ambiguity*: The correct answers are only evident after the whole pair of questions are revealed together. Trichelair et al. [24] classified problems into two groups: *associative* and *non-associative*, depending on whether one answer candidate obviously associates with the clause containing the pronoun.

2.3   Current Approaches

There are two strands of approaches tackling WSC: model-free and model-based. In this paper, a method is considered model-based if (1) It could manifest traits of a representation of the world in understanding the sentences and knowledge, in a human-comprehensible manner and (2) Such representations would indeed be used in answering the question while the reasoning steps are also interpretable.

Impressive progress has been made by end-to-end model-free approaches on WSC, especially using large-scale neural LMs [16,20,24]. These approaches typically employ neural language models such as GPT-2 [16] and RoBERTa [12], which are pre-trained using large corpora for the language modeling task. In doing so, the commonsense hidden in the corpora is believed to be mined. Moreover, these LMs are suitable for fine-tuning on datasets similar to the WSC. When the RoBERTa LM was fine-tuned on WinoGrande, a large-scale WSC-like dataset, it showed promising results on the SuperGLUE-WSC, achieving accuracy above 90% [20]. This LM also holds the current SOTA performance on WSC273 with an accuracy of 87.55% [28].

On the model-based side, structured representations are utilized to provide interpretable answers. Schüller [22] pointed out that for some cases in WSC, world knowledge is not enough to deduce the correct answer as pragmatics is in play. Sentences and knowledge are represented using graphs based on syntactic analysis. Using the relevance theory as a reasoning backend, 4 problems were solved. Sharma et al. [23] further proposed to hunt for similar sentences online as a source of knowledge. Golovin et al. [5] employed a logic of conditional belief, based on the assumption that humans solve WSC problems by picturing different possible scenarios and then choosing the most plausible one among them. They utilized existing NLP tools to automatically translate sentences into relational triples while extracting rules from the ConceptNet [9], a semantic network containing triples about commonsense concepts. Although their approach demonstrated human-understandable justification, the accuracy was not on par with their LM-based counterparts. These attempts are limited at least in two aspects for the WSC problems: 1) graphs and triples might not be expressive enough; 2) the source of knowledge might not be comprehensive. Without proper representation for complicated situations and knowledge, the effectiveness of reasoning is much hindered.

It is also noteworthy that there are approaches trying to combine neural networks and logical frameworks. Prakash et al. [15] used syntactic information of similar sentences from the internet as a source to construct alignment between original WSC sentences and web-searched sentences. They also used the BERT LM to adjust the alignment, before using a probabilistic soft logic framework to answer the questions. Such methods do not align completely with either side but they provide valuable lessons. While both sides have their merits, we believe it is their issues that are the keys that might lead us to a systematic approach for the WSC, and even the higher goal of reaching human-level intelligence.

2.4   Have LM-Based Approaches Already Solved WSC?

As LM-based approaches reach comparable human-level accuracies, concerns have been raised about their true understanding of commonsense.

Lack of Interpretability. Due to the neural network nature, the commonsense learned by and the reasoning process of LMs are not human-interpretable. Without a proper model about the world, often found in Bayesian Networks or logical approaches, the performance of LMs might be mere "likelihood of combinations of words in corpora" [18]. An example could be seen from [7], where the BERT LM achieved 72.5% on WSC273 when fine-tuned on both WSCR and MaskedWiki, two related datasets. Oddly, fine-tuning only on MaskedWiki didn't improve the performance at all, while fine-tuning only on WSCR boosted the accuracy from 61.9% to 71.4%. The spurious results, combined with the uninterpretable nature, are not convincing evidence of machine commonsense.

Lack of Robustness. Researchers have discovered that model-free approaches could suffer from simple adversarial examples in the task of natural language inference [6,26]. Trichelair et al. [24] came up with adversarial WSC examples where the two parties are swapped from the original sentences, thus changing the answers accordingly. They discovered that LMs could not *consistently* cope with such examples.

Lack of Understanding the Reasons. While humans are capable of not only correctly answer WSC problems, but also providing convincing explanations or reasons for their judgement, LMs seem to lack such capability. In [28], the authors curated both positive and negative explanations for choosing the correct answers to WSC problems. The experiments showed that LMs could not effectively distinguish the explanations, as the accuracy on the new task dropped to around 55% at best.

We attribute these deficiencies to the model-free nature of LMs. Without a proper representation of the world and natural language text, it is not surprising that these methods rely exclusively on superficial features of the text. Fine-tuning on WSC-like datasets improves the performance, and yet it's unclear how to interpret how they employ common sense instead of exploiting artifacts in datasets. It is reasonable to hypothesize that until methods adopt proper world models, a satisfying solution to the WSC is beyond reach.

3   Representing and Reasoning with WSC Using First-Order Logic: Our Exploration

In this section, we introduce our exploration to represent WSC in the situation calculus and to reason with a first-order theorem prover. The motivations are: 1) identify the key challenges for KR&R presented by the WSC, and 2) examine whether FOL is a suitable representation and reasoning scheme for WSC. Therefore we adopt the ideal condition where both language understanding and knowledge acquisition are done manually. In this way, our investigation would not be bottlenecked. We found that 1) FOL could be an approximate representation language for WSC, albeit not perfect; 2) the reasoning power of FOL theorem provers is sufficient.

We choose the *situation calculus* (SC) [17], a variant of FOL, as the representation language. Compared to generic FOL, SC provides special constructs that enable better descriptions for dynamic worlds. This decision aligns with our observation that many WSC problems involve action and change. We carefully avoid its second-order components, so our approach only uses FOL.

3.1 Preliminaries of the Situation Calculus

SC is a three-sorted language that contains *objects*, *actions* or *situations*. Actions and situations enable us to represent the changing world in a more appropriate way. Actions are what change the world, and they are characterized by *precondition* and *effect axioms*. For example, the action *fitInto* requires its first argument to be a container and the second argument to be not too large. Effect axioms could be systematically transformed into *successor state axioms* (SSAs) [17].

A situation is a sequence of actions, describing the history of how the world changes. The initial situation, S_0, is an empty sequence of action. The special function $do(a, s)$ yields the successor situation s after performing action a. $Poss(a, s)$ states that action a could be performed in situation s, on top of which, $Exec(s)$ states that the sequence of actions in s could be performed in according order. Relational fluents are situation-dependent relations.

In order to formalize WSC problems, we require a number of axioms besides our own formalizations. The basic axioms Σ include the properties of $Exec$ (axioms 1), the unique name axioms (UNAs) for situations, actions, and constants[1].

$$Exec(S_0). \; Exec(do(a, s)) \equiv Exec(s) \wedge Poss(a, s). \tag{1}$$

Besides the basic axioms, our work requires precondition and effect axioms to characterize actions. For each action A, a single action precondition axiom is of the form: $Poss(A(\boldsymbol{x}, s) \equiv \Pi_A(\boldsymbol{x}, s)$, where $\Pi_A(\boldsymbol{x}, s)$ is an FOL formula with free variables among $\boldsymbol{x}$, s. For an action A that might change a relational fluent F, we use positive or negative effect axioms of the form:

$$\varepsilon_F^+(\boldsymbol{x}, \boldsymbol{y}, s) \rightarrow F(\boldsymbol{x}, do(A(\boldsymbol{y}, s)) \tag{2}$$

$$\varepsilon_F^-(\boldsymbol{x}, \boldsymbol{y}, s) \rightarrow \neg F(\boldsymbol{x}, do(A(\boldsymbol{y}, s)) \tag{3}$$

where $\varepsilon_F^+(\boldsymbol{x}, \boldsymbol{y}, s)$ and $\varepsilon_F^-(\boldsymbol{x}, \boldsymbol{y}, s)$ are FOL formulae whose free variables are among $\boldsymbol{x}$, $\boldsymbol{y}$, s. Using SC, we obtain formalization of each problem with four parts: 1) Basic axioms, 2) Problem formulation, 3) Commonsense knowledge rules and 4) Answer candidates: A_1 and A_2.

Let KB denote the set of axioms from the first three parts. The reasoning task is to decide whether $KB \models A_1$ or $KB \models A_2$, where $\models$ denotes entailment in first-order logic. We will use a first-order theorem prover for this purpose.

3.2 Formalization in the Situation Calculus

1. Causation: Action and Change. Many WSC problems involve action and change. For example, consider WSC-29:

---

[1] Formulae in this paper are all universally quantified. For brevity, we omit the UNAs.

Example 2. The police left the house and went into the garage, [where/after] they found the murder weapon. Where did they find the murder weapon? **Answers**: garage/house.

This problem involves three events: "leave the house", "go into the garage" and "find the murder weapon", where certain actions change the location of "the police". The preconditions reveal the answer to the question. The pair of special words is *"where"* and *"after"*. They decide the temporal order of these events, showing where the murder weapon was found. We use the following symbols:

- Constants: *Police, House, Garage, Weapon*;
- Actions: $leave(x,p)$, $enter(x,p)$, $findIn(x,y,s)$;
- Fluents: $Found(x,y,s)$, $Inside(x,p,s)$.

Our formulation for the *"where"* case:

- $Inside(Police, House, S_0)$;
- $S_1 = do(leave(Police, House), S_0)$;
- $S_2 = do(enter(Police, Garage), S_1)$;
- $S_3 = do(findIn(Police, Weapon), S_2)$;
- $Exec(S_3)$.

The $findIn$ action takes place after the police enters the garage. From common sense, leaving and entering places alter the location of subjects, and the subject and object of the action $findIn$ must be in the same place. While Liu et al. [11] reported that a subset of WSC problems involve explicit causations, their approach required the presence of *causal cues* (e.g., "because", "so"). In contrast, situation calculus enables us to model direct causations systematically with precondition and effect axioms: actions change the truth of fluents, and conditions on fluents cause actions to happen. Our formalization for the commonsense knowledge:

- $y \neq z \rightarrow \neg(Inside(x,y,s) \land Inside(x,z,s))$;
- $Inside(x,p,s) \rightarrow \neg Inside(x,p,do(leave(x,p),s))$;
- $\neg Inside(x,p,s) \rightarrow Inside(x,p,do(enter(x,p),s))$;
- $Poss(find(x,y),s) \equiv \exists p.Inside(x,p,s) \land Inside(y,p,s)$;
- $Found(y,do(find(x,y),s))$.

Finally the answer candidates are formalized as $A_1 = Found(Weapon, S_0)$ and $A_2 = Found(Weapon, S_3)$.

2. Frame Problem. This refers to the problem in representing the effects of actions in logic without having to list exhaustively all the "non-effects" of actions.

Example 3. Jane knocked on the door, and Susan answered it. She invited her to come [out/in]. Who invited whom? **Answers**: Jane invited Susan/Susan invited Jane.

Clearly "knocking on the door" wouldn't change the location for both parties. Neither does "answering the door". With a large domain with much more actions and fluents, the frame problem poses as a serious challenge. Luckily, Reiter [17] proposed a solution[2] to this problem via the SSAs. We formalize the SSAs for the actions *comeIn*, *comeOut* and the fluent *Inside*: $Inside(x, do(a, s)) \equiv a = comeIn(x) \vee Inside(x, s) \wedge a \neq comeOut(x)$.

3. Abduction/Deduction. We observe two types of reasoning problems: *abduction* and *deduction*. For abductive problems, we no longer validate whether the answer candidates are entailed. Instead, the candidates ϕ_1 and ϕ_2 are the potential explanations. Our observation from the problem would be explained by one of them, thus we check whether $KB \cup \{A_1\} \models O$ or $KB \cup \{A_2\} \models O$, where O is the observation. This demands our formalization to specify the observation explicitly. For example:

Example 4. John couldn't see the stage with Billy in front of him because he is so [short/tall]. Who is so [short/tall]?
Answers: John/Billy.

When abduction is needed, we manually introduces the symbol *Observe* to specify the observation as:

$$Observe(\neg Exec(see(John, Stage), S_0)).$$

Together with the KB, the candidate $Short(John)$ or $Tall(Billy)$ would explain this observation.

4. Abnormality and Nonmonotonic Reasoning. Nonmonotonic reasoning is a vital part of commonsense reasoning [13], enabling us to cope with defeasible inferences where conclusions could be retracted given more information. Levesque [10] suggested that nonmonotonic reasoning would be necessary for WSC. For certain problems, violations of normality are needed. Notice that in the following example, the results of "convince" are negative:

Example 5. Sid explained his theory to Mark but he couldn't [convince/understand] him. Who did not [convince/understand] whom?
Answers: Sid did not convince Mark/Mark did not convince Sid.

Usually, when someone explains a theory thoroughly, the other party would understand/be convinced. We observe the opposite in this example, where something went wrong.

We introduce a predicate $Ab(c)$ to state the current context c is abnormal, which is then utilized in problem formulation and commonsense knowledge. In

---

[2] This solution only applies to deterministic actions without ramification; In our cases, we have no trouble with this limitation.

this example, we establish the abnormal negative effects of the action $explainTo$ for predicates *Convinced* and *Understand* as commonsense:

$$Ab(c) \leftrightarrow \neg convinced(x, y, do(explainTo(x, y, c), s)).$$

For problems that need abnormality, we include $Ab(C)$ in the formulation.

3.3   Solving with the Theorem Prover

To simulate the way humans solve the WSC, we collect all the commonsense knowledge into a single knowledge base. Given a WSC problem, an important issue is to extract the relevant knowledge. We make iterative calls to an FOL theorem prover to validate whether the extracted commonsense knowledge is enough to come up with the solution. The intuitive idea is as follows: 1) For each WSC problem, retrieve the basic axioms, the problem formulation, and the answer candidates; 2) Extract nonlogical symbols from the formulae, establishing a vocabulary, based on which extract commonsense knowledge formulae mentioning such symbols, forming a set of knowledge while at the same time enlarging the vocabulary by adding new symbols introduced by the extracted knowledge formulae; 3) Invoke the theorem prover to check whether the problem could be solved with current knowledge; 4) Repeat steps 2 to 4 until it is solved.

Let F denote the set of axioms for the basic axioms and problem formulation, K denote the set of knowledge formulae, O denote the observations if *Observe* is present. For deductive problems, we validate if $S \cup K \models A_1$ and $S \cup K \models A_2$. If exactly one holds, then we successfully deduce the correct candidate. For abductive cases, we check for both $S \cup K \cup \{A_1\} \models O$ and $S \cup K \cup \{A_2\} \models O$. Similarly, abduction is successful if and only if exactly one of them holds.

To handle the potential abnormality, preparation is done before invoking the theorem prover. At each iteration, check whether the current set of knowledge formulae involves the atom $Ab(c)$. If yes, we need to make sure the problem formulation mentions $Ab(C)$. For abnormal problems, $Ab(C)$ is already present; If $Ab(C)$ is not present, we add $\neg Ab(C)$.

In our experiment, we utilize the efficient first-order theorem prover Z3 [4]. All but 2 problems in the public collection of the WSC are correctly solved using our formalization. For those two exceptions, our system encounters either conflicting or insufficient knowledge formulae.

4   Discussion

In this section, we reflect on our FOL exploration and summarize the challenges and issues of formalizing WSC from the perspective of KR&R. We also lay out the conjectured desiderata for a systematic solution to the WSC.

4.1   Challenges and Issues of Formalizing WSC

Generality of Commonsense Knowledge. In our formalization, there are few reusable commonsense knowledge rules, as the problems are concerning different scenarios. Instead of exhaustively constructing all possible commonsense rules, it is essential to obtain knowledge that could generalize.

The Frame, Ramification and Qualification Problems. While our approach employs the SSAs to partially solve the frame problem, it does not cater for actions with ramification, that is, indirect effects. Currently, we didn't run into ramification problems in our exploration. However, future formalization might encounter this issue. On the other hand, the qualification problem refers to the difficulty to list all the preconditions. In Example 2, the police leaving the house must depend on the fact that there are no criminals shooting at them from the doorway. Using precondition axioms, we ignore such possibilities.

Contexts and Non-monotonic Reasoning. Generality also requires the realization of contexts [14]. Shifting among different contexts is a common challenge in commonsense reasoning. Our exploration only uses contexts to signal the abnormality. A proper formalization of contexts and their interactions is required.

Mental States: Intentions, Knowledge, and Beliefs. Numerous problems in the WSC involve the social interactions of people, which inevitably calls for special treatments. In one of the problems: *"Susan knew that Ann's son had been in a car accident, so she told her about it"*, both intentions and beliefs are involved. We simply emulate the above reasoning with situation calculus sentences without modeling them using proper constructs.

Flexible Representation. While we demonstrate the power of FOL to solve WSC, it only approximates the many different logic constructs used in commonsense knowledge. The lack of expressiveness and the rigidness of FOL compared to natural language result in rules that are often awkward and contrived. It is obvious that commonsense reasoning requires a more flexible representation.

Different Types of Inference. Exact and sound reasoning might be only a part of what we consider commonsense reasoning. People adopt inexact reasoning, such as inference by analogy or inference by association. There are WSC problems that are associative, allowing humans or even statistical systems to exploit shallow linguistic features to answer correctly [24]. Rather than relying on either precise reasoning or inexact reasoning, we believe future approaches should consider the full spectrum of inference between them.

Language Understanding and Knowledge Acquisition. Our approach currently avoids these two important tasks. Our laborious efforts in formalizing WSC reflect that the great challenges for solving WSC are often skipped or underestimated in model-based approaches. However, these might represent the core issues in achieving human-level intelligence.

4.2 Spectrum Between Model-Free and Model-Based Approaches

While both strands of methods suffer from their own problems, their issues might lead us to a systematic solution for WSC. For model-free approaches, the lack of world models impairs its interpretability for both language understanding and inference, while the rigidness of logical approaches prevents automatic acquisitions of commonsense knowledge. Although we do not yet have a working system to address these issues, it is possible to list desirable ingredients for future research based on our reflections.

- Model-based language understanding and reasoning modules. This doesn't exclude a neural implementation. Rather we encourage neural approaches to incubate the ability to create world models in order to overcome the issues of brittleness.
- Flexible representation and reasoning that could enable automatic acquisitions of knowledge and tractable inference. While formal languages and exact reasoning are too rigid in some cases, the model-free LMs or even graph structures might not be adequate in others. A multi-layer framework with different representations and reasoning is called for.

In addition to resolving the pronouns in WSC problems, systems with these ingredients should have little trouble providing enough detailed explanations behind their decisions.

5 Conclusion

The recent advance of model-free approaches had shown promising results in answering WSC questions. We focused instead on their lack of interpretability and attribute the limitations to their model-free nature. We investigated the KR&R issues behind the WSC by formalizing them using FOL. Although the reasoning power was enough for our formalization, we believe it requires a more flexible representation and a wide range of inference in order to encompass the commonsense in the WSC. In light of this, we postulated the essential ingredients for a systematic solution: model-based understanding and reasoning, with a full spectrum of suitable representation and reasoning. Hopefully, our efforts would illustrate a rough direction and call for the community to re-visit the pioneers' works on common sense, towards solving the WSC.

Acknowledgement. We thank Prof. Yongmei Liu for her guidance and insightful advice, and we thank Yu Dong for his effort. We acknowledge support from the National Natural Science Foundation of China (No. 61572535) and the Guangdong Basic and Applied Basic Research Foundation (2020A1515010642).

References

1. Bender, D.: Establishing a human baseline for the Winograd schema challenge. In: MAICS, pp. 39–45 (2015)
2. Davis, E., Marcus, G.: Commonsense reasoning and commonsense knowledge in artificial intelligence. Commun. ACM **58**(9), 92–103 (2015)
3. Davis, E., Morgenstern, L., Ortiz, C.: The Winograd schema challenge (2016). https://cs.nyu.edu/~davise/papers/WinogradSchemas/WS.html
4. de Moura, L., Bjørner, N.: Z3: an efficient SMT solver. In: Ramakrishnan, C.R., Rehof, J. (eds.) TACAS 2008. LNCS, vol. 4963, pp. 337–340. Springer, Heidelberg (2008). https://doi.org/10.1007/978-3-540-78800-3_24
5. Golovin, D., Claßen, J., Schwering, C.: Reasoning about conditional beliefs for the Winograd schema challenge. In: COMMONSENSE 2017 (2017)
6. Gururangan, S., Swayamdipta, S., Levy, O., Schwartz, R., Bowman, S.R., Smith, N.A.: Annotation artifacts in natural language inference data. In: NAACL-HLT, pp. 107–112 (2018)
7. Kocijan, V., Cretu, A., Camburu, O., Yordanov, Y., Lukasiewicz, T.: A surprisingly robust trick for the Winograd schema challenge. In: ACL, pp. 4837–4842 (2019)
8. Lake, B.M., Ullman, T.D., Tenenbaum, J.B., Gershman, S.J.: Building machines that learn and think like people. Behav. Brain Sci. **40**, e253 (2017)
9. Lenat, D.B.: CYC: a large-scale investment in knowledge infrastructure. Commun. ACM **38**(11), 32–38 (1995)
10. Levesque, H.J., Davis, E., Morgenstern, L.: The Winograd schema challenge. In: KR 2012(2012)
11. Liu, Q., Jiang, H., Ling, Z.H., Zhu, X., Wei, S., Hu, Y.: Combing context and commonsense knowledge through neural networks for solving Winograd schema problems. In: 2017 AAAI Spring Symposium Series (2017)
12. Liu, Y., et al.: RoBERTa: a robustly optimized BERT pretraining approach. arXiv:1907.11692 (2019)
13. McCarthy, J.: Generality in artificial intelligence. Commun. ACM **30**(12), 1030–1035 (1987)
14. McCarthy, J.: Notes on formalizing context. In: Proceedings of the 13th International Joint Conference on Artificial Intelligence - Volume 1, IJCAI 1993, pp. 555–560. Morgan Kaufmann Publishers Inc., San Francisco (1993)
15. Prakash, A., Sharma, A., Mitra, A., Baral, C.: Combining knowledge hunting and neural language models to solve the Winograd schema challenge. In: ACL, pp. 6110–6119 (2019)
16. Radford, A., Wu, J., Child, R., Luan, D., Amodei, D., Sutskever, I.: Language models are unsupervised multitask learners. OpenAI Blog **1**(8), 9 (2019)
17. Reiter, R.: Knowledge in Action: Logical Foundations for Specifying and Implementing Dynamical Systems. MIT Press, Cambridge (2001)
18. Richard-Bollans, A., Álvarez, L.G., Cohn, A.G.: The role of pragmatics in solving the Winograd schema challenge. In: COMMONSENSE 2017 (2017)
19. Russell, S.J., Norvig, P.: Artificial Intelligence - A Modern Approach. Third International Edition. Pearson Education, London (2010)
20. Sakaguchi, K., Bras, R.L., Bhagavatula, C., Choi, Y.: Winogrande: an adversarial Winograd schema challenge at scale. In: AAAI 2020, pp. 8732–8740 (2020)
21. Sap, M., Rashkin, H., Chen, D., LeBras, R., Choi, Y.: SocialIQA: commonsense reasoning about social interactions. In: EMNLP (2019)

22. Schüller, P.: Tackling Winograd schemas by formalizing relevance theory in knowledge graphs. In: KR 2014 (2014)
23. Sharma, A., Vo, N.H., Aditya, S., Baral, C.: Towards addressing the Winograd schema challenge - building and using a semantic parser and a knowledge hunting module. IJCAI **2015**, 1319–1325 (2015)
24. Trichelair, P., Emami, A., Trischler, A., Suleman, K., Cheung, J.C.K.: How reasonable are common-sense reasoning tasks: a case-study on the Winograd schema challenge and SWAG. In: EMNLP-IJCNLP, November 2019
25. Trinh, T.H., Le, Q.V.: A simple method for commonsense reasoning. arXiv (2018)
26. Tsuchiya, M.: Performance impact caused by hidden bias of training data for recognizing textual entailment. In: LREC 2018 (2018)
27. Wang, A., et al.: SuperGLUE: a stickier benchmark for general-purpose language understanding systems. In: NeurIPS 2019, pp. 3261–3275 (2019)
28. Zhang, H., Zhao, X., Song, Y.: WinoWhy: a deep diagnosis of essential common-sense knowledge for answering Winograd schema challenge. In: ACL 2020, pp. 5736–5745 (2020)

The Novel Efficient Transformer for NLP

Benjamin Mensa-Bonsu$^{(\boxtimes)}$, Tao Cai$^{(\boxtimes)}$, Tresor Y. Koffi, and Dejiao Niu

Jiangsu University, Zhenjiang, Jiangsu, China
5102181306@stmail.ujs.edu.cn, caitao@ujs.edu.cn

Abstract. Reducing the numerical precision of weights and activations of deep neural networks have proven to be a stunningly efficient way of deploying deep networks on edge devices with limited resources. With the advent of the Transformer model, several quantization techniques have been proposed to reduce the computation and model size. However, these existing quantization techniques use fixed bit-width assignments, which result in a significant degradation in the accuracy of the model. We present in this work an efficient Transformer based on our novel multi-layer quantization technique, which reduces the precision of data based on the characteristics of weights and activations in each layer of the Transformer architecture while at the same time preserving the model's structure. The WMT2014 DE-EN and WMT2014 FR-EN datasets are used to evaluate. The results show that our efficient Transformer achieves 4x compression with improved accuracy and an overall reduction in the training time overhead. By comparing with existing state-of-the-art techniques, we further proved that with a minimum of 3-bit and a maximum of 8-bit quantization, comparable state-of-the-art BLEU scores can be obtained.

Keywords: Natural language processing · Transformer · Multi-layer quantization · Machine translation

1 Introduction

Natural language processing (NLP) tasks including machine translation [4], speech recognition [16] and sentiment analysis [20] have over the years produced excellent results by employing Recurrent Neural Networks (RNNs), Long Short-Term Memory (LSTM) [10], and Gated Recurrent Unit (GRU) models. These models though effective in many NLP tasks, however, had a major limitation, which is their inability to deal with long-range dependencies. Further research has lead to the recent development of the Transformer model [17] that extensively employs the self-attention mechanism instead of RNNs, and has achieved state-of-the-art accuracy in several natural language processing tasks. The Transformer model's successes can largely be attributed to its superior capability in capturing long-distance dependencies and the use of millions of parameters during training, hence making the Transformer a very deep model. The deeper the learning model, the better the accuracy [2], but this also gives rise to many new

© Springer Nature Switzerland AG 2021
H. Qiu et al. (Eds.): KSEM 2021, LNAI 12816, pp. 139–151, 2021.
https://doi.org/10.1007/978-3-030-82147-0_12

challenges as deeper models have an extensive memory requirement and also consume a significant amount of system resources in terms of time and power.

With these drawbacks, it is impractical to deploy the Transformer model on embedded devices that have limited computational resources and memory capacity. A growing body of research is currently dedicated to discovering various methods to significantly reduce the model size and inference time for the Transformer model with very little or no degradation in the model's accuracy. A compression technique like Pruning [22] which involves removing redundant or unimportant weights to achieve a sparse compact network for inference, has been proposed. Other techniques like network Quantization [14], and the combinations of these approaches have all been proposed in current literature to address the low latency, memory capacity, and power efficiency requirements of the Transformer. Though pruned Transformer models have been proven to be effective in model size reduction with preserved accuracy [18], its iterative nature requires excessive prune–retrain cycles with additional hyperparameter adjustments. The Transformer quantization method, on the other hand, uses fixed bit-width [1] to reduce the precision of the neural network parameters from single-precision (FP32) to lower bit representations with a trade-off in accuracy.

In this work, we provide a novel *multi-layer quantization* (abbreviated as MLQ) technique that stores the Transformer model in low bit precision based on the characteristics of the weights and activations of each layer of the model's architecture. We also provide a simplified overall training architecture that preserves the model structure and reduces the overall training time of the Transformer model. With the proposed MLQ, we achieved state-of-the-art BLEU performance on WMT2014 DE-EN and WMT2014 FR-EN datasets with a 4x compression rate. Our core contributions are as follows:

- We propose a novel MLQ technique to achieve a highly compressed model and simplify the Transformer's overall training architecture and training time. This leads to a negligible loss in accuracy.
- We perform a sensitivity analysis of each layer of the Transformer architecture before quantization. This analysis forms the basis for accurate bit-width selection for weights and activations of the Transformer model.
- Unlike traditional pruning and quantization methods, a new weight classification algorithm that classifies weights in each layer of the Transformer based on the weights' characteristics is given to avoid removing parameters before quantization and maintain the whole structural information of the model.
- An activation deduction module that combines with the weight classification algorithm is also introduced to ensure activations are quantized based on their characteristics in each layer of the Transformer model.

The rest of this paper is organized as follows. In Sect. 2, we describe the related work, followed by the analysis of the current Transformer in Sect. 3. We present our novel efficient quantization technique in Sect. 4 and perform related experiments in Sect. 5. Finally in Sect. 6 we provide the conclusion.

2   Related Work

The study of low-precision methods for training deep neural networks is an active research area due to the increasing time and energy cost of training large-scale deep learning models. In the pursuit of enhancing compute efficiency, [8] trained a deep neural network with minimal loss in accuracy, using a 16-bit fixed-point representation. Near state-of-the-art results on MNIST, CIFAR-10, and SVHN datasets were obtained in [6] in constraining weights to either +1 or −1 during propagation. Consequent research in reducing precision below half-precision led to DoreFa-Net [21], and a binarized neural network [11] each producing a version of AlexNet [12] which quantizes the weights and activations of the neural networks using different bit-widths of 1 and 2, respectively. Model weights, activations, and gradients were proven to be capable of being stored in half-precision [14] without any further adjustments in hyperparameters, but further research in [7] suggested that quantizing to an ultra-low bit precision introduces quantization noise into the model, causing significant degradation in performance of the model. In addressing the accuracy drawback in quantization, stochastic rounding using 16-bit fixed-point representation [8] has been applied with little degradation in the accuracy.

In relation to machine translation tasks, a distributed training of OpenSeq2Seq [13] in a mixed-precision manner was designed to give a state-of-the-art performance at 1.5-3x less training time. A combination of iterative magnitude pruning [9] with quantization algorithm based on k-means clustering resulted in transformers.zip [3] with high-performance percentage. Recently, the Lite Transformer [19] has been designed with a Long-Short Range attention mechanism to support deployment on edge devices. However, its compression algorithm combines quantization with pruning, which we avoid because pruning has the potential of distorting model structure and increasing overall training time, as proven in this work. In this work, we perform a varied bit-width quantization, which, unlike current existing quantization techniques, does not remove weights from the network. We also do not use a fixed INT8 bit-width but rather introduce new algorithms to classify weights and activations into important or less important parameters before selectively quantizing them.

3   Analysis of the Current Transformer

The Transformer architecture as proposed by [17] for machine translation is composed of an encoder-decoder structure with multi-head attention arranged in N layers. The input token vectors to each layer are projected by a self-attention into a set of keys K, queries Q, and values V. A scaled dot product attention is then used to compare and combine them using the dimension of the keys given as d_k:

$$Attention(Q, K, V) = softmax\left(\frac{QK^T}{\sqrt{d_k}}\right) V \qquad (1)$$

Multi-head self-attention is obtained by concatenating the multiple self-attention heads h times with a linear matrix projection W_O:MultiHead(Q, K, V) = Concat $(head_1, head_2, .., head_h)$ W_O, where:

$$head_i = Attention(QW_1, KW_2, VW_3) \tag{2}$$

The W_i represents the learned linear transformations $W_i : d_{model} \rightarrow$ d*. The outputs of multi-head attention go through a 2-layer position-wise feed-forward network with ReLU in between:

$$FFN(x) = W_2ReLu(W_1x + b_1) + b_2 \tag{3}$$

The major challenge associated with the current Transformer architecture has to do with how to effectively encode arbitrarily long contexts into its fixed size parameter representation during training. A challenge that is popularly known as context-fragmentation. A better solution to address this compute-intensive process will be to evaluate the weights and activations in a low-bit representation using the proposed quantization algorithm in this paper.

3.1   Analysis of the Current Training Architecture of Transformer

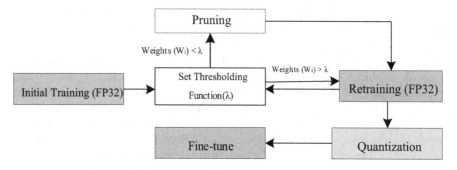

Fig. 1. The current pruning and quantization training architecture for the Transformer.

Aside from the current challenges with quantizing the Transformer, the overall existing low precision training architecture in itself has significant drawbacks. It can be observed from Fig. 1 that the model is first trained in high precision (FP32), after which a thresholding function is invoked to separate weights. Prior to quantization, the training architecture follows a rigorous train-prune-retrain cycle, which requires paying close attention to the hyperparameter adjustments; this results in an increase in the training time. This traditional pruning follows a salience based method to set to zero and remove redundant weights (or connections) from the neural network based on their weight's magnitudes and Hessian function of the loss with respect to the weights, which is defined as follows:

$$S_c = \begin{cases} W_{ij} \\ A \end{cases} as \quad A = \frac{W_{ij}^2 H_{jj}}{2} \tag{4}$$

S_c represents the salience score for the weight matrix W_{ij} with Hessian matrix H_{jj}. This method, though effective in reducing model size, has adverse effects on the model structure and overall accuracy of the Transformer. Aside from the weights, quantizing activations is also crucial. Activations of full precision have the potential of spreading in a wide range; therefore, proper distribution and assessment of activations need to be done prior to quantization to prevent the activation distribution from exploding in value.

4   The Novel Efficient Transformer for NLP

4.1   The Novel Training Architecture for Efficient NLP Transformer

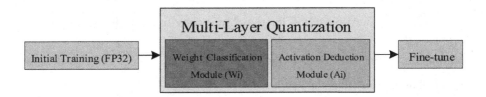

Fig. 2. The proposed simplified training architecture for the Transformer.

To reduce the training time and maintain the accuracy of the Transformer, we propose a novel MLQ technique composed of weight classification and activation deduction modules. The weight classification module analyzes the sensitivity of weights in each layer of the Transformer, while the activation deduction module, on the other hand, deduces the entropy of activations in each layer as the basis for quantization. These modules together provide a solid basis for the novel quantization of weights and activations, making sure each layer is not quantized "too much or too little" but efficiently with accuracy preserved.

4.2   The Weight Classification

We design the weight classification rule to distinguish the important degree of weights. This provides the basis for using different bit assignments for different weight sensitivities. The Hessian value H is directly proportional to the importance of the weights; therefore, in the weight classification, we define an optimal salient threshold value where all weights with the magnitude below the threshold would be considered less important. As shown in Algorithm 1, we define our magnitude by looping through each layer of the Transformer architecture,

---

Algorithm 1. Weight Classification

Procedure: $classifyWeights(M_{FP})$ ▶ M_{FP} is the full precision (FP32) model

Initialize model layers to be M_L

Initialize $\sigma, W_{imp}, W_{Limp}$ to represent Std Dev of each layer weights, Important weights and Less Important weights respectively.

foreach layer L in M_L **do**   ▶ loop through layer weights

$\quad \sigma = findStd((L(W))$

$\quad\quad th \leftarrow mul(\sigma, q)$ ▶ define the threshold

if $|W| > th$ **then**

$\quad W_{imp} \leftarrow M_L(W)$

end if

if $|W| < th$ **then**

$\quad W_{Limp} \leftarrow M_L(W)$

end if

end foreach

Update model weights (M_{FP}) with W_{imp}, W_{Limp}

return M_{FP}

---

calculate the standard deviation for that layer, then multiply it by the quality parameter q.

From Eq. 4, our salience criterion is updated as: $S_c = \begin{cases} q\sigma_{ij} \\ A \end{cases}$ which defines our thresholding function $th(.)$ to be:

$$th(W_{ij}) = \begin{cases} W_{ij} & if \quad |W_{ij}| > \dfrac{q\sigma_{ij}}{\dfrac{W_{ij}^2 H_{jj}}{2}} \\[3em] W_{zj} & if \quad |W_{ij}| \leq \dfrac{q\sigma_{ij}}{\dfrac{W_{ij}^2 H_{jj}}{2}} \end{cases} \tag{5}$$

The thresholding function $th(W_{ij})$ in Eq. 5 above is used to classify the weights in each layer of the Transformer as important or less important weights, after which bit-width assignment is performed based on the weight's class. Important weights are lightly quantized to prevent loss of data and quantization errors whilst less important weights are heavily quantized to achieve a more compressed model with high accuracy. Our MLQ relies on this weight classification to determine the extent to which weights are to be quantized for each layer.

4.3   The Activation Deduction

The activation deduction follows a similar process as that of the weights. We are, however, the first to apply this idea with the Transformer model in a machine translation task by introducing and combining an L_2 regularization factor with the thresholding function to act as a penalty during training to prevent the activations from exploding in value. To calculate the entropy, we consider the elements of each layer's activations $A_{ij}, i \in 1, 2, .., k$ as random variables of an underlying distribution p_i, then the entropy H^i for the ith layer is given as $\mathrm{H}^i = -\Sigma p_i(A_{ij}) \log(p_i(A_{ij}))$. The activation deduction function for each layer becomes:

$$th(A_{ij}) + L_2 = \begin{cases} A_{ij} & if \quad \|A_{ij}\| > \mathrm{H}^i \\ A_{zj} & if \quad \|A_{ij}\| \leq \mathrm{H}^i \end{cases} \tag{6}$$

where $L_2 = (\gamma)\dfrac{1}{N} \sum_{i=1}^{k} \|A_{ij}\|^2$ and γ and $\mathbf{N}$ represent the parameters to control regularization and batch size respectively. The clamp function is then used to associate all the values outside the (X_{min}, X_{max}) range, depending on the value of x which is the input to the layer; $clamp(x; \alpha, \beta) = min(max(x, \alpha)\beta)$. Softmax divisions and outputs are also computed in low precision for faster inference. The output of the Scaled Dot-Product utilizes low matrix computations in our proposed algorithm, therefore permitting loss to be calculated through forward propagation with quantized weights.

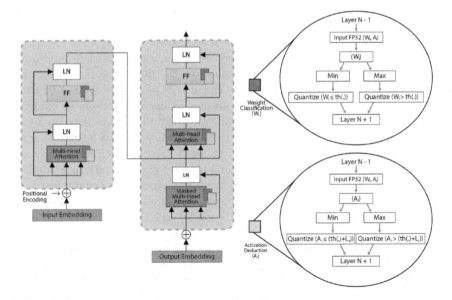

Fig. 3. MLQ of transformer for NLP. Weight classification (W_i) analyses weight characteristics whilst the activation deduction (A_i) analyses the characteristics of activations in each **N**th layer of the Transformer architecture.

4.4   Multi-layer Quantization (MLQ) Algorithm

We perform an initial few epochs training of the model in high precision (FP32) to learn language embedding. This serves as a preparatory period to set a quantization reference for the weight classification and activation deduction modules. After this preparatory period, the bit-width for weights and activations are determined, and a fine-tuned quantized network is derived by scaling all entries of the input matrix to the close interval [0,1]. We determine the weight bit-width for the nth layer using the weight classification algorithm while quantizing the activations using the activation deduction algorithm. The MLQ technique is then applied with the step size between two quantized values dynamically deduced to re-scale the weights and activations in the range that can be represented by the desired integer bit-width. Important weights and high entropy activations are given defined quantization endpoints that will conserve as much information in order not to distort accuracy. On the other hand, less important weights and low entropy activations are assigned higher endpoints to reduce precision heavily. Unlike existing uniform quantization approaches, the weight classification and activation deduction does an initial work of projecting a degree of relevance on each weight or activation respectively and produce a desired bit-width $\boldsymbol{b}$. For the real value $\boldsymbol{x}$, and the desired bit-width $\boldsymbol{b}$, the Quantized function $\boldsymbol{Q(x)}$ is given as:

$$Q_b(X) = \frac{1}{2^b - 1} round((2^b - 1)X) + \frac{1}{2} \tag{7}$$

We can infer from Eq. 3 that the position-wise feed-forward layers of the Transformer consist of a ReLU function between two linear transformations. Our quantization module, therefore, targets all inputs to the network and re-scales the output of the ReLU computations to the range $[\alpha\beta]$ being represented by the n bits integer. The summation operations are not quantized because, at inference time, its computation does not produce any extra gains. All inputs to the multi-head attention in both the encoders and decoders are quantized by assessing the sensitivity of the keys K, queries Q, and values V, respectively. We enforce our MLQ on the fully connected and embedding layer's weights, which make up 99% of the Transformer's weights, except for the biases since they occupy just 0.1% of the total weights. This helps to reduce the model size by 4x with a speedup in training overhead. We fine-tune the new model on a few epochs train to reach convergence.

In each feed-forward and multi-attention layer of the Transformer, we convert the FP32 weight matrices, inputs, and activation tensors to lower bit representations while replacing all the core computations (FP32 MatMuls) of the Transformer to lower bits as well. From Fig. 3 (left), it can be observed that the architecture of the Transformer model is composed of different layers. Each layer has its varied characteristics based on its weights and activations, therefore applying quantization to suit these varied characteristics is optimal for efficiency.

5 Experiments and Results

The proposed MLQ method in this work is evaluated using the base Transformer model [17] with characteristics of 6 layers encoder-decoder structure, d_{model} of 512 with 8 heads, and d_{ff} of 2048, as our precision reference and an initial set of model parameters.

5.1 WMT 2014 DE-EN

Layer Sensitivity. The WMT2014 DE-EN data set contains 4.5M sentence pairs. We use *newstest2013* as the development set and *newstest2014* as test set, and report BLEU scores using $multi - bleu.perl$. This experiment analyzes the sensitivity of each layer of the Transformer and how it responds to our MLQ scheme. Given Table 1, to arrive at the optimum quantization schedule, we experiment on various bit quantization combinations and choose the minimum number of quantization bits for each layer such that overall model accuracy in terms of BLEU scores becomes high. From Table 1, a fixed n-bit quantization, where n < 8 (n = 4), will result in very low accuracy. Within the layers, the Important parameters (Imp) are more sensitive to quantization resulting in severe accuracy degradation when quantized to n < 8. This layer sensitivity analysis helps us to assign the number of bits for each layer's weights and activations accordingly. For the important weights and activations, we quantize with n = 8 while quantizing the less important ($LessImp$) weights and activations to n = 3. This gives us a deeply compressed model with preserved accuracy.

Table 1. Layer sensitivity analysis of the transformer using WMT2014 DE-EN dataset.

Multi-head		FeedForward		BLEU
#Bits (Imp)	#Bits (Less Imp)	#Bits (Imp)	#Bits (Less Imp)	
4	4	4	4	24.64
8	8	8	8	28.7
4	8	4	8	26.7
8	3	8	3	**27.9**

Training Time Overhead. We further compare the training time of our MLQ's training architecture to other existing quantization schemes. We automate the overall training process involved in Transformer quantization by setting a fixed number of training epochs (400). This experiment's focus is not on accuracy since few epochs are run; the focus, however, is to validate how changes in the model structure affect the training times of the various quantization schemes. From Fig. 4, it can be observed that all the quantization schemes use almost equal training time during the initial few training epochs. This is

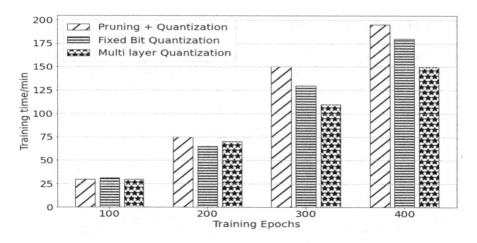

Fig. 4. Training time comparison of our MLQ with other quantization methods.

because quantization techniques learn word embeddings from the dataset at this stage. Between 100–200 epochs, weights less than the defined threshold is being calculated, which increases the training time for the *Pruning + Quantization* (P+Q) technique. The *Fixed Bit Quantization* (FBQ) also begins calculating the X_{min} and X_{max} for various weights, while our classification algorithms are in session for MLQ. The period between 200–300 epochs is the most crucial and time-consuming stage of the entire training process. Unimportant weights are being shed off in the P+Q technique, while all weights and activations are uniformly compressed in the FBQ technique. This is also the stage where our MLQ technique analysis the characteristics of each layer of the model prior to quantization. The MLQ has the least wall clock minutes in training time after 400 epochs due to its simplified training architecture. This is followed by the FBQ, which trails slightly behind ours due to the re-adjustment of weights and activations after a uniform quantization. The Pruning process has been completed successfully, and quantization therefore follows, accounting for the longer training time in P + Q. This trend continues till the end of the training.

5.2   WMT2014 FR-EN

The WMT2014 FR-EN dataset contains 36M sentence pairs. Our MLQ strategy targets weight matrices and activations that incur heavy matrix multiplications. These weight matrices account for 99% of the total parameters of the model. We begin the quantization of the activations after a fixed number of steps (3000). The purpose of this is to ensure that a more stable stage of the network has been reached and the estimated ranges do not exclude a significant fraction of values.

We compared our MLQ strategy to other previous Transformer quantization methods, as shown in Table 2. All models have the base Transformer configuration with results from WMT14 train sets and report tokenized-BLEU

Table 2. Performance comparison of our MLQ with other current quantization methods.

Method	Precision	BLEU		Compression
		EN-DE	FR-EN	
Vaswani et al., 2017 [17]	Full	27.3	38.1	1x
Bhandare et al., 2019 [1]	8	27.3	–	≤2.1x
Prato et al., 2020 [15]	8	27.6	39.9	3.91x
Chung et al., 2020 [5]	2.6	27.1	38.0	11.8x
Multi-layer Quant.	Mixed	27.9	39.9	4.0x

on *newstest*2014. Our work attains reasonable accuracy as compared to the reported BLEU of full precision models and other uniform bit quantization methods. The compressed model sizes of all compared models are reported, and the BLEU scores on the test set using the highest validation accuracy checkpoint with multiple training steps are computed. We trained the models once and validated them after every training epoch. The direct quantization process in TensorFlow by [1] did not report the number of training steps, which resulted in their compression rates. The results obtained in [15] were closely related to ours; however, our MLQ reasonably outperforms their work in terms of compression ratio due to the varied bits used in our approach. The extremely low bit quantization in [5] reported a high compression rate with as low as 2.6 bits, but with an expected trade-off in accuracy as compared to our method.

6 Conclusion

In this work, we proposed a novel multi-layer quantization technique that quantizes the Transformer model for NLP by analyzing the characteristics of weights and activations in each layer of the Transformer model. Important weights and activations are lightly quantized, while less important weights and activations are highly quantized to give a 4x compressed model with preserved accuracy. We further complemented our novel method with experimental results and analysis to confirm its superior accuracy in terms of BLEU scores with existing state-of-the-art quantization techniques.

Acknowledgement. This work was funded by the National Natural Science Foundation of China, Grant Number 61806086, and the Project of National Key R&D Program of China, Grant Numbers 2018YFB0804204 and 2019YFB1600500.

References

1. Bhandare, A., et al.: Efficient 8-bit quantization of transformer neural machine language translation model. arXiv preprint arXiv:1906.00532 (2019)

2. Brock, A., Donahue, J., Simonyan, K.: Large scale GAN training for high fidelity natural image synthesis. arXiv preprint arXiv:1809.11096 (2018)
3. Cheong, R., Daniel, R.: transformers.zip: compressing transformers with pruning and quantization. Technical report, Stanford University, Stanford, California (2019)
4. Cho, K., van Merriënboer, B., Bahdanau, D., Bengio, Y.: On the properties of neural machine translation: encoder-decoder approaches. In: Proceedings of SSST-8, 8th Workshop on Syntax, Semantics and Structure in Statistical Translation (2014)
5. Chung, I., et al.: Extremely low bit transformer quantization for on-device neural machine translation. In: Findings of the Association for Computational Linguistics: EMNLP 2020 (2020)
6. Courbariaux, M., Bengio, Y., David, J.P.: BinaryConnect: training deep neural networks with binary weights during propagations. In: Proceedings of the 28th International Conference on Neural Information Processing Systems (2015)
7. Fan, A., et al.: Training with quantization noise for extreme model compression. arXiv e-prints arXiv:2004.07320 (2020)
8. Gupta, S., Agrawal, A., Gopalakrishnan, K., Narayanan, P.: Deep learning with limited numerical precision. In: Proceedings of the 32nd International Conference on International Conference on Machine Learning - Volume 37, pp. 1737–1746 (2015)
9. He, Q., et al.: Effective quantization methods for recurrent neural networks. arXiv:1611.10176 (2016)
10. Hochreiter, S., Schmidhuber, J.: Long short-term memory. Neural Comput. 9(8), 1735–1780 (1997)
11. Hubara, I., Courbariaux, M., Soudry, D., El-Yaniv, R., Bengio, Y.: Binarized neural networks. In: Proceedings of the 30th International Conference on Neural Information Processing Systems, pp. 4114–4122 (2016)
12. Krizhevsky, A., Sutskever, I., Hinton, G.E.: ImageNet classification with deep convolutional neural networks. In: Advances in Neural Information Processing Systems, vol. 25. Curran Associates, Inc. (2012)
13. Kuchaiev, O., Ginsburg, B., Gitman, I., Lavrukhin, V., Case, C., Micikevicius, P.: OpenSeq2Seq: extensible toolkit for distributed and mixed precision training of sequence-to-sequence models. In: Proceedings of Workshop for NLP Open Source Software (NLP-OSS), pp. 41–46 (2018)
14. Micikevicius, P., et al.: Mixed precision training. In: International Conference on Learning Representations (2018)
15. Prato, G., Charlaix, E., Rezagholizadeh, M.: Fully quantized transformer for machine translation. In: Findings of the Association for Computational Linguistics: EMNLP 2020, pp. 1–14 (2020)
16. Saini, P., Kaur, P.: Automatic speech recognition: a review. Int. J. Eng. Trends Technol. 4(2), 1–5 (2013)
17. Vaswani, A., et al.: Attention is all you need. In: Proceedings of the 31st International Conference on Neural Information Processing Systems, pp. 6000–6010 (2017)
18. Voita, E., Talbot, D., Moiseev, F., Sennrich, R., Titov, I.: Analyzing multi-head self-attention: specialized heads do the heavy lifting, the rest can be pruned. In: Proceedings of the 57th Annual Meeting of the Association for Computational Linguistics (2019)
19. Wu, Z., Liu, Z., Lin, J., Lin, Y., Han, S.: Lite transformer with long-short range attention. In: 8th International Conference on Learning Representations (2020)

20. Zhang, L., Wang, S., Liu, B.: Deep learning for sentiment analysis: a survey. Wiley Interdiscip. Rev. Data Min. Knowl. Discov. **8**(4), e1253 (2018)
21. Zhou, S., Wu, Y., Ni, Z., Zhou, X., Wen, H., Zou, Y.: DoReFa-Net: training low bitwidth convolutional neural networks with low bitwidth gradients. arXiv preprint arXiv:1606.06160 (2016)
22. Zhu, M., Gupta, S.: To prune, or not to prune: exploring the efficacy of pruning for model compression. In: 6th International Conference on Learning Representations, ICLR 2018 (2018)

Joint Entity and Relation Extraction for Long Text

Dong Cheng, Hui Song$^{(\boxtimes)}$, Xianglong He, and Bo Xu

School of Computer Science and Technology, Donghua University, Shanghai, China
{2191920,2191924}@mail.dhu.edu.cn, {songhui,xubo}@dhu.edu.cn

Abstract. Extracting relation triplets from unstructured text has been well studied in recent years. However, previous works focus on solving the relation overlapping problem, and few of them deal with the long text relation extraction. In this work, we introduce a novel end-to-end joint entity and relation extraction model, namely, LTRel, which is capable of extracting relation triplets from long text based on a cross-sentence relation classification algorithm. On the other hand, due to the importance of entity recognition to the entire end-to-end model, we refine the entity tagging scheme and the feature representation of TPLinker, which save the memory space and computation, and also improve the accuracy. We evaluate our model on two public datasets: the English dataset NYT and the Chinese dataset DuIE2.0 proposed by Baidu, both of which are better than state-of-the-art on F1 score, especially significant on the Chinese dataset with a higher proportion of long text samples.

Keywords: Long text · Relation extraction · End-to-end model · Triplets · Chinese dataset · Cross-sentence

1 Introduction

The task of relation extraction is to identify relation triplets from unstructured texts. A relation triplet consists of pairs of entities mentions with semantic relations, i.e., triplet such as (subject, relation, object). The traditional pipeline methods first extract named entities, and then classify the relation types between candidate entity pairs. However, this kind of models ignore the close connection and interaction between the two subtasks, may leading to error propagation [6]. End-to-end relation extraction models [9, 14] extracting all triplets of entities and relationships in one sentence simultaneously achieve significant performance improvements in both named entity recognition and relation classification.

Recent methods focus on solving the relation overlapping problem which improve the performance greatly. However, they rarely deal with long text relationship extraction methods, and not suitable for too long text. For the mainstream text encoder BERT [19] is a text-length limited model, and the complexity of the relation extraction decoder is usually the square of the text length which also limits the sentence length. Some extraction methods, such as TPLinker [15], employ the sliding window mechanism to translate the problem into multi-sentence extraction, but missing the two types of relation triplets shown as in Fig. 1.

© Springer Nature Switzerland AG 2021
H. Qiu et al. (Eds.): KSEM 2021, LNAI 12816, pp. 152–162, 2021.
https://doi.org/10.1007/978-3-030-82147-0_13

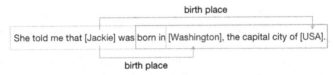

Fig. 1. An example of sliding window method which failed to extract two kinds of relational triplets. The yellow and blue boxes are two windows with a window size of 8 words and a step size of 6. The interval between the subject and the object of one triplet, *(Jackie, birth place, Washington)*, is smaller than the window size 8, but the step size is so large that there is no window that contains both entities. The interval of the other triplet *(Jackie, birth place, USA)* is 10 which is larger than the window size, that is, the maximum text length span. (Color figure online)

In this paper, we propose a novel end-to-end model LTRel for long texts relation extraction which translates the problem into two sentence pairs relation extraction. Our methodology encodes the entities once and classify the relation types within any two sub-sentence based relational graphs [16]. LTRel views the short text relation extraction based on BERT encoder as a special case of two different sentences, without increasing the computational complexity.

In addition, we found that the entity recognition subtask has a great impact on performance. The existing methods suffer with the following problems. GraphRel [16] annotates the entities with BIOES, which cannot handle the nested entity problem. TPLinker [15] identify entities with pointer networks to solve the nested entity problem increasing the complexity of the model to the square of the text length. In the paper, we ignore the invalid negative samples when constructing the entity tagging matrix to reduce the computational complexity and enhance the entity pair semantic representation when judging whether a span is an entity, which is significantly helpful in Chinese.

With LTRel, our contribution in threefold:

- We propose a new end-to-end relation extraction algorithm for long texts, the F1 in the Chinese data set reaches 72.3%, improving the state-of-the-art method +2.2%. (refer the calculating method of others)
- A cross-sentence relation classification algorithm is developed to identify the relation of the entities between two different sentences.
- We optimize the tagging scheme and the entity feature representation of TPLinker, which save the memory space and computation, and also improve the accuracy.

We evaluate our model on two public datasets: the English dataset NYT [18] and the Chinese dataset DuIE2.0 proposed by Baidu, both of which are better than state-of-the-art on F1 score.

2 Related Work

Relation extraction from unstructured texts is a well-studied task in natural language processing field. Early works [1–5] address this task with pipeline method. They first extract named entities with an entity recognition algorithm, and then identify the candidate entity pairs if any relation exists with a relation classification algorithm. The pipeline methods do not only ignore the close connection and interaction between the two subtasks of named entity recognition and relation classification, but also easily cause error propagation [6].

Many end-to-end joint entity and relation extraction models are investigated in recent studies [7, 8], which integrate entity and relation information in a shared model but fail to deal with the relation overlapping problem. To address this problem, a variety of works end-to-end relation extraction methods [9–13] for the problem of relation overlapping have been proposed. Nowadays, the problem of relation overlapping can be solved very well, for example, by establishing a relation specific tagging scheme, and the accuracy of relation triplets has reached more than 90% [14–17], which has almost reached the limit in this field.

GraphRel [16] is an end-to-end relation extraction model with graph convolutional networks. It adds dependency information to the encoding layer through GCN, but the dependency information from the NLP tools often contains a lot of error. Its entity recognition subtask uses BIOES sequence labeling method, but it cannot solve the problem of nested entities. Its relation classification method is worth noting, which converts the pairwise combination of tokens into a matrix, and classifies the relations of each element in the matrix. However, it treats the relationship classification task as a multi-class single-label task, which makes the relation overlapping problem of EPO completely unsolvable.

TPLinker [15] has been improved on the basis of GraphRel and achieved state-of-the-art in experimental performance. The entity recognition model is built with a pointer network of entity span. Although it solves the nested entity problem of GraphRel, the complexity has also increased from n to n square. On the other hand, whether it is the entity or the pointer network of the relationship in the model, only two tokens in the token pair are considered to classify, and other information in the span is ignored.

3   Methodology

To extract triplets from a long text (the length is N), it is divided into k sub-sentence with the maximum encoding token length n. LTRel model performs entity recognition on each sub-sentence to get candidate entities, then implements a cross-sentence relation classification for any two sub-sentences. After traversing all the sub-sentence combinations, potential relation triplets in the complete long sentence could be obtained. Relation extraction with only one sub-sentence ($N < n$) is regarded as a special case, and the extraction step performs only once. The framework of our methodology is show as Fig. 2.

The entity recognition part of the model is constructed based on TPLinker [15] and improved in two aspects. We enhance the feature representation of the entity token pair and neglect the invalid negative sample in the entity pair matrix, the storage space and the calculation cost are reduced and the accuracy of the model increase simultaneously.

The cross-sentence relation classification refers to identifying whether there is a certain relationship between two entities in different sentence. This step repeats $k \times k$ times to traverse all sub-sentence combination.

The specific implementation of the model is presented in the following sections.

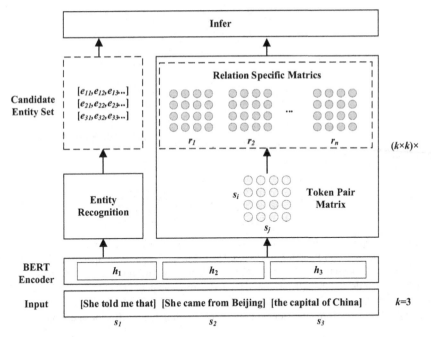

Fig. 2. The framework of LTREL model for long text relation extraction

3.1 Long Text Segmentation

When we split the text simply by length n, an entity mention may be divided into two sub-sentences, resulting in entity recognition errors. In order to solve this problem, we add heuristic rule what is truncating the sentence at the token like punctuation tokens. The specific method is to first determine the head position i of the entire clause, and then locates the tail position at $i + n$. If the token at that position is a punctuation token, then truncating the sentence there. If not, locate the tail position to the previous position. Continue to judge and repeat until you find a suitable token to truncate the sentence. To align the different lengths of the divided sub-sentences, we pad each sub-sentence to a same fixed length n.

3.2 Entity Recognition

The entity recognition network is developed based on TPLinker [15], and is improved from two aspects: entity token pair matrix representation and tag matrix.

3.2.1 Entity Tagging Scheme

The entity tagging method based on entity span solves the nested entity problem which BIOES sequence tagging fail, at the expense of the complexity increasing from $O(n)$ to $O(n^2)$. An entity tagging matrix of shape $n \times n$ is built to indicate whether the row token to the column token is an entity span as shown in Fig. 3.

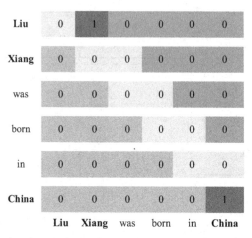

Fig. 3. An example of entity tagging matrix, *Liu Xiang* and *China* are two entities. Then the element in the 0th row and 1st column is marked as 1 which means that the span from *Liu* to *Xiang* (row to column) is an entity, and *China* is the same. The gray part of the lower left triangle in the matrix is the area deleted in TPLinker, and the red part of the upper right triangle is proposed to be cut down in our work. The maximum entity length is set to 2, which means the span whose length is greater than 2 is not considered in the entity tagging matrix. (Color figure online)

For the head of the entity cannot stand behind the tail of the entity, TPLinker crops the lower left triangular part of the entity tagging matrix H ($i > j$).We further remove the invalid negative samples (not in an entity span) in the matrix from the intuition that the too long spans are impossible to be an entity mention. For example, a span from the first token of the sentence to the end of the sentence is obviously impossible to be an entity. The maximum entity length m is set by statistics. Any $h_{i,j}$, *where* $j - i + 1 > m$, is discarded, which further cuts down a large quantity of worthless negative samples and reduce the data storage and the calculation cost.

3.2.2 Entity Token Pair Matrix Representation

Given a sentence, we first encode it with BiLSTM or BERT, and get the vector representation $\{h_1, h_2, \ldots h_n\}$. We form h_i and h_j for the embedding of any two tokens to generate their token pair embedding expression $h_{i,j}$. If there is no restriction on the order of i and j, then a token pair expression can be obtained and regarded as a matrix $H_{n \times n}$.

$$h_{i,j} = \sigma\left(\omega_h \cdot \left[h_i; h_j\right] + b_h\right) \tag{1}$$

Forwarding the matrix H to a dense layer and a sigmoid layer, the model predicts whether the (i, j) is an entity span from the i-th token to the j-th token.

$$P_e(i, j) = Sigmoid(W_{es} \cdot \left(ReLU\left(W_{er} \cdot h_{i,j} + b_{er}\right) + b_{es}\right) \tag{2}$$

To enhance semantic representation of an entity pair embedding, we replace the existing 2-components vector with a 5-components one. Except the information of the first and last tokens of the entity, we add three parts: the average representation of all the token in the entity span, the token before the first one, and the token after the end of the entity span, which is depicted as:

$$h_{i,j} = \sigma \left(W_h \cdot \left[h_i; h_j; h_{i \to j}; h_{i-1}; h_{j+1} \right] + b_h \right), \ where \ h_{i \to j} = \frac{1}{j-i+1} \sum_{k=i}^{j} h_k \quad (3)$$

These new components are meaningful for the following reasons: for entities with more than two tokens, each token contributes to the semantic representation to distinguish it from other parts of sentence. And the token pre-order and post-order of the entity span sometimes serve as an indicator for judging an entity span. For example, in Chinese text, tokens "《" and "》" are used before and after the entities like books and songs.

3.3 Cross-Sentence Relation Classification

Previous works infer the relation type of entities in one sentence, which employ GCN to represent relation-token information, and then predict the relation as a multi-label multi-classification problem. We further expand the idea to deal with relation classification between two sentences, then one sentence issue is a special case of our methodology.

3.3.1 Relation Tagging Scheme

Given two sentences $\{w_1^1, w_2^1, \dots w_n^1\}$ and $\{w_1^2, w_2^2, \dots w_n^2\}$ are denoted as s_1, s_2, respectively.

For r types of relationships, we generate r relationship label matrices with the same size as the token pair label matrix. Its rows correspond to the representation of the first sentence, and its columns correspond to the second sentence. The element value of the matrix is 0 or 1 representing whether there is relationship between two entities. For example, there is a triplet (w_i^1, r_k, w_j^2), under the of, then the (i,j) element of the k-th relation label matrix is marked as 1. The remaining elements are marked as 0. An example is shown in Fig. 4.

We do not make any reduction in the relation tagging scheme, and keep these matrices size as $n \times n$.

3.3.2 Relation Token Pair Representation

For the relation token pair matrix, the row of it corresponds to the tokens of s_1, and the column corresponds to the tokens of s_2. The sentences encoding as h_i^1 and g_j^2, the token pair representation $g_{i,j}$ is calculated as follows:

$$g_{i,j} = \sigma \left(W_g \cdot \left[h_i^1; g_j^2 \right] + b_g \right) \quad (4)$$

Forwarding token pair matrix G to a dense layer and a sigmoid layer, the model predicts whether there is relation between the i-th token from s_1 and the j-th token from s_2.

$$P_r(i,j) = Sigmoid \left(W_{rs} \cdot \left(ReLU \left(W_{rr} \cdot g_{i,j} + b_{rr} \right) + b_{rs} \right) \right) \quad (5)$$

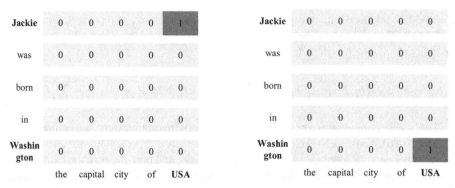

Fig. 4. Two sentences "Jackie was born in Washington" and "the capital city of USA". There are two relation triplets (*Jackie, birth_place, USA*) and (*Washington, the capital of, USA*). The left picture is the relation label matrix under the ***birth_place*** relation, and the right picture is the matrix under the ***capital of*** relation.

3.4 End-To-End Model Loss Function

We use cross-entropy as the categorical loss function during training. For entity loss, we feed in an entity tagging matrix as the ground truth of the $P_e(i, j)$ for each entity span (w_i, w_j). For relation loss, the ground truth of $P_r(i, j)$ is the relation label matrices. The total loss of the end-to-end model is calculated as the sum of entity loss and relation loss:

$$loss_{all} = loss_{entity} + loss_{relation} \tag{6}$$

3.5 Long Text Relation Extraction Inference

For the given two sentences, the candidate entities set E_1, E_2 of two sentences are first identified, which containing n_1, n_2 entities. Combine the entities in E_1 and E_2 to obtain a total of $n_1 \times n_2$ entity pairs (subject and object pairs).

For any entity pair (e_i^1, e_j^2) and relation r_k, the entity length of the subject and object are l_1 and l_2 respectively, we retrieve the sub-matrix of size $l_1 \times l_2$ in the relation prediction matrix to find if any element value equal to 1, then the triplet (e_i^1, r_k, e_j^2) is extracted.

4 Experiment

4.1 Datasets

In order to verify the performance of our model, we conduct experiments on two public datasets, namely the English dataset NYT [18] and the Chinese dataset DuIE2.0 proposed by Baidu.

NYT is a remotely supervised and labeled English data set. It contains 24 pre-defined relationship, 56,000 training sets, 5,000 validation sets, and 5,000 test sets.

DuIE2.0 is the largest Chinese relation extraction dataset in industry field proposed in the 2020 Language and Intelligent Technology Competition. The labeling method is also remote supervision, the data size is nearly 200,000 samples.

4.2 Implementation Details

Our model is developed with the deep learning framework Pytorch, and the network weight optimizer is Adam. Similar to related work [14, 16], we set the maximum length of the encoding sentence to 100, the threshold of the two-class probability to 0.5, and learning rate is 1e−5. For the English and Chinese dataset, the maximum entity lengths are 10 and 44.

4.3 Evaluation Standard

In previous work, there are two labeling standards for loss calculation and performance evaluation.

– Partial matching, only the end of the entity is labeled.
– Exact matching, the entire entity span is labeled.

Our experimental evaluation standard is exact match, that is, if all three parts of an extracted triplet are correct, it is a positive answer.

4.4 Result Analysis

4.4.1 Model Performance on NYT Dataset

On the English data set NYT, we reproduce the baseline algorithms GraphRel and TPLinker (SOTA method on NYT and WebNLG datasets). The entity recognition algorithm described in Sect. 3.2 is named as *Enhanced pointer network*, and the relation classification in Sect. 3.3 named as *CSRel_EPO*. Table 1 summarize experiments on different models we conducted, and the F1 is the average of five training procedure.

GraphRel uses the BiLSTM as encoder, and classifies the relation with the softmax activation function, which is impossible to deal with the relation overlapping problem of the EPO. We replace its encoding layer with Bert_base, and the relation classification method of our CSRel_EPO, which increase the F1 score of the relation triplets by more than 20%.

We also reproduced the current SOTA end-to-end relationship extraction model TPLinker, and the F1 score of the relation triplets reach 90.4% in our experimental environment, which fail reach 92.0% described in the original paper. Our model LTRel_1 combines the entity recognition method of TPLinker and our CSREL_EPO, then the performance is almost the same as that of TPLinker. Sample statistics shows that there are few long texts in NYT dataset, not much improvement room leaves for CSREL_EPO.

LTRel_2 employ the enhanced point network and CSREL_EPO, the F1 of the relation triplets is further improved. At the same time the quantity of samples that need to be calculated and predicted is much less than that of LTREL_1, in terms of the calculation

Table 1. Performance comparison of models on NYT

Model	Encoder	Entity recognition	Relation classification	Relation triplets F1
GraphRel	BiLSTM	BIOES	Softmax	61.9%
GraphRel_EPO	Bert_base	BIOES	CSRel_EPO	83.4%
TPLinker*	Bert_base	Pointer network	Pointer network	90.4%
LTRel_1	Bert_base	Pointer network	CSRel_EPO	90.5%
LTRel_2	Bert_base	Enhanced pointer network	CSRel_EPO	90.8%

space of the entity model. Here is a practical example: we set the longest encoding length as 100, and the size of the token pair matrix without any reduction is 10,000. In TPLinker, the lower left triangle part of the matrix is discarded, which is equivalent to cutting half of the labeled samples, the size reduces to about 5,000. Our method takes the maximum entity length as 11, and further reduces the size of the labeled sample to about 1,000.

4.4.2 Model Performance on DuIE Dataset

We select the best-performing algorithm on the English dataset LTRel_2 to evaluate the Chinese dataset Baidu DuIE2.0. Due to a lot of text length in the Chinese dataset, we compare our method with sliding window, the result shows nearly 2.2% improvement of F1 (shown in Table 2).

For Chinese, the information around the entity can often play an important role in indicating the span of the entity than in English. The LTREL with five-part information embedding can further improve the F1 of the relation triples.

Table 2. Performance comparison of models on DuIE2.0

Model	Entity pair embedding	Relation triplets F1
TPLinker_Sliding window	Two components	70.1%
LTREL_2C	Two components	71.8%
LTREL_5C	Five components	72.3%

In addition, we evaluate the performance of LTRel's relational triplets on single-sentence triplets and cross-subsentence triplets on DuIE2.0, and the F1 are 72.7% and 69.9%, which shows our long text model achieves nearly the same performance on both kind of task.

5 Conclusion

In this paper, we introduce a novel end-to-end joint entity and relation extraction model which is suitable for sentences of any length. Previous sliding window mechanism splits long text into separate samples, ignoring the semantic relation of the text, fail with some cases. We propose a cross-sentence relation classification algorithm which translating the problem into multiple sentence pairs relation extraction. Moreover, we refine the entity tagging scheme and feature representation of TPLinker, which reduces the memory space and computation cost with certain performance improvement. Experimental results show that the F1 of our model LTRel in the Chinese data set reach-es 72.3%, improving the previous method +2.2.

References

1. Zelenko, D., Aone, C., Richardella, A.: Kernel methods for relation extraction. J. Mach. Learn. Res. **3**(3), 1083–1106 (2003)
2. Zhou, G., Su, J., Zhang, J., Zhang, M.: Exploring various knowledge in relation extraction. In Proceedings of ACL. In: Proceedings of the 43rd Annual Meeting of the Association for Computational Linguistics, ACL 2005, pp. 427–434. Association for Computational Linguistics, Michigan (2005)
3. Mintz, M., Bills, S., Snow, R., Jurafsky, D.: Distant supervision for relation extraction without labeled data. In: Proceedings of the 47th Annual Meeting of the Association for Computational Linguistics, ACL 2009, pp. 1003–1011. Association for Computational Linguistics, Singapore (2009)
4. Chan, Y., Roth, D.: Exploiting syntactico-semantic structures for relation extraction. In: Proceedings of the 49th Annual Meeting of the Association for Computational Linguistics, ACL 2011, pp. 551–560. Association for Computational Linguistics, Portland (2011)
5. Gormley, M.R., Yu, M., Dredze, M.: Improved relation extraction with feature-rich compositional embedding models. In: Proceedings of the 2015 Conference on Empirical Methods in Natural Language Processing, EMNLP 2015, pp. 1774–1784. Association for Computational Linguistics, Portugal (2015)
6. Li, Q., Ji, H.: Incremental joint extraction of entity mentions and relations. In: Proceedings of the 52nd Annual Meeting of the Association for Computational Linguistics, ACL 2014, pp. 402–412. Association for Computational Linguistics, Baltimore (2014)
7. Gupta, P., Schtze, H., Andrassy, B.: Table filling multi-task recurrent neural network for joint entity and relation extraction. In: Proceedings of COLING 2016, the 26th International Conference on Computational Linguistics, pp. 2537–2547. The COLING 2016 Organizing Committee, Japan (2016)
8. Zheng, S., Wang, F., Bao, H., Hao, Y., Zhou, P., Xu, B.: Joint extraction of entities and relations based on a novel tagging scheme. In: Proceedings of the 55th Annual Meeting of the Association for Computational Linguistics, ACL 2017, pp. 1227–1236. Association for Computational Linguistics, Vancouver (2017)
9. Tan, Z., Zhao, X., Wang, W., Xiao, W.: Jointly extracting multiple triplets with multilayer translation constraints. In: Proceedings of the AAAI Conference on Artificial Intelligence, AAAI 2019, pp. 7080–7087. Natural Language Processing, Atlanta (2019)
10. Takanobu, R., Zhang, T., Liu, J., Huang, M.: A hierarchical framework for relation extraction with reinforcement learning. In: Proceedings of the AAAI Conference on Artificial Intelligence, pp. 7072–7079. Natural Language Processing, Atlanta (2019)

11. Li, X., et al.: Entity relation extraction as multi-turn question answering. In: Proceedings of the 57th Annual Meeting of the Association for Computational Linguistics, ACL 2019, pp.1340–1350. Association for Computational Linguistics, Italy (2019)

12. Sun, C.: Joint type inference on entities and relations via graph convolutional networks. In: Proceedings of the 57th Annual Meeting of the Association for Computational Linguistics, ACL 2019, pp.1361–1370. Association for Computational Linguistics, Italy (2019)

13. Yu, B., et al.: Joint extraction of entities and relations based on a novel decomposition strategy. arXiv:1909.04273 (2020)

14. Wei, Z., Su, J., Wang, Y., Tian, Y., Chang, Y.: A novel cascade binary tagging framework for relational triple extraction. In: Proceedings of the 58th Annual Meeting of the Association for Computational Linguistics, ACL 2020, pp. 1476–1488. Association for Computational Linguistics, Spain (2020)

15. Wang, Y., Yu, B., Zhang, Y., Liu, T., Zhu, H., Sun, L.: TPLinker: single-stage joint extraction of entities and relations through token pair linking. In: Proceedings of the 28th International Conference on Computational Linguistics, COLING 2020, pp. 1572–1582. International Committee on Computational Linguistics, Spain (2020)

16. Fu, T., Li, P., Ma, W.: Graphrel: modeling text as relational graphs for joint entity and relation extraction. In: Proceedings of the 57th Annual Meeting of the Association for Computational Linguistics, ACL 2019, pp. 1409–1418. Association for Computational Linguistics, Italy (2019)

17. Sui, D., Chen, Y., Liu, K., Zhao, J., Zeng, X., Liu, S.: Joint entity and relation extraction with set prediction networks. arXiv:2011.01675 (2020)

18. Riedel, S., Yao, L., McCallum, A.: Modeling relations and their mentions without labeled text. In: Machine Learning and Knowledge Discovery in Databases, European Conference, ECML-PKDD 2010. Springer-Verlag, Spain (2010)

19. Devlin, J., Chang, M., Lee, K., Toutanova, K.: Bert: pre-training of deep bidirectional transformers for language understanding. In: Proceedings of the 2019 Conference of the North American Chapter of the Association for Computational Linguistics, NAACL 2019, pp. 4171–4186. Association for Computational Linguistics, Minnesota (2019)

Evaluating Dataset Creation Heuristics for Concept Detection in Web Pages Using BERT

Michael Paris[1]([✉])[ID] and Robert Jäschke[1,2][ID]

[1] Berlin School for Library and Information Science,
Humboldt-Universität zu Berlin, Berlin, Germany
{michael.paris,robert.jaeschke}@hu-berlin.de
[2] L3S Research Center Hannover, Hanover, Germany

Abstract. Dataset creation for the purpose of training natural language processing (NLP) algorithms is often accompanied by an uncertainty about how the target concept is represented in the data. Extracting such data from web pages and verifying its quality is a non-trivial task, due to the Web's unstructured and heterogeneous nature and the cost of annotation. In that situation, annotation heuristics can be employed to create a dataset that captures the target concept, but in turn may lead to an unstable downstream performance. On the one hand, a trade-off exists between cost, quality, and magnitude for annotation heuristics in tasks such as classification, leading to fluctuations in trained models' performance. On the other hand, general-purpose NLP tools like BERT are now commonly used to benchmark new models on a range of tasks on static datasets. We utilize this standardization as a means to assess dataset quality, as most applications are dataset specific. In this study, we investigate and evaluate the performance of three annotation heuristics for a classification task on extracted web data using BERT. We present multiple datasets, from which the classifier shall learn to identify web pages that are centered around an individual in the academic domain. In addition, we assess the relationship between the performance of the trained classifier and the training data size. The models are further tested on out-of-domain web pages, to asses the influence of the individuals' occupation and web page domain.

Keywords: Dataset · Generation · Heuristic · Bias · Quality · Web archive · Classification

1 Introduction

Dataset generation for a specific machine learning task is time-consuming when done by humans and takes even more time in the case of manual sample creation. Since the release of BERT [9] many variations of pre-trained NLP language models have been published, which alleviate the stress on optimizing the architecture

© Springer Nature Switzerland AG 2021
H. Qiu et al. (Eds.): KSEM 2021, LNAI 12816, pp. 163–175, 2021.
https://doi.org/10.1007/978-3-030-82147-0_14

for many NLP tasks and increased the focus on dataset generation. Specifically, aspects of dataset curation [23] gain growing attention as a consequence of this development. In this context, datasets used to train a concept classifier allow the model to learn a representation through annotated examples. Furthermore, tasks comprising the classification of an abstract concept rely on heuristics for their a priori definition to create such annotated examples. This increases the likelihood of unintended bias, depending on how the annotators or curators interpret these heuristics. The accompanying indefiniteness can lead to different training datasets, which in turn would lead to diverging classifications of the model on new data. Uncertainties have generally been analyzed as a model-dependent phenomenon, such that specific datasets were created to probe the behavior of BERT [7] or improve on the learned decision boundary [13]. On the one hand, improving the model through diversification of the data samples improves the quality of the decision boundary by means of a more detailed representation of the concept. On the other hand, this approach changes nothing about the architecture of the model, implying that heuristics determine the representation of the concept within the dataset learned by the model. In addition to the challenge of creating refined datasets through heuristics, a semantic concept drift may occur over time, thereby altering the initially captured concept. Especially for rapidly changing web concepts, adjusting individual data samples quickly becomes unfeasible.

In contrast to the current approach, in which datasets are used to analyze or improve a language model, we use BERT to measure how well different heuristics for annotation reflect a particular concept. We use raw web archives as data source, present a pipeline that simplifies the creation of datasets for NLP language models, and compare the performance and limitations of the heuristics.

Our approach allows researchers to leverage their domain knowledge of an existing dataset to train an NLP classifier and extract subsets relevant for their research objective. Specifically, our contribution comprises

1. *the creation of datasets using three different heuristics,*
2. *a pipeline for the application and comparison of these heuristics, and*
3. *insights into the dataset creation quality, measured using BERT.*[1]

This paper is organised as follows: Sect. 2 discusses related work, Sect. 3 presents the data creation process, training of the models, and approaches to investigate their performance, Sect. 4 presents the results, and Sect. 5 discusses possible explanations and pitfalls of these.

2   Related Work

The Web as a dataset resource has been frequently discussed and used by the community [11,21]. To a large degree the datasets created for the use in linguistics and natural language processing (NLP) rely on (semi-)structured and homogeneous data (e.g., Wikipedia) [16,25,30]. But most of the Web is only available

---

[1] Code and data are available at https://github.com/parismic/EvaluateHeuristics/.

in an unstructured form and is thus less accessible to non-technical research fields. Non-expert researchers working with unstructured data are therefore limited to data resources such as Twitter [4] or news articles [26]. These resources do not require a large overhead of frameworks or custom designed tools to yield datasets appropriate for specific research questions [18].

Web archives, for which various tools already exist, could be a rich resource for the curation of derived datasets, if the effort to accumulate research-related content from millions of web pages could be reduced [26]. Some tools aim to lower the threshold for such instances with a focus on reproducibility and best practices [3,15]. In many of these cases the desired collection of web pages depends on the textual information presented. This requires boiler plate removal approaches to extract the information from the heterogeneously structured pages on the Web. Advances in boiler plate removal allow high accuracy in the automatic extraction of main content sections [27].

The processing of common NLP tasks has fundamentally changed after the release of BERT [9], after which many other general NLP tools have followed. Without the requirement to deal with the architecture of the system, the importance of dataset quality becomes more pronounced [5]. For common NLP tasks it is desired to gauge the quality of the trained model on samples outside the distribution through contrast sets [12]. In a sense, the incomplete information about the decision boundary in [12] stems from the heuristics used for the creation of the dataset.

These heuristics are often manifested with methods for assembling datasets, from 1) **existing resources** (e.g., author names from a digital library to label persons) [24], 2) **manual annotation** [1], and 3) **weak supervision** (e.g., structured information on Wikipedia for labeling financial events [10] or regular expressions to identify or extract samples). In those methods, a bias [20] of the dataset creator is carried into the heuristics, which should at least be coherent across the different dataset creation approaches. Further, bias enters the dataset on the level of the annotator or sample creator to an extent that the annotator can be identified on the basis of the sample itself [13].

This study aims to highlight another aspect of bias introduced to the dataset depending on the creation approach and definiteness of the concept itself. Specifically, we provide an exemplary case study for the concept of a *person-centric web page*.

3   Datasets and Experiments

This section details the dataset creation process for the concept of *person-centric (PC) web pages* in the academic context for the training, evaluation, testing, and validation of the classifiers. In general, we assume that a human observer can recognize whether a web page is *PC* and contains information about a person on the basis of the main content and not the style or navigation. We limit our investigation to content presented in natural language texts on web pages. The overall procedure will extract and boiler-plate web pages from a large web crawl and associate a class label with the boiler-plated content. The content together with the annotations will be used to fine-tune a pre-trained BERT model. This is followed by an evaluation of the model on test sets, which are subsets of all fine-tuning datasets to express the coherence between heuristics.

3.1   Datasets

We utilize several datasets to define and investigate what constitutes a *PC* web page in the academic context and to investigate the divergence between commonly used heuristics (i.e., *human annotation, weak annotation from existing resources*, and *weak annotation with regular expressions*) for creating training data for a binary classifier.

The datasets named in the remainder of this work as *DBLP, Manual, RegEx,* and *Wikidata* were created on the basis of the 2019-06 snapshot of the "German Academic Web" (GAW) [22] which will be referred to as *crawl*. The snapshot was created on the basis of a URL seed list containing all home pages of German academic institutions with the right to award a doctorate degree at that time. This *crawl* contains WARC records [14] of web pages reachable within 20 link hops from the domains of the seeds.

An additional dataset *Wikidata$_{Q5}$* for the validation of the classifier performance was created on the basis of URLs of the `official websites` (P856) associated with all entities of `instance` (P31) `human` (Q5) on Wikidata [28]. For all these entities the corresponding `occupation` (P106) was extracted and WARC records were created for the listed official websites on 2021-01-28 using the library scrapy-warcio.[2]

Pre-processing. We restricted the *crawl* to records of MIME type[3] *text/html* and HTTP response code *200*. After that, the HTML for all WARC records was extracted and processed using the boiler plate removal tool Web2Text [27] trained on the CleanEval [2] dataset. This process enables a robust extraction of the main textual content of a web page without the noise introduced by headers, side panels, navigation, etc. or any knowledge of the structure of the web page. This step is applied to all extracted WARC records and is followed by the removal of duplicates and the removal of identical text samples from the pairwise larger dataset, yielding non-overlapping datasets (i.e., for datasets $\tilde{D}_1$ and D_2, where $|\tilde{D}_1| > |D_2|$, $\tilde{D}_1$ is transformed to $D_1 = \tilde{D}_1 \setminus D_2$).

Dataset Enrichment and Annotation. Due to an expected low frequency of the *PC* concept in a random subset of the *crawl*, an enrichment process was applied to increase its frequency. For that, a dataset was created such that from each seed institution in the *crawl* three annotators independently navigated to web presences of research groups of that institution and extracted common base URL

---

[2] https://github.com/internetarchive/scrapy-warcio.

[3] Multipurpose Internet Mail Extensions – a standard for naming different types of content.

paths of the staff. Specifically, this was done by collecting URLs of staff members and extracting the longest common URL prefixes. The annotators were instructed to cover different fields of research to ensure a contextual diversity, such that the classifier would not instead focus on a particular research domain. However, diversification was not specified in any narrow terms to mimic an application scenario in which an unknown bias may affects the dataset. All URLs starting with an element from the list of common URL prefixes of staff members were extracted from the *crawl* and comprise the *enrichment* dataset. This process aims to increase the frequency of *PC* web pages without specifically excluding non-*PC* web pages.

In the four months following the completion of the crawl, the same annotators had to decide whether a page is *PC* on the basis of the displayed content in a web browser and label it as such. If all three annotators agreed, then the respective label was used as annotation, URLs not present at annotation time were removed from further processing and all others were considered to be *not PC*.

***Manual* Dataset.** The *Manual* dataset was created in a two-step process. First, 2,000 random records from the *crawl* and 1,274 records from the *enrichment* dataset were selected. Next, these 3,274 records were annotated, whereby the annotator agreement yielded a $\kappa_{\text{FLEISS}} = 0.844$. The resulting *Manual* dataset contains 1,407 non-*PC* and 606 *PC* samples, of which 68 originated from the 2,000 randomly selected records.

***RegEx* Dataset.** To construct a dataset which reduces annotation cost and leverages the structure of the *crawl* we constructed a dataset by utilizing common patterns in URLs of *PC* pages using regular expressions. The regular expressions act as a weak annotation mechanism to classify records of the *crawl* based on their URL. If any of the following regular expressions matched against substrings of the last path element[4] in the URL path, the record was annotated as *PC*: `mitarbeite`, `angestellte`, `group`, `gruppe`, `staff`, `~[a-z]`, `people`, `team`, `kolleg`, `lehrend`, `beschaeftigte`.

The non-*PC* records were extracted by only considering URLs which did not match any of the mentioned regular expressions *anywhere* in the URL. We select a subset such that the ratio of *PC* and non-*PC* records is equal to that ratio in the *Manual* dataset and refer to the resulting dataset as *RegEx*.

***DBLP* Dataset.** For many concepts there are datasets available which already provide a level of proximity to the desired concept for classification. In the case of *PC* web pages, DBLP [17] provides a frequently used dataset which extensively covers researchers from computer science and their associated web pages. We used these URLs in the DBLP dump of 2020-10-01 to identify and annotate records in the *crawl* as *PC*. All URLs associated with a person and contained within the *crawl* were selected and amounted to 1,859 weakly-annotated *PC* samples. Non-*PC* samples were constructed by employing the same method as

---

[4] That is, the string confined by the last and second to last '/' in the SURT format of the URL.

for the *RegEx* dataset, whereby the ratio of *PC* and non-*PC* samples equal that in the *Manual* dataset.

Wikidata-Derived Datasets. Wikidata provides an additional resource for the selection of *PC* web pages, as well as rich ontological structure to validate the scope of the trained classifiers. As such, it allows us to investigate the heuristics in terms of the entities' occupation and region. Analogous to the *DBLP* dataset, the existing WARC records in the *crawl* associated with the aforementioned URLs were extracted, comprising the weakly-annotated *Wikidata* dataset of 293 *PC* samples. To validate results and determine limitations of the classifiers, we categorized all occupations in *Wikidata$_{Q5}$* as *academic*, if they or an immediate sub-class have an occupation of 1) researcher, 2) knowledge worker, 3) scientist, 4) scholar, or 5) university-teacher, thus allowing us to observe the preference of the classifier given that the *crawl* focuses on the academic web.

Table 1. Total counts of the records in the datasets at different phases of the cleaning process. The difference between the sum of records in the train and test set in relation to the pre-processed dataset stems from the removal of identical text-label pairs within and between the datasets.

	URLs	URLs$_{on\ seeds}$	WARCs	Pre-proc.	Train		Test	
			PC		*PC*	non-*PC*	*PC*	non-*PC*
DBLP	234,291	4,439	2,759	1,859	1,669	3,881	121	281
Manual	-		800	2,013	484	1,126	121	281
RegEx	-		1,135,899	-	4,840	11,260	-	-
Wikidata	159,431	531	388	293	-	-	254	589

3.2 BERT as a Measurement Tool for Heuristics

With the rise of powerful general-purpose language models following BERT [9] a shift occurred from the traditional NLP pipeline towards a dataset-focused approach. Allowing users to quickly fine-tune a pre-trained model for a given task alleviates the previously required considerations about the model architecture and allows users to focus on issues like dataset curation. In general, these models are evaluated on established datasets, thereby testing their performance on tasks defined through the dataset, while maintaining stable performance across different dataset for the same task. Due to this stability these models can be used to evaluate the coherence and performance of a dataset in capturing a concept, and in turn the heuristics underlying the annotation process.

Fine-Tuning BERT. We used hugginface's pretrained multilingual-cased BERT implementation [29] trained on cased text in the top 104 languages. We fine-tuned for 4 epochs, using batch size 32, with learning rate 2×10^5

on the Adam optimizer with weight decay [19] and maximum sequence length of 128 word pieces. The optimal number of epochs was determined by finding a model with minimal validation loss using the standard fine-tuning approach. From the four datasets (*Manual, DBLP, RegEx, Wikidata*) we constructed three training sets and three test sets as presented in Table 1. For each sample size the pre-trained model was fine-tuned for 10 different random seeds, used in the selection of the sub-samples and initialization of the system. This was done to determine the robustness of the model inherited from the training dataset by determining the fluctuation with varying training sample sizes.

3.3 Complementarity

We also investigate the improvement achievable by one classifier to another [6]. This provides another perspective on how the heuristics for constructing the training datasets complements another. Given the prediction results of two binary classifiers A and B, we can determine the complementary recall $R_{\mathrm{comp}} = 1 - \frac{|B_{\mathrm{wrong}} \cap A_{\mathrm{wrong}}|}{|A_{\mathrm{wrong}}|}$ and precision $P_{\mathrm{comp}}(A, B) = 1 - \frac{|B_{\mathrm{wrong}} \cap A_{\mathrm{wrong}}|}{|A_{\mathrm{wrong}}|}$ [8].[5]

4 Results

The following results present the performance of the fine-tuned classifiers based on the datasets described in Sect. 3.1. As a starting point, we present the F1 score as a function of the fine-tuning sample size as described in Sect. 3.2.

4.1 Robustness and Sample Size

We observe in Fig. 1 that the F1 scores diverge with increasing sample size for the classifiers trained on the *DBLP* and *Manual* datasets when tested on the respective other. The classifier trained on the *RegEx* dataset displays a comparable performance for a sample size of 1,600 to the *DBLP* and *Manual* classifiers tested on the *Manual* and *DBLP* datasets, respectively. With an increasing sample size the *RegEx*-trained classifier outperforms the other classifiers when tested on *non-native*[6] test data. The general performance of the regular expression approach shows a score between 0.83 and 0.86 on *Wikidata*. A significant drop in the variance of the models' F1 scores occurs between sample sizes of 200 to 400 and 400 to 600 for the datasets *DBLP*, *Manual* and *RegEx*, respectively. The *Manual*-trained model generally performs better than the *DBLP*-trained model when tested on the respective other test set.

---

[5] Where 'wrong' refers to the falsely classified PC items for recall, and the falsely classified non-PC items for precision, respectively.

[6] Test data which does not originate from the same distribution as the training dataset.

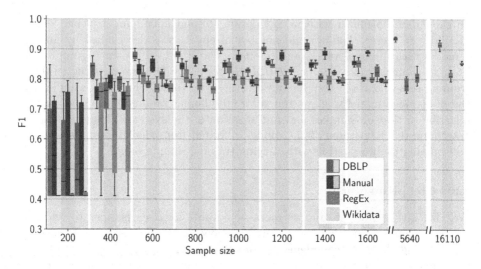

Fig. 1. Performance of the trained classifiers in terms of the F1 score as a function of the fine-tuning sample size and the source of the test data. For each training sample size a classifier was trained and evaluated for 4 epochs on 10 different seeds (solid colors, boxplot) and tested on 3 datasets (translucent colors, background stripes).

4.2 Context Dependence

To determine the dependence of the trained model on the context, we investigate the occupational dependence as a proxy for the context of the concept. Since negative samples are unavailable, the recall is presented in Fig. 2 instead of the F1 score. It illustrates the influence of the epoch given the test data of *Wikidata*$_{Q5}$. A strong discrepancy is displayed between the recall of computer-scientist, researcher, and university-teacher and all other occupations. Out of the distinct occupations, the *DBLP*-trained classifier performs best on the computer-scientist occupation. This occupation also presents the largest spread between the examined classifiers. On a large scale, only a minor dependence is observed with regard to the training epochs for the same training dataset. An improvement can be observed at epoch = 4 (•) for the *RegEx*-trained classifier and a general deterioration for the *DBLP* and *Manual*-trained classifier relative to the epoch with minimal validation loss (▲).

4.3 Domain Dependence

Following the results in Fig. 2, a limitation of the trained classifiers could also arise from regional differences associated with the top-level domain (TLD). Therefore, Fig. 3 presents the TLD dependence of the recall with respect to the fine-tuning dataset. This is presented for the academic occupations (★) in contrast to all occupations (■). A clear shift in recall can be observed when *academic* occupations are classified independently of the TLD. This shift averages

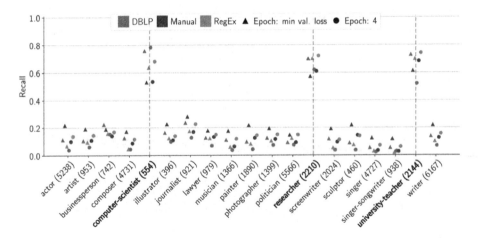

Fig. 2. Recall by occupation for the classifier after epochs: 4 (•) and epoch in which the validation loss reached the minimum (▲). The number following the occupation expresses the samples size for that occupation.

for all classifiers in *all* occupations at $R = 0.23$ and in the *academic* occupations at $R = 0.56$. Within the two different categories we can observe that in most TLDs the *Manual* and *DBLP* classifier perform best in *all* (■) and *academic* (★) occupations, respectively. Since the *GAW* is focused on Germany it contains a language bias. This could cause the performance of the trained classifier to vary in its ability to determine the correct results in another language setting. Another issue could be variations specific to each TLD, like the page structure or language, which could limit the applicability of this approach.

4.4 Complementarity

Since we would like to not only investigate the quality of the initial heuristics on the classifier's performance but also how much these diverge, it is necessary to determine the recall complementarity (cf. Sect. 3.3) of the predictions. We perform this on the *Wikidata* dataset, as this is a *non-native* dataset for either of the classifiers. Table 2 can be understood as the relative improvement of classifier A by classifier B. Under the same training conditions, the classifiers retain a significant discrepancy in between the potential improvement in recall (Table 2a) provided by *DBLP* towards *Manual* and *RegEx* and the inverse. Unlike in the case of complementary precision (Table 2b), in which a closer symmetry can be observed.

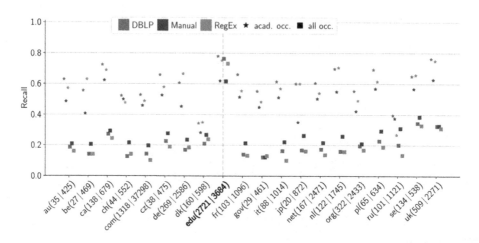

Fig. 3. Recall for the 20 most frequently occurring top-level domains depending on the underlying association with an academic occupation (see Sect. 3.1) in contrast to all occupations. The numbers after the domain express the sample size for the *academic* and *all* occupations, respectively.

Table 2. Complementarity measures on *Wikidata*. Classifiers were trained on 1,600 training samples.

<table>
<tr><td colspan="4">(a) Recall R_{comp}</td><td colspan="4">(b) Precision P_{comp}</td></tr>
<tr><td>A \ B</td><td>DBLP</td><td>Manual</td><td>RegEx</td><td>A \ B</td><td>DBLP</td><td>Manual</td><td>RegEx</td></tr>
<tr><td>DBLP</td><td>0.0</td><td>23.8</td><td>23.8</td><td>DBLP</td><td>0.0</td><td>52.8</td><td>52.8</td></tr>
<tr><td>Manual</td><td>52.9</td><td>0.0</td><td>36.8</td><td>Manual</td><td>39.3</td><td>0.0</td><td>53.6</td></tr>
<tr><td>RegEx</td><td>**56.2**</td><td>41.1</td><td>0.0</td><td>RegEx</td><td>54.1</td><td>**64.9**</td><td>0.0</td></tr>
</table>

5   Discussion and Conclusion

This study aims to provide insights into the relationship between dataset coherence regarding a specific concept and creation heuristics measured with BERT. We found a divergence between creation heuristics (Fig. 1), which is larger than the variation within a heuristic, but nonetheless all heuristics perform similar on any *non-native* dataset. We further observed that the bias of *DBLP*, being focused on computer science, is inherited by the classifier (Fig. 2) and that the general definition of the *PC* concept associated with the *Manual* dataset yields the most reliable recall across all occupations and domains (Fig. 3). This coincides with the bias observed during the annotation of the *Manual* dataset, in which samples presenting publication lists of and articles about a single person were labeled as *PC*. The most effortless approach, utilizing regular expressions, provides a surprisingly reliable solution to the task. But this comes at the cost of an in-depth domain knowledge of the URL structure in the crawl. As such knowledge is often present with researchers analysing specific web archives it could be translated to other tasks.

Some of the problems that lead to a reduction in performance in all classifiers can be found in the annotator agreement and in the boiler-plating mechanism, as well as in the fact that web data is quite noisy. In addition, URLs associated with a person in databases such as DBLP or Wikidata sometimes do not point to a *PC* web page, but to a more general home page or the page of a research group. Such an inaccuracy in the weak annotation stems from the assumption that all official and DBLP-listed web pages are associated with a human entity, and can be regarded as a drawback of the use of existing resources. Overall, we find that the usefulness of focused web archives are the user-made semantic decisions in the structure of URLs, which can be leveraged by experts. Such expert decisions could be used to update rules for evolving concepts, thereby mitigating the influence of concept drift. A follow-up study might use this work for the analysis of the web-related interactions between identified individuals.

Acknowledgments. Parts of this research were funded by the German Federal Ministry of Education and Research (BMBF) in the REGIO project (grant no. 01PU17012D).

References

1. Al-Smadi, M., Qawasmeh, O., Talafha, B., Quwaider, M.: Human annotated Arabic dataset of book reviews for aspect based sentiment analysis. In: 3rd International Conference on Future Internet of Things and Cloud, pp. 726–730. IEEE (2015)
2. Baroni, M., Chantree, F., Kilgarriff, A., Sharoff, S.: Cleaneval: a competition for cleaning web pages. In: Proc. of the International Conference on Language Resources and Evaluation. LREC, European Language Resources Association (2008)
3. Ben-David, A., Amram, A.: Computational methods for web history. The SAGE handbook of web history, pp. 153–167 (2019)
4. Blank, G.: The digital divide among Twitter users and its implications for social research. Soc. Sci. Comput. Rev. **35**(6), 679–697 (2017)
5. Bommasani, R., Cardie, C.: Intrinsic evaluation of summarization datasets. In: Proceedings of the Conference on Empirical Methods in Natural Language Processing, pp. 8075–8096. EMNLP, Association for Computational Linguistics (2020)
6. Brill, E., Wu, J.: Classifier combination for improved lexical disambiguation. In: Annual Meeting of the Association for Computational Linguistics, pp. 191–195. Association for Computational Linguistics (1998)
7. Câmara, A., Hauff, C.: Diagnosing BERT with retrieval heuristics. In: Jose, J.M., et al. (eds.) ECIR 2020. LNCS, vol. 12035, pp. 605–618. Springer, Cham (2020). https://doi.org/10.1007/978-3-030-45439-5_40
8. Derczynski, L.: Complementarity, F-score, and NLP evaluation. In: Proc. of the International Conference on Language Resources and Evaluation, pp. 261–266. LREC, European Language Resources Association (2016)

9. Devlin, J., Chang, M.W., Lee, K., Toutanova, K.: BERT: pre-training of deep bidirectional transformers for language understanding. In: Proceedings of the Conference of the North American Chapter of the Association for Computational Linguistics: Human Language Technologies. NAACL, Association for Computational Linguistics, Minneapolis, Minnesota (2019)
10. Ein-Dor, L., et al.: Financial event extraction using wikipedia-based weak supervision. In: Proceedings of the Second Workshop on Economics and Natural Language Processing (2019)
11. Ferrari, A., Spagnolo, G.O., Gnesi, S.: Pure: a dataset of public requirements documents. In: International Requirements Engineering Conference (2017)
12. Gardner, M., et al.: Evaluating models' local decision boundaries via contrast sets (2020), arxiv:2004.02709
13. Geva, M., Goldberg, Y., Berant, J.: Are we modeling the task or the annotator? an investigation of annotator bias in natural language understanding datasets (2019), arXiv:1908.07898
14. International Internet Preservation Consortium (IIPC): The WARC Format 1.1. https://iipc.github.io/warc-specifications/specifications/warc-format/warc-1.1/#warc-file-name-size-and-compression, [Online; Last accessed 11 Mar 2021]
15. Kiesel, J., Kneist, F., Alshomary, M., Stein, B., Hagen, M., Potthast, M.: Reproducible web corpora: interactive archiving with automatic quality assessment. J. Data ad Inf. Quality **10**(4), 1–25 (2018)
16. Lehmann, J., et al.: DBpedia – a large-scale, multilingual knowledge base extracted from Wikipedia. Semantic Web **6**(2) (2015)
17. Ley, M.: DBLP: some lessons learned. Proc. VLDB Endowment **2**(2), 1493–1500 (2009)
18. Lin, J., Milligan, I., Wiebe, J., Zhou, A.: Warcbase: scalable analytics infrastructure for exploring web archives. J. Comput. Cultural Heritage **10**(4), 1–30 (2017)
19. Loshchilov, I., Hutter, F.: Decoupled weight decay regularization. In: International Conference on Learning Representations (2019)
20. Lu, K., Mardziel, P., Wu, F., Amancharla, P., Datta, A.: Gender bias in neural natural language processing. In: Nigam, V., et al. (eds.) Logic, Language, and Security. LNCS, vol. 12300, pp. 189–202. Springer, Cham (2020). https://doi.org/10.1007/978-3-030-62077-6_14
21. Mohammad, S.M.: NLP scholar: a dataset for examining the state of NLP research. In: Proceedings of the Language Resources and Evaluation Conference. ELRA (2020)
22. Paris, M., Jäschke, R.: How to assess the exhaustiveness of longitudinal web archives. In: Proceedings of the Conference on Hypertext and Social Media. ACM (2020)
23. Peng, Y., Yan, S., Lu, Z.: Transfer learning in biomedical natural language processing: an evaluation of bert and elmo on ten benchmarking datasets. arXiv preprint arXiv:1906.05474 (2019)
24. Qian, Y., Zheng, Q., Sakai, T., Ye, J., Liu, J.: Dynamic author name disambiguation for growing digital libraries. Inf. Retrieval J. **18**(5), 379–412 (2015). https://doi.org/10.1007/s10791-015-9261-3
25. Strube, M., Ponzetto, S.P.: Wikirelate! computing semantic relatedness using wikipedia. AAAI **6**, 1419–1424 (2006)
26. Vlassenroot, E., et al.: Web archives as a data resource for digital scholars. Int. J. Digital Humanities **1**(1), 85–111 (2019). https://doi.org/10.1007/s42803-019-00007-7

27. Vogels, T., Ganea, O.-E., Eickhoff, C.: Web2Text: deep structured boilerplate removal. In: Pasi, G., Piwowarski, B., Azzopardi, L., Hanbury, A. (eds.) ECIR 2018. LNCS, vol. 10772, pp. 167–179. Springer, Cham (2018). https://doi.org/10.1007/978-3-319-76941-7_13

28. Vrandečić, D., Krötzsch, M.: Wikidata: a free collaborative knowledgebase. Commun. ACM **57**(10), 78–85 (2014)

29. Wolf, T., et al.: Transformers: State-of-the-art natural language processing. In: Proceedings of the Conference on Empirical Methods in Natural Language Processing, pp. 38–45. EMNLP, Association for Computational Linguistics (2020)

30. Zesch, T., Müller, C., Gurevych, I.: Extracting lexical semantic knowledge from Wikipedia and Wiktionary. LREC **8**, 1646–1652 (2008)

Panoptic-DLA: Document Layout Analysis of Historical Newspapers Based on Proposal-Free Panoptic Segmentation Model

Min Lu, Feilong Bao$^{(\boxtimes)}$, and Guanglai Gao

College of Computer Science, Inner Mongolia University, Inner Mongolia Key
Laboratory of Mongolian Information Processing Technology National and Local
Joint Engineering Research Center of Intelligent Information Processing Technology
for Mongolian, Hohhot, China
{csfeilong,csggl}@imu.edu.cn

Abstract. In this paper, we introduce a novel historical newspaper layout analysis model named Panoptic-DLA. Different from the previous works regarding layout analysis as a separate object detection or semantic segmentation problem, we define the layout analysis task as the proposal-free panoptic segmentation to assign a unique value to each pixel in the document image, encoding both semantic label and instance id. The model consists of two branches: the semantic segmentation branch and the instance segmentation branch. Firstly, the pixels are separated to "things" and "stuff" by semantic classification taking the background as "stuff", and content objects such as images, paragraphs, etc., as "things". Then the predicted "things" are grouped further to their instance ids by instance segmentation. The semantic segmentation branch adopted DeepLabV3+ to predict pixel-wise class labels. In order to split adjacent regions well, the instance segmentation branch produce a mountain-like soft score-map and a center-direction map to represent content objects. The method is trained and tested on a dataset of historical European newspapers with complex content layout. The experiment shows that the proposed method achieves the competitive results against popular layout analysis methods. We also demonstrate the effectiveness and superiority of the methods compared to the previous methods.

Keywords: Document Layout Analysis · Historical newspapers · Panoptic segmentation · Soft score-map · Panoptic-DLA

1 Introduction

Document Layout Analysis (DLA) is a critical and fundamental step in any document understanding system. Its goal is to split a document image into regions of

This work is partially supported by the National Key Research and Development Program of China (No.2018YFE0122900), China National Natural Science Foundation (No. 61773224, No. 61866030, No. 62066033).

H. Qiu et al. (Eds.): KSEM 2021, LNAI 12816, pp. 176–190, 2021.
https://doi.org/10.1007/978-3-030-82147-0_15

interest and classifies them, e.g. text, image, etc. Compared to the segmentation of contemporary document images, page segmentation of historical document images pose particular challenges due to the low quality of print, the large size of images and the very tight layout. This paper aims to create a general model to solve the layout parsing of historical newspapers.

In recent years, deep learning-based approaches have shown great power in the field of page segmentation. The methods typically applied in DLA can be divided into two categories: the segmentation-based method and the regression-based method. The segmentation-based method is intended to label each pixel with a semantic class by producing per-class binary prediction maps for input document image in a bottom-up manner. [12] adopted DeepLab [4] to perform a semantic segmentation procedure with connected component analysis in post-processing part. However, as mentioned in the work [12], the connected component analysis made some merging errors for its weakness in splitting close adjacent regions. Therefore, separate segmentation-based method can not be directly applied to historical newspapers with close content layout. The regression-based method, actually the proposal-based instance segmentation method, generates region bounding boxes by regressing the coordinates of the proposed boxes in a top-down manner. As well-established object detection models like Faster R-CNN [20], RetinaNet [13], and Mask R-CNN [9] have achieved excellent performance in various benchmarks [14], they were all successfully applied in page segmentation works. However, their performances are highly limited by the quality of predicted bounding boxes which are sensitive to hyper-parameters such as class score threshold, scale ratios and quantity of predefined anchors. The regression of bounding boxes may inevitably lead to overlaps and missed detection of boundary pixels or that of whole content region even.

The common drawback in the previous methods is over-simplified supervision. The common observation is that most page regions are quadrilateral and a few of headings and images are curved. The shape and location information which is supposed to be useful has been successfully utilized to represent objects in the scene text detection methods [15,27]. However, the previous methods for DLA, aiming for differentiating positive proposal or pixels from the background rather than generating an object mask of a specific shape, ignore the consideration of such kind of information and therefore did not make full use of the given data. In addition, a remarkable feature of the document page we need to take into consideration is that content objects cover the whole page extensively. In other words, without considering background noise or artifact after binarization, each foreground pixel should be classified into a page region. Therefore, in order to reduce missing rate, it is reasonable to segment foreground and background pixels firstly and then label all pixels in foreground regions to their specific instances.

Based on the above considerations, we decided to use the bottom-up method to design a document-specific segmentation model which is not restricted by the bounding box prediction and can segment the adjacent areas well. The model is based on proposal-free panoptic segmentation model named Panoptic-DLA which predicts per-pixel semantic class and instance id, taking background as "stuff" and other objects of interest as "things". In particular, following the design of Panoptic-DeepLab [6], the model trains two branches in parallel. One is the semantic segmentation branch aiming to segment "stuff" and "things" in per-pixel level. The other is the instance segmentation branch, which dedicates to group predicted "things" further to their instance ids. Dual-Atrous Spatial Pyramid Pooling (ASPP) and dual-decoder modules were adopted to semantic segmentation and instance segmentation respectively. The semantic segmentation branch adopts the typical semantic segmentation model, DeepLabV3+ [5]. To encode location and shape information into the data, inspired by [27], the instance segmentation branch builds Region Center-Border Probability map (RCBP) and Region Center Direction (RCD) map to the represent object and pixel direction instead of center-regression process in Panoptic-DeepLab [6]. Values for the border/center pixels is 0/1 and the values of other pixels gradually decay from center to border in RCBP map, and the rising direction of RCBP can be used to group pixels. RCD predicts the vectors of border pixels which direct from the pixels to the regional center. The method is trained and tested on historical European newspapers [8] and historical Japanese newspapers [22]. The main contribution is as follows:

- We provide a proposal-free page segmentation model named Panoptic-DLA for historical newspaper layout analysis. It can segment foreground pixels and background pixels well, so that as more foreground pixels as possible are detected to participate in the instance segmentation task.
- TextMountain score maps are utilized into the model to encode the location and shape information, as well as to separate the close adjacent regions well.
- This is the first work on historical European newspaper layout analysis, and experiments show that the proposed method works pretty well.

In the following sections, we introduce the related work firstly, then propose our method, describe the experiments, and close the paper with a conclusion at last.

2   Related Work

Traditional page segmentation methods can be categorized as top-down, bottom-up methods for both contemporary and historical documents analyzing tasks. Top-down approaches such as projection profile analysis [11], recursive x-y cuts [17] and white space analysis [2], process the whole image and recursively subdivide it into smaller blocks to isolate the desired part. It resorts to projection profile, Hough transform, Gaussian filters and generally assumes that gap between adjacent text-lines is significant and the text lines are reasonably straight, which may not be faithful in historical documents. Bottom-up methods use simple rules, analyzing the geometric relationships between neighboring blocks such as the distance or the overlap to aggregate elements into regions. Elements can be any part of a page image such as pixels, patches or connected components [1,19]. Although these methods are simple and efficient for some specific situations, with the requirement of prior knowledge about the documents, such as text-line, inter-spaces, text orientation, etc. most of them cannot be easily generalized to various layout situations.

Deep learning methods can also be categorized as top-down and bottom-up method. The top-down method turned the page segmentation task to object detection problem. [18] did the layout analysis for historical palm-leaf manuscript and early paper documents from Indian subcontinent by employing the Mask R-CNN [9]. The object detectors [9,13,20] are always treated as evaluation methods for building layout analysis datasets [22,26]. The bottom-up methods were mainly designed for layout parsing tasks [3,23] which just need to annotate the different semantic regions without further instance segmentation. Chen et al. [3] generates the image patches by using the superpixels algorithm and then classified them by a simple CNN with only one convolution layer. Wick et al. [23] classified the each pixel into the background and other text types using a U-Net [21] structure model without any pre-processing steps such as superpixel generation. As the binary semantic map tends to link adjacent regions together, some excellent works involving a soft probability map [15,27] have been proposed in the scene text detection field. [15] propose to perform soft pyramid label between 0 and 1 in text field based on Mask R-CNN [9]. The value of the pyramid label is determined by the distance to the boundary of the text box. After plane clustering algorithm, pyramid shaped text box with 3D coordinate is constructed, which predicts more accurate text box and improve the robustness to imprecise bounding box prediction. TextMountain [27] models the text shape as a mountain whose peak is text center and foot is text border.

The framework of our method follows the design of Panoptic-DeepLab [6]. It adopts the dual context and decoder structures specific to semantic segmentation and instance segmentation, respectively. The semantic segmentation branch was designed as a typical semantic segmentation model. The instance segmentation branch of Panoptic-DeepLab involved simple class-agnostic instance center regression, as well as the offset regression from each pixel to its corresponding center. The grouping in inference is extremely simple by assigning the pixels to their closest predicted center. For encoding location and shape information and split adjacent pixels in proposal-free manner, we adopt the shape modeling idea in TextMountain [27] instead of center regression heads in the instance segmentation.

3   Methodology

This section described the Panoptic-DLA in detail. We firstly introduce basic architecture and segmentation heads including Region Semantic Segmentation map (RS), Region Center-Border Probability map (RCBP) and Region Center Direction map (RCD). Then we describe how to group pixels with the output of the model and merge the semantic and instance information in inference.

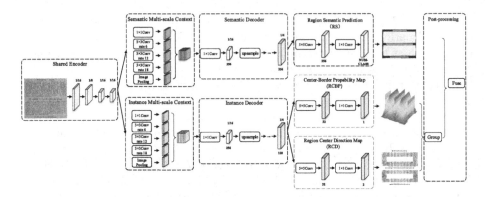

Fig. 1. The Panoptic-DLA is the modification of Panoptic-DeepLab by replacing center prediction and regression maps with RCBP and RCD in instance segmentation branch as framed with red dotted boxes. It adopts decoupled context and decoupled decoder modules for semantic segmentation and instance segmentation predictions respectively. The predicted semantic segmentation and class-agnostic instance segmentation are then fused to generate the final layout segmentation result.

3.1 Architecture

Panoptic-DLA consists of three components as illustrated in Fig. 1: (1) an encoder backbone shared for both semantic segmentation and instance segmentation, (2) dual-ASPP modules and dual-decoder modules specific to each task, and (3) semantic segmentation and instance prediction heads.

Basic Architecture: The encoder backbone with atrous convolution is shared for two branches. Separate ASPP and a light-weight decoder module consisting of a single convolution during each upsampling stage are used to semantic segmentation and instance segmentation, based on the assumption that the two branches need different context information and decoding information.

Semantic Segmentation Head: The semantic segmentation head predicts the per-pixel semantic class including both background ("stuff") and foreground regions ("things"). The weighted bootstrapped cross entropy loss [25] is employed for semantic segmentation.

Class-Agnostic Instance Segmentation Head: The instance segmentation head predicts both RCBP and RCD. RCBP is the mountain-like score map where the pixels at the regional center are set to higher values and those on regional border lower values. For simplicity, the content region in this paper is defined as the minimum circumscribed rectangle of the instance region mask. The label of the point is calculated as the proportion of the shortest distance to the height of the rectangle. The higher the proportion, the closer the location is to the regional center, and the higher value should be assigned to the pixel, vice versa. As illustrated in Fig. 2, the RCBP of x can be can be formulated as:

$$RCBP_x = \frac{2 \times min(\|a_1\|, \|a_2\|, \|a_3\|, \|a_4\|)}{h_x} \qquad (1)$$

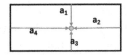

Fig. 2. The vertical lines of four sides.

where a_i is a vertical vector from i-th side to point x, $\|a_i\|$ is the length of a_i. h_x indicate the height of rectangle which can be calculated as minimum distance from a point to two opposite sides, that is, $min(\|a_1\| + \|a_3\|, \|a_2\| + \|a_4\|)$. For achieving better performance on network training, RCD is also predicted as introduced in [27]. The direction vector is calculated as:

$$v_x = \sum_{i=1}^{4} \left[\frac{h_x}{2} - \|a_i\| \right]_+ \times \frac{a_i}{\|a_i\|} \tag{2}$$

where $[z]_+$ represents max $(z, 0)$. It is considered that each side has a thrust to push the point to the center, and the pushing direction is from the sides to the point. The closer to the side, the greater the thrust is. The thrust will disappear if the distance exceeds half the altitude. RCD adopts the unit vector u_x, represented as $u_x = \frac{v_x}{\|v_x\|}$. It can help with separating adjacent regions by assigning totally different RCD values to pixels on the intersection edges of two adjacent regions. We expand objects by one pixel for the RCBP and RCD algorithms can not represent narrow regions (height less than 2) and edge pixels.

L_1 Loss is used in this task and only the labels on the foreground regions are calculated. The loss of RCBP and RCD can be formulated as Eq. 3 and Eq. 4:

$$L_{RCBP} = \frac{\sum_x |RCBP_x - RCBP_x^*|}{\sum_x RS_x^*} \tag{3}$$

$$L_{RCD} = \frac{\sum_x RS_x^*(RCBP_x < \gamma)|u_x - u_x^*|}{\sum_x RS_x^*(RCBP_x < \gamma)} \tag{4}$$

where RS_x^* is region semantic value, which is 0 or 1 value, indicating background and foreground pixels respectively. $RCBP_x$ and $RCBP_x^*$ represent the prediction and ground truth of the RCBP. L_{RCD} is only valid on border region lower than center threshold γ which is set to 0.6. u_x and u_x^* are prediction and ground-truth of RCD respectively. The overall loss function can be formulated as:

$$L = L_{RS} + \lambda_1 L_{RCBP} + \lambda_2 L_{RCD} \tag{5}$$

where L_{RS}, L_{RCBP} and L_{RCD} are the loss functions of semantic segmentation, RCBP and RCD, respectively. λ_1 and λ_2 are the balancing factors of the tasks. By default, we set λ_1 to 5 and λ_2 to 2.5.

3.2   Layout Segmentation

After RS, RCBP and RCD are obtained, the rest is to group the predicted foreground pixels to their instance class and then combine with semantic segmentation to get the final layout segmentation result, as detailed below.

Instance Grouping: Firstly, the mountain peak is generated by $RCBP_x > \gamma$. Each peak is assigned to an individual class id as they represent center points of distinct instance. Then each pixel on mountain foot is grouped to their peak according to the rising direction of probability growth in RCBP or the RCD vector direction. The oriented graph is generated as follows: For RCBP, the largest point in 8-neighbor of each pixel is selected as the next point; For RCD, we choose the vector with angles smaller than $3/8\pi$ as the next vector. Each point's direction is deterministic, so this task can be efficiently solved in parallel by assigning to all points the values of their next points recurrently until their values are no longer changed. The unlabeled pixels are regrouped according to their semantic class and 8-neighbor pixels.

Semantic Labeling: On the basis of given semantic segmentation results and class-agnostic instance segmentation results, the semantic label of the predicted instance mask is inferred from the majority vote of the corresponding predicted semantic label. For the undetected and unclassified foreground pixels in instance grouping, we mark them further in parallel by recurrently assigning them the same instances of the points with the same semantic class among their 8-neighbor pixels.

4   Experiment

4.1   Dataset Setting

We experiment the method on the typical western and Asian language newspapers: historical European newspaper dataset (ENP) [8] and historical Japanese newspaper dataset (HJ) [22]. ENP dataset comprising over 500 page images with a total of 17 page content objects. All page images in the dataset are either 300dpi or 400dpi. 520 pictures pages are selected finally after filtering out some rough annotations, and 10 content types are recorded among them without considering the low frequency objects (number<38) and the "Table" object. Table 1 presents the distribution of a variety of page content objects in the ground truth. According to the number of page objects in each page, the newspaper pages can be divided into four intervals. Table 2 shows the quantity of pages in different interval: 0~50, 50~100, 100~200, and 200+. Maximum objects count is 823 and the minimum is 2. The numbers of training set, verification set and test set are 410, 30 and 80. They were split in the same proportion of objects counts as the total set.

HJ dataset is the large Asian historical newspaper dataset available. The experiment tested on the main pages. The main pages were annotated as hierarchical content structure including 7 classes: Body, Rows, Title Region, Title, Subtitle, Text Region and Other. Each page has rows vertically stacked in page. Texts are vertically written in text regions and are read from right to left. They are horizontally arranged within each row. "Body" covers all the content regions. "Title Region" is further split into "Title" and "Subtitle" blocks. For our method assigns only one label to each pixel without overlapping, we choose the general

Table 1. Contents of ground truth set (520 pages).

Page Content	Abbreviation	Count	Page Content	Abbreviation	Count
Graphics	Graph.	832	Heading	Hdg	6,224
Caption	Cap.	150	Image	Img	636
Drop-capital	DrCap.	750	Paragraph	Para.	37,360
Separator	Sep.	12,950	Page-number	PgN.	241
Header	Hdr	573	Footer	Ft.	65

Table 2. Dataset splits used for training and inference.

Set	0~50	50~100	100~200	200+	All
Total	189	140	104	87	520
Train	148	111	82	69	410
Valid	11	8	6	5	30
Test	30	21	16	13	80

semantic level: Text Region and Title Region. The higher level: Row and Body and lower semantic regions: Title and Subtitle are not considered in the work. We train the model from scratch without pretraining. The numbers of training, verification and test set are 1481, 308, and 308. They were split as [22].

4.2 Experimental Settings

We report foreground pixel-leveled metric [23] by calculating foreground pixels in the binarized page. Firstly we get class-wise average performance at the document level and then average it across all the documents containing the corresponding classes. Compared to the standard object detection metric AP, it enables researchers to compare the methods on their ability to segment foreground objects rather than on their ability to learn and possibly overfit the peculiarities of an ambiguous hand-made ground truth segmentation. The 'poly' learning rate policy [16] is applied with an initial learning rate of 0.001. We resize the image to 1200 pixels at the longest size and perform random scale data augmentation during training with batch size 4. The optimization adopt Adam [10] without weight decay. The training iterations is 200K. Xception-71 [7] is employed as the backbone. The implementation is based on Detectron2 [24]. The whole experiments are conducted on 2 NVIDIA P40 GPUs.

4.3 Results and Analysis

In this section, we introduce the ablation experiments and comparisons with famous object detectors on 2 historical newspaper datasets. Overall performances are shown in Table 3 and Table 5. Performances of each content objects are reported in Table 4. On the whole, the segmentation effect of Japanese newspaper page is better than that of European page. The main reason is that HJ dataset is larger, with simpler layout and has fewer categories to segment than ENP dataset.

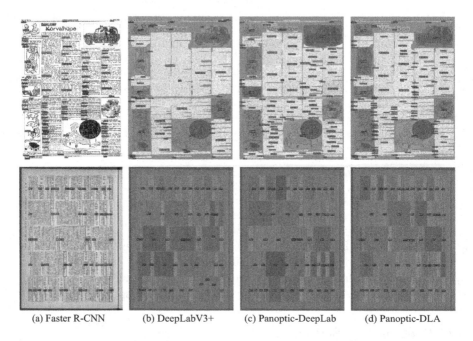

(a) Faster R-CNN   (b) DeepLabV3+   (c) Panoptic-DeepLab   (d) Panoptic-DLA

Fig. 3. Visualization of comparison results. The first row shows the segmentations of one historical European newspaper page. The second row shows the results of the historical Japanese newspaper page segmentation. From left to right: results by Faster R-CNN, DeepLabV3+, Panoptic-DeepLab and the proposed method. In the latter three segmentation images in column, the background pixels are colored in red, each content object is marked with distinct color. The colors of the regions with the same semantic class are similar with each other. (Color figure online)

Ablation Experiment. The single semantic segmentation model DeepLabV3+, Panoptic-DeepLab and the proposed method with three kinds of post-processing were trained and evaluated for comparison. All methods share the same backbone. DeepLabV3+ predicts the per-class probability maps and generate bounding boxes by connected component analysis on each probability map. While it performs pretty well on detection of the objects which locate far from each other, it has difficulty in handling the close adjacent regions with the same semantic label.

Table 3. Ablation experiment. DeepLabV3+ is the semantic segmentation module without instance segmentation. Panoptic-DeepLab applied center prediction and off-set regression process in instance segmentation. The proposed method evaluated with three kinds of post-processing. "Regroup" means the relabeling operation for unlabeled foreground pixels after RCBP or RCBP with RCD.

Method	Post-Process			ENP			HJ		
	RCBP	RCD	Regroup	P	R	F	P	R	F
DeepLabV3+				59.50	60.56	60.03	88.02	87.80	87.91
Panoptic-DeepLab				54.85	42.93	48.16	95.91	96.34	96.12
Panoptic-DLA(a)	√			76.89	55.66	64.58	99.76	99.46	99.61
Panoptic-DLA(b)	√	√		76.57	55.76	64.53	99.76	99.46	99.61
Panoptic-DLA(c)	√		√	75.87	57.64	65.51	99.75	99.54	99.64

Without affecting the reading order, the merging of the same semantic regions is forgivable, such as the merging of the upper and lower regions in European newspaper pages. However, it can be seen from the Fig. 3 that DeepLabV3+ even merged the left and right regions of European newspaper page, as well as the upper and lower regions of Japanese newspaper page mistakenly. This directly broken the readability of the newspaper content. In ENP dataset, the merging error usually occurs as the merging of upper and lower paragraphs owing to "Separator" laying between left and right regions. The proposed method greatly reduces the merging error by RCBP and RCD module. For European newspaper segmentation, Table 4 shows that fmeasure (92.74%) of "Paragraph" by our method is 49.19% higher than DeepLabV3+ and the overall performance

Table 4. Foreground pixel-wise metrics on each content type.

Method		ENP										HJData	
		Graph	Cap.	Hdg	PgN	DrCap	Img	Ft.	Sep.	Para.	Hdr	Tit.	Txt
DeepLab-v3	P	28.61	36.67	72.92	62.03	59.10	65.16	63.72	63.78	62.09	80.96	94.93	81.12
	R	20.02	48.50	70.85	67.49	41.76	81.20	66.09	68.47	62.25	66.32	94.39	81.21
	F	23.55	41.76	71.87	64.64	48.93	72.30	64.88	66.04	62.16	72.91	94.65	81.16
Panoptic-DeepLab	P	36.90	46.26	62.95	74.78	0.00	76.00	54.40	59.73	84.69	52.83	99.18	99.72
	R	11.10	36.15	43.53	55.00	0.00	73.93	38.95	16.25	86.38	68.05	99.06	99.78
	F	17.06	40.58	51.46	63.38	–	74.95	45.39	25.54	85.52	59.48	99.11	99.74
Panoptic-DLA	P	47.07	66.21	75.79	64.57	88.24	82.76	84.69	71.43	93.33	84.48	99.75	99.75
	R	15.27	57.64	71.25	50.02	18.12	83.70	59.59	48.98	92.17	79.73	99.18	99.90
	F	23.05	61.62	73.44	56.37	30.06	83.22	69.95	58.11	92.74	82.03	99.46	99.83
Retinanet	P	38.96	57.11	68.79	82.56	63.10	84.91	63.99	64.56	89.20	74.96	99.51	90.86
	R	18.94	47.46	57.28	53.72	19.23	82.53	56.90	42.08	87.65	70.28	99.71	99.52
	F	25.48	51.83	62.50	65.08	29.47	83.70	60.23	50.95	88.34	72.54	99.60	94.99
Faster R-CNN	P	74.84	64.12	79.97	81.09	80.48	79.99	82.80	70.89	89.95	83.67	99.76	99.74
	R	20.81	44.59	66.43	51.24	22.53	79.42	32.36	46.95	90.78	72.13	99.16	99.92
	F	32.56	52.60	72.57	62.79	35.20	79.70	46.53	56.48	90.36	77.47	99.46	99.83
Mask R-CNN	P	52.04	61.46	74.81	76.22	97.86	80.35	69.75	68.84	91.36	89.65	99.01	99.74
	R	21.61	46.93	72.76	56.43	21.69	82.33	54.64	45.01	90.49	82.69	99.19	99.85
	F	30.53	53.22	73.77	64.84	35.50	81.32	61.27	54.43	90.92	86.02	99.09	99.79

is 9.1% higher than that. For Japanese newspaper segmentation, the proposed method get 13.34% higher fmeasure in overall.

Panoptic-DeepLab adds the instance segmentation part of center-point prediction and offset regression to contribute to the division of adjacent regions. As seen in Table 3, the segmentation of Japanese newspapers has been significantly improved as well as the performance on "Paragraph" in ENP dataset as shown in Table 4. On the overall, however, Panoptic-DeepLab got the lowest performance among segmentations of European newspaper pages. The content regions mostly present quadrilateral shapes, but as seen in Fig. 3, European newspaper segmentations by Panoptic-Deeplab tends to present irregular shapes and takes some common-sense mistakes as (1) dividing an area into multiple areas; (2) regarding the discontinuous area as one area, etc. The main reason should be that the small dataset cannot support the model to learn shape and position information. The problem is considerably alleviated after encoding the information in the target data in our methods. Most of the detected areas by the proposed method are continuous, and the shape tends to be more regular. The results confirm that encoding shape and location information into the data in the instance segmentation branch is extremely useful to represent content objects, especially for the small datasets.

In addition, in order to verify the role of RCD and "Regroup" process in the post-processing stage, the experiments of RCBP, RCBP with RCD, and RCBP with "Regroup" were carried out for comparison. Seen from the Table 3 on ENP dataset, the performance of RCBP with RCD is lower than single RCBP. Nevertheless, "Regroup" did the contribution by scoring 1.44% higher fmeasure on average. So we adopt the RCBP with "Regroup" as post-processing method for ENP segmentation, while the "Regroup" doubled the post-processing time. The whole post-processing time cost about 1s~2s per-image of 1200*840 size. For HJ dataset, we adopt the model with single RCBP, because "Regroup" just made slightly small contribution.

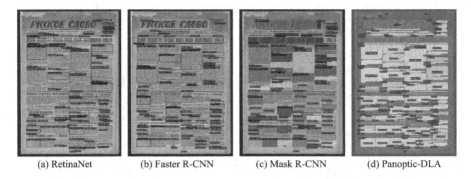

(a) RetinaNet	(b) Faster R-CNN	(c) Mask R-CNN	(d) Panoptic-DLA

Fig. 4. Visualization of comparison results with object detectors. From left to right: the segmentation of Retinanet, Faster R-CNN, Mask R-CNN and the proposed method.

Comparison with Other Detection Methods. The Faster R-CNN, Mask R-CNN and RetinaNet were also trained for comparison. They adopted ImageNet-pretrained neural network with the backbone of ResNet-50-FPN. The detectors performed pretty well on Japanese newspaper pages owing to their large data and regularly shaped content objects. The proposed method performs comparably with the best RCNN detectors on both datasets. The missed detection and overlapping errors are the tough and inevitable issues in the whole field of regression-based detection. For European newspapers, missed detections are always focused on the border pixels of the content objects (see Fig. 3). However, at some time, the detectors may miss the whole regions as illustrated in Fig. 4. The proposed method can ensure as many foreground pixels as possible to be segmented from background pixels. So as shown in Table 4, the recall of the "Paragraph" in our method scores 1.53% higher than the best "Paragraph" detector Faster R-CNN, and get 0.31% higher recall than Mask R-CNN in overall on ENP dataset.

Table 5. Comparison with object detector methods.

Data	Method	AP	AP_{50}	AP_{75}	AP_s	AP_m	AP_l	P	R	F
ENP	Faster R-CNN	20.28	33.33	21.08	14.07	25.32	26.48	78.78	52.72	63.17
	Mask R-CNN	21.09	33.56	22.62	13.56	27.62	28.01	76.23	57.45	65.52
	RetinaNet	17.22	28.75	18.42	11.99	23.55	25.56	68.81	53.92	60.25
	Panoptic-DLA	18.82	29.34	19.80	11.21	20.46	28.76	75.85	57.64	65.51
HJ	Faster R-CNN	94.17	98.41	98.29	–	90.27	96.75	99.75	99.54	99.64
	Mask R-CNN	94.23	98.93	98.26	–	90.44	97.14	99.37	99.52	99.44
	RetinaNet	94.41	98.86	98.68	–	89.68	97.08	95.18	99.61	97.34
	Panoptic-DLA	95.11	98.91	98.27	–	91.57	97.13	99.75	99.54	99.64

Additionally, we also test the AP metric for object detectors and the proposed method to explore their specific tasks they are suitable to evaluate. As seen in Table 5, the segmentation effect of object detectors is very impressive. They are better at detecting small objects and slender objects than the proposed methods, and the proposed method performs best at detecting large objects. From the point of view of overall performance on HJ dataset, RetinaNet performs best among the three detectors. However, when measured by foreground pixels, Faster R-CNN get the highest performance and RetinaNet performs the worst. The difference between the two evaluation methods indicates that the fitting ability of the bounding box can not be directly determined as the detection ability in layout analysis task. For instance, in natural object detection, the prediction which deviated from ground truth object boxes will still be seen as true positive in the range keeping IoU higher than a specific threshold. Nevertheless, even being set the highest IoU as 0.95, it has great possibility to cause the text of line to be cropped out which seriously affects the underlying work such as OCR.

So pixel-level evaluation is better when conducting strict comparisons between detection methods. Certainly, AP is the better choice to reveal the detection performance at bounding box-level. The IoU can be appropriately increased to the range such as from 0.75 to 0.95. It is more suitable to evaluate rectangular objects in well-annotated document pages instead of historical documents which include some skewed and irregular content objects.

5   Conclusion

In this study, we presented the proposal-free layout segmentation method for historical newspaper page. For document page segmentation task, we hope our work could inspire re-thinking of the importance of separating foreground and background pixels by semantic segmentation module. Besides, the instance segmentation branch also verified that shape and location information of pixels are common but useful to represent content objects. There are still some deficiencies in our method. On the one hand, misclassification of boundary pixels is still the difficult point. On the other hand, the post-processing methods are simple but time-consuming. In the future, we will integrate some lightweight algorithms such as randomized neural networks to accelerate the model training efficiency and explore an end-to-end system to avoid the post-processing stage.

References

1. Boulid, Y., Souhar, A., Elkettani, M.Y.: Arabic handwritten text line extraction using connected component analysis from a multi agent perspective. In: 2015 15th International Conference on Intelligent Systems Design and Applications (ISDA), pp. 80–87. IEEE (2015)
2. Breuel, T.M.: Two geometric algorithms for layout analysis. In: Lopresti, D., Hu, J., Kashi, R. (eds.) DAS 2002. LNCS, vol. 2423, pp. 188–199. Springer, Heidelberg (2002). https://doi.org/10.1007/3-540-45869-7_23
3. Chen, K., Seuret, M., Hennebert, J., Ingold, R.: Convolutional neural networks for page segmentation of historical document images. In: 2017 14th IAPR International Conference on Document Analysis and Recognition (ICDAR), vol. 1, pp. 965–970. IEEE (2017)
4. Chen, L.C., Papandreou, G., Kokkinos, I., Murphy, K., Yuille, A.L.: Deeplab: semantic image segmentation with deep convolutional nets, atrous convolution, and fully connected crfs. IEEE Trans. Pattern Anal. Mach. Intell. **40**(4), 834–848 (2017)
5. Chen, L.C., Zhu, Y., Papandreou, G., Schroff, F., Adam, H.: Encoder-decoder with atrous separable convolution for semantic image segmentation. In: Proceedings of the European Conference on Computer Vision (ECCV), pp. 801–818 (2018)
6. Cheng, B., et al.: Panoptic-deeplab: a simple, strong, and fast baseline for bottom-up panoptic segmentation. In: Proceedings of the IEEE/CVF Conference on Computer Vision and Pattern Recognition, pp. 12475–12485 (2020)
7. Chollet, F.: Xception: deep learning with depthwise separable convolutions. In: Proceedings of the IEEE Conference on Computer Vision and Pattern Recognition, pp. 1251–1258 (2017)

8. Clausner, C., Papadopoulos, C., Pletschacher, S., Antonacopoulos, A.: The enp image and ground truth dataset of historical newspapers. In: 2015 13th International Conference on Document Analysis and Recognition (ICDAR), pp. 931–935. IEEE (2015)

9. He, K., Gkioxari, G., Dollár, P., Girshick, R.: Mask R-CNN. In: Proceedings of the IEEE International Conference on Computer Vision, pp. 2961–2969 (2017)

10. Kingma, D.P., Ba, J.: Adam: A method for stochastic optimization. arXiv preprint arXiv:1412.6980 (2014)

11. Li, S., Shen, Q., Sun, J.: Skew detection using wavelet decomposition and projection profile analysis. Pattern Recogn. Lett. **28**(5), 555–562 (2007)

12. Li, Y., Zou, Y., Ma, J.: DeepLayout: a semantic segmentation approach to page layout analysis. In: Huang, D.-S., Gromiha, M.M., Han, K., Hussain, A. (eds.) ICIC 2018. LNCS (LNAI), vol. 10956, pp. 266–277. Springer, Cham (2018). https://doi.org/10.1007/978-3-319-95957-3_30

13. Lin, T.Y., Goyal, P., Girshick, R., He, K., Dollár, P.: Focal loss for dense object detection. In: Proceedings of the IEEE International Conference on Computer Vision, pp. 2980–2988 (2017)

14. Lin, T.-Y., et al.: Microsoft COCO: common objects in context. In: Fleet, D., Pajdla, T., Schiele, B., Tuytelaars, T. (eds.) ECCV 2014. LNCS, vol. 8693, pp. 740–755. Springer, Cham (2014). https://doi.org/10.1007/978-3-319-10602-1_48

15. Liu, J., Liu, X., Sheng, J., Liang, D., Li, X., Liu, Q.: Pyramid mask text detector. arXiv preprint arXiv:1903.11800 (2019)

16. Liu, W., Rabinovich, A., Berg, A.C.: Parsenet: Looking wider to see better. arXiv preprint arXiv:1506.04579 (2015)

17. Nagy, G., Seth, S., Viswanathan, M.: A prototype document image analysis system for technical journals. Computer **25**(7), 10–22 (1992)

18. Prusty, A., Aitha, S., Trivedi, A., Sarvadevabhatla, R.K.: Indiscapes: Instance segmentation networks for layout parsing of historical indic manuscripts. In: 2019 International Conference on Document Analysis and Recognition (ICDAR), pp. 999–1006. IEEE (2019)

19. Rajput, G., Ummapure, S.B., Patil, P.N.: Text-line extraction from handwritten document images using histogram and connected component analysis. Int. J. Comput. Appl. **975**, 8887 (2015)

20. Ren, S., He, K., Girshick, R., Sun, J.: Faster R-CNN: towards real-time object detection with region proposal networks. IEEE Trans. Pattern Anal. Mach. Intell. **39**(6), 1137–1149 (2016)

21. Ronneberger, O., Fischer, P., Brox, T.: U-Net: convolutional networks for biomedical image segmentation. In: Navab, N., Hornegger, J., Wells, W.M., Frangi, A.F. (eds.) MICCAI 2015. LNCS, vol. 9351, pp. 234–241. Springer, Cham (2015). https://doi.org/10.1007/978-3-319-24574-4_28

22. Shen, Z., Zhang, K., Dell, M.: A large dataset of historical Japanese documents with complex layouts. In: Proceedings of the IEEE/CVF Conference on Computer Vision and Pattern Recognition Workshops, pp. 548–549 (2020)

23. Wick, C., Puppe, F.: Fully convolutional neural networks for page segmentation of historical document images. In: 2018 13th IAPR International Workshop on Document Analysis Systems (DAS), pp. 287–292. IEEE (2018)

24. Wu, Y., Kirillov, A., Massa, F., Lo, W.Y., Girshick, R.: Detectron2. https://github.com/facebookresearch/detectron2 (2019)

25. Yang, T.J., et al.: Deeperlab: single-shot image parser. arXiv preprint arXiv:1902.05093 (2019)

26. Zhong, X., Tang, J., Yepes, A.J.: Publaynet: largest dataset ever for document layout analysis. In: 2019 International Conference on Document Analysis and Recognition (ICDAR), pp. 1015–1022. IEEE (2019)
27. Zhu, Y., Du, J.: Textmountain: accurate scene text detection via instance segmentation. Pattern Recogn. **110**, 107336 (2021)

Improving Answer Type Classification Quality Through Combined Question Answering Datasets

Aleksandr Perevalov[1(✉)] and Andreas Both[1,2]

[1] Anhalt University of Applied Sciences, Köthen (Anhalt), Germany
{aleksandr.perevalov,andreas.both}@hs-anhalt.de
[2] DATEV eG, Nuremberg, Germany
andreas.both@datev.de

Abstract. Understanding what a person is asking via a question is one of the first steps that humans use to find the corresponding answer. The same is true for Question Answering (QA) systems. Hence, the quality of the expected answer type classifier (EAT) has a direct influence on QA quality. Many research papers are aiming at improving short text classification quality, however, there is a lack of focus on the impact of training data characteristics on the classification quality as well as effective reuse of datasets through their augmentation and combination. In this work, we propose an approach of analyzing and improving the EAT classification quality via a combination of existing QA datasets. We provide 4 new question classification datasets based on several well-known QA datasets as well as the approach to unify its class taxonomy. We made a sufficient amount of experiments to demonstrate several valuable insights related to the impact of training data characteristics on the classification quality. Additionally, an embedding-based approach for automatic data labeling error detection is demonstrated.

Keywords: Expected answer type classification · Textual data augmentation · DBpedia ontology · Knowledge base question answering

1 Introduction

The text classification task holds a significant role in Question Answering (QA) systems where typically a question is provided as input using natural language. Previous research shows that the prediction of the expected answer type (EAT or target type) of a question has a direct positive impact on the QA system's quality [6,11,12]. Consequently, high-precision models have to be provided in order to increase the overall QA quality.

In this paper, we follow the hypothesis that a high-quality EAT classifier will lead to an improved answer quality of a QA system. While improving the classification quality through effective reuse of the existing datasets, we address the issue of generalization, i.e., we aim for a classifier that can be easily used

© Springer Nature Switzerland AG 2021
H. Qiu et al. (Eds.): KSEM 2021, LNAI 12816, pp. 191–204, 2021.
https://doi.org/10.1007/978-3-030-82147-0_16

for different knowledge domains. Hence, the robustness of the approach is a topic in this work as well as the characteristics of datasets that are used for training such classifiers. Additionally, an in-depth analysis of possible flaws and errors will be done to contribute to a better understanding of corresponding challenges and datasets. These efforts are dedicated to our long-term research agenda of providing reusable components for QA systems that can be combined while aiming for an increased QA quality.

In this paper we address the following research questions:

RQ1: Can the EAT classification quality be increased by combining previously isolated datasets?

RQ2: What are the characteristics of (in-)appropriate training datasets?

RQ3: Is it possible to automatically detect labeling errors in the data?

Our work has the following contributions: (1) We proposed an approach for improving the EAT classification quality based on effective reuse of existing datasets. (2) We derived 4 new question classification datasets based on LC-QuAD, QALD, WebQuestions, and SimpleQuestions and demonstrate how to unify the datasets to combine them together (Sect. 4). (3) We found, empirically evaluated, and reported several insights from the influence of the training data on classification quality. (4) We demonstrated an approach for automatically detect labeling errors in the text classification datasets.

The paper is organized as follows: In Sect. 2 we describe the related work. We conceptually describe the approach that we follow in this work in Sect. 3. In Sect. 4 the datasets and the data preparation process are described. After that, we show our experimental setting (Sect. 5). The analysis of the experimental results is provided in Sect. 6. Conclusions are given in Sect. 7.

2   Related Work

As the main challenge of the classification of short texts (such as questions) is obviously the shortness and sparsity of the data, the approach based on combining of knowledge bases and neural networks was proposed in [29]. The approach is based on linking a word to a concept in a knowledge base (KB) to retrieve more information (also known as background knowledge).

Another solution for the described problem was to use a set of unstructured data to pre-train the embedding layer of the model. Such unsupervised approaches are presented in the following game-changing publications: word2vec [18], Global Vectors (GloVe) [20], and fastText [9].

In recent years, the transformer-based models are holding a significant part in the whole NLP industry and research community. Such models as ELMo [22], ULM-FIT [8], BERT [8], and XLNet [31] have achieved state-of-the-art results in many language-understanding tasks (cf. [26]). Based on top of this progress, several works related to the data augmentations and characteristics were published. In [33] the BERT-based text classification model BERT4TC is proposed via constructing so-called "auxiliary sentences". The work [34] presents an approach for data augmentation based on enriching the corpus and short texts with

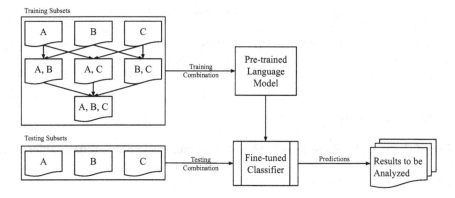

Fig. 1. General idea of the data combination approach

hidden topics. The authors of the publication [16] study and summarize augmentation methods to improve the question classification. In [32] an approach of transforming a question to its generalized form via replacing named entities with corresponding types from a knowledge base is presented. Recently, a challenge on answer type classification (SMART Task) [17] has shown that transformers are demonstrating the highest results in this task [19,23]. There also an approach was introduced that is based on English data augmentation using machine translation [21]. Additionally, the results of the SMART challenge clearly show that rule-based answer type classifiers are non-competitive in terms of quality (e.g., [25]) while also being able to show a comprehensive error analysis.

The majority of the research regarding text classification does not consider the training data unification, transformation, and augmentation techniques. Besides, we were unable to find publications describing the influence of the training data characteristics on the particular model as well as the effect of combining previously isolated datasets to improve classification quality. We exploit this research gap in this work.

3   Approach

The majority of research studies describe new model architectures or improvements of the existing ones to increase the quality of the text classification task (cf. Sect. 2). In our approach, we concentrate on the effective usage of the existing datasets through their combination.

To describe the impact of particular dataset properties on the classification quality, we create all possible combinations of the considered datasets. For example, if a set of three datasets is given $\{A, B, C\}$, then the *power set of non-empty elements* is used. All elements of the power set are used independently for the classifier training. For the evaluation, the corresponding test subsets of $\{A, B, C\}$ are used. Hence, for the evaluation 21 (7 training combinations, i.e., power set * 3 test datasets) experiments need to be executed and analyzed (see Fig. 1).

The classifier is a pre-trained language model that we fine-tune and evaluate on our datasets. The model configuration is fixed, i.e., we do not fine tune, change the architecture, or optimize the hyperparameters of the model. This approach allows us to see the individual impact of each dataset's characteristics on the classification quality while analyzing results of different dataset combinations.

4   Data Preparation

Most of the considered datasets are based on a particular KB and have different structures. We transform and unify the data, s.t., it is applicable for the question classification task.

4.1   Datasets Overview

In our work we used the following datasets: Large-scale Complex Question Answering Dataset version 1 [27] (LC-QuAD), 9th Edition of Question Answering over Linked Data Challenge [28] (QALD), Cognitive Computation dataset [14] (TREC), WebQuestions [1], and SimpleQuestions [2].

LC-QuAD is a QA dataset with 4,900 pairs of questions and corresponding SPARQL queries over on DBpedia. LC-QuAD does not have an answer type label that is required for our task. Therefore, add it to the dataset by querying the KB. LC-QuAD is widely used in the process of QA systems development (cf. [5,24]).

QALD-9 is the 9th version of Question Answering over Linked Data (QALD) dataset that consists of 558 questions. For every question instance: textual representations in multiple languages (we use the English representation), the corresponding SPARQL query, the answer entity URI, and the answer type are available. The dataset has become a benchmark for many research studies in QA (e.g., [4,7]).

TREC (also known as CogComp) is a question classification dataset which contains 6,000 questions and its' classes. The dataset is a long-established text classification benchmark in the research community (e.g., [10,13]). The taxonomy of the dataset was mapped to the unified taxonomy defined in the next subsection.

WebQuestions is a QA dataset that contains 5,812 questions with a textual answer list for each one. The dataset is widely used for evaluation of QA systems [30]. The given dataset is built on the Freebase[1] KB.

SimpleQuestions is a large dataset for answering simple questions. The dataset consists of 108,442 questions written in natural language by humans and the corresponding triples: subject, predicate, and object represented by URIs from the Freebase KB. The SimpleQuestions dataset as well as WebQuestions were used for creation and evaluation of QA systems (e.g., [3,15]).

---

[1] https://developers.google.com/freebase/.

Table 1. Overview of the unified datasets

Name	Class taxonomy	Classes	Original size	Processed size	Data loss
LC-QuAD-train	DBpedia	20	3922	1868	−2570
LC-QuAD-test		20	978	462	
QALD-train	DBpedia	19	408	393	−24
QALD-test		12	150	141	
TREC-train	TREC[a]	19	5500	3703	−1062
TREC-test		19	500	1235	
WebQuestions-train	Freebase	27	3024	2965	−96
WebQuestions-test		22	2788	2751	
SimpleQuestions-train	DBpedia	20	75910	41346	−49304
SimpleQuestions-test		21	32532	17792	

[a] https://cogcomp.seas.upenn.edu/Data/QA/QC/definition.html

4.2 Unification of Classes Taxonomy

The unified class taxonomy is mandatory for the considered datasets to ensure comparability. After reviewing the existing datasets and their data sources, we have decided to use the DBpedia Ontology top-level classes[2] as the target ontology (i.e., all questions will be transferred to a representation matching the DBpedia Ontology). Additionally, we added primitive answer type classes to the taxonomy in order to cover such questions as "How many people live in Germany" (Number), "Was Angela Merkel born in Hamburg?" (Boolean), and so on. In total, we obtained 54 classes in the answer type classification taxonomy, some examples are: dbo:Agent, dbo:Place, dbo:Work, dbo:Activity, dbo:Disease, dbo:Language, dbo:Currency, dbo:EthnicGroup, Number, Text (String), Boolean, and DateTime.

4.3 Retrieving Answer Type Classes Using SPARQL

The datasets LC-QuAD, QALD, WebQuestions, and SimpleQuestions do not have a direct answer type label referring to the DBpedia Ontology. Instead, these datasets provide for each question a SPARQL query, URIs, and textual representations of answers (see Subsect. 4.1 for details). Thus, we have to retrieve the answer type using a linked data approach.

Our data transformation pipeline consists of the following 2 steps: (1) retrieve an answer entity for the question from the knowledge base, (2) retrieve an answer type for the answer entity from a knowledge base. For example, the SPARQL queries in Listing 1 are intended to compute the answer type of the question "Where was Barack Obama born?".

```
# first step: get the answer (dbr:Hawaii)
SELECT ?answer WHERE {
    dbr:Barack_Obama dbo:birthPlace ?answer .
```

[2] https://wiki.dbpedia.org/services-resources/ontology.

```
}
# second step: get the answer type (dbo:Place)
SELECT ?answerType WHERE {
    dbr:Hawaii rdf:type ?answerType .
    # all non-top level DBpedia Ontology classes are excluded
}
```

Listing 1. Retrieving answer type via 2-step pipeline using SPARQL over DBpedia

We run our 2-step pipeline for LC-QuAD and QALD as they are providing SPARQL queries that are used to retrieve the correct answers from DBpedia.

The SimpleQuestions dataset provides the results in the form of answer entities (URIs) pointing to the Freebase. Hence, only the second step needs to be executed. To link the Freebase entities to DBpedia we used the owl:sameAs property which is contained in DBpedia entities. However, not all entities are interlinked that is why the approach led to the loss of some data of ca. 42%.

The WebQuestions dataset contains only answer labels. This situation leads to a high ambiguity while trying to identify the (correct) answer resource in DBpedia. Therefore, despite a high required time investment, we manually labeled the data to ensure a high quality of the dataset.

The TREC dataset already has a question classification structure. The taxonomy of the classes represents an answer type of questions on two class levels: upper (6 classes) and lower (50 classes). The upper classes are more general (e.g., ENTITY, LOCATION) and incorporate itself the lower ones which are more specific (e.g., group, individual, city). The given lower-level taxonomy was mapped to the DBpedia class taxonomy that is used in our work, because its detailing level is more consistent.

The overview of the created datasets is shown in Table 1. The data loss (i.e., the answers could not be mapped to DBpedia entities) is significant for LC-QuAD (56%) and SimpleQuestions (45%). However, we assume that the dataset size is large enough for the model training, because for LC-QuAD the overall number of data items is still in the same order of magnitude as TREC-train and SimpleQuestions-train is still the largest dataset. Additionally, the different numbers of instances in the taxonomy classes are recognizable. In Sect. 6, we will discuss the impact of the situation on the cross-dataset training process.

5   Experiments

As described in Sect. 3 we used the power set of all considered datasets to train a model (i.e., there are 31 training sets) and tested it using the 5 corresponding test sets. In our experiments, 3 different pre-trained models were used: `bert-base-cased`, `roberta-base`, `distilbert-base-uncased`. These models were selected as the top-3 most downloadable models in the Hugging Face repository[3]. The hyperparameters were not changed, the exact values, as well as the other experimental settings and datasets are present in our repository[4].

---

[3] https://huggingface.co/models.
[4] https://github.com/Perevalov/eat_classification_ksem2021.

Table 2. Average quality of the models aggregated by the number of the datasets in a training combination (F1 score, %).

Model	Std. err. (SE)	Number of training datasets				
		1	2	3	4	5
bert-base-cased	$SE < 1\%$	71.97 ± 0.44	77.50 ± 0.45	83.22 ± 0.45	86.13 ± 0.46	88.08 ± 0.44
	$SE \leq 100\%$	55.95 ± 3.27	76.70 ± 0.68	82.15 ± 0.60	85.75 ± 0.57	88.08 ± 0.44
roberta-base	$SE < 1\%$	44.19 ± 0.42	78.17 ± 0.58	81.32 ± 0.51	82.61 ± 0.57	86.49 ± 0.47
	$SE \leq 100\%$	46.40 ± 1.49	72.99 ± 1.18	79.88 ± 1.19	83.33 ± 1.23	85.75 ± 0.99
distilbert-base-uncased	$SE < 1\%$	56.54 ± 0.54	77.60 ± 0.53	81.49 ± 0.56	85.80 ± 0.49	89.88 ± 0.45
	$SE \leq 100\%$	52.99 ± 2.42	75.19 ± 0.82	80.98 ± 0.72	85.03 ± 0.71	87.43 ± 0.83

Based on the results we build a consolidated evaluation table[5]. It is worth to mention that corresponding training and test datasets (i.e., X-train and X-test) are not intersecting (which is true for all considered datasets).

Additionally, the average F1 score of the models grouped by number of the datasets in a training combination was analyzed. Hence, each group x (where $x \in \{1, 2, 3, 4, 5\}$) is a set of all training combinations created by merging x datasets. In Table 2 the corresponding results are presented. Detailed insights from the evaluation are described in the following section.

6   Analysis and Discussion

Despite different standard error threshold selection, there is a consistent quality improving trend corresponding with the addition of external datasets (cf. Table 2). While answering RQ1, it is worth to underline that the more datasets are combined to create a training set, the more robust are the results w.r.t. the standard error.

There is often an intuitive opinion that increase of training data size always leads to directly proportional quality growth. The conducted experiments have shown that it is not always the case. In the following subsections, we analyze the reasons for such behavior.

6.1   Effect of Class Distribution Mismatch

To give details of the conducted experiments and its results, we firstly analyze the correlation between the class distribution similarity (CDS) and the quality of a particular experimental result. The CDS was measured using Kullback–Leibler divergence (KLD), where the test set distribution is considered as the original (P) and the train set distribution is the one that we are comparing to (Q). The resulting matrix of CDS presented in Fig. 2.

The main diagonal of the matrix in the figure shows that train and test splits of a corresponding dataset appear typically to be similar. Interestingly, this is not the case for the QALD. The average F1 score of the experiment where the

---

[5] The complete experimental results are available as online appendix at footnote 4.

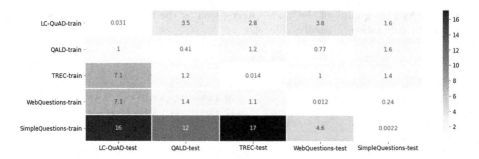

Fig. 2. KLD matrix between train (P) and test (Q) class distributions

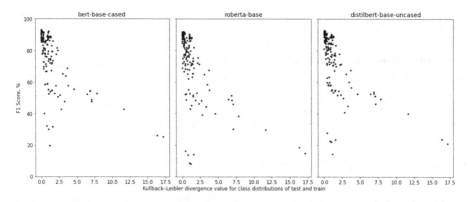

Fig. 3. Visualization of correlation between F1 score and KLD values for train and test class distributions.

model was trained using QALD-train and testing on QALD-test is $27.96 \pm 7.76\%$ which is obviously low and has high variance. It correlates with high KLD value. Additionally, QALD is the smallest dataset among all. On the opposite side, the TREC dataset has the most similar train and test sets. The average F1 score of the respective experiment is $90.23 \pm 0.57\%$ which is relatively high and supports our assumption on correlation between CDS and quality.

We used a KLD matrix to show all train (31) and test (5) combinations. There, the correlation between the KLD matrix values and the corresponding experimental results (F1 score) is calculated (the KLD values and experimental results are ordered by the train-test tuples respectively). The obtained correlation coefficients for all 3 classifiers are: $-0.62, -0.59, -0.60$ (all significant at $p < 0.00001$). Thus, *there is a strong negative correlation between KLD values and F1 scores.* The visual representation of the correlation is given in Fig. 3.

The statement above can be interpreted as follows: the more training set's class distribution differs from the test set's ones, the lower will be the classification quality. Hence, the QALD-test dataset is not reflecting completely the characteristics of QALD-train dataset w.r.t. the class distribution, i.e., QALD-test is not a well-suited test for QALD-train which is leading to a lower F1 score.

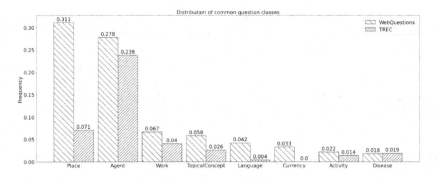

Fig. 4. Visual distribution comparison

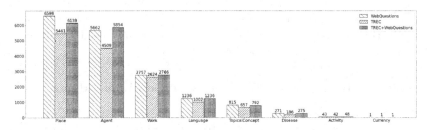

Fig. 5. Correctly classified questions (test data: SimpleQuestions-test)

While answering RQ2, *we suggest to the research community to use KLD as a measure for optimal training dataset selection.*

6.2 Impact of Class Distribution on Class-Wise Accuracy

Despite the fact that addition of training data improves the quality on the average, there are 25.16%, 9.68%, and 21.29% (for used models respectively) of experiments resulting quality decrease while using more than 1 training dataset.

Consider the particular example of the distribution-accuracy correlation with 3 combinations: WebQuestions, TREC and TREC ∪ WebQuestions. All the considered combination were tested on SimpleQuestions-test. At first, the visual class distribution has to be taken into an account (see Fig. 4).

The figure shows that the distribution of two datasets is not similar for almost all classes. Most visible for the class dbo:Place which is *significantly imbalanced* (however, for other classes the share is different with more than an order of magnitude, e.g., dbo:Language and dbo:Currency). The main idea behind the combination of datasets is to make "weak" classes "stronger" while assuming that the quality will increase and the trained models will become more robust. Let us compare the correctly classified questions after making a combination TREC ∪ WebQuestions using SimpleQuestions-test to test the model.

The visual comparison on Fig. 5 shows that after appending WebQuestions to TREC the number of correctly classified questions for class dbo:Place was increased from 5461 to 6139 (+12.42%). However, if we take another point of view: After TREC was appended to WebQuestions the number of correctly classified questions was decreased from 6598 to 6139 (−6, 96%).

The "synergy effect" of appending datasets is reached with such classes as dbo:Agent, dbo:Work, dbo:Language, dbo:Disease and dbo:Activity. For all these classes the number of correctly classified questions was increased in both point of views.

Consequently, the increase of classification quality using combinations is achieved through "strengthening" infrequent classes in the training data. Specifically, combining datasets may improve classification if a significant difference in class distribution between training and testing sets is observed. On the other side, combining datasets may lead to a quality decrease (e.g., class dbo:Place on Fig. 5) because the "perfect balance" is violated. We assume that *the class distribution of a training dataset must exactly match to the one in a testing dataset* (see RQ2). However, this topic requires additional research on different models and datasets with proper validation techniques.

6.3   Labeling Errors Estimation with Question Embeddings

Despite our data preparation process was consistent (see Sect. 4), we still admit that data labeling errors may took place. To analyze these errors, we have created an automatic approach of labeling errors detection using question embeddings. The intuition behind the approach is to utilize the ability of neural models to capture the semantics of text in form of embeddings. Hence, we assume that all semantically similar questions have close embeddings in vector space. Knowing such property of a model, we can easily search for labeling errors.

The approach has the following steps: (1) fine-tune a language model on a training dataset, (2) use the fine-tuned model to generate embeddings for the dataset, (3) define the class centers in embedding space based on the generated embeddings, (4) for each question, discover if its embedding is closer to the class center different from the currently assigned one, (5) mark all questions found in the previous step as wrongly labeled.

For the purpose of error estimation, the `distilbert-base-uncased` model was used. The model was fine-tuned on the combination of: LC-QuAD, QALD, TREC, WebQuestions, and SimpleQuestions training subsets. Thereafter, the datasets listed above were analyzed for labeling errors using the described approach. The following error rate (and absolute values) results were obtained: LC-QuAD-train – 1.28% (24), QALD-train – 3.56% (14), TREC-train – 3.37% (125), WebQuestions-train – 3.54% (105), SimpleQuestions-train – 3.63% (1501). Where error rate is a ratio of number of errors to a total number of examples in a dataset. More detailed results by classes are shown in Fig. 6.

The approach is able to correct the estimated errors in the data automatically. For example, in the dataset QALD-train the question "How many museums does Paris have?" is labeled with dbo:Place, while the suggested class is `Number`. In the same dataset the question "Who is 8th president of US?" is labeled as `String` while our automatic process suggests the class dbo:Agent. In WebQuestions-train

Fig. 6. Estimated labeling error rates (%) by classes for each dataset

"who is ruling tunisia now?" is labeled with dbo:Activity while our approach is suggesting the EAT class dbo:Agent.

There were also false suggestions results. For example, for the question "what nationality is jermaine paul?" of WebQuestions-train the class dbo:Place was suggested (however, the correct class is dbo:EthnicGroup). According to manual inspection of the results, the majority of false suggestions (ca. 60–70%) happen due to not precisely define class taxonomy definition.

Hence, *the demonstrated approach is able not only estimate labeling errors in the dataset but also to correct them* (see RQ3). We provide the full list of questions considered as wrongly labeled as well as suggested correct classes as an online appendix[6]. Though, the effectiveness of such approach as well as the influence of labeling errors on the classification quality has to be evaluated in details, which is not covered by this paper and will be part of future research.

7   Conclusion and Future Work

In this work, we proposed an approach for improving EAT classification quality and reported results from an analysis of the impact of training data characteristics on classification quality.

The following novel contributions are provided: (1) an approach for EAT classification quality improvement was proposed, (2) 4 new question classification datasets are derived and published online, (3) the influence of training data characteristics on classification quality was studied, and (4) an approach for automatic detection of labeling errors in textual data was shown.

For the future work, we set the following research tasks: (1) the derived datasets are based on DBpedia top-level classes are very general, thus, the most specific classes has to be obtained, (2) the proposed data combining approach should be tested on the recently published SMART dataset [17], (3) the proposed labeling errors detection approach should be validated by rerunning the experiments, (4) the EAT classification task needs to be extended to a multilingual setting, (5) estimate and optimize the time complexity of the dataset

---

[6] The full list of questions considered as wrongly labeled is available at footnote 4.

combination approach, and (6) the approach has to be extended to other class taxonomies or a Zero-shot learning approach might be used.

References

1. Berant, J., Chou, A., Frostig, R., Liang, P.: Semantic parsing on freebase from question-answer pairs. In: Proceedings of the 2013 Conference on Empirical Methods in Natural Language Processing, pp. 1533–1544 (2013)
2. Bordes, A., Usunier, N., Chopra, S., Weston, J.: Large-scale simple question answering with memory networks. arXiv preprint arXiv:1506.02075 (2015)
3. Diefenbach, D., Lopez, V., Singh, K., Maret, P.: Core techniques of question answering systems over knowledge bases: a survey. Knowl. Inf. Syst. **55**(3), 529–569 (2017). https://doi.org/10.1007/s10115-017-1100-y
4. Diefenbach, D., Singh, K., Both, A., Cherix, D., Lange, C., Auer, S.: The Qanary ecosystem: getting new insights by composing question answering pipelines. In: Cabot, J., De Virgilio, R., Torlone, R. (eds.) ICWE 2017. LNCS, vol. 10360, pp. 171–189. Springer, Cham (2017). https://doi.org/10.1007/978-3-319-60131-1_10
5. Dubey, M., Banerjee, D., Chaudhuri, D., Lehmann, J.: EARL: joint entity and relation linking for question answering over knowledge graphs. In: Vrandečić, D., et al. (eds.) ISWC 2018. LNCS, vol. 11136, pp. 108–126. Springer, Cham (2018). https://doi.org/10.1007/978-3-030-00671-6_7
6. Garigliotti, D., Hasibi, F., Balog, K.: Target type identification for entity-bearing queries. In: Proceedings of the 40th International ACM SIGIR Conference on Research and Development in Information Retrieval (2017)
7. Höffner, K., Walter, S., Marx, E., Usbeck, R., Lehmann, J., Ngonga Ngomo, A.C.: Survey on challenges of question answering in the semantic web. Seman. Web **8**(6), 895–920 (2017)
8. Howard, J., Ruder, S.: Universal language model fine-tuning for text classification. In: Proceedings of the 56th Annual Meeting of the Association for Computational Linguistics (Volume 1: Long Papers), Melbourne, Australia, pp. 328–339. Association for Computational Linguistics (July 2018). https://doi.org/10.18653/v1/P18-1031
9. Joulin, A., Grave, E., Bojanowski, P., Mikolov, T.: Bag of tricks for efficient text classification. In: Proceedings of the 15th Conference of the European Chapter of the Association for Computational Linguistics: Volume 2, Short Papers, pp. 427–431. Association for Computational Linguistics, Valencia, Spain (April 2017), https://www.aclweb.org/anthology/E17-2068
10. Kalchbrenner, N., Grefenstette, E., Blunsom, P.: A convolutional neural network for modelling sentences. In: Proceedings of the 52nd Annual Meeting of the Association for Computational Linguistics (Volume 1: Long Papers), Baltimore, Maryland, pp. 655–665. Association for Computational Linguistics (June 2014). https://doi.org/10.3115/v1/P14-1062
11. Kamath, S., Grau, B., Ma, Y.: Verification of the expected answer type for biomedical question answering. In: 2018 Companion Proceedings of the The Web Conference (2018)
12. Kamath, S., Grau, B., Ma, Y.: Predicting and integrating expected answer types into a simple recurrent neural network model for answer sentence selection. Computación y Sistemas **23**(2019)

13. Kim, Y.: Convolutional neural networks for sentence classification. In: Proceedings of the 2014 Conference on Empirical Methods in Natural Language Processing (EMNLP), pp. 1746–1751. Association for Computational Linguistics, Doha, Qatar (2014). https://doi.org/10.3115/v1/D14-1181

14. Li, X., Roth, D.: Learning question classifiers. In: The 19th International Conference on Computational Linguistics, COLING 2002 (2002)

15. Lukovnikov, D., Fischer, A., Lehmann, J., Auer, S.: Neural network-based question answering over knowledge graphs on word and character level. In: Proceedings of the 26th International Conference on World Wide Web, WWW '17, Republic and Canton of Geneva, CHE, pp. 1211–1220. IW3C2 (2017). https://doi.org/10.1145/3038912.3052675

16. Marivate, V., Sefara, T.: Improving short text classification through global augmentation methods. In: Holzinger, A., Kieseberg, P., Tjoa, A.M., Weippl, E. (eds.) CD-MAKE 2020. LNCS, vol. 12279, pp. 385–399. Springer, Cham (2020). https://doi.org/10.1007/978-3-030-57321-8_21

17. Mihindukulasooriya, N., Dubey, M., Gliozzo, A., Lehmann, J., Ngomo, A.C.N., Usbeck, R.: SeMantic AnsweR Type prediction task (SMART) at ISWC 2020 Semantic Web Challenge. CoRR/arXiv abs/2012.00555 (2020). https://arxiv.org/abs/2012.00555

18. Mikolov, T., Sutskever, I., Chen, K., Corrado, G.S., Dean, J.: Distributed representations of words and phrases and their compositionality. In: Burges, C.J.C., Bottou, L., Welling, M., Ghahramani, Z., Weinberger, K.Q. (eds.) Advances in Neural Information Processing Systems, vol. 26. Curran Associates, Inc. (2013). https://proceedings.neurips.cc/paper/2013/file/9aa42b31882ec039965f3c4923ce901b-Paper.pdf

19. Nikas, C., Fafalios, P., Tzitzikas, Y.: Two-stage semantic answer type prediction for question answering using BERT and class-specificity rewarding. In: Proceedings of the SeMantic AnsweR Type prediction task (SMART), ISWC 2020. CEUR Workshop Proceedings, vol. 2774, pp. 19–28. CEUR-WS.org (2020). http://ceur-ws.org/Vol-2774/paper-03.pdf

20. Pennington, J., Socher, R., Manning, C.: GloVe: global vectors for word representation. In: Proceedings of the 2014 Conference on Empirical Methods in Natural Language Processing (EMNLP), , Doha, Qatar, pp. 1532–1543. Association for Computational Linguistics (October 2014). https://doi.org/10.3115/v1/D14-1162

21. Perevalov, A., Both, A.: Augmentation-based answer type classification of the SMART dataset. In: Proceedings of the SeMantic AnsweR Type prediction task (SMART), ISWC 2020. CEUR Workshop Proceedings, vol. 2774, pp. 1–9. CEUR-WS.org (2020). http://ceur-ws.org/Vol-2774/paper-01.pdf

22. Peters, M., et al.: Deep contextualized word representations. In: Proceedings of the 2018 Conference of the North American Chapter of the Association for Computational Linguistics: Human Language Technologies, Volume 1 (Long Papers), New Orleans, Louisiana, pp. 2227–2237. Association for Computational Linguistics (June 2018). https://doi.org/10.18653/v1/N18-1202

23. Setty, V., Balog, K.: Semantic answer type prediction using BERT IAI at the ISWC SMART task 2020. In: Proceedings of the SeMantic AnsweR Type prediction task (SMART), ISWC 2020. CEUR Workshop Proceedings, vol. 2774, pp. 10–18. CEUR-WS.org (2020). http://ceur-ws.org/Vol-2774/paper-02.pdf

24. Singh, K., et al.: Why reinvent the wheel: let's build question answering systems together. In: Proceedings of the 2018 World Wide Web Conference. pp. 1247–1256, WWW '18. International World Wide Web Conferences Steering Committee (2018). https://doi.org/10.1145/3178876.3186023

25. Steinmetz, N., Sattler, K.: COALA - a rule-based approach to answer type prediction. In: Proceedings of the SeMantic AnsweR Type prediction task (SMART), ISWC 2020. CEUR Workshop Proceedings, vol. 2774, pp. 29–40. CEUR-WS.org (2020). http://ceur-ws.org/Vol-2774/paper-04.pdf
26. Sun, C., Qiu, X., Xu, Y., Huang, X.: How to fine-tune BERT for text classification? arXiv abs/1905.05583 (2019)
27. Trivedi, P., Maheshwari, G., Dubey, M., Lehmann, J.: LC-QuAD: a corpus for complex question answering over knowledge graphs. In: d'Amato, C., et al. (eds.) ISWC 2017. LNCS, vol. 10588, pp. 210–218. Springer, Cham (2017). https://doi.org/10.1007/978-3-319-68204-4_22
28. Usbeck, R., Gusmita, R.H., Ngomo, A.N., Saleem, M.: 9th challenge on question answering over linked data (QALD-9) (invited paper). In: Joint proceedings of the 4th Workshop on Semantic Deep Learning (SemDeep-4) and NLIWoD4: Natural Language Interfaces for the Web of Data (NLIWOD-4) and 9th Question Answering over Linked Data challenge (QALD-9) co-located with 17th International Semantic Web Conference (ISWC 2018), Monterey, California, United States of America, 8–9 October 2018, vol. 2241, pp. 58–64. CEUR Workshop Proceedings (2018)
29. Wang, J., Wang, Z., Zhang, D., Yan, J.: Combining knowledge with deep convolutional neural networks for short text classification. In: Proceedings of the 26th International Joint Conference on Artificial Intelligence, IJCAI-17, vol. 350, pp. 2915–2921 (2017). https://doi.org/10.24963/ijcai.2017/406
30. Wen, T.H., et al.: A network-based end-to-end trainable task-oriented dialogue system. In: Proceedings of the 15th Conference of the European Chapter of the Association for Computational Linguistics: Volume 1, Long Papers, Valencia, Spain, pp. 438–449. Association for Computational Linguistics (April 2017). https://www.aclweb.org/anthology/E17-1042
31. Yang, Z., Dai, Z., Yang, Y., Carbonell, J., Salakhutdinov, R., Le, Q.V.: XLNet: generalized autoregressive pretraining for language understanding. In: Advances in Neural Information Processing Systems, vol. 32. Curran Associates, Inc. (2019)
32. Yavuz, S., Gur, I., Su, Y., Srivatsa, M., Yan, X.: Improving semantic parsing via answer type inference. In: Proceedings of the 2016 Conference on Empirical Methods in Natural Language Processing, Austin, Texas, pp. 149–159. Association for Computational Linguistics (November 2016). https://doi.org/10.18653/v1/D16-1015
33. Yu, S., Su, J., Luo, D.: Improving BERT-Based text classification with auxiliary sentence and domain knowledge. IEEE Access 7, 176600–176612 (2019). https://doi.org/10.1109/ACCESS.2019.2953990
34. Zhang, H., Zhong, G.: Improving short text classification by learning vector representations of both words and hidden topics. Knowl. Based Syst. 102, 76–86 (2016). https://doi.org/10.1016/j.knosys.2016.03.027

FOBA: Flight Operation Behavior Analysis Based on Hierarchical Encoding

Tongyu Zhu$^{(\boxtimes)}$ and Zhiwei Tong$^{(\boxtimes)}$

SKLSDE Lab, Beihang University, Beijing, China
zhutongyu@nlsde.buaa.edu.cn, tzw@buaa.edu.cn

Abstract. Through analyzing flight data we can detect pilot's improper operation, which effectively improves flight safety. This paper proposes an approach to convert multivariate flight data into symbol series and an auto-regressive semantic understanding model. Our model can predict what kind of pilot operation or aircraft status should appear at the next time step according to data at the current time step. Furthermore, we proposed a prediction model for unsafe event predicting based on our semantic understanding model. The experiment results show that our prediction model outperforms well known classifiers. Finally, experiments show that our model has the application value of correcting pilot operation.

Keywords: Behavior encoding · Deep learning · Flight Event Predict

1 Introduction

In critical flight stages, such as taking-off and landing, pilot's improper operations are the direct factor leading to flight events. Flight Operation Quality Assurance (FOQA) [1] is a system that helps airlines and pilots to detect wrong aircraft operations and improve flight safety. FOQA systems collect high frequency flight data from Quick Access Recorder which is one kind of onboard flight data recorder to detect abnormal operation after flight. In general, FOQA systems apply the industrial standard "Exceedance Detection" algorithms which uses a list of specified parameters and their thresholds to identify known unsafe events [2]. In recent years, machine learning methods have been gradually introduced to explore the causes of those flight events and predict potential risk [3,5,6].

While the above-mentioned work has been proved to be effective, All the detection methods are aimed at exceedance events, not for describing and understanding the semantics and effects of operation behavior. Relations between control actions and events are not found.

In view of the above problem, we propose a Flight Operation Behavior Analysis (FOBA) framework based on flight operation behavior coding and understanding, which can predict unsafe event. The framework include Flight Operation Behavior Encode (FOBEC), Flight Operation Behavior Understand

© Springer Nature Switzerland AG 2021
H. Qiu et al. (Eds.): KSEM 2021, LNAI 12816, pp. 205–217, 2021.
https://doi.org/10.1007/978-3-030-82147-0_17

(FOBU) and Flight Event Predict (FEP) component. The main contributions of this study can be summarized as follows:

1. This paper proposes a hierarchical coding scheme, named FOBEC, of operation behavior, and contains independent information about pilot behavior, flight control and outside airflow.
2. We propose an auto-regressive semantic understanding model FOBU and a hard landing prediction model FEP.
3. We propose a pilot operation correction method based on our framework FOBA.

The rest of this paper is organized as follows: Sect. 2 is about the current techniques of flight event detection. Section 3 introduces our flight operation behavior encoding method and flight operation behavior understanding approach. And, Sect. 4 we give a case study on how to apply the behavior understanding model to predict a unsafe event and correct pilot operation. Then, Sect. 5 presents our dataset and experimental results. Finally, conlusion is given in Sect. 6.

2   Related Work

Flight event detection is the most important part of FOQA program. The existing FOQA systems use exceedance events methods to find flight events and statistical methods to detect the fleet's flight risk [4]. Some research showed flight behavior analysis and methods based on machine learning could detect flight event better.

2.1   Flight Operation Quality Assurance

Digital flight data is available on all modern aircrafts. Once collected, it is translated into engineering units (e.g., feet, knots, degrees), analyzed and stored by the Flight Data Monitoring(FDM) tool in the airline database. Nicolas Maille [3] discusses the design of an analysis process using a flight decomposition relying on crew activities and including discrete parameters that reflect crew actions. Dimitry Gorinevsky et al. [6] describes an application of data mining technology called Distributed Fleet Monitoring, which transforms the data into a list of abnormally performing aircraft, abnormal flight-to-flight trends, and individual flight anomalies by fitting a large scale multi-level regression model to the entire data set. Alvin Megatroika et al. [7] compared two models of aircraft operation anomaly detection. It is concluded that both models could detect anomalies within FOQA data and the one-class SVM outperforms self-organizing map neural network in number of anomalies found, however in runtime length, self-organizing map neural network performs better.

Junjie Liu et al. [8] taking the 2011 to 2014 ASRS flight fatigue events as samples to do semantic network analysis. The results show that the correlation research on nodes of flight fatigue events not only can effectively analyze the related reasons with strong correlation, but also judge the correlation among various causes.

2.2   Behavior Modeling

S. Sekizawa et al. use markov process to model driving behavior [9]. Their model succeeded in recognizing pilot behavior. To model pilot behavior, the key point is to extract the hidden motivation behind it. Hidden markov model can express the hidden state. However, landing process is a stable process with fixed rules or phases, and the pilots always behave with the same intention to keep the aircraft stable. HMM's probability-based transferring doesn't work for such a background.

Considering that QAR data are time series and the record of each parameter forms a curve, methods of clustering curves based on shapes have being adopted to evaluate landing processes. X. Li et al. focused on shape of data curves and clustered data based on curves [10]. They adopted their model on classifying types of hard landing and achieved high accuracy. However, their model can only be applied on data where hard landing actually happens. They didn't perform classifying between normal landing and hard landing to prove their model's ability to describe normal landing processes.

Y. Wang et al. use recurrent neural network to detect semantic-level driving characteristics [11]and have realized identification of drivers. However, their work is limited to analyzing a whole process, not a single time point. Meanwhile, their work uses data of cars which is far less complex than that of flights.

2.3   Machine Learning on Landing Events

For landing events prediction, hard landing prediction is a typical flight landing event prediction task. Previous studies mainly focus on using statistical machine learning algorithm and feature engineering. Qiao et al. [12] used RBF neural network to predict hard landing, which involved a k-means clustering of the model parameters. Qian et al. [13] extracted statistical information on several key flight variables, such as mean, standard deviation, median, maximum, then used kmeans to cluster these feature information and applied these clustered results to predict hard landing. Holmes et al. [14] focused on the use of Gaussian process regression for the prediction of loads on the components of a landing gear. Tong et al. [15] used long short-term memory and 15 most relevant parameters with feature engineering to establish a deep hard landing prediction model. Because hard landing samples account for only a small percentage,training data is always unbalanced. In order to maintain a balanced training data, existing studies mainly use a small training set to do a specific predicting,thus hinder the performance of machine learning model and fail to fully characterize the whole landing phase.

3   Approach

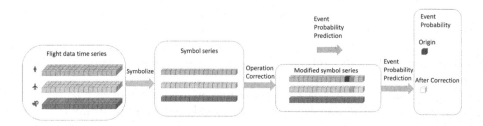

Fig. 1. Illustration of FOBA's architecture

The structure of FOBA framework is shown in Fig. 1. We formulate flight data as multivariate time series. Suppose one flight process data has T time steps and D features, it can be represented as $\mathbf{X} = \{x_{ij}\}$ where $x_{ij} \in \mathbb{R}, i \in \{1, 2, ..., T\}, j \in \{1, 2, ..., D\}$. Specifically, all parameters can be partitioned into three groups: aircraft status related parameters such as pitch angle, environmental condition related parameters such as wind speed and pilot operation related parameters such as pitch operation.

3.1   Symbolic Representation

Given a multivariate time series $x_{ij} \in \mathbb{R}$, the task is to get a suitable symbolic representation of it.

We use Symbolic Aggregate Approximation (SAX) to convert flight time series into symbolic representation. We separate parameters into three groups corresponding to aircraft status, pilot operation and environment condition.

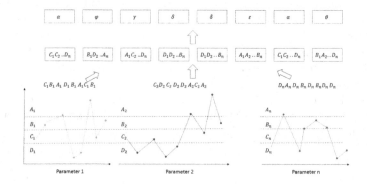

Fig. 2. The distribution of all values of a parameter in the data set

For each parameter, SAX is used to get a symbolic representation of it. Firstly, Z-normalization is applyed. For each parameter p, time series $[x_1^p, x_2^p, ..., x_T^p]$, has a mean of zero and a standard deviation. Then, some breakpoints are pre-defined. Breakpoints can be seen as a list of numbers $B = \beta_1, ..., \beta_{a-1}$, where a is how many equal areas are partitioned of a $N(0, 1)$ Gaussian curve. These are also called quantiles of a distribution.

The symbolic representation forms a set of tokens corresponding to each parameter. We partition this set into three subsets, corresponding to pilot operation, aircraft status and environmental status. For each subset, the tokens form a sequence and again mapped into a unique token. Thus, a flight time series can be converted into three strings. Formally, P_t^i means the token of the i-th parameter at time step t in a landing time series. A data point at time t in a landing time series can be represented as a vector $[P_t^1, P_t^2, ..., P_t^D]$. Three parameter subsets are predefined as U^A, U^E, U^P. This point can then be represented as three token string. For example, tokens of aircraft status parameters at time t can be represented as a string $P_t^1 P_t^2 ... P_t^d$ where $P_t^i \in U^A, d = |U^A|$. Each token string is then mapped into a unique token. For example, above mentioned $P_t^1 P_t^2 ... P_t^d$ is mapped into a single symbol s_t^A. Finally, each landing time series is transformed into three strings:

$$S^A = (s_1^A, s_2^A \cdots s_T^A),$$
$$S^E = (s_1^E, s_2^E \cdots s_T^E), \tag{1}$$
$$S^P = (s_1^P, s_2^P \cdots s_T^P).$$

The process through which raw data of parameters from U^i is transformed into S^i, where $(i \in \{A, E, P\})$, is shown in Fig. 2.

3.2 Definition of FOBU

Flight process has a natural sequential ordering and follows some rules. Each sub-phase has standard aircraft status. In addition, pilots have to obey the pre-designed rules of operation. Previous aircraft status and environmental condition determine the pilot operation at next step, while previous pilot operation and environmental condition determine the current aircraft status.

Considering these characteristics of flight, we propose a deep auto-regressive aircraft landing model named Flight Operation Behavior Understanding. This model regresses through predicting the aircraft status and the pilot operation according to the previous flight data. Figure 3 shows the architecture of FOBU. Symbolic representation data is fed into FOBU. The model is optimized on Next Status Prediction (NSP) task. The goal of NSP is to predict symbols of aircraft status and pilot operation at the current time step according to previous symbol data. This is useful when we try to simulate the whole flight process. Formally, s_t^A is a symbolic representation corresponding to the aircraft status at time step t, s_t^E is a symbolic representation corresponding to the environmental condition at time step t, s_t^P is a symbolic representation corresponding to the pilot operation at time step t. Given the previous $t - 1$ data, the model tries to

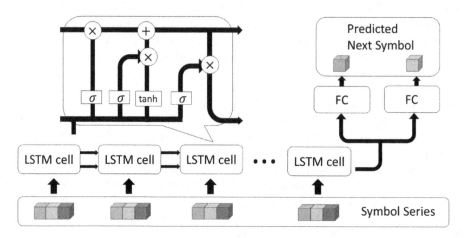

Fig. 3. The general model architecture of FOBU. The flight multivariate time series is partitioned into three groups corresponding to pilot operation, aircraft status and environmental condition. Each group of parameters is transformed into symbolic representation. long short-term memory(LSTM) is used to encode previous flight status and predict the pilot operation token and aircraft status token at the current time step.

predict the next aircraft status and pilot operation:

$$s_t^A = F_A(s_{[1:t-1]}^A, s_{[1:t-1]}^E, s_{[1:t-1]}^P),$$
$$s_t^P = F_P(s_{[1:t-1]}^A, s_{[1:t-1]}^E, s_{[1:t-1]}^P). \tag{2}$$

However ,symbolic representation of the environment condition is not to be predicted s_t^E because it is a objective factor. FOBU gives the joint probabilities over the pilot operational sequence and aircraft status sequence:

$$p(s^A) = \prod_{t=1}^{T} p(s_t^A | s_1^A, s_1^E, s_1^P, ..., s_{t-1}^A, s_{t-1}^E, s_{t-1}^P),$$
$$p(s^P) = \prod_{t=1}^{T} p(s_t^P | s_1^A, s_1^E, s_1^P, ..., s_{t-1}^A, s_{t-1}^E, s_{t-1}^P). \tag{3}$$

In this paper, we use Long-Short Term Memory(LSTM) as the main model. We modify the update process to adapt to multiple sequence input. At each time step t we have input s_t^A, s_t^E, s_t^P. An embedding layer coverts each token into a dense vector x_t^A, x_t^E, x_t^P. Aircraft status, pilot operation and environmental condition use different embedding look-up tables. The inference process is as follows:

$$f_t = \sigma(W_f[x_t^A, x_t^P, x_t^E] + U_f h_{t-1} + b_f),$$
$$i_t = \sigma(W_i[x_t^A, x_t^P, x_t^E] + U_i h_{t-1} + b_i),$$
$$o_t = \sigma(W_o[x_t^A, x_t^P, x_t^E] + U_o h_{t-1} + b_o),$$
$$\widetilde{C_t} = \tanh(W_c[x_t^A, x_t^P, x_t^E] + U_c h_{t-1} + b_c), \tag{4}$$
$$C_t = f_t \odot C_{t-1} + i_t \odot \widetilde{C_t},$$
$$h_t = o_t \odot \tanh(C_t),$$

where W_f, W_o, W_i, W_c, U_f, U_o, U_i, U_c are model parameters. Each time step will have an output h_t. We use two matrices corresponding to aircraft status and pilot operation to do classification. The probability distribution of the aircraft status p_t^A and The probability distribution of the pilot operation p_t^P at next time step will be

$$p_t^A = W_A h_t,$$
$$p_t^P = W_P h_t, \tag{5}$$

where W_A and W_P are $M \times N_A$, $M \times N_P$ metrics, h_t is a M-dim vector. M is the size of h_t, N_A is the amount of symbols for aircraft status, N_P is the amount of symbols for pilot operation. We can get the normalized score through a softmax function.

The loss function for pre-training aircraft landing model is defined as:

$$L_a(x) = - \sum_{t=1}^{T} \log p(x_t^A | h_{t-1}, x_{[1:t-1]}^A, x_{[1:t-1]}^P, x_{[1:t-1]}^E)$$
$$- \sum_{t=1}^{T} \log p(x_t^P | h_{t-1}, x_{[1:t-1]}^A, x_{[1:t-1]}^P, x_{[1:t-1]}^E). \tag{6}$$

4   Case Study

In this chapter, we introduce how to use FOBU and FEP to help predict flight events. In this paper, hard landing prediction is chosen as the flight events prediction task.

4.1   Landing Events Prediction

For a flight time series, FOBU will produce a representation at each time step which contains high-dimensional features. By adding a classification layer on the top of the last time-step representation h_T, we try to get the prediction result:

$$p(y = 1) = \sigma(h_T W_h), \tag{7}$$

where W_h is the model parameters at the fine-tuning stage. The final loss is cross entropy loss calculated as

$$L_c(x) = \frac{1}{N} \sum_{i=1}^{N} y_i \log(\sigma(h_T W_h)) + (1 - y_i) \log(1 - \sigma(h_T W_h)), \tag{8}$$

where y_i is the label of the i-th sample indicating whether hard landing happens.

4.2   Attention Mechanism

To further reinforce our model's expression of the whole flight process, we add attention mechanism to our model. Attention mechanism is an effective architecture and has been widely used in many applications. It can also give insight in which part of input is important to the final decision through attention score. Vector W_a and b_a is the attention parameter, the attention score at time step t can be calculated as:

$$a_t = \tanh\left(W_a h_t + b_a\right). \tag{9}$$

The final representation for hard landing classification h is

$$h = \sum_{t=1}^{T} \widetilde{a_t} h_t, \tag{10}$$

where $\widetilde{a_t}$ is a_t after softmax, h_t is flight status of time t. Through applying attention mechanism, we find that the last 5 time steps tend to have bigger attention value. This means that the last few seconds of the landing process are very important in determining whether a hard landing occurs.

4.3   Pilot Operation Correction Algorithm

The goal of pilot operation correction is to find a method of modification of pilot operation, so as to reduce the probability of hard landing prediction of the original hard landing sample. The implementation of pilot operation correction can help analyze what operation can reduce the probability of hard landing in a given state. The implementation of the pilot operation correction algorithm is based on three characteristics of FOBU:

1. FOBU is trained in a self-regression manner and can predict future landing state symbols based on a given landing status symbol sequence, which provides the basis for modifying subsequent sequence regeneration after pilot operation.
2. FOBU is trained on a large number of normal landing samples, and the model can infer the operation that the pilot usually takes at the current moment under a given aircraft landing sequence, which is the result of learning from a large number of samples, which provides a reasonable basis for the pilot's operation correction.
3. The performance of the hard landing prediction model based on the aircraft landing model has been significantly improved, which supports the prediction of the hard landing probability after the pilot's operation has been corrected.

Based on the above characteristics, this paper puts forward the pilot opera-tion correction algorithm. The pilot operation correction based on the aircraft landing model FOBU is divided into three parts: operation modify, aircraft land-ing process inference, and Hard landing prediction of modified landing sequence.

1. Operation Modify

   Select moment t to modify the pilot's operation, then input the symbol sequence of the previous $t-1$ moments into FOBU, which predicts the prob-ability distribution of the pilot's operation for each symbol at moment t. We sort these pilot action symbols by probability value and select the most confident pilot operation symbols as alternative corrections.

2. Aircraft landing process inference

   After modifying the pilot operation at moment t, the aircraft state sequence and the pilot operation sequence after moment t should be updated, while the environment sequence remain unchanged. We use FOBU to predict the sequence of aircraft state and the sequence of pilot operations after the moment t to generate a sequence of corrected pilot operations.

3. Hard landing prediction of modified landing sequence

   After obtaining the inferred sequence after the pilot's operation correction, these sequences are input into FEP, and the probability of hard landing pre-diction is obtained.

5   Experiment and Results

In this section, we will introduce the experiment result of training FOBU. We will also show the experimental results of using FEP to predict hard landing com-pared to other methods. Finally, we provide experiment result of pilot operation correction.

5.1   Dataset

This paper uses real flight data from QAR provided by China Academy of Civil Aviation Science and Technology. The data contains more than 50000 flight data dated from 2016 to 2018. Each flight data contains more than 600 parameters. All aircraft types in this dataset are A320 series.

Data of landing phase is extracted from the whole flying data. The data we choose as landing data begins at 250 ft altitude and ends after touching down, since this is the major period which may influence the landing quality and have time to adjust aircraft for pilot before touching down.

We split the 52887 normal landing data into three groups. The first group contains approximately 50,000 landing samples to train FOBU. The second and third groups are for hard landing prediction experiment. The second group con-tains 156 hard landing samples and 156 normal landing samples as the hard landing prediction training sets, and the third group contains 112 hard landing samples and 112 normal landing samples as the validation sets.

5.2   Training FOBU

Data is preprocessed to symbolic representation as introduced before. We choose Adam as the optimizer and set the initial learning rate to 0.0003. The perplexity is used as the metric. Perplexity is a measurement of how well a probability distribution or probability model predicts a sample. A low perplexity indicates the probability distribution FOBU performs well in predicting next symbol. The final perplexity is the sum of the pilot operation perplexity and the aircraft status perplexity. We use different training data sizes to analyze how training data size affects FOBU's performance. The FOBU trained on the whole training set, around 50000 samples, gets a perplexity (pilot operation perplexity plus aircraft status perplexity) of 161.76.

5.3   Hard Landing Predict with FEP

We fine-tune the FOBU to realize FEP. The basic version is to use the last hidden state of FOBU as the features for classification. Another version is to use attention mechanism and the state of each time step to generate features. In order to compare our proposed method with the traditional hard landing prediction method, we built some baselines using feature engineering and machine learning algorithm. New features we build include the average value, max value. Finally, we extracted 548 features in total. We use these features to train support vector machine(SVM), logistic regression(LR) naive bayes(NB) and Decision Tree. Up-Sampling abbreviated as US is applied for imbalanced training data. We meanwhile use FEP on hard landing prediction tasks without pre-training to see

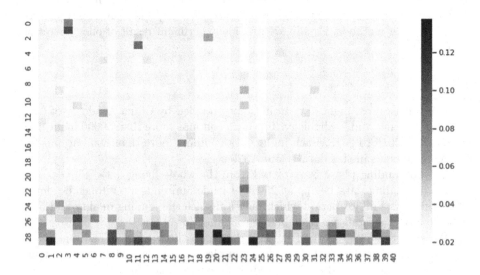

Fig. 4. Landing sequence attention score. The columns are different time steps. The rows are different samples. Darker color means the attention score is higher

the bonus gained from pre-training. The metrics of hard landing prediction are precision, recall and F-Score.

The experimental results are shown in Table 1. Firstly, the result of our proposed method gets significant improvement on hard landing prediction task compared with traditional methods. FEP based on FOBU gets 8% improvement on F-Score. Secondly, without FOBU, the performance of FEP on hard landing prediction drops significantly, which proves that by training on large scale flight data in our proposed way, FOBU can automatically learn valuable knowledge of flight rules and high level representation to characterize the flight process. In addition, knowledge can be transferred to hard landing prediction task.

Table 1. Hard landing prediction experiment result

Model	Precision	Recall	F-Score
NB	0.497	0.817	0.618
LR	0.549	0.325	0.408
SVM(rbf kernel)	0.532	0.342	0.416
SVM(linear kernel)	0.523	0.183	0.272
Decision Tree	0.667	0.583	0.622
US-SVM(Linear)	0.550	0.183	0.275
US-SVM(rbf)	0.531	0.142	0.224
US-LR	0.553	0.392	0.459
US-NB	0.684	0.667	0.675
FEP	0.713	0.642	0.675
FEP on FOBU	**0.795**	0.742	0.767
FEP on FOBU with Attention	0.780	**0.767**	**0.773**

5.4 Pilot Operation Correction

In this section, we introduce experiment results of using trained FOBU and FEP to analyze landing process and correct pilot operation. We input all hard landing samples into FEP and get the attention score of each time step. The attention score shows how much this time step influences the final hard landing. Figure 4 shows the result of some samples. We can see that most of the hard landing samples have a high correlation with the last 5 time steps. This means hard landing is mostly caused by factors in the last few seconds.

For each hard landing sample, we change the pilot operation token at one of the last 5 time steps. The pilot operation token is changed by sampling from the distribution at the current time step given by the trained FOBU. The following sequence is generated by trained FOBU. The completed sequence is fed into FEP which gives the predicted hard landing probability. We collect some pilot operation changes which can decrease the hard landing prediction score significantly.

Table 2 shows the changing sets. The token is converted to its original parameter SAX symbolic representation. For example, "0013" means the parameter RUDDERPEDAL has symbol "0",RUDDERANGLE has symbol "0", PITCHS-STICK has symbol "1", the ROLLSSTICK has symbol "3".

Table 2. Operation correction experiment result

Case Id	Original	Modified	Original prob	Modified Prob	Reduced prob
1	0013	0012	0.759	0.243	0.516
2	0312	0012	0.834	0.330	0.504
3	4423	4412	0.756	0.285	0.471
4	4111	4412	0.756	0.452	0.304
5	4322	4422	0.896	0.590	0.306
6	0312	0412	0.785	0.470	0.315
7	4222	4212	0.777	0.467	0.310
8	0022	0012	0.812	0.584	0.228
9	4004	4012	0.715	0.463	0.252
10	4421	4422	0.814	0.598	0.216

The results show that some modification of the pilot operation at specific time point can significantly decrease the probability of hard landing occurrence. The change from "0013" to "0012" means decreasing the ROLLSSTICK operational value a little to avoid hard landing.

6 Conclusion

In this paper, we propose a framework to do flight operation behavior analysis called FOBA. Main model of FOBA called FOBU can extract representation and learn rules of flight automatically from large scale flight data. The FEP based on FOBU shows significant improvement on a case of hard landing prediction task after fine-tuning, which proves the ability of FOBA applyed on specific flight event. Finally we showed some cases based on experiments where FOBA is used to correct pilot operation effectively.

References

1. Halford, C., Harper, M.: Asias: aviation safety information analysis and sharing. In: 2008 IEEE/AIAA 27th Digital Avionics Systems Conference, pp. 2-C. IEEE (October 2008)
2. Mitchell, K., Sholy, B., Stolzer, A.J.: General aviation aircraft flight operations quality assurance: overcoming the obstacles. IEEE Aerosp. Electr. Syst. Mag. **22**(6), 9–15 (2007)

3. Maille, N.: On the use of data-mining algorithms to improve FOQA tools for airlines. In: 2013 IEEE Aerospace Conference, pp. 1–8. IEEE (March 2013)

4. Zhao, X., Zhou, X., Zhang, X.: Research on flight parameters based on statistical theory. In: 2019 IEEE 1st International Conference on Civil Aviation Safety and Information Technology (ICCASIT), pp. 515–518. IEEE (October 2019)

5. Nanduri, A., Sherry, L.: Anomaly detection in aircraft data using Recurrent Neural Networks (RNN). In: 2016 Integrated Communications Navigation and Surveillance (ICNS), pp. 5C2-1. IEEE (April 2016)

6. Gorinevsky, D., Matthews, B., Martin, R.: Aircraft anomaly detection using performance models trained on fleet data. In: 2012 Conference on Intelligent Data Understanding, pp. 17–23. IEEE (October 2012)

7. Megatroika, A., Galinium, M., Mahendra, A., Ruseno, N.: Aircraft anomaly detection using algorithmic model and data model trained on FOQA data. In: 2015 International Conference on Data and Software Engineering (ICoDSE), pp. 42–47. IEEE (November 2015)

8. Liu, J., Du, Y., Zhang, R.: Correlation analysis of semantic network nodes in flight fatigue events. In 2019 IEEE 1st International Conference on Civil Aviation Safety and Information Technology (ICCASIT), pp. 114–119. IEEE (October 2019)

9. Sekizawa, S., et al.: Modeling and recognition of driving behavior based on stochastic switched ARX model. IEEE Trans. Intell. Transp. Syst. 8(4), 593–606 (2007)

10. Li, X., Shang, J., Zheng, L., Liu, D., Qi, L., Liu, L.: CurveCluster: automated recognition of hard landing patterns based on QAR curve clustering. In: 2019 IEEE SmartWorld, Ubiquitous Intelligence & Computing, Advanced & Trusted Computing, Scalable Computing & Communications, Cloud & Big Data Computing, Internet of People and Smart City Innovation (SmartWorld/SCALCOM/UIC/ATC/CBDCom/IOP/SCI), pp. 602–609. IEEE (August 2019)

11. Wang, Y., Ho, I. W.H.: Joint deep neural network modelling and statistical analysis on characterizing driving behaviors. In: 2018 IEEE Intelligent Vehicles Symposium (IV), pp. 1–6. IEEE (June 2018)

12. Qiao, X., Chang, W., Zhou, S., Lu, X.: A prediction model of hard landing based on RBF neural network with K-means clustering algorithm. In: 2016 IEEE International Conference on Industrial Engineering and Engineering Management (IEEM), pp. 462–465. IEEE (December 2016)

13. Qian, S., Zhou, S., Chang, W.: An improved aircraft hard landing prediction model based on panel data clustering. In: 2017 29th Chinese Control And Decision Conference (CCDC), pp. 438–443. IEEE (May 2017)

14. Holmes, G., Sartor, P., Reed, S., Southern, P., Worden, K., Cross, E.: Prediction of landing gear loads using machine learning techniques. Struct. Health Monit. 15(5), 568–582 (2016)

15. Tong, C., et al.: An innovative deep architecture for aircraft hard landing prediction based on time-series sensor data. Appl. Soft Comput. 73, 344–349 (2018)

An Event Detection Method Combining Temporal Dimension and Position Dimension

Zehao Yu[✉]

School of Computer Science, Beijing University of Posts and Telecommunications, Beijing 100876, China
1147711288@qq.com

Abstract. Increasing numbers of tweets streaming data present both challenges and opportunities to improve event detection approach. So, it is important to propose a method that can solve some challenges. One such challenge is to automatically detect a set of events from large texts dynamically. The unique features of tweets, such as short and noisy content, diverse and fast changing topics, and large data volume, make event detection a challenge. Many previous works on event detection focused on supervised methods that did not take temporal information of the text and the position information of the words into account simultaneously. In this paper, we propose an unsupervised approach for event detection from tweets or texts that incorporates information from all positions of a word's occurrences into a biased PageRank and the temporal information into the tweets or texts. Our proposed model obtains remarkable improvements in performance over three event detection methods called Joint Model, Globe Vector- Latent Dirichlet Allocation, and Language Independent Neural Network that do not take into account word positions and temporal information for this task. Specifically, on three datasets of tweets and texts. Our method achieves higher precision and less time cost. Our experiments on three datasets of tweets and corpora show that our proposed model obtains better results than the latest three event detection methods Joint Model, GV-LDA, LINN Through quantitative analysis and qualitative analysis in our paper, we can have a better understanding of our proposed method.

Keywords: Event detection · Temporal information · Position information · Unsupervised model

1 Introduction

With the ever-increasing volume of data, it is increasingly challenging to stay up-to-date with trends in many fields. Automatically detecting events from large texts is an important but a hard assignment. The traditional algorithms for event detection can only reach an accuracy at a low level. That leads to event detection techniques desire much more room for improvement. Many approaches to event detection have been proposed in supervised method and unsupervised method.

All the mentioned traditional algorithms have demonstrated desirable accuracy for event detection field. However, the above event detection methods can only detect events

H. Qiu et al. (Eds.): KSEM 2021, LNAI 12816, pp. 218–227, 2021.
https://doi.org/10.1007/978-3-030-82147-0_18

in documents that do not vary from time. In the real world, the documents change dynamically that lead to the events in documents are evolving according to time. While detection for an evolving event focuses on paying more attention to new documents.

During our study, an enhanced event detection approach combining temporal dimension and word position dimension, the algorithm takes the temporal information of events into account and can capture new events among the texts. The algorithm also jointly uses words' position information and the words' frequency in texts. The approach we proposed are evaluated experimentally, our method is more effective than traditional methods.

Section 2 introduces the other works related to event detection in recent years. Section 3 introduces an event detection approach we proposed combining temporal dimension and position dimension. Section 4 show experimental results of event detection approach we proposed. In the last, Sect. 5 introduces the future work.

Our contributions are shown as below, we proposed a graph-based ranking method exploiting the information supplied by the positions of every word int the text and the information supplied by the temporal dimension that every text belongs to. Our method that incorporates information from all positions of a word's occurrences in the text and temporal information of the text into a biased PageRank to score topic words that are later used to score and rank the topic words in the texts.

2 Related Work

We introduce some event detection approaches in recent years. In the statement [1], events are detected by clustering a large volume of data. An improved event detection algorithm based on emotions and word co-occurrence detection was proposed in the statement [2]. HUPC was introduced in the statement [3] to detect coherent events and new emerging events simultaneously. The authors in the statement [4] proposed a three-layer hybrid event detection method. Authors in the statement [5] proposed a scalable and modular topic modeling method to detect subevents and labelled the events more accurately. The authors in the statement [6] proposed GV-LDA model which combines global vector model with LDA to tackle problem of sparseness of words in microblog event detection.

Feng et al. in the statement [7] combined CNN with other features. Chen and Xu in the statement [8] proposed an event detection method called DMCNN. Cao and Li in the statement [9] applied active learning in event detection, which achieved better results when compared to traditional systems. The authors in statement [10] proposed a special architecture in event detection, they introduced an incremental beam-search algorithm in conjunction with structured perceptron.

In the statement [11], the authors proposed a method that can detect events in real time, but the method needs predefined topic words for the event. The authors in the statement [12] and authors in the statement [13] proposed a method for detecting events in continuous-time event sequences. Chen et al. in the statement [14] proposed an event detection method called LIPED.

Qiu et al. [15] introduce a mobile-cloud framework to provide fine-grained permission authorization service for IoT devices. Tao and Qiu et al. [16] introduced contributions include combining syntax and semantic validations, designing and implementing a reusable software component to implement this integrated validation process, and supporting invoking this integrated validation through the more flexible observer pattern.

The authors in [17] use a Kullback-Leibler random sample partition data model to generate a set of disjoint data blocks, where each block is a good representation of the entire data set, it could reduce the model building time in parallel computation environment by using less than 15% of the entire data, the authors in [18] proposed F-RVFL algorithm that show better generalization performance on classification problems, the authors in [19] proposed IF-RVFL is a semi-supervised learning algorithm using the self-training strategy, which can make full use of a large number of unlabeled samples to improve the performance of the model. Qiu et al. [20] proposed a smart personal health advisor based on deep analytics of big data and an intelligent review spam detector [21] in cloud infrastructures for various big data applications [22, 23].

3 Proposed Methodology

We proposed our event detection approach combining temporal dimension and word position features. By using our methodology, we can detect events that containing topic words more accurately and dynamically than traditional methods. The framework of our methodology was shown in the Fig. 1.

The preprocessing step in Fig. 1 was shown in Fig. 2 in details. First, a tweet or a text is split into sentences, then sentences are tokenized, and conduct part of speech tagging by using the Stanford POS-tagger for English, after removing plurals for tagged nouns. Finally, only adjectives and nouns are considered as valid words for ranking as candidate topic words.

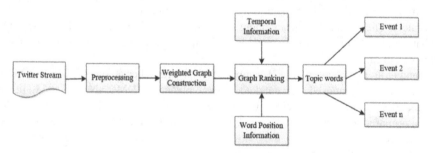

Fig. 1. The framework of our methodology

The creation of our methodology focuses on the ranking method in Fig. 1, we take the temporal dimension and word position information into account when calculating the ranking scores. The graph-based ranking method is fully unsupervised, the great advantage of this approach is that it can reduce the human labelling work. The original PageRank algorithm ranks vertices of a directed unweighted graph. In a directed graph

Fig. 2. The flowchart of preprocessing step

$G = (V, E)$, For a given vertex V_i, let $In(V_i)$ be the set of vertices that point to it, and let $Out(V_i)$ be the set of vertices that V_i points to. The score of V_i is defined as follows:

$$S(V_i) = (1 - d) + d * \sum_{j \in In(V_i)} \frac{1}{|Out(V_j)|} S(V_j) \tag{1}$$

where d is a damping factor, the value of d is between 0 and 1. We set $d = 0.85$.

In the paper, we adopt a formula for graph-based ranking that incorporates the edge weights when computing the value of a node in the graph. The formula is defined as follows in Eq. (2):

$$WS(V_i) = (1 - d) + d * \sum_{V_j \in In(V_i)} \frac{w_{ji}}{\sum_{V_k \in Out(V_j)} w_{jk}} WS(V_j) \tag{2}$$

In the formula (2), we also set the value of d to 0.85.

Word Position Information. The word position information aimed at extracting words of high frequency and their positions in a text or a tweet. The relative position of every word in a tweet or text is an important feature in our event detection method, many traditional methods have missed this important information when extracting events from tweet stream. In our method, we take into account all positions of a word's occurrences in the tweet or text when measuring the word position information.

Next, we will show how to measure the word position information. After preprocessing we extract nouns and adjectives as candidate words. We weigh each candidate word with its inverse position in the text or tweet before any preprocessing are applied. When the same word appears multiple times in the tweet or text, we will assign the sum of all its position weight to measure the candidate word position information in the Tweet. Let us take an example, if a word appears on the following positions: 2nd, 4th, 8th in tweet or text, its weight is calculated as follows: $1/2 + 1/4 + 1/8 = 0.875$. By using this method can we get all the weights of candidate words in the tweet or text. Then we normalize the weights for every candidate word in Eq. (3):

$$\tilde{p} = \left[\frac{p_1}{p_1 + p_2 + \ldots + p_{|V|}}, \frac{p_2}{p_1 + p_2 + \ldots + p_{|V|}}, \ldots \frac{p_{|V|}}{p_1 + p_2 + \ldots + p_{|V|}} \right] \tag{3}$$

Temporal Information. The temporal information is essential when detecting the latest events. we aim to take into account the temporal information of each text or tweet and put more focus on the events in new tweets or texts.

We call the value u_i, Since exponential average is extensively used in time-series prediction, its value reduces exponentially depending on time, so we choose to decay the weights exponentially depending on time, the Eq. (4) illustrates the process:

$$u_i = DecayRate^{(t_j - t_i)/30} \tag{4}$$

where t_j represents the current time of the candidate word in a tweet or text, t_i represents the first appearance in the first tweet or text, $(t_j - t_i)$ represents the time gap in days, in our paper we set the value of *DecayRate* to 0.5.

In our method, since we take both the candidate word's temporal information and word position in the tweet or text into account, we modify the Weighted graph-based Ranking in Eq. (2), the formula (5) shown below illustrates our modifications.

$$S(v_i) = (1 - d) * \tilde{p}_1 + d * \sum\nolimits_{v_j \in Adj(v_i)} \frac{u_i \cdot w_{ji}}{O(v_j)} S(v_j) \tag{5}$$

where $O(v_j) = \sum_{v_k \in Adj(v_j)} w_{jk}$, $\tilde{p}_i$ represents the weight for vertex v_i in the vector $\tilde{p}$ as shown in Eq. (3), we set the value of d to 0.85, u_i can be calculated by using Eq. (4), w_{ji} represents the number of the co-occurrence of the two candidate words v_i and v_j within a window of w in the tweet or text. In our paper we set the window size of w to 2.

In our paper, the candidate word' scores can be calculated by using Eq. (5) recursively, when the difference between two consecutive iterations is less than 0.0001 or a number of 100 iterations is reached the calculation can stop.

Forming Candidate Topic Words. After each candidate word in the graph is weighted a score by the Eq. (5), candidate words that have adjacent positions in a tweet or text are concatenated into phrases.

The candidate words ending with an adjective is not allowed, and only the candidate words ending with a noun are collected as candidate topic words for the text or tweet. The score of a candidate topic word p_i is computed by summing all the values of the candidate words contained in the candidate topic word.

$$\textit{Candidate topic word Score}(p_i) = \sum\nolimits_{v_j \in p_i} \textit{Word Score}(v_j) \tag{6}$$

All the candidate topic words in a tweet t_0 are ranked in decreasing order of the candidate topic word scores, then select the top n candidate topic words as the topic words of t_0. n ranges from 1 to 20 in our paper.

4   Experiments and Results

We evaluate the empirical performance of our event detection method combining with temporal information and word position information.

4.1   Experimental Settings

Datasets. In order to demonstrate the efficiency of our approach on tweets, the three datasets below will be used in the experiments.

Tweets2011 collection is a standard tweet stream published in TREC 2011 microblog track, each tweet contains a user id and a timestamp.

We also filter out duplicate tweets and tweets than only have one word, the tweet2011 dataset was reduced to the size of 4,230,578 tweets and 98,857 distinct words.

Wikipedia Data. The Wikipedia data are based on the Wikipedia dump released on 30 Jan, 2010, which contains 3,246,821 articles and 266,625,017 hyperlinks.

TDT1 Corpus. The TDT1 corpus contains a set of texts (15,863). A set of 25 target events were defined. All documents were tagged by the tagger, only nouns in the documents were used in the experiment.

Baseline Methods. In order to demonstrate the advantage of our approach, we compared our approach with other three event detection methods on the datasets described above:

Joint Model (Li and Ji, 2014), a joint structured perception approach.
GV-LDA (Li and Yu,2018), a method proposed in the statement [6] which combines global vector model and Latent Dirichlet Allocation (LDA), train global vector model over tagged corpus to get word vectors.
Language-Independent Neural Network (Feng and Huang, 2016), a method proposed in the statement [7].

4.2 Quantitative Analysis

In our experiment, we select top-10 topic words in each tweet or document. Then we compute the precision for our method and the three baseline methods on the three datasets. We call the three baseline methods in brief as Joint Model, GV-LDA, LINN. The results are shown in Table 1 and Fig. 3.

Table 1. Precision comparison of joint model, GV-LDA, LINN, and our method on three datasets

Model	Precision on Tweets2011	Precision on Wikipedia data	Precision on TDT1 corpus
Joint model	0.326	0.775	0.769
GV-LDA	0.168	0.636	0.625
LINN	0.407	0.823	0.801
Our method	0.469	0.851	0.826

We find that our method outperforms Joint Model, GV-LDA, and LINN on the three datasets. The improvements show the advantage of our method's consideration of temporal information and word position information when calculating scores of topic words. From Table 1 and Fig. 3, we can also draw conclusions below. The LINN method performs better Joint Model and GV-LDA lies in that LINN can take word semantic information into consideration and avoid the errors occurring from using NLP tools that may deteriorate the performance for event detection, GV-LDA makes the worst performance, which is just a variation of traditional LDA method, missing much semantic information, it also inherits the drawbacks from LDA. Joint Model perform better than GV-LDA lies in that it mines various entity mentions and relations share linguistic and logical constraints that cannot be found by GV-LDA, which leads to higher precision

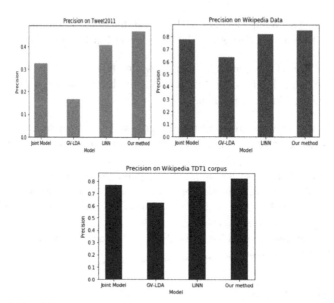

Fig. 3. Precision comparison of joint model, GV-LDA, LINN, and our method

than GV-LDA. Uniquely, our method works well because it does not only rely on the local semantic context of a unit (vertex), but rather taking into account the whole semantic information recursively drawn from the entire tweet or text (graph), which is very important to event detection. Tweets are dynamically when new tweets coming in, so the new events should be captured, only our method considers the temporal information and capture the latest events that match the ground truth. Word position information is also a crucial information should be taken into account in the field of event detection. By taking into account the word position information, we can assign higher score to the important words than can represent the topic, which leads to the topic words we select can convey the topic. The other three methods also do not take the word position information into account.

We can also find that all the methods performing on the Tweet2011 do not get high accuracy above 0.5, the best accuracy achieved by our method is 0.469 on Tweet2011, while on the other two datasets Wikipedia Data and TDT1 corpus all the methods get better performance than on Tweet2011, even the GV-LDA get accuracy above 0.6. The reason behind that lie in that in the Tweet2011 datasets, there is no category information for documents. The other two datasets have good ground truth, accurate category information.

For efficiency comparison, we list the average running time (per iteration) of Joint Model, LINN, GV-LDA, and our method in our experiments on the dataset Tweets2011 in Table 2 and Fig. 4. We can see that the running time of our method is always less than the other three methods over different topic numbers.

The LINN has the highest time cost in the methods, because neural network needs much time for training, and the Bi-LSTM also occupies much time for computation. GV-LDA is a variation of LDA, it costs less time than Joint Model and LINN. LINN costs the time is almost two times of GV-LDA. The running time of LINN is always four times of our method on different topic numbers (K).

As can be seen from Table 2 and Fig. 4, our approach has great time saving advantage over other three methods on different topic numbers in Tweet2011. Because Join Model, GV-LDA, and LINN are all supervised methods, which need much time for processing training sets. Our method is an unsupervised method based on variation of graph-based ranking algorithm, which do not need much time for training and can reach fast convergence when computing.

Table 2. Time cost (seconds) per iteration of joint model, GV-LDA, LINN, and our method on Tweets2011 collection

Topic number K	50	100	150	200	250
Joint model	50.16	82.56	130.77	158.54	203.62
GV-LDA	40.07	76.45	115.16	149.68	186.77
LINN	80.45	150.56	233.6	298.67	385.68
Our method	20.46	38.56	57.37	75.66	95.88

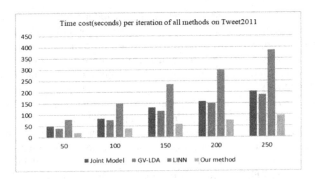

Fig. 4. Time cost (seconds) per iteration comparisons

5 Conclusion

We proposed a novel unsupervised graph-based algorithm when detecting events in tweets or texts, which incorporates both the position of words, word frequency and temporal information in a tweet or text into a biased PageRank. To our knowledge, we are the first to integrate the position information and temporal information in event detection field. Specifically, unlike supervised approaches that cost much time and achieve relatively low precision, we showed that our method achieves better performance on event detection precision and time costs.

Our experiments on three datasets of tweets and corpora show that our proposed model obtains better results than the latest three event detection methods Joint Model,

GV-LDA, LINN. In our future work, we will explore the effectiveness of using more features from tweets (e.g., retweet rate and hashtags) in our method, in addition in order to better reflect real events, topics can be linked with named entities such that each topic is forced to contain a certain number of entities. We extend event detection by allowing each text or tweet to have local events and shared events.

References

1. Sankaranarayanan, J., Samet, H., Teitler, B.E., Lieberman, M.D., Sperling, J.: TwitterStand: news in Tweets. In: Proceedings of the ACM SIGSPATIAL (2009)
2. Tian, L., Gong-De, G.: Bursty topic detection based on word co-occurrence and emotions. Computer Systems & Applications (2016)
3. Huang, J., Peng, M., Wang, H.: Topic detection from large scale of microblog stream with high utility pattern clustering. In: 8th ACM Workshop on Ph. D. Workshop in Information and Knowledge Management (2015)
4. Geng, X., Zhang, Y., Jiao, Y., et al.: A novel hybrid clustering algorithm for topic detection on Chinese microblogging. IEEE Trans. Comput. Soc. Syst. **6**(2), 289–300 (2019)
5. Nolasco, D., Oliveira, J.: Subevents detection through topic modeling in social media posts. Future Gener. Comput. Syst. **93**(APR), 290–303 (2019)
6. Li, S., Li, W., Yu, Z.: Research on microblog topic detection based on GV-LDA. Software Guide (2018)
7. Feng, X., Qin, B., Liu, T.: A language-independent neural network for event detection. Sci. China (Inf. Sci.) **61**(9), 1–12 (2018). https://doi.org/10.1007/s11432-017-9359-x
8. Chen, Y., Xu, L., Liu, K., Zeng, D., Zhao, J.: Event extraction via dynamic multi-pooling convolutional neural networks. In: 53rd Annual Meeting of the Association for Computational Linguistics and the 7th International Joint Conference on Natural Language Processing, vol. 1, pp. 167–176 (2015)
9. Cao, K., Li, X., Fan, M., Grishman, R.: Improving event detection with active learning. In: Recent Advances in Natural Language Processing, pp. 72–77, Hissar, Bulgaria (2015)
10. Li, Q., Ji, H.: Incremental joint extraction of entity mentions and relations. In: 52nd Annual Meeting of the Association for Compu. Linguistics (Volume 1: Long Papers) (2014)
11. Sakaki, T., Okazaki, M., Matsuo, Y.: Earthquake shakes Twitter users: real time event detection by social sensors. In: 19th International Conference on World Wide Web, pp. 851–860 (2010)
12. Li, C., Sun, A., Datta, A.: Twevent: segment-based event detection from Tweets. In: CIKM, pp. 155–164 (2012)
13. Liu, S., Hauskrecht, M.: Detection of Outlier Events in Continuous-Time Event Sequences (2019)
14. Chen, C., Chen, M.C., Chen, M.S.: An adaptive threshold framework for event detection using HMM-based life profiles. ACM Trans. Inf. Syst. **27**(2), 63–97 (2009)
15. Dai, W., Qiu, M., Qiu, L., Chen, L., Wu, A.: Who moved my data? privacy protection in smartphones. IEEE Commun. Mag. **55**(1), 20–25 (2017)
16. Tao, L., Golikov, S., Gai, K., Qiu, M.: A reusable software component for integrated syntax and semantic validation for services computing. In: IEEE Symposium on Service-Oriented System Engineering, pp. 127–132 (2015)
17. Wei, C., Zhang, J., Valiullin, T., et al.: Distributed and parallel ensemble classification for big data based on Kullback-Leibler random sample partition. In: ICA3PP 2020, pp. 448–464
18. Cao, W., Gao, J., Ming, Z., et al.: Fuzziness based random vector functional-link network for semi-supervised learning. In: IEEE International Conference on Computational Science and Computational Intelligence (CSCI) (2018)

19. Cao, W., Yang, P., Ming, Z., et al.: An improved fuzziness based random vector functional link network for liver disease detection. In: IEEE 6th International Conference on Big Data Security on Cloud (BigDataSecurity/HPSC/IDS) (2020)
20. Chen, M., Zhang, Y., Qiu, M., Guizani, N., Hao, Y.: SPHA: smart personal health advisor based on deep analytics. IEEE Commun. Mag. **56**(3), 164–169 (2018)
21. You, L., Peng, Q., Xiong, Z., He, D., Qiu, M., Zhang, X.: Integrating aspect analysis and local outlier factor for intelligent review spam detection. Future Gener. Comput. Syst. **102**, 163–172 (2020)
22. Dai, W., Qiu, L., Wu, A., Qiu, M.: Cloud infrastructure resource allocation for big data applications. IEEE Trans. Big Data **4**(3), 313–324 (2016)
23. Qiu, M., Ming, Z., Wang, J., Yang, L.T., Xiang, Y.: Enabling cloud computing in emergency management systems. IEEE Cloud Comput. **1**(4), 60–67 (2014)

Local Feature Normalization

Ning Jiang[1]([✉]) [iD], Jialiang Tang[1] [iD], Wenxin Yu[1] [iD], and Jinjia Zhou[2] [iD]

[1] School of Computer Science and Technology,
Southwest University of Science and Technology, Mianyang, China
`jiangning@swust.edu.cn`
[2] Graduate School of Science and Engineering, Hosei University, Tokyo, Japan

Abstract. In deep learning, Batch Normalization (BN) is a widely used fundamental technique in Convolutional Neural Networks (CNNs) to improve the training speed and generalization capability of CNNs due to its effectiveness and simplicity. However, BN only focuses on global features and normalizes the whole feature map while ignoring the importance of the local feature. In this paper, we proposed the local feature normalization layer (LFN) to solve this problem by enhancing the features' local area competition. These CNNs with LFN can leverage local regions with rich feature information. After normalized by LFN, if a feature of the local region is more expressive, its value will be bigger, and conversely, the value will be smaller. We also discussed how to use LFN better in CNNs in detail and solve some algorithm conflict problems. The LFN layer should be used after the ReLU in the first few layers. And LFN should not be used in front of the Max-pooling layer. Experimental results show that various CNN+LFN achieved better accuracy on the image classification tasks CIFAR dataset and ImageNet dataset than the same neural network with other popular normalization methods.

Keywords: Convolutional neural networks · Local feature normalization · Model optimization · Batch normalization · Image classification

1 Introduction

Batch normalization (BN) [8] is a fundamental component of existing advanced deep neural networks, which has promoted the recent success of deep learning and had broad application to computer vision fields such as image classification [7,17], object detection [4,14], and image segmentation [12,20]. BN improves the neural network's performance by first calculating the means and deviations of the features in mini-batch input features and then utilizing the calculated means and deviations to normalize the features. Despite the success of BN, there is also some inadequacy of BN. The first is BN only focuses on the normalization of the whole features alone the mini-batch. When the batch data distribution is not consistent with the overall training data, it will lose efficacy. It leads the neural network with BN to often need a big batchsize to get high performance, which

H. Qiu et al. (Eds.): KSEM 2021, LNAI 12816, pp. 228–239, 2021.
https://doi.org/10.1007/978-3-030-82147-0_19

increases the memory consumption of the neural network. And the second is BN ignores the local information of the features. For the features, each local region may have a different value. The difference between these local regions means the difference in the contribution to the network's final performance.

There are some methods to solve the first problem of BN, Layer Normalization (LN) [1] and Instance Normalization (IN) [18] solve the problem by avoiding normalizing along the batch dimension. Group normalization (GN) [19] divides the channels of features into groups and normalizes the features within each group. However, these methods also ignore the importance of local features. This paper proposes the local feature normalization layer (LFN) to solve the second problem existing in BN, which carries out normalization operations at local regions of the features. Different from local response normalization (LRN) [10], which uses only a few pixels around a pixel to implement normalization, we normalize all pixels at the same location of each channel. Figure 1 shows the way to normalize the features of existing normalization methods and our proposed LFN. The main idea of our proposed LFN is to augment the competitiveness of the local features by highlight these more expressive local regions between features. Different from BN implement normalize on a whole feature, we normalize the local features repeatedly. More specifically, we first extract the local features at the same position between features as a set of vectors, and then we normalize the vector. After normalized by LFN, local regions with large values will be more expressive, and the local regions with small values will be inefficient. In most cases, we will also add a BN and Rectified Linear Unit (ReLU) [5] at the front of LFN. The BN can speed up the convergence. The ReLU can remove negative incentives of the local feature by removing the negative local feature to zero. By adding a local feature normalization layer to a neural network, the neural network can better use the local region information and achieve better performance. The contributions of our proposed method are summarized as follows:

1. We analyzed the problems of the BN neglect local feature and proposed a local feature normalization (LFN) layer to solve this problem. The LFN layer can be widely used to improve the accuracy of existing neural network models(prove in Sect. 4.3).
2. Through a large number of experimental verification and analysis, we propose how to use the LFN layer to neural networks (see Sect. 4.2 for details).
3. Through extensive experiments, the LFN proved its effectiveness on different classification tasks (CIFAR10 [9], CIFAR100, and ImageNet [3]).

The rest of the paper is summarized as follows. The Sect. 2 introduces the related work of this paper. Section 3 describes in detail how to implement LFN. Section 4 verifies the effectiveness of LFN through a large number of experiments. Section 5 concludes the paper.

2 Related Work

The related work of this paper mainly includes convolutional neural networks, neural network normalization methods.

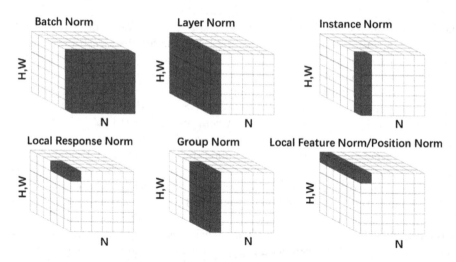

Fig. 1. A series of normalization methods. Each subplot represents a feature map tensor, N is the batch axis, C is the channel axis, and (H, W) is the spatial axes. The pixels in blue are these features that are normalized together. (Color figure online)

Convolutional Neural Networks. In recent years, convolutional neural networks have demonstrated their outstanding capabilities. In 2012, AlexNet [10] first apply these components such as Rectified Linear Unit (ReLU) [5] and local response normalization (LRN) to the neural network. In 2014, Simonyan et al. [15] proposed the deeper convolutional neural network named VGGNet and prove that the depth of the network has a significant impact on the performance of the network. Then GoogleNet [17] proposed to increase the width of the network to design a sparse network structure that only contains 1/12 parameters of AlexNet and achieves state-of-art performance. ResNet [6] solves the problem of gradient disappearance through deep residual learning, which increases the depth of the network to thousands of layers and further improves the performance.

Normalization. Many normalization methods have been proposed to optimize the training of neural networks. Local response normalization (LRN) is first introduced in AlexNet [10] to prevent the problem of overfitting. But LRN is rarely be used and is largely replaced by some algorithms like dropout [16] and data augmentation. Compared with LRN, a series of global normalization methods achieve better results. By calculating the means and variances alone the mini-batch features, Ioffe et al. [8] proposed the batch normalization (BN). BN normalize the neurons in the features to achieve global normalization and successful in speeding up the training of neural network and effective to prevent the overfitting. Instance Normalization (IN) [18] implements normalization to a single image in a batch, instead of normalization of all images in the batch like BN. Wu et al. [19] proposed the Group Normalization (GN) to divide the features into multiple groups according to the channel and normalize them on each group, and successfully getting rid of the limitation of batchsize in BN. Switchable Nor-

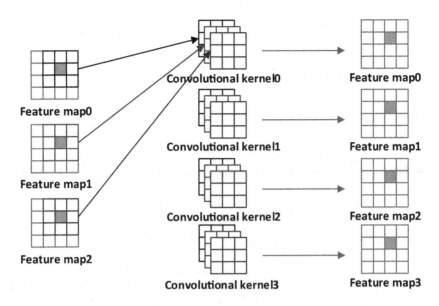

Fig. 2. The calculation process of the pixel at the same position between features in the convolution layer. The pixels at the same position on each feature map will be input into the convolution kernel to get a group of new pixels. (Color figure online)

malization (SN) [13] incorporated some normalization algorithms and proposed a normalization method that could learn adaptively and overcame the shortcomings of these algorithms to a certain extend. Positional Normalization (PN) [11] is similar to our, which regularizes the entire feature map along the channel. Still, they neglect the local competition of the feature. And PN only applies to generative adversarial networks to achieve satisfactory performance and unable to improve other tasks' ability.

3 Approach

In this section, we will first elaborate on how to process local features and how to implementation LFN. Then we derive the gradient of LFN step by step. In the end, we describe how to use the LFN layer in CNNs.

3.1 Local Cross Kernel Features

In the CNNs, each convolution layer is a feature extractor for multiple patterns. As shown in Fig. 2, for a fixed pixel in three input features (green pixel in the left of Fig. 2), four different convolution kernels (middle of Fig. 2) are used to calculate with multiple pixel points around this green pixel, then four result values (green pixel in right of Fig. 2) are obtained. These four result values are the likelihood values of the four patterns corresponding to this fixed pixel.

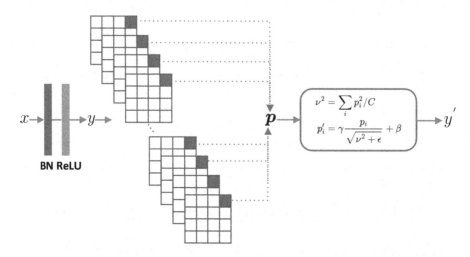

Fig. 3. The process of the LFN to normalize the feature. The input x first through the BN, ReLU in turn to obtain y, y contains $H \times W$ number of local feature vector p, the LFN is normalizing p along the channel dimension to get the normalized feature y'.

The higher the likelihood value of a pattern, the higher the matching value between the pixel and the pattern. The feature vector composed of these four likelihood values is the Local Cross Kernel Feature of this fixed pixel. Simultaneously, 16 pixels of the whole feature are convoluted one by one, and 16 likelihood values of the same model are connected, respectively. Four by four feature matrices corresponding to 4 patterns (right of Fig. 2) can be obtained.

3.2 Local Features Normalization

To better explain our method, we set the feature map processed by the convolutional layer as a 4D tensor $x \in R^{B \times C \times H \times W}$, B is the batchsize, C is the channel number of x, and H, W are the width and height of x respectively. LFN aims to enhance the competition between the local positions of the features, which means it is necessary to highlight the local areas with large feature values while lowering the local areas with small feature values. Different from the Position Normalization (PN) [11], which implements normalization to the whole feature map along the channel through the same way of BN [8]. We carry out normalization in a different way from BN alone the channel, which is more beneficial to highlight the local features and achieves the better performance (see in Sect. 4.4). Specifically, as shown in Fig. 3, the input $x \in R^{B \times C \times H \times W}$ passes through the BN layer and Relu in turn to get the output $y \in R^{B \times C \times H \times W}$. We set the local feature value vector as $p = \{p_1, p_2, \cdots, p_C\}$, p represents a vector composed of pixels at the same position in each channel of the feature y. y contains $H \times W$ number of such local feature value vector. In the first, we calculate the mean square of p as follows:

$$\nu^2 = \sum_{i=1}^{C} p_i^2/C \tag{1}$$

The mean square is more efficient to highlight the competition of local features and the p is normalized through:

$$p_i' = f(p_i) = \frac{p_i}{\sqrt{\nu^2 + \epsilon}} \tag{2}$$

the ϵ is a small positive constant to prevent the error of division by zero. We also add two learnable parameters to ensure the non-linear of the Eq. 2 to improved the Eq. 2:

$$p_i' = f(p) = \gamma \frac{p_i}{\sqrt{\nu^2 + \epsilon}} + \beta \tag{3}$$

By repeating the Eq. 3 $H \times W$ times alone the features y, LFN can be applied to normalize the entire features y.

3.3   Gradients of LFN Layer

In this section, we will derive the expression of the gradient of the neural network using the LFN layer. A set of features $y = \{y_1, y_2, \cdots, y_c\}$ passes through the LFN layer (Eq. 3) to get the output $y' = \{y_1', y_2', \cdots, y_c'\}$. For ease of explanation, we set the Eq. 3 as $y' = f(y)$, and the gradients is $\frac{\partial f}{\partial y'}$. The γ and β in Eq. 3 are vectors of size C, the C is the number of channels, and y_i' is the vector of per-channel activations of the ith local point. So, the gradients of γ and β are described as:

$$\left(\frac{\partial f}{\partial \gamma}, \frac{\partial f}{\partial \beta}\right) = \left(\sum_{i=1}^{C} \frac{\partial f^T}{\partial y_i'} y_i, \sum_{i=1}^{C} \frac{\partial f}{\partial y_i'}\right) \tag{4}$$

Through the Eq. 3, can get the gradients of y: $\frac{\partial f}{\partial y} = \gamma \frac{\partial f}{\partial y'}$. In the end, the gradients that back-propagation of the LFN layer can be formalized as:

$$\frac{\partial f}{\partial y} = \frac{1}{\sqrt{\nu^2 + \epsilon}} \left(I - \hat{y}\hat{y}^T\right) \frac{\partial f}{\partial y} \tag{5}$$

3.4   How to Use LFN

In this section, we will show how to use the LFN layer in the convolutional blocks. Take the VGGNet as an example, the VGGNet is composed of more stacked convolutional blocks, each block contains two convolutional layers (CONV), batch normalization layers (BN), and Rectified Linear Unit (ReLU). The data input into the block is through CONV→BN→ReLU→CONV→BN→ReLU sequentially. As shown in Fig. 4, we insert LFN at different positions of the convolution block.

LFN[1]: The LFN layer is inserted behind the two BN layers.

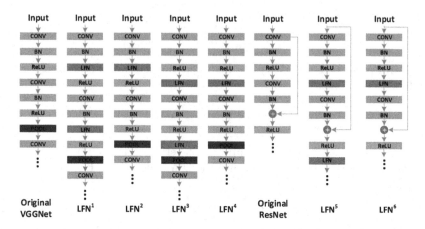

Fig. 4. The diagram of how to use the LFN layer in the convolutional block.

LFN^2: The LFN layer is only inserted behind the first BN layer.
LFN^3: The LFN layer is used behind the two ReLU layers.
LFN^4: The LFN layer is used behind the first ReLU layers.

For the LFN layer to use in ResNet, the ResNet block contains the same kind and number of layers of VGGNet block, but there is a residual connection in the residual block. There are two ways to use the LFN in the residual block.

LFN^5: The LFN layer is inserted behind the two ReLU layers.
LFN^6: The LFN layer is only inserted behind the first ReLU layer.

In Sect. 4.2, we have proved that LFN4 and LFN6 achieve the best results in VGGNet and ResNet through a large number of experiments. Its shows that the LFN is better to use at the behind of the ReLU, because the ReLU can remove negative incentives of the input features by removing the negative values in the features. And LFN is not suitable to use at the front of the max-pooling due to it would greatly change the value in the feature and harm the normalization of LFN. In the end, LFN is not used behind the residual connection, because the identity mapping of the residual connection is conflicts with the normalization of LFN.

4   Experiments

In this section, we will perform a series of experiments on the CIFAR [9] and ImageNet [3] datasets to demonstrate the effectiveness of our proposed method local feature normalization (LFN) layer.

Datasets. The CIFAR dataset is composed of 32×32 pixel RGB images, including 50,000 training samples and 10,000 test samples. The CIFAR-10 dataset contains 10 categories of images and the CIFAR-100 dataset contains 100 categories of images. The ImageNet dataset is a large-scale image recognition dataset, which consists of 256×256 pixel RGB images of 1,000 categories. There are about 1.28

Table 1. Classification result of VGGNet on the CIFAR dataset. Accuracy† means the accuracy improved of experimental VGGNet.

LFN Type	CIFAR-10		CIFAR-100	
	Accuracy	Accuracy†	Accuracy	Accuracy†
Original	93.31%	\	73.26%	\
1LFN	93.46%	0.15%	73.99%	0.73%
2LFN	**93.68%**	**0.37%**	**74.43%**	**1.17%**
3LFN	93.65%	0.35%	73.54%	0.28%
4LFN	93.47%	0.16%	73.62%	0.36%
5LFN	93.33%	0.02%	73.52%	0.26%

million images in the training dataset, 50,000 images in the validation dataset, and 50,000 images in the testset.

Training Setups. For the training on the CIFAR dataset, experimental CNNs are optimized using stochastic gradient descent (SGD) [2] and the learning rate, weight decay, and the momentum are set as 0.1, 1×10^{-4} and 0.9, respectively. The batchsize is fixed as 128 and each CNN training 150 epoch on the CIFAR dataset. When training on the ImageNet dataset, we set the learning rate as 0.01 and batchsize is 32, each CNN training 100 epoch. Other setups are the same as that of CIFAR datasets.

4.1 Different Settings of LFN

In this part, we chose the 16-layer VGGNet16 [15] as the model to implement experiments on CIFAR datasets. VGGNet16 includes five VGG blocks, one of the blocks is composed of a different number of 3×3 convolutional kernel layers and a Max-pooling layer, the batch normalization layer (BN) and Rectified Linear Unit (ReLU) are used after each convolutional layer of VGGNet16 in turn. We added LFN to the first one, two, three, four, and five VGG blocks.

Table 1 shows the results of VGGNet16 with the LFN layer, the nLFN (n = 1, 2, 3, 4, 5) means uses the LFN at the first n blocks of VGGNet. VGGNet16 achieves better results with LFN in all positions than without LFN. When experimenting on the CIFAR-10 dataset, the VGGNet16 uses LFN in the first two layers made the highest accuracy of 93.68%, which is 0.37% higher than the accuracy of VGGNet16 without LFN (93.31%). And the VGGNet16 with LFN in the first two blocks gets a significant accuracy of 74.43% on the CIFAR-100 dataset, which is 1.17% higher than the VGGNet16 without LFN. The experimental results show that the improvement of the VGGNet16 with LFN is more evident on the CIFAR-100 dataset. The CIFAR-100 dataset contains more categories and has fewer images in each category, and it leads to the overfitting of neural network train on CIFAR-100 is worse than that of the CIFAR-10 dataset. So, the experimental results show that LFN is beneficial for solving the overfitting.

Table 2. Classification result of various positions to apply LFN in CNNs.

LFN Type	CIFAR-10		CIFAR-100	
	Accuracy	Accuracy$^\uparrow$	Accuracy	Accuracy$^\uparrow$
VGGNet16	93.31%	\	73.26%	\
VGGNet16+LFN[1]	93.35%	+0.04%	73.31%	+0.50%
VGGNet16+LFN[2]	93.54%	+0.23%	74.19%	+0.93%
VGGNet16+LFN[3]	93.39%	+0.08%	73.32%	+0.06%
VGGNet16+LFN[4]	**93.68%**	**+0.37%**	**74.43%**	**+1.17%**
ResNet18	93.92%	\	76.53%	\
ResNet18+LFN[5]	93.72%	−0.20%	76.42%	−0.11%
ResNet18+LFN[6]	**94.96%**	**+1.04%**	**77.33%**	**+0.91%**

4.2 How to Use LFN Layer

In this section, we will explain how to use the LFN. We select the VGGNet16 and ResNet18 to train on the CIFAR datasets. The LFN will apply in the first two blocks of the VGGNet16 and ResNet18. As described in Sect. 3.4, VGGNet16 uses four ways to use the LFN layer as LFN[1−4], and ResNet18 uses two ways to use the LFN layer as LFN[5] and LFN[6]. Table 2 exhibition the classification results of the different positions to use the LFN layer. For the experiment of VGGNet, We can find that all the neural networks with LFN layers perform better than the neural network without LFN layers. In detail, placing the LFN layer after ReLU performs better than putting it between BN and ReLU, and not use the LFN layer in the front of the Max-pooling layer performs better than that used. When the LFN layer is placed after ReLU and the LFN layer is not used before the Max-pooling layer, the VGGNet16 has achieved the highest accuracy, 93.68% on the CIFAR-10 dataset, and 74.43% on the CIFAR-100 dataset. For the experiment of ResNet18, the ResNet18 with the LFN after each ReLU layer drop slightly, its because used the LFN after the residual connection damage the identity mapping of the residual block. But the ResNet18 with the LFN[6] achieves an obviously improvement, obtains 94.96% and 77.33% accuracy on the CIFAR-10 and CIFAR-100 datasets. Compare to the original ResNet18, the accuracy of ResNet18 improved 1.04% and 0.91% on the CIFAR-10 and CIFAR-100 datasets.

4.3 Experiments on Different Models

To verify the effectiveness of LFN more broadly, we use various neural network models to implement extensive experiments on CIFAR datasets. We choose AlexNet, VGGNet11, VGGNet13, VGGNet16, and ResNet18, ResNet34 as our experimental models. AlexNet (without the maxpooling layer) uses LFN at each convolution layer, LFN located after BN and ReLU. The VGGNet uses LFN the same as LFN[4] and the ResNet uses LFN the same as LFN[6]. The experimental

Table 3. Results of various neural networks on CIFAR dataset.

Algorithm	CIFAR-10			CIFAR-100		
	No LFN	LFN	Accuracy†	No LFN	LFN	Accuracy†
AlexNet	84.65%	86.72%	2.07%	56.42%	61.84%	5.42%
VGGNet11	91.17%	91.86%	0.69%	70.19%	71.91%	1.72%
VGGNet13	93.12%	93.85%	0.73%	73.16%	75.21%	2.05%
VGGNet16	93.31%	93.63%	0.32%	73.26%	74.43%	1.17%
ResNet18	93.92%	94.96%	1.04%	76.53%	77.33%	0.80%
ResNet34	94.85%	95.58%	0.73%	77.34%	78.47%	1.13%

Table 4. Results of ResNet with various normalization on the CIFAR dataset.

Dataset	Model	BN [8]	IN [18]	GN [19]	PN [11]	SN [13]	LFN
CIFAR-10	ResNet18	93.92%	92.94%	92.76%	94.02%	94.73%	**94.96%**
	ResNet34	94.85%	93.27%	93.46%	94.27%	95.01%	**95.58%**
CIFAR-100	ResNet18	75.63%	72.27%	73.40%	75.74%	76.64%	**77.33%**
	ResNet34	77.34%	73.82%	73.57%	76.26%	77.05%	**78.47%**

results are shown in Table 3. In the experiments, all neural networks using LFN achieved better performance than without LFN, which demonstrates that our LFN can be widely applied to the existing neural network model to promote the ability of models. And similar to the experiment of Sect. 4.1, in all neural networks, LFN performs better on CIFAR-100 than that on CIFAR-10. It is worth noting that the LFN has a more considerable effect on improving the performance of smaller neural network models. For example, when training VGGNet on the CIFAR-100 dataset, the VGGNet13 achieved an accuracy improvement of 2.05%, which is significantly higher than the accuracy improvements obtained by VGGNet16 (1.17%). And the accuracy of the VGGNet13 with LFN (75.21%) exceeded the accuracy of the VGGNet16 with LFN(74.43%). It is very encouraging that when applying the LFN to AlexNet, a very significant improvement of accuracy has been achieved, a 2.07% accuracy improvement on the CIFAR-10 dataset, and a 5.42% accuracy improvement on the CIFAR-100 dataset.

4.4   Comparison with Other Normalization Layers

In this part, we will compare our proposed Local Feature Normalization (LFN) layer with other normalization algorithms. We select ResNet34 and ResNet18 as our neural network to train on the CIFAR dataset. ResNet18 and ResNet34 use the batch normalization (BN) [8], group normalization (GN) [19], instance normalization (IN) [18], switchable normalization (SN) [13], position normalization (PN) [11] and our LFN to training on the CIFAR dataset. Table 4 displays the classification result of ResNet18 and ResNet34 which use the different normalization algorithms. We can see that ResNet18 and ResNet34 with our proposed

Table 5. Classification result of CNNs on the ImageNet dataset.

Model	Top1 Accuracy			Top5 Accuracy		
	None	BN	LFN	None	BN	LFN
VGGNet16	71.59%	73.36%	**73.97%**	90.38%	91.51%	**91.85%**
ResNet18	\	69.71%	**70.13%**	\	89.07%	**89.33%**
ResNet34	\	73.31%	**73.67%**	\	91.42%	**91.67%**

LFN all achieved the highest performance on the CIFAR dataset, ResNet18 gets a 94.96% accuracy on the CIFAR-10 dataset and gets a 77.33% accuracy on the CIFAR-100 dataset. The ResNet34 gets 95.58% and 78.47% accuracy on the CIFAR-10 and CIFAR-100 datasets respectively.

4.5 Experiments on ImageNet

In this section, we will experiment on the ImageNet to future demonstrate the capability of LFN. The VGGNet16, ResNet18 and ResNet34 are used as networks, the VGGNet16 uses the LFN[4], the ResNet18 and ResNet34 use the LFN[6].

Table 5 shows the classification results of the experiment on ImageNet dataset. All the neural networks with LFN get a salient improvement. The VGGNet16 with LFN achieves the top-1 accuracy of 73.97% and top-5 accuracy of 91.90%, which 2.38% and 1.47% higher than that of VGGNet16 without BN, 0.61% and 0.34% higher than that of the VGGNet16 with BN. The BN is a fundamental element of the ResNet, so BN is used by default in ResNet. ResNet18 achieves 70.13%(improved 0.42%) top-1 accuracy and 89.33%(0.26%) top-5 accuracy, ResNet34 gets the top-1 accuracy of 73.67%(0.36%) and the top-5 accuracy of 91.67%(0.25). Experimental results show that LFN is more effective to improve the performance of CNNS on a large datasets.

5   Conclusion

In this work, we propose the local feature normalization layer (LFN) to promote the competitiveness between local features of the neural network. And we proposed how to use LFN in the neural networks by extensive experimental analysis. The experimental results show that our LFN can improve the performance of experimental neural networks (AlexNet, VGGNet, ResNet, etc.) on the benchmark image classification tasks. And these CNNs with LFN achieve better accuracy than that of these CNNs with other exiting normalization algorithms. We believe that through further theoretical analysis of LFN, there will be more improvements and applications of LFN.

Acknowledgement. This research is supported by Sichuan Science and Technology Program (No. 2020YFS0307, 2020YFG0430), SWUST Doctoral Foundation under Grant 19zx7102.

References

1. Ba, J.L., Kiros, J.R., Hinton, G.E.: Layer normalization. arXiv preprint arXiv:1607.06450 (2016)
2. Bottou, L.: Stochastic gradient descent tricks (2012)
3. Deng, J., et al.: Imagenet: A large-scale hierarchical image database. In: 2009 IEEE Conference on Computer Vision and Pattern Recognition, pp. 248–255. IEEE (2009)
4. Girshick, R., Donahue, J., Darrell, T., Malik, J.: Rich feature hierarchies for accurate object detection and semantic segmentation. In: Proceedings of the IEEE Conference on Computer Vision and Pattern Recognition, pp. 580–587 (2014)
5. Glorot, X., Bordes, A., Bengio, Y.: Deep sparse rectifier neural networks. In: Proceedings of the Fourteenth International Conference on Artificial Intelligence and Statistics, pp. 315–323 (2011)
6. He, K., Zhang, X., Ren, S., Jian, S.: Deep residual learning for image recognition. In: 2016 IEEE Conference on Computer Vision and Pattern Recognition (CVPR) (2016)
7. Huang, G., Liu, Z., Van Der Maaten, L., Weinberger, K.Q.: Densely connected convolutional networks. In: Proceedings of the IEEE Conference on Computer Vision and Pattern Recognition, pp. 4700–4708 (2017)
8. Ioffe, S., Szegedy, C.: Batch normalization: accelerating deep network training by reducing internal covariate shift (2015)
9. Krizhevsky, A., Hinton, G., et al.: Learning multiple layers of features from tiny images (2009)
10. Krizhevsky, A., Sutskever, I., Hinton, G.E.: Imagenet classification with deep convolutional neural networks. In: Advances in Neural Information Processing Systems, pp. 1097–1105 (2012)
11. Li, B., Wu, F., Weinberger, K.Q., Belongie, S.: Positional normalization (2019)
12. Long, J., Shelhamer, E., Darrell, T.: Fully convolutional networks for semantic segmentation. In: Proceedings of the IEEE Conference on Computer Vision and Pattern Recognition, pp. 3431–3440 (2015)
13. Luo, P., Ren, J., Peng, Z., Zhang, R., Li, J.: Differentiable learning-to-normalize via switchable normalization. arXiv preprint arXiv:1806.10779 (2018)
14. Ren, S., He, K., Girshick, R., Sun, J.: Faster R-CNN: Towards real-time object detection with region proposal networks. In: Advances in Neural Information Processing Systems, pp. 91–99 (2015)
15. Simonyan, K., Zisserman, A.: Very deep convolutional networks for large-scale image recognition. arXiv preprint arXiv:1409.1556 (2014)
16. Srivastava, N., Hinton, G., Krizhevsky, A., Sutskever, I., Salakhutdinov, R.: Dropout: a simple way to prevent neural networks from overfitting. J. Mach. Learn. Res. **15**(1), 1929–1958 (2014)
17. Szegedy, C., et al.: Going deeper with convolutions. In: Proceedings of the IEEE Conference on Computer Vision and Pattern Recognition, pp. 1–9 (2015)
18. Ulyanov, D., Vedaldi, A., Lempitsky, V.: Instance normalization: The missing ingredient for fast stylization. arXiv preprint arXiv:1607.08022 (2016)
19. Wu, Y., He, K.: Group normalization. In: Proceedings of the European Conference on Computer Vision (ECCV), pp. 3–19 (2018)
20. Yu, F., Koltun, V.: Multi-scale context aggregation by dilated convolutions. arXiv preprint arXiv:1511.07122 (2015)

Combining Knowledge with Attention Neural Networks for Short Text Classification

Wei Li and Li Li[✉]

School of Computer and Information Science,
Southwest University, Chongqing, China
liwei666@email.swu.edu.cn, lily@swu.edu.cn

Abstract. Text classification has emerged as an important research area over the last few years in natural language processing (NLP). Different from formal documents and paragraphs, short texts are more ambiguous, due to the lack of contextual information and the data sparsity problem, which poses a great challenge to traditional classification methods. In order to solve this problem, conceptual knowledge is introduced to enrich the information of short texts. However, this method assumes that all knowledge is equally important which is not conducive to distinguishing short texts classification. In addition, it also brings knowledge noise to the text, and causes the degradation of classification performance. To measure the importance of concepts to short texts, the paper introduces the attention mechanism. Text-Relevant-Concept (T-RC) is utilized to resolve the ambiguity of concepts and choose the most appropriate meaning to align short text. We employ Concept-Relevant-Concept (C-RC) to handle conceptual hierarchy and the relative importance of the concept. We investigate a model combining Knowledge with Attention Neural Networks (CK-ANN). Experiments show that CK-ANN outperforms state-of-the-art methods on text classification benchmarks, which proves the effectiveness of our method.

Keywords: Text classification · Knowledge · Attention mechanism · Natural language processing · Neural networks

1 Introduction

Text classification is a fundamental task in Natural Language Processing (NLP), and it is classified into categories based on certain characteristics of the sentence. It work extensively in multiple fields such as sentiment analysis [1], web search [2], and language inference [3]. Currently, existing text classification algorithms are divided into traditional machine learning and deep learning. Traditional machine learning such as clustering, support vector machine [4], Bayes, etc. Owing to the effectiveness of deep learning, various neural networks and

© Springer Nature Switzerland AG 2021
H. Qiu et al. (Eds.): KSEM 2021, LNAI 12816, pp. 240–251, 2021.
https://doi.org/10.1007/978-3-030-82147-0_20

pre-trained models have good performance in text classification, such as Convolutional Neural Networks (CNN), Recurrent Neural Networks (RNN), Bidirectional Encoder Representation from Transformers (BERT) [5], and so on.

These methods show excellent performance in paragraphs and documents. But, short texts suffer from the data sparsity, since they have not enough background knowledge, so they do not perform well on short texts. To address this problem, various text representation models are applied in the current research work to obtain more information of different granularity from short text. Text representation plays a vital role in text classification, especially in the short text where text is usually short.

Text representation models can be grouped into explicit representation and implicit representation which are based on the different ways of leveraging external sources [6]. For explicit representation, which makes efficient utilize multiple features from various aspects (e.g. knowledge bases, POS tagging, and dependency parsing). The other is implicit representation, which uses Neural Language Model (NLM) to transform words into an implicit semantic space and quantize them as vectors [7]. When short texts use implicit representation, short texts are usually conve rted to implicit space and represented as dense vectors, which can capture more abundant information from context and promote text understanding with the help of the deep neural network. However, implicit representation also have some disadvantages: it do not perform well on new and rare words, which is very important for short text information extraction and understanding.

In this paper, we propose a model to integrate the explicit and implicit representation of short texts into a unified neural network. We use knowledge base (KB) such as Yago, Freebase, and Probase [8] to enrich short text representation solving the problem of data sparsity. The information in KBs is helpful for classification. For example, given a short text S1: *"The impact of Double-Twelfth Incident on China"*, the implicit model regard *"Double-Twelfth Incident"* as a new word, hence cannot capture that *"Double-Twelfth Incident"* is a *historical event* which plays a vital role to classify the short text into the class *history*. We take advantage of *isa* relation and associate each short text with its relevant concepts in the KB by conceptualization. The Model integrates concept information as prior knowledge into text understanding. Intuitively, although the use of prior knowledge enrich semantic information, then there are two main problems that have been cited here. First, conceptualization introduce incorrect concepts, due to the polysemy of concepts and the ambiguity of entities, which not help to distinguish categories in text classification, or even lead to performance degradation. Second, we should consider the conceptual hierarchy and the relative importance of the concept. Let us consider an example. In the short text S2: *"Jobs is one of the co-founders of Apple"*, we can find from KB that the concepts *fruit, mobile phone*, and *Technology Company* belongs to *"Apple"*. Obviously, *fruit* is not a suitable concept for the short text, which just verified the first point. In addition, we acquire the concepts *inventor, entrepreneur*, and *person* of *Jobs* from KB. Although they are all correct concepts, *entrepreneur* are more specific than *person* and *inventor*, and in this case should be assigned a greater weight.

To address these problems and achieve a better performance, we combine the attention mechanism and neural networks to propose the CK-ANN model. Specifically, we first preprocess the text, which is to obtain the entity words of the short text, and conceptualize the entity from KBs by the knowledge retrieval module to obtain the corresponding conceptual knowledge. Second, we use the input layer to get word vectors for text and concepts, respectively. Third, We use the attention layer to combine short text representation and concept representation to obtain context-relevant concepts, which supplement text information. Final, we study how to incorporate context-relevant concepts into our classification model. The main contributions of this paper are summarized as follows:

- We propose combining Knowledge with Attention Neural Networks (CK-ANN). This model assimilates into prior knowledge to enrich the semantic information of short texts.
- We Introducing the attention mechanism to solve the problem of knowledge noise and different hierarchy of knowledge. By combining these two aspects, the appropriate weight of the concept is finally obtained to measure the importance of knowledge for short text.
- We conduct experiments on four text classification datasets and the results show that CK-ANN achieves the best performance than state-of-the-art methods.

2   Related Work

2.1   Short Text Understanding

Every day, billions of short texts are being produced, including search queries, ad keywords, tags, tweets, etc. First of all, the short text does not always conform to grammatical rules. What's more, short texts contain limited context, resulting in the sparseness of the text. The majority of search queries contain less than 5 words. On account of the above reasons, short texts cause the significant amount of ambiguity, which makes them extremely difficult to handle. This has aroused great enthusiasm among researchers. Most researchers use external knowledge to handle the problem of insufficient background information related to texts. These approaches can be classified into two categories: Explicit Representation Model (ERM) and Implicit Representation Model (IRM).

2.2   Traditional Text Classification

Traditional text classification methods pay attention to more feature engineering which is used to represent texts and machine learning algorithms are harnessed as the classifiers, such as Support Vector Machine and Naive Bayes. In these feature designs, the feature designs widely used by most researchers are bag-of-words and TF-IDF. Bag-of-words and TF-IDF both use statistical methods to convert text into vector space, but both ignore the importance of word order. In addition, More complex features are used by researchers to improve classification performance, such as part-of-speech tags, noun phrases, and tree kernels. However, the common problem faced by these methods is severe data sparsity.

2.3 Neural Text Classification

Recently, with the development of deep learning, neural network methods form a new trend in text classification. First, kim et al. [1] used word2vec to transform the text into a vector space, employed CNN to encode the text, which extract text's n-grams features features to achieve sentence classification. Subsequently, the researchers designed a character-level CNN to extract character-level information. And the combined word-level [9] and character-level capture more information that is conducive to the task.

Wang et al. [4] used concepts obtained from the knowledge base to rich the text information, and then took them as features to improve short text classification. They proposed a concept-based similarity mechanism to classify a given short text into the most similar category. Finally, The acquired conceptual knowledge and text encoding were fed into the vector space and feed to the SVM classifier for text classification. The model that combines explicit representation and implicit representation to represent text was proposed by Wang et al. [10]. They used concept knowledge to enhance semantics, and used character convolution neural network to capture the features of unknown words. Xu et al. [11] proposed model to solve the polysemy problem of words in different contexts and improved the performance of classification.

3 Method

In this paper, we propose a CK-ANN shown in Fig. 1, which can incorporate concepts into neural networks for short text classification. But in the process of integration, we consider the relative importance of the text to the concept and between concepts. Before explaining the model in detail, we give a brief overview for our model. The architecture of our proposed model consists of four parts. It has a text representation, knowledge retrieval, concepts represention, one output layer. The output of the output layer is the probability distribution of the class label. First of all, we need to formulate for the problem. We use the formula $p\left(y_i|s_i;\theta\right)$ to represent the probability of the text class y_i, where θ is the parameters in the model and s_i is the sentence, denoted as S = $\{\,w_1, w_2, \cdots, w_n\,\}$ with w_i denoting to the position of i-th word in the sentence.

3.1 Knowledge Retrieval

The function of this module is to retrieve the corresponding relevant knowledge from the KB, according to the input text. The knowledge we are interested in this paper is the relationship of *isA*, and other semantic relations *isPropertyOf* should be applied to similar methods in future research. Specifically, we can get a related concept set C through this module according to the input short text s. In order to achieve this goal, we need to carry out a two-step strategy, named entity linking and conceptualization. Entity linking plays a vital role in NLP, which is used to find entities mentioned in short texts [12]. We use existing

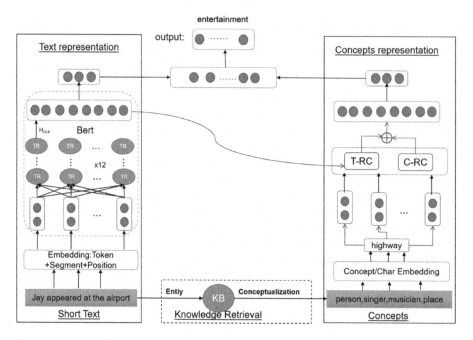

Fig. 1. Model architecture. The input short text is *"Jay appeared at the airport"*. The concepts include *person, singer, musician, place*. The class label is *entertainment*.

entity extraction solutions [13] to get the short text entity set E. Then, for each entity e∈ E we get its conceptual knowledge from KB, such as YAGO, Probase [8], and CN-Probase [14]. The technology proposed by Wang et al. [15] use to conceptualize services for each entity. For instance,given a short text *"Jobs is one of the co-founders of Apple"*, we obtain the entity set E = {*Jobs, co-founder, Apple*} by entity linking. Then, we conceptualize the entity *Apple* and acquire its concept set C = {*fruit, company, food, brand, manufacturer*} from Probase. We get the weight of the relevance between the conceptualization and the entity, and we rank this weight to select the top K. If the entity cannot find the corresponding knowledge in KB, then we treat it as a concept and put itself in the concept set C.

3.2 Input Layer

The input layer is composed of two parts, one is the input of short text, and the other is the input of conceptual knowledge. Here we denote short text S of length n and concept set C of size m.

For short text, since we use the Bert model to extract text representation information, our input must match Bert. We use WordPiece embeddings with a 30,000 token vocabulary to express words of short text. The first token of every sequence is always a special classification token [CLS]. The final hidden state corresponding to this token is used as a text representation for downstream tasks.

At last, the input embeddings shown in Fig. 2, $V^w \in R^{n \times d}$ are the sum of the token embeddings, the segmentation embeddings and the position embeddings.

For the input of conceptual knowledge, we use two types of embedding including word embedding and character embedding. Combining character embedding is conducive to the representation of new words. The character embedding layer uses Convolutional Neural Networks (CNN) to obtain a high-dimensional vector. In short, it is to map each word to a high-dimensional vector space, which is a fixed-size vector. Word embedding use pre-trained word vectors named Glove[1] [16] to obtain the word embedding. Given a word x, we can get $x_w \in R^{d1/2}, x_c \in R^{d1/2}$ from word embedding and character embedding respectively. Finally, the output of x is the concatenation $[x_w; x_c] \in R^{d1}$. Following, We fuse characters and word embedding vectors by using a two-layer Highway Network. Highway Network calculation method is as follows:

$$V^c = t \odot g\left(W_h X + b_h\right) + (1 - t) \odot X \tag{1}$$

$$t = \sigma\left(W_t X + b_t\right) \tag{2}$$

For the letter representation in the formula, we state that g is a nonlinear function (tanh), t is referred to as the transform gate, and $(1 - t)$ as the carry gate. W_t and W_h are weight matrices, and b_t and b_h are bias vectors. $X \in R^{m \times d1}$ is the concepts subset representation after the word embedding and the embedding vector are concatenated. Here we denote concepts vector $V^c \in R^{m \times d1}$.

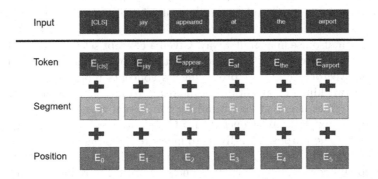

Fig. 2. Input of short text

3.3   Text Representation

The input layer takes a sequence of N tokens $(w_1, \cdots, w_n)$ as inputs, and computes output of d-dimensional representations $V^w \in R^{n \times d}$. We input V^w into the encoder to obtain sentence-level text representation. For the text encoder,

---

[1] https://nlp.stanford.edu/projects/glove/.

we use Transformer architecture [17] in the same way as Bert. In this paper, we choose Bert-base as the main component of the text representation, since it is composed of transformers, it can capture rich semantic information. Compared with CNN and RNN, transfomer breaks through the shortcomings of RNN that cannot be calculated in parallel, and solves the problem that CNN cannot capture long-term dependence. In this paper, the sentence is fed into the pre-training Bert, and bert is employed to obtain the semantic information of the sentence context. We denote the number of layers (i.e., Transformer blocks) as L, the hidden size as H, and the number of self-attention heads as A. Then, We use the parameters[2] of bert-base to initialize the component. The size of this parameter is 110M. Finally we obtain the sentence-level text representation $H_{[CLS]} \in R^d$, which is the output of the hidden state of the last layer of the special classification token [CLS]. Next, we use a linear formula to reduce the dimensionality of the $H_{[CLS]}$ vector, which is to get the text representation $q \in R^{d2}$, since the dimensionality of $H_{[CLS]}$ is too high. The conversion formula is as follows:

$$q = f(W_1 H_{[CLS]} + b_1) \tag{3}$$

Here $W_1 \in R^{d2 \times d}$ denotes the weight matrix, $f(.)$ is a non-linear function, and b1 is the offset.

3.4   Concepts Representation

External knowledge, such as a knowledge base, is used to acquire prior knowledge and represented by a set C, which improves the rich information and makes it easier for the machine to complete specific tasks. In this paper, we use conceptual knowledge to demonstrate our approach. There is no doubt that other prior knowledge can also use in a similar way. Given a concept set C of size m denoted as $(c_1, c_2, \cdots, c_m)$, where V_i^c obtained from the output of the input layer is the i-th concept vector, we aim at producing its concepts representation p. First, we propose two kinds of attention mechanisms to measure the importance of each concept, since it is very significant for conceptual representation. Next, we will introduce Text-Relevant-Concept (T-RC) attention, which is based on graph attention [18]. The purpose of T-RC is to measure the semantic similarity of the i-th concept to the short text representation q, since the entity has ambiguity and the additional knowledge has knowledge noise. In order to reduce this influence, T-RC is necessary. The calculation formula for T-RC attention is as follows:

$$\alpha_i = \frac{q\,\sigma(W_2 V_i^c + b_2)}{\sum_{j \in N} q\,\sigma(W_2 V_j^c + b_2)} \tag{4}$$

The weight of attention α_i is semantic similarity for i-th concept towards the short text. A larger α_i means that i-th concept provides more useful information for short text. Here V_i^c is the i-th concept vector, q is the short text representation, and $W_2 \in R^{d1 \times d2}$ is a weight matrix. $\sigma(.)$ named sigmod is a non-linear

---

[2] https://huggingface.co/bert-base-uncased.

activation function, where b_2 is the offset, and softmax work for normalizing attention weights of each concept.

What's more, It plays an important role in enriching text semantic information that we should consider the hierarchy of concepts and the relative importance between concepts. We propose Concept-Relevant-Concept (C-RC) attention based on self-attention [17]. The vector representation V^c of the given concept matrix set C. According to V^c we can get query vectors $Q \in R^{m \times d1}$, keys $K \in R^{m \times d1}$ and values $V \in R^{m \times d1}$. C-RC uses the scaled dot-product attention, which is a variant of dot-product (multiplicative) attention. We need to calculate the dot product between Q and K, and then in order to prevent the result from being too large, we will use the d1 as the scaling factor:

$$\beta = Attention(Q, K, V) \tag{5}$$

$$= softmax(\frac{QK^T}{\sqrt{d1}})V \tag{6}$$

We output $\beta \in R^{m \times d1}$ to denote the attention representation of each concept relative to the whole concept set. Finally, the attention weight of the concept to the short text and the vector of the concept to the whole concept set are employed to calculate the weighted sum of the concept vector, thereby generating a semantic vector $p \in R^{d1}$ representing the concepts:

$$p = \sum_{i=1}^{m}(\alpha_i V_i^c + \beta_i) \tag{7}$$

3.5 Ouput Layer

Finally, We concatenate the text representation output q and the concept representation output p into a vector as the input of a Multi-Layer Perceptron (MLP) to compute the category score. Then, we use softmax to convert the value of the vector into a probability distribution, which calculation is as follows:

$$p(y_i|s_i) = \frac{exp(y_i)}{\sum_{i=1}^{c} exp(y_i)} \tag{8}$$

When the model is training, we indicate that all parameters are θ. We take the cross-entropy loss as our loss function. Given the training set $T = (s_i, y_i)$, s_i represents the input text of the i-th sample, and y_i represents the label corresponding to the i-th sample. The definition of this loss function is as follows:

$$J(\theta) = -\sum_{i=1}^{|T|} \log p(y_i|s_i; \theta) \tag{9}$$

4   Experiment

In this chapter, first, we will give some super parameter settings during the experiment. What's more, we mainly introduce the comparison model we selected, as well as the public datasets. We compared our method with several state-of-the-art neural network based methods. Then, we conducted ablation experiments to analyze the effects of various components of our proposed model.

Table 1. The statistics of dataset.

Datasets	Classes	Trainning/Test set	Avg. Len	Vocabulary Size
TREC	6	5952/500	10	9170
MR	2	8530/2132	20	18,764
TagMyNews	7	18434/4609	20	34,130
Snippets	8	9872/2468	13	30,645

4.1   Datasets and Experiment Setup

To demonstrate the effectiveness of our model, We conducted full experiments on four widely used datasets: TREC, MR, TagMyNews, Snippets. The detailed information of the data set is shown in Table 1.

TREC [3]. This is a common question dataset, which contains 6 different types of questions such as person, location, digital information, etc.

MR. We use this dataset for sentiment classification, since it is about movie reviews. which involves detecting positive/negative comments on movies.

Snippets. This dataset is adopted from Phan et al. [19]. It is a compilation of search snippets for the google search. There are a total of eight labels such as health, sports, etc.

TagMyNews. We use news titles as this benchmark dataset released by Vitale et al. [20]. This data set contains English news from the Internet.

4.2   Baseline Methods

In this section, we will introduce a variety of benchmark methods to compare with our method, which are described in detail as follows:

Bow+SVM. Bow+SVM is based on the traditional algorithm svm as a classifier proposed by Chris Manning et al. [21]. The main idea of this method is that it takes unigram of the texts as features. The uniform frequency determines the weight of each feature.

---

[3] http://cogcomp.cs.illinois.edu/Data/QA/QC/.

TextCNN. TextCNN [1] use CNN as a classifier to extract features based on pre-trained word vectors. It is a multi-channel structure and is a powerful benchmark model in classification methods.

DE-CNN. DE-CNN [11] incorporate context-relevant knowledge into a convolutional neural network for short text classification.

KPCNN. KPCNN [10] is based on pre-training word vectors, adding external knowledge based on text information, and using a combination of word-level CNN and character-level CNN to classify text.

STCKA. STCKA [22] retrieves external knowledge to increase semantics, and uses attention mechanism to measure the importance of knowledge.

Bert. Bert [5] is a pre-trained language model that can be trained on a large number of expectations and can be applied to many downstream tasks such as question answering, classification, etc.

When our model is training, we set the batch size to 32. For the entire model, we use the Adam optimizer with the a learning rate of 5e−5, and dropout rate is 0.5. We set the maximum input length to 32 words. If a word cannot be found in the alphabet, we will initialize its embedding randomly. In the knowledge retrieval module, the knowledge base we use is Probase. The specific parameters of the encoder bert in the text representation module are set as L = 12, H = 768, A = 12. There are also some hyperparameter settings as follows: K = 5, d = 768, d1 = 300, d2 = 384.

Table 2. Accuracy of compared models on different datasets.

Model	TREC	MR	TagMyNews	Snippets
Bow+SVM	85.66	77.52	–	–
TextCNN	93.4	82.45	81.98	94.81
DE-CNN	94.62	84.6	–	–
KPCNN	93.46	83.25	82.38	94.98
STCKA	94.23	84.31	83.15	95.09
Bert	97.82	86.21	87.94	96.72
CK-ANN	**98.83**	**87.05**	**88.59**	**97.02**

4.3   Results and Analysis

The accuracy of prediction is used as an evaluation metric, which is Stanford's metric and widely used by researchers. The experiment results are shown in Table 2. We can clearly see from the experimental results that our effect is better than the benchmark model. In other words, introduce conceptual information as the prior knowledge, and make T-RC and C-RC two kinds of attention to

Table 3. Various parts of ablation research.

Methods	TREC
Bert+Concepts	95.33
Bert+Concepts+T-RC	96.83
Bert+Concepts+C-RC	97.40
CK-ANN	**98.83**

measure the importance of conceptual knowledge, which can improve the performance of short text classification in the deep learning model.

We perform ablation studies on the TREC to dive into the effectiveness of different components in our model. The result is displayed in Table 3. We first explored the different effects of the two types of attention in the experiment. We select Bert+Concepts as the baseline. Baseline simply connection text and concept sent into Bert together. From the results, we can find that the introduced knowledge has many noise, which not only does not help the classification but reduces the performance. After adding T-RC and C-RC to bert, it has improved compared to the baseline.

5   Conclusion

In this article, we proposed a novel method CK-ANN that takes advantage of external knowledge combined with neural networks for short text classification. We solved the problem of sparsity of short text data by conceptualizing them, with the help of the well-known knowledge base. We also solved the problem of knowledge noise caused by the introduction of conceptual knowledge. First, we use Bert to obtain the short text representation. Then, we utilizes two attention to extracts those text-relevant concepts and concepts aware, which obtain the final representation of the concept. We classified a short text based on the short text and its relevant concepts.

Acknowledgement. This research was supported by NSFC (Grants No. 61877051). Li Li is the corresponding author for the paper.

References

1. Kim, Y.: Convolutional neural networks for sentence classification. In: EMNLP, pp. 1746–1751. ACL (2014)
2. Rakhshani, H., et al.: Neural architecture search for time series classification. In: IJCNN, pp. 1–8. IEEE (2020)
3. Chen, Q., Zhu, X., Ling, Z., Inkpen, D., Wei, S.: Neural natural language inference models enhanced with external knowledge. In: ACL (1), pp. 2406–2417. Association for Computational Linguistics (2018)

4. Wang, F., Wang, Z., Li, Z., Wen, J.: Concept-based short text classification and ranking. In: CIKM, pp. 1069–1078. ACM (2014)

5. Devlin, J., Chang, M., Lee, K., Toutanova, K.: BERT: pre-training of deep bidirectional transformers for language understanding. In: NAACL-HLT (1), pp. 4171–4186. Association for Computational Linguistics (2019)

6. Wang, H.: Understanding short texts. In: Ishikawa, Y., Li, J., Wang, W., Zhang, R., Zhang, W. (eds.) APWeb 2013. LNCS, vol. 7808, p. 1. Springer, Heidelberg (2013). https://doi.org/10.1007/978-3-642-37401-2_1

7. Bengio, Y., Ducharme, R., Vincent, P., Janvin, C.: A neural probabilistic language model. J. Mach. Learn. Res. 3, 1137–1155 (2003)

8. Wu, W., Li, H., Wang, H., Zhu, K.Q.: Probase: a probabilistic taxonomy for text understanding. In: SIGMOD Conference, pp. 481–492. ACM (2012)

9. Johnson, R., Zhang, T.: Deep pyramid convolutional neural networks for text categorization. In: ACL (1), pp. 562–570. Association for Computational Linguistics (2017)

10. Wang, J., Wang, Z., Zhang, D., Yan, J.: Combining knowledge with deep convolutional neural networks for short text classification. In: IJCAI, pp. 2915–2921. ijcai.org (2017)

11. Xu, J., et al.: Incorporating context-relevant concepts into convolutional neural networks for short text classification. Neurocomputing 386, 42–53 (2020)

12. Moro, A., Raganato, A., Navigli, R.: Entity linking meets word sense disambiguation: a unified approach. Trans. Assoc. Comput. Linguistics 2, 231–244 (2014)

13. Ferragina, P., Scaiella, U.: TAGME: on-the-fly annotation of short text fragments (by wikipedia entities). In: CIKM, pp. 1625–1628. ACM (2010)

14. Chen, J., et al.: Cn-probase: a data-driven approach for large-scale Chinese taxonomy construction. In: ICDE, pp. 1706–1709. IEEE (2019)

15. Wang, Z., Wang, H., Wen, J., Xiao, Y.: An inference approach to basic level of categorization. In: CIKM, pp. 653–662. ACM (2015)

16. Pennington, J., Socher, R., Manning, C.D.: Glove: Global vectors for word representation. In: EMNLP, pp. 1532–1543. ACL (2014)

17. Vaswani, A., et al.: Attention is all you need. In: NIPS. pp. 5998–6008 (2017)

18. Lv, S., et al.: Graph-based reasoning over heterogeneous external knowledge for commonsense question answering. In: AAAI, pp. 8449–8456. AAAI Press (2020)

19. Phan, X.H., Nguyen, M.L., Horiguchi, S.: Learning to classify short and sparse text & web with hidden topics from large-scale data collections. In: WWW, pp. 91–100. ACM (2008)

20. Vitale, D., Ferragina, P., Scaiella, U.: Classification of short texts by deploying topical annotations. In: Baeza-Yates, R., et al. (eds.) ECIR 2012. LNCS, vol. 7224, pp. 376–387. Springer, Heidelberg (2012). https://doi.org/10.1007/978-3-642-28997-2_32

21. Wang, S.I., Manning, C.D.: Baselines and bigrams: Simple, good sentiment and topic classification. In: ACL (2), pp. 90–94. The Association for Computer Linguistics (2012)

22. Chen, J., Hu, Y., Liu, J., Xiao, Y., Jiang, H.: Deep short text classification with knowledge powered attention. In: AAAI, pp. 6252–6259. AAAI Press (2019)

A Dialogue Contextual Flow Model for Utterance Intent Recognition in Multi-turn Online Conversation

Zhenyu Zhang[(✉)], Tao Guo, Ling Jiang, and Manchang Gu

XiaoduoAI Company, Chengdu, China

Abstract. There are many intents of dialogues that cannot be recognized due to the contextual features of conversation, resulting in service failure for online chatting robots. Current methods leverage memory networks or machine reading comprehension (MRC) for multi-turn conversation intent recognition. We proposed a novel model for dialogue intent recognition, which leverages the advantages of MRC and memory networks. The model uses a self-attention and co-attention based contextual flow block to aggregate the dialogue utterances for intent recognition. We built a Chinese multi-turn dialogue dataset and designed a multi-task learning method to train the model. The experiment results are exciting, where the proposed model gets 82.75% accuracy and 78.13% F1 score. Those results show promising feasibility to apply our method in online chatting robot.

Keywords: Intent recognition · Multi-turn conversation · Contextual modeling · Chatting robot · Deep learning

1 Introduction

The user intent recognition is very important for chatting robot in e-commerce. There have been many research works in the user intent recognition [1,17,19]. However, most of those researches are focused on single utterance recognition, which firstly recognizes the intent from an utterance and then responds an answer to customer from a knowledge base [12]. Although some researches improve the chatting service [2,25] via conversation estimation, the literature of intent recognition for multi-turn conversation is still poorly explored, which also improves service quality. There are two major difficulties for the multi-turn dialogue intent recognition: case **a**) the history conversation utterances can influence the intent of the last utterance; case **b**) the intent of the last utterance cannot be directly recognized without attending to previous utterances. Therefore single utterance intent recognition method will conclude a wrong intent in case **a** or result in a failed prediction in case **b**. Figure 1 shows an example of such difficulties, where the dialogues are from the leading Chinese online shopping platform Taobao[1]

---

[1] www.taobao.com.

© Springer Nature Switzerland AG 2021
H. Qiu et al. (Eds.): KSEM 2021, LNAI 12816, pp. 252–263, 2021.
https://doi.org/10.1007/978-3-030-82147-0_21

Fig. 1. The problem of intent recognition (Color figure online)

and the utterances are translated into English. Each dialogue is assigned with 2 intents: 1) yellow one is recognized with only the last utterance; 2) green one is recognized with the history utterances. The intent of the last utterance in **Dialogue A.** is quite different when attend to conversation history (case **a**), while the intent in **Dialogue. B** is recognized as "unknown" without attending to history conversation (case **b**).

In order to deal with the multi-turn conversation intent recognition problem, the researchers have proposed several useful methods. Those research works can be classified into 2 categories, i.e., memory networks [22] based methods and machine reading comprehension (MRC) [4] based methods. The prototype memory networks [22] leverage the memory slots to maintain the input facts to predict answers. The end-to-end memory networks [20] and the dynamic memory networks [11] are proposed to improve performance. For MRC based methods, there are many published multi-turn dialogue datasets including CoQA [18], QuAC [5], DoQA [3], etc. However, memory networks based methods barely concern directly selecting contextual related history utterances while it's hard to obtain topic-related passages for MRC based methods. In this paper, we propose a contextual flow model to address those problems.

Our co-attention and self-attention based contextual flow model (ACFlow) consists of three parts that are utterance encoder, attention-flow layer, and multi-task learning header. The utterance encoder encodes an utterance into a dense vector. The attention-flow layer leverages the dense vector to generate dialogue representation vector. We train ACFlow model with the multi-task learning header. Besides, we build a Chinese multi-turn dialogue dataset (CMTD) that consists of about 900K labelled dialogues from Tabao. Our major contributions are summarized as follows:

- We build a Chinese multi-turn dialogue dataset (CMTD) that consists of about 900K labeled samples.
- We build a self-attention and co-attention based contextual flow model (ACFlow) to recognize the user intent in multi-turn conversation.
- We compare our method with previous methods in CMTD and the results are exciting. Our proposed model achieved 82.75% accuracy score and 78.13% F1 score.

We describe how the CMTD is built in Sect. 2. We describe the ACFlow model in Sect. 3. We show the experimental results in Sect. 4. We analyze the threats of our work in Sect. 5 and show the related works in Sect. 6. We conclude the paper in Sect. 7.

2   Chinese Multi-turn Dialogue Datset

In order to get a basic understanding of online chatting data, we sampled 1000 users and checked their chatting utterances in one month. We found that the average duration of each dialogue is 4.68 h and the average time gap between two dialogues is 6.01 h. The average utterances in one dialogue is 8.59. We denote the history utterances as **dialogue context** and last utterance as **question**. The dialogue context is necessary for 72% of the dialogues to recognize intent, where 43.7% dialogues belong to case **a** (refer to Sect. 1) and 28.3% belong to case **b**.

For dialogue construction, we set two limits for one dialogue: duration within 6 h and utterances count within 10. Then we collected the chatting history of all available users within two months and sampled over 900K dialogues. We hired workers to label dialogues as shown in Table 1. The term "proofs" is the relevant utterances to the last utterance (i.e., the 2nd and 3rd utterances is relevant). The term "type" is dialogue context type, where there are 3 types that are **a**, **b** (refer to Sect. 1) and **u** (the dialogue context is unnecessary). *snick* and *cnick* is the customer and customer service staff. Each dialogue is labelled by 3 workers and we drop the dialogues with fewer than 2 same labelling results. The intent is a brief and abstract description. We normalized the description of similar intents into one intent and removed the intents that occur fewer than 20 times. Finally, we get **1536 unique intents** and one special intent "unknown intent".

Table 1. The illustration of one labelled dialogue

Utterances	Proofs	Type	Intent
cnick: Why is the price cheaper than before?	-	-	-
snick: We only keep price for 30 d.	-	-	-
snick: It has been more than 30 d since your order.	-	-	-
cnick: Does it have to be within 30 d?	2,3	b	Problem for price keeping days

Our statistics about CMTD show that 45.1% dialogues belong to case **a** and 24.6% belong to case **b**, which is compatible with the dialogues of 1000 manually checked users thus demonstrates the dialogue construction settings are rational. We also normalized the utterances of our dataset (remove pictures, url links and emotion flags; keep one copy of duplicate utterances).

3   Attention-Based Contextual Flow Model

In this section, we firstly introduce the proposed attention based contextual flow model. Then, we describe the multi-task oriented training.

3.1   The Proposed Model

The attention based contextual flow model (ACFlow) is illustrated in Fig. 2. The model consists of three major components: 1) the LSTM-CNN based utterance encoder, 2) the co-attention and self-attention based contextual flow block (ACF-Block), and 3) the multi-task oriented learning header. The input to the model is firstly processed by a sentencepiece tokenizer [10] following the tutorial[2]. We feed the **dialogue context** (i.e., $u1$, $u2$, $u3$) and the **question** (i.e., q that denotes the last utterance) to the encoder. For the LSTM-CNN encoder, we adopt the network structure proposed in [28] which combines BLSTM-2DPooling and BLSTM-2DCNN to extract feature vector for each utterance. The feature vectors are then feed to ACF-Block which consists of context-question attention layer, self-attention layer and question-context attention layer. Equation 1 denotes the context-question attention (C-Q attention) layer. For each utterance (u_i) of dialogue context, we concatenate it with the question and apply a nonlinear attention to get question aggregated representation u_i^1. The $W_{cq} \in R^{2d \times d}$ and $b_{cq} \in R^d$ are learned parameters.

$$u_i^1 = tanh(W_{cq} * [q; u_i] + b_{cq}), \ 1 \leq i \leq N \tag{1}$$

The self-attention layer shown in Eq. 2 uses dialogue context to get a contextual representation (u_i^2), where $W_{self} \in R^{d \times d}$ is learnable.

$$u_i^2 = \sum_{i=1}^{i=N} attn_{ij} * u_j^1, \text{ where}$$

$$score_{ij} = \frac{(u_i^1 * W_{self} * u_j^1)}{\sum_{k=1}^{k=N} u_i^1 * W_{self} * u_k^1}, \ attn_{ij} = \frac{exp(score_{ij})}{\sum_{k=1}^{k=N} score_{ik}}. \tag{2}$$

The question-context attention layer (Q-C attention) shown in Eq. 3 incorporates the contextual information into the question representation to get the feature vector $vec_{feature}$ via a dot attention. The $W_{qc} \in R^{d \times d}$ and $b_{qc} \in R^d$ are learned parameters.

$$vec_{feature} = (W_{qc} * q + b_{qc}) + \sum_{i=1}^{i=N} dot(W_{qc} * q + b_{qc}, u_i^2) * u_i^2 \tag{3}$$

Therefore, we finished computing the co-attention between question and context together with the self-attention in one ACF-Block. Our model consists of 3 ACF-Blocks.

---

[2] https://github.com/google/sentencepiece. We train a unigram based tokenizer in CMTD where the vocabulary size is 50K. The sentencepiece tokenizer splits a Chinese utterance into pieces and encode each piece with a unique integer.

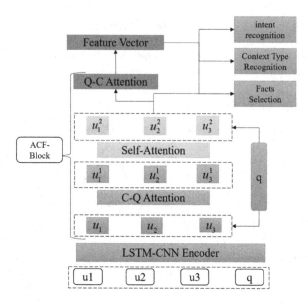

Fig. 2. Overview of ACFlow

3.2 The Multi-task Oriented Training

We designed a multi-task learning method for ACFlow model, where the multi-task learning header consists of the intent recognition, dialogue context type recognition and facts selection (refer to Eq. 4, 5 and 6 respectively).

As shown in Eq. 4, we feed feature vector ($vec_{feature}$) to a feed-forward layer (ff) for the intent recognition task and apply a softmax to the output and get the cross entropy (CE) loss on CMTD (D), where x_k and $intent_k$ denote the dialogue and the intent. The θ_{acflow} and θ_{ff} denote the parameters of ACFLow model and feed-forward layer.

$$Loss1(\theta_{acflow}, \theta_{ff}) = \sum_{x_k, intent_k \in D} CE(intent_k, ff(vec_{feature}, \theta_{ff})) \quad (4)$$

For the dialogue context type recognition task, we labelled 3 types of dialogue context that are a, b and u as mentioned in Sect. 2. As shown in Eq. 5, we concatenate the question with the feature vector ($[q; vec_{feature}]$) and apply a feed-forward layer with a softmax activation. We compute the cross-entropy of the output to get $Loss2$.

$$Loss2(\theta_{acflow}, \theta_{ff}) = \sum_{x_k, type_k \in D} CE(type_k, ff([q; vec_{feature}], \theta_{ff})) \quad (5)$$

For the facts selection task, we treat this as a sequence labelling problem. We apply the conditional random field (CRF) layer [13] on the N utterances (u_i^2) of dialogue context to predict true/false relevance of each utterance. As shown in

Eq. 6, the tag_k is a sequence of 0/1 where $sel_i = 0$ denotes u_i is irrelevant. We apply the log-likelihood maximization strategy to get $Loss3$.

$$Loss3(\theta_{acflow}, \theta_{crf}) = \sum_{x_k, tag_k \in D} -MLE(tag_k, crf(u_1^2, u_2^2, ..., u_N^2, \theta_{crf}))$$

$$tag_k = (sel_1, sel_2, ..., sel_n), where\ sel_i \in \{0, 1\} \tag{6}$$

Finally, we get the total loss as shown Eq. 7. We use the LAMB optimizer [24] to train our model with the $Loss_{multi-task}$, where $\lambda_1, \lambda_2, \lambda_3$ are hyperparameters tuned via grid search.

$$Loss_{multi-task}(\theta_{acflow}, \theta_{header}) = \lambda_1 * Loss1 + \lambda_2 * Loss2 + \lambda_3 * Loss3$$

$$where\ 1 = \lambda_1 + \lambda_2 + \lambda_3\ \wedge\ \lambda_1, \lambda_2, \lambda_3 \geq 0 \tag{7}$$

4 Experiments and Discussion

In this section, we firstly introduce experimental design. Then we discuss the experimental results.

4.1 Experimental Design

Our evaluation focuses on the following research questions:

RQ1: How effective is the ACFlow Model? We compared the ACFlow model with some state-of-the-art models in multi-turn dialogue intent recognition. The compared models are:

- **BERT-NLI**: The BERT-wwm model [6] is pre-trained Chinese language model with whole word masking strategy. We concatenate the dialogue context utterances and treat the multi-turn intent recognition problem as a natural language inference (NLI) problem.
- **E2EMN**: the end-to-end memory networks [20] proposed by Microsoft.
- **DMN**: the dynamic memory network [11], which updates the memory iterative with a dynamic gate via attention mechanism.
- **KVNet**: the key-value network [23], which selects relevant history utterances to generate a feature vector.
- **DANet**: the deep utterance aggregation model [27], which aggregate both word-level and utterance-level information.

All the above research works are published together with source code.

RQ2: How effective is the model design of ACFlow? Our ACFlow consists of Q-C attention, C-Q attention and dialogue context self-attention (refer to Sect. 3). We evaluated the model accuracy under the following setups:

- directly use question (q) as feature vector ($vec_{feature}$).
- remove the Q-C attention and use $[avg(\sum_{i=1}^{i=N} u_i^2); q]$ ([.;.] denotes the concatenation operation) as the feature vector.

- remove the self-attention for dialogue context utterances vectors.
- replace the self-attention with a Bi-LSTM layer.
- remove the C-Q attention layer.

RQ3: How effective is the multi-task learning? We leveraged multi-task learning to train the ACFlow model with 3 tasks that are intent recognition, context type recognition and facts selection. We removed some learning tasks and get the intent recognition accuracy so as to observe the effectiveness of the learning tasks.

Evaluation Metrics. Assume there are M intents and the model prediction is a confusion matrix A, where A_{ij} represents count of samples whose intent is i and the predicted intent is j. The accuracy score is computed by Eq. 8. The F1 score is computed by Eq. 9, where the *precision(c)* and *recall(c)* represent the precision and recall of intent c respectively. The higher accuracy and F1 scores refer to better model prediction.

$$\text{Accuracy} = \frac{\Sigma_i A_{ii}}{\Sigma_i \Sigma_j A_{ij}}. \tag{8}$$

$$F1 = \frac{2 * precision * recall}{precision + recall}, \text{where}$$
$$\text{precision} = \frac{1}{M} \sum_{c=1}^{c=M} \frac{A_{cc}}{\Sigma_i A_{ic}}, \ \text{recall} = \frac{1}{M} \sum_{c=1}^{c=M} \frac{A_{cc}}{\Sigma_j A_{cj}}. \tag{9}$$

Experimental Setup. CMTD dataset contains 1536 intents and 900K samples; we split them into 2 parts: 90% as training dataset and 10% as testing dataset. We trained ACFlow and all the comparative models on the train dataset and evaluated them on the testing dataset. The batch size is 1024 (except for BERT-NLI whose batch size is 128) and learning rate is 1e−4 with LAMB optimizer [24]. We trained the models for 20 epochs with 500 warm-up steps.

4.2   Experimental Results for RQ1

Table 2 shows the evaluation scores of different models and the **ACFlow** model outperforms the other models significantly. ACFlow model outperforms the best comparative model (DMN) by 4.71% accuracy score and 2.12% F1 score. We observed that the BERT-NLI method achieves the lowest scores, which shows that the multi-turn dialogue intent recognition cannot be treated as a natural language inference problem. The dialogue context cannot be well represented via simply concatenation.

We also observed that the attention based model outperforms the non-attention based models. E2EMN and KVNet do not apply attention mechanism for context representation while the DMN, DANet and ACFlow leverage the

Table 2. The evaluation of different models

Model	Accuracy	F1
BERT-NLI	0.6624	0.5768
E2EMN	0.7361	0.6949
DMN	0.7854	0.7601
KVNet	0.7002	0.6425
DANet	0.7695	0.7110
ACFlow	**0.8275**	**0.7813**

attention mechanism for dialogue context representation. Compared with the other attention based model, our model leverage both the co-attention and self-attention, which we believe is necessary for dialogue context representation and question information incorporation.

4.3 Experimental Results for RQ2

Table 3. Model design evaluation of ACFlow

Model Ablation	Accuracy
Directly q	0.4394
No Q-C attention	0.7906
No self-attention	0.7833
Replace self-attention	0.8203
No C-Q attention	0.8165
ACFlow	0.8275

As shown in Table 3, removing each attention layer in ACFlow model will result in accuracy score drop. Without any attention module, the model directly use the question to predict the intent which cannot access the dialogue context. Therefore, only the samples of type u (refer to Sect. 2) can be recognized.

We get 79.06% accuracy score after removing the Q-C attention module. Without Q-C attention, the dialogue context vectors are averaged and concatenated with q to get feature vector, where each history utterance is of same importance. Therefore, the Q-C attention is important for selecting proper utterances. We get 78.33% accuracy score after removing the self-attention module. The self-attention module can build the relation between the context and generate a global dialogue context representation. Without the self-attention, only local context utterances information is accessed. We get 82.03% accuracy score after replacing the self-attention module with a Bi-LSTM layer, which can process time-series sequence thus able to handle global context information. However, the Bi-LSTM is non-superior to the self-attention because it achieves lower accuracy score and is also much less computation efficient than self-attention. We get 81.65% accuracy score after removing the C-Q attention module. Without C-Q attention, the dialogue context utterances are not able to attend the question (q). The experiment results demonstrate that we need to attend the question (q) to get a better dialogue context representation for intent recognition.

4.4 Experimental Results for RQ3

Table 4. Multi-task learning evaluation

Training task	Accuracy
IntR	0.7969
IntR+DCTR	0.8033
IntR+FactSel	0.8152
ACFlow	0.8275

As shown in Table 4, the model accuracy score drops to 79.69% without multitask learning strategy. The term **IntR** refers to intent recognition task, **DCTR** refers to dialogue context type recognition task, and **FactSel** refers to facts selection task. **FactSel** is very crucial to our model as it can help the model focus on the most relevant dialogue context utterances, which might be responsible for the parameters of C-Q attention and self-attention in ACFlow model. **DCTR** can help the model learn to aggregate the information from context to the question q, which might be responsible to the Q-C attention in ACFflow model. The experiment results demonstrate the effectiveness of the multi-task learning for the dialogue intent recognition.

5   Threats to Validity

Despite of the exciting results, there are still works left to be improved in future:

- We leverage a LSTM-CNN encoder to encode each utterance, while the transformer encoder [21] has achieved great success in NLP in recent years. Also, the utterances in CMTD is within 30 words and [9] shows there is little difference for short text classification between transformer and RNN. Our work lacks exploration of using other encoders, which is left as a future work.
- The CMTD dataset now contains many private information of online customers, which makes it hard for publishment. We are working on data desensitization and the dataset will become available in future.

6   Related Works

In this section, we focus on introducing the memory networks and machine reading comprehension methods used for multi-turn dialogue intent recognition.

6.1   Memory Networks

Facebook AI proposed the memory networks [22] to leverage the memory slots to maintain the input facts and then predict answers for user questions. Later the end-to-end memory networks [20] using deep learning was proposed by Microsoft for multi-hop inference in conversation. Ankit Kumar et al. [11] proposed the dynamic memory networks that can update the memory state in each episode. IBM researchers incorporated the reinforcement learning into memory networks [15]. Tsinghua researchers then proposed a domain aware multi-decoder for task oriented conversation [26]. Xu et al. proposed the key-value network [23] that can significantly expand the input size. Zhang et al. [27] builds a deep utterance aggregation model to incorporate the dialogue context information into the last utterance. Some recent researches found that the feed-forward part of transformer [21] is similar to memory networks [8]. However, current memory network based methods barely concerned directly select contextual related history utterances.

6.2   Machine Reading Comprehension

The machine reading comprehension (MRC) has achieved great success since BERT was released [7], which achieved semi-human level score in SQUAD [16]. In the literature of multi-turn dialogue, there are many MRC based dataset that prospers many related researches, which includes CoQA [18], QuAC [5], DoQA [3], etc. Those dataset usually consists of a topic passage of the dialogue and the conversation utterances. MRC method is used to select text-spans to answer question concerning either the topic passage or the conversation history. Alibaba Group incorporates history utterance embedding [14] into BERT model to find answer for user question. ACFlow model is also designed to select utterances as facts to help recognize intent.

7   Conclusion

In this paper, we proposed a contextual flow (ACFlow) model for multi-turn dialogue intent recognition. We also built a Chinese multi-turn dialogue dataset that contains about 900K labelled samples. Our model outperforms several state-of-the-art methods and improves the accuracy score a lot. We also experimented the ablations of the ACF-Block and multi-task learning header to explore the rational design of the model for the literature of multi-turn dialogue intent recognition. Our work can help researchers to explore more efficient multi-turn dialogue model in future. And the ACFlow model can be applied to the online chatting robot for better customer service.

Acknowledgment. This work is funded by the XiaduoAI company and the customer intent recognition model is now applied to the shopping dialog robot of XiaoduoAI.

References

1. Ahmad, W.U., Bai, X., Peng, N., Chang, K.W.: Learning robust, transferable sentence representations for text classification. arXiv preprint arXiv:1810.00681 (2018)
2. Bao, W., Wen, H., Li, S., Liu, X., Lin, Q., Yang, K.: GMCM: graph-based micro-behavior conversion model for post-click conversion rate estimation. In: Huang, J., et al. (eds.) Proceedings of the 43rd International ACM SIGIR Conference on Research and Development in Information Retrieval, SIGIR 2020, Virtual Event, China, 25–30 July 2020, pp. 2201–2210. ACM (2020)
3. Campos, J.A., Otegi, A., Soroa, A., Deriu, J., Cieliebak, M., Agirre, E.: DoQA-accessing domain-specific FAQs via conversational QA. arXiv preprint arXiv:2005.01328 (2020)
4. Chen, D., Fisch, A., Weston, J., Bordes, A.: Reading Wikipedia to answer open-domain questions. arXiv preprint arXiv:1704.00051 (2017)
5. Choi, E., et al.: QuAC: question answering in context. arXiv preprint arXiv:1808.07036 (2018)
6. Cui, Y., Che, W., Liu, T., Qin, B., Wang, S., Hu, G.: Revisiting pre-trained models for Chinese natural language processing. arXiv preprint arXiv:2004.13922 (2020)
7. Devlin, J., Chang, M., Lee, K., Toutanova, K.: BERT: pre-training of deep bidirectional transformers for language understanding. In: Proceedings of the 2019 Conference of the North American Chapter of the Association for Computational Linguistics: Human Language Technologies, pp. 4171–4186. Association for Computational Linguistics (2019)
8. Geva, M., Schuster, R., Berant, J., Levy, O.: Transformer feed-forward layers are key-value memories. arXiv preprint arXiv:2012.14913 (2020)
9. Hu, Z., et al.: Texar: a modularized, versatile, and extensible toolkit for text generation. In: ACL 2019, System Demonstrations (2019)
10. Kudo, T.: Subword regularization: improving neural network translation models with multiple subword candidates. In: Gurevych, I., Miyao, Y. (eds.) Proceedings of the 56th Annual Meeting of the Association for Computational Linguistics, pp. 66–75. Association for Computational Linguistics (2018)
11. Kumar, A., et al.: Ask me anything: dynamic memory networks for natural language processing. In: International Conference on Machine Learning, pp. 1378–1387. PMLR (2016)
12. Liu, X., Zhang, Y., Liao, Y., Jiang, L.: Dynamic updating of the knowledge base for a large-scale question answering system. ACM Trans. Asian Low Resour. Lang. Inf. Process. 19(3), 45:1–45:13 (2020). https://doi.org/10.1145/3377708
13. Ma, X., Hovy, E.H.: End-to-end sequence labeling via bi-directional LATM-CNNs-CRF. In: Proceedings of the 54th Annual Meeting of the Association for Computational Linguistics, ACL 2016, Volume 1: Long Papers, Berlin, Germany, 7–12 August 2016. The Association for Computer Linguistics (2016)
14. Qu, C., Yang, L., Qiu, M., Croft, W.B., Zhang, Y., Iyyer, M.: Bert with history answer embedding for conversational question answering. In: Proceedings of the 42nd International ACM SIGIR Conference on Research and Development in Information Retrieval, pp. 1133–1136 (2019)
15. Rajendran, J., Ganhotra, J., Singh, S., Polymenakos, L.: Learning end-to-end goal-oriented dialog with multiple answers. arXiv preprint arXiv:1808.09996 (2018)

16. Rajpurkar, P., Zhang, J., Lopyrev, K., Liang, P.: SQuAD: 100,000+ questions for machine comprehension of text. arXiv preprint arXiv:1606.05250 (2016)
17. Ravuri, S.V., Stolcke, A.: Recurrent neural network and LSTM models for lexical utterance classification. In: 16th Annual Conference of the International Speech Communication Association, INTERSPEECH 2015, Dresden, Germany, 6–10 September 2015, pp. 135–139. ISCA (2015)
18. Reddy, S., Chen, D., Manning, C.D.: CoQA: a conversational question answering challenge. Trans. Assoc. Comput. Linguist. **7**, 249–266 (2019)
19. Shao, Z., Li, X., Guo, Y., Zhang, L.: Influence of service quality in sharing economy: Understanding customers' continuance intention of bicycle sharing. Electron. Commer. Res. Appl. **40**, 100944 (2020)
20. Sukhbaatar, S., Szlam, A., Weston, J., Fergus, R.: End-to-end memory networks. arXiv preprint arXiv:1503.08895 (2015)
21. Vaswani, A., et al.: Attention is all you need. In: Advances in Neural Information Processing Systems 30: Annual Conference on Neural Information Processing Systems 2017, Long Beach, CA, USA, 4–9 December 2017, pp. 5998–6008 (2017)
22. Weston, J., Chopra, S., Bordes, A.: Memory networks. arXiv preprint arXiv:1410.3916 (2014)
23. Xu, K., Lai, Y., Feng, Y., Wang, Z.: Enhancing key-value memory neural networks for knowledge based question answering. In: Proceedings of the 2019 Conference of the North American Chapter of the Association for Computational Linguistics: Human Language Technologies, Volume 1 (Long and Short Papers), pp. 2937–2947 (2019)
24. You, Y., Li, J., Hseu, J., Song, X., Demmel, J., Hsieh, C.: Reducing BERT pre-training time from 3 days to 76 minutes. CoRR abs/1904.00962 (2019)
25. Zhang, W., et al.: Large-scale causal approaches to debiasing post-click conversion rate estimation with multi-task learning. In: The Web Conference 2020, WWW 2020, Taipei, Taiwan, 20–24 April 2020, pp. 2775–2781. ACM/IW3C2 (2020)
26. Zhang, Y., Ou, Z., Yu, Z.: Task-oriented dialog systems that consider multiple appropriate responses under the same context. In: Proceedings of the AAAI Conference on Artificial Intelligence, vol. 34, pp. 9604–9611 (2020)
27. Zhang, Z., Li, J., Zhu, P., Zhao, H., Liu, G.: Modeling multi-turn conversation with deep utterance aggregation. arXiv preprint arXiv:1806.09102 (2018)
28. Zhou, P., Qi, Z., Zheng, S., Xu, J., Bao, H., Xu, B.: Text classification improved by integrating bidirectional LSTM with two-dimensional max pooling. In: Proceedings of the 26th International Conference on Computational Linguistics, COLING 2016, Technical Papers, Osaka, Japan, 11–16 December 2016, pp. 3485–3495. ACL (2016)

An Empirical Study on Effect of Semantic Measures in Cross-Domain Recommender System in User Cold-Start Scenario

Yuhan Wang, Qing Xie$^{(\boxtimes)}$, Lin Li, and Yongjian Liu

School of Computer Science and Technology, Wuhan University of Technology, Wuhan, China
{wyh0520,felixxq,cathylilin,liuyj}@whut.edu.cn

Abstract. Cold-start problem is one of the fatal problems in recommender system. The development of cross-domain recommender system (CDRS) provides feasibility to deal with the problem, while it needs to handle heterogeneous information when linking different domains. Some existing semantic measures based on Linked Open Data (LOD) are likely to play a positive role in this research area. According to the different LOD information used, we analyze two classes of semantic measures (similarity and relatedness) to explore the relationship between LOD-based domain correlation and user interests, and study the performance of different semantic measures on a cross-domain recommendation framework. Through experiments on a real-world dataset, this work has identified that the similarity measures can accurately capture the user's existing interests while the relatedness measures can produce diverse recommendations. Besides, by comparing with some representative methods, the experiment demonstrated that the cross-domain recommendation method could provide users with satisfactory recommendations even in the cold-start scenario.

Keywords: Cold-start · Linked open data · Cross-domain recommender system · Semantic measures

1 Introduction

Recommender systems play an important role in various applications, aiming to help users discover items of potential interest. The primary source in personalized recommendation tasks is user historical behaviors. However, for cold-start users who entered the system for the first time, missing historical behavior usually results in performance degradations. Recently, cross-domain recommender system (CDRS) has attracted growing attention. The main idea of CDRS is to analyze user preferences collected from auxiliary (source) domain to guide recommendation tasks in target domain. It is beneficial for discovering broader user preferences and obtaining more detailed user profiles. Therefore, CDRS could increase the possibility of solving the cold start problem.

Supported by the Fundamental Research Funds for the Central Universities (WUT: 2020III008GX).

The core task of CDRS is the transfer and utilization of knowledge between target and source domains. However, different domains usually differ greatly in data structures such as user profiles and item attributes, which makes CDRS unable to map or correlate these heterogeneous data directly. Several collaborative filtering approaches employ existing techniques to model information from source and target domains, such as matrix factorization [21], tensor factorization [7], or clustering [17]. These flexible frameworks work well in general scenarios, but they are not suitable for new users with uncertain interests. There are also some researches based on semantic relations, which construct semantic networks by introducing external knowledge bases [4,12]. They are effective in solving data sparsity, cold-start, and data heterogeneity issues. However, dealing with the entire network structure requires learning a mass of parameters, which may lead to inefficient training.

Linked Open Data (LOD) is a recent community-driven effort that provides access to a large amount of diverse and structured data [2]. These data come from different sources covering various domains. So CDRS can extensively benefit from the reliable and rich content provided by LOD. Various semantic measures have been proposed in existing works to estimate the relationship between entities in LOD. According to the different types of LOD information used, they can be divided into two main classes. The first class of measures evaluates the similarity of resources by comparing their descriptions or contents in LOD [13], while the second is mainly based on the concept of connectivity to evaluate the relatedness between resources [14–16]. In this paper, we expect to study the effect of different measures in CDRS, so as to provide users with satisfactory recommendations. In general, we exploit a cross-domain recommendation framework (see Fig. 1, more details in Sect. 3.1), which adopts LOD-based semantic calculation and matrix factorization. Specifically, the framework aims to address the cold-start problem of target users and the heterogeneity of information across domains. It first investigates the semantic correlation found in LOD datasets (e.g., DBpedia) to connect domains, then brings the inter-domain correlation into the joint matrix factorization model to generate recommendations.

In order to improve the user experience in recommender system, it is necessary to correctly predict users' various interests. Yet only considering recommendation accuracy is not enough, as it may cause the risk of dull recommendations. For capturing more aspects of user interest, it is essential for the recommender to improve the recommendation diversity. Diversity does not simply mean different item genres (types) in the recommendation list. It should also consider additional properties, such as the frequency of genres being represented, and the different importance of genres to user interests. Some frequently used metrics [25,27] do not adequately consider these properties. Therefore, we propose a diversity metric on top of the basic concept of BinomDiv [24]. Our proposed metric uses the genre data available to estimate both the coverage and non-redundancy of the recommendation results in the evaluation.

The main contributions of this paper are summarized as follows. Firstly, we construct a cross-domain recommendation framework to address the cold-start problem and cross-domain information heterogeneity, then evaluate several semantic measures based on different types of LOD information, so as to explore the relationship between the LOD-based domain correlation and user preference. Secondly, we design a metric for evaluating the diversity of recommendation results, and apply it in the empirical study on a real-world dataset. Thirdly, we compare the performance of different semantic measures in experiments, and validate the effectiveness of cross-domain recommendation method in new user scenarios.

The remaining part of the paper is organized as follows: Sect. 2 contains a review of works related to CDRSs and semantic measures. Section 3 formally defines the recommendation framework in three parts: an overview, a detailed introduction of involved LOD-based semantic measures and matrix factorization models. In Sect. 4, we present comprehensive empirical experiments on a real-world dataset to compare the performance of two classes of semantic measures and different recommendation algorithms, then discuss the results in detail. Finally, Sect. 5 concludes this paper and reveals the practical significance.

2   Related Works

2.1   Knowledge Linkage for Cross-Domain Recommendation

The core task of CDRS is the transfer and exploitation of knowledge between source and target domain. However, due to the disparity of data structure in different domains, CDRS should take into account first how to make multi-source data available for generating recommendations.

A common way to address the heterogeneity of multiple domains is to identify relatedness between their features. One solution explores inter-domain mapping to link different domains, and the identification of the relatedness can usually make use of some common knowledge, such as common item attributes [3], association rules [1]. Another solution establishes connections between different domains by calculating the relation between domains, based on user-contributed tags [20] or constructing semantic networks [12]. However, generally common knowledge is not always available. Besides, the workload of constructing the semantic network is usually heavy and may cause computational issues.

With the introduction of Linked Open Data (LOD), information from multiple domains can be extracted and stored in formal and structured representations, which can be well managed by the recommendation system. Therefore, there have been some works using LOD to connect resources and concepts in different domains, such as [5,9,19]. Our research also exploits LOD to pre-calculate the correlation between items in a CDRS. It can connect different domains while avoiding handling the entire network structure, which improves recommendation performance and calculation efficiency.

2.2   Semantic Similarity/Relatedness Measures on Linked Open Data

There are two classes of semantic measurement methods: similarity and relatedness. Similarity refers to the specific quantified value of resemblance between concepts or entities/resources (including words, short texts, and documents), while relatedness shows the degree of correlation between them. The semantic measure is significant for users to obtain the desirable resources rapidly and accurately. It is essential for applications such as data clustering, QA systems, intelligent retrieval, social network analysis, and recommendation.

When the similarity measure is applied in the recommender system, it is usually based on the general principle of collaborative filtering. Meymandpour et al. [13] proposed a similarity measure, PICSS (Partitioned Information Content-based Semantic Similarity), which considers the variability in link types and the direction of relations in multiple LOD datasets. Regarding the semantic relatedness measures, Passant [14] introduced a distance function named LDSD (Linked Data Semantic Distance), which uses the number of direct and indirect paths between resources to compute the semantic distance. Resim (Resource Similarity) [15] is derived from LDSD, which satisfies several fundamental axioms of semantic similarity. We will explore these two classes of measures in CDRS to estimate their importance in cross-domain recommendation.

3   The Cross-Domain Recommendation Model

3.1   Overview

First, we introduce the cross-domain recommender system exploited in this work, based on LOD semantic correlation analysis. Figure 1 shows its overall architecture.

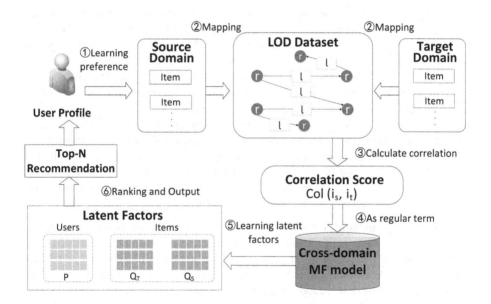

Fig. 1. Overview of the recommender architecture.

Considering a new user u, who has few interactions in the target domain, but has some historical records in the source (auxiliary) domain, the goal of the system is to learn his preferences and provide personalized recommendations in the target domain. First, we obtain the historical records of u from the source domain database, which represent his interests, and are denoted as $I(u) = \{i_1, i_2, \ldots\}$. Then these recorded items are mapped into the corresponding entities/resources in the LOD graph by SPARQL queries. In this work, we use DBpedia as the LOD dataset, which is a multi-domain repository providing semantic relations and structure-based Wikipedia knowledge representation. The resources in DBpedia are connected via a set of links identified by their URI. So we can obtain the correlation between different resources without domain restrictions. By using semantic similarity/relatedness calculation measures (as described in Sect. 3.2), we can obtain the correlation score between items from source and target domains, which is formulated as follows:

$$col_{ij} = col(i_S, i_T) \tag{1}$$

Next, the cross-domain matrix factorization (MF) models [5] use correlation scores as a regularization term to learn the feature vectors of users and items in the latent factor space. In Fig. 1, P, Q_S and Q_T are matrices containing the latent vectors as rows of users, source domain items, and target domain items, respectively. Finally, applying the user vector $p_u \in R^K$ and the target domain item vector $q_i \in R^K$, the model will output a Top-N recommendation list for user u.

3.2 Measuring Semantic Similarity/Relatedness Between LOD Entities

The primary problem faced by cross-domain recommendations is domain heterogeneity. This work solves this problem by using LOD datasets, which contain multi-domain knowledge. LOD is designed as a graph structure, and the resources in the graph structure are semantically connected by links. Denote the LOD graph as $G = (R, L, T)$, where R and L are sets of resources and links respectively. T is a set of triples, where $t = < l_k, r_i, r_j >$ represents a triple that resource r_i is connected to resource r_j by l_k.

After mapping the items from different domains to the corresponding LOD resources, we can link domains by calculating the correlation between the resources. Semantic correlation can be divided into two classes: similarity and relatedness. Similarity considers the common properties of resources to compare their resemblance. Relatedness analyzes the resource connectivity to measure the correlation between resources, and takes into account functional or lexical relations [11]. Next, we summarize several LOD-based semantic measures compared in our empirical study.

TF-IDF. [5] is a similarity measure that has been applied in recommender systems. Based on the metadata obtained from LOD, it compares the semantically enriched item profile established for each item. These metadata are some specific information related to the recommendation domain. For example, we select the genre relation (dbo: literaryGenre) in the book domain and the actor relation (dbo: starring) in the movie domain from DBpedia. The similarity between two items is calculated as the cosine similarity of their weighted TF-IDF vectors.

PICSS. [13] is a measure that combines feature-based and content-based approaches. PICSS defines an LOD resource as a set of its features, which are denoted by the triples related to the resource in LOD. The core idea of PICSS is to compare the similarity of different resources by the information content of features. Tversky ratio model [23] is employed to calculate the similarity between resources. This measure considers both the shared and different features between resources, and adjusts the contribution of features in the similarity calculation based on the information richness.

LDSD. [14] relies on the LOD relations to measure the correlation between resources. It is based on the idea: if the resources are connected closely by the links, their relatedness scores should be high. LDSD uses both direct and indirect links to calculate the resource correlation. Generally speaking, LDSD is a weighted measure designed to reduce the impact of the most popular links.

Resim. [15, 16] improved LDSD to satisfy the three fundamental axioms of similarity measures: "equal self-similarity", "symmetry", and "minimality".

Table 1 summarizes the above measures and compares the LOD information used.

Table 1. Summary of semantic measures.

Approach	LOD information		Type of correlation	
	Content	Links	Similarity	Relatedness
PICSS	✓		✓	
TF-IDF	✓		✓	
LDSD		✓		✓
Resim		✓		✓

3.3   Cross-Domain Matrix Factorization Model

To employ the cross-domain correlation to the recommendation algorithm, we choose to use cross-domain MF models [5], which jointly employ user records and item metadata to provides Top-N recommendations. The cross-domain MF models are based on iMF [8], and suitable for recommender systems with positive-only feedback. iMF automatically learns user and item latent factor by minimizing the loss function about the mean square error of the score prediction, as follows:

$$\mathcal{L}(\mathbf{P}, \mathbf{Q}) = \sum_{u} \sum_{i} c_{ui} \left(x_{ui} - \langle \mathbf{p}_u, \mathbf{q}_i \rangle \right)^2 + \lambda \left(\|\mathbf{P}\|^2 + \|\mathbf{Q}\|^2 \right) \tag{2}$$

where $\mathbf{P}$ and $\mathbf{Q}$ respectively represent two matrix containing the latent vectors of users and items. Let k_{ui} be the number of interactions between user u and item i. x_{ui} indicates user preferences, and $x_{ui} = 1$ when $k_{ui} > 0$, otherwise $x_{ui} = 0$. c_{ui} measures the confidence of the interaction, and is calculated by $c_{ui} = 1 + \alpha * k_{ui}$, where α is a scaling parameter.

Extending iMF to cross-domain recommender system, [5] proposed and verified the superior performance of NeighborMF and CentroidMF, which are based on different hypotheses about the relationship between the latent factors of the source and target domain items. Consider a group of users overlap between the domains, defined as $\mathbf{U} = \mathbf{U}_S \cup \mathbf{U}_T$. $\mathbf{I} = \mathbf{I}_S \cup \mathbf{I}_T$ represents the set of all items from source and target domain. These models aim to learn vectors in latent space, where $\mathbf{p}_u$ for $u \in \mathbf{U}$, $\mathbf{q}_i$ for $i \in \mathbf{I}_S$, and $\mathbf{q}_j$ for $j \in \mathbf{I}_T$. We apply them in our cross-domain recommendation framework.

NeighborMF is based on the hypothesis that the feature vectors of similar items should be closer to each other in the latent space. This hypothesis uses the correlation matrix **Col** to proportionally regularize the item latent vector using its source neighbor items. Accordingly, semantically correlated items should have similar potential parameters.

CentroidMF is based on the hypothesis that the latent vector of target item is closer to the centroid (average) of its neighbor items. It concerns additional consideration: When neighbor source items are vastly different, NeighborMF may have difficulty regularizing target items to approach all of its neighbor items simultaneously. Therefore, this model does not use neighbor source domain items individually in regularization, but the centroid approach to make the latent vector of item j close to the average of the latent vectors of $N(j)$.

4   Experiment

In this section, we first introduce the datasets, and then describe the simulation of the cold start scenario and the evaluation metrics. After that, we summarize the baseline methods for comparison with the evaluation metrics. We conduct a series of quantitative and qualitative analyses to compare the performance of different semantic measures, and verify the positive effect of the proposed cross-domain recommendation model.

4.1   Data Description

The experiments are conducted on the dataset provided by The Information Retrieval Group[1]. It contains the Facebook users' interaction records and the information of the relevant items. We take a two-step process on the original dataset. First, we filter out users and items with less than 10 interactions, which can alleviate data sparsity to achieve more precise performance [22]. Second, we further filter the items unable to be queried in DBpedia. Table 2 shows the details of the dataset.

Table 2. Statistics of the dataset.

Dataset	Users	Items	Interactions	Sparsity	Genres	Overlap users
Movies	57,008	5,383	1,495,145	99.51%	2,203	6231
Books	7,084	4,411	108,554	99.65%	1,034	

4.2   Evaluation Methodology and Metrics

We simulate the experience of new users in an offline environment [10]. In the beginning, we keep all the data in the source domain to the training data, and further split the data in the target domain. For splitting target data, the first step is to divide target

---

[1] http://ir.ii.uam.es/.

users into five equal-sized groups. In each fold of cross-validation, we keep four groups of data to the training data, while using the fifth group as test users. In the second step, we randomly select *ProfileSize* records of the test users as training data and the rest as test data. It aims to simulate a new user with only *ProfileSize* interactions in the target domain. In our experiments, we choose *ProfileSize* = 1 to simulate that the target user has only one historical record. Finally, the training set contains three types of data: all the data of source users, the data of the target training users, and the *ProfileSize* data of the target test user. The test data contains the records of test users, excluding the *ProfileSize* used for training.

We evaluate the performance of the experiment from two aspects: accuracy and diversity. For accuracy, we use the common metric *Mean Reciprocal Rank(MRR)*. For diversity, we use our proposed metric *WBinomDiv* that considers multiple diversity-related properties. *WBinomDiv* is proposed based on *BinomDiv* [24], which is defined by two sub-metrics using genre data:

$$BinomDiv(R) = Coverage(R) * NonRed(R)$$

where *Coverage* shows how well the recommended list covers the genres of user interest. *NonRed* represents the non-redundancy of the recommended list. If the recommended list over-represents a particular genre, *NonRed* will penalize the diversity score of the list. However, we found that *BinomDiv* is strongly influenced by the collected genre data, and the number of genres significantly relates to the difference of value range between the two sub-metrics. Suppose there are two recommendation list l_1 and l_2, we define this difference as:

$$Difference\,(l_1, l_2) = \left| \frac{Coverage\,(l_1) - Coverage\,(l_2)}{NonRed\,(l_1) - NonRed\,(l_2)} \right| \tag{3}$$

By changing the total number of genres, we calculate the diversity of these two lists. Figure 2 shows the relationship between the number of genres and *Difference*. We can observe a clear trend of decreasing showing a significant negative correlation: With the increase in the number of genres, the significant decrease recorded in *Difference* is far less than 1, indicating that the difference of value range between the two sub-metrics is not at the same magnitude.

To eliminate the bias caused by this different variable range, we define the improved diversity metric as *WBinomDiv*:

$$WBinomDiv(R) = \varphi_C(Coverage(R)) * \varphi_N(NonRed(R)) \tag{4}$$

where φ_C and φ_N are scaling functions, which are selected according to the number of genres. In our experiments, we choose $\varphi_C(x) = x$ and $\varphi_N(y) = e^{0.01*y}$.

4.3 Baselines and Parameter Settings

The baseline models compared in the experiments are summarized as follows:

- *Pop*: This non-personalized method only considers the popularity of the item. Popularity is defined by the number of user-inspired behaviors (such as likes and ratings) on items. We randomly selected 10 items out of the Top-30 Popularity as the recommendations.

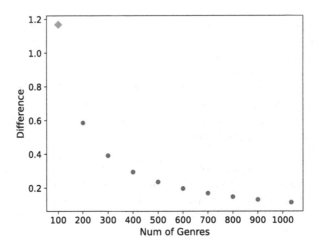

Fig. 2. *Difference* for different number of genres.

- *UserCF*: The User-based Collaborative Filtering method makes recommendations based on the interests of the target user and neighbor users. We choose Jaccard similarity to get neighbor users.
- *ItemCF*: Item-based Collaborative Filtering uses the user's historical behavior to recommend similar items that they have expressed interest in before. Jaccard similarity is used to obtain similar items.
- *iMF* [8]: This is a representative matrix factorization algorithm for implicit feedback data. It considers all user-item pairs, including those with no interaction records.
- *BPR* [18]: Bayesian Personalized Ranking is a representative personalized learn-to-ranking framework. It focuses on the user's rating difference for different items. We used the method implemented by LibRec [6].
- *KGAT* [26]: Knowledge Graph Attention Network (KGAT) is a single-domain recommendation framework based on knowledge graph and attention mechanism. It directly models the high order relations between users and items with embedding propagation.

We also train the model of *UserCF/ItemCF/iMF* in cross-domain scenarios, and use the prefix *CD-* to indicate these cross-domain versions.

In the parameter setting, we refer to the optimal parameters published by [5,6] and [26]. For *UserCF*, the number of neighborhoods is set to 50. For *iMF*, the latent feature number is fixed at 10, the regularization is 10^{-5}, and the learning rate is 6. For *BPR*, the learning rate and regularization are both set to 0.01, and the factor number is 10. For *KGAT*, the learning rate 0.0001, the node dropout ratio 0.1, the layers size are [64,32,16], and the embedding size is 64. Besides, Table 3 shows the parameter settings for the cross-domain MF models.

Table 3. Parameter setting for cross-doamin MF models.

Method	K	λ	α	λ_c	N	Norm
NeighborMF	14	1	1	1	80	TRUE
CentroidMF	14	0.1	1	0.5	10	TRUE

4.4 Performance Comparison on Semantic Measures

We first compare the performance of the chosen semantic similarity (*TF-IDF* and *PICSS*) and relatedness (*Resim* and *LDSD*) calculation measures on cross-domain MF models. Besides, we set *Random* measure as a baseline, which contains correlation scores generated randomly from 0 to 1.

Figure 3 shows accuracy and diversity results obtained with the different correlation measures. First, what stands out in Fig. 3(a) is that PICSS has achieved the best accuracy on the two MFs. On NeighborMF, the relative improvements are 0.2% (TF-IDF), 0.6% (LDSD), and 5.5% (Resim); on CentroidMF, the improvements are 0.1% (TF-IDF), 0.2% (LDSD), 0.1% (Resim). TF-IDF and LDSD showed sub-optimal performance. Surprisingly, Resim is observed to perform very poorly on NeighborMF, even if it is improved based on LDSD. A possible explanation may be that Resim aims to ensure "minimality", so it further distinguishes the relevance between resources. However, the weakness of NeighborMF is that when neighbor source domain items are mutually diverse, the regularization of NeighborMF may be difficult to achieve the desired effect. Finally, it shows that all correlation measures outperformed significantly *Random* measure (except NeighborMF). Figure 3(b) shows the diversity results. First, it is intuitive that *Random* method shows better performance than other measures on both MFs. Secondly, it is apparent from the chart that the diversity of LDSD is higher than the other measures. TF-IDF has a less effective effect, and PICSS and Resim show moderate diversity. It is worth noting that the PICSS on NeighborMF has the highest accuracy, but the lower diversity. It is almost certainly a trade-off between accuracy and diversity.

These results provide important insights into further analysis of similarity and relatedness measures. The comparison in MRR reveals similarity (PICSS and TF-IDF) can provide more accurate recommendations than relatedness measures (Resim and LDSD). There are several reasonable explanations for this result. Similarity mainly regards the LOD content data. The main idea is that resources with more shared features are more similar. While relatedness singly relying on the resource connectivity may not always reflect the actual similarity between resources. Therefore, resources with high similarity can be substitutes for each other, but related resources may not. On the other hand, *WBinomDiv* result presents the average performance of relatedness is superior to similarity in diversity. This result can be explained as relatedness pays more attention to the links connections, so it is more likely to choose LOD resources with various descriptions.

We introduce a case study from the experiment to further illustrate the results (as shown in Fig. 4). The selected user has expressed interest in *HarryPotter* book, the system recommends the *Harry Potter* series of movies by semantic similarity. While the relevance of works selected by the relatedness may be latent. For example, relatedness between *How to Train Your Dragon* and *Harry Potter* mainly depends on the common

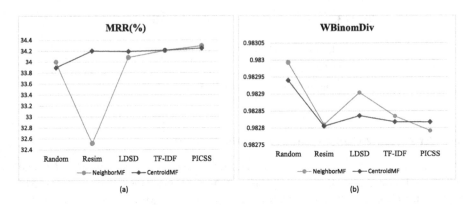

Fig. 3. Performances of the different correlation measures in accuracy and diversity. (a) shows the comparison on metric MRR and (b) shows the comparison on WBinomDiv.

cultural element of "Dragon". The result may exactly match old users, who expect to watch other enjoyable movies. Here we propose a suggestion that the recommendation system can choose certain correlation measures according to the length of time the user has settled. For new users, accurate prediction with similarity can make them quickly settle down in the system; while old users may need more serendipitous items, so switching to relatedness will improve satisfaction.

For the comparison of the next experiment, we evaluate the comprehensive performance of measures using *TradeOff*:

$$TradeOff(m) = \frac{MRR(m)}{avg\_MRR} + \frac{WBinomDiv(m)}{avg\_WBinomDiv} \tag{5}$$

Table 4 shows *TradeOff* of different measures. We can observe that PICSS is outstanding on both NeighborMF and CentroidMF. We will experiment with these two methods in the next session, and denote them as NeighborMF-PICSS and CentroidMF-PICSS.

Table 4. Trade-off between accuracy and diversity of different methods

Method	PICSS	TF-IDF	LDSD	Resim	Random
NeighborMF	**2.0088**	2.0063	2.0027	1.9565	2.0026
CentroidMF	**2.0075**	2.0064	2.0057	2.0060	1.9970

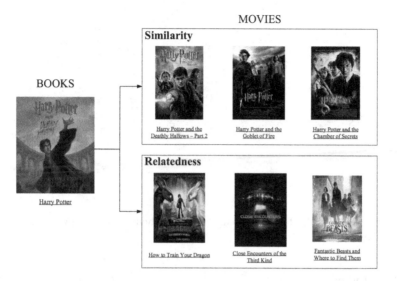

Fig. 4. A case study that shows the difference between similarity and relatedness measures, finding the most related MOVIES for the user based on their interests in the BOOKS domain.

4.5 Performance Comparison on Recommendation Algorithms

Figure 5 shows the accuracy and diversity of different recommendation methods. First, we point out the incomplete recommendations of *UserCF* and *CD-UserCF*. Although the effect of *UserCF* is better than *CD-UserCF*, the former can only provide recommendations for 54.2% of users on average, while the latter can provide 79.2% of users. The rest of the methods can generate results for 100% of users. We can see that compared to the single-domain methods (*ItemCF/UserCF/iMF*), their cross-domain versions perform better. At the same time, the results show that the single-domain recommendation methods *BPR* and *KGAT* perform poorly, which also proves the effectiveness of the cross-domain method in solving the cold start problem. Secondly, NeighborMF-PICSS and CentroidMF-PICSS are superior in accuracy and diversity compared to other methods. The reason is MF-Correlation method employs an external knowledge base to calculate the correlation of cross-domain items, and then uses the correlation as the regularization of the joint MF, which helps to generate more precise user vectors. In this way, the model can accurately and broadly capture user interests, even if there are only a few interaction records in the target domain. Overall, the experiment proves the effectiveness of MF-Correlation.

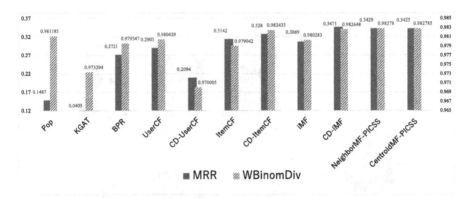

Fig. 5. Performances of the different recommendation methods in accuracy(MRR) and diversity (WBinomDiv)

5   Conclusions

The purpose of this study is to explore the relationship between LOD-based inter-domain correlation and user interests. From the perspective of accuracy and diversity, we studied the performance of different correlation measures in a cross-domain recommendation framework. In the new user scenario simulated by a real dataset, it is proved that the similarity measures can bring higher accuracy and the relatedness measures have a positive contribution to diversity. Besides, the comparison of different recommendation methods demonstrates the effectiveness of the proposed methods. The insights gained from this study may contribute to the design of a dynamic recommender system, which adopts different strategies for different users according to User Active Time. New users gain trust from recommendations calculated by the similarity measures, as it accurately captures users' preferences, thereby increasing user engagement in the system. After a period, the system can switch to relatedness measures to provide diverse items to stimulate the user's interest.

References

1. Azak, M., Birturk, A.: Crossing framework a dynamic infrastructure to develop knowledge-based recommenders in cross domains. In: Proceedings of the 6th International Conference on Web Information Systems and Technologies, pp. 125–130 (2010)
2. Bizer, C., Heath, T., Berners-Lee, T.: Linked data: The story so far. In: Semantic services, interoperability and web applications: emerging concepts, pp. 205–227. IGI global (2011)
3. Chung, R., Sundaram, D., Srinivasan, A.: Integrated personal recommender systems. In: Proceedings of the Ninth International Conference on Electronic Commerce, pp. 65–74 (2007)
4. Fernández-Tobías, I., Cantador, I., Kaminskas, M., Ricci, F.: A generic semantic-based framework for cross-domain recommendation. In: Proceedings of the 2nd International Workshop on Information Heterogeneity and Fusion in Recommender Systems, pp. 25–32 (2011)

5. Fernández-Tobías, I., Cantador, I., Tomeo, P., Anelli, V.W., Di Noia, T.: Addressing the user cold start with cross-domain collaborative filtering: exploiting item metadata in matrix factorization. User Model. User-Adap. Inter. **29**(2), 443–486 (2019)
6. Guo, G., Zhang, J., Sun, Z., Yorke-Smith, N.: Librec: a java library for recommender systems. In: UMAP Workshops, vol. 4. Citeseer (2015)
7. Hu, L., Cao, J., Xu, G., Cao, L., Gu, Z., Zhu, C.: Personalized recommendation via cross-domain triadic factorization. In: Proceedings of the 22nd International Conference on World Wide Web, pp. 595–606 (2013)
8. Hu, Y., Koren, Y., Volinsky, C.: Collaborative filtering for implicit feedback datasets. In: 2008 Eighth IEEE International Conference on Data Mining, pp. 263–272. IEEE (2008)
9. Jayaratne, L.: Content based cross-domain recommendation using linked open data. GSTF J. Comput. **5**(3), 7–15 (2017)
10. Kluver, D., Konstan, J.A.: Evaluating recommender behavior for new users. In: Proceedings of the 8th ACM Conference on Recommender Systems, pp. 121–128 (2014)
11. Likavec, S., Osborne, F., Cena, F.: Property-based semantic similarity and relatedness for improving recommendation accuracy and diversity. Int. J. Seman. Web Inf. Syst. (IJSWIS) **11**(4), 1–40 (2015)
12. Loizou, A.: How to recommend music to film buffs: enabling the provision of recommendations from multiple domains. Ph.D. thesis, University of Southampton (2009)
13. Meymandpour, R., Davis, J.G.: A semantic similarity measure for linked data: an information content-based approach. Knowl.-Based Syst. **109**, 276–293 (2016)
14. Passant, A.: Measuring semantic distance on linking data and using it for resources recommendations. In: AAAI Spring Symposium: Linked Data Meets Artificial Intelligence, vol. 77, p. 123 (2010)
15. Piao, G., Ara, S., Breslin, J.G.: Computing the semantic similarity of resources in DBpedia for recommendation purposes. In: Qi, G., Kozaki, K., Pan, J.Z., Yu, S. (eds.) JIST 2015. LNCS, vol. 9544, pp. 185–200. Springer, Cham (2016). https://doi.org/10.1007/978-3-319-31676-5_13
16. Piao, G., Breslin, J.G.: Measuring semantic distance for linked open data-enabled recommender systems. In: Proceedings of the 31st Annual ACM Symposium on Applied Computing, pp. 315–320 (2016)
17. Ren, S., Gao, S., Liao, J., Guo, J.: Improving cross-domain recommendation through probabilistic cluster-level latent factor model. In: Proceedings of the AAAI Conference on Artificial Intelligence (2015)
18. Rendle, S., Freudenthaler, C., Gantner, Z., Schmidt-Thieme, L.: Bpr: Bayesian personalized ranking from implicit feedback. arXiv preprint arXiv:1205.2618 (2012)
19. Sansonetti, G., Gasparetti, F., Micarelli, A.: Cross-domain recommendation for enhancing cultural heritage experience. In: Adjunct Publication of the 27th Conference on User Modeling, Adaptation and Personalization, pp. 413–415. UMAP 2019 Adjunct, Association for Computing Machinery, New York (2019)
20. Shi, Y., Larson, M., Hanjalic, A.: Tags as bridges between domains: improving recommendation with tag-induced cross-domain collaborative filtering. In: Konstan, J.A., Conejo, R., Marzo, J.L., Oliver, N. (eds.) UMAP 2011. LNCS, vol. 6787, pp. 305–316. Springer, Heidelberg (2011). https://doi.org/10.1007/978-3-642-22362-4_26
21. Singh, A.P., Gordon, G.J.: Relational learning via collective matrix factorization. In: Proceedings of the 14th ACM SIGKDD International Conference on Knowledge Discovery and Data Mining, pp. 650–658 (2008)
22. Sun, Z., et al.: Are we evaluating rigorously? benchmarking recommendation for reproducible evaluation and fair comparison. In: Fourteenth ACM Conference on Recommender Systems, pp. 23–32 (2020)

23. Tversky, A.: Features of similarity. Psychol. Rev. **84**(4), 327 (1977)
24. Vargas, S., Baltrunas, L., Karatzoglou, A., Castells, P.: Coverage, redundancy and size-awareness in genre diversity for recommender systems. In: Proceedings of the 8th ACM Conference on Recommender Systems, pp. 209–216 (2014)
25. Vargas, S., Castells, P.: Rank and relevance in novelty and diversity metrics for recommender systems. In: Proceedings of the fifth ACM Conference on Recommender Systems, pp. 109–116 (2011)
26. Wang, X., He, X., Cao, Y., Liu, M., Chua, T.S.: Kgat: knowledge graph attention network for recommendation. In: Proceedings of the 25th ACM SIGKDD International Conference on Knowledge Discovery & Data Mining, pp. 950–958 (2019)
27. Ziegler, C.N., McNee, S.M., Konstan, J.A., Lausen, G.: Improving recommendation lists through topic diversification. In: Proceedings of the 14th International Conference on World Wide Web, pp. 22–32 (2005)

Community Enhanced Course Concept Recommendation in MOOCs with Multiple Entities

Binglong Ye[1], Shengyu Mao[1], Pengyi Hao[1(✉)], Wei Chen[2], and Cong Bai[1]

[1] School of Computer Science and Technology, Zhejiang University of Technology, Hangzhou, China
haopy@zjut.edu.cn
[2] State Key Lab of CAD&CG, Zhejiang University, Hangzhou 310058, China

Abstract. Massive Open Online Courses (MOOCs) are becoming a new way of education in the world, providing people with a large number of open courses to facilitate their access to knowledge. However, there are many courses and different course focuses influence people's choice, which reduces the enthusiasm of online learning. To fill this gap, course concept recommendation is researched to help people better access the courses they are interested in. In this paper, we propose community enhanced course concept recommendation with multiple entities (CERec-ME). A series of heterogeneous graphs of multiple entities (e.g., users, videos, teachers, courses, concepts) in MOOCs are constructed based on meta-paths that are defined as the relationships among entities. Under different meta-paths, a set of feature representations for users and concepts are generated respectively by using graph convolutional networks (GCN). In order to extract more reasonable node representations from neighborhood nodes in a GCN, a high-level semantic of graph is explored by defining community structure and measuring the similarities of nodes in the community. The CERec-ME is an end-to-end framework. The parameters in CERec-ME are optimized through a novel loss function which is able to consider information about the community structure along with information about the node neighborhoods. Experiments are conducted on two public real-world datasets XuetangX and MOOCCube, showing that CERec-ME is more effective for knowledge concept recommendation compared with state-of-the-art baseline methods.

Keywords: Course concept recommendations · Graph convolutional networks · Community analysis · Moocs · Graph embedding

1 Introduction

MOOCs have become very popular among students [9]. MOOCs have revolutionized the entire field of education by opening online resources to the world and providing new educational opportunities [21]. This new form of online learning has been described as an extension of e-learning and distance education [1].

H. Qiu et al. (Eds.): KSEM 2021, LNAI 12816, pp. 279–293, 2021.
https://doi.org/10.1007/978-3-030-82147-0_23

Most universities have adopted online education, especially in 2020, when the epidemic is severe. So it can be predicted that MOOCs will remain important for learning in all fields in the coming years.

Although the size of MOOCs and the number of students are increasing, MOOCs still have some difficulties. (i) In the course videos of MOOCs, there are often a large number of course concepts that require prerequisite courses. Students do not understand these concepts and do not know which prerequisite courses they need to take [13]. (ii) The content and focus of courses in the same category in MOOCs vary, for example, in the course of advanced mathematics, some courses focus on geometry and some courses focus on calculus [3]. These problems do not attract students to continue learning efficiently on the platform, resulting in low course completion rate [20]. Therefore, MOOCs need to better understand and capture students' interests and recommend more appropriate courses for them, which is the purpose of course recommendation.

Course recommendation methods can be divided into two categories: (i) one is collaborative filtering (CF) based recommendation, which considers the course selection behavior of the target user and finds out the course selection behavior of similar users and predicts the target user's rating of the corresponding course [14,16], or considers the target user's rating of certain courses and then predicts similar courses with high similarity. These methods suffer from the problem of sparsity, which limits the recommended performance. (ii) Another is graph-based approaches, which considers various entities in MOOCs, forms a graph based on the connections among them, then learns the graph representation of each entity, and finally use matrix factorization to make course recommendations [3,22]. However, the common graph representation may aggregate some unuseful neighbor information on the current node, resulting in less accurate node representation, therefore, the results of recommendation are not satisfied.

Here, we introduce the concept of community structure [12] to compensate for the shortcomings of graph representation. In this paper, we propose Community Enhanced Course concept Recommendation in MOOCs with Multiple Entities (CERec-ME), which is an end-to-end framework. We use meta-paths as guides to capture information in heterogeneous graphs and learn the node representation of users and course concept on the graph by graph convolutional network. To make the node representation of entities more complete, we add modularity that can measure the strength of community structure to the graph convolutional network to maintain community information. Here, we consider the modularity and node representations in a loss function as a way to make it possible to update the node representation while taking into account the community structure information. Finally, we take into account the node representation of users and course concepts in the matrix factorization to obtain the rating matrix, and optimize the parameters by a new loss function to obtain the final recommendation list. The main contributions of this paper can be summarized as follows: (i) We propose a new loss function for taking the community structure information of the graph into account in the node representation of the graph. This results in a more complete representation of the nodes. (ii) We conducted extensive experimental studies using two public datasets collected from the real world in order to fully evaluate the performance of the proposed model. The effectiveness of the present method is demonstrated compared to a series of baseline methods.

2   Related Works

Collaborative Filtering based methods, consider the similarity between users or the similarity between courses. Tan et al. proposed an association rule-based recommendation to calculate the similarity between users [16]. Kabbur et al. proposed the factored item similarity models (FISM), which used the product of two low-dimensional latent factor matrices to represent the item-item similarity matrix [8]. Pang et al. proposed a multi-layer bucketing recommendation (MLBR) method, which used Jaccard distance to describe the similarity between two learners [14]. He et al. proposed a neural attention item similarity model (NAIS) for item-based CF. The key was an attention network that distinguishes which history items in a user's profile are more important for prediction [5]. He et al. proposed a neural network based collaborative filtering (NCF), which can express and generalize matrix factorization in its framework and use a multi-lyer prceptron to learn the user-item interaction function [6]. Elbadrawy and Karypis introduced matrix factorization (MF) into course recommendation and proposed a neighborhood-based collaborative filtering method for users [2]. This MF-based approach was improved by Thanh Nhan et al. who used a collaborative filtering method based on k nearest neighbors (kNN) to improve the performance of matrix factorization [17]. However, in the face of a large number of users and items, it is easy to cause the sparsity problem of the user-item matrix, because it is impossible for users to have a rating for all items.

Graph Based Methods. MOOCs platform contains a series of entities (course, video, user, etc.) and relationships (course-user, course-video, etc.), which can form a graph-structured entity relationship network. Zhu et al. constructed the graph structure with information about students, courses, and students' ratings of courses, and used a random walk-based approach to learn the vectorized representation of student entities, finally used a matrix factorization-based approach to predict students' ratings of courses [22]. Gong et al. proposed a method using Graph Convolutional Network(GCN), which constructs different entity types in MOOCs into the network and learns graph representations of entities through meta-paths thereby capturing contextual information. [3]. Wang et al. proposed a graph neural network based approach and employed two aggregation methods to handle the user's sequence neighbors [18]. However, these graph-based methods suffer from incomplete graph representation of entities and therefore affect the performance of recommendations.

3   Proposed Method

3.1   Problem Statement

The goal is to output scores of a series of course concepts for a user and then get a recommendation list - the top N highest scoring courses. More formally,

Table 1. Notations and descriptions

Notation	Descriptions	Notation	Descriptions
MP	Set of meta-path	A_{MP}	Set of adjacency matrix Corresponding to the meta-path
F^u	The content feature of user entities	F^k	The content feature of course of course concept entities
A	The adjacency matrix	$\tilde{D}$	The degree matrix
h^l	l-th layer of entity representation	W^l	Weights of l-th GCN layer
$e^u_{MP_m}$	The representation of user entities on the m-th meta-path	$e^k_{MP_m}$	The representation of course concept entities on the m-th meta-path
E^u	The final representation of user entities	E^k	The final representation of course concept entities
δ	The hyperparameter that controls the impact of community structure	x_u	The latent factor of user u
y_k	The latent factor of course concept k	t_u, t_k	The matrix to ensure the E^u and E^k in the same space
z	Denotes the number of meta-path	$\hat{r}_{u,k}$	The predicted rating of user u to course concept k
$r_{u,k}$	The true rating of user u to course concept k	β_u, β_k	The turning parameter
n_1, n_2	The matrix dimension	d_1, d_2, D	The matrix dimension

given multiple types of data X = user (U), course (C), video (V), teacher (T), course concept (K), a prediction function f is used to learn and then generate a recommendation list Y for the target user's course concept K (e.g., Python, Python crawler, etc.), $f : X \to Y = \{k_j | k_j \in K, j < N\}$. The notations used in this paper are shown in Table 1.

3.2   Entity Content Description and Extraction

In general, the names of course concepts are almost generalizations of course concepts (e.g., Python, Python crawler, C++, binary tree, chain table, etc.), and they contain rich semantic information. Therefore, we generated word embeddings for each course concept and treated it as a content feature. We compose a corpus of different course concepts with the size of n_1, and construct a two-dimensional matrix in the form of one-hot encoding, where each row represents a course concept and each column has a value of 0 or 1. The two-dimensional matrix formed by the corpus of course concepts has the size of $n_1 \times n_1$, which is then passed through a $n_1 \times d_1$ neural network for dimensionality reduction, to obtain the content features $F^k \in \mathbb{R}^{n_1 \times d_1}$ of the course concepts. d_1 denotes the dimension after dimensionality reduction, $d_1 < n_1$. Specifically, we use Word2vecotr [11] to generate word embeddings. Similarly, for users, we generate their content features $F^u \in \mathbb{R}^{n_2 \times d_2}$ in the same way.

3.3   Meta-path Based Entity Relationship Extraction

Using the word vector of course concepts as content features can represent the information of course concepts well. In addition there is rich contextual information in MOOCs, such as relationships between multiple entities (e.g. user:001 watched video:v_002 and video:v_010, which were created by teacher:t_003; this behavior indicates that these two videos are connected). Considering the need to describe multiple entities and their complex relationships in a suitable way, we construct a heterogeneous graph to describe users, course concepts and their corresponding heterogeneous relationships.

A heterogeneous graph [15] can be defined as a $G = \{V, E\}$, V and E are sets of nodes and edges of multiple entity types, respectively, and the type of nodes + the type of edges >2. In this study, a heterogeneous graph includes five entity types (e.g., user (U), course (C), video (V), teacher (T), and course concept (K). Followed by [3], the relationships between $\{U, C, V, T\}$ are described as: (1) The adjacency matrix of course concepts clicked by the user. When user i clicked course concept j in his learning process, the corresponding value in this matrix is 1, otherwise, 0. (2) The adjacency matrix where the user has learned the course. If the user i is learning the course j, its corresponding value in this matrix is 1, otherwise, 0. (3) The adjacency matrix where the user has watched the video. If the user i has watched the video j, the corresponding value in this matrix is 1, otherwise, 0. (4) The adjacency matrix where the user has studied the course of a certain teacher. If the user i has studied the course taught by a certain teacher j, the corresponding value in this matrix is 1, otherwise, 0.

Meta-paths [4] are used to describe composite relationships between multiple entities in a heterogeneous graph. A typical meta-path between two users can be described as $U \xrightarrow{click} K \xrightarrow{click^{-1}} U$, which indicates that two different users are related because they clicked on the same course concept. $U \xrightarrow{learn} C \xrightarrow{taught\ by} T \xrightarrow{taught\ by^{-1}} C \xrightarrow{learn^{-1}} U$, which indicates that two users are related by paths containing different courses taught by the same teacher. It can be noted that in the heterogeneous graph, the potential meta-paths can be infinite, but not all of them are related to the target task. Therefore, we design the required meta-paths from the heterogeneous graph and obtain the set of meta-paths $MP = \{MP_1, MP_2, MP_3...MP_z\}$, z denotes the number of meta-paths. According to the obtained meta-paths, all related entities are connected on the heterogeneous graph to obtain subgraphs, and the adjacency matrix of meta-paths is formed according to the subgraphs, and the values in the matrix

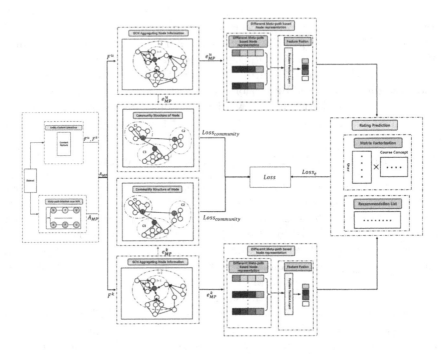

Fig. 1. The overall framework of CERec-ME.

are the entity relationship weights corresponding to the edges between two entities, and repeat the above operation until all adjacency matrices are obtained
$A_{MP} = \{A_{MP_1}, A_{MP_2}, A_{MP_3} \cdots A_{MP_z}\}$.

3.4 Community Enhanced Course Concept Recommendation

After obtaining the content features F^k, F^u and the adjacency matrix set A_{MP},
we put them into the graph convolutional neural network to learn the potential
entity representations. The whole system structure is given in Fig. 1. It mainly
includes entity representation and community structure, whole feature representation under a set of meta-paths, and rating prediction, which is an end-to-end
framework with three loss functions. We employ the graph convolutional network
layers as follows:

$$h^{l+1} = \sigma\left(\left(Ph^l\right)W^l\right) \tag{1}$$

h^{l+1} represents the node representation of an entity. In particular, h^0 is the input
we provide at the beginning, and in addition we provide the adjacency matrix
A, where A is one of the A_{MP}. $P = \tilde{D}^{-1/2}\tilde{A}\tilde{D}^{-1/2}$, $\tilde{A} = A + I$, which represents
the adjacency matrix A plus its identity matrix I, $\tilde{D} = diag\left(\tilde{A}\mathbf{1}\right)$, $\mathbf{1}$ is the
all-ones vector, $\tilde{D}_{i,i} = \sum_j \tilde{A}_{i,j}$. Also $\sigma(\cdot)$ denotes the activation function, where
$ReLU(\cdot) = max\{0, \cdot\}$. l denotes the lth layer of graph convolution. W^l is the

trainable shared weight matrix of the l-th layer. The information of neighboring nodes is aggregated through a graph convolution layer, and the node representation of the course concept entity obtained after three layers graph convolutional layer, it can be shown as

$$e^k = ReLU\left(\left(Ph^2\right)W^2\right) \tag{2}$$

Similarly, we let F^u go through the above graph convolutional network with three layers and get user representation e^u.

However, the above process ignores the measurement of community structure and cannot consider the relationship between communities. Community structure is the high-level semantic of graph. The connections between nodes in a community are dense, and the connections between nodes in different communities are sparse. Therefore, the representation of nodes in the same community should be more similar than nodes belonging to different communities [10]. For example, courses in the same category should be more closely connected to each other and courses in different categories should be more distant from each other. When making course recommendations, courses that are similar are more likely to be recommended. Therefore, to make the graph representation of entities more complete, we introduce modularity that can measure the strength of community structure and merge it into a unified loss function for optimization. Modularity is a measure of the strength of community structures [12], by defining the modularity matrix $B \in \mathbb{R}^{n \times n}$, where $B_{ij} = A_{ij} - k_i k_j / 2r$. A_{ij} denotes the weight of the edges between node i and node j, k_i and k_j denote the degree of the two nodes respectively, and r denotes the total number of edges in this network. Modularity actually measures the difference between the number of edges within a community and the expected number of edges in an equivalent random network. Finally to obtain the community information, we define the following loss function:

$$Loss_{com_k} = 1/(2r)e^{k\,T}B\,e^k \tag{3}$$

When the value of $Loss_{com_k}$ is larger, the strength of the community structure is stronger, which indicates the quality of community division is better. Similarly, we can obtain $Loss_{com_u}$.

Since each meta-path corresponds to an adjacency matrix, we repeat the above steps to obtain $e^k_{MP} = \left\{e^k_{MP_1}, e^k_{MP_2}, ..., e^k_{MP_z}\right\}$ and $e^u_{MP} = \left\{e^u_{MP_1}, e^u_{MP_2}, ..., e^u_{MP_z}\right\}$. They correspond to the representation of nodes under different meta-paths.

However, different users have different preferences in MOOCs, some prefer certain teachers' classes and some prefer certain types of videos, so the same user may have stronger performance under one meta-path relationship but weaker performance under another meta-path relationship. So we use a fusion method that allows it to focus on entity representation under other meta-paths when generating fusion weights. This leads to better recommendation rating of course concepts through potential connection information among users. The formula

Algorithm 1. Generating the representations of course concept entities

---

Input: the given adjacency matrix set A_{MP};
the content feature matrix F^k of course concept entities.
Parameter: Optional list of parameters
Output: The final node representations of course concept entities E^k.

1: Let $e_{MP}^k = \{\}$;
2: **for** each $A_{MP_1} \in A_{MP}$ **do**
3:     Calculate $\tilde{A}, \tilde{D}, P$ according to Formula 1;
4:     Let $h^0 \Leftarrow F^k$;
5:     Calculate h^1 by Formula 1;
6:     Calculate h^2 by Formula 1;
7:     Calculate e^k by Formula 2;
8:     Add e^k to e_{MP}^k;
9:     Calculate $Loss_{com_k}$ by Formula 3;
10: **end for**
11: **for** each $e_{MP_i}^k \in e_{MP}^k$ **do**
12:     Calculate $\alpha_{MP_i}^k$ by Formula 5;
13: **end for**
14: Generate E^k by Formula 4;
15: **return** E^k.

---

for the final entity representation is defined as:

$$E^k = \sum_{i=1}^{z} \alpha_{MP_i}^k e_{MP_i}^k \qquad (4)$$

where $\alpha_{MP_i}^k$ is the attention weight under each meta-path and E^k is the final entity representation of course concept. For each meta-path, a second attention object is created for it, which is used to simultaneously associate information on other meta-paths to generate more appropriate attention weights, as follows.

$$\alpha_{MP_i}^k = softmax(v(tanh(w_1 e_{MP_i}^k \gamma + w_2 u_{MP_i}(1-\gamma) + b))) \qquad (5)$$

Where $u_{MP_i} = \left(\sum_{j \neq i}^{z} e_{MP_j}^k \right) / (z-1)$ is the second attention object generated under the ith meta-path, $e_{MP_j}^k$ is the entity representation under the associated other meta-paths, γ is a hyperparameter to control the ratio of the attention of the entity under the current meta-path to the second entity generated when generating the attention weights, and v, w_1, w_2, b are trainable parameters. The weight scoring is generated by a $tanh()$ function and finally normalized by a $softmax$ function to obtain the weight representation of each meta-path. Similarly, we can obtain E^u. The algorithm of obtaining entity representation is given in Algorithm 1 by taking E^k as an example.

Based on the course concept representation E^k and the user representation E^u, we use an extended matrix factorization approach to make course concept recommendations for users. We treat the number of times that a user clicks on a course concept as a rating matrix. According to the matrix factorization, it needs to decompose the rating matrix into two low-order matrices $\hat{r}_{u,k} = x_u^T y_k$, the potential factors $x_u \in \mathbb{R}^{D \times n_2}$ and $y_k \in \mathbb{R}^{D \times n_1}$ of the user and the low-dimensional features of the course concept, where D is the dimension of the potential factors x_u and y_k, $D < n_1$, and $D < n_2$. The user entity E^u and the course concept entity E^k are put into the prediction rating matrix,

$$\hat{r}_{u,k} = x_u^T y_k + \beta_u \cdot E^u{}^T t_k + \beta_k \cdot t_k^T E^k \tag{6}$$

where the trainable parameters t_k, t_u are used to ensure that E^u, E^k are in the same dimensional space and β_u, β_k are tuning parameters. In order to obtain the appropriate score prediction, we minimize the optimization function of matrix factorization to tune the potential factors x_u and y_k for the low-dimensional features of user and course concepts, and finally obtain the rating matrix $\hat{r}_{u,k}$ with the following optimization function.

$$Loss_e = \overset{min}{U, K} \sum_{u=1}^{n_2} \sum_{k=1}^{n_1} (r_{u,k} - \hat{r}_{u,k})^2 / (n_1 \times n_2) \tag{7}$$

Combined with the loss about the community structure $Loss_{com_k}$ and $Loss_{com_e}$, the final optimized loss function is as follows.

$$Loss = Loss_e + \delta(Loss_{com_k} + Loss_{com_e}) \tag{8}$$

In this way, community structure information and neighborhood information are merged into a unified loss function. δ is a hyperparameter to control the effect of community structure on node representation. Finally, each user's course concepts are sorted from the largest to the smallest according to the rating matrix, and the top K courses are recommended to the user.

4   Experiments

4.1   Datasets

To validate the effectiveness of the proposed method, we use two datasets. (i) Dataset 1: We use real data from the XuetangX MOOC platform. This dataset package treats students' course selection behaviors from October 1st, 2016 to December 30th, 2017 as the training set. It treats students' course selection behaviors on January 1st, 2018 and March 31st, 2018 as the test set. It contains 9,986 MOOC courses, 43,405 videos, 1,029 course concepts, and 9,986 real MOOC users. In addition, the dataset includes relationships such as user-course, course-video, course-course concept, etc. (2) Dataset 2: MOOCCube [19] contains 706 MOOC courses, 38,181 videos, 114,563 course concepts, and 199,199 real MOOC users. The data source also contains a large-scale concept map and related academic papers as a resource for further exploitation. The concept map information was obtained from Baidubaike, Wikipedia, and Termonline. The data on courses and student activities were obtained from the real environment of XuetangX. The Academic resources were provided by Aminer, an academic project that provides a comprehensive search and mining service for researchers' social networks. These data went through three stages of automated filtering, crowdsourced annotation and expert annotation to form the MOOCCube.

4.2   Evaluation Metrics

The common metrics are used to evaluate all the methods. Hit Ratio of top-K items (HR@K) is a recall-based metric that indicates the percentage of top-k items in all courses of the test set that interact with the user. NDCG@K(Normalized Discounted Cumulative Gain) [7] is a precision-based metric that evaluates the difference between the ranked list and the real interaction list of the user, $NDCG@K = 1/Z \sum_{i=1}^{K}((2^{r_i} - 1)/(\log_2(i+1)))$, where Z denotes the normalization factor and r_i denotes the ith item of the recommendation list. If the item at that position is in the user's real list, r_i is 1, otherwise it is 0. The MRR(Mean Reciprocal Rank) [5] is defined as, $MRR = 1/rank_i$, where $rank_i$ denotes the rank position of the first recommended course for the i-th user in the ground-truth list. In addition, the AUC (Area Under Curve) below the ROC (Receiver Operating Characteristic) curve is also used. In the following experiments, we calculate each metric for each user, then take the average of all the users in the test.

4.3   Evaluation of Different Meta-paths Combinations

In this section, we analyze the performance of the model under different meta-paths combinations. For dataset 1, we design four kinds of meta-paths, including, $MP_1 : U \to K \xrightarrow{-1} U$, $MP_2 : U \to C \xrightarrow{-1} U$, $MP_3 : U \to V \xrightarrow{-1} U$, $MP_4 : U \to C \to T \xrightarrow{-1} C \xrightarrow{-1} U$. The effect of the combination under different meta-paths is shown in Table 2. For dataset 2, we design two meta-paths, including $MP_2 : U \to C \xrightarrow{-1} U$, $MP_3 : U \to V \xrightarrow{-1} U$. The results are shown in Table 3.

We can see that in the two datasets, the individual meta-paths show different effects. In dataset 1, the effect ranking is $MP_3 > MP_1 > MP_2 > MP_4$, and in dataset 2, the effect ranking is $MP_3 > MP_2$. The combination of multiple meta-paths has better effect than using single meta-path. In dataset 1, it is clear that different meta-path combinations have different effects (e.g. $MP_1 \& MP_3 > MP_1 \& MP_2$, $MP_1 \& MP_2 \& MP_3 > MP_1 \& MP_2 \& MP_4$). For example, in dataset 1, the combination of MP_3 and MP_1 gives 2.0% to 3.0% higher AUC than either meta-path alone, and adding meta-paths to the original base meta-path combination gives better results. In addition, the best results can be obtained by including all the meta-path combinations in each dataset.

Comparing the two datasets, we find that the number of videos and courses in dataset 2 is smaller than that in dataset 1. The corresponding result obtained from dataset 2 is also lower than that of dataset 1. This is because there are more

Table 2. Results of different meta path combinations under dataset 1.

Meta-path	HR@5	NDCG@5	MRR	AUC
MP1	0.5486	0.4061	0.3785	0.8894
MP2	0.4658	0.3272	0.3184	0.8648
MP3	0.5953	0.4284	0.4056	0.8953
MP4	0.4394	0.3082	0.3042	0.8551
MP1&MP2	0.5724	0.4009	0.3781	0.8956
MP1&MP3	0.6151	0.4312	0.4145	0.9164
MP1&MP4	0.6025	0.4212	0.3945	0.8966
MP2&MP3	0.6112	0.4384	0.4091	0.9120
MP2&MP4	0.4591	0.3267	0.3257	0.8543
MP3&MP4	0.6086	0.4304	0.4085	0.8923
MP1&MP2&MP3	0.6502	0.4621	0.4284	0.9289
MP1&MP2&MP4	0.6105	0.4413	0.4128	0.9088
MP1&MP3&MP4	0.6354	0.4484	0.4174	0.9201
MP2&MP3&MP4	0.6167	0.4459	0.4187	0.9098
MP1&MP2&MP3&MP4	**0.6532**	**0.4712**	**0.4453**	**0.9412**

Table 3. Results of different meta path combinations under Dataset 2.

Meta-path	HR@5	NDCG@5	MRR	AUC
MP2	0.4475	0.3214	0.3075	0.8468
MP3	0.5462	0.4056	0.3879	0.8664
MP2&MP3	**0.5685**	**0.4188**	**0.4012**	**0.8823**

connections between users and videos and courses in dataset 1 comparing with dataset 2, and the GCN aggregates neighborhood nodes better, therefore the node representation obtained is more complete, thus improving the performance of recommendations.

4.4 Evaluation of Model Parameters

We investigated the impact of different GCN layers, shown in Fig. 2. Figure 2 (a) and (b) correspond to dataset 1 and dataset 2, respectively. We can clearly see the impact of different layers. The results show that the best results are obtained when the number of layers is three in both datasets. We also investigate the hyperparameter δ that controls the degree of influence of the community structure, as shown in Fig. 3. Figure 3 (a) and (b) correspond to dataset 1 and dataset 2, respectively. We found that $\delta \in [0, 1]$ works well when the δ is 0.5 for dataset 1 and 0.6 for dataset 2. When δ is too large, the neighborhood information will be ignored and the recommendation will be effected.

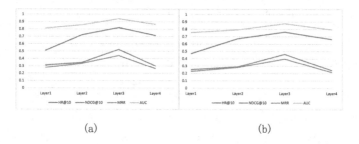

(a)   (b)

Fig. 2. The performance of different layers under dataset 1 and dataset 2.

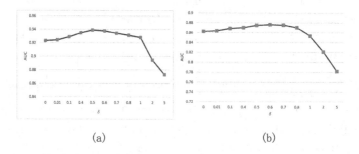

(a)   (b)

Fig. 3. The performance of different δ under dataset 1 and dataset 2.

4.5   Comparison with Other Methods

For evaluating the proposed CERec-ME, we compare the following methods. MLP [6] applied multi-layer perceptron in user representation and course concept representation to learn the probability of recommending course concept. FISM [8] was an collaborative filtering algorithm based on user's historical behavior and target course concepts. NAIS [5] was an collaborative filtering algorithm based on attention mechanism to distinguish the weights of various online learning actions. ACKRec [3] was an graph neural network based approach for knowledge concept recommendation in MOOCs. For MLP, FISM, and NAIS, we constructed the

Table 4. Results of different baseline methods under dataset 1.

Method	HR@1	HR@5	HR@10	HR@20	NDCG@5	NDCG@10	NDCG@20	MRR	AUC
MLP	0.0660	0.3680	0.5899	0.7237	0.2231	0.2926	0.3441	0.2146	0.8595
FISM	0.1410	0.5849	0.7489	0.7610	0.3760	0.4203	0.4279	0.3293	0.8532
NAIS	0.078	0.4112	0.6624	0.8649	0.2392	0.3201	0.3793	0.2392	0.8863
ACKRec	0.2645	0.6470	0.8122	0.9255	0.4635	0.5170	0.5459	0.4352	0.9232
CERec-ME	**0.2732**	**0.6532**	**0.8221**	**0.9388**	**0.4712**	**0.5284**	**0.5598**	**0.4453**	**0.9412**

rating matrix of user-course concept from the dataset as the historical interaction of users follwered by the instructions of them. For ACKRec, based on its steps,

Table 5. Results of different baseline methods under dataset 2.

Method	HR@1	HR@5	HR@10	HR@20	NDCG@5	NDCG@10	NDCG@20	MRR	AUC
MLP	0.0537	0.3421	0.5764	0.7015	0.2031	0.2762	0.3216	0.2088	0.8123
FISM	0.1213	0.5635	0.7324	0.7502	0.3647	0.4026	0.4133	0.3018	0.8109
NAIS	0.064	04032	0.6426	0.8516	0.2216	0.3064	0.3597	0.2210	0.8453
ACKRec	0.2428	0.5594	0.7523	0.8421	0.4122	0.4514	0.4911	0.3944	0.8624
CERec-ME	**0.2482**	**0.5685**	**0.7686**	**0.8596**	**0.4188**	**0.4652**	**0.5056**	**0.4012**	**0.8823**

we construct the corresponding user features and course concet features and their corresponding adjacency matrices as inputs. For fair comparison, we select the most appropriate parameters to obtain the best results for these methods. From Table 4 and Table 5, it can be seen that CERec-ME and ACKRec perform much better than MLP, FISM, NAIS. The AUC of CERec-ME is about 5.5% to 8.8% higher than MLP, FISM and NAIS in dataset, and about 1.3.7% to 7.1% higher than them in dataset 2. Since CERec-ME considers community structure, an important graph information, to make the graph node representation better and more conducive to capturing the heterogeneous relationships in MOOCs data, CERec-ME is about 1.33% higher than ACKRec under the HR@20 criterion, and 1.39% and 1.80% higher under the NDCG@20 and AUC criteria, respectively, in dataset 1. In dataset 2, CERec-ME is about 1.75% higher than ACKRec under the HR@20 criterion, and 1.45% and 1.99% higher under the NDCG@20 and AUC criteria, respectively.

5   Conclusions

In this paper, a course concept recommendation model for multiple entity relations based on community structure is proposed, which is an end-to-end graph neural network. To capture the information between multiple entity relationships on MOOCs platform, we construct a heterogeneous graph of multiple entity types on MOOCs platform, which could be viewed as a composition of multiple entity relationships. Meta-paths are used as a guide to capture information between multiple entities through GCN, taking into account also the community structure information between entities, in order to learn a more complete graph representation of entities. To verify the effectiveness of the proposed method, we conduct experiments on XuetangX MOOC and MOOCCube. The results have shown that the method outperforms the state-of-the-art methods.

Acknowledgements. This work is supported by National Natural Science Foundation of China under grants No. 61801428 and U1908210, and Natural Science Foundation of Zhejiang Province of China under grants No. LR21F020002.

References

1. Almatrafi, O., Johri, A., Rangwala, H.: Needle in a haystack: identifying learner posts that require urgent response in mooc discussion forums. Comput. Educ. **118**, 1–9 (2018)
2. Elbadrawy, A., Karypis, G.: Domain-aware grade prediction and top-n course recommendation. In: ACM Conference on Recommender Systems, pp. 183–190 (2016)
3. Gong, J., et al.: Attentional graph convolutional networks for knowledge concept recommendation in moocs in a heterogeneous view. In: ACM SIGIR, pp. 79–88 (2020)
4. Gori, M., Monfardini, G., Scarselli, F.: A new model for learning in graph domains. IEEE Int. Joint Conf. Neural Netw. **2**, 729–734 (2005)
5. He, X., He, Z., Song, J., Liu, Z., et al.: Nais: neural attentive item similarity model for recommendation. IEEE Trans. Knowl. Data Eng. **30**(12), 2354–2366 (2018)
6. He, X., Liao, L., Zhang, H., Nie, L., Hu, X., Chua, T.S.: Neural collaborative filtering. In: International Conference on World Wide Web, pp. 173–182 (2017)
7. Järvelin, K., Kekäläinen, J.: IR evaluation methods for retrieving highly relevant documents, pp. 41–48. ACM SIGIR (2000)
8. Kabbur, S., Ning, X., Karypis, G.: Fism: factored item similarity models for top-n recommender systems. In: ACM SIGKDD, pp. 659–667 (2013)
9. King, C., Robinson, A., Vickers, J.: Targeted mooc captivates students. Nature **505**(7481), 26–26 (2014)
10. Liu, Y., et al.: Community enhanced graph convolutional networks. Pattern Recogn. Lett. **138**, 462–468 (2020)
11. Mikolov, T., Chen, K., Corrado, G., Dean, J.: Efficient estimation of word representations in vector space. In: International Conference on Learning Representations (2013)
12. Newman, M.E.: Modularity and community structure in networks. Natl. Acad. Sci. U.S.A. **103**(23), 8577–8582 (2006)
13. Pan, L., Li, C., Li, J., Tang, J.: Prerequisite relation learning for concepts in moocs. In: Annual Meeting of the Association for Computational Linguistics, pp. 1447–1456 (2017)
14. Pang, Y., Jin, Y., Zhang, Y., Zhu, T.: Collaborative filtering recommendation for mooc application. Comput. Appl. Eng. Educ. **25**(1), 120–128 (2017)
15. Shi, C., Hu, B., Zhao, W.X., Philip, S.Y.: Heterogeneous information network embedding for recommendation. IEEE Trans. Knowl. Data Eng. **31**(2), 357–370 (2018)
16. Tan, H., Guo, J., Li, Y.: E-learning recommendation system. Int. Conf. Comput. Sci. Softw. Eng. **5**, 430–433 (2008)
17. Thanh-Nhan, H.L., Nguyen, H.H., Thai-Nghe, N.: Methods for building course recommendation systems. In: KES, pp. 163–168 (2016)
18. Wang, J., Xie, H., Wang, F.L., Lee, L.K., Au, O.T.S.: Top-n personalized recommendation with graph neural networks in moocs. Comput. Educ. Artif. Intell. **2**, 100010 (2021). https://doi.org/10.1016/j.caeai.2021.100010
19. Yu, J., et al.: Mooccube: a large-scale data repository for nlp applications in moocs. In: Annual Meeting of the Association for Computational Linguistics, pp. 3135–3142 (2020)
20. Zhang, H., Sun, M., Wang, X., Song, Z., Tang, J., Sun, J.: Smart jump: Automated navigation suggestion for videos in moocs. In: International Conference on World Wide Web Companion, pp. 331–339 (2017)

21. Zhang, J.: Can moocs be interesting to students? an experimental investigation from regulatory focus perspective. Comput. Educ. **95**, 340–351 (2016)
22. Zhu, Y., Lu, H., Qiu, P., Shi, K., Chambua, J., Niu, Z.: Heterogeneous teaching evaluation network based offline course recommendation with graph learning and tensor factorization. Neurocomputing **415**, 84–95 (2020)

AABC:ALBERT-BiLSTM-CRF Combining with Adapters

JiaYan Wang[1,2], ZiAng Chen[1,2], JuChuan Niu[1,2], and YongGang Zhang[1,2(✉)]

[1] College of Computer Science and Technology, Jilin University,
Changchun 130012, China
zhangyg@jlu.edu.cn
[2] Key Laboratory of Symbolic Computation and Knowledge Engineering,
Ministry of Education, Jilin University, Changchun, China

Abstract. Pre-training models (PTMs) are language models pre-trained on a large corpus, which can learn general language representations through training tasks within the model. PTMs complete various NLP tasks by connecting with downstream models. PTMs can avoid building new models from the beginning. Therefore, they are widely used in the NLP field. In order to achieve the goal of completing multiple tasks with merely one model, the scale of PTM has been rising. However, the larger scale brings a larger amount of parameters, which also means more parameters to be adjusted in the future. Therefore, this article proposes a new AABC (Adapters-ALBERT-BiLSTM-CRF) model which is introduced Adapters on ALBERT. The Adapters remain unchanged during the pre-training phase and only adjusting the Adapters module can achieve the best effect during the fine-tuning. In order to verify the reduction of the model's adjustment parameters, AABC experimented on three tasks: named entity recognition (NER), sentiment analysis (SA), and natural language inference (NLI). Tests results show that the AABC model performs better than the BERT model on classification tasks with types less than five. Also, AABC is better than the rival model in terms of tuning parameters. On the 7 datasets of SA and NLI tasks, the average parameter counts of AABC is only 2.8% of BERT-BiLSTM-CRF. Experimental results demonstrate that the proposed method a potential classification model.

Keywords: Adapters · Pre-training models · Fine-tune · Named entity recognition

1 Introduction

With the proposal of the Transformer [1] model by Google in 2017, it is possible for us to fulfill mutil tasks with one simple model. The current mainstream operation method is to download and fine-tune a pre-trained model containing hundreds of millions or even billions of parameters, and then connect downstream models on the basis of the pre-trained model, aiming to complete various NLP

© Springer Nature Switzerland AG 2021
H. Qiu et al. (Eds.): KSEM 2021, LNAI 12816, pp. 294–305, 2021.
https://doi.org/10.1007/978-3-030-82147-0_24

tasks. But storage and training of such large pre-training models are expensive, which seriously hinders the development of pre-training models in a more regular direction. The latest development of the NLP field based on the transformer language models [2] has achieved pre-training on a large amount of text data. These models are fine-tuned for target tasks, achieving the SOTA on most tasks [3,4].

Adapters [5], as a convenient and portable fine-tune strategy, have been introduced into the language model, which can achieve same performance as the fully fine-tuned model on most tasks [6]. They consist of a set of additional network layers on each encoder of Transformer. These newly added network layers are retrained, while the trained parameters of the pre-training model remain frozen during fine-tuning. Researchers can effectively share parameters between tasks by training many task-specific and language-specific adapters for the same model. Adapters module research has recently achieved excellent results in multitasking and cross-language transfer learning [7,8]. However, it is not easy to reuse and share the Adapters module. Their architectures are different in details, and they are all related to the structure of the pre-trained model, downstream tasks, and language.

The structure of the article is as follows. First, it introduces the theoretical knowledge of each part of the AABC model, and then analyses the experimental results on NER, SA and NLI tasks. Finally it summarizes the work of the full text. Our main work is to combine ALBERT with the Adapters which is trying to create a more generalized pre-training model. This model can maintain a balance between efficiency and performance when facing different tasks.

2   Related Work

Transfer learning is a machine learning method which uses the model developed by task A as a starting point and applies it to task B. Pre-training models have been widely used in fields of CV and NLP. These pre-training models have consumed huge time resources and computing resources during training, and transfer learning can transfer the learned knowledge to related tasks.

In the past two years, it seems that transfer learning has become a necessary technology due to pre-training models such as BERT and GPT [9] that have been widely used. There are two types of transfer learning: One is feature-based transfer learning. Feature-based transfer learning means that we learn word embedding vectors from existing models, and then use the word embedding vectors as the input of the new model for further training. The other is model transfer learning. The transfer learning of a model refers to keeping some parameters unchanged on the basis of the model which is trained on other datasets, and adjusting another part of the parameters. The constant parameters are generally the bottom layer parameters, and the adjusted parameters are generally the top layer parameters. However, as the number of parameters decreases, there is an obvious trade-off between performance and parameter efficiency.

When dealing with specific tasks, fine-tuning aims to use its labeled samples to adjust the parameters of the pre-training model. For instance, BERT can be applied to determine whether two sentences have same semantics. The input is two sentences, and the corresponding encoding representation of each sentence is obtained through BERT. We can use the first hidden layer's node to predicate the classification, and calculate the probability whether the two sentences are synonymous sentences by this classification. We also need to add linear layer and softmax are calculated to obtain the distribution of the classification labels. The loss can be passed back to BERT to fine-tune the network. It is also possible to design a new network for a specific task, and use the pre-training result as its input.

3   AABC Model

3.1   Adapters

The main method of transfer learning is to fine-tune the weight of the pre-training model. The Adapters module has been introduced as an alternative method and applied in the fields of computer vision and NLP [10–12]. Adapters module is essentially composed of a neural network [13]. It exist in a large pre-training model with parameters Θ by introducing a small number of parameters Φ. When the parameters Θ in the pre-training model are fixed, the parameters Φ in the Adapters module are learned through the target task. Therefore, the Adapters module learns the coding representation of a specific task from the hidden layer of the pre-trained model. The current work mainly focus on training the Adapters module for each task separately, which makes parallel training and weight combination possible. In the field of NLP, the application of Adapters is mainly based on the Transformer architecture.

3.2   ALBERT

The release of BERT refreshed the NLP task rankings. But the large-scale model also brings other problems. ALBERT divides these problems into two categories: memory limitations and model degradation. In BERT and some other pre-training models, such as XLNet [14] and RoBERTa [15], the dimension E of WordPiece Embedding and the dimension H of the hidden layer are bound. WordPiece Embedding is intended to learn context-free expressions, while the hidden layer aims to learn contextual expressions. Unbinding the WordPiece Embedding size E and the hidden layer size H can make the use of the model parameters required for modeling more effective. We add a matrix which has the dimension E. From an experimental view, this operation can reduce the impact of vocabulary on the scale of the model. In the field of NLP, the vocabulary is generally large, so it can be imagined that such an improvement in the unbinding effect is outstanding. The specific method is to decompose the word embedding vector matrix, transforming the large matrix into two small matrices.

This operation can significantly reduce the number of parameters that we need to transfer words to embedding vectors. The second solution to the problem is cross-layer parameter sharing. All parameters of each Transformer module are shared, so that the parameters no longer increase as more layers are stacked to the model. The essence of Next Sentence Prediction(NSP) used in BERT is to integrate the two tasks of topic prediction and coherence prediction. Consistency prediction is the main core task, which can learn the information in the sentence. ALBERT changed NSP to Sentence Order Prediction(SOP). Its positive sampling method is the same as BERT, but the negative sample is changed to two sentences in inverted order, which forces the model to learn the fine-grained distinction of text.

3.3 BiLSTM

Recurrent Neural Network (RNN) is a neural network that can process serialized text data. However, RNN will not work well due to the problems of gradient disappearance and gradient explosion [16] in practice. Long short-term memory network (LSTM) [17] captures the long-distance dependence of the context by merging storage units. The LSTM controls the percentage of the information passed to memory cell, also controls the ratio of the previous state information to be gotten rid of.

For a given sentence (x1, x2,..., xn) containing n words, each word is represented as a d-dimensional vector. LSTM calculates the representation of the context $\overrightarrow{h_t}$ starting from the left side to the right side of the sentence on each word t. In order to add useful information, the contextual representation $\overleftarrow{h_t}$ starting from the right side also needs to be calculated. The calculation of is achieved by utilizing the reverse direction LSTM. This set of forward and backward LSTMs is called bidirectional LSTM [18]. The word representation output by BiLSTM is obtained by concatenating the left and right context representations of the word.

3.4 CRF

For sequence labeling tasks, taking the correlation of multiple state labels into consideration can improve the efficiency of decoding. CRF can define its own feature function set. Each feature function in the function set takes the label sequence as input and the extracted features as output. This can not only express the dependence between observations, but also express the complex dependence between observations and multiple states. Therefore, adding the CRF layer after the BiLSTM layer is beneficial to improve the effect. During training and decoding phase, CRF adopts the Viterbi algorithm.

3.5 AABC

Although the ABC model performs well on the NER task, its pre-training part ALBERT model still has shortcomings. ALBERT does not change the common problem that all pre-training models require large-scale adjustment of parameters during fine-tuning. Therefore, we propose the AABC model on the basis of the ABC model. The Adapters layer is added to ALBERT. Only adjust the parameters in the Adapters layer can adapt more tasks. In the parameter sharing mechanism of the ALBERT model, the number of parameters is compressed. But the introduction of the Adapters module can increase the diversity of parameters.

The main purpose of the AABC model is to balance the amount of parameters and performance. The introduction of the Adapters module can indirectly compensate for the hidden depth of the ALBERT model.

Since the AABC model is modified on the basis of ABC, it shares similar overall structure with ABC model. The difference is that the AABC model adds the Adapters module inside ALBERT. The Adapters module remains unchanged during the model training and only exists as a network layer in the neural network. We complete various tasks by adjusting the parameters in the Adapters to produce results comparable to the original model. There have been many researches on the structure of Adapters module in the past two years, and we mainly refer to the model structure of Houlsby and Pfeiffer et al. in the experiments. The arrangement of Adapters is shown in Fig. 1 left. According to the experimental results, we chose to place the Adapters module between the first feed-forward layer and the layer normalization layer. The model is firstly calculated by the multi-head attention mechanism, then passed through the network layer to the Adapters module, and finally normalized by Layer Normalization with residual connection calculation. The structure of the Adapters module is shown in Fig. 1 right. The internal structure of the module is not complicated. The input vector enters the feed-forward layer, and then has its dimension changed through the mapping and the non-linear transformation with the external residual calculation. The final output is a vector with same dimension as input. From a macro perspective, adding the Adapters module is equivalent to stacking more network layers and enhancing the learning ability.

In theory, the value of the CRF layer is to increase constraints and improve the performance of the model on sequence labeling tasks. For SA and NLI tasks, whether the CRF layer makes sense is worth thinking about. So we added ablation learning, and found that the presence or absence of the CRF layer has little effect on the experimental results. In order to continue the entire AABC model structure, we chose to retain the CRF layer.

4 Experiments

4.1 Datasets

NER. Named Entity Recognition (NER) refers to identifying entities with specific meanings in texts, including names of persons, places, organizations, proper nouns, etc. We select five named entity recognition datasets for this paper, as shown in Table 1. Both CoNLL2003 [19] data set and WeiboNER dataset [20] contain four entity types, including place name (LOC), organization name (ORG), person name (PER), and other (MISC). The ResumeNER dataset [21] contains eight entity types, while the MSRA dataset has three entity types. Since

MSRA does not have a validation set, 10% of the test set is randomly selected as the validation set.

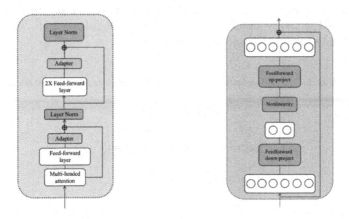

Fig. 1. The position of adapters in the model.

Table 1. The introduction of natural language inference datasets

Dataset		Train	Dev	Test
CoNLL2003	tok	203k	51k	46k
OntoNotes5.0	tok	1.2M	178K	49K
WeiboNER	tok	1855	379	405
ResumeNER	tok	124.1K	13.9K	15.1K
MSRA	tok	2169.9K	–	172.6K

SA. Sentiment analysis is also called opinion mining. The definition of SA is to analyze people's opinions, sentiment, appraisal, attitude and emotion of an entity expressed through text. The entities here can be products, services, organizations, individuals, events, and various topics. In the experiments, we use IMDb and SST-2 datasets.

NLI. Natural language inference(NLI) mainly focus on the mission to judge the semantic relationship between two sentences (Premise, Hypothesis) or two words. In order to ensure that the model focus on semantic understanding, the task eventually changes into a classification task. There are three categories ("Entailment", "Contradiction", "Neutral") in this task. NLI is a classification task which uses the accuracy rate to evaluate the quality of the model. Therefore, we can focus on semantic understanding and semantic representation. If a model can generate a full sentence representation vector, we can easily apply this part of the results to other tasks such as dialogue, question and answer, etc. All this shows that NLI is a very significant and very meaningful research. The datasets we used in the experiments are shown in Table 2.

Table 2. The introduction of natural language inference datasets

	Train	Dev	Test	Test
SNLI	550k	10k	10k	46k
QNLI	105k	5.4k	5.4k	149K
MNLI	393k	9.8k	20k	405
RTE	2.5k	277	3k	15.1K
WNLI	634	71	146	172.6K

4.2 Training

Since the ALBERT model is the result of the distillation of the BERT model, this article mainly compares the effects and parameters of ALBERT and BERT after adding the Adapters module. However, The BiLSTM-CRF model is the best NER model before the pre-training model is popular, so it is selected as a fixed downstream model The model applies the SGD strategy to train itself, and trains up to 30 epochs. Training will stop when the named entity recognition results begin to converge. If the learning rate remain unchanged for 5 consecutive epochs, the learning rate will be reduced by half. And following the method of Chen [22], Dropout is introduced in the input layer of BiLSTM. CRF module refers to literature[23].

In order to make the experiment more convincing, I followed the two corpus BOOKCORPUS [24] and English Wikipedia [25], pretrained by BERT as well. The word embedding layer size we use is 30,000 dimensions like BERT, and sentence fragments are used to slice sentences like XLNet [26]. In the mask mechanism, we use the n-gram mask mechanism [27], and n is generated randomly. We set n is 3 according to the experiment results. The formula is as follows:

$$p(n) = \frac{1/n}{\sum_{k=1}^{n} 1/k} \tag{1}$$

All model updates use the 4096 batch size and the LAMB optimizer with a learning rate of 0.00176. Since we are modifying the model on the basis of ALBERT, the parameters of the pre-training model share same settings with the original ALBERT. The maximum character length in the training sample is 128, batch size is 8, epoch is 50, and BiLSTM layers number is 100. The ratio of training set, validation set, and test set is 75%: 10%: 15%. For the optimization part, I chose Adam [28]. The learning rate gradually increased in the first 10% of the training rounds, and then gradually decayed. The ultimate goal is to expect that under the same performance as the original model, AABC's number of parameters is small.

4.3   Results

The experiment mainly revolves around the BERT-BiLSTM-CRF (BERT-BC) and ABC models, and compares the effects of the two models on three tasks after adding the Adapters module. The experimental results are based on the F1 value, accuracy rate and the final parameter quantity.

Due to the large number of Attention computer systems in the model and the non-sharing of parameters between layers, the amount of parameters of BERT-BC is very large (here, we use BERT-base and ALBERT-base as experimental model). Due to the parameter sharing mechanism of ALBERT, the amount of parameters is only 11% of BERT under same number of layers. Therefore, the ABC model is more portable than the BERT-BC, judging the scale of model. Table 3 lists the results and the average fine-tuning parameters of the four models on five NER public datasets. On the CoNLL2003 dataset, the F1 value of the ABC model is the highest. On the complex datasets such as OntoNotesv5 and WeiboNER, BERT-BC works better. Due to the complexity of these two datasets, the model does require a large number of parameters and a large number of hidden layers during the training process. Blindly compressing the amount of model parameters will weaken the model's ability to learn semantic features. Therefore, BERT-BC works better on these two datasets. On the ResumeNER and MSRA datasets, AABC works better. But in terms of average tuning parameters, AABC is the lowest, only 12.5% of BERT-BC. The experimental results show that the model does require a lot of calculations and large quantities of adjustment on parameters for semantic learning.

Table 3. The results on NER task.

	BERT-BC	Adapters-BERT-BC	ABC	AABC
CoNLL2003	92.07%	92.06%	92.65%	92.20%
OntoNoteV5	90.07%	88.26%	89.88%	86.31%
WeiboNER	63.17%	62.15%	62.94%	60.98%
ResumeNER	96.33%	95.82%	96.48%	96.59%
MSRA	93.76%	93.43%	93.89%	94.38%
ParamsAve	160M	80M	40M	20M

Table 4 lists the results of the four models on the SA and NLI tasks. Among them, the first two lines are SA datasets, the evaluation index is the F1 value; the three to seven lines are NLI task datasets, the evaluation index is the accuracy rate. The last line is the average tuning parameter. The results show that the Adapters-BERT-BC model achieves outstanding performance on the IMDb and RTE datasets, and the AABC model performs best on the other five datasets. In terms of average tuning parameters, the AABC model contains only 5M, which is 2.8% of the Adapters-BERT-BC. Table 5 takes the SNLI dataset as an example. However, ALBERT completely beats BERT in terms of model size due to operations such as parameter sharing which is only 8.3% of BERT. After adding the two models to the Adapters module, the performance has been improved. In the comparison of parameters, the advantages of AABC are more obvious. AABC only uses 3M parameters to achieve an accuracy of 87.43%, while Adapters-BERT-BC still has 36M which is three times of ALBERT-Adapters. It can be concluded that the AABC model achieves the goal of the smallest parameter amount on the NLI task.

But the AABC model also has shortcomings. As the number of parameters decreases, there is an obvious trade-off between performance and parameter efficiency. The goal of Adapters is to use the least amount of parameters to achieve the best results. It should be noted that in some experiments, the effect of adding the Adapters module is not ideal. Analysis of the reason is that the learning of natural language does require some parameter training. The complexity of natural language requires models to spend time and space to learn. When the number of parameters is too small, the model does not have good semantic learning ability and cannot learn deep features according to the context.

Table 4. The results on SA and NLI tasks.

	BERT-BC	Adapters-BERT-BC	ABC	AABC
IMDb	92.62%	**93.26%**	92.25%	93.20%
SST-2	93.68%	93.45%	95.53%	**96.12%**
QNLI	90.44%	90.75%	90.86%	**90.98%**
RTE	62.93%	**66.47%**	65.73%	65.19%
WNLI	86.09%	86.32%	86.40%	**86.58%**
MNLI	82.45%	85.35%	89.82%	**90.69%**
SNLI	86.08%	87.39%	86.92%	**87.43%**
ParamsAve	120M	40M	15M	**5M**

Table 5. The results on SNLI dataset.

SNLI	Contradiction	Entail	Neutral	Accuracy	Params
BERT-BC	87.73%	88.04%	82.39%	86.08%	108M
ABC	88.48%	87.91%	83.45%	86.92%	12M
Adapters-BERT-BC	89.44%	**88.94%**	**83.69%**	87.39%	36M
AABC	**89.57%**	88.89%	83.66%	**87.43%**	**3M**

5 Concluion and Future

In this paper, we added the Adapters module on the basis of the ABC model and proposed the AABC model. AABC is used to solve the problem that the ABC model has too much adjustment parameters when facing different tasks. Experiments proved that the AABC model can effectively reduce the tuning parameter while maintaining the same performance through three classification tasks. Compared with BERT-BC, the average tuning parameters of AABC on a total of 7 datasets were reduced to 2.8% of the original model. Although the pre-trained model has proven its ability on many NLP tasks, challenges still exist due to the complexity of the language. The AABC is still no way to be SOTA in complex datasets. How to find a balance between the amount of parameters and performance is the main research direction in the future. On the other hand, due to the rapid update iteration of natural language, many new words will emerge over time. The language model cannot infer new meanings based on the originally learned semantics in the first time. If the model can be made intelligent enough to learn the meaning of new words without additional data training, then the research of NLP will be raised to a higher level.

Acknowledgements. This work is supported by the National Natural Science Foundation of China (61373052), the 13th five year plan science and technology project of Jilin Provincial Department of Education (JJKH20200995KJ) and the Natural Science Foundation of Jilin Province (20200201447JC).

References

1. Vaswani, A., et al.: Attention is all you need. In: Advances in Neural Information Processing Systems 30: Annual Conference on Neural Information Processing Systems 2017, pp: 5998–6008 (2017)
2. Devlin, J., Chang, M., Lee, K., Toutanova, K.: BERT: pre-training of deep bidirectional transformers for language understanding. In: NAACL-HLT, pp. 4171–4186 (2019)
3. Liu, Y., et al.: RoBERTa: a robustly optimized BERT pretraining approach. arXiv preprint arXiv:1907.11692 (2019)
4. Conneau, A., et al.: Unsupervised cross-lingual representation learning at scale. In: Proceedings of the 58th Conference of the Association for Computational Linguistics, pp: 8440–8451 (2020)

5. Houlsby, N., et al.: Parameter-efficient transfer learning for NLP. In: Proceedings of the 36th International Conference on Machine Learning, ICML 2019, pp. 2790–2799 (2019)

6. Peters, M.E., Ruder, S., Smith, N.A.: To tune or not to tune? adapting pretrained representations to diverse tasks. In: Proceedings of the 4th Workshop on Representation Learning for NLP, pp: 7–14 (2019)

7. Pfeiffer, J., Kamath, A., Ruckle, A., Cho, K., Gurevych, I.: AdapterFusion: Non-destructive task composition for transfer learning. arXiv preprint arXiv:2005.00247 (2020)

8. Pfeiffer, J., Vulic, I., Gurevych, I., Ruder, S.: MAD-X: An Adapter-based Framework for Multi-task Cross-lingual Transfer. In: Proceedings of the 2020 Conference on Empirical Methods in Natural Language Processing, pp. 7654–7673 (2020)

9. Radford, A., Narasimhan, K., Salimans, T., Sutskever, I.: Improving language understanding by generative pre-training (2018)

10. Rebuffifi, S.A., Bilen, H., Vedaldi, A.: Learning multiple visual domains with residual adapters. In: Advances in Neural Information Processing Systems 30: Annual Conference on Neural Information Processing Systems 2017, pp. 506–516 (2017)

11. Bapna, A., Firat, O.: Simple, scalable adaptation for neural machine translation. In: Proceedings of the 2019 Conference on Empirical Methods in Natural Language Processing and the 9th International Joint Conference on Natural Language Processing, pp. 1538–1548 (2019)

12. Wang, R., et al.: K-adapter: Infusing knowledge into pre-trained models with adapters. arXiv preprint arXiv:2002.01808 (2020)

13. Ustun, A., Bisazza, A., Bouma, G., Noord, G.: UDapter: language adaptation for truly universal dependency parsing. In: Proceedings of the 2020 Conference on Empirical Methods in Natural Language Processing, pp. 2302–2315 (2020)

14. Yang, Z., Dai, Z., Yang, Y., Carbonell, J., Salakhutdinov, R.R., Le, Q.V.: XLNet: Generalized autoregressive pretraining for language understanding. In: NeurIPS, pp. 5754–5764 (2019)

15. Liu, Y., et al.: RoBERTa: a robustly optimized BERT pre-training approach. arXiv preprint arXiv:1907.11692 (2019)

16. Bengio, Y., Simard, P., Frasconi, P.: Learning long-term dependencies with gradient descent is difficult. IEEE Trans. Neural Net. **5**(2), 157–166 (1994)

17. Hochreiter, S., Schmidhuber, J.: Long short-term memory. Neural Comput. **9**(8), 1735–1780 (1997)

18. Graves A., Schmidhuber, J.: Framewise phoneme classification with bidirectional LSTM networks. In: IEEE International Joint Conference on Neural Networks, pp. 2047–2052 (2005)

19. Chieu, H.L., Ng, H.T.: Named entity recognition with a maximum entropy approach. In: Proceedings of the Seventh Conference on Natural Language Learning, pp. 160–163 (2003)

20. Peng, N., Dredze, M.: Named entity recognition for Chinese social media with jointly trained embeddings. In: Empirical Methods in Natural Language Processing, pp. 548–554 (2015)

21. Zhang, Y., Yang, J.: Chinese NER using lattice LSTM. In: Proceedings of the 56th Annual Meeting of the Association for Computational Linguistics (vol. 1: Long Papers), pp. 1554–1564 (2018)

22. Chen, X., Qiu, X., Zhu, C., Liu, P., Huang, X.: Long short term memory neural networks for Chinese word segmentation. In: Empirical Methods in Natural Language Processing, pp. 1197–1206 (2015)

23. Peng, N., Dredze, M.: Named entity recognition for Chinese social media with jointly trained embeddings. In: Proceedings of the Conference on Empirical Methods in Natural Language Processing, pp. 548–554 (2015)
24. Zhu, Y., et al.: Aligning books and movies: Towards story-like visual explanations by watching movies and reading books. In: Proceedings of the IEEE International Conference on Computer Vision, pp. 19–27 (2015)
25. English Wiki. https://www.enwiki.org/w/Main_Page. Accessed 1 Jun 2021
26. Kudo, T., Richardson, J.: SentencePiece: a simple and language independent subword tokenizer and detokenizer for neural text processing. In: Proceedings of the 2018 Conference on Empirical Methods in Natural Language Processing: System Demonstrations, pp: 66–71 (2018)
27. Joshi, M., Chen, D., Liu, Y., Weld, D.S., Zettlemoyer, L., Levy, O.: SpanBERT: Improving pre-training by representing and predicting spans. arXiv preprint arXiv: 1907.10529 (2019)
28. Kingma, D., Ba, J.: Adam: a method for stochastic optimization. arXiv preprint arXiv:1412.6980 (2014)

Q-Learning with Fisher Score for Feature Selection of Large-Scale Data Sets

Min Gan[1] and Li Zhang[1,2(✉)]

[1] School of Computer Science and Technology and Joint International Research Laboratory of Machine Learning and Neuromorphic Computing, Soochow University, Jiangsu, China
zhangliml@suda.edu.cn
[2] Provincial Key Laboratory for Computer Information Processing Technology, Soochow University, Jiangsu, China

Abstract. Feature selection is to select some useful features from candidate ones, which is one of the main methods for data dimension reduction. Because general feature selection methods are directly performed based on given data sets at hand, it is time-consuming for them to deal with large-scale data sets. To solve this issue, this paper proposes a novel feature selection method, called Q-learning with Fisher score (QLFS), for large-scale data sets. QLFS adopts the framework of Q-learning of reinforcement learning (RL) and takes Fisher score (FS), a filtering method for feature selection, as the internal reward. Here, FS is modified to calculate the ratio of the between-class and within-class distances for a feature subset instead of the ratio for a single feature. By selecting part of the training samples in each episode, QLFS can perform batch learning and then deal with large-scale data sets in batch. Experimental results on several large-scale UCI data sets show that QLFS not only improves the classification performance but also has an advantage of training speed compared with other methods.

Keywords: Feature selection · Fisher score · Q-learning · Large-scale

1 Introduction

Due to the curse of dimensionality [12], how to effectively reduce the dimension of data is an essential issue in high-dimensional data processing. Feature selection is one kind of main methods for data dimension reduction. Its purpose is to select some useful features from the candidates and form the optimal feature subset with the best discrimination ability for subsequent tasks [1,9]. According to the relationship between feature selection methods and learners, methods for

Supported by the Natural Science Foundation of the Jiangsu Higher Education Institutions of China under Grant No. 19KJA550002, the Six Talent Peak Project of Jiangsu Province of China under Grant No. XYDXX-054, and the Priority Academic Program Development of Jiangsu Higher Education Institutions.

H. Qiu et al. (Eds.): KSEM 2021, LNAI 12816, pp. 306–318, 2021.
https://doi.org/10.1007/978-3-030-82147-0_25

feature selection can be divided into three types: filter, wrapper and embedded [20].

With the advent of the big data era, the number of data samples is also growing, which would result in large-scale data sets. This brings a new challenge to the existing feature selection methods [13,22]. Fortunately, Moran et al. [15] proposed a new feature selection method named curious feature selection (CFS) that is a kind of intrinsically motivated learning methods. CFS applies a reinforcement learning method to feature selection, so that feature selection can respond to the change of data structure, and automatically update and select with the increase of data. CFS provides an idea of dealing with large-scale data sets in batch. However, CFS is a kind of wrapper methods that are bound to a learner. Thus, the performance of CFS mainly depends on the chosen learner. Moreover, the selected features are not general.

To remedy it, this paper proposes a filter feature selection method that combines Q-learning with Fisher score, called Q-learning with Fisher score (QLFS). Fisher score, a kind of filter methods, originally treats each feature independently when measuring the importance of features by calculating the ratio of between-class and within-class distances. Here, we modify Fisher score and make it measure the importance of feature subsets instead of features. QLFS uses the modified Fisher score as the intrinsic reward and sets a threshold to determine that the reward is positive or negative. In the Q-value table, QLFS takes the number of selected features as the state and the feature to be selected next as the action. In each episode of QLFS, we can use a part of training samples for feature selection. In this way, QLFS can handle a large-scale data set in batch.

The rest of this paper is organized as follows. In Sect. 2, we briefly introduce the related work, including Q-learning, CFS and classical Fisher score. In Sect. 3, we combine modified Fisher score with Q-learning and propose a new filter method for feature selection. Section 4 gives experiments on some large-scale UCI data sets. Finally, conclusions are drawn in Sect. 5.

2   Related Work

2.1   Reinforcement Learning

Reinforcement learning (RL) is inspired by the behaviorism theory in psychology [21], which is applied in various fields [3,4]. In the process of interaction with an environment, an agent learns the strategy by receiving the action reward from the environment to achieve the maximum return or achieve the specific goal. In many applications, the RL environment can be formulated as a Markov decision process (MDP) [17]. In MDP, a set of states and a set of actions would interact with the environment, in which we can adopt these actions to control the change of states and get the corresponding rewards. Most learning algorithms for MDPs compute the optimal policy by learning a value function that represents the estimate of how advantageous it is for the agent to be in a certain state or to perform a certain action in a given state.

Q-learning, a basic and popular algorithm based on Markov decision-making process, is a model-free RL algorithm that does not require prior knowledge but directly interacts with the environment to optimize its behavior [6]. In Q-learning, Q-value is the evaluation of state behavior pairs, that is, the expectation of income getting by a certain action in a certain state at a given moment. The main idea behind the algorithm is to construct a Q-value table with all state behavior pairs and then select the strategy that can obtain the maximum profit according to Q-values. The Q-value update rule for the next state is

$$Q_{T+1}(s_t, a_t) = (1 - \alpha)Q_T(s_t, a_t) + \alpha(r_t + \max_a Q_T(s_{t+1}, a)), \tag{1}$$

where α is the learning rate, T is the number of iterations, s_t is the current state, a_t is the action taken in s_t, s_{t+1} is the next state after taking a_t in s_t and r_t is the reward.

2.2   Curious Feature Selection

CFS proposed by Moran et al. is a novel feature selection method with intrinsically motivated learning [15], which is based on the curiosity loop [7,8] and formed by Q-learning. CFS can learn the data structure in large and varied data sets.

In CFS, both the state space and the action space are equal to the data feature space. Specifically, CFS takes the current selected feature as the state and the next selected feature as the action. CFS divides a data set into small chunks with a constant size and takes these chunks as episodes for curiosity loops.

The intrinsic reward of CFS is based on the performance of a learner. First, a feature subset is formed by selecting a specific action in the current state. Then, the learner constructs a model using this feature subset. Next, we can obtain the prediction error in the verification set using the trained model. The difference between the current and the previous prediction errors is regarded as the reward to update the Q-value table. The process would be repeated until terminating condition is satisfied.

2.3   Fisher Score

Fisher score, a classical supervised method for feature selection, seeks features that can make the within-class scatter minimum and the between-class scatter maximum. Assume that there is a set of labeled samples $\{(\mathbf{x}_i, y_i)\}_{i=1}^n$, where $\mathbf{x}_i = [x_{i1}, x_{i2}, \cdots, x_{im}]^T \in \mathbb{R}^m$, $y_i \in \{1, 2, \cdots, c\}$ is the label of $\mathbf{x}_i$ to indicate its category, m is the dimension of samples, and c is the number of classes. Fisher score first assigns a score to each feature and then selects the optimal feature subset according to these scores. The score of the k-th feature can be computed independently as

$$F(k) = \frac{\sum_{i=1}^c n_i(\mu_{f_k}^i - \mu_{f_k})^2}{\sum_{i=1}^c n_i(\sigma_{f_k}^i)^2}, \tag{2}$$

where n_i is the number of samples belonging to the i-th class, $\mu^i_{f_k}$ and $\sigma^i_{f_k}$ are respectively the mean and variance of the k-th feature in the i-th class, and μ_{f_k} is the mean of the k-th feature in all classes.

3   Q-Learning with Fisher Score (QLFS)

The framework of QLFS is shown in Fig. 1, which is mainly divided into three parts: episode generation, episode training and feature selection. This section introduces the three parts in details.

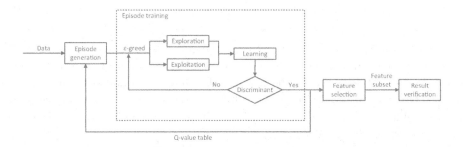

Fig. 1. Framework of QLFS.

3.1   Episode Generation

By using the concept of episodes in RL, QLFS can deal with large-scale data sets. An episode is the process from the beginning to the end of a strategy executed by an agent interacting with the environment in the general RL setting.

Generally, a large-scale data set can be divided into multiple data subsets equally. QLFS can learn a new policy to update the Q-value table using one subset in an episode. In addition, each episode needs its own parameters: learning rate α and probability ϵ. Both parameters should be monotonically decreased with the increase of episodes so that the values in the Q-value table gradually converge. In this way, multiple subsets can be trained in multiple episodes.

In the following experiment of this paper, $Maxitr$ episodes were trained in each data set. The ϵ and α for T-th episode are set as follows:

$$\epsilon = \begin{cases} 0.9, & \text{if } T < MaxItr/4 \\ 0.6, & \text{if } T < MaxItr/2 \\ 0.3, & \text{if } T < 3 * MaxItr/4 \\ 0.1, & \text{otherwise} \end{cases}, \qquad \alpha = \epsilon/10. \tag{3}$$

3.2   Episode Training

State and Action. The basic RL model consists of the environment, the agent state set S and the action set A that can be taken under states. In QLFS, we set states in S according to the number of features selected in the current feature subset; that is, each state represents the cardinal of the current feature subset. We have

$$s \in S = \{0, 1, 2, \ldots, m-1\}. \tag{4}$$

The action space is equal to the data feature space; that is, each action represents the next feature to be selected. Namely,

$$a \in A = \{f_1, f_2, \cdots, f_m\}, \tag{5}$$

where f_i is the i-th feature.

Each state has a set of available actions that is a subset of A. In the actual training, we need to manually remove some selected features to form the current candidate subset A', because the features that have been added to the subset cannot be selected repeatedly. Without loss of generality, let F_{sel} be the selected feature subset in the current state. Then the current candidate subset $A' = A - F_{sel}$. According to states and actions, we construct a Q-value table with the size of $m \times m$. This Q-value table is shared in each episode and is gradually stable with iterations.

Intrinsic Reward. In order to consider the association between features and adapt to the framework of Q-learning, we modify Fisher score to make it evaluate feature subsets instead of features. Let B be a feature subset. Then, the modified Fisher score of B is defined as:

$$J(B) = \frac{\sum_{i=1}^{c} n_i \|\boldsymbol{\mu}_B^i - \boldsymbol{\mu}_B\|^2}{\sum_{i=1}^{c} n_i (\boldsymbol{\sigma}_B^i)^2}, \tag{6}$$

where n_i is the number of the i-th class, $\boldsymbol{\mu}_B^i$ and $\boldsymbol{\sigma}_B^i$ are respectively the mean vector and variance matrix of the i-th class with all features in B, and $\boldsymbol{\mu}_B$ is the mean vector of the all classes with all features in B.

In Eq. (6), the numerator and the denominator denote the scatters of between-class and within-class in the subspace B, respectively. Compared to Eq. (2), the modified Fisher score focuses on the discriminant ability of a feature subset instead of a single feature. The higher the modified Fisher score $J(B)$ is, the stronger discriminant ability the feature subset B has.

Let t be the iteration number. The modified Fisher score would generate a series $\{J(B_t)\}$, $t = 0, 1, \cdots, m-1$. For this series, we have some properties shown in Theorem 1.

Theorem 1. *Given the series $\{J(B_t)\}$ generated by the modified Fisher score, the following properties hold on for B_t and B_{t+1}:*

- $B_0 = \emptyset$;

- $B_t \subset B_{t+1}, t = 0, \cdots, m-1;$
- $J(B_{t+1}) \leq J(B_t), t = 1, \cdots, m-1.$

The detailed proof can be referred to [5]. According Theorem 1, $J(B_1)$ reaches the maximum value. There is only one feature in B_1, where $J(B_1) = \max_{k=1,\cdots,m}(F(k))$. In the current iteration, a feature should be selected from candidates to the set B_t and then a new set B_{t+1} would be formed. This feature should make $J(B_{t+1})$ maximum. That is to say, the later features are added, the less important they are to the construction of the optimal feature subset. If the score $J(B_t)$ drops to a certain extent, the rest candidates can be discarded. To implement this thought, we set a threshold to stop the process of feature selection. Let $\lambda * \max_{k=1,\cdots,m}(F(k))$ be the threshold, where $\lambda \in (0,1)$. The internal reward formula can be expressed as

$$Reward_t = J(B_t) - \lambda * \max_{k=1,\cdots,m}(F(k)). \tag{7}$$

When $J(B_t)$ drops to a certain extent, the reward is negative. In other words, the selection process can be stopped prematurely if the Q-value corresponding to the highest score is negative.

Exploration and Exploitation. In the training process, how to choose the action under the current state is based on the ϵ-greedy scheme that is to randomly select any optional action under a certain probability, called exploration; otherwise select the action with the largest Q-value in the current state, called exploitation. The ϵ-greedy scheme can be defined as:

$$a_t = \begin{cases} \text{random}(A'), & \text{if } random(0,1) < \epsilon \\ \text{argmax}(Q(s_t)), & \text{otherwise} \end{cases}, \tag{8}$$

where ϵ is the probability of selecting a random action (from the actions available) in the exploration model, $\text{random}(A')$ is to choose an action randomly from A', $random(0,1)$ is randomly generating a real number between 0 and 1, and $\text{argmax}(Q(s_t))$ is to select the action with the largest value of $Q(s_t)$.

In the process of exploration and exploitation, one episode contains at most m rounds. After each episode, a complete feature selection strategy can be generated based on the Q-value table. The specific training process is shown in Algorithm 1.

3.3   Feature Selection

The Q-value table obtained from each episode would be shared, which can be taken out at any time for feature selection without specific iteration stop conditions.

The process of feature selection is similar to that of episode training except for the ϵ-greed scheme; that is, feature selection uses only exploitation without exploration. During the process of feature selection, we pick up the action with the largest Q-value in the current state.

4   Experiments

We test the ability of our method to select discriminant features and compare it with other supervised algorithms on four large-scale UCI data set [2]. Compared methods include max-relevance and min-redundancy (mRMR) [16], Chi-square test (Chi2) [14], Fisher socre (FS) [9], a feature selection method based on the monarch butterfly optimization and Fisher criterion (GCMBO-FC) [18], CFS [15] and our proposed method. KNN is used to classify data processed by feature selection algorithms, where the parameter K of KNN is 5.

All experiments are implemented in JetBrains PyCharm 2019.2.2 or in MAT-LAB R2016a on a PC with an Inter Core I5 processor and 16 GB RAM.

Algorithm 1. Training of Q-value table in QLFS

Input: Data set $X = \{(\mathbf{x}_i, y_i)\}_{i=1}^{n}$;
      Shared Q-value table $\mathbf{Q}$;
      Number of training samples in each episode N_{epi};
      Discount factor γ;
      Ratio of threshold λ
      Maximum number of iterations $MaxItr$;

Output: Q-value table, $\mathbf{Q}$

1: Initialize $\mathbf{Q} = \mathbf{1}_{m*m}$, where $\mathbf{1}_{m \times m}$ is the $m \times m$ matrix of all ones;
2: **repeat**
3:     Get the current episode data set X_{epi};
4:     Initialize the current feature subset $F_{sel} = \emptyset$ of this episode, the candidate feature subset $F_{available} = \{f_1, f_2, \cdots, f_m\} - F_{sel}$ and the initial state $s_t = 0$;
5:     Get the probability ϵ and the learning rate α by Eq.(3);
6:     **repeat**
7:         Select an action a_t for the current state s_t by Eq. (8);
8:         Calculate the modified Fisher score of the feature subset $F_{sel} \cup \{a_t\}$ by Eq. (6) and the intrinsic reward corresponding to this selection by Eq. (7);
9:         Update the Q-table by Eq. (1);
10:        Update $F_{sel} = F_{sel} \cup \{a_t\}$, $F_{available} = F_{available} - \{a_t\}$ and the current state $s_t = s_t + 1$;
11:    **until** $F_{available} = \emptyset$;
12: **until** $MaxItr$.

4.1   Experimental Setting

In experiments, the number of maximum episodes $MaxItr$ in QLFS and CFS is set to be 2000 and the number of samples in each episode N_{epi} is 100. For each data set, we randomly divide the data set into $MaxItr$ subsets and supplement them using the previous subsets. Ensure that all kinds of samples in each subset are evenly distributed. Each algorithm uses the same subset sequence.

In order to avoid contingency, we divide every data set 20 times according to training and test in the proportion 4:1. In addition, all sample features have been normalized.

We show the results from three aspects: (1) the performance of QLFS vs. different λ; (2) results of QLFS and other feature selection methods when $\lambda = 0.2$, where the threshold of CFS is 0 and the selected feature number of other methods is the same as that of QLFS; (3) the running time of each algorithm with the increase of sample numbers. The final classification results are the average ones.

4.2   Information of Data Sets

Here, we conduct experiments on four large-scale data sets: Crowdsourced Mapping (shorted for Map) [11], Online Shoppers Purchasing Intention (shorted for Shopper) [19], MAGIC Gamma Telescope (Shorted for Telescope) [10], and Default of Credit Card Clients (Shorted for Client) [23]. The data information is summarized in Table 1.

Table 1. Information of UCI data sets

Data sets	Samples	Features	Classes
Map	10845	29	6
Shopper	12330	18	2
Telescope	19020	11	2
Client	30000	24	2

4.3   Influence of Parameter λ

First, we observe the effect of parameter λ on the classification performance. The parameter λ varies in the set $\{0.15, 0.2, 0.25, 0.3, 0.35\}$.

The prediction accuracy of KNN vs. episodes ($\times 20$) under different λ is shown in Fig. 2. From results of these four data sets, we can see that different data sets have different optimal λ. When λ is too small, QLFS takes almost all features as the optimal feature subset, which loses the significance of feature selection. When λ is too large, QLFS may select fewer features and exclude some useful features, which cannot achieve good performance. It can be seen from Fig. 2 that although the classification performance greatly depends on λ, a satisfactory result could be obtained in a certain range of λ. For example, λ for Map can be set to 0.15 to 0.2, and for Shopper, Telescope and Client can be 0.2 to 0.3.

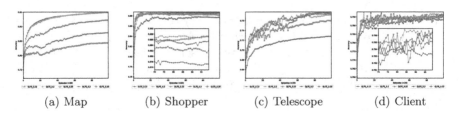

(a) Map   (b) Shopper   (c) Telescope   (d) Client

Fig. 2. Accuracy of KNN vs. episodes ($\times 20$) under different λ on (a) Map, (b) Shopper, (c) Telescope, and (d) Client.

We take the average on the last five nodes (or last 100 episodes) as the final results for different λ, which is shown in Table 2. From this table, we can see that the optimal λ of QLFS may be 0.2 or 0.25. However, no matter what the value is, QLFS has a good stability.

Table 2. Average accuracy (%) over last 100 episodes using different λ

λ	Map	Shopper	Telescope	Client
0.15	$94.88\% \pm 0.39$	$87.71\% \pm 0.68$	$72.80\% \pm 0.53$	$79.33\% \pm 0.44$
0.20	$\mathbf{95.00}\% \pm 0.40$	$\mathbf{88.72}\% \pm 0.39$	$77.15\% \pm 1.14$	$\mathbf{79.61}\% \pm 0.47$
0.25	$92.23\% \pm 1.72$	$\mathbf{88.72}\% \pm 0.52$	$\mathbf{77.73}\% \pm 1.21$	$79.60\% \pm 0.47$
0.30	$87.82\% \pm 2.04$	$88.53\% \pm 0.62$	$77.41\% \pm 1.30$	$79.55\% \pm 0.52$
0.35	$84.31\% \pm 1.60$	$88.19\% \pm 0.65$	$76.00\% \pm 1.14$	$79.54\% \pm 0.64$

4.4   Accuracy Comparison

We compare QLFS with CFS and other classical feature selection methods(Chi2, mRMR, FS and GCMBO-FC). The prediction results of KNN classification after using different feature selection methods are given in Fig. 3.

Compared with both Chi2 and mRMR, the classification accuracy of KNN with the feature subset selected by QLFS is much higher under the same number of features. Compared with FS, the modified FS is effective for measuring the importance of feature subsets. By adopting the Q-learning framework, although only a few samples are used for each episode, QLFS retains the advantage of modified FS in terms of accuracy curve and final effect on the whole. Moreover, QLFS is more effective than GCMBO-FC in improving FS.

Compared with CFS, QLFS is more stable. Because CFS depends on learners and the number of samples in each episode is small, CFS has a large occasionality during the verification of feature subset. On both Telescope and Client data sets, CFS still fluctuates a lot even at the end of training.

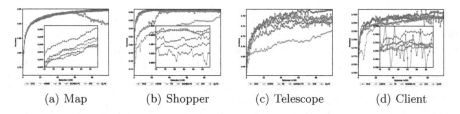

| (a) Map | (b) Shopper | (c) Telescope | (d) Client |

Fig. 3. Accuracy of KNN vs. episodes ($\times 20$) obtained by different feature selection methods on (a) Map, (b) Shopper, (c) Telescope, and (d) Client.

We take the average on the last five nodes (or last 100 episodes) as the final results for different feature selection methods, which is shown in Table 3. In terms of average accuracy, QLFS has the best results on all four data sets. Observation on standard deviation indicates that CFS is the most unstable algorithm. Although QLFS is a batch learning method, its stability is better than classical methods, and is even the best on three data sets.

Table 3. Average accuracy (%) over last 100 episodes using different feature selection methods

Method	Map	Shopper	Telescope	Client
Chi2	$94.59\% \pm 0.57$	$88.41\% \pm 0.45$	$74.71\% \pm 1.40$	$79.30\% \pm 0.45$
mRMR	$94.68\% \pm 0.45$	$86.89\% \pm 2.47$	$73.00\% \pm 2.03$	$79.35\% \pm 0.39$
FS	$94.55\% \pm 0.64$	$88.65\% \pm 0.46$	$75.72\% \pm 1.21$	$79.36\% \pm 0.44$
GCMBO-FC	$94.75\% \pm 0.44$	$88.55\% \pm 0.61$	$75.45\% \pm 1.39$	$79.29\% \pm 0.42$
CFS	$89.87\% \pm 3.10$	$88.13\% \pm 0.67$	$75.12\% \pm 3.41$	$79.24\% \pm 1.16$
QLFS	$\mathbf{95.00\%} \pm 0.40$	$\mathbf{88.72\%} \pm 0.39$	$\mathbf{77.15\%} \pm 1.14$	$\mathbf{79.61\%} \pm 0.47$

4.5   Running Time Comparison

As shown in Fig. 4, we record the running time of each feature selection method at different time points to observe the influence of the size of training set on compared methods.

CFS and QLFS, which are combined with reinforcement learning, retain the results of previous learning and do not need to re-train the previous trained data, so their running time does not increase linearly. The curves of running time obtained by other algorithms increase almost linearly with the increase of training samples. Owing to the long running time of mRMR and GCMBO-FC, no or only part results are shown in Fig. 4.

Since CFS is embedded with a learner, its running time depends not only on the number of samples in each episode, but also on the number of features in verification. With the increase of episodes in CFS, the Q-values in some cases begin to be less than the threshold; that is, the training process is easy to be stopped, so that the running time of single episode begin to decline. The running time of CFS, for example, is decreased from 0.048s to 0.018s for Map in episodes.

Like FS, QLFS is a filter method for feature selection and calculates a score for each feature in each episode. Thus, QLFS only depends on the number of samples and the number of all features in the current episode. Different from CFS and classical algorithms, the training time of QLFS is almost stable at a small value from the beginning. For example, the running time of QLFS on Map is stable at 0.017s, and on Shopper 0.0093s in each episode.

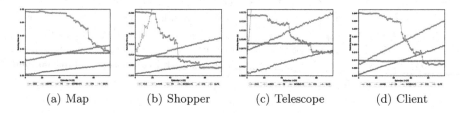

| (a) Map | (b) Shopper | (c) Telescope | (d) Client |

Fig. 4. Running time (s) vs. episodes (×20) obtained by different feature selection methods on (a) Map, (b) Shopper, (c) Telescope, and (d) Client.

4.6   Experimental Summary

The performance of QLFS is mainly related to the parameter λ. At present, we have not found a good way for estimating the value of λ, but we can easily find an applicable range of λ. In this range, QLFS is not very sensitive to λ and can achieve good selection results. QLFS improves the performance of feature selection by modifying FS from only considering single feature to considering the whole feature subset. After adopting the Q-learning framework, QLFS still retains its original advantages and has not been destroyed by batch processing. QLFS as a filter method is more stable than CFS.

In terms of running time, QLFS retains the running speed of previous learning. When the data set is expanded, it does not need to relearn the learned data. The strategy of learning only a part of data in each episode makes the learning time of QLFS stable and shorter. Therefore, QLFS has some advantages over classical feature selection methods.

5   Conclusion

Inspired by CFS, we proposed QLFS based on FS and Q-learning. QLFS can preserve the basic idea of FS that selects features with the greater between-class scatter and the smaller within-class scatter. During the calculation of Fisher scores, QLFS considers the data distribution of the selected feature subset rather than a single feature. QLFS redesigns the Q-value table and changes the intrinsic reward from the wrapper type to the filter type. In experiments, we test the influence of λ on feature selection and prove the superiority of QLFS compared with other algorithms in terms of the accuracy of subsequent classification.

Meanwhile, QLFS does not need to understand the overall situation of the data set and uses only a part of samples in each episode. Even so, QLFS is fast and stable. Therefore, QLFS can be applied to online learning as well as batch learning. In the future, we can further improve the online learning ability of QLFS. Although QLFS achieves good performance in our experiments, there is still some issues in QLFS. One issue is how to confirm the value of λ. We need a more effective way to design a threshold for different data sets. The other is that there may exist better filter methods that can be combined with Q-learning or other RL methods. In the following research, we can try to combine more classical filtering methods with reinforcement learning, not only the collocation of FS and Q-learning.

Acknowledgments. This work was supported in part by the Natural Science Foundation of the Jiangsu Higher Education Institutions of China under Grant No. 19KJA550002, by the Six Talent Peak Project of Jiangsu Province of China under Grant No. XYDXX-054, by the Priority Academic Program Development of Jiangsu Higher Education Institutions, and by the Collaborative Innovation Center of Novel Software Technology and Industrialization.

References

1. Chandrashekar, G., Sahin, F.: A survey on feature selection methods. Comput. Electr. Eng. **40**(1), 16–28 (2014)
2. Dua, D., Graff, C.: UCI machine learning repository (2017). http://archive.ics.uci.edu/ml
3. Gai, K., Qiu, M.: Optimal resource allocation using reinforcement learning for iot content-centric services. Appl. Soft Comput. **70**, 12–21 (2018)
4. Gai, K., Qiu, M.: Reinforcement learning-based content-centric services in mobile sensing. IEEE Netw. **32**(4), 34–39 (2018)
5. Gan, M., Zhang, L.: Iteratively local fisher score for feature selection. Appl. Intell. 1–15 (2021). https://doi.org/10.1007/s10489-020-02141-0
6. Goldberg, Y., Kosorok, M.R.: Q-learning with censored data. Ann. Stat. **40**(1), 529–560 (2012)
7. Gordon, G., Ahissar, E.: Hierarchical curiosity loops and active sensing. Neural Netw. **32**, 119–129 (2012)
8. Gordon, G., Fonio, E., Ahissar, E.: Learning and control of exploration primitives. J. Comput. Neurosci. **37**(2), 259–280 (2014). https://doi.org/10.1007/s10827-014-0500-1
9. Guyon, I., Elisseeff, A.: An introduction to variable and feature selection. J. Mach. Learn. Res. **3**(3), 1157–1182 (2003)
10. Heck, D., Knapp, J., Capdevielle, J., Schatz, G., Thouw, T., et al.: Corsika: a monte carlo code to simulate extensive air showers. Rep. fzka **6019**(11), 1–90 (1998)

11. Johnson, B.A., Iizuka, K.: Integrating openstreetmap crowdsourced data and land-sat time-series imagery for rapid land use/land cover (lulc) mapping: Case study of the laguna de bay area of the philippines. Appl. Geogr. **67**, 140–149 (2016)
12. Keogh, E., Mueen, A.: Curse of dimensionality. Ind. Eng. Chem **29**(1), 48–53 (2009)
13. Li, J., Liu, H.: Challenges of feature selection for big data analytics. IEEE Intell. Syst. **32**(2), 9–15 (2017)
14. Liu, H., Setiono, R.: Chi2: feature selection and discretization of numeric attributes. In: Proceedings of 7th IEEE International Conference on Tools with Artificial Intelligence, pp. 388–391. IEEE (1995)
15. Moran, M., Gordon, G.: Curious feature selection. Inf. Sci. **485**, 42–54 (2019)
16. Peng, H., Long, F., Ding, C.: Feature selection based on mutual information criteria of max-dependency, max-relevance, and min-redundancy. IEEE Trans. Pattern Anal. Mach. Intell. **27**(8), 1226–1238 (2005)
17. Puterman, M.L.: Markov Decision Processes: Discrete Stochastic Dynamic Programming. Wiley, Hoboken (2014)
18. Qi, X., Liu, X., Boumaraf, S.: A new feature selection method based on monarch butterfly optimization and fisher criterion. In: 2019 International Joint Conference on Neural Networks (IJCNN), pp. 1–6. IEEE (2019)
19. Sakar, C.O., Polat, S.O., Katircioglu, M., Kastro, Y.: Real-time prediction of online shoppers' purchasing intention using multilayer perceptron and lstm recurrent neural networks. Neural Comput. Appl. **31**(10), 6893–6908 (2019)
20. Stańczyk, U.: Feature evaluation by filter, wrapper, and embedded approaches. In: Stańczyk, U., Jain, L.C. (eds.) Feature Selection for Data and Pattern Recognition. SCI, vol. 584, pp. 29–44. Springer, Heidelberg (2015). https://doi.org/10.1007/978-3-662-45620-0_3
21. Sutton, R.S., Barto, A.G.: Reinforcement Learning: An Introduction. MIT press, MIT Press, Cambridge (2018)
22. Wang, H., Xu, Z., Fujita, H., Liu, S.: Towards felicitous decision making: An overview on challenges and trends of big data. Inf. Sci. **367**, 747–765 (2016)
23. Yeh, I.C., Lien, C.H.: The comparisons of data mining techniques for the predictive accuracy of probability of default of credit card clients. Expert Syst. Appl. **36**(2), 2473–2480 (2009)

The Modularity of Inconsistent Knowledge Bases with Application to Measuring Inconsistency

Kedian Mu[✉]

School of Mathematical Sciences, Peking University, Beijing 100871,
People's Republic of China
mukedian@math.pku.edu.cn

Abstract. Inconsistency is one of the important issues in knowledge systems, especially with the advent of the world wide web. Given a context of inconsistency characterization, not all the primitive conflicts in an inconsistent knowledge base are independent of one another in many cases. The primitive conflicts tightly associated with each other should be considered as a whole in handling inconsistency. In this paper, we consider the modularity of inconsistency arising in a knowledge base, which provides a promising starting point for parallel inconsistency handling in very large knowledge bases. Then we propose a modularity-based approach to measuring inconsistency for knowledge bases.

Keywords: Inconsistency · Modularity · Conflict modules · Knowledge bases · Inconsistency measuring

1 Introduction

Inconsistency arises easily in knowledge-based systems when knowledge is gathered from heterogeneous or distributed sources. A growing number of theories and techniques for analyzing and resolving inconsistency have been proposed so far in a variety of application domains. In particular, measuring inconsistency has been considered as a promising starting point for better handling inconsistency in many real-world applications recently [13].

A knowledge base (a finite set of propositional formulas) in a propositional logic is inconsistent if there exists a formula such that both the formula and its negation can be derived from the knowledge base. The occurrence of inconsistency in a knowledge base is disastrous, since any proposition can be derived from that knowledge base. In order to analyze and resolve the inconsistency in a knowledge base, we often need to characterize the inconsistency within some specific context in many cases. For example, the set of minimal inconsistent subsets of an inconsistent knowledge base can be considered as a characterization of inconsistency in the sense that one needs to remove only one formula from each minimal inconsistent subset to resolve inconsistency [20]. Here a minimal inconsistent subset refers to an inconsistent subset without an inconsistent proper

© Springer Nature Switzerland AG 2021
H. Qiu et al. (Eds.): KSEM 2021, LNAI 12816, pp. 319–332, 2021.
https://doi.org/10.1007/978-3-030-82147-0_26

subset. Besides this, the set of propositional variables assigned to the designated truth value of *both true and false* in some paraconsistent models such as the $\mathsf{LP_m}$ model in Priest's Logic of Paradox (LP for short) [18] can be considered as a characterization of inconsistency in a context of atom-based analysis of inconsistency [4,6,12]. Here we use the term of primitive conflict introduced in [1] to denote such features of an inconsistent knowledge base used to characterize inconsistency in a given context.

Given a context of inconsistency characterization, if we look inside the set of primitive conflicts, we can find that not all the primitive conflicts are independent of one another for some inconsistent knowledge bases. Some primitive conflicts may be tightly associated with each other for some given knowledge base. For example, in the context of characterizing inconsistency by minimal inconsistent subsets, the association among some minimal inconsistent subsets of a knowledge base due to their overlaps has been considered in some approaches to measuring inconsistency based on minimal inconsistent subsets [7-10,15].

Such associations among primitive conflicts bring a natural partition of the set of primitive conflicts such that only primitive conflicts in the same cluster are associated with one another under the given context of inconsistency characterization. To illustrate this, consider knowledge bases $K = \{a \wedge c, \neg a, b, \neg b, c, \neg c, \neg a \vee b, d, \neg d\}$ under the context of characterizing the inconsistency with minimal inconsistent subsets. Note that K has five minimal inconsistent subsets $\{a \wedge c, \neg a\}$, $\{b, \neg b\}$, $\{a \wedge c, \neg a \vee b, \neg b\}$, $\{c, \neg c\}$, and $\{d, \neg d\}$. The first three minimal inconsistent subsets of K are tightly associated with one other because both $\{a \wedge c, \neg a\}$ and $\{b, \neg b\}$ overlap $\{a \wedge c, \neg a \vee b, \neg b\}$. Then it is intuitive to consider that K has three separate clusters of primitive conflicts, which arise from the three separate parts $\{a \wedge c, \neg a, b, \neg b, \neg a \vee b\}$, $\{c, \neg c\}$ and $\{d, \neg d\}$ of K, respectively. The first cluster consists of the first three minimal inconsistent subsets, while the other two clusters consists of the last two minimal inconsistent subsets, respectively. On the other hand, within the context of atom-based characterization in the framework of LP, it is intuitive to divide $\{a, b, c, d\}$ (atoms assigned to the designated truth value) into two clusters, i.e., $\{a, b, c\}$ and $\{d\}$. Correspondingly, K can be divided into two subsets, i.e., $\{d, \neg d\}$ and $K \setminus \{d, \neg d\}$.

In such cases, it is advisable to take into account the separate clusters of primitive conflicts instead of individuals to handle the inconsistency in a knowledge base. Moreover, such a consideration provides a promising starting point for handling the inconsistency in a knowledge base in a parallel way, because any two primitive conflicts from different clusters are independent of each other. This is attractive to inconsistency handling for very large knowledge bases.

In this paper, we focus on taking such a partition of an inconsistent knowledge base into account in characterizing and handling inconsistency for that base. At first, we propose a notion of module to split an inconsistent knowledge base into several parts such that each inconsistent part (module) has only one block of primitive conflicts under a given context of inconsistency characterization. Moreover, we show that there exists a unique module-based partition for a knowledge base under the given context. Then we propose a modularity-based framework for measuring the inconsistency in a knowledge base, which allows us to integrate the inconsistency assessments for modules of the base to assess the inconsistency of the whole knowledge base in a flexible way.

The rest of this paper is organized as follows. In Sect. 2 we introduce some necessary notions about inconsistency characterization. In Sect. 3 we propose the notion of module of a knowledge base, and then we give some instances. In Sect. 4 we propose a modularity-based framework for measuring the inconsistency in a knowledge base. In Sect. 5 we compare our work with some very closely related work. Finally, we conclude this paper in Sect. 6.

2 Preliminaries

We use a finite propositional language in this paper. Let $\mathcal{P}$ be a finite set of propositional atoms (or variables) and $\mathcal{L}$ a propositional language built from $\mathcal{P}$ and two propositional constants $\top$ (true) and $\bot$ (false) under connectives $\{\neg, \wedge, \vee\}$. We use $a, b, c, \cdots$ to denote the propositional atoms, and $\alpha, \beta, \gamma, \cdots$ to denote the propositional formulas.

A *knowledge base* K is a finite set of propositional formulas. For two knowledge bases K and K' such that $K \cap K' = \emptyset$, we use $K + K'$ instead of $K \cup K'$ to denote the union of K and K'.

K is *inconsistent* if there is a formula α such that $K \vdash \alpha$ and $K \vdash \neg\alpha$, where $\vdash$ is the classical consequence relation. We abbreviate $\alpha \wedge \neg\alpha$ as $\bot$ when there is no confusion. Then we use $K \vdash \bot$ (resp. $K \nvdash \bot$) to denote that a knowledge base K is inconsistent (resp. consistent). An inconsistent subset K' of K is called a *minimal inconsistent subset* of K if no proper subset of K' is inconsistent. We use $\mathsf{MI}(K)$ to denote the set of all the minimal inconsistent subsets of K. A formula in K is called a *free formula* if this formula does not belong to any minimal inconsistent subset of K [4]. We use $\mathsf{FREE}(K)$ to denote the set of free formulas of K. Evidently, $K = (\bigcup \mathsf{MI}(K)) \cup \mathsf{FREE}(K)$, where $\bigcup \mathsf{MI}(K) = \cup_{M \in \mathsf{MI}(K)} M$.

Given a knowledge base K, a subset R of K is called a *minimal correction subset* of K if $K \setminus R \nvdash \bot$ and for any $R' \subset R$, $K \setminus R' \vdash \bot$. We use $\mathsf{MC}(K)$ to denote the set of all the minimal correction subsets of K.

It is well known that an inconsistent knowledge base K has no classical model. Some paraconsistent models have been established for inconsistent knowledge bases. Without loss of generality, we introduce the $\mathsf{LP_m}$ model, one of the simple but representative paraconsistent models [4,6,12], in this paper.

The $\mathsf{LP_m}$ model [18] of knowledge bases is given in the framework of Priest's Logic of Paradox (LP for short) [19]. Roughly speaking, Priest's Logic of Paradox provides three-valued models for inconsistent knowledge bases by expanding the classical truth values $\{\mathsf{T}, \mathsf{F}\}$ to the set $\{\mathsf{T}, \mathsf{F}, \{\mathsf{T}, \mathsf{F}\}\}$, in which the third truth value $\{\mathsf{T}, \mathsf{F}\}$ (also abbreviated as B in [6,12]) is considered intuitively as both true and false [18]. Here we use the following notations and the concepts about the $\mathsf{LP_m}$ model used in [6]. An interpretation ω for $\mathsf{LP_m}$ models maps each propositional variable to one of the three truth values $\mathsf{T}, \mathsf{F}, \mathsf{B}$ such that

– $\omega(\text{true}) = T$, $\omega(\text{false}) = F$,
– $\omega(\neg\alpha) = B$ if and only if $\omega(\alpha) = B$, $\omega(\neg\alpha) = T$ if and only if $\omega(\alpha) = F$,
– $\omega(\alpha \wedge \beta) = \min_{\leq_t}\{\omega(\alpha), \omega(\beta)\}$, $\omega(\alpha \vee \beta) = \max_{\leq_t}\{\omega(\alpha), \omega(\beta)\}$,

where $F <_t B <_t T$. Then the set of models of a formula α is defined as $\mathsf{Mod}_{\mathsf{LP}}(\alpha) = \{\omega | \omega(\alpha) \in \{T, B\}\}$. Further, the set of models of a knowledge base K is defined as $\mathsf{Mod}_{\mathsf{LP}}(K) = \{\omega | \omega \in \mathsf{Mod}_{\mathsf{LP}}(\alpha) \text{ for all } \alpha \in K\}$.

Let ω be an interpretation and K a knowledge base, then we use $\omega!(K)$ to denote the set of propositional variables of K assigned to B by ω. Based on $\omega!(K)$, we can define the minimal models of K w.r.t. $\omega!(K)$ as follows:

$$\mathsf{MinMod}_{\mathsf{LP}}(K) = \{\omega \in \mathsf{Mod}_{\mathsf{LP}}(K) | \forall \omega' \in \mathsf{Mod}_{\mathsf{LP}}(K), \omega!(K) \not\subset \omega'!(K)\}.$$

The probability distribution on the language $\mathcal{L}$ presented in [16,17] is defined as follows: a function $P : \mathcal{L} \mapsto [0, 1]$ is a probability function on $\mathcal{L}$ if P satisfies

– if $\models \alpha$, then $P(\alpha) = 1$,
– if $\models \neg(\alpha \wedge \beta)$, then $P(\alpha \vee \beta) = P(\alpha) + P(\beta)$.

Probability distributions over a knowledge base describe how plausible each formula can be true. Note that there is no probability distribution such that the probability of each formula of K is 1 if $K \vdash \bot$.

3   Conflict Modules

In this section, we propose a notion of conflict modules to characterize an inconsistent knowledge base. We start with the notion of partition of a knowledge base.

Let K be a knowledge base, a set $\mathcal{B} = \{B^{(i)} | \emptyset \subset B^{(i)} \subseteq K\}_{i=0}^m$ with $B^{(i)} \cap B^{(j)} = \emptyset$ for $i \neq j$ of subsets of K, is called a partition of K if $\sum_{i=0}^m B_i = K$.

Let K be a knowledge base and $\mathcal{A}(K)$ the set of atoms of formulas in K. A set $\{A^{(i)} | \emptyset \subset A^{(i)} \subseteq \mathcal{A}(K)\}_{i=0}^m$ with $A^{(i)} \cap A^{(j)} = \emptyset$ for $i \neq j$ of subsets of $\mathcal{A}(K)$, is called a partition of $\mathcal{A}(K)$ if $\sum_{i=0}^m A_i = \mathcal{A}(K)$. Such a partition may be considered as a kind of language split used in belief change in some sense. Let $\emptyset \subset A \subseteq \mathcal{A}(K)$, we use $\mathcal{F}(A)$ to denote the set of formulas containing at least one variable of A in K.

We can also split a knowledge base into several parts according to the separation of their atoms. Let K be a knowledge base, a partition $\mathcal{B} = \{B^{(i)} | \emptyset \subset B^{(i)} \subseteq K\}_{i=0}^m$ of K, is called an A-partition of K if $\mathcal{F}(\mathcal{A}(B_i)) = B_i$ for all $0 \leq i \leq m$. Evidently, if $\{B^{(i)}\}_{i=0}^m$ is an A-partition of K, then $\{\mathcal{A}(B^{(i)})\}_{i=0}^m$ is a partition of $\mathcal{A}(K)$.

Further, if a partition $\mathcal{B}$ of K satisfies a given constraint such as $\mathcal{F}(\mathcal{A}(B_i)) = B_i$, then we call $\mathcal{B}$ a *constrained partition*. Essentially, an A-partition of K is a constrained partition of K. A partition $\mathcal{B}_1$ of K is a *refinement* of a partition $\mathcal{B}_2$ of K if every element of $\mathcal{B}_1$ is a subset of some element of $\mathcal{B}_2$.

Here we use $\mathcal{C}_\mu(K)$ to denote the set of primitive conflicts of K under the context μ of inconsistency characterization. For example, if we use minimal inconsistent subsets to characterize the inconsistency of K, then the set of primitive conflicts of K is exactly $\mathsf{MI}(K)$. Now we are ready to define the conflict modules of a knowledge base.

Definition 1. *Let K be an inconsistent knowledge base and μ a context of inconsistency characterization. Then a set $\{K^{(i)}|K^{(i)} \subseteq K\}_{i=1}^m$ of subsets of K with $K^{(i)} \cap K^{(j)} = \emptyset$ for $i \neq j$, is called the set of conflict modules of K w.r.t. μ, if*

(1) $K^{(i)} \vdash \bot$, $i = 1, 2, \ldots, m$,

(2) $\mathcal{C}_\mu(\sum_{l=1}^{k} K^{(i_l)}) = \sum_{l=1}^{k} \mathcal{C}_\mu(K^{(i_l)})$ for all $1 \leq i_1 < \cdots < i_k \leq m$,

(3) $\mathcal{C}_\mu(\sum_{i=1}^{m} K^{(i)}) = \mathcal{C}_\mu(K)$,

(4) for each $K^{(i)}$, there is no constrained partition of $K^{(i)}$ w.r.t. μ, or for each partition $\{K_1^{(i)}, K_2^{(i)}\}$ of $K^{(i)}$, $\mathcal{C}_\mu(K_1^{(i)}) + \mathcal{C}_\mu(K_2^{(i)}) \subset \mathcal{C}_\mu(K^{(i)})$.

Here (1) states that each conflict module of K is inconsistent. (2) states that any union of conflict modules cannot bring any new primitive conflict under the context μ. This essentially ensures that the primitive conflicts in different conflicts modules exactly belong to different blocks of primitive conflicts under the context μ. (3) states that all the primitive conflicts in K are distributed over the conflicts modules of K. (4) states that each conflict module is a unity in characterizing inconsistency under the context μ.

Just for simplicity, the set of conflict modules of a consistent knowledge base is considered as $\emptyset$. If the set of conflict modules of an inconsistent knowledge base K is $\{K\}$, then we call K *a modular knowledge base*. We call $K \setminus \sum_{i=1}^{m} K^{(i)}$ the conflict-free module of K. We use $K^{(0)}$ to denote the conflict-free module of K. Evidently, if K is consistent, its conflict-free module is itself. From now on, we call the partition $\{K^{(i)}\}_{i=0}^m$ the set of modules of K.

Proposition 1. *Let K be an inconsistent knowledge base and μ a context of inconsistency characterization. Then there is a unique set of conflict modules of K w.r.t. μ.*

Proof. Let $\{K_1^{(i)}\}_{i=1}^m$ and $\{K_2^{(j)}\}_{j=1}^n$ be two different sets of conflict modules of K. Without loss of generality, suppose that $K_1^{(1)}$ is covered by $K_2^{(1)}$ and $K_2^{(2)}$, i.e., $K_1^{(1)} \subseteq K_2^{(1)} \cup K_2^{(2)}$ and $K_1^{(1)} \cap K_2^{(1)} \neq \emptyset$, $K_1^{(1)} \cap K_2^{(2)} \neq \emptyset$.

If there is no constrained partition of $K_1^{(1)}$ w.r.t. μ, then consider $\alpha_1 \in K_1^{(1)} \cap K_2^{(1)}$ and $\alpha_2 \in K_1^{(1)} \cap K_2^{(2)}$, then $\alpha_1 \in K_2^{(1)}$ and $\alpha_2 \in K_2^{(2)}$. This contradicts that α_1 and α_2 must be in the same part when we partition K in the context μ.

If there is at least one constrained partition of $K_1^{(1)}$ w.r.t. μ, then there exists at least one primitive conflict $C \in \mathcal{C}_\mu(K_1^{(1)})$ such that $F(C) \cap K_2^{(1)} \neq \emptyset$

and $F(C) \cap K_2^{(2)} \neq \emptyset$, where $F(C)$ is the set of formulas involved in C. So, $C \notin C_\mu(K_2^{(1)})$ and $C \notin C_\mu(K_2^{(2)})$, but $C \in C_\mu(K_2^{(1)}+K_2^{(2)})$. Therefore, $C_\mu(K_2^{(1)})+C_\mu(K_2^{(2)}) \subset C_\mu(K_2^{(1)}+K_2^{(2)})$. This contradicts that $\{K_2^{(j)}\}_{j=1}^n$ is also a set of modules of K w.r.t. μ. Therefore, $\{K_1^{(i)}\}_{i=1}^m = \{K_2^{(j)}\}_{j=1}^n$. □

Here we give some instances of conflicts modules. Consider the case μ_M where the inconsistency of a knowledge base is characterized by minimal inconsistent subsets of K. We define a relation R_{μ_M} over $\bigcup \mathsf{MI}(K)$ as follows: $(\alpha, \beta) \in R_{\mu_M}$ if and only if there exists a sequence $\alpha_0, \cdots, \alpha_n$ of formulas in $\bigcup \mathsf{MI}(K)$ with $\alpha_0 = \alpha$ and $\alpha_n = \beta$ such that α_{i-1} and α_i belong to the same minimal inconsistent subset for all $1 \leq i \leq n$. Evidently, R_{μ_M} is an equivalence relation. We use $[\alpha]_{\mu_M}$ to denote the equivalence class α belongs to, i.e., $[\alpha]_{\mu_M} = \{\beta \in \bigcup \mathsf{MI}(K) | (\alpha, \beta) \in R_{\mu_M}\}$. Then the set of conflict modules of K w.r.t. μ_M is given as the quotient set of $\bigcup \mathsf{MI}(K)$ by R_{μ_M}.

Proposition 2. *Let K be an inconsistent knowledge base. Then*

- *the set of conflict modules of K w.r.t. μ_M is given as $\{[\alpha]_{\mu_M} | \alpha \in \bigcup \mathsf{MI}(K)\}$;*
- *the conflict-free module $K^{(0)} = \mathsf{FREE}(K)$.*

Proof. Given $K \vdash \bot$, suppose that $\{[\alpha_1]_{\mu_M}, \ldots, [\alpha_m]_{\mu_M}\}$ is the quotient set of $\bigcup \mathsf{MI}(K)$ by R_{μ_M}. It can be easily shown that the quotient set satisfies conditions (1)-(3) of definition of conflict modules. For the condition (4), any split of $[\alpha_i]_{\mu_M}$ can break at least one minimal inconsistent subset, then $\mathsf{MI}(S_1) + \mathsf{MI}(S_2) \subset \mathsf{MI}([\alpha_i]_{\mu_M})$ for any partition $\{S_1, S_2\}$ of $[\alpha_1]_{\mu_M}$. Therefore, $\{[\alpha]_{\mu_M} | \alpha \in \bigcup \mathsf{MI}(K)\}$ is the set of conflict modules of K w.r.t. μ_M, and $K^{(0)} = \mathsf{FREE}(K)$. □

Example 1. Consider $K_1 = \{a, \neg a, \neg a \vee b, \neg b \wedge d, \neg d \wedge e, c, \neg c, e \vee f, g\}$. Then $\mathsf{MI}(K_1) = \{M_1, M_2, M_3, M_4\}$, where $M_1 = \{a, \neg a\}$, $M_2 = \{a, \neg a \vee b, \neg b \wedge d\}$, $M_3 = \{\neg b \wedge d, \neg d \wedge e\}$, and $M_4 = \{c, \neg c\}$. The set of conflict modules of K_1 with regard to μ_M is $\{\{a, \neg a, \neg a \vee b, \neg b \wedge d, \neg d \wedge e\}, \{c, \neg c\}\}$, and the corresponding conflict-free module of K_1 is $\{e \vee f, g\}$. The set of minimal inconsistent subsets of K_1 can be divided into two blocks, i.e., $\{M_1, M_2, M_3\}$ and $\{M_4\}$.

Now we give an A-partition of K based on the dependence of formulas on atoms. We define a relation R_A over K as follows: $(\alpha, \beta) \in R_A$ if and only if there exists a sequence $\alpha_0, \cdots, \alpha_n$ of formulas in K with $\alpha_0 = \alpha$ and $\alpha_n = \beta$ such that α_{i-1} and α_i have at least one common atom for all $1 \leq i \leq n$. Evidently, R_A is an equivalence relation. We use $[\alpha]_A$ to denote the equivalence class α belongs to, i.e., $[\alpha]_A = \{\beta \in K | (\alpha, \beta) \in R_A\}$. Evidently, $\mathcal{F}(\mathcal{A}([\alpha]_A)) = [\alpha]_A$. Then $\{[\alpha]_A | \alpha \in K\}$ is exactly an A-partition of K.

Consider an atom-based case μ_L where the inconsistency of a knowledge base is characterized by the set of propositional variables assigned to B by minimal $\mathsf{LP_m}$ models, that is, $C_{\mu_L}(K) = \{a \in \mathcal{A}(K) | \exists \omega \in \mathsf{MinMod_{LP}}(K) s.t. \omega(a) = \mathsf{B}\}$. Then the set of conflict modules of K w.r.t. μ_L can be given by the following proposition.

Proposition 3. *Let K be an inconsistent knowledge base. Then*

– *the set of conflict modules of K w.r.t. μ_L is given as*

$$\{[\alpha]_A | \alpha \in K \text{ s.t. } [\alpha]_A \vdash \bot\};$$

– *the conflict-free module $K^{(0)} = \sum_{[\alpha]_A \nvdash \bot} [\alpha]_A.$*

Proof. Let K be an inconsistent knowledge base and $\alpha \in K$ such that $[\alpha]_A \vdash \bot$. Then for any $\beta \in K$ such that $\beta \notin [\alpha]_A$, then it holds that $b \notin \mathcal{C}_{\mu_L}([\alpha]_A)$ for all $b \in \mathcal{A}(\{\beta\})$. Then it is easy to check that the conditions (1), (2), and (3) of the definition of conflict modules are satisfied. Note that for any proper subset $S \neq \emptyset$ of $[\alpha]_A$, $\mathcal{F}(\mathcal{A}(S)) \neq S$. So, the condition (4) is also satisfied. $\square$

Example 2. Consider K_1 again. The set of conflict modules of K_1 with regard to either μ_L is $\{\{a, \neg a, \neg a \vee b, \neg b \wedge d, \neg d \wedge e, e \vee f\}, \{c, \neg c\}\}$, and the corresponding conflict-free module of K_1 is $\{g\}$.

The corresponding partition of atoms is $\{\{a, b, d, e, f\}, \{c\}, \{g\}\}$. The set of atoms assigned to B by minimal LP_m models can be split into two blocks, i.e., $\{a, d\}$ and $\{c\}$.

Consider a case μ_P of probability-based inconsistency characterization where the primitive conflicts are represented by minimal P-inconsistent subsets. Here a subset S of K is called a P-inconsistent subset of K if $\mathcal{F}(\mathcal{A}(S)) = S$, and there is no probability distribution P on S such that $P(\alpha) = 1$ for all $\alpha \in S$. A P-inconsistent subset S is called a minimal P-inconsistent of K if no proper subset of S is P-inconsistent. Then the set of conflict modules of K w.r.t. μ_P can be given by the following proposition.

Proposition 4. *Let K be an inconsistent knowledge base. Then*

– *the set of conflict modules of K w.r.t. μ_P is given as*

$$\{[\alpha]_A | \alpha \in K \text{ s.t. } [\alpha]_A \vdash \bot\};$$

– *the conflict-free module $K^{(0)} = \sum_{[\alpha]_A \nvdash \bot} [\alpha]_A.$*

Proof. Let K be an inconsistent knowledge base and $\alpha \in K$. Note that $[\alpha]_A$ is a minimal P-inconsistent subset iff $[\alpha]_A \vdash \bot$. $\square$

However, for any context μ_A of atom-based or valuation-based or paraconsistent models-based inconsistency characterization, the set of conflict modules of K w.r.t. μ_A is exactly $\{[\alpha]_A | \alpha \in K \text{ s.t. } [\alpha]_A \vdash \bot\}$.

4   Module-Based Inconsistency Assessment

The modularity of inconsistent knowledge bases provides a good starting point to measure inconsistency in a parallel way. Given a context of inconsistency characterization, the primitive conflicts of an inconsistent knowledge base are distributed over the conflict modules of that base. Moreover, the primitive conflicts in each conflict module exactly comprise a separate block. Then a desirable inconsistency measure should take into account the inconsistency assessment of each module as well as the way to integrate the assessments of these modules in order to assess the inconsistency of the whole knowledge base. To this end, we first give a general framework to define an inconsistency measure based on modules of a knowledge base.

Definition 2. *Let K be a knowledge base. Then the inconsistency measure for K with regard to μ, denoted $I_\mu(K)$, is a module-based measure if*

$$I_\mu(K) = \delta(I_\mu(K^{(0)}), I_\mu(K^{(1)}), \cdots, I_\mu(K^{(m)})), \tag{1}$$

where $\{K^{(i)}\}_{i=1}^m$ (possibly empty) is the set of conflict modules of K with regard to μ, and δ is an operation for integrating the measures of modules with $\delta(x) = x$.

Now we give some existing instances of module-based measures.

- The measure $I_{MI}(K)$ presented in [6] is defined as the number of minimal inconsistent subsets of K. Then by Proposition 2, $I_{MI}(K) = \sum_{i=0}^m I_{MI}(K^{(i)})$.
- The measure $I_{dr}(K)$ presented in [14] is defined as the smallest size of minimal correction subsets of K. Then by Proposition 2, $I_{dr}(K) = \sum_{i=0}^m I_{dr}(K^{(i)})$.
- The measure $I_{LP_m}(K)$ presented in [4,6] is defined as the normalized minimum number of variables assigned inconsistent truth values in $\mathsf{LP_m}$ models (with regard to $|\mathcal{P}|$). Then by Proposition 3, $I_{LP_m}(K) = \sum_{i=0}^m I_{LP_m}(K^{(i)})$.
- *The maximal η-consistency* presented in [11] is one of the most representative of probability-based measures. For $0 \leq \eta \leq 1$, a knowledge base K is η-consistent if there exists a probability function P such that $P(\alpha) \geq \eta$ for all $\alpha \in K$. Furthermore, K is maximally η-consistent if K is η-consistent, and for all $\gamma > \eta$, K is not γ-consistent. If we define $I_{pr}(K) = \eta$ if K is maximally η-consistent, then by Proposition 4, $I_{pr}(K) = \min_{0 \leq i \leq m} I_{pr}(K^{(i)})$.

The behavior of the module-based inconsistency measure depends on properties of assessments for modules as well as characteristics of the integration operation δ. Just for simplicity, we assume that any inconsistency measure discussed from now on is a non-negative inconsistency measure such that the higher the inconsistency value, the more inconsistent a knowledge base is.

In order to characterize a module-based inconsistency measure, we consider the following postulates about the integration operation δ firstly. Let $x_i \geq 0$ for $i \geq 0$,

- *0-Invariance:* $\delta(x_0, x_1, \cdots, x_m) = \delta(x_1, \cdots, x_m)$ if $x_0 = 0$.
- *M-Monotony:* $\delta(x_0, \cdots, x_m) \leq \delta(x_0, \cdots, x_m, x_{m+1})$ for $0 \leq m$.
- *R-Monotony:* $\delta(x_0, \cdots, x_i, x_{i+1}, \cdots, x_m) \leq \delta(y, x_{i+1}, \cdots, x_m)$ if $\delta(x_0, \cdots, x_i) \leq y$.

Essentially, the property of 0-Invariance says that the variables with the value 0 play no role in the integration of nonnegative variables under δ. The property of M-monotony says that the result of integration under δ cannot decrease as we extend the set of variables to be integrated. The property of R-monotony says that replacing a set of variables with some variable greater than the integration of these variables cannot make the result of integration under δ decrease.

Evidently, both $\delta(x_0, x_1, \cdots, x_m) = \sum_{i=0}^{m} x_i$ and $\delta(x_0, x_1, \cdots, x_m) = \max_{0 \le i \le m} x_i$ satisfy all the three postulates.

Then we consider the properties of inconsistency assessment for modules and modular knowledge bases.

- *Consistency*: $I_\mu(K^{(i)}) = 0$ if and only if $i = 0$.
- *$\subseteq$-Monotony*: $I_\mu(K) \le I_\mu(K')$ for two modular knowledge bases K and K' such that $K \subseteq K'$.
- *Reinforcement*: Suppose that $K_1, \ldots, K_{n-1}$, and K_n are modular knowledge bases with regard to μ such that $\sum_{i=1}^{n-1} K_i \subseteq K_n$, then

$$\delta(I_\mu(K_1), \cdots, I_\mu(K_{n-1})) \le I_\mu(K_n).$$

- *M-Dominance*: Let $\mathcal{B}_\beta$ and $\mathcal{B}_\alpha$ be the sets of modules of $K \cup \{\beta\}$ and $K \cup \{\alpha\}$ for two formulas α and β not in K, respectively, then $\delta(I_\mu(K')|K' \in \mathcal{B}_\alpha \setminus \mathcal{B}_\beta) \ge \delta(I_\mu(K'')|K'' \in \mathcal{B}_\beta \setminus \mathcal{B}_\alpha)$ if $\alpha \vdash \beta$ and $\alpha \not\vdash \bot$.

The property of Consistency says that only the conflict-free module has null inconsistency assessment. However, it is exactly the property of consistency presented in [6]. The property of $\subseteq$-monotony says that the inconsistency measure for modular knowledge bases is monotonic w.r.t. set inclusion. The property of Reinforcement says that the inconsistency assessment of a modular knowledge base obtained by connecting a number of smaller disjoint modular knowledge bases is not less than the result of integration of assessments of these smaller modular knowledge bases. The property of M-Dominance states the result of integration of new modules cannot be less than that of the modules disappeared by replacing a formula with another logically stronger formula.

Besides the property of Consistency presented in [6], the properties of Monotony, Free Formula Independence, and Dominance presented in [4–6], and the property of Safe Formula Independence (also termed as Weak Independence in [21]) presented in [6] are considered as representative ones for characterizing inconsistency measures. In detail, let I be an inconsistency measure, then

- *Consistency* : $I(K) = 0$ if and only if K is consistent.
- *Monotony*: $I(K \cup K') \ge I(K)$.
- *Free Formula Independence*: If $\alpha \in \mathsf{FREE}(K \cup \{\alpha\})$, then $I(K \cup \{\alpha\}) = I(K)$.
- *Dominance*: If $\alpha \notin K$ and $\alpha \vdash \beta$ and $\alpha \not\vdash \bot$, then $I(K \cup \{\alpha\}) \ge I(K \cup \{\beta\})$.
- *Safe Formula Independence*: If $\mathcal{A}(\{\alpha\}) \cap \mathcal{A}(K) = \emptyset$ and $\alpha \not\vdash \bot$, then $I(K \cup \{\alpha\}) = I(K)$.

Here we adopt the revised form of Dominance presented by [2].

However, the following propositions show that the postulates of the integration operation and the properties of inconsistency measures for modules and modular knowledge bases guarantee the satisfaction of these representative properties by the module-based inconsistency measure.

Proposition 5. *If I_μ satisfies $I_\mu(K^{(0)}) = 0$, and δ satisfies 0-Invariance, then $I_\mu(K \setminus K^{(0)}) = I_\mu(K)$.*

Proof. Let $\{K^{(i)}\}_{i=1}^m$ be the set of conflict modules of K, then if $I_\mu(K^{(0)}) = 0$, $I_\mu(K) = \delta(0, I_\mu(K^{(1)}), \cdots, I_\mu(K^{(m)}))$. Further, by 0-Invariance, $I_\mu(K) = \delta(I_\mu(K^{(1)}), \cdots, I_\mu(K^{(m)})) = I_\mu(K \setminus K^{(0)})$. □

Corollary 1. *If $I_{\mu M}$ satisfies $I_{\mu M}(K^{(0)}) = 0$, and δ satisfies 0-Invariance, then $I_{\mu M}$ satisfies the property of Free Formula Independence.*

Proof. If α is a free formula of $K \cup \{\alpha\}$, then $(K \cup \{\alpha\})^{(0)} = K^{(0)} \cup \{\alpha\}$. Then by Proposition 5, $I_{\mu M}(K \cup \{\alpha\}) = I_{\mu M}(K \cup \{\alpha\} \setminus K \cup \{\alpha\}^{(0)}) = I_{\mu M}(K \setminus K^{(0)}) = I_{\mu M}(K)$. □

Corollary 2. *If $I_{\mu L}$ satisfies $I_{\mu L}(K^{(0)}) = 0$, and δ satisfies 0-Invariance, then $I_{\mu L}$ satisfies the property of Safe Formula Independence.*

Proof. Note that α is a safe formula of K, then α is also a free formula of K. □

Proposition 6. *If I_μ satisfies $\subseteq$-Monotony and Reinforcement, and δ satisfies M-monotony and R-monotony, then I_μ satisfies the property of Monotony.*

Proof. Let $\{(K)^{(i)}\}_{i=0}^m$ and $\{(K \cup K')^{(j)}\}_{j=0}^n$ be sets of modules of K and $K \cup K'$, respectively. Moreover, suppose that for $j > k$, $(K \cup K')^{(j)} \cap (K)^{(i)} = \emptyset$ for all $i = 1, 2, \cdots, m$. Suppose that $x_i = I_\mu((K)^{(i)})$ and $y_j = I_\mu((K \cup K')^{(j)})$. Then if $(K)^{(i)}$ is not a module of $K \cup K'$, then there exists some $(K \cup K')^{(j)}$ such that $(K)^{(i)} \subset (K \cup K')^{(j)}$. Suppose that $(K)^{(j_1)}, \cdots, (K)^{(j_l)} \subset (K \cup K')^{(j)}$. Then by Reinforcement, it holds that $\delta(x_{j_1}, \cdots, x_{j_l}) \leq y_j$. Further, by R-monotony, it holds that $\delta(x_1, \cdots, x_{j_1}, \cdots, x_{j_l}, \cdots, x_m) \leq \delta(x_1, \cdots, y_j, \cdots, x_m)$. Then by M-monotony, $\delta(x_1, \cdots, x_m) \leq \delta(x_1, \cdots, x_m, y_k, y_{k+1}, \cdots, y_n)$. Further, by $\subseteq$-Monotony and the two inequalities above, it holds that $\delta(x_1, \cdots, x_m) \leq \delta(y_1, \cdots, y_{k-1}, y_k, y_{k+1}, \cdots, y_n)$. □

Proposition 7. *If I_μ satisfies $\subseteq$-Monotony, M-Dominance and Reinforcement, and δ satisfies M-monotony and R-monotony, then I_μ satisfies the property of Dominance.*

Proof. Let $\mathcal{B}_\beta$ and $\mathcal{B}_\alpha$ be the sets of modules of $K \cup \{\beta\}$ and $K \cup \{\alpha\}$ for two formulas α and β not in K, respectively, then $I_\mu(K \cup \{\alpha\}) = \delta(I_\mu(K')|K' \in \mathcal{B}_\alpha)$ and $I_\mu(K \cup \{\beta\}) = \delta(I_\mu(K')|K' \in \mathcal{B}_\beta)$.

Let K_α be the module of $K \cup \{\alpha\}$ such that $\alpha \in K_\alpha$. Then $I_\mu(K \cup \{\alpha\}) = \delta(I_\mu(K_\alpha), I_\mu(K')|K' \in \mathcal{B}_\alpha \setminus \{K_\alpha\})$. Note that $I_\mu(K_\beta) \leq \delta(I_\mu(K'')|K'' \in \mathcal{B}_\beta \setminus \mathcal{B}_\alpha)$ and $I_\mu(K_\alpha) = \delta(I_\mu(K'')|K'' \in \mathcal{B}_\alpha \setminus \mathcal{B}_\beta) \geq \delta(I_\mu(K'')|K'' \in \mathcal{B}_\beta \setminus \mathcal{B}_\alpha)$. Therefore, $I_\mu(K \cup \{\alpha\}) \geq \delta(I_\mu(K'')|K'' \in (\mathcal{B}_\beta \setminus \mathcal{B}_\alpha) + \mathcal{B}_\alpha \setminus \{K_\alpha\})$. So, $I_\mu(K \cup \{\alpha\}) \geq I_\mu(K \cup \{\beta\})$. □

Lastly we give two new instances of module-based inconsistency measure guided by these postulates.

Definition 3. *Let K be a knowledge base and $\{K^{(i)}\}_{i=0}^m$ the set of modules of K with regard to μ_M. Then the inconsistency measure $I_{\max}(K)$ for K is defined as $I_{\max}(K) = \max\limits_{0 \leq i \leq m} I_{dr}(K^{(i)})$.*

Essentially, $I_{\max}(K)$ use the maximum value of modules of K as the inconsistency value of the whole knowledge.

Proposition 8. *$I_{\max}$ satisfies the properties of Consistency, Free Formula Independence, Safe Formula Independence, Monotony, and Dominance.*

Proof. Note that proofs for Consistency, Free Formula Independence, Safe Formula Independence and Monotony are trivial. Here we just focus on Dominance. Let $\alpha \notin K$ and $\alpha \vdash \beta$ and $\alpha \not\vdash \bot$. Let K_α (resp. K_β) be a module of $K \cup \{\alpha\}$ (resp. $K \cup \{\beta\}$) such that $\alpha \in K_\alpha$ (resp.$\beta \in K_\beta$). Let $K_1, K_2, \ldots, K_m$ be the modules of $K \cup \{\beta\}$ such that $K_i \cap K_\alpha \neq \emptyset$ and $K_i \neq K_\beta$ for all $i = 1, 2, \cdots, m$.

Let R be the smallest correction subset of K_α. If $\alpha \notin R$, then R is also a (not necessarily minimal) correction subset of $K_\beta \cup K_1 \cup \cdots \cup K_m$. If $\alpha \in R$, then $R \cup \{\beta\} \setminus \{\alpha\}$ is a correction subset of $K_\beta \cup K_1 \cup \cdots \cup K_m$. So, $I_{dr}(K_\alpha) \geq I_{dr}(K_\beta \cup K_1 \cup \cdots \cup K_m)$. Therefore, $I_{\max}(K \cup \{\alpha\}) \geq I_{\max}(K \cup \{\beta\})$. □

Definition 4. *Let K be a knowledge base and $\{K^{(i)}\}_{i=0}^m$ the set of modules of K with regard to μ_M. Then the inconsistency measure $I_e(K)$ for K is defined as*

$$I_e(K) = \delta_e(I_e(K^{(0)}), \cdots, I_e(K^{(m)})) = \begin{cases} \prod\limits_{i=1}^m I_e(K^{(i)}), & \text{if } m \geq 1 \\ 0, & \text{otherwise.} \end{cases}$$

where $I_e(K^{(0)}) = 0$ and $I_e(K^{(i)}) = e^{I_{dr}(K^{(i)})}$ for $1 \leq i \leq m$.

Note that $I_e(K^{(i)}) > 1$, then we have the following result.

Proposition 9. *I_e satisfies the properties of Consistency, Free Formula Independence, Safe Formula Independence, Monotony, and Dominance.*

The proof is similar to the proof above. So we omit it.

5   Comparison and Discussion

Splitting an inconsistent knowledge into their modules provides a promising starting point for handling inconsistency for big knowledge bases in a parallel way. Note that the notion of conflict module is based on the association among primitive conflicts under a given context of inconsistency characterization.

Within the context μ_M where the inconsistency is characterized by minimal inconsistent subsets, the notion of strong-partition presented in [7] and the notion of MIS partition presented in [9] are similar to that of the set of conflict modules. All the three notions take into account the association among minimal inconsistent subsets of an inconsistent knowledge base. But they are different from one another in essence. The MIS-partition is a partition of the set of minimal inconsistent subsets. Instead, both the set of modules and the strong partition are partitions of the whole knowledge base. Note that the set of conflict modules must cover all the minimal inconsistent subsets as well as their associations. So, all the blocks of minimal inconsistent subsets remain unchanged in conflict modules. However, this does not hold for strong partition. To illustrate this, consider $K = \{a, \neg a, b, \neg b, \neg a \vee b\}$, then the conflict module of K is itself, while the strong partition of K is $\{\{a, \neg a\}, \{b, \neg b\}, \{\neg a \vee b\}\}$. On the other hand, the MIS-partition also tends to break the associations among minimal inconsistent subsets. Consider K again. The MIS-partition of $\mathsf{MI}(K)$ is $\{\{\{a, \neg a\}, \{b, \neg b\}\}, \{\{a, \neg a \vee b, \neg b\}\}\}$. Such a partition breaks the block consists of all the three minimal inconsistent subsets.

In addition, the language splitting-based belief revision [3] seems similar to the modularity of inconsistent knowledge base. However, the language splitting-based belief revision aims to isolate local relevant information to new information when the new information brings conflicts to the old belief base, whilst we split an inconsistent knowledge base into several separate parts according to the distribution of all primitive conflicts given a context of inconsistency characterization.

The modularity-based framework for measuring the inconsistency in a knowledge base consists of two parts, i.e., inconsistency assessments for conflict modules and the integration operation over them. The sum operation is an usual one for integrating a set of variables. In this case, it is advisable to adapt the properties about additivity such as MinInc Separation presented in [6], Ind-decomposability presented in [7], and Sub-Additivity presented in [9] to ones in terms of modules.

6   Conclusion

We have proposed the notion of conflict modules to capture the association among primitive conflicts as well as all the primitive conflicts of a knowledge base under a given context of inconsistency characterization. The association among primitive conflicts makes primitive conflicts comprise separate blocks, each of which should be considered as a whole in inconsistency handling. Given a knowledge base, each of conflict modules exactly contains one block of primitive conflicts of that base, moreover, all the primitive conflicts are distributed over the conflict modules.

Then we have proposed a flexible framework for measuring inconsistency of a knowledge based on modularization of that knowledge base, which consists of two parts, i.e., inconsistency assessments for conflict modules and the integration operation over them. Some intuitive postulates about integration operation and properties for inconsistency assessment for modules have been proposed to characterize the framework.

Acknowledgements. This work was partly supported by the National Natural Science Foundation of China under Grant No.61572002, No. 61690201, and No. 61732001.

References

1. Besnard, P.: Revisiting postulates for inconsistency measures. In: Fermé, E., Leite, J. (eds.) JELIA 2014. LNCS (LNAI), vol. 8761, pp. 383–396. Springer, Cham (2014). https://doi.org/10.1007/978-3-319-11558-0_27
2. Besnard, P.: Basic postulates for inconsistency measures. In: Hameurlain, A., Küng, J., Wagner, R., Decker, H. (eds.) Transactions on Large-Scale Data- and Knowledge-Centered Systems XXXIV. LNCS, vol. 10620, pp. 1–12. Springer, Heidelberg (2017). https://doi.org/10.1007/978-3-662-55947-5_1
3. Hansson, S.O., Wassermann, R.: Local change. Studia Logica **70**(1), 49–76 (2002). https://doi.org/10.1023/A:1014654208944
4. Hunter, A., Konieczny, S.: Shapley inconsistency values. In: Doherty, P., Mylopoulos, J., Welty, C. (eds.) KR2006, pp. 249–259. AAAI Press (2006)
5. Hunter, A., Konieczny, S.: Measuring inconsistency through minimal inconsistent sets. In: Brewka, G., Lang, J. (eds.) KR08, pp. 358–366. AAAI Press (2008)
6. Hunter, A., Konieczny, S.: On the measure of conflicts: Shapley inconsistency values. Artif. Intell. **174**(14), 1007–1026 (2010)
7. Jabbour, S., Ma, Y., Raddaoui, B.: Inconsistency measurement thanks to mus decomposition. In: Bazzan, A.L.C., Huhns, M.N., Lomuscio, A., Scerri, P. (eds.) AAMAS 2014, Paris, France, 5–9 May, 2014, pp. 877–884. IFAAMAS/ACM (2014)
8. Jabbour, S., Ma, Y., Raddaoui, B., Sais, L., Salhi, Y.: On structure-based inconsistency measures and their computations via closed set packing. In: Weiss, G., Yolum, P., Bordini, R.H., Elkind, E. (eds.) AAMAS 2015, Istanbul, Turkey, 4–8 May, 2015, pp. 1749–1750. ACM (2015)
9. Jabbour, S., Ma, Y., Raddaoui, B., Sais, L., Salhi, Y.: A MIS partition based framework for measuring inconsistency. In: Baral, C., Delgrande, J.P., Wolter, F. (eds.) KR 2016, Cape Town, South Africa, 25–29 April, 2016, pp. 84–93. AAAI Press (2016)
10. Jabbour, S., Sais, L.: Exploiting MUS structure to measure inconsistency of knowledge bases. In: Kaminka, G.A., et al. (eds.) ECAI 2016. Frontiers in Artificial Intelligence and Applications, vol. 285, pp. 991–998. IOS Press (2016)
11. Knight, K.: Measuring inconsistency. J. Philos. Logic **31**(1), 77–98 (2002)
12. Konieczny, S., Lang, J., Marquis, P.: Quantifying information and contradiction in propositional logic through epistemic actions. In: Gottlob, G., Walsh, T. (eds.) Proceedings of the 18th International Joint Conference on Artificial Intelligence (IJCAI2003), pp. 106–111. Morgan Kaufmann (2003)

13. Liu, W., Mu, K.: Introduction to the special issue on theories of inconsistency measures and their applications. Int. J. Approx. Reasoning **89**, 1–2 (2017)
14. Mu, K.: Responsibility for inconsistency. Int. J. Approx. Reasoning **61**, 43–60 (2015)
15. Mu, K.: Measuring inconsistency with constraints for propositional knowledge bases. Artif. Intell. **259**, 52–90 (2018)
16. Paris, J.: The Uncertain Reasoner's Companion: A Mathematical Perspective, Cambridge Tracts in Theoretical Computer Science 39. Cambridge University Press (1994)
17. Paris, J., Vencovska, A.: Proof systems for probabilistic uncertain reasoning. J. Symbolic Logic **63**(3), 1007–1039 (1998)
18. Priest, G.: Minimally inconsistent LP. Studia Logica **50**(1), 321–331 (1991)
19. Priest, G.: The logic of paradox. J. Philos. Logic **8**(1), 219–241 (1979)
20. Reiter, R.: A theory of diagnosis from first principles. Artif. Intell. **32**(1), 57–95 (1987)
21. Thimm, M.: Measuring inconsistency in probabilistic knowledge bases. In: UAI 2009, Montreal, Canada, June 2009, pp. 530–537. AUAI Press (2009)

Collaborative Embedding for Knowledge Tracing

Jianwen Sun[1], Jianpeng Zhou[2], Kai Zhang[2(✉)], Qing Li[1], and Zijian Lu[2]

[1] National Engineering Laboratory for Educational Big Data,
Central China Normal University, Wuhan, China
sunjw@ccnu.edu.cn, viven_a@mail.ccnu.edu.cn
[2] National Engineering Research Center for E-Learning, Central China Normal
University, Wuhan, China
zhangkai@mail.ccnu.edu.cn, {hi.zhou,ronghwa_lu}@mails.ccnu.edu.cn

Abstract. Knowledge tracing predicts students' future performance based on their past performance. Most of the existing models take skills as input, which neglects question information and further limits the model performance. Inspired by item-item collaborative filtering in recommender systems, we propose a question-question Collaborative embedding method for Knowledge Tracing (CoKT) to introduce question information. To be specific, we incorporate student-question interactions and question-skill relations to capture question similarity. Based on the similarity, we further learn question embeddings, which are then integrated into a neural network to make predictions. Experiments demonstrate that CoKT significantly outperforms baselines on three benchmark datasets. Moreover, visualization illustrates that CoKT can learn interpretable question embeddings and achieve more obvious improvement on AUC when the interaction data is more sparse.

Keywords: Knowledge tracing · Question embedding · Collaborative embedding · Bipartite graph · Student assessment

1 Introduction

Knowledge Tracing (KT) is an essential task in intelligent tutoring systems, which aims at tracing students' knowledge states over time and predicting the probability they answer new questions correctly. KT can model the learning processes and facilitate personalized learning guidance (e.g. skip easy questions and delay difficult questions) to improve learning efficiency and experience.

Researchers have proposed varied KT models including probability based models [1], factor analysis models [10] and deep models [6,13]. In this paper, we focus on the type of deep models, which take advantage of recent advances in deep learning and have achieved great success in KT [6,13]. Generally, most deep KT models input skills and estimate the mastery of skills, rather than assess students' capability to answer specific questions correctly. Thus they are defined

© Springer Nature Switzerland AG 2021
H. Qiu et al. (Eds.): KSEM 2021, LNAI 12816, pp. 333–342, 2021.
https://doi.org/10.1007/978-3-030-82147-0_27

as skill-level models [4]. These models use only skills to represent questions, which makes them unable to distinguish questions that share the same skills but vary in other aspects such as difficulty [3,8].

To distinguish different questions, a straightforward method is to input questions instead of skills in these models. However, since many questions are just attempted by few students, it's difficult for KT model to capture the characteristics of these questions and make accurate predictions on the probability of answering these questions correctly. This problem is known as the sparsity issue and also discussed in [4,8,11,12,14].

To address the sparsity issue, our basic idea is to introduce question similarity. The underlying assumption of this idea is that if two questions are answered by the same student with the same response (both correct or both incorrect) or they share the same skills, then they are regarded to be similar. Besides, the probability of the same student correctly answering similar questions is close. Thus, based on the question similarity, KT model can make more accurate predictions on the questions which have few training records and thereby suffer less from the sparsity issue. Therefore, we propose a Collaborative embedding method for Knowledge Tracing (CoKT) to mine question similarity from accessible data and further learn the question embeddings. Technically, we firstly construct two graphs based on student-question interactions and question-skill relations respectively. Secondly, we generate question node sequences that contain the question similarity from the two graphs. Finally, we transfer the similarity into question embeddings through skip-gram algorithm.

Our contributions are as follows: 1) We propose an approach for extracting question similarity to enhance question representation. 2) To our knowledge, we are the first to use student-question interaction graph to learn question embeddings. 3) Our method significantly improves the prediction performance of KT models, and can learn interpretable question embeddings and alleviate the sparsity issue.

2   Related Work

2.1   Knowledge Tracing

Since taking only skills as input limits model performance, several works proposed to take advantage of question information as a supplement. According to the type of question information they mainly use, we classify these works into two categories. One category of models utilize intrinsic information of questions such as text descriptions and difficulty. For example, [3,9] encode text descriptions into question embeddings to capture the individual characteristics of questions. [5] calculates question difficulty and utilizes it to distinguish the questions sharing the same skills. The other category of models mainly focus on interactive information among students, questions and skills, such as student-question interactions and question-skill relations. For instance, [11] uses the relations between questions and skills as a constraint to train question embeddings. [4] use the relations between questions and skills to construct a bipartite graph and capture the implicit similarity between questions. In our work, we utilize not only question-skill relations but also student-question interactions to mine collaborative information of questions, and then learn question embeddings based on node2vec algorithm.

2.2 Item-Item Collaborative Filtering

Item-item collaborative filtering [7] is a technique in recommender systems, which utilizes users' ratings on items to calculate the similarity between items (collaborative) and then recommends candidate items to users based on the similarity between candidate items and users' already-rated items (filtering). Inspired by the idea, we mine the similarity between questions from student-question interactions and question-skill relations (collaborative), and then transfer the similarity information into question embeddings (embedding).

3   Problem Formulation

3.1   Knowledge Tracing

Knowledge tracing can be formalized as: given a student's historical interaction sequence $X = \{(q_1,r_1),(q_2,r_2),\ldots,(q_t,r_t)\}$ and q_{t+1}, where (q_t,r_t) represents the question q_t and response $r_t \in \{0,1\}$ (0 represents wrong response and 1 represents correct response) at step t, the goal is to predict the probability that the student correctly answers the next question q_{t+1}, $P(r_{t+1}=1|X,q_{t+1})$.

3.2   Student-Question Interaction Graph

Let $U = \{u_i\}_{i=1}^{N_u}$ be the student set and $Q = \{q_j\}_{j=1}^{N_q}$ be the question set, where N_u and N_q are respectively the number of student and the number of question. Usually, each student u_i answers some questions $\{q_1, ..., q_{m_i}\}$ correctly and answers other questions $\{q_1, ..., q_{n_i}\}$ incorrectly, where m_i and n_i are respectively the number of questions the student u_i answers correctly and incorrectly. We denote the student-question interactions as a student-question interaction graph $G_{uq} = \{(u, r_{uq}, q)|u \in U, q \in Q\}$, where $r_{uq} = 1$ if the student u answers the question q correctly, otherwise $r_{uq} = 0$.

3.3   Question-Skill Relation Graph

Additionally, let $S = \{s_k\}_{k=1}^{N_s}$ be the skill set, where N_s is the number of skill. Generally, one question q_j corresponds to one or more skills $\{s_1, ..., s_{n_j}\}$, where n_j is the number of skills related to question q_j. We denote the question-skill relations as a question-skill relation graph $G_{qs} = \{(q, r_{qs}, s)|q \in Q, s \in S\}$, where $r_{qs} = 1$ if the question q is labeled with the skill s.

4   Method

The overall framework of CoKT is illustrated in Fig. 1, which consists of four modules: Pre-training Module, Fusion Module, Knowledge State (KS) Module and Prediction Module. The highlight of CoKT lies in the Pre-training Module.

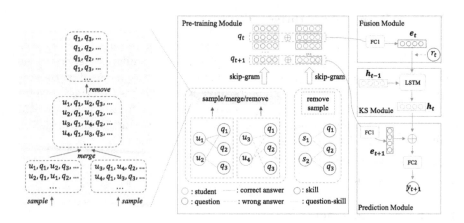

Fig. 1. The overall framework of CoKT.

4.1   Pre-training Module

Bipartite Graph Construction. According to the definition in Sect. 3.2, we use student-question interactions in train dataset to build the student-question graph. Intuitively, two questions answered by the same student with different responses are less likely to be similar, so the coexisting of correct and wrong interactions in one graph may bring more noise than benefits. For this reason, we separate the student-question graph into two bipartite graphs, each of which contains either correct interactions or wrong interactions. And they are respectively denoted as G_{uq}^c and G_{uq}^w. Likewise, according to the definition in Sect. 3.3, we construct the question-skill bipartite graph with question-skill relations. Based on the constructed graphs, we will generate question node sequences and further learn question feature vectors (see Algorithm 1 for an overall view).

Node Sequence Generation. We sample node sequences on the bipartite graphs and process them to get homogeneous question node sequences. Under our assumption of question similarity, similar questions have common user or skill neighbors, so in the sampled question node sequences the more similar two questions are, the closer they are and the more frequently they co-occur.

For the student-question graph, we adopt the following strategy. Firstly, we *sample* node sequences on G_{uq}^c and G_{uq}^w separately with a biased random walk procedure, following node2vec [2], to get two groups of node sequences. Then, we *merge* these two groups of node sequences. Finally, we *remove* non-question nodes in the sequences, because we just focus on capturing the similarity between question nodes. For the question-skill graph, we simply *sample* node sequences and *remove* non-question nodes. Until now, we get two sets of question node sequences which are respectively derived from the student-question graph and the question-skill graph.

Feature Vector Learning. We do the following operations on the two sets of processed sequences separately so as to obtain two feature vectors for each question: slide a fixed-size window over the set of sequences to obtain the neighbors of each node, and then apply skip-gram algorithm, which maximizes the co-occurrence probability between the nodes and their neighbors, to learn the feature vector of each node.

Algorithm 1: Pre-training Algorithm

Input: student-question graph $G_{uq}^c = (V_u \cup V_q, E_{uq}^c)$ and $G_{uq}^w = (V_u \cup V_q, E_{uq}^w)$, question-skill graph $G_{qs} = (V_q \cup V_s, E_{qs})$, window size w, embedding size d, walks per node r, walk length l, return p, in-out q

Output: question feature vectors $\Phi_{uq} \in R^{|V_q| \times d}$, $\Phi_{qs} \in R^{|V_q| \times d}$

1   // for student-question graph
2   $W_{uq}^c = \text{node2vecWalks}(G_{uq}^c, r, l, p, q)$
3   $W_{uq}^w = \text{node2vecWalks}(G_{uq}^w, r, l, p, q)$
4   $W_{uq} = \text{Merge}(W_{uq}^c, W_{uq}^w)$
5   $W_{uq} = \text{Remove}(W_{uq})$
6   $\Phi_{uq} = \text{SkipGram}(w, d, W_{uq})$
7   // for question-skill graph
8   $W_{qs} = \text{node2vecWalks}(G_{qs}, r, l, p, q)$
9   $W_{qs} = \text{Remove}(W_{qs})$
10   $\Phi_{qs} = \text{SkipGram}(w, d, W_{qs})$
11   return Φ_{uq}, Φ_{qs}

12 **Def Merge**(*walks* W_{uq}^c, W_{uq}^w):
13   Initialize W_{uq} to W_{uq}^c
14   **for** *walk* in W_{uq}^w **do**
15   append *walk* to W_{uq}
16   **return** W_{uq}
17 **Def Remove**(*walks* W):
18   Initialize W' to empty
19   **for** *walk* in W **do**
20   delete non-question nodes from *walk*
21   append *walk* to W'
22   **return** W'

4.2 Fusion Module

In the Fusion Module, for the sake of getting the embedding e_t of each question as well as feature crossing and dimension reduction, the two feature vectors of the question are concatenated and followed by a non-linear layer. Furthermore, to combine the question and response, we concatenate the question embedding e_t and zero vector $\mathbf{0} = (0, 0, ..., 0)$ with the same d dimensions of question embedding to obtain the combined input vector $x_t \in \mathbf{R}^{2d}$ as implemented in [3]:

$$x_t = \begin{cases} [e_t \oplus \mathbf{0}], \ r_t = 1 \\ [\mathbf{0} \oplus e_t], \ r_t = 0 \end{cases} \tag{1}$$

where $\oplus$ is the operation that concatenates two vectors.

4.3   Knowledge State Module

In the Knowledge State (KS) Module, for each time step t, the knowledge state is defined as the hidden state h_t and updated based on the current input vector x_t and the previous state h_{t-1} in a recurrent formula:

$$h_t = LSTM(x_t, h_{t-1}; \theta_h) \tag{2}$$

where θ_h are the parameters of LSTM.

4.4   Prediction Module

The Prediction Module estimates an interaction function between the knowledge state vector and the next question's embedding, which can be learned with a neural network, to calculate the predictive probability y_{t+1} that a student answers the next question correctly. Referring to [3], we take the calculation as:

$$\begin{aligned} o_{t+1} &= \text{ReLU}\left(\mathbf{W}_1 \cdot [h_t \oplus e_{t+1}] + \mathbf{b}_1\right) \\ y_{t+1} &= \text{Sigmoid}\left(\mathbf{W}_2 \cdot o_{t+1} + \mathbf{b}_2\right) \end{aligned} \tag{3}$$

where o_{t+1} denotes the overall representation of next question and knowledge state, and $\mathbf{W}_1$, $\mathbf{W}_2$, $\mathbf{b}_1$ and $\mathbf{b}_2$ are the parameters.

4.5   Optimization

To train CoKT (except for pre-training module), we use Adam gradient descent algorithm by minimizing the cross entropy loss between the predictive probabilities and the true labels of the student's responses. Formally, let y_{t+1} be the predictive probability and r_{t+1} be the true label at t-th step, and thus the loss function is defined as:

$$\mathcal{L} = -\sum_{t=0}^{T-1} (r_{t+1} \log y_{t+1} + (1 - r_{t+1}) \log(1 - y_{t+1})) \tag{4}$$

5   Experiments

5.1   Experimental Settings

Datasets. We conduct our experiments on three commonly-used datasets in KT and the detailed statistics of datasets are reported in Table 1.

For all datasets, we remove records without skills and combine multiple skills into a new joint skill for skill-level DKT and DKVMN models. For student response sequences that are shorter than 3, we just drop them because too short sequences are meaningless. And for those that are longer than 200, we break them up into several shorter ones for computational efficiency reason. For each dataset, we split 80% of all the sequences as training set, 20% as test set.

Table 1. Datasets statistics.

	ASSIST09	ASSIST12	EdNet
#students	3,852	27,485	5,000
#questions	17,737	53,065	12,161
#skills	123	265	189
#exercises	282,619	2,709,436	676,974
Questions per skill	173	200	147
Skills per question	1.197	1.000	2.280
Attempts per question	16	51	56
Attempts per skill	2,743	10,224	8,420

Baselines. The baselines are as follows: DKT [6], which takes one-hot encoding of skills as input and represents knowledge state with a single hidden vector in recurrent neural network, DKVMN [13], which uses memory network to store knowledge state of each concept separately instead of using a single hidden vector, and DKT-Embed, which is our question-level extension (input questions instead of skills) to DKT and generates input vectors by an embedding layer.

We also compare three simplified versions of CoKT: CoKT-NoStu, which removes the student-question graph from CoKT, CoKT-NoSkill, which removes the question-skill graph from CoKT, and CoKT-Embed, which removes the two graphs and learns question embeddings merely by an embedding layer.

5.2   Prediction Task

We use AUC (Area Under the Curve) as the metric to evaluate the performance of all KT models on predicting binary-valued student responses to future questions. The higher the AUC, the better the model performs. Each experiment is repeated 5 times, and the average performance is reported. Table 2 reports the AUC results of all models, and we find several observations as below.

1) CoKT and CoKT-NoSkill outperform baselines on all datasets. Particularly, CoKT achieves 4.6% absolute AUC improvement on average in comparison with DKT and DKVMN.

2) The performance of CoKT is better than CoKT-NoStu, which implies that the student-question graph can provide plentiful similarity information among questions to improve KT models.

3) By comparing skill-level DKT and question-level DKT-Embed, we note that DKT-Embed underperforms DKT on ASSIST09, but outperforms DKT on ASSIST12 and EdNet, which indicates that they may either suffer from the sparsity issue or the issue caused by inputting only skills. The supremacy of CoKT on all datasets confirms its efficacy in tackling both the issues.

4) In terms of input information, both CoKT-Embed and CoKT-NoSkill utilize only student-question interactions, but CoKT-NoSkill which incorporates embedding model (node2vec) performs much better. This demonstrates a

promising application of embedding models to explicitly learn question embeddings in KT.

Table 2. The AUC over three datasets.

Model	ASSIST09	ASSIST12	EdNet
DKT	0.7561	0.7286	0.6822
DKVMN	0.7550	0.7283	0.6967
DKT-Embed	0.7268	0.7431	0.7191
CoKT-Embed	0.7535	0.7591	0.7384
CoKT-NoStu	0.7620	0.7338	0.7108
CoKT-NoSkill	0.7835	0.7737	0.7452
CoKT	0.7928	0.7802	0.7464

5.3 Question Embedding Visualization

We use t-SNE to project high-dimensional question embeddings to 2-D points, colored according to their skills. We select the 20 skills with the largest number of related questions and then visualize the embeddings of the questions that related to any of these skills. Figure 2 clearly shows that questions with the same skills are close to each other, and questions that do not share common skills are well separated, which indicates that our method can preserve the skill-level similarity among questions into interpretable question embeddings.

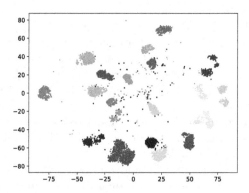

Fig. 2. Visualization of the embeddings of questions and related skills

5.4   The Sparsity Issue

We hold the view that the sparsity issue occurs when many questions have few attempts. In this way, KT model can not fully capture those questions' characteristics during the training process, so the AUC of those questions are relatively lower and ultimately reduce the overall AUC of model. We conduct an experiment to verify this explanation and show that CoKT has the ability to alleviate the sparsity issue. Specifically, we first calculate each question's attempt number in train dataset and AUC in test dataset, and then group questions according to their attempt number. After that, we calculate each group's average attempt number and the mean of the group of AUC values. Finally, we observe how the mean AUC of each group varies with its average attempt number. Figure 3 demonstrates that: 1) The mean AUC increases with the number of attempts, which indicates that fewer attempts on questions result in lower AUC; 2) in the range of low attempt number, CoKT gains more obvious improvement over DKT-Embed. This means that CoKT can improve the AUC of questions that have few attempts, which shows its capability to alleviate the sparsity issue.

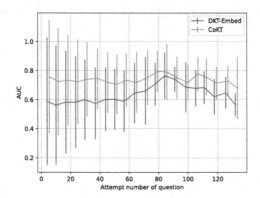

Fig. 3. The mean AUC varies with the average attempt number of questions (the smaller the attempt number is, the more sparse the group of data is).

6   Conclusion

In this paper, we addressed the problem caused by using only skills to represent questions in KT models. We proposed a novel model CoKT, which extracts question similarity from student-question interactions and question-skill relations to enhance question representation. Experiments showed that CoKT significantly outperforms baselines and can alleviate the sparsity issue. In future work, we intend to exploit richer interactive information such as exercise duration to describe student-question interactive process more precisely.

Acknowledgements. This research is supported by National Natural Science Foundation of China (62077021, 62077018, 61807012), Humanity and Social Science Youth Foundation of Ministry of Education of China (20YJC880083), and Teaching Research Funds for Undergraduates and Postgraduates of CCNU.

References

1. Corbett, A.T., Anderson, J.R.: Knowledge tracing: modeling the acquisition of procedural knowledge. User Model. User-Adapt. Interact. **4**(4), 253–278 (1994)
2. Grover, A., Leskovec, J.: node2vec: scalable feature learning for networks. In: Proceedings of the 22nd ACM SIGKDD International Conference on Knowledge Discovery and Data Mining, pp. 855–864 (2016)
3. Liu, Q., et al.: EKT: exercise-aware knowledge tracing for student performance prediction. IEEE Trans. Knowl. Data Eng. **33**(1), 100–115 (2019)
4. Liu, Y., Yang, Y., Chen, X., Shen, J., Zhang, H., Yu, Y.: Improving knowledge tracing via pre-training question embeddings. In: Proceedings of the Twenty-Ninth International Joint Conference on Artificial Intelligence, IJCAI-20, pp. 1577–1583 (2020)
5. Minn, S., Desmarais, M.C., Zhu, F., Xiao, J., Wang, J.: Dynamic student classiffication on memory networks for knowledge tracing. In: Yang, Q., Zhou, Z.-H., Gong, Z., Zhang, M.-L., Huang, S.-J. (eds.) PAKDD 2019. LNCS (LNAI), vol. 11440, pp. 163–174. Springer, Cham (2019). https://doi.org/10.1007/978-3-030-16145-3_13
6. Piech, C., et al.: Deep knowledge tracing. Adv. Neural Inf. Process. Syst. **28**, 505–513 (2015)
7. Sarwar, B., Karypis, G., Konstan, J., Riedl, J.: Item-based collaborative filtering recommendation algorithms. In: Proceedings of the 10th International Conference on World Wide Web, pp. 285–295 (2001)
8. Sonkar, S., Waters, A.E., Lan, A.S., Grimaldi, P.J., Baraniuk, R.G.: qDKT: Question-centric deep knowledge tracing. In: Proceedings of the 13th International Conferenceon Educational Data Mining (2020)
9. Tong, H., Zhou, Y., Wang, Z.: Exercise hierarchical feature enhanced knowledge tracing. In: Bittencourt, I.I., Cukurova, M., Muldner, K., Luckin, R., Millán, E. (eds.) AIED 2020. LNCS (LNAI), vol. 12164, pp. 324–328. Springer, Cham (2020). https://doi.org/10.1007/978-3-030-52240-7_59
10. Vie, J.J., Kashima, H.: Knowledge tracing machines: factorization machines for knowledge tracing. Proc. AAAI Conf. Artif. Intell. **33**, 750–757 (2019)
11. Wang, T., Ma, F., Gao, J.: Deep hierarchical knowledge tracing. In: Proceedings of the 12th International Conference on Educational Data Mining (2019)
12. Yang, Y., et al.: GIKT: a graph-based interaction model for knowledge tracing. In: Machine Learning and Knowledge Discovery in Databases (2020)
13. Zhang, J., Shi, X., King, I., Yeung, D.Y.: Dynamic key-value memory networks for knowledge tracing. In: Proceedings of the 26th international conference on World Wide Web, pp. 765–774 (2017)
14. Zhang, N., Du, Y., Deng, K., Li, L., Shen, J., Sun, G.: Attention-based knowledge tracing with heterogeneous information network embedding. In: Li, G., Shen, H.T., Yuan, Y., Wang, X., Liu, H., Zhao, X. (eds.) KSEM 2020. LNCS (LNAI), vol. 12274, pp. 95–103. Springer, Cham (2020). https://doi.org/10.1007/978-3-030-55130-8_9

Construction and Analysis of Cross-Regional Emergency Collaboration Network Model

Yunlei Zhang[✉], Xiangyao Ma, Huayu Guan, and Ling Wang

North China Institute of Science and Technology, Sanhe, Hebei, China
zhangyunlei@ncist.edu.cn

Abstract. In recent years, the impact of accidents and disasters in the region has expanded, and many places are unable to handle major accidents and disasters alone, requiring cross-regional collaboration. To address the difficult issues of reasonable and effective allocation of various emergency resources such as funds and materials in the process of cross-regional collaboration, in this paper, we introduce a network model to construct an emergency collaboration network by linking the emergency response center, rescue sites and affected sites. Using the network analysis method, including the key node analysis, community discovery and so on, to assist in solving the problems of emergency material allocation and emergency rescue partner discovery. Finally, the visualization technology is used to show the emergency coordination network to the emergency managers, so as to assist their emergency decision-making.

Keywords: Cross-regional · Emergency collaboration · Complex network

1 Introduction

In recent years, with the rapid development of China's regional integration, the collaborative development between regions is more and more close, and the influence of regional accidents and disasters is gradually expanding. Many places can not deal with major accidents and disasters alone, and need cross regional collaborative processing, such as the catastrophic flood in the Yangtze River Basin in 1998, the snow and ice disaster in 2008, the "5. 12" earthquake in Wenchuan, the typhoon "litchi horse" which seriously affected the southeast coast in 2019, and the New Coronavirus infection in early 2020, in China. In the face of these major disasters, the related regions need unified coordination and joint response. However, the collaboration mechanism of cross-regional emergency management in China has just started. In the process of response, there are some problems, such as the lack of cross-regional early warning mechanism, weak ability of joint response and so on. Therefore, how to maintain the cross-regional accurate and dynamic emergency collaboration ability all the time, and have the emergency rescue ability to quickly respond and resolve the risk when the risk comes, so as

© Springer Nature Switzerland AG 2021
H. Qiu et al. (Eds.): KSEM 2021, LNAI 12816, pp. 343–350, 2021.
https://doi.org/10.1007/978-3-030-82147-0_28

to build an efficient collaborative emergency system to deal with cross-regional accidents and disasters, has become a major practical problem that emergency managers urgently need to study and solve.

In this paper, we studied cross-regional collaborative comprehensive risk prevention method. The reasonable and effective allocation of funds, materials and other emergency resources is not only the difficulty of emergency management, but also an important guarantee of cross-regional emergency collaboration construction. Firstly, we analyze the relationship among the response center, the rescue site and the disaster site of each region, construct the emergency collaborative network with the specific situation of each region, and analyze the optimal emergency resource allocation scheme. Secondly, combined with the historical disaster data of the emergency collaborative network, the key regions in the network are determined to assist the decision-making of material reserve. Thirdly, according to the network model, emergency management departments at all levels and their related departments need to make use of their own resources and form a partnership to further assist emergency decision-making. Finally, we visualize the emergency collaborative network to assist the emergency managers to make decisions.

The structure of this paper is as following: Sect. 1 discusses the introduction, in Sect. 2 a comparative study is made on related works to cross-regional emergency collaboration network model. Section 3 elaborates the proposed model. Finally, in Sect. 4, we conclude the work and disscuss the future work.

2   Related Works

Nagurney et al. [10] integrated a variety of commodity trading modes into the Supply Chain Supernetwork equilibrium model, and discussed the influence of the Internet on the Supply Chain Supernetwork equilibrium. Cruz et al. [4] put forward a super network dynamic model of global supply chain with social network involving financial engineering method. In the field of supply chain, Xu et al. [1] considered that different consumers have different preferences for the attributes of product quality or brand, studied the Supply Chain Supernetwork equilibrium conditions under multi-user and multi criteria random selection. Zhu et al. [7,8] analyzed the interaction between the disaster risk environment and the dynamic allocation of emergency resources by using the super network theory, in which the disaster risk degree and the number of emergency resources allocation were taken as the network flow of the disaster network and the emergency network respectively. Cao et al. [5,9] put forward the super network structure and model of multi-level urban agglomeration emergency coordination, which is composed of rescue sites, transit sites and disaster affected sites, aiming at the situation of cross city disasters or resource shortage in a single city, and used the stochastic equilibrium assignment theory to study the random selection of multiple emergency allocation methods in decision-making. In view of the disasters that affect many different regions, considering the difference of disaster rescue, Zhu [6] built a cross-regional collaborative emergency rescue path selection model considering efficiency and fairness, taking the shortest total rescue time and the lowest deprivation cost as multiple objectives. According to the characteristics of proximity similarity and regional difference in disaster distribution in Beijing, Tianjin and Hebei, Qu et al. [3] proposed a new model of regional collaborative response to natural disasters under the overall planning of Beijing, Tianjin and Hebei from the perspective of integrating emergency resources and collaborative response to emergencies.

In summary, there are few researches on the application of complex network theory to solve the cross-regional emergency collaborative decision-making problem. However, it is possible to build emergency collaborative network to solve the issues in cross-regional emergency collaboration. In this paper, we explore emergency collaborative network in key rescue sites discovery, rescue partnership discovery and visualization of the emergency collaborative network.

3   Constructing and Analyzing Cross-Regional Emergency Collaboration Network Model

The construction of emergency collaborative network is the basis. In this paper, we integrate the historical accident data of each region, the traffic data between them, the response center in each region, the location data of the rescue site and so on. The emergency collaborative network consists of nodes and edges. The response centers, rescue sites and affected sites are taken as nodes in the network, and the traffic data between them are taken as edges. The cost of transport between them are taken as the weights of edges in the network. The historical disaster data of each region are taken as the attributes of the nodes.

3.1   Constructing Cross-Regional Emergency Collaboration Network

Obtaining the Accidents Data. We crawled accidents in coal mine safety production from 2008 to 2021, which includes about 1000 accidents[1]. We obtained 179 regions which are at the level of county and district. Accidents data includes time, location and casualties. We take these regions as the nodes in the network, and take accidents data as the attributes of the node. We parse the accidents data according to the process as Fig. 1 shows.

Obtaining the Expressway Data. The expressway data between the accident places are obtained as the connecting edge between the nodes in the emergency collaborative network, and the distance is used as the weight of the connecting edge. Here, we get the distance between cities by calling Tencent location service.

---

[1] http://www.mkaq.org/sggl/shigukb/.

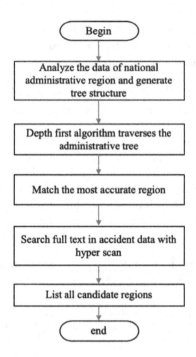

Fig. 1. The flowchart of extracting information of the accidents.

Constructing the Network. In the process of network construction, the obtained disaster sites are taken as nodes, and the distance between the them which is obtained by calling Tencent location service is taken as the connecting edge. If the distance between any two disaster sites is added to the network as an edge, a complete graph is constructed, that is, there are connected edges between any two nodes. Obviously, the complete graph is not what the rescue managers want, which increases too much noisy information; Each time the edge with the smallest traffic distance is selected to connect the unconnected disaster sites. If there are n disaster sites, then n-1 edges are needed to connect all the disaster sites. At this time, the connected network is a network with the least edges, which is called the minimum spanning tree. Obviously, this kind of network is not what the rescue managers want, because there is only one path between any two disaster sites. If there is one edge is missing on the path, the network will not be connected and rescue cannot be implemented; In order to add appropriate redundant edges in the network, the following adjustments are made when constructing the minimum spanning tree: the edge with the minimum traffic distance is selected to connect two nodes each time, and if the degree of one of the two nodes is less than the specified value, the edge is added to the network. The construction process is shown in Fig. 2. Here, we set the threshold value of 5 to construct the traffic network of the disaster area, which contains 179 nodes and 685 edges.

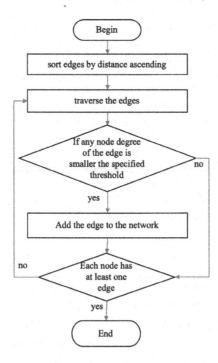

Fig. 2. The flowchart of constructing network.

3.2   Key Rescue Sites Discovery

It is far from enough and unscientific to only use the administrative level of cities and towns to select key rescue sites. Although the administrative level of some cities and towns is relatively low and the transportation facilities are not perfect, they are traffic fortresses. To pass through other cities and towns, they must pass through here. Such cities and towns play an important role in the transportation network. In the selection of key rescue sites, the traffic location of towns must be considered. Only by selecting these towns can we ensure the most possible successful rescue. Generally, the node degree and node betweenness of town nodes are selected to measure the location of town in the transportation network. On the basis of constructing the emergency collaborative network, the key nodes in the emergency collaborative network are analyzed by using the key node analysis method, which is used as the key place for emergency rescue or response. At the same time, the key node is the key of emergency rescue, and the emergency resources can be stored in this location during resource allocation.

The degree of the city is the numbers of cities it connected. It is calculated by formula (1)

$$k_i = \sum_j e_{ij} = \sum_j e_{ji} \qquad (1)$$

where i and j indicate nodes, k_i indicates the degree of node i, j is the adjacent node of i, e_{ij} indicates the edge between node i and j.

The betweenness of the city is the proportion of the shortest path connecting any two cities passing through the city. The betweenness is larger, the city is more important. It is calculated by formula (2)

$$B_i = \frac{\sum_{j,k \in V, j \neq k} n_{jk}(i)}{\sum_{j,k \in V, j \neq k} n_{jk}} \qquad (2)$$

where V indicates the node set, i, j, k indicate the node in the network, B_i indicates the betweenness of node i, $n_{jk}(i)$ indicates the number of shortest path between node j and k passing node i.

We list the top 10 cities with the highest degree and betweenness in Table 1.

Table 1. The key rescue sites discovered by different metrics.

Ranking	Degree	Betweenness
1	Changchun, Jilin	Zhangjiakou, Hebei
2	Wuzhong, Ningxia	Xilinguole, Neimenggu
3	Changchun, Jilin	Zhangjiakou, Hebei
4	Shenyang, Liaoning	Tongchuan, Shanxi
5	Loudi, Hunan	Chongqing
6	Xiangtan, Hunan	Yanan, Shanxi
7	Gongyi, Henan	Xinzhou, Shanxi
8	Jinzhong, Shanxi	Dazhou, Sichuan
9	Zhuzhou, Hunan	Guangyuan, Sichuan
10	Tonghua, Jilin	Baoji, Shanxi

3.3 Rescue Partner Sites Discovery

In cross-regional emergency collaborative decision-making, constrained by geographical location, resource allocation and other conditions, it will lead to different resource allocation in each region, so each region needs to help each other to coordinate emergency. On the basis of the emergency collaborative network, we can use the community discovery methods to find the rescue partner sites, which are closely related. So that in the same community area as a partnership, we can establish a collaborative emergency mechanism, and then achieve rapid and low-cost emergency rescue. In this paper, we adopt famous community detection method Louvain [2] to find rescue partners.

We found cross-regional partnerships, for example, Heihe City in Heilongjiang Province and Hulunbuir city in Inner Mongolia Autonomous Region are in the same community. Fuxin, Jinzhou and Huludao in Liaoning Province and Tang-shan and Qinhuangdao in Hebei Province are in the same community. Xuzhou in Jiangsu Province and Zaozhuang in Shandong Province are in the same com-munity. Shangqiu in Henan Province and Bozhou, Fuyang and Suzhou in Anhui Province are in the same community. All of them are suggested as rescue part-nership to deal with the disaster or accident together.

3.4   Visualization System of Assistant Decision-Making

In the visualization results, the size of the node indicates its importance in emergency response. Color out the partners of the same kind. The above visual effects assist emergency managers to make decisions. An example is shown in Fig. 3.

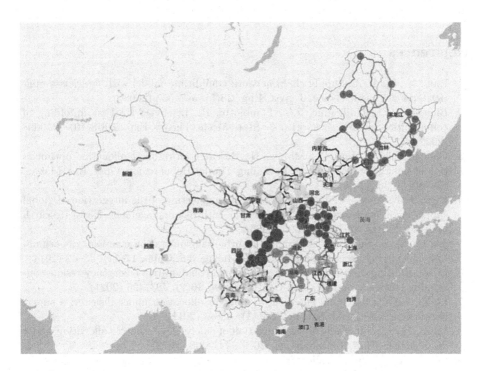

Fig. 3. An example of visualization.

4   Conclusion and Discussion

When major natural disasters and major accidents occur, many local govern-ments can not deal with them alone, and need cross-regional collaborative emer-gency response. Aiming at the problem of selecting key nodes and discovering partner relationship in cross-regional emergency cooperation, we use complex network to model historical accident data and traffic data. Then key nodes and partners is discovered through node centrality and community discovery methods in complex network. Finally, the analysis results is presented to emergency managers through visualization technology to assist decision-making in emergency response. At present, the data source of analysis is relatively less, and the integration of more data sources may be one of the future work. The current visualization is only static, and the dynamic display of more information may be the future work.

Acknowledgements. This work was supported in part by the North China Institute of Science and Technology Higher Education Research Program under Grants #HKJYZD202112, and Science and Technology Research and Development Program under Grant #2021011004.The authors are grateful for the anonymous reviewers whose comments helped improve and clarify this manuscript.

References

1. Bing, X., Daoli, Z.: Supply chain network equilibrium model with multiclass multicriteria stochastic choice. J. Syst. Eng. **23**(5), 547–553 (2008)
2. Blondel, V.D., Guillaume, J.L., Lambiotte, R., Lefebvre, E.: Fast unfolding of communities in large networks. J. Stat. Mech. Theory Exp. **2008**(10), P10008 (2008)
3. Chongchong, Q., Jing, W., Mingke, H.: Research on resource allocation optimization of synergetic development in Beijing-Tianjin-Hebei region. Oper. Res. Manag. Sci. **30**(1), 36–42 (2021)
4. Cruz, J.M., Anna, N., Tina, W.: Financial engineering of the integration of global supply chain networks and social networks with risk management. Naval Research Logistics (NRL) **53**(7), 674–696 (2006)
5. Jie, C., Li, Z.: Super-network model of urban agglomeration emergency coordination considering decision preferences. J. Manag. Sci. China **17**(11), 33–42 (2014)
6. Li, Z.: Routing optimization of cross-regional collaborative emergency rescue considering efficiency and fairness. Control Decis. **36**(2), 483–490 (2021)
7. Li, Z., Jie, C.: Study on emergency resources allocation under disaster: a supernetwork perspective. J. Soft Sci. **26**(11), 42–46 (2012)
8. Li, Z., Jie, C.: Supernetwork optimization of emergency resources allocation under disaster risk. Chin. J. Manag. Sci. **20**(6), 141–148 (2012)
9. Li, Z., Jie, C.: Urban agglomeration coordination for emergency resources allocation: a supernetwork structure perspective. Manag. Rev. **27**(07), 207–217 (2015)
10. Nagurney, A., Loo, J., Dong, J., Zhang, D.: Supply chain networks and electronic commerce: a theoretical perspective. Netnomics **4**(2), 187–220 (2002)

Residual Gated Recurrent Unit-Based Stacked Network for Stock Trend Prediction from Limit Order Book

Xuerui Lv[1] and Li Zhang[1,2]($^{\boxtimes}$) (iD)

[1] School of Computer Science and Technology, Joint International Research
Laboratory of Machine Learning and Neuromorphic Computing, Soochow University,
Suzhou 215006, Jiangsu, China
20194227038@stu.suda.edu.cn, zhangliml@suda.edu.cn
[2] Provincial Key Laboratory for Computer Information Processing Technology,
Soochow University, Suzhou 215006, Jiangsu, China

Abstract. The fluctuation of financial assets is non-stationary and non-linear, so the stock trend prediction is a hard task. Limit order book (LOB) takes an important role in the order-driven market. Investors can make decisions referring to LOBs, which affects the movement of stock prices. Existing networks with a recurrent structure cannot learn temporal features well for the analysis of LOBs. To remedy it, this paper proposes a stacked residual gated recurrent unit (SRGRU) network to forecast the stock trend by utilizing high-frequency LOBs. SRGRU contains multiple residual gated recurrent unit (RGRU) blocks that are stacked to increase the depth of the network and improve the generalization ability. RGRU, which is designed based on gated recurrent unit (GRU), can learn temporal features and prevent the degradation of a network caused by deepening it. Experiments are conducted on FI-2010. The results show that SRGRU goes beyond the state-of-the-art models.

Keywords: Microstructure market data · Financial time series · Limit order book · Deep learning · Stacked residual network · Gated recurrent unit

1 Introduction

In the real world, people make all kinds of investments to create wealth. The essence of investment is to predict the investment target, and the error rate of prediction greatly affects the return of investment. The combination of financial

This work was supported in part by the Natural Science Foundation of the Jiangsu Higher Education Institutions of China under Grant No. 19KJA550002, by the Six Talent Peak Project of Jiangsu Province of China under Grant No. XYDXX-054, by the Priority Academic Program Development of Jiangsu Higher Education Institutions, and by the Collaborative Innovation Center of Novel Software Technology and Industrialization.

© Springer Nature Switzerland AG 2021
H. Qiu et al. (Eds.): KSEM 2021, LNAI 12816, pp. 351–363, 2021.
https://doi.org/10.1007/978-3-030-82147-0_29

time series and machine learning technologies can assist people to judge the future trend of stocks, so as to reduce the risk of investment. Various financial time series produced from the securities market are the main embodiment of asset values. As a kind of financial time series, limit order book (LOB) data plays a crucial role in the order-driven financial market transactions [1]. The LOB data is the integration of unfilled entrustment orders, from which investors can obtain real-time market trading information. LOB is also an important reference index for investors to make investment decisions. Investors can submit a limit order, a market order, or a cancellation order according to their subjective judgment. These orders all can dynamically transform the LOB data. Therefore, the trend analysis of LOBs is of great significance.

Existing literature showed that it is helpful for price discovery to analyze LOBs of stocks by using machine learning models [2]. Many algorithms have been proposed for the trend analysis of LOBs. For example, Ntakaris et al. [3] used a ridge regression (RR) model and a single hidden-layer feedforward neural (SLFN) network to forecast the trend of mid-price, while they achieved a weak performance on LOB data. Tsantekidis et al. [4] used one simple long short term memory (LSTM) model to predict the price movement of high frequency financial time series. Their experiment results on limit order book data show that LSTM is superior to support vector machine (SVM) and multilayer perception (MLP). Zhang et al. [5] developed a deep convolutional neural network (DeepLOB) according to the structural features of LOBs. DeepLOB can extract feature maps from prices and volumes. Tran et al. [6] proposed a bilinear network combined with the attention machine. They believed that the temporal attention-augmented bilinear layers (TABN) can highlight the attention of time information. Both DeepLOB and TABN deal with the basic features of LOBs, ignoring the extension of basic features. However, the existing convolutional neural network (CNN) models for LOBs [5,7] have a large number of parameters and high computational difficulty.

In other domains, it is proved that recurrent neural network (RNN) has the memory ability that can connect the front and back parts of a sequence [8]. For example, RNN can learn the contextual relevance of the text [9]. Besides, the shared weight mechanism of RNN can reduce the parameters of the model. Both LSTM [10] and gated recurrent unit (GRU) network [11,12] can solve the gradient vanishing problem of RNN, while GRU has fewer parameters than LSTM. The bi-directional recurrent network was introduced to learn the contextual connection of texts because the beginning and end of a sentence influence each other [13]. Nevertheless, it is possible that the historical data of the time series can affect the future trend, the future trend will not affect the historical data that has already occurred. The bi-directional recurrent network is not applicable to the prediction of LOBs. Residual learning framework was proposed for image classification [14], which can transmit signals directly from the low level to the high level to prevent network degradation.

Following the idea of GRU and residual learning framework, we present a novel stacked residual gated recurrent unit (SRGRU) network to better forecast

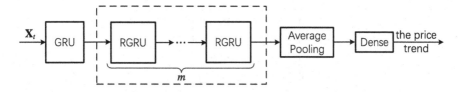

Fig. 1. General framework of the proposed SRGRU.

the future stock trend based on LOBs in this paper. The contributions of this paper are as follows:

- On the basis of gated recurrent unit (GRU), an RGRU is proposed to learn temporal features and prevent the degradation of network.
- By using RGRU and a stacked method, a novel SRGRU network is proposed to judge the stock movement on LOBs. SRGRU can capture the global temporal information through the RGRU layers and deepen the network to enhance performance through the stacked way.
- SRGRU deals with basic features and extended features to fit the dynamicity of LOBs.

The remainder of the paper is as follows. Section 2 describes our network architecture. Section 3 introduces the basic features and extended features of LOB data. Section 4 provides an exhaustive description of experiments and results. Section 5 makes a summary and gives possible extensions for the future work.

2   Method

This section proposes the SRGRU network and describes it in detail. The general framework of SRGRU is shown in Fig. 1. As we can see that SRGRU contains one GRU layer, m RGRU blocks, an average pooling layer and a dense layer. The input data $\mathbf{X}_t$ of SRGRU consists of basic and extended features from LOBs. The output at the end of SRGRU is the price trend.

Let $\{\mathbf{X}_t, \mathbf{Y}_t\}_{t=1}^{N}$ be the input pair of SRGRU, where N is the number of samples, $\mathbf{X}_t \in \mathbb{R}^{k \times c}$ is an input sample of SRGRU and has the form

$$\mathbf{X}_t = [\mathbf{x}_{t-k+1}, \cdots, \mathbf{x}_t]^T \tag{1}$$

$\mathbf{x}_t \in \mathbb{R}^c$ is a feature vector with c features, k is the number of recent feature vectors, and $\mathbf{Y}_t \in \mathbb{R}^{3 \times 1}$ is the label vector of $\mathbf{X}_t$,

$$\mathbf{Y}_t = \begin{cases} [1, 0, 0]^T, & if \quad l_t = 1 \\ [0, 1, 0]^T, & if \quad l_t = 0 \\ [0, 0, 1]^T, & if \quad l_t = -1 \end{cases} \tag{2}$$

l_t denotes the price trend of $\mathbf{x}_t$. Generally, the price trend of "up", "stationary" and "down" denote "$l_t = 1$", "$l_t = 0$" and "$l_t = -1$", respectively.

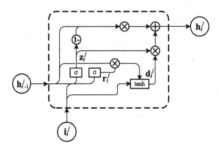

Fig. 2. Architecture of a GRU.

2.1   Gated Recurrent Unit

GRU is a recurrent hidden unit of the gate recurrent neural network [15]. The architecture of a GRU is given in Fig. 2. A GRU has two inputs: $\mathbf{h}_{t-1}^{j}$ and $\mathbf{i}_{t}^{j}$ and one ouput $\mathbf{h}_{t}^{j}$. There is an update gate $\mathbf{z}_{t}^{j}$, a reset gate $\mathbf{r}_{t}^{j}$ and a hidden state $\mathbf{d}_{t}^{j}$, which can capture the long term time dependence. For the jth hidden unit, the calculation process of the activation vector $\mathbf{h}_{t}^{j}$ at time t can be describe as:

$$\mathbf{z}_{t}^{j} = \sigma(\mathbf{W}_{z} \cdot [\mathbf{h}_{t-1}, \mathbf{i}_{t}])^{j} \tag{3}$$

$$\mathbf{r}_{t}^{j} = \sigma(\mathbf{W}_{r} \cdot [\mathbf{h}_{t-1}, \mathbf{i}_{t}])^{j} \tag{4}$$

$$\mathbf{d}_{t}^{j} = \tanh(\mathbf{W} \cdot [\mathbf{r}_{t} \odot \mathbf{h}_{t-1}, \mathbf{i}_{t}])^{j} \tag{5}$$

$$\mathbf{h}_{t}^{j} = \mathbf{z}_{t}^{j} \odot \mathbf{d}_{t}^{j} + (1 - \mathbf{z}_{t}^{j}) \odot \mathbf{h}_{t-1}^{j} \tag{6}$$

where $\odot$ is the element-wise multiplication, $\mathbf{z}_{t}^{j}$ is the update gate, $\mathbf{r}_{t}^{j}$ is the reset gate, σ is the sigmoid function, $\mathbf{W}_{z}$, $\mathbf{W}_{r}$ and $\mathbf{W}$ are the weight matrices.

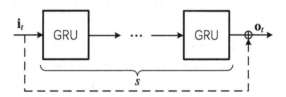

Fig. 3. Structure of RGRU block.

2.2   Residual Gated Recurrent Unit Block

Residual connection makes an easy element-wise addition for the input and the final output of some weight layers. This addition operation can keep the parameters invariant, which does not increase the calculation intensity but greatly improve the efficiency of models. We design a residual GRU (RGRU) block and take it as our baseline block. As shown in Fig. 3, RGRU contains s GRU layers, where $s \in \mathbb{Z}^+$. RGRU can be described as follow:

$$\mathbf{o}_t = f^s(\mathbf{i}_t) \oplus \mathbf{i}_t \tag{7}$$

where $\oplus$ denotes the element-wise addition, $\mathbf{i}_t$ is the input vector of the residual block, $f^s(\cdot)$ is the output of s GRU layers, and $\mathbf{o}_t$ is the output of the RGRU block.

2.3 Stacked Strategy for SRGRU

The stacked strategy is to stack multiple identical blocks for the purpose of enhancing the performance. As shown in Fig. 1, the SRGRU network stacks m identical RGRU blocks with GRU layers. SRGRU includes $s \times m$ GRU layers, which means one RGRU block contains s GRU layers.

In order to stack RGRU blocks better, we add a GRU layer at the start of our model. The output shape of RGRU is the same as that of the input matrix according to Eq. 7. The size of the input matrix $\mathbf{X}_t$ is $k \times (12n + 6)$. The output shape of the first GRU layer is $k \times g$. The input and output shape of all residual blocks are $k \times g$, where g is the unit number of each GRU layer in our network. At the back of m RGRU blocks, we use the average pooling layer to deal with the feature matrix of time dependence. Since all values in the feature matrix have great significance, our model do not use the maximum pooling layer. The maximum pooling layer chooses the maximum value of the sampling kernel, which discards the values at other positions in the sampling kernel. At the end of SRGRU, the dense layer output the price trend of stocks.

3 Data Preprocessing

3.1 Limit Order Book Data

An LOB contains n-level ask limit orders and n-level bid limit orders. A limit order for an asset is a submission to buy or sell the underlying asset with a specified price and specified volume. The more detailed information about LOBs can reference Ref. [1]. The activities of a limit order contain submissions, cancellations, and executions. LOBs would be reconstructed when these activities happen.

Prices and volumes in an LOB are basic features. It is not comprehensive to use only basic information. Therefore, we extend the features of LOBs and divide features into two groups: the basic and the extended ones.

Basic Features. The basic features of an n-level LOB consist of $2n$ prices and $2n$ volumes. Let $\mathbf{v}_t^o = [P_{t_1}^{ask}, V_{t_1}^{ask}, P_{t_1}^{bid}, V_{t_1}^{bid}, \cdots, P_{t_n}^{ask}, V_{t_n}^{ask}, P_{t_n}^{bid}, V_{t_n}^{bid}]^T \in \mathbb{R}^{4n}$ be a basis feature vector, where $P_{t_i}^{bid}, V_{t_i}^{bid}, P_{t_i}^{ask}$, and $V_{t_i}^{ask}$ are the i-level price and volume of bid orders and the i-level price and volume of ask orders, respectively.

Extended Features. The activities of limit orders can update the distribution of LOBs and cause the dynamical change of LOBs. which can be reflected by extended features. Usually, the extended features of an n-level LOB contain the distribution features and the dynamical features. Let $\mathbf{v}_t^e = [\mathbf{a}_{t_1}^T, \mathbf{a}_{t_2}^T, \mathbf{a}_{t_3}^T, \mathbf{a}_{t_4}^T, \mathbf{b}_{t_1}^T, \mathbf{b}_{t_2}^T]^T \in \mathbb{R}^{8n+6}$ be an extended feature vector, where $\mathbf{a}_{t_i}$ and $\mathbf{b}_{t_i}$ denote the distribution features and the dynamical features, respectively, whose detailed representations are described as follows:

$$
\begin{cases}
\mathbf{a}_{t_1} = \left[(P_{t_1}^{ask} - P_{t_1}^{bid}), (P_{t_1}^{ask} + P_{t_1}^{bid})/2, \cdots, (P_{t_n}^{ask} - P_{t_n}^{bid}), (P_{t_n}^{ask} + P_{t_n}^{bid})/2\right]^T \\
\mathbf{a}_{t_2} = \left[|P_{t_n}^{ask} - P_{t_1}^{ask}|, |P_{t_n}^{bid} - P_{t_1}^{bid}|, |P_{t_2}^{ask} - P_{t_1}^{ask}|, |P_{t_2}^{bid} - P_{t_1}^{bid}|, \cdots, |P_{t_n}^{ask} \right. \\
\qquad \left. -P_{t_{n-1}}^{ask}|, |P_{t_n}^{bid} - P_{t_{n-1}}^{bid}|\right]^T \\
\mathbf{a}_{t_3} = \left[\frac{1}{n}\sum_{i=1}^{n} P_{t_i}^{ask}, \frac{1}{n}\sum_{i=1}^{n} P_{t_i}^{bid}, \frac{1}{n}\sum_{i=1}^{n} V_{t_i}^{ask}, \frac{1}{n}\sum_{i=1}^{n} V_{t_i}^{bid}\right]^T \\
\mathbf{a}_{t_4} = \left[\sum_{i=1}^{n}(P_{t_i}^{ask} - P_{t_i}^{bid}), \sum_{i=1}^{n}(V_{t_i}^{ask} - V_{t_i}^{bid})\right]^T
\end{cases}
\tag{8}
$$

and

$$
\begin{cases}
\mathbf{b}_{t_1} = \left[dP_{t_1}^{ask}/dt, dP_{t_1}^{bid}/dt, \cdots, dP_{t_n}^{ask}/dt, dP_{t_n}^{bid}/dt\right]^T \\
\mathbf{b}_{t_2} = \left[dV_{t_1}^{ask}/dt, dV_{t_1}^{bid}dt, \cdots, dV_{t_n}^{ask}/dt, dV_{t_n}^{bid}/dt\right]^T
\end{cases}
\tag{9}
$$

where $\mathbf{a}_{t_1}$ is a vector that represents the price spread of the same level and the mid-price of multiple levels, which can reflect the relative distribution of ask and bid orders; $\mathbf{a}_{t_2}$ is a vector that represents the price spread of the i-level and the n-level, and the price spread of the adjacent level; $\mathbf{a}_{t_3}$ is a vector that represents the average price and the average volume of orders; $\mathbf{a}_{t_4}$ is a vector that represents the cumulative price spread, which can reflect the imbalance degree of ask and bid orders; $\mathbf{b}_{t_1}$ is a vector that represents the price derivative of each level; $\mathbf{b}_{t_2}$ is a vector that represents the volume derivative of each level.

Vector to Image. Let $\mathbf{x}_t = [\mathbf{v}_t^o, \mathbf{v}_t^e]^T \in \mathbb{R}^{(12n+6)}$ be a feature vector that contains the basic features and the extended features. The future trend of stocks at time t is closely related to the historical LOBs time series. We make samples be similar to images through merging the feature vectors from time $(t - k + 1)$ to time t, where k is the length of the historical time interval. The input sample that likes an image is denoted as $\mathbf{X}_t \in \mathbb{R}^{k \times (12n+6)}$ for SRGRU.

4   Experiments and Results

4.1   Evaluation Metrics

We evaluate NEM with four metrics: "Accuracy", "Precision", "Recall" and "F1-score", which are the most common indicators for trend analysis. For each class, the four metrics are respectively defined as follows:

$$\text{Accuracy} = \frac{TP + TN}{TP + FN + FP + TN} \tag{10}$$

$$\text{Precision} = \frac{TP}{TP + FP} \tag{11}$$

$$\text{Recall} = \frac{TP}{TP + FN} \tag{12}$$

$$\text{F1-score} = \frac{2 \times \text{Precision} \times \text{Recall}}{\text{Precision} + \text{Recall}} \tag{13}$$

where TP, FN, FP and TN present the true positives, false negatives, false positives and true negatives, respectively. We use the average evaluation metrics of three labels ("up", "stationary" and "down"). In addition, F1-score is a comprehensive index that can fairly measure the performance of methods even in case of sample imbalance. Thus, we take it as the main evaluation index in our experiments.

4.2   Data Description and Settings

FI-2010 was provided by Ntakaris et al. [3] that contains ten consecutive trading days from June 1 to June 14, 2010. The LOB time series of five stocks in FI-2010 were derived from the Nasdaq Nordic stock market and is divided into ten folds with five class of prediction horizons $H \in \{10, 20, 30, 50, 100\}$. Following the convention [6], we use the z-score normalization on data and have two setups for data: Setup1 and Setup2, where Setup1 uses nine folds as the training set and one fold as the test set, and Setup2 uses seven folds as the training set and one fold as the test set.

SRGRU is implemented in Python and trained by Keras based on TensorFlow on the machine with Intel-Core-i5-9500-CPU and 16G. FI-2010 contains 10-level limit orders, so the number of features is 126. The unit number of a GRU layer is 16. The activation functions are ReLU and softmax for the hidden layers and the last layer, respectively. The optimization algorithm for our model is the Adam algorithm. Additionally, we set "epsilon" to 1, the learning rate to 0.01. We take the cross-entropy loss as the loss function and "Loss" and "Accuracy" as the metrics for training. It is difficult to achieve quality improvement if the training epochs are less than 50. Therefore, we train SRGRU with a mini-batch of 64 samples and 200 epochs on FI-2010. In experiments, we use two kinds of RGRU blocks for experiments: SRGRU-1 and SRGRU-2. For SRGRU-1, we have $m = 6$ and $s = 1$. For SRGRU-2, we have $m = 3$ and $s = 2$.

4.3   Experimental Results

Parameter Analysis. First, we observe the effect of the parameter k on the performance of SRGRU. Here, SRGRU-1 is tested. The parameter k takes value

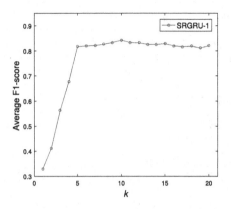

Fig. 4. Average F1-score vs. k obtained by SRGRU-1 when $H = 50$.

Fig. 5. Training and validation losses obtained by three models.

Table 1. Comparison between different LSTMs and GRUs on Setup1

Method	Accuracy (%)	Precision (%)	Recall (%)	F1-score (%)
1-layer LSTM	88.94	82.00	66.33	71.98
2-layer LSTM	89.74	82.67	69.67	74.95
6-layer LSTM	90.12	85.33	70.00	75.81
1-layer GRU	89.43	83.67	68.33	74.00
2-layer GRU	90.16	84.33	70.33	75.86
6-layer GRU	90.39	85.33	70.33	76.27
SRLSTM-1	90.10	83.33	72.33	77.01
SRLSTM-2	89.97	83.67	70.00	75.45
SRGRU-1	**90.75**	**85.67**	**72.67**	**77.97**
SRGRU-2	90.52	85.00	72.00	77.41

in the set $\{1, 2, \cdots, 20\}$ for experiments on FI-2010. We use the average F1-score of Setup1 and Setup2 to determine the optimal value of k. As shown in Fig. 4, we can obviously observe that F1-score rises rapidly when $k < 5$ and slowly decreases when $k > 10$, which indicates that it is difficult to learn the pattern of price movement with too few or too many historical data. Therefore, we use $k = 10$, which can make SRGRU-1 achieve the best performance.

Comparison with LSTM and GRU Networks. To evaluate SRGRU on Setup1, we construct six different models using GRU or LSTM, including 1-layer LSTM, 1-layer GRU, 2-layer LSTM, 2-layer GRU, 6-layer LSTM, and 6-layer GRU. In fact, SRGRU can be regarded as a network framework. Because LSTM has a similar role as GRU, we construct a novel stacked residual LSTM

(SRLSTM) by replacing the GRU layer with the LSTM one in our method. According to the setting part, we define two type models for SRLSTM similar to SRGRU: SRLSTM-1 and SRLSTM-2.

Experimental results are shown in Table 1, where the best results among compared methods are in bold type. We can observe that networks with GRU are much better than ones with LSTM, which indicates that it is wise to choose GRU as our basic layer. In addition, we find that the greater the number of LSTM layers is, the higher F1-score of the corresponding model has. Similar conclusion can be drawn for GRU networks. SRLSTM does not have obvious advantage over GRU networks. However, SRGRU is obviously superior to GRU. Among four stacked networks, SRGRU-1 has the best performance in four metrics, followed by SRGRU-2. This implies that the residual structure can increase the important information forgotten by the network.

Comparison with the Dropout Method. The dropout method is the most common method to prevent overfitting. Thus, we add the dropout method to the 6-layer GRU to improve its performance. Here, we compare three methods: 6-layer GRU, 6-layer GRU with dropout, and SRGRU-1. As shown in Fig. 5, we display the relationship between "Loss" and the number of epochs, where 6-layer GRU is shorted for GRU, and 6-layer GRU with dropout for GRU with dropout.

For the 6-layer GRU, there has a greater and greater difference between validation loss and training loss as increasing the number of epochs. In other words, the 6-layer GRU exists overfitting. Fortunately, the 6-layer GRU with dropout can relieve this phenomenon. Although the dropout method greatly avoids the issue of overfitting, it makes training loss greater. In addition, we find that SRGRU-1 has the lowest training loss among three methods and has a compared validation loss to the dropout method. Namely, SRGRU can avoid overfitting to some degree.

Comparison with the Existing Models. We perform SRGRU-1 and SRGRU-2 on Setup1 and Setup2 and compare them with the existing models.

For Setup1, models used to compare with SRGRU contain SLFN [3], multi-linear discriminant analysis (MDA), TABN [6], N-BoF [17], T-LoBoF [18] and DeepLOB [5]. Their results are shown in Table 2, where the best results for each H are in bold and "-" means that the corresponding reference does not provide experimental results. Among the compared models, we notice that SRGRU-1 and SRGRU-2 generally outperform other models. This suggests that the stacked residual structure can learn great representations for the LOB time series. When $H = 10$, SRGRU-2 obtains the best accurary (90.52%) and precision (85.00%), which is much higher than those of DeepLOB (78.91% and 78.47%). In addition, SRGRU-1 outperforms SRGRU-2 by about 0.80% in terms of the average F1-score.

For Setup2, the models used to compare with SRGRU are SVM [4], MLP [4], CNN-I [7], CNN-II [16] and DeepLOB [5]. Their results are shown in Table 3, where the best results for each H are in bold and "-" means that

Table 2. Comparison of the existing models on Setup1

Method	Accuracy (%)	Precision (%)	Recall (%)	F1-score (%)
Prediction horizon $H = 10$				
SLFN	64.30	51.20	36.60	32.70
MDA	71.92	44.21	60.07	46.06
TABN	78.01	72.03	74.06	72.84
MCSDA	83.66	46.11	48.00	46.72
N-BoF	62.70	42.28	61.41	41.63
T-LoBoF	–	47.80	68.25	51.58
DeepLOB	78.91	78.47	**78.91**	**77.66**
SRGRU-1	90.45	84.50	72.75	77.55
SRGRU-2	**90.52**	**85.00**	72.00	77.41
Prediction horizon $H = 50$				
SLFN	47.30	46.80	46.40	45.90
MDA	–	–	–	–
TABN	74.81	74.58	74.27	74.32
MCSDA	–	–	–	–
N-BoF	56.52	47.20	58.17	46.15
T-LoBoF	–	51.56	65.81	53.73
DeepLOB	75.01	75.10	75.01	74.96
SRGRU-1	**90.53**	**86.67**	**83.33**	**84.90**
SRGRU-2	90.15	86.00	82.67	84.27
Prediction horizon $H = 100$				
SLFN	47.70	45.30	43.20	41.00
MDA	–	–	–	–
TABN	74.07	73.51	73.80	73.52
MCSDA	–	–	–	–
N-BoF	56.43	47.27	54.99	46.86
T-LoBoF	–	–	–	–
DeepLOB	76.66	76.77	76.66	76.58
SRGRU-1	**90.12**	**86.33**	**84.00**	**85.11**
SRGRU-2	88.99	85.00	82.00	83.47

the corresponding reference does not provide experimental results. We observe that the four indexes of SRGRU-1 and SRGRU-2 are much better than the LSTM model, which indicates the stacked structure and the residual module are greatly improve the prediction performance. SRGRU-1 achieves a better F1-score (84.28%) than that of DeepLOB (80.35%) when $H = 50$. Besides, we notice that SRGRU achieves the best results compared with these five deep learning methods, which means that SRGRU is more suitable for time series learning.

Table 3. Comparison of the existing models on Setup2

Method	Accuracy (%)	Precision (%)	Recall (%)	F1-score (%)
Prediction horizon $H = 10$				
MLP	–	60.78	47.81	48.27
LSTM	–	75.92	60.77	66.33
CNN-I	–	65.54	50.98	55.21
CNN-II	–	45.00	56.00	44.00
DeepLOB	84.47	84.00	**84.47**	**83.40**
SRGRU-1	90.47	84.00	74.11	78.31
SRGRU-2	**90.49**	**85.00**	72.00	77.26
Prediction horizon $H = 20$				
MLP	–	65.20	51.33	51.12
LSTM	–	70.52	59.60	62.37
CNN-I	–	67.38	54.79	59.17
CNN-II	–	–	–	–
DeepLOB	74.85	74.06	74.85	72.82
SRGRU-1	89.33	**84.67**	75.67	79.49
SRGRU-2	**89.50**	**84.67**	**76.00**	**79.57**
Prediction horizon $H = 50$				
MLP	–	67.14	55.21	55.95
LSTM	–	68.50	60.03	61.43
CNN-I	–	67.12	55.58	59.44
CNN-II	–	47.00	56.00	47.00
DeepLOB	80.51	80.38	80.51	80.35
SRGRU-1	**90.06**	**86.00**	**82.67**	**84.28**
SRGRU-2	90.01	85.67	**82.67**	84.11

Comparison of the Average Execution Time. In the subsection, we list the average execution time of TABN [6], LSTM [4], DeepLOB [5], SRGRU-1 and SRGRU-2 under the same environment in Table 4, where "Backward" denotes the average backward time of training a single sample, and "Forward" denotes the average forward time for predicting the trend of a single sample. We also list the number of parameters. The proposed SRGRU-1 and SRGRU-2 have the same number of parameters, which are less than that of DeepLOB. Although the number of SRGRU layers is about 4 times that of LSTM, the average computation time of "Backward" is only about 1.57 times that of LSTM.

Table 4. Comparison of the execution time

Method	Backward (ms)	Forward (ms)	Number of parameters
TABN	0.0583	0.0695	1,1344
LSTM	0.1561	0.0543	10,304
DeepLOB	2.8293	1.2250	142,435
SRGRU-1	0.2461	0.1566	16,419
SRGRU-2	0.2621	0.1425	16,419

5   Conclusion

We proposed SRGRU to predict the price movement with LOBs. Extensive experiments were conducted on the FI-2010 dataset. The similar models of LSTM and GRU were analyzed, which proved that the proposed model was the optimal one. According to different data partitions, we constructed two experimental setups: Setup1 and Setup2. Experimental results on both Setup1 and Setup2 showed that SRGRU outperforms the state-of-the-art model (DeepLOB) in performance indexes of accuracy and F1-score. SRGRU also had a shorter average execution time and fewer parameters compared with DeepLOB.

In the experiment, we found that when $H = 10$, the proportion of the three types of samples was extremely imbalanced ("up": "stationary": "down"$= 1 : 4 : 1$). We think that the imbalance situation leads to a poor performance of SRGRU. To further improve the performance of SRGRU, we plan to solve the issue of class imbalance in future work.

References

1. Cont, R.: Statistical modeling of high-frequency financial data. IEEE Signal Process. Mag. **28**(5), 16–25 (2011)
2. Wei, L., Shi, L.: Investor sentiment in an artificial limit order market. Complexity **2020**(8581793), 1–10 (2020)
3. Ntakaris, A., Magrisv, M., Kanniainen, J., et al.: Benchmark dataset for mid-price forecasting of limit order book data with machine learning methods. J. Forecast. **37**(8), 852–866 (2018)
4. Tsantekidis, A., Passalis, N., Tefas, A., et al.: Using deep learning to detect price change indications in financial markets. In: 25th European Signal Processing Conference (EUSIPCO), pp. 2511–2515 (2017)
5. Zhang, Z., Zohren, S., Roberts, S.: DeepLOB: deep convolutional neural networks for limit order books. IEEE Trans. Signal Process. **11**(67), 3001–3012 (2019)
6. Tran, D.T., Iosifidis, A., Kanniainen, J., et al.: Temporal attention-augmented bilinear network for financial time-series data analysis. IEEE Trans. Neural Netw. Learn. Syst. **5**(30), 1407–1418 (2018)
7. Tsantekidis, A., Passalis, N., Tefas, A., et al.: Forecasting stock prices from the limit order book using convolutional neural networks. In: 2017 IEEE 19th Conference on Business Informatics (CBI), pp. 7–12 (2017)

8. Lipton, Z.C., Kale, D., Wetzel, R.: Directly modeling missing data in sequences with RNNs: improved classification of clinical time series. In: Proceedings of the 1st Machine Learning in Health Care (MLHC), pp. 253–270 (2016)

9. Meng, Z., Mou, L., Jin, Z.: Hierarchical RNN with static sentence-level attention for text-based speaker change detection. In: Proceedings of the 2017 ACM on Conference on Information and Knowledge Management (CIKM), pp. 2203–2206 (2017)

10. Huang, T., Shen, G., Deng, Z.H.: Leap-LSTM: Enhancing long short-term memory for text categorization. In: Proceedings of the Twenty-Eighth International Joint Conference on Artificial Intelligence (IJCAI), pp. 5017–5023 (2019)

11. Poon, H.K., Yap, W.S., Tee, Y.K., et al.: Hierarchical gated recurrent neural network with adversarial and virtual adversarial training on text classification. Neural Netw. **119**, 299–312 (2019)

12. Zhang, X., Shen, F., Zhao, J., et al.: Time series forecasting using GRU neural network with multi-lag after decomposition. In: International Conference on Neural Information Processing (ICONIP), pp. 523–532 (2017)

13. Sun, C., Liu, Y., Jia, C., Liu, B., Lin, L.: Recognizing text entailment via bidirectional LSTM model with inner-attention. In: Huang, D.-S., Hussain, A., Han, K., Gromiha, M.M. (eds.) ICIC 2017. LNCS (LNAI), vol. 10363, pp. 448–457. Springer, Cham (2017). https://doi.org/10.1007/978-3-319-63315-2_39

14. He, K., Zhang, X., Ren, S., et al.: Deep residual learning for image recognition. In: 2016 IEEE Conference on Computer Vision and Pattern Recognition (CVPR), pp. 770–778 (2010)

15. Cho, K., Merriënboer, B., Gulcehre, C., et al.: Learning phrase representations using RNN encoder-decoder for statistical machine translation. In: Proceedings of the 2014 Conference on Empirical Methods in Natural Language Processing (EMNLP), pp. 1724–1734 (2014)

16. Tsantekidis, A., Passalis, N., Tefas, A., et al.: Using deep learning for price prediction by exploiting stationary limit order book features. Appl. Soft Comput. **93**(106401), 1–10 (2020)

17. Passalis, N., Tsantekidis, A., Tefas, A., et al.: Time-series classification using neural bag-of-features. In: 2017 25th European Signal Processing Conference (EUSIPCO), pp. 301–305 (2017)

18. Passalis, N., Tefas, A., Kanniainen, J., et al.: Deep temporal logistic bag-of-features for forecasting high frequency limit order book time series. In: 2019 IEEE International Conference on Acoustics, Speech and Signal Processing (ICASSP), pp. 7545–7549 (2019)

A Social Attribute Inferred Model Based on Spatio-Temporal Data

Tongyu Zhu[1]([✉]), Peng Ling[1]([✉]), Zhiyuan Chen[1], Dongdong Wu[2],
and Ruyan Zhang[2]

[1] Beihang University, Beijing, China
{zhutongyu,opbird,waker}@buaa.edu.cn
[2] Beijing Emergency Management Information Center, Beijing, China

Abstract. Understanding the social attributes of urban residents, such as occupations, settlement characteristics etc., has important significance in social research, public policy formulation and business. Most of the current methods for obtaining people's social attributes by analyzing of social networks cannot reflect the relationship between the occupational characteristics and their daily movements. However, the current methods of using spatio-temporal data analysis are limited by the characteristics of the samples, and focus more on travel patterns and arrival time predictions. Based on coarse-grained CDR (Call Detail Record) data, this paper proposes an approach to infer occupation attribute by analyzing the travel patterns of personnel and incorporating more enhanced information. Finally we uses the CDR data of 6 million people to analyze and extract two types of people: college students in Beijing and urban hummingbirds and the F1 score of our proposed model is more than 0.95.

Keywords: Sptio-temporal data · Travel patterns · Social attribute · Time-series data classification · Semi-supervised model

1 Introduction

Understanding the demographic characteristics of urban residents, such as occupations, settlement characteristics and other social attributes, has important significance in social research, public policy formulation, and business. However, this type of data is difficult to collect from the public, usually through the census, and the update rate is low. Or adopt the method of questionnaire survey, with low sampling rate and large deviation.

The location tracking functionality of modern mobile devices provides unprecedented opportunity to the understanding of individual mobility in daily life [1]. With the popularity of mobile devices, more detailed data about personal activities or status can be collected more effectively and frequently. Nunes

This work is supported by the Science and Technology Program of Beijing (Z181100009018010).

H. Qiu et al. (Eds.): KSEM 2021, LNAI 12816, pp. 364–375, 2021.
https://doi.org/10.1007/978-3-030-82147-0_30

et al. [2] used the MIT reality mining proximity trace to detect, track and investigate social group's evolution throughout time. The bus smart card data from a large population can record human daily activities at an individual level with high spatial and temporal resolutions, which could reveal personal interests and travel patterns of passengers [3]. What APPs installed on one's smartphone, i.e., APP list, convey lots of information regarding his/her personal attributes, such as gender, occupation, income, and preferences. Zhao et al. [4] developed an attribute-specific representation to describe user attributes from an APP list. Some specific features or behavior or mobility patterns can be detected with mobile phone data. Xu at el. [5] attempt to reveal to what extent the job change occasion can be predicted based on the career mobility and daily activity patterns at the individual level, by aggregating the work experiences and check-in records of individuals. Although the above research can obtain personal details, it relies on the mobile phone user authorization of the respondent, so it is more used by social software companies such as FB and WeChat etc. Shibasaki et al. [6] analyzed human behavior in Bangladesh using "Call Detail Records" of mobile devices for classifying people life patterns and understanding the patterns in relation with income index and proximity to cities etc. Hu et al. [7] examine and compare lifestyle behaviors of people living in cities of different sizes, utilizing freely available social media data as a large-scale, low-cost alternative to traditional survey methods. The research quantitatively compare the behaviors of individuals of living in big cities like New York City to those living in small cities such as Rochester.

In summary, there is no research attempting to obtain social attributes of people, such as occupations, through mobile location data. In this paper, we propose an approach that can use millions of anonymous users' CDR data and adopt a deep learning method to obtain a person's occupational attributes based on his coarse-precision movement data. The main contributions of paper are third-folds:

- It develops a purely data-driven social attribute classification approach, which makes full use of spatial-temporal data, free of any survey data or census data. To our best knowledge, we are the first one to map the trajectory data to personal social attribute.
- We propose a data mining model, in which we combine personal travel features with corresponding regional features to enhance the information contained in travel trajectories, to better describe human travel behaviors. The problem of without a large number of labeled data is solved in a semi-supervised way in our approach.
- Expensive experiments covering 6 million people, accounting for one third of Beijing's permanent population, are conducted in our model. We take students and urban hummingbirds as examples, respectively corresponding to resident sensitive and mobile sensitive and the results show that the model leads to significant performance improvement especially when the training dataset is fully expanded.

2   Related Work

2.1   Human Mobility

Human trajectories show a high degree of temporal and spatial regularity [8]. Researchers have made advancements in developing methods to adopt spatio-temporal data to understand human mobility and travel [8,9] Xia et al. [10] propose an integrated analysis method to find the characteristics of human mobility. Jiang et al. [11] provided an innovative data mining framework that synthesizes the state-of-the-art techniques in extracting mobility patterns from raw mobile phone CDR data. Merkebe [12] use mobile data to derive country-wide mobility patterns. Researchers identify significant locations of users such as home, work, or other and found 28 trip type combinations.

Previous works have studied the problem of human mobilitypatterns mapping from spatio-temporal data. However, these works have not solved how to mine the relationship between social attributes and travel data.

2.2   Social Attribute

Social community detection dividing users into densely knitted or highly related groups with each group well separated from the others. Aylani et al. [13] use a new parameter Common Social Activity (CSA) to find community for a selected seed user along with other activity parameter. Chunaev et al. [14] propose a unified weight-based model with proper normalisation that generalises some of weight-based models known so far. Gu et al. [15] propose a social community detection scheme for mobile social networks based on social-ware, including social attribute similarity, node interest similarity and node mobility.

Previous works pay attention to find various community, while ignore that people gather in community mainly because of social attribute. Therefore, we take the social attribute as the starting point and study the characteristics of their respective communities.

2.3   Travel Pattern

Recently, there is a bunch of research focusing on travel pattern recognition. Chen J et al. [16] compared the classification results of three machine learning models: support vector machines, decision trees and convolutional neural networks. Xiao et al. [17] uses the continuous hidden Markov model to infer travel modes. Li et al. [18] constructed a spatially embedded network to model the mobility interactions in urban space and then utilized the community detection method to reveal the sub-regional structures in individual travel modes and as well as the aggregated one.

Poi data greatly enriches human behavior semantics. Zhang et al. [19] studies the effect of city structure on travel pattern at a refined level with the availability of detailed POIs (Points of Interest) data. Zhu et al. [20] propose a pattern and preference-aware travel route recommendation scheme base on different kinds of POI category.

The results mentioned above ignore the close connection between people's travel pattern and social attribute. Social attribute is the deep semantics of travel pattern. For example, student always travel regularly, while urban hummingbirds do the opposite. Based on this, we have conducted in-depth research on the social attributes of people.

3 Methodology

In this section, we first give the definition of the problem, and then introduce the framework we propose.

3.1 Framework Overview

The goal of the framework is to build a social label classification model based on massive spatio-temporal data, maping the user's trajectory to social attribute label.

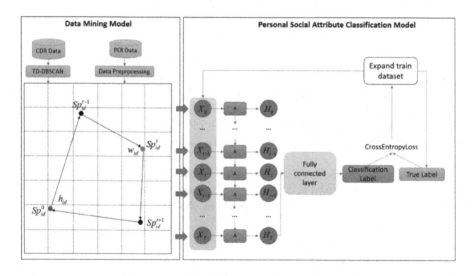

Fig. 1. The framework overview

As shown in Fig. 1, the framework we proposed can be divided into two parts: (1)*Data Mining Model*: the ST-DBSCAN algorithm [21] is used to extract users' stay points using mobile phone data and then the long-term stay point and the home stay points are mined. Then the POI data and users' stay points data are used to generate area features which are combined with users' stay points to better describe users' behaviors;(2) *Social Label Classification Model*:

368 T. Zhu et al.

a time series classification model based on Long Short-Time Memory is applied to classify different social labels. As a result of the lack of a large number of users' social attribute label data, a semi-supervised method is used for training. The training dataset is expanded by self-training. In particular, the first-generation classifier trained with a small amount of labeled data is used to obtain pseudo labels, and the high-confidence pseudo labels are marked as hard labels and added to the training set according to the rules.

3.2 Data Mining Model

Data Mining Model is designed to better describe travel behaviors of different users based on the spatio-temporal data. The result consists of two parts: individual travel feature and area feature.

The raw data of mobile phone records is $\boldsymbol{R_{id}}$, where $R_{id} = \{r_{id}^1, r_{id}^2, \ldots, r_{id}^N\}$ is a set of N records. A record r_{id}^i is defined as a 4-tuple(id, ts, te, loc), where id represents the user uniquely identified by the mask generated by the mobile phone number, ts represents the time of the event, te represents the end time of the event, loc represents the corresponding location.

To obtain the user's stay points collection $\boldsymbol{Sp_{id}}$ from the mobile phone CDR data, we use a clustering algorithm named ST-DBCAN.

$$Sp_{id} = \text{stdbscan}(\boldsymbol{Sp_{id}}, \varepsilon_s, \varepsilon_t), \tag{1}$$

where $\boldsymbol{Sp_{id}} = \{sp_{id}^1, sp_{id}^2, \ldots, sp_{id}^N\}$ is a set of N stay point, and one stay point r_{id}^i is defined as a 4-tuple(id, ts, te, loc).ε_s and ε_t represent the spatial threshold and time threshold in ST-DBSCAN algorithm.

Taking the advantage of $\boldsymbol{Sp_{id}}$, we can extract all stay periods in various locations. Calculate the length of stay in each location during rest and working hours, and take the longest stay point as the place of residence h_{id} and work w_{id}.

Personal travel characteristics $\boldsymbol{p_{id}}$ are used to describe personal travel behavior, where $\boldsymbol{p_{id}} = \{p_{id}^1, p_{id}^2, \ldots, p_{id}^T\}$ is a time series. The feature at time t is defined as $\boldsymbol{p_{id}^t}$, which consists of three parts as shown in Eq. 2.

$$p_{id}^t = \{td_{id}^t, dh_{id}^t, il_{id}^t\}. \tag{2}$$

Supposing that the user stays at Sp^t at time t and the user stays at point Sp^{t-1} at time $t-1$.td_{id}^t is defined as the travel distance from time $t-1$ to time t.dh_{id}^t is defined as the distance from home at time t.il_{id}^t is defined as whether it is in the working position at time t. The calculation process is as follows.

$$td_{id}^t = dis(Sp^t, Sp^{t-1}), \tag{3}$$

$$dh_{id}^t = dis(Sp^t, h_{id}), \tag{4}$$

$$il_{id}^t = \begin{cases} 1, Sp^t \in w_{id} \\ 0, Sp^t \notin w_{id} \end{cases}. \tag{5}$$

In the aspect of area data mining, the entire city is divided into several 1 km * 1 km grid areas and the POI data are used to significantly enrich the information in the areas of stay points. However, there are hundreds of categories in the poi data which are too complex to analyze. We have remapped the POI types in the original data to seven categories: catering, business, famous tourist sites, workspace, residence, education and logistics.

As the number of POI types is different, it is necessary to set a factor for each type to avoid errors caused by uneven distribution of the number of different type poi data in the original data. The factor and score for different POI types is calculated as follows:

$$\sigma_i = \frac{\sum_{k=1}^{m} n_k}{n_i},$$

$$n_i^{z'} = \sigma_i \times n_i^z,$$

$$s_i^z = \frac{n_i^{z'}}{\sum_{k=1}^{m} n_k^{z'}},$$

(6)

where n_i represents the POI number of type i, σ_i represents the factor of type i. n_i^z represents the POI number of type i in area z. $n_i^{z'}$ represents the amount after correction. s_i^z represents the score of type i in area z.

Since most of the stays in life are exceed 30 min, we take 30 min as the time interval to generate 48 sampling moments one day for each user. Supposing that the user stays at area z at time t, the area features z^t are defined as Eq. 7.

$$z^t = \left\{ z_t^n, z^w, z^h, z^s, z^d \right\},$$

(7)

where z_t^n represents the number of people in the area z at time t. z^h and z^w represents the number of residents and workers in area. z^s represents POI distribution in area, the calculation process is shown in Eq. 8. z^d represents average length of stay of all people in the area z, the calculation process is shown in Eq. 9.

$$z^d = \frac{\sum_{sp_j.loc \in z} sp_j.te - sp_j.ts}{|\{sp_k, sp_k.loc \in z\}|},$$

(8)

$$z^s = \left\{ s_1^z, s_2^z, \dots, s_7^z \right\}.$$

(9)

Supposing user stay at area z at time t, the final travel features are as follows.

$$X_{id}^t = \{p_{id}^t, z^t\}$$

$$= \left\{ \underbrace{dh_{id}^t, td_{id}^t, il_{id}^t}_{personel\ travel\ feature} \quad , \quad \underbrace{z_t^n, z^w, z^h, z^s, z^d}_{correspoinding\ area\ feature} \right\}.$$

(10)

3.3   Personal Social Attribute Classification Model

The personal social attribute classification model is designed to learn a good mapping from the input temporal features to the final classification label. Different from a supervised model with a large amount of labeled data, our proposed model can expand the train dataset by adding rules to choose hard labels from pseudo labels in the process of self-training.

The proposed model is based on LSTM which works well in temporal feature classification and the cross entropy loss function is used to evaluate the classification results. In the aspect of training, we take manually labeled data as the initial training dataset and expand the training dataset by self-training in Algorithm 1.

Algorithm 1. Training Data Expansion

Input:
　　labeled data $L = \{(x_1, y_1), (x_2, y_2), \ldots, (x_m, y_m)\}$;
　　unlabeled data $S = \{s_1, s_2, \ldots, s_n\}$;
　　the initial model m,the minimum size of the training data num_{min};

Output:
　　the expanded label data L', the updated model m';
　1: train the initial model m with dataset L;
　2: calculate the loss function $loss(x, y) = -\log\left(\frac{\exp(x[y])}{\sum_j x[j]}\right)$;
　3: update the model m by the back propagation to m'.
　4: **while** $|L| < num_{min}$ **do**
　5: 　　**for** s_i in S **do**
　6: 　　　$out_i = softmax(m'(s_i))$;
　7: 　　　$pseudolabel_i = j$　$s.t.\forall t \in out_i, t \leq out_i[j]$
　8: 　　　**if** $out_i[pseudolabel_i] \geq \varepsilon$ **and satisfy rules　then**
　9: 　　　　$L = L \cup \{(s_i, pseudolabel_i)\}$
　10: 　　**end if**
　11: 　**end for**
　12: **end while**
　13: $L' = L, m' = m$
　14: **return** L', m';

Algorithm 1 includes two parts: LSTM model training and training set expansion, where the time complexity mainly depends on the latter. In the worst case, the number of cycles in the training set expansion is equal to the number of unlabeled data, and the time complexity of a single cycle is a constant level. Therefore, the time complexity of Algorithm is $O(n_S)$, where n_S is the number of unlabeled data.

In the training set expansion, taking students and urban hummingbirds as examples, the selection rules for pseudo labels with high-confidence are in the followings.

$$\delta_j = \frac{\sum_{s \in Sp} (s.te - s.ts) \cdot s^j_{z(s)}}{\sum_{s \in Sp} s.te - s.ts}, j = 1, 2, ..., m, \tag{11}$$

$$\lambda = \sum_{i=0}^{|Sp|-1} dis(SP_i, SP_{i+1}). \tag{12}$$

In the Formula 11, 12, we use the length of stay as the weight to calculate the user's POI score δ. and the total distance of the user λ. The candidates with the student pseudo label are supposed to stay longer in the education area, which means $\delta_j > \overline{\delta_j}$ In addition, the candidates with the urban hummingbirds pseudo label are supposed to travel a long distance on each day that means $\lambda > \overline{\lambda}$. In a word, the proposed semi-supervised model needs some rules to figure out the hard labels to be added to the training data from numbers of pseudo labels.

4 Experiments

4.1 Data and Pre-processing

The data in our experiments includes the mobile phone CDR data and the POI data. The CDR data contains 6 millions of anonymous users and two hundred thousand base stations. The POI dataset contains location information of 1.3 million points of interest. In the data preprocessing, active users are filtered out according to the update interval of the CDR data and the incorrect data caused by the long-distance base station jitter is eliminated.

4.2 Results Analysis

People with different social attributes have different travel modes. For example, students have relatively short travel distances, most activities on campus, and regular travel characteristics; while urban hummingbirds such as freight and express delivery have long and irregular travel distances. Therefore, we selects students and urban hummingbirds as typical research objects.

For students, we get the gathering place of students in our experiments. The result in Fig. 2 shows that we can correctly identify most of the students' gathering places as school buildings or dormitories and the students' activities are highly clustered. The matching rate of students' gathering places with real schools is more than 85%.

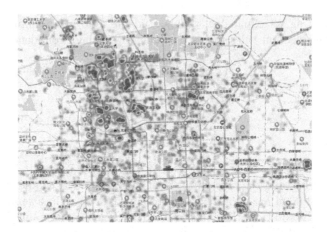

Fig. 2. The recognition result of student gathering place.

For urban hummingbirds, we identified that their main gathering place is in the suburbs south of the city as shown in Fig. 3. There are many points of interest similar to logistics centers or wholesale markets around their gathering places and their daily travel distance and number of stay points are much higher than the average.

Fig. 3. The recognition result of urban hummingbird gathering place.

4.3   Performance Comparison

We compare the proposed social label classification model with five baselines, which are introduced as follows.

- **CNN** (Convolutional Neural Network:) The convolutional neural network (CNN, or ConvNet) is a class of deep neural networks, most commonly applied to analyzing visual imagery and time series.
- **RNN** (Recurrent Neural Network:) Recurrent Neural Network can be used in classification, including pattern and sequence recognition, novelty detection and sequential decision making.
- **SVM:** The SVM algorithm has been widely applied in the classification. In our baseline, we take the better effect of the linear-svm and the rbf-svm.
- **Decision Tree:** Decision trees used in data mining are of two main types: classification tree or regression tree analysis. We take the classification tree as our baseline.
- **Random Forest:** Random forests are an ensemble learning method for classification by constructing a multitude of decision trees at training time and outputting the class that is the mode of the classes.

The results of different baselines and our proposed model on Test Set is shown in the Table 1. From these results, it can be concluded that the LSTM model has a better effect on the class that requires long-term observation. For most models, the classification effect of urban hummingbirds is not ideal. The F1 scores of our proposed model with different training data set sizes is shown in Fig. 4.

Table 1. Final results of various models on Test Set.

Model	Accuracy	Class	Precision	Recall	F1 Score
SVM	0.75	STU	0.9705	0.6282	0.7627
		UHB	0.5	0.0366	0.0683
		Others	0.6443	0.9760	0.7762
Decision tree	0.87	STU	0.9550	0.9671	0.9610
		UHB	0.2511	0.2738	0.2619
		Others	0.8743	0.8513	0.8626
Random forest	0.88	STU	0.95	0.9397	0.9448
		UHB	0	0	0
		Others	0.8287	0.9460	0.8801
RNN	0.85	STU	0.8864	0.9188	0.9023
		UHB	0	0	0
		Others	0.7988	0.8769	0.8360
CNN	0.89	STU	0.9776	0.9262	0.9512
		UHB	0	0	0
		Others	0.8175	0.9774	0.8903
LSTM	**0.98**	STU	0.9744	0.9944	0.9843
		UHB	0.9950	0.9804	0.9876
		Others	0.9941	0.9736	0.9838

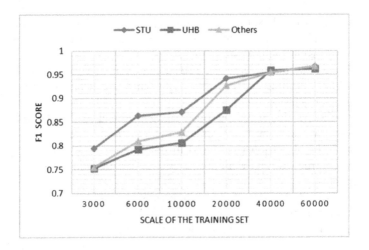

Fig. 4. F1 scores with different training data sizes.

5   Conclusions

In this paper, we proposed a purely data-driven social attribute inferred approach free of any survey data or census data. In particular, a spatio-temporal data was proposed to better describe human travel behaviors and generate travel features with behavioral semantics. The proposed semi-supervised social attribute classification model was used to map these spatial-temporal trajectory to social labels. In addition, we gave our method to get the hard labels to expand the train data from the pseudo labels. Experimental results on the test dateset proved that our model outperforms several baseline models and the F1 score of our model exceeds 0.95, especially when the data set is expanded sufficiently.

References

1. Do, T.M.T., Gatica-Perez, D.: The places of our lives: visiting patterns and automatic labeling from longitudinal smartphone data. IEEE Trans. Mob. Comput. **13**(3), 638–648 (2013)
2. Nunes, I.O., de Melo, P.O.V., Loureiro, A.A.: Group mobility: detection, tracking and characterization. In: 2016 IEEE International Conference on Communications (ICC), pp. 1–6. IEEE, May 2016
3. Zhang, Y., Aslam, N.S., Lai, J., Cheng, T.: You are how you travel: a multi-task learning framework for Geodemographic inference using transit smart card data. Comput. Environ. Urban Syst. **83**, 101517 (2020)
4. Zhao, S., et al.: Mining user attributes using large-scale app lists of smartphones. IEEE Syst. J. **11**(1), 315–323 (2016)
5. Xu, H., Yu, Z., Xiong, H., Guo, B., Zhu, H.: Learning career mobility and human activity patterns for job change analysis. In: 2015 IEEE International Conference on Data Mining, pp. 1057–1062. IEEE, November 2015

6. Shibasaki, M., Witayangkurn, A., Rahman, M.M.: Comparison of life patterns from mobile data in Bangladesh. In: 2019 First International Conference on Smart Technology and Urban Development (STUD), pp. 1–7. IEEE, December 2019
7. Hu, T., Bigelow, E., Luo, J., Kautz, H.: Tales of two cities: using social media to understand idiosyncratic lifestyles in distinctive metropolitan areas. IEEE Trans. Big Data 3(1), 55–66 (2016)
8. Gonzalez, M.C., Hidalgo, C.A., Barabasi, A.L.: Understanding individual human mobility patterns. Nature 453(7196), 779–782 (2008)
9. Zhou, X., Zhao, Z., Li, R., Zhou, Y., Palicot, J., Zhang, H.: Human mobility patterns in cellular networks. IEEE Commun. Lett. 17(10), 1877–1880 (2013)
10. Xia, F., Wang, J., Kong, X., Wang, Z., Li, J., Liu, C.: Exploring human mobility patterns in urban scenarios: a trajectory data perspective. IEEE Commun. Mag. 56(3), 142–149 (2018)
11. Jiang, S., Ferreira, J., González, M.C.: Activity-based human mobility patterns inferred from mobile phone data: a case study of Singapore. IEEE Trans. Big Data 3(2), 208–219 (2017)
12. Demissie, M.G., Phithakkitnukoon, S., Kattan, L., Farhan, A.: Understanding human mobility patterns in a developing country using mobile phone data. Data Sci. J. 18(1) (2019)
13. Aylani, A., Goyal, N.: Community detection in social network based on useras social activities. In: 2017 International Conference on I-SMAC (IoT in Social, Mobile, Analytics and Cloud) (I-SMAC), pp. 625–628. IEEE, February 2017
14. Chunaev, P., Nuzhdenko, I., Bochenina, K.: Community detection in attributed social networks: a unified weight-based model and its regimes. In: 2019 International Conference on Data Mining Workshops (ICDMW), pp. 455–464. IEEE, November 2019
15. Gu, K., Liu, D., Wang, K.: Social community detection scheme based on social-aware in mobile social networks. IEEE Access 7, 173407–173418 (2019)
16. Chen, J., Qi, K., Zhu, S.: Traffic travel pattern recognition based on sparse global positioning system trajectory data. Int. J. Distrib. Sensor Netw. 16(10), 1550147720968469 (2020)
17. Xiao, G., Cheng, Q., Zhang, C.: Detecting travel modes from smartphone-based travel surveys with continuous hidden Markov models. Int. J. Distrib. Sensor Netw. 15(4), 1550147719844156 (2019)
18. Li, W., Xu, M., Xia, H.: Revealing the spatial structure of human mobility in diverse travel modes. In: 2018 International Conference on Computational Science and Computational Intelligence (CSCI), pp. 1093–1098. IEEE, December 2018
19. Zhang, S., Liu, X., Tang, J., Cheng, S., Wang, Y.: Urban spatial structure and travel patterns: analysis of workday and holiday travel using inhomogeneous Poisson point process models. Comput. Environ. Urban Syst. 73, 68–84 (2019)
20. Zhu, L., Yu, L., Cai, Z., Zhang, J.: Toward pattern and preference-aware travel route recommendation over location-based social networks. J. Inf. Sci. Eng. 35(5) (2019)
21. Birant, D., Kut, A.: ST-DBSCAN: an algorithm for clustering spatial-temporal data. Data Knowl. Eng. 60(1), 208–221 (2007)

Chinese Judicial Summarising Based on Short Sentence Extraction and GPT-2

Jie Liu, Jiaye Wu, and Xudong Luo$^{(\boxtimes)}$

Guangxi Key Laboratory of Multi-Source Information Mining and Security,
College of Computer Science and Information Engineering,
Guangxi Normal University, Guilin, Guangxi, China
luoxd@mailbox.gxnu.edu.cn

Abstract. This paper studies the compilation of judicial case summarisation in China. Judicial case summaries are made through the abridgement, generalisation, and summarisation of court verdicts. It is a time-consuming, inefficient manual process done by legal professionals. The automatic generation of such summaries could save much time of legal professionals. Court verdicts are generally lengthy, exceeding the maximum word limit for inputs into pre-trained models. Through the observation and analysis of existing data sets, this paper conducts further treatment of these datasets. The dataset of one court verdict is split into five via phrase extraction to obtain the extracts of five key components of a court verdict and the corresponding manual summaries. In this way, we convert one text summarisation problem into five text compression and integration problems for sentences of five different categories. We adopt the GPT-2 pre-trained model, which excels in text generation, to conduct text compression and integration. From that, key points for compression of various parts of the verdict are obtained, which are eventually put together to obtain the summary of the court verdict. This paper divides datasets using extractive algorithms and compresses and integrates them using abstractive algorithms. Our experiments show that our approach proposed by this paper performs well.

1 Introduction

Automatic text summarisation is an important means of obtaining key information from texts. Text summarisation generates a summary containing all essential information from the original document [1]. Although many models have been applied to the summary task, for the summary task, due to the different structure of the text content, it is difficult to find a general model that can achieve better results in many kinds of texts. Legal information in the public domain Increasingly, it is also necessary to make corresponding efforts to process and obtain legal-related information according to a user's needs [12], so this paper sets application scenarios and researches legal abstracts.

To solve some legal problems, lawyers usually need to refer to previous judgments and may spend a lot of time reading judgment documents instead of

© Springer Nature Switzerland AG 2021
H. Qiu et al. (Eds.): KSEM 2021, LNAI 12816, pp. 376–393, 2021.
https://doi.org/10.1007/978-3-030-82147-0_31

solving the problem. So, the automatic generation of judicial abstracts can save a lot of legal workers' time. A judicial summary is the compression and summary of the content of the trial documents. The automatic judicial summary is also very suitable for ordinary people. It is getting more accessible for people to obtain legal documents, but legal documents are usually long and full of legal clauses. These terms help understand the case. There are certain obstacles. After the summary is automatically generated, the user's willingness to query legal information will also be significantly improved [12], and at the same time, criminals can be punished quickly according to the situation of the case.

In this paper, we analyse the existing judicial summary dataset and finds that the length of a judgment document is too long, with an average length of more than 2,000, far exceeding the usual text processing tasks. The data is semi-structured to a certain extent, and we use a combination of extraction and generation for summarising. Inspired by the idea of the Divide-and-Conquer Algorithm, the original dataset was further processed and divided. By adjusting the dataset, a more difficult problem is decomposed into five relatively simple sub-problems. Also, different models are trained for other parts of a judgment document, and the abstract is generated in a targeted manner to be precise and intelligent and achieve a considerable improvement in the effect. Using cutting-edge advanced technology in natural language processing, the pre-trained language model generates outstanding GPT-2 [21] for sentence compression and fusion. Compared with the direct extraction, the generative formula makes the generated summary more fluent and achieves a similar effect as the manual summary.

The main contributions of this paper are as follows: (1) Little research is on Chinese judicial summarising, but ours in this paper does it. (2) Our further processing and segmenting the actual dataset and training different models for different content in a judgment document achieve accurate intelligence and improve the effect of the summarising significantly. (3) We use GPT-2, instead of directly extracting abstracts composed of critical sentences from judgment documents, to achieve similar effects to artificial abstracts. (4) We integrate the extraction method with the generation method in the automatic text summarisation, so taking their respective advantages to make the final result very good. (5) Not only can our method save many legal professionals' time, but it can also automatically extract the plot characteristics of massive judgment documents, which provides strong support for the intelligent learning of future judgment results and other legal-related tasks.

The rest of this paper is organised as follows. Section 2 recaps the basic principle of the GPT-2 p model. Section 3 discusses our dataset processing and short sentence extraction. Section 4 discusses how to compress a legal document and generates its summary. Section 5 presents our experimental evaluation of our method. Section 6 discusses the related work. Finally, Sect. 7 concludes this paper with future work.

2 Prelimimary

This section recaps the basic idea of the GPT-2 pre-trained model, which our work in this paper will base on.

The GPT-2 pre-trained model is the second generation of GPT, which is stacked by the Transformer's decoder module. The encoder module includes a feedforward neural network layer and a self-attention layer with a mask, which can process sequences of up to 1024 words. Each word passes through all the decoder modules along with its previous path. Its model framework is the same as GPT, but it adds a normalisation layer on the top layer, initialises the strategy, and expands the vocabulary. GPT-2 has a large scale, and the smallest GPT-2 also needs at least 500 MB of storage space to store all its parameters. The text it generates exceeds people's expectations in terms of contextual coherence and emotional expression.

GPT-2 uses a masked self-attention, and it is not allowed to see the information of the word on its right. And it adopts an autoregressive mechanism to make it perform well in the text generation effect. Like most pre-trained models, use unsupervised pre-training and then use supervised fine-tuning. In the unsupervised learning process, a multi-layer Transformer decoder is used, and the optimisation task is a language model.

First, given an unlabeled large corpus, denoting each sequence as $U =< u_1, \cdots, u_n >$, GPT-2 trains a language model by maximising the likelihood function:

$$L_1(u) = \sum_i \log P(u_i \mid u_{i-k}, \cdots, u_{i-1}; \Theta). \tag{1}$$

When learning a language model, the calculation process from input to output is:

$$h_0 = UW_e + W_p, \tag{2}$$
$$h_l = \text{transformer\_block}(h_l - 1) \, \forall i \in [1, n], \tag{3}$$
$$P(u) = \text{softmax}(W_n W_e^T), \tag{4}$$

where k is the size of the context window, W_e is the word vector matrix, W_p is the position embedding matrix, $U = \{u_{-k}, \cdots, u_{-1}\}$ is the vocabulary vector of the left window, and n is the number of layers of Transformer.

After obtaining the Transformer-based model, for a specific task, on dataset C, assuming that the input and output are x and y respectively, add another layer to the output of Tansformer:

$$P(y \mid x^1, \cdots, x^m) = \text{softmax}(h_l^m W_y), \tag{5}$$

so as to get a new loss function:

$$L_2(C) = \sum_{(x,y)} \log P(y \mid x^1, \cdots, x^m). \tag{6}$$

3   Dataset

This section will discuss the dataset we will use for training.

3.1   Dataset Observation and Analysis

The dataset used in this paper is from the "Law Research Cup" Judicial Summarising Track, which the Beijing Judicial Big Data Institute provides and marks. It contains 13,531 judgments and the corresponding judicial summaries. At the same time, each document is divided into many short sentences with the tag of 0 or 1, where 0 means unimportant short sentences, and 1 means meaningful short sentences. The average number of input words is 2,568, the maximum number of words is 13,064. The average number of output words is 283, and the maximum is 474 words.

Table 1. Dataset D_1

Id	Paper	Abstract
5cec68aadcbea086 a5b4b6eccb58a88f	The civil judgment of the first instance in the tort liability dispute between Tang Mingliang, He Weihua, and Shenzhen Huaming Weidian Automobile Service Co., Ltd.	The plaintiff and the defendant in a dispute over tort liability

We try to perform the binary classification and sequence-to-sequence model directly, but the effect is not satisfactory. In a summary of a judgment document, the sample distribution in the judgment document is not uniform. The unimportant sentences are ten times more than the important sentences, so the effect of binary classification extraction is not ideal. Directly adopting the sequence-to-sequence generative model requires a particularly long training time, because the input text is too long. Further, we find that an artificial summary can be roughly divided into four to five parts: dispute type, litigation request, defendant's defence (not every document has it), the trial investigation and the judgment. They are condensed and summarised from the sentences from different parts of the judgment document.

3.2   Dataset Division and Processing

The judge clerk is long and complex. The artificially summarised abstract is divided into five parts by keyword positions, rules, and so on. For each part, the corresponding part is extracted from the judgment document. The results of the two parts are directly related to the subsequent algorithm. Through observation, we find that we can use rules to realise the preliminary extraction work through a program. After the initial extraction, through manual observation, there will

Table 2. Dataset D_2

Id	Paper	Abstract
1f3ce8e247e402fb 816ff030c66d8dde	The plaintiff Xu Shaoqin filed a lawsuit with this court: 1. Request to inherit two houses from the inheritance of the father and mother, deposit 40,000 yuan and interest, divide the father's funeral expenses and funeral subsidy of 137,007 yuan; 2. Request the defendant to bear litigation costs	The plaintiff requested: request to inherit two houses, deposits, and interest from the inheritance of the father and mother, and divide the funeral expenses and funeral subsidy of the father

Table 3. Dataset D_3

Id	Paper	Abstract
c30010092b8d48c3 ac6c5bc644b0b96a	The defendant Zhong Zhixiang argued that it is a fact that the rent is in arrears, and we have negotiated with the plaintiff about the rent. In recent years, the business has not been good and the rent cannot be paid. I paid for all the decorations of the venue we rented	The defendant argued that he could not pay the rent and could pay part of the rent, but the plaintiff disagreed

Table 4. Dataset D_4

Id	Paper	Abstract
2f7360ce46586be8 aa4ccbc9bc04b2be	This court believes that the small loan contract signed by the Plaintiff Postal Savings Jianli Sub-branch and the defendant's Zhang Lixiong and Tan Yuexi represents the true intentions of both parties and is legal and valid, and this court recognizes it. The Plaintiff Postal Savings Jianli Sub-branch issued the loan in accordance with the contract, and the defendant's Zhang Lixiong and Tan Yuexi should repay the principal and interest of the loan as agreed. Their failure to perform their obligations as agreed in the contract constitutes a breach of contract and shall bear the liability for breach of contract in accordance with the law. Therefore, the plaintiff's request of the Defendants Zhang Lixiong and Tan Yuexi to repay the loan principal, interest, and penalty interest according to the contract was supported by this court	Upon review, the loan contract between the defendant and the plaintiff was legal and valid, and the plaintiff issued the loan to the defendant in accordance with the contract. The defendant shall be liable for breach of contract if it fails to repay the loan within the time limit

Table 5. Dataset D_5

Id	Paper	Abstract
6ca8fc47698ce689 b296a254a8a20fe3	In summary, in accordance with paper 112 of the "General Principles of the Civil Law of the People's Republic of China", paper 3, paper 11, paper 16, paper 17, and paper 18 of the "Inheritance Law of the People's Republic of China", According to paper 142 of the "Civil Procedure Law of the People's Republic of China", the judgment is as follows: confirm that the "will" involved in the case made on March 27, 2017, is an invalid will. The case acceptance fee of 100 yuan was jointly borne by the defendants Liu 5 and Liu 6	In accordance with paper 112 of the "General Principles of the Civil Law of the People's Republic of China", papers 3, 11, 16, 17 and 18 of the "Inheritance Law of the People's Republic of China", "The Chinese People According to paper 142 of the Civil Procedure Law of the Republic, the judgment confirms that the "will" involved in the case is invalid

still be some problematic data. For example, such as the extracted data is empty, or too long, too short, and so on. Thus, we further process the data, plus corresponding constraints and restrictions. However, some data may be lost in the process, although the result after extraction is more accurate.

First, we divide the first dataset D_1. This part of the content is mainly the type of judgment. This dataset is very easy to extract. It is enough to extract the first sentence from the judgment document and the manual summary, as shown in Table 1.

For the second part of the litigation request, we compose it into dataset D_2, which appear in almost all judgment documents and contain obvious keywords, such as "claims", "appeals", "Request for order", "Request for court", and other keywords. By searching via keywords, we can find the litigation request part in the judgment document. Since this part is extracted roughly, we can extract it as comprehensively as possible. For the part of the litigation request in the manual summary, we can find it by its location. Most of them are located after the first sentence and before the trial is found out. Of course, there is also a small part in the first sentence, which can be intercepted by some keywords, and finally constitutes a dataset D_2, as shown in Table 2.

It is more difficult to extract the third part (the defendant argument) from the judgment document than the previous two. This part does not exist in all judgment documents and sometimes appears in the judgment document, but it is not summarised in the manual summary. The corresponding sentence can be found through keywords such as "defence". However, sometimes it is difficult to determine its length in the judgment document, so the front part of it is intercepted through keywords such as "review". The corresponding part in the manual summary can still be extracted by means such as location. So we can get D_3, as shown in Table 3.

The fourth part is the trial and identification, which is the most challenging part. Its content is often more than a thousand words, and there will be a lot of redundancy in all extraction. After careful observation and analysis, we find that the keyword "this court thinks" can be further narrowed. However, there are still many redundancies, and sometimes "this court thinks" appears in the judgment document more than once. For this, we adopt the LEAD3 method, which is simple but very effective in the text abstract, selects the first three sentences starting from "this hospital thinks" to extract, and at the same time adds keywords for interception. For the manual summary of the trial investigation part, it can be extracted by keywords and location information. For example, dataset D_4 is extracted as shown in Table 4.

For the fifth part of the judgment result, we can extract it more easily by keywords such as "the judgment is as follows". Of course, the length uncertainty problem may also occur. At this time, we still use the LEAD3 method to make specific improvements. We can extract the judgment result part directly according to the location, such as dataset D_5 as shown in Table 5.

In short, after the dataset is divided and processed, we can get the data sets D_1, D_2, D_3, D_4, and D_5. Each data set D_i contains a sequence of U_i and a sequence of Y_i. The sequence of U_i represents the sequence of judgment documents, i.e., $U_i = < u_1^i, \cdots, u_m^i >$; the sequence of Y_i represents manual summary, i.e., $Y_i = < y_1^i, \cdots, y_n^i >$.

4   Text Compression

After extracting five different datasets, since the fragments extracted from the judgement document will still have a lot of redundancy, we need to compress and merge the sentences to obtain a more similar result to the manual summary. Through the investigation and comparison of various options, we chose the GPT-2 pre-trained model for text compression.

4.1   Sentence Compression and Fusion

After the dataset is divided, the input length is greatly reduced, which solves the problem of the input length limitation of the pre-trained model. A divided dataset is composed of different fragments in the judgment document. We use sentence compression and sentence fusion technology to generate a more compact summary for a better summarising effect. There are many ways to achieve sentence compression, such as deleting words [15] from a sentence, or replacing, reordering, or inserting words in a sentence [5]. Sentence fusion technology is to merge two or more related sentences that contain overlapping content to get a sentence. In this paper, we use GPT-2 to achieve sentence compression and fusion.

4.2   GPT-2 Model

For the five datasets, we use the same model structure because the tasks are the same, but the parameters are different. For each dataset D_i, we use the pre-trained model for fine-tuning, and the objective function is as follows:

$$L_2\left(D_i\right) = \sum_{\left(U_i, Y_i\right)} \log P\left(y_1^i, y_2^i, ... y_n^i \mid u_1^i, u_2^i, ... u_m^i\right), \tag{7}$$

$$P\left(y_1^i, y_2^i, ... y_n^i \mid u_1^i, u_2^i, ... u_m^i\right) = \text{softmax}\left(h_l^m W_y\right). \tag{8}$$

For each input, using the pre-trained language model, we can directly select the output vector h_l^m of the last time step of the last layer of Transformer, and then follow it with a fully connected layer, where W_y is the parameter matrix of the newly introduced fully connected layer.

For the decoder, we use stochastic decoding [3], including temperature sampling, Top-k sampling, and nuclear sampling. The temperature sampling uses the temperature t, which makes the distribution more inclined to high probability events, which implicitly weakens the effect of the tail distribution. In the decoding process of Top-k sampling, select the most likely top k tokens from $P\left(u^i \mid u_{1:t-1}^i\right)$, add their probabilities to get $P' = \sum_{i=1}^{K} P\left(u^i \mid u_{1:t-1}^i\right)$; then calculate $P\left(u^i \mid u_{1:t-1}^i\right)$ as follows:

$$P'\left(u^i \mid u_{1:t-1}^i\right) = \frac{P\left(u^i \mid u_{1:t-1}^i\right)}{P'}, \tag{9}$$

where $u^i \in V^{(k)}$; and finally from $P'\left(u^i \mid u_{1:t-1}^i\right)$ sample a token as output. Nuclear sampling is based on Top-k sampling, which sets $P' = \sum_{i=1}^{K} P\left(u^i \mid u_{1:t-1}^i\right)$ as a pre-defined good constant $P' \in (0,1)$, and the selected tokens are different according to the changes in the sub-historical distribution.

4.3   Fusion

Different models can be obtained through datasets $D_1, \cdots, D_5$. For each model, we choose the best effect to fuse, and finally stitch each part of the output. The process is shown in Fig. 1. The model structure of GPT-2 is shown in Fig. 2. In the training process, we first use the Wiki Chinese dataset to train GPT-2. After the training, we can get a general language model and then use the unprocessed data to perform a pre-training with the general language model. This step can improve the effectiveness of the subsequent dataset training. After the pre-training, we train the divided datasets separately. Figure 3 shows the training process, and Algorithm 1 shows its idea.

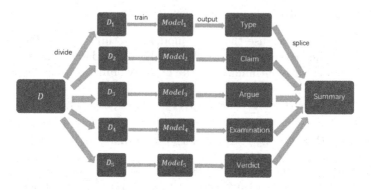

Fig. 1. Model structure

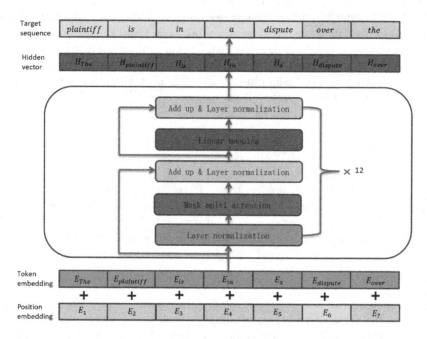

Fig. 2. Gpt-2 model structure

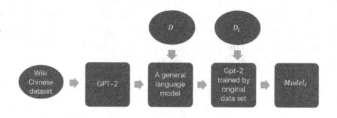

Fig. 3. Training process

Algorithm 1. General idea

Input:
  Raw data D,the Wiki Chinese dataset:WC, Smaple: S
Output:
  The prediction result:$summary$;
1: $D_1,D_2,D_3,D_4,D_5=$ extract(D);
2: call(GPT-2);
3: $language\_model=$Train(GTP-2, WC);
4: $pre\_training\_model=$Train($language\_model$, D);
5: $train\_D_1,train\_D_2,train\_D_3,train\_D_4,train\_D_5=$Read_train$(D_1,D_2,D_3,D_4,D_5)$;
6: $model\_1, model\_2, model\_3, model\_4, model\_5=$Train($pre\_training\_model,train\_D_1$, $train\_D_2,train\_D_3,train\_D_4,train\_D_5$)
7: $valid\_D_1,valid\_D_2,valid\_D_3,valid\_D_4,valid\_D_5=$Read_valid$(D_1,D_2,D_3,D_4,D_5)$;
8: $model\_1, model\_2, model\_3, model\_4, model\_5=$Train($model\_1,model\_2,model\_3,model\_4,$ $model\_5,valid\_D_1,valid\_D_2,valid\_D_3,valid\_D_4,valid\_D_5$)
9: $model\_1, model\_2, model\_3, model\_4, model\_5=$Adjus_parameters($model\_1,model\_2,model\_3,$ $model\_4,model\_5$);
10: $model\_1, model\_2, model\_3, model\_4, model\_5=$Select_best($model\_1,model\_2,model\_3,model\_4,$ $model\_5$);
11: Call($model\_1, model\_2, model\_3, model\_4, model\_5$);
12: $result\_1,result\_2,result\_3,result\_4,result\_5=$Test ($model\_1, model\_2, model\_3, model\_4, model\_5,$ S);
13: summary=Splice($result\_1,result\_2,result\_3,result\_4,result\_5$)
14: **return** $summary$;

5 Experiment

This section presents an experimental evaluation of our system.

5.1 Experimental Setup

The dataset contains a total of 13,531 samples, which are divided into a training set, a validation set, and a test set according to the ratio of 8:1:1 (*i.e.*, they contain 10825, 1353, and 1353 samples, respectively). We divide the dataset to five datasets. The valid data is shown in Table 6.

Table 6. Dataset information

Dataset	Number of training samples
D_1	9484
D_2	10773
D_3	7194
D_4	10038
D_5	9422

After the dataset is divided and processed, we use GPT2-Chinese [7] to train a general model on the Wiki Chinese corpus and uses HuggingFace's transformers [25] to implement the writing and training of the GPT2 model text compression task. The weight of the general model is used as the initial stage of the text

Table 7. Output and label

Dataset	Output	Label
D_1	The plaintiff is in a dispute over the loan contract	The plaintiff was in a dispute over the loan contract
D_2	The plaintiff filed a lawsuit request: the defendant repays the plaintiff's loan and interest, penalty interest, and compound interest; the plaintiff enjoys the priority right of compensation for the defendant's mortgaged house	The plaintiff requested to order the defendants Yang Ke and Tan Zhenyi to repay the principal and interest of the loan to the plaintiff; the plaintiff was ordered to have priority in compensation for the mortgaged housing provided by the two defendants
D_3	The defendant argued that: the plaintiff had resigned voluntarily and should not pay economic compensation	The defendant argued that the plaintiff resigned voluntarily and should not pay economic compensation, and the other claims were rejected according to law without basis
D_4	Upon review, the personal house/car loan and guarantee contracts signed by the plaintiff and the defendant are legal and valid. The defendant's failure to repay the loan and interest as stipulated in the contract constitutes a breach of contract and shall bear the liability for breach of contract. The plaintiff has the right to declare that the remaining loans expire early, Requiring the defendant to repay the principal and interest of the loan and enjoy the priority right of repayment of the mortgage	The defendant's Yang Ke and Tan Zhenyi did not respond. In this case, the "Personal House/Car Loan and Guarantee Contract" concluded by the plaintiff and the defendant is a valid contract. The plaintiff issued the loan as agreed upon after the contract was signed, but the defendant failed to repay the principal and interest of the loan as agreed. This is a breach of contract and the plaintiff has the right to demand a declaration The remaining loans expired early, and the defendant was required to repay the principal and interest of the loan and enjoy the priority right of repayment of the mortgage
D_5	Therefore, in accordance with paper 75 of the "General Principles of the Civil Law of the People's Republic of China", paper 64 and paper 144 of the "Civil Procedure Law of the People's Republic of China", the Supreme People's Court on the Application of the Civil Procedure Law of the People's Republic of China According to paper 90 of the Interpretation, the judge rejected the plaintiff's claim	According to the "General Principles of Civil Law", "Civil Procedure Law", and "Interpretation of the Supreme People's Court on the Application of the Civil Procedure Law of the People's Republic of China", the verdict: dismissed the plaintiff's claim

compression task. First, each part of the dataset is input for training separately, the entire dataset is input for fine-tuning, and then the fine-tuned model is used for each sub-dataset for training and fine-tuning. The loss function is the cross-

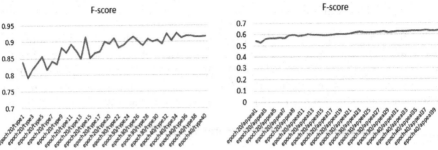

Fig. 4. D_1 results in different epochs

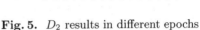

Fig. 5. D_2 results in different epochs

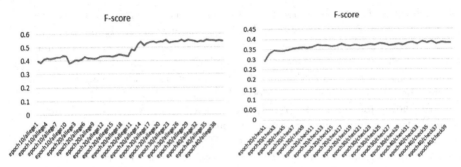

Fig. 6. D_3 results in different epochs

Fig. 7. D_4 results in different epochs

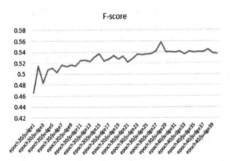

Fig. 8. D_5 results in different epochs

entropy loss function. It is used to obtain five GPT-2 text compression models with different parameters. In-text generation, to achieve better results, we use temperature sampling, Top-k sampling, and nuclear sampling strategies. Since the intermediate decoding uses a random sample, the content generated each time cannot be guaranteed to be consistent. As a result, we can run it several times and take the one with the highest ROUGE (Recall-Oriented Understudy for Gisting Evaluation) score [16].

388   J. Liu et al.

5.2   Model Evaluation

We use ROUGE for evaluation. The ROUGE score can be calculated by comparing the automatically generated summary with the reference summary. Specifically, ROUGE-1 (R_1) evaluates the matching of one-tuples, ROUGE-2 (R_2) measures the matching of two-tuples, ROUGE-L (R_L) measures the longest common subsequence. Finally, we use their f-scores to calculate the total score as follows:

$$0.2 \times \text{f-score}(R_1) + 0.4 \times \text{f-score}(R_2) + 0.4 \times \text{f-score}(R_L).$$

5.3   Results and Analysis

For each datasets D_i, the output and labels are as shown in Table 7. For each dataset D_i, Figs. 4, 5, 6, 7 and 8 show the changes in the result of F under different epochs. From these figures, we can see that different epochs have a significant impact on the effect of the final model for the five datasets. And the larger the epoch, the better its effect. However, after increasing to a certain extent, the effect of adjusting the epoch becomes smaller.

After adjusting the model parameters and analysing the results of each part generated, it can be found that the two parts of the litigation request and the judgment have been fine-tuned after the GPT-2 has been able to obtain better results. However, for the two parts of the argument and the trial investigation, there are still some problems. After further analysis, we find that the argumentation part does not appear in every document, and the argumentation sometimes appears during the manual summarising, and sometimes it is omitted directly. The sample data for this part is too small, resulting in poor results. For the part found in the trial, the effect is not good due to the different lengths and the difficultly to determine the location. If the quality of the extracted data can be improved (*i.e.*, the quality of the divided dataset is better), better results can be obtained.

At the same time, we analyse time complexity, including the time used to extract different types and the time used for one epoch when GPT-2 is used for training for different types. As shown in Table 8, the time required to extract the data sets D_1, D_2, D_3, D_4, and D_5 is very short. In the training process with GPT-2, the longer the input data length, the longer the training time. For issues such as resource allocation, we can get celebrities through literature [6,8,9].

For the final result, compared with common algorithms, the experimental result is as shown in Table 9. It can be seen that in the case of combining rule extraction with GPT-2, the quality of text summarisation is much better than using some text summarisation algorithms directly for automatic summarisation. Although the Lead algorithm works better in some situations, it still has certain flaws for such long-length judgment documents. The Textrank algorithm is a sorting algorithm based on graphs, and its effect is still lacking in the extraction of the text summary of the judgment document. BERT [13] is a well-known pre-trained model for natural language processing, but it is more suitable for tasks such as text classification. By directly extracting rules, we can roughly

Table 8. Running time

Program	Running time
Get D_1,D_2,D_3,D_4,D_5,	0:00:05.783941
Train GPT-2 model with D_1	0:02:15.946246
Train GPT-2 model with D_2	0:06:54.258672
Train GPT-2 model with D_3	0:01:51.761168
Train GPT-2 model with D_4	0:06:54.258672
Train GPT-2 model with D_5	0:05:04.323781

Table 9. Algorithm comparison

Model	ROUGE-1	ROUGE-2	ROUGE-L	F-score
Lead3	0.36109	0.20334	0.23829	0.24887
Texttrank	0.30219	0.161156	0.19773	0.204154
BERT	0.216	0.14864	0.18528	0.176768
BERT binary classification	0.53022	0.43194	0.46449	0.46462
Rule extraction	0.58134	0.4364	0.46288	0.47598
Rule extraction+GPT-2	0.66166	0.5136	0.55687	0.56052

reduce the text, but if we want to be more streamlined, we need to integrate it with generative algorithms. Finally, we integrate rule extraction with GPT-2, and find it works very well.

6 Related Work

This section compares related research with ours, including text summarising, pre-trained models, and legal text summarising.

6.1 Text Abstract

Automated summarisation can be divided into extractive summarising and abstract summarising according to the output. The main extraction methods include the empirical Lead3 algorithm, the Summarunner algorithm [18] based on traditional supervised learning, and the deep learning algorithm BertSum [17] based on supervised learning and so on. The extraction method has a low error rate in grammar and syntax, guarantees a certain effect, and has advantages in efficiency, but the abstract's smoothness is a big problem. It is generally regarded as a seq2seq problem for abstract abstracts, and an output sequence is obtained through the input sequence. In terms of abstract text, Chopra, Auli, and Rush [4] propose a data-driven method for sentence summarisation, using a local attention-based model [24] in the traditional encoder-decoder model proposes a layered decoding algorithm. Liu and Manning [22] propose an attention mechanism-based Seq2Seq model that adds Copy and Coverage mechanisms, pre-training and fine-tuning, and so on. Compared with extractive text summarisation, abstract text summarisation is closer to manual summarisation. However, they have some problems such as long training time, duplication of generated text, and grammatical errors.

Different from those above, we integrate extractive algorithms and abstract algorithms. First, we use an extraction algorithm to extract some essential parts. After dividing the dataset, the length of the text input is greatly changed, and the training time of the subsequent generation algorithm is changed. To merge the generation algorithm, we use a pre-trained model, which improves efficiency and has a low grammatical error rate.

6.2 Pre-trained Model

The pre-trained model in natural language processing can learn general language representation (*i.e.*, good word embeddings). Some models of this kind are ELMO [19], OpenAI GPT [20], and BERT. They are all contextual word embeddings, which dynamically change with different contexts, and can perform word embedding representations well (very beneficial to downstream natural language processing tasks). Specifically for sequence-to-sequence natural language generation tasks, Microsoft Research Asia propose MASS [23], and Google develops a pre-trained generative summarising model (PEGASUS) [27] by extracting blank sentences. Although the training cost of a pre-trained model is small, the pre-trained model can achieve faster convergence speed, and efficiently improve the natural language processing task's perforce, especially when the training dataset is small.

To reduce the required computing resources and accelerate the training speed, in this paper we use the GPT-2 pre-training generative model, which outperforms other pre-trained models in text generation tasks. Kieuvongngam, Tan, and Niu [14] use GPT-2 for Medical summarising task. Their models provide abstract and comprehensive information based on the keywords extracted from the original papers. However, we apply GPT-2 to legal summarising task and summarise a judicial document through important sentences in the document.

6.3 Legal Text Summarising

Galgani *et al.* [10] propose a hybrid legal summarisation method, which integrates manually created knowledge base rules with machine learning to do the automatic summarisation task. Anand and Wagh [2] use the simple general technology of neural network to complete the summarising task of Indian legal judgment documents. Specifically, they use the LSTM network and word and sentence embedding to capture semantics. Yamada *et al.* [26] propose an annotation scheme, which describes the argument structure of the judgment document, establishes a legal argument corpus in the Japanese judgment document, and moved towards a structure-based summarising. Kanapala *et al.* [11] treat legal document summarising as a binary optimisation problem, and use a gravitational search algorithm to solve the problem.

Differently from previous work that uses some of the machine learning methods, we use deep learning to select attributes automatically. Compared with the use of sequence models such as LSTM, we use a more advanced pre-training language model, which can generate better results and is more efficient. Many researchers have proposed different algorithms for text summarising tasks in different languages, but few of them studied Chinese judicial summarising. Instead, in this paper, we develop an accurate and efficient Chinese judicial abstract generation system by considering Chinese judgment documents' characteristics.

7   Conclusion

The legal summarising is a significant research topic. Our work in this paper is different from the general extractive summarising model that treats text sentences as a binary classification problem. We divided the sentences in a judicial document into multiple categories by using an extraction algorithm, constructed various datasets, and then used GPT-2 to perform compression and fusion processing, respectively. Specifically, we trained corresponding models for different parts of judgment documents, and obtained five GPT-2 compression generation models with different parameters, thereby improving the quality of the generated summary. However, there is still a lot of work to be studied in the follow-up, such as the more intelligent realisation of sentence extraction, the use of different models for different datasets, the extraction of similar cases, and prediction of judgment results.

Acknowledgements. This work was supported by the National Natural Science Foundation of China (No. 61762016), and a research fund of Guangxi Key Lab of Multi-Source Information Mining & Security (No. 19-A-01-01).

References

1. Allahyari, M., et al.: Text summarization techniques: a brief survey. Int. J. Adv. Comput. Sci. Appl. **8**(10), 397–405 (2017)
2. Anand, D., Wagh, R.: Effective deep learning approaches for summarization of legal texts. J. King Saud Univ. Comput. Inf. Sci. (2019). https://www.sciencedirect.com/science/article/pii/S1319157819301259
3. Brown, T., et al.: Language models are few-shot learners. In: Larochelle, H., Ranzato, M., Hadsell, R., Balcan, M.F., Lin, H. (eds.) Advances in Neural Information Processing Systems, vol. 33, pp. 1877–1901 (2020)
4. Chopra, S., Auli, M., Rush, A.M.: Abstractive sentence summarization with attentive recurrent neural networks. In: Proceedings of the 2016 Conference of the North American Chapter of the Association for Computational Linguistics: Human Language Technologies, pp. 93–98 (2016)
5. Cohn, T., Lapata, M.: Sentence compression beyond word deletion. In: Proceedings of the 22nd International Conference on Computational Linguistics, pp. 137–144 (2008)

6. Dai, W., Qiu, L., Wu, A., Qiu, M.: Cloud infrastructure resource allocation for big data applications. IEEE Trans. Big Data **4**(3), 313–324 (2016)
7. Du, Z.: GPT2-Chinese: Tools for training GPT2 model in Chinese language (2019). https://github.com/Morizeyao/GPT2-Chinese
8. Gai, K., Qiu, M.: Reinforcement learning-based content-centric services in mobile sensing. IEEE Netw. **32**(4), 34–39 (2018)
9. Gai, K., Qiu, M., Zhao, H., Sun, X.: Resource management in sustainable cyber-physical systems using heterogeneous cloud computing. IEEE Trans. Sustain. Comput. **3**(2), 60–72 (2017)
10. Galgani, F., Compton, P., Hoffmann, A.: Combining different summarization techniques for legal text. In: Proceedings of the Workshop on Innovative Hybrid Approaches to the Processing of Textual Data, pp. 115–123 (2012)
11. Kanapala, A., Jannu, S., Pamula, R.: Summarization of legal judgments using gravitational search algorithm. Neural Comput. Appl. **31**(12), 8631–8639 (2019)
12. Kanapala, A., Pal, S., Pamula, R.: Text summarization from legal documents: a survey. Artif. Intell. Rev. **51**(3), 371–402 (2019)
13. Devlin, J., Chang, M. W., Lee, K., Toutanova, K.: BERT: pre-training of deep bidirectional transformers for language understanding. Universal Language Model Fine-tuning for Text Classification, p. 278 (2018)
14. Kieuvongngam, V., Tan, B., Niu, Y.: Automatic text summarization of covid-19 medical research articles using BERT and GPT-2. arXiv preprint arXiv:2006.01997 (2020)
15. Knight, K., Marcu, D.: Summarization beyond sentence extraction: a probabilistic approach to sentence compression. Artif. Intell. **139**(1), 91–107 (2002)
16. Lin, C.-Y.: ROUGE: a package for automatic evaluation of summaries. In: Text Summarization Branches Out, pp. 74–81 (2004)
17. Liu, Y.: Fine-tune BERT for extractive summarization. arXiv preprint arXiv:1903.10318 (2019)
18. Nallapati, R., Zhai, F., Zhou, B.: SummaRuNNer: a recurrent neural network based sequence model for extractive summarization of documents. In Proceedings of the 31st AAAI Conference on Artificial Intelligence, pp. 3075–3081 (2017)
19. Peters, M., et al.: Deep contextualized word representations. In: Proceedings of the 2018 Conference of the North American Chapter of the Association for Computational Linguistics: Human Language Technologies, vol. 1, pp. 2227–2237 (2018)
20. Radford, A., Narasimhan, K., Salimans, T., Sutskever, I.: Improving language understanding by generative pre-training. https://s3-us-west-2.amazonaws.com/openai-assets/research-covers/language-unsupervised/language_understanding_paper.pdf, 2018
21. Radford, A., Wu, J., Child, R., Luan, D., Amodei, D., Sutskever, I.: Language models are unsupervised multitask learners. OpenAI Blog **1**(8), 9 (2019)
22. See, A., Liu, P.J., Manning, C.D.: Get to the point: summarization with pointer-generator networks. In: Proceedings of the 55th Annual Meeting of the Association for Computational Linguistics, vol. 1, pp. 1073–1083 (2017)
23. Song, K., Tan, X., Qin, T., Lu, J., Liu, T.-Y.: MASS: masked sequence to sequence pre-training for language generation. In: International Conference on Machine Learning, pp. 5926–5936. PMLR (2019)
24. Tan, J., Wan, X., Xiao, J.: Abstractive document summarization with a graph-based attentional neural model. In Proceedings of the 55th Annual Meeting of the Association for Computational Linguistics, vol. 1, pp. 1171–1181 (2017)
25. Wolf, T., et al.: HuggingFace's transformers: state-of-the-art natural language processing. arXiv preprint arxiv:abs/1910.03771 (2019)

26. Yamada, H., Teufel, S., Tokunaga, T.: Building a corpus of legal argumentation in Japanese judgement documents: towards structure-based summarisation. Artif. Intell. Law **27**(2), 141–170 (2019)
27. Zhang, J., Zhao, Y., Saleh, M., Liu, P.: PEGASUS: pre-training with extracted gap-sentences for abstractive summarization. In: International Conference on Machine Learning, pp. 11328–11339. PMLR (2020)

Extracting Anomalous Pre-earthquake Signatures from Swarm Satellite Data Using EOF and PC Analysis

Maja Pavlovic, Yaxin Bi$^{(\boxtimes)}$, and Peter Nicholl

School of Computing, Faculty of Computing, Engineering and the Built Environment,
Ulster University, Belfast, UK
{Pavlovic-M,y.bi,p.nicholl}@ulster.ac.uk

Abstract. The goal of this work is to utilize the General Empirical Orthogonal Function (EOF) and Principal Component Analysis (PCA) to detect potential earthquake pre-cursory variations in Earth's ionosphere-lithosphere geomagnetic system and observe their spatial-temporal signatures along seismotectonic fault lines. Two major earthquake episodes in China have been selected for this study: an M6.0 earthquake, which occurred on 19th January 2020 at ENE of Arzak, and another M6.3 earthquake, occurring on 22nd July 2020 in western Xizang. The spatial-temporal variability patterns in an ~ 800 km radius of earthquake epicentres were calculated from geomagnetic data recorded by SWARM satellites A, B and C. The results of EOF spatial components and associated time-series principal components (PCs) revealed anomalous patterns along and on borders of the local tectonic fault lines and around earthquake epicentres. The Planetary A and K geomagnetic storm indices did not show abnormal activities around the same time periods. This could suggest a pre-cursory connection between the detected geomagnetic anomalies and these earthquakes.

Keywords: Empirical orthogonal function · Principal components · Geomagnetism precursors · Anomaly detection · SWARM data · Earthquakes

1 Introduction

The connection between preceding anomalous geomagnetic variations in lithosphere and ionosphere, and major earthquake events has been widely reported in the literature [2, 6, 9]. However, associated spatial-temporal signatures that could be used for near-time earthquake prediction have not been well characterized to date.

Major earthquakes result from a sudden release of pre-built stress along the fault lines of tectonic plates in Earth's lithosphere [1]. Pre-earthquake geomagnetic anomalies, observed in lithosphere and ionosphere, can occur due to complex interactions between lithosphere, atmosphere, and ionosphere, the mechanisms of which are outlined [14, 15]. Earth's magnetic field consists of: (a) the main field of our planet's outer liquid core, (b) external contributions from ionosphere and magnetosphere, ranging hundreds to thousands of kilometers in altitude, and (c) lithospheric field, the weakest source,

© Springer Nature Switzerland AG 2021
H. Qiu et al. (Eds.): KSEM 2021, LNAI 12816, pp. 394–405, 2021.
https://doi.org/10.1007/978-3-030-82147-0_32

effectively, a residual from the main and the external fields [18]. It is subject to complex interactions between these components and other sources, the strongest impact of which is seen in solar wind related activity, commonly measured by geomagnetic storm activity indices K and A.

Electromagnetic data observed by low earth orbiting (LEO) satellites is frequently used to examine geomagnetic signatures of large-scale lithospheric structures [18]. However, extracting unambiguous pre-earthquake geomagnetic signatures is complicated by physical complexity of the planetary magnetic field, interaction of its components and problems with data quality and sparsity [5].

Development of various anomaly detection (AD) methods, such as Geometric Moving Average Martingale (GMAM), HOT-SAX, CUSUM-EWMA (CE), and Fuzzy shape-based AD have greatly improved the understanding of the problem [4, 11]. Despite this, an earthquake pre-cursory spatial-temporal geomagnetic signature has not been unequivocally described yet.

The EOF and PC analysis has proven extremely successful in other geoscience domains, such as meteorology and oceanography [8, 13, 16]. It was used in detecting ionospheric pre-earthquake anomalies from the total electron content (TEC) data [3], measuring external magnetic field variations on decadal scale from ground observatories [17], and analyzing ionospheric peak electron density of height parameters [12]. In these studies, such analysis was used to extract spatial variability patterns of the physical variable of interest and observe how it changes with time. From the computational efficiency point of view, this method can compress large datasets into several key features that can easily be handled in further analysis and, thus, also offers an operational advantage [10].

In the context of large-scale tectonic fault structures, as observed by LEO satellites, review of the literature published to date, has not identified application of EOF and PCA in investigation of pre-earthquake geomagnetic signature properties, or interactions between Earth's external and lithospheric magnetic fields.

The primary goal of this study was to establish a method baseline and evaluate its capability in identifying anomalous pre-earthquake geomagnetic patterns for LEO datasets. This was accomplished by: (a) identifying significant EOF and PC components from SWARM satellite geomagnetic data on a short- and long-term scale, (b) analyzing the extracted components in the seismotectonic and solar activity context to minimize the impact of other potential anomaly sources on our calculations, and (c) evaluating the outcome results and areas for future investigation.

The data, earthquake locations, seismotectonic settings, solar activity context, and analytical background of the EOF and PCA are outlined in Sect. 2. Results are presented and discussed in Sect. 3, and conclusions are summarized in the final section. A detailed comparison with other AD methods applied to this problem will form a part of a separate study.

2   Data and Methods

2.1   Geomagnetic Data Sources and Earthquake Locations

Geomagnetic data from the SWARM satellite trio A, B, and, C, was used for this research. The satellite constellation orbits the Earth at heights of 462 km (A & C) and 510 km (B).

Two earthquake events have been used for this study: (a) an M6.0 earthquake with epicenter at 39.835°N, 77.108°E, 86 km ENE of Arzak, on 19th January 2020, and (b) another M6.3 earthquake, at 33.144°N, 86.864°E in western Xizang, China, on 22nd July 2020. Their seismotectonic settings were obtained from the USGS, as shown in Fig. 1. The analysis was conducted on a short- and long-term timeline: (a) from 28th October 2019 to 24th January 2020, for the Arzak earthquake, and from 4th May to 27th July 2020 for the Xizang earthquake, and (b) from 1st January 2019 to 24th January 2020 for Arzak, and from 20th July 2019 to 27th July 2020 for Xizang. The spatial-temporal variability patterns in an ~ 800 km radius of earthquake epicentres were calculated from geomagnetic data, collected at 1 Hz by the Vector Field Magnetometers of SWARM A, B and C.

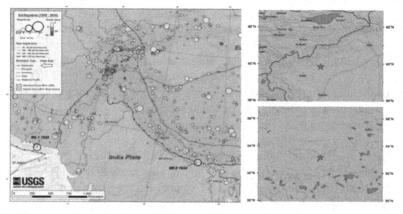

Fig. 1. Seismotectonic setting in > 1000 km radius of earthquake epicenters, showing fault line locations (left). Arzak (top right), and Xizang (bottom right) earthquake epicenters. Source: USGS.gov

The planetary 24-h A indices and eight 3-hourly K indices were used to examine the impact of solar activity on the geomagnetic dataset, as standard measures of geomagnetic storm conditions. Their values are derived in real-time from the network of western hemisphere ground-based magnetometers and provided by the National Geophysical Data Centre at NOAA. K indices range from 'very quiet' to 'extremely disturbed', on a scale of 0 to 9. A indices use a descriptive range on a scale of 0 to 400, where the value of 30 means a local geomagnetic storm has occurred.

2.2 Empirical Orthogonal Function and Principal Component Analysis

EOF and PCA extracts dominant spatial-temporal variability patterns from a dataset, by performing a decomposition of data into orthogonal basis functions determined directly from the data. These functions are, generally, acquired by calculating the covariance matrix eigenvectors of a dataset. Various well-known, standardized procedures for this calculation have been provided in the literature [8, 10, 20], and, thus, only a brief mathematical summary is given here.

Data matrix $X_{M \times N}$, measured N times on M locations is decomposed into n EOF spatial patterns and PC time series as:

$$X_{M \times N} = \Sigma_{i=1}^{n} PC(i) \times EOF(i) \tag{1}$$

It was shown that Singular Value Decomposition (SVD) of a given, centered, data matrix $X = U \Lambda V^T$, directly provides values for the PCs ($U\Lambda$), and EOFs (columns of V). The variance of each PC is given in the squared diagonal values of Λ.

For this study we used a SWARM geomagnetic dataset and removed the Earth's main field contribution, as modelled by CHAOS-7 [7]. A geomagnetic residual $\left|\overrightarrow{B_{GR}}\right|$, is defined as the difference between a total geomagnetic field measured in the NEC coordinate system $\left|\overrightarrow{B_{NEC}}\right|$, and the Earth's main magnetic field, as estimated by the CHAOS model $\left|\overrightarrow{B_{MChaos}}\right|$:

$$\left|\overrightarrow{B_{GR}}\right| = \left|\overrightarrow{B_{NEC}}\right| - \left|\overrightarrow{B_{MChaos}}\right| \tag{2}$$

The goal is to extract the key patterns of the geomagnetic residual and determine how much of its total variance is described by each pattern.

In general, the EOF method requires M fixed measurements taken N times. In our case, SWARM measurements are taken every second, in low resolution mode. This yields $24 \times 60 \times 60 = 86400$ measurements in a 24-h period, during one satellite orbit pass. However, the satellites are not geostationary and measurement locations per each pass are not strictly identical. To counter this, a grid map of linearly interpolated measurements has been created. Every grid point on the map represents an artificial, fixed, measurement location, so that values on each pass can be used from the corresponding exact locations.

Gaps in the data have been noted, due to occasional problems with satellite operation. Where these gaps were abundant in the observed region, days with missing values were omitted from processing.

Data analysis, EOF and PC component calculation was carried out in following steps:

a) Data pre-processing:
    $\left|\overrightarrow{B_{GR}}\right|$ data grid was organized into an 86400×24 matrix, and linearly interpolated onto an (X_q, Y_q) geospatial grid of arbitrary resolution, with an ~ 800 km radius around earthquake epicenter. This resulted in an $\left(\left|\overrightarrow{B_{GR}}\right|\right)_{M \times N} = B_{i,j}, i = 1 \ldots M, j = 1 \ldots N$ matrix, where X_q, Y_q are latitude and longitude, $M = X_q x Y_q$, and N is a number of days,

b) $\left(\left|\overrightarrow{B_{GR}}\right|\right)_{M \times N}$ data matrix was centered and normalized by removing the average values and dividing by standard deviation,

c) Singular value decomposition was performed on $\left(\left|\overrightarrow{B_{GR}}\right|\right)_{M \times N}$, and a total of N PC and EOF components were extracted.

The centered and normalized, truncated geomagnetic residual can be reconstructed from any k selected components:

$$\left(\left|\overrightarrow{B_{GR}}\right|\right)_{M \times N}(k) = PC(k) \times EOF(k) \tag{3}$$

The goal is to determine the best k, namely how many EOF and PCs can be used to capture the maximum significant amount of total variance in the data. At the height of satellite location, geomagnetic signal from Earth's lithosphere, where the earthquakes originate, is weak in comparison with other contributing sources. This complicates the problem of distinguishing between the noise and the anomaly. Iterative adding of components showed that the truncated reconstructed geomagnetic residual stabilized only after the 8th component, as illustrated in Fig. 2, amounting to total data variance threshold between 93.6% and 98.6%, depending on the dataset.

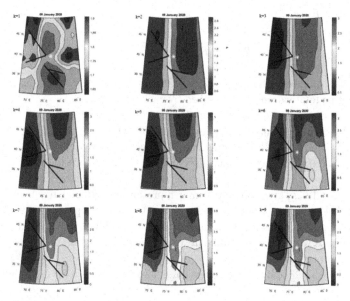

Fig. 2. Iterative geomagnetic residual reconstruction around Arzak earthquake, from k = 1 to 9, 9th January 2020, SWARM A, short-term. Black lines are known fault lines approximations based on seismotectonic information, and yellow star marks the earthquake epicenter. (Color figure online)

Usually, the number of significant components would be selected by simply setting a total amount of data variance threshold at 90% or 95% and applying either Monte-Carlo [20] significance testing or observing the cumulative sum of variance scree plot. This would result in 3 to 5 components, which is not enough to capture all variations with significant impact on the geomagnetic residual. Such observation implies that contributions from lower components (EOF and PCs 4–8) can strongly impact the total geomagnetic residual, and, therefore, ionosphere dynamics, despite their individual, relatively low share in total data variance.

3 Evaluation and Results

3.1 Arzak Earthquake

EOF and PC Analysis
Iterative analysis of the reconstructed geomagnetic residual shows that the first 8 calculated EOF and PC components strongly affect the total geomagnetic residual. For short-term SWARM A, B, and C data, this accounts for 97.5%, 97.9% and 97.8% of the total variance of the original calculated geomagnetic residual, respectively, over the area of Arzak earthquake epicenter. In the long-term timeline analysis, this captures 98.6%, 98%, and 98.5% of the total variance of the original residual for SWARM A, B, and C.

The eight significant EOF components, representing the spatial distribution of each individual component oscillation, are illustrated in Fig. 3(a), for short-term period analysis, and in Fig. 4(a), for long-term analysis of SWARM A data. The percentages in which each of the individual components contributes to the total amount of variance in the data are calculated from the squared diagonal values of Λ, obtained from the SVD of the data matrix $\left(\left|\overrightarrow{B_{GR}}\right|\right)_{M \times N}$. These values are shown on top of each EOF component, in Fig. 3(a).

The first, dominant oscillation, captures 76.3% of the total geomagnetic residual variance, in short-range, and 82.5% in long-range. This reflects a dominance of higher-altitude, ionospheric, geomagnetic contributions.

The eight significant PC time series are illustrated in Fig. 3(b), for short-term period analysis, and in Fig. 4(b), for long-term analysis of SWARM A data.

In an imminent period of two weeks before the earthquake, a moderate to strong anomalous pattern in short-term is visible on 9th January 2020, on two bottom fault lines, (EOF and PC 1 and 8), around the earthquake epicenter (EOF and PC 6), and on top faults (EOF and PC 2) in SWARM A. Similar behavior was observed in SWARM C, while SWARM B showed no visually distinctive variability on the date.

A dominant EOF and PC 1 component shows a strong oscillatory pattern north and south of the earthquake epicenter, with strongest dips in PC 1 amplitude present on 11th November, in a period between 21st and 24th November, 19th December, and 9th January. The corresponding temporal variability can be noted in PC 2 and 3, but with different spatial distribution, as illustrated by EOF 2 and 3. No correspondence has been found between these oscillations and periods of heightened solar activity, indicated by values of planetary indices A and K, shown in Fig. 5(a) and (b). Pre-earthquake geomagnetic anomalies have been reported in the literature, up to approximately one month prior to earthquake occurrence. Other possible geomagnetic contributions can result from interference of ionospheric and magnetospheric currents. These influences could, in the future, be evaluated by using other geomagnetic indices, in addition to A and K, such as Dst index. For better evaluation, the behavior of EOF and PC components was observed in longer term, in a period of one year before the earthquake occurrence.

Looking at Fig. 4(b), for long-term analysis, the strongest anomalous patterns in SWARM A were observed on 1st September, 28th September, and 25th October 2019, in EOF and PC 1 and 2. Heightened solar activity, characterized by a rise in planetary indices A and K values, as shown in Fig. 5(a), and (b), has been identified in the corresponding time-period. From this, we can conclude that these anomalous patterns are most likely related to corresponding large-scale solar activity. The impact of other influences in long-term analysis, only becomes pronounced in anomalous pattern in EOF and PC 8, on 9th January 2020, 10 days before earthquake occurrence. Similar behavior is observed in SWARM C, while in SWARM B, no imminent, potential pre-earthquake anomalies can be identified upon inspection.

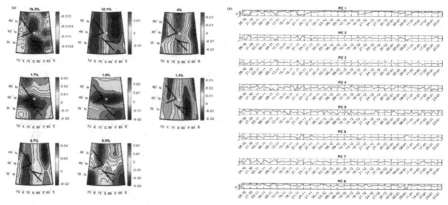

Fig. 3. Short-term analysis around Arzak earthquake epicenter: (a) EOF, and (b) PC from SWARM A. Black lines are fault lines approximations based on seismotectonic information, and yellow star marks the earthquake epicenter. (Color figure online)

3.2 Xizang Earthquake

EOF and PC Analysis

In short-term analysis, the first 8 EOF and PC components account for 97.7%, 93.6%, and 97.6% of the total variance of the original geomagnetic for SWARM A, B, and C. In long-term, the first 8 components can be used to reconstruct 98.4%, 96.9%, and 98.3%, of the total variance of original residual in SWARM A, B and C, respectively. EOF and PC components for SWARM A, in short- and long- term analysis are shown in Figs. 6 and 7, in analogy with illustrations from Arzak case.

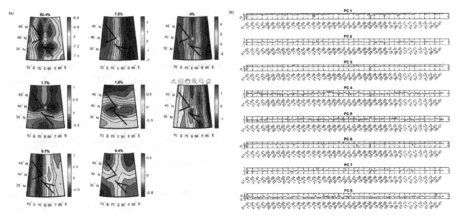

Fig. 4. Long-term analysis around Arzak earthquake epicenter: (a) EOF, and (b) PC from SWARM A. Black lines are fault lines approximations based on seismotectonic information, and yellow star marks the earthquake epicenter. (Color figure online)

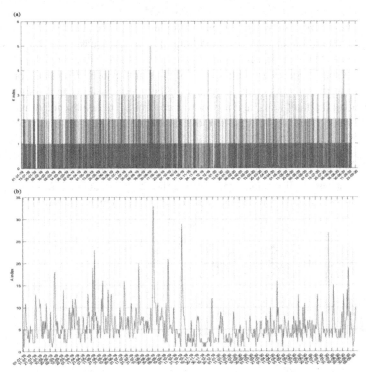

Fig. 5. (a) K and (b) A planetary indices, indicative of periods of heightened solar activity. Source: NGDC.NOAA.gov

Most distinctive anomalous pattern in short-term analysis is visible on 14th July 2020, close to earthquake epicenter, across EOF and PC 1 and 3. EOF and PC 2 shows a strong anomaly along the bottom part of the fault lines and along edges of both fault lines in EOF and PC 5. In EOF and PC 6, 2nd July can be distinguished as anomalous pattern, 13th July in EOF and PC 5 and 6, and 15th July is in EOF and PC 5. SWARM C shows a similar pattern, with a more moderate variation in EOF and PC 1 and 5, during the same dates. Unlike the Arzak episode, in this case, SWARM B exhibits strong anomalous variations on the top fault in EOF and PC 1 and around epicenter in EOF and PC 2, on 14th July.

As with the Arzak earthquake, in long-term observations, PC patterns are strongly influenced by solar activity. The impact of heightened geomagnetic activity indices captured in August, September, and October 2020, and described in section on Arzak earthquake episode (Fig. 5), can also be seen across PC 1, 2, and 3 of SWARM A, B, and C around Xizang area. However, more anomalous patterns are seen in February and April 2020, across EOF and PC 1 and 2 of SWARM A, B, and C, which show no clear connection to geomagnetic storm indices. Strong anomalous pattern is again visible on 14th July in EOF and PC 3 around earthquake epicenter, and in EOF and PC 6 and EOF and PC 7 on left edges of the fault lines in SWARM A and C.

Unlike the Arzak case, where the oscillatory pattern, unrelated to solar activity, can be seen in a period longer than one month before the earthquake, the most distinctive anomaly with a clear peak in activity is distinctly visible on 14th July, 8 days before the earthquake event. This appears across most of the significant EOF and PC components, in both short-term, and long-term analysis. EOF components show an associated spatial signature along the fault lines, and around the epicenter. In the absence of related solar activity, they contribute to the argument of this anomaly to be a pre-earthquake related pattern.

It should be emphasized that a geo-tectonic setting of each earthquake is specific to the area, and likely impacts the interactions between lithosphere and ionosphere, thus carrying important implications in interpreting the identified anomalous patterns. However, because these mechanisms are not yet clearly understood, no unequivocal assertions

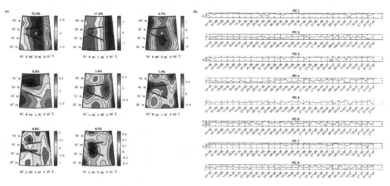

Fig. 6. Short-term analysis around Xizang earthquake epicenter: (a) EOF, and (b) PC from SWARM A. Black lines are fault lines approximations based on seismotectonic information, and yellow star marks the earthquake epicenter. (Color figure online)

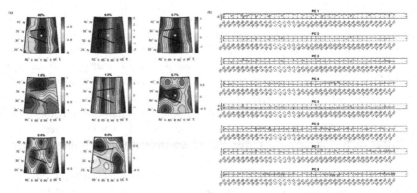

Fig. 7. Long-term analysis around Xizang earthquake epicenter: (a) EOF, and (b) PC from SWARM A. Black lines are fault lines approximations based on seismotectonic information, and yellow star marks the earthquake epicenter. (Color figure online)

can be made. The primary goal of this study was to examine if, and how, the EOF and PC computational analysis tool, can be applied to the problem of identifying potential pre-earthquake anomalous patterns. More investigation is underway to determine means of quantifying the strength of anomalous patterns identified across individual EOF and PC components, in comparison to a standard, non-anomalous oscillatory response.

4   Conclusions

The study results show that potential anomalous pre-earthquake patterns can be identified for both earthquake episodes through 8 significant EOF and PC components. When this information is observed in the context of seismotectonic earthquake setting, and side by side with geomagnetic activity indices, this may provide an indication on whether a particular anomaly can be regarded as an earthquake pre-cursor. However, it is possible that not all pre-cursor anomalies will exhibit a clearly recognizable large-scale seismotectonic spatial signature, and some observed anomalies may arise from other interference sources or from artificial data processing noise.

Although physical interpretation of individual EOF and PC components needs to be treated cautiously and requires further investigation, our primary goal had been met.

EOF and PC analysis had identified 9th January 2020 for Arzak, and 14th July 2020 for Xizang, as potential earthquake pre-cursory anomalies. Geomagnetic storm indices A and K had showed no distinctive solar activity during, and up to, a few weeks prior to the earthquake occurrences. EOF spatial signatures, in short-term, show the anomalous patterns had been distributed along fault lines and around earthquake epicenters, in both cases. This could be a strong indication of large-scale seismotectonic pre-earthquake related geomagnetic activity. In the long-term analysis, the first few components exhibit most distinctive solar activity associated patterns, possibly overshadowing other sources of lower amplitude geomagnetic variability.

Despite the arguments favoring the extracted patterns to be pre-earthquake related, a measure of difference between a standard, non-anomalous EOF and PC component behavior, and pre-earthquake anomalous response pattern requires clarification. The longest period analyzed in this study only extends to one full year prior to earthquake occurrence. A longer period of observations over the same area would likely prove informative in identifying other typical anomalous patterns, not necessarily earthquake related, and in identifying a more accurate standard, non-anomalous behavior. However, there was a limit of the data availability at the time this study was conducted.

A further study was carried out to examine if anomaly detection from significant PC components can be improved by means of applying a simple Long/Short-Term Memory Neural Network for training and prediction and utilizing error estimation between predicted and calculated PC values. The current results are not presented here, due to space limitations.

Acknowledgment. This work is partially supported by the project of "Seismic Deformation Monitoring and Electromagnetism Anomaly Detection by Big Satellite Data Analytics with Parallel Computing" (ID: 59308) under the Dragon 5 program, a largest cooperation between European Space Agency and Ministry of Science and Technology of China.

References

1. Agnew, D.C.: History of seismology. In: Lee, W., Jennings, P., Kisslinger, C., Kanamori, H. (eds.) International Handbook of Earthquake and Engineering Seismology, Part A, vol. 81A, p. 1200. Elsevier Press, Amsterdam (2002)
2. Cicerone, R.D., Ebel, J.E., Britton, J.: A systematic compilation of earthquake precursors. Tectonophysics **476**, 371–396 (2009). https://doi.org/10.1016/j.tecto.2009.06.008
3. Chang, X., Zou, B., Guo, J., Zhu, G., Li, W., Li, Wu.: One sliding PCA method to detect ionospheric anomalies before strong earthquakes: cases study of Qinghai, Honshu, Hotan and Nepal earthquakes. Adv. Space Res. **59**(8), 2058–2070 (2017). https://doi.org/10.1016/j.asr.2017.02.007 (ISSN 0273-1177)
4. Christodoulou, V., Bi, Y., Wilkie, G.: A fuzzy shape-based anomaly detection and its application to electromagnetic data. IEEE J. Sel. Top. Appl. Earth Obs. Remote Sens. **11**, 3366–3379 (2018)
5. Christodoulou, V., Bi, Y., Wilkie, G.: A tool for Swarm satellite data analysis and anomaly detection. PLoS ONE **14**(4), e02120982019 (2019). https://doi.org/10.1371/journal.pone.0212098
6. De Santis, A., Marchetti, D., Pavón-Carrasco, F.J., et al.: Precursory worldwide signatures of earthquake occurrences on swarm satellite data. Sci. Rep. **9**, 20287 (2019). https://doi.org/10.1038/s41598-019-56599-1
7. Finlay, C.C., et al.: The CHAOS-7 geomagnetic field model and observed changes in the South Atlantic anomaly. Earth Planet. Space **72**(1), 1–31 (2020). https://doi.org/10.1186/s40623-020-01252-9
8. Hannachi, A., Joliffe, I.T., Stephenson, D.: Empirical orthogonal functions and related techniques in atmospheric science: a review. Int. J. Climatol. **27**, 1119–1152 (2007). https://doi.org/10.1002/joc.1499
9. Huang, F., et al.: Studies on earthquake precursors in China: a review for recent 50 years. China, Geodesy Geodyn. **8**, 1–12 (2017)

10. Jolliffe, I.T., Cadima, J.: Principal component analysis: a review and recent developments. Phil. Trans. R. Soc. A **374**, 20150202 (2016). https://doi.org/10.1098/rsta.2015.0202
11. Kong, X., Bi, Y., Glass, D.H.: Detecting seismic anomalies in outgoing long-wave radiation data. IEEE J. Sel. Top. Appl. Earth Obs. Remote Sens. **8**(2), 649–660 (2015). https://doi.org/10.1109/JSTARS.2014.2363473
12. Lin, J., et al.: Empirical orthogonal function analysis and modeling of the ionospheric peak height during the years 2002–2011. J. Geophys. Res. Space Phys. **119**, 3915–3929 (2014). https://doi.org/10.1002/2013JA019626
13. Ludwig, F.L., Horel, J., Whiteman, C.D.: Using EOF analysis to identify important surface wind patterns in mountain valleys. J. Appl. Meteorol. **43**, 969–983 (2004). https://doi.org/10.1175/1520-0450(2004)043
14. Molchanov, O., Fedorov, E., Schekotov, A., Gordeev, E., Chebrov, V., et al.: Lithosphere-atmosphere-ionosphere coupling as governing mechanism for preseismic short-term events in atmosphere and ionosphere. Nat. Hazards Earth Syst. Sci. **4**(5/6), pp.757–767. Copernicus Publications on behalf of the European Geoscience Union (2004)
15. Pulinets, S., Ouzounov, D.: Lithosphere–Atmosphere–Ionosphere coupling (LAIC) model – an unified concept for earthquake precursors validation. J. Asian Earth Sci. **41**(4–5), 371–382 (2011). https://doi.org/10.1016/j.jseaes.2010.03.005 (ISSN 1367-9120)
16. Roundy, P.E.: On the interpretation of EOF analysis of ENSO, atmospheric Kelvin waves, and the MJO. J. Clim. **28**(3), 1148–1165 (2015). https://doi.org/10.1175/JCLI-D-14-00398.1
17. Shore, R.M., Whaler, K.A., Macmillan, S., Beggan, C., Velímský, J., Olsen, N.: Decadal period external magnetic field variations determined via eigenanalysis. JGR Space Phys. **121**(6), 5172–5184 (2016). https://doi.org/10.1002/2015JA022066
18. Thébault, E., Purucker, M., Whaler, K.A., Langlais, B., Sabaka, T.J.: The magnetic field of the earth's lithosphere. Space Sci. Rev. **155**, 95–127 (2010). https://doi.org/10.1007/s11214-010-9667-6
19. Thébault, E., Vigneron, P., Langlais, B., Hulot, G.: A Swarm lithospheric magnetic field model to SH degree 80. Earth Planet. Space **68**(1), 1–13 (2016). https://doi.org/10.1186/s40623-016-0510-5
20. Von Storch, H., Zwiers, F.W.: Statistical Analysis in Climate Research. Cambridge University Press (2003)

Hierarchical Multi-label Text Classification: Self-adaption Semantic Awareness Network Integrating Text Topic and Label Level Information

Rui Zhao, Xiao Wei[✉], Cong Ding, and Yongqi Chen

School of Computer Engineering and Science, Shanghai University, Shanghai, China
{zhaorui1513,xwei,mollydc,MrChenYQ}@shu.edu.cn

Abstract. Hierarchical multi-label text classification is used to assign documents to multiple categories stored in a hierarchical structure. However, the existing methods pay more attention to the local semantic information of the text, and make insufficient use of the label level information. In this paper, we propose a new self-adaption semantic awareness network integrating text topic and label level information. Compared with the existing methods, our method has two contributions: (1) On the basis of the traditional text encoder, we add the global topic information of the text and the hierarchical information of the label, describe the text from different levels and effectively use the correlation between the labels. (2) We design an adaptive fusion strategy that adaptively retains information helpful for classification from three different levels of features and exploits their mutual influence. Experimental results on two benchmark datasets show that our model is better than the state-of-the-art methods on six metrics, especially in the prediction of low-frequency labels with sparse samples.

Keywords: Hierarchical multi-label text classification · Self-adaption semantic fusion · Global topic information · Label correlation

1 Introduction

Text classification can generally be divided into two types: multi-class classification and multi-label classification. Hierarchical multi-label text classification (HMTC) is a special type of multi-label text classification. The classification hierarchy is usually expressed as a label tree, and the classification result corresponds to one or more nodes in the tree. At the same time, two conditions need to be met simultaneously: (1) If a text has a label C, it also has all the ancestor labels of C implicitly in the label tree; (2) When predicting the label of a text, it must also meet the hierarchical restriction that the text cannot appear to hit the labels that not belong to the ancestors of C. Figure 1 shows an example of book advertisement text classification with a four-level hierarchical category structure in the BGC dataset.

© Springer Nature Switzerland AG 2021
H. Qiu et al. (Eds.): KSEM 2021, LNAI 12816, pp. 406–418, 2021.
https://doi.org/10.1007/978-3-030-82147-0_33

Text : ... Francine Prose, O, The Oprah MagazineBrutally honest and rich in detail, this posthumously published diary of a twenty-seven-year-old Vietcong woman doctor, saved from destruction by an American soldier, gives us fresh insight into the lives of those fighting on the other side of the Vietnam War. It is a story of the struggle for one's ideals amid the despair and grief of war, but most of all, it is a story of hope in the most dire circumstances."As much a drama of feelings as a drama of war."—Seth Mydans, New York Times"A book to be read by and included in any course on the literature of the war. ...

Classification result :
(Hit the following label)

H_1:Nonfiction

H_2:History | Biography & Memoir

H_3:Military History

H_4:1950 – Present Military History

Fig. 1. Example of book advertisement text classification in HMTC problem.

So far, HMTC methods can be divided into two types: local approaches and global approaches. The global approaches aggregated different levels of labels and used a single classifier to make predictions, transforming the HMTC problem into a flat MTC problem, such as TextRCNN [10], capsule network [1], LSAN [19] et al. The local approaches constructed multiple hierarchical classifiers, and each classifier was responsible for predicting the label of the corresponding level. Representative methods included Parabel [16], HFT-CNN [17], HARNN [6], HiAGM [23] et al. Until now, the use of label semantic information and hierar-chical structure information is still relatively superficial. The semantic feature extraction of the text is not sufficient, and the topic feature of the text is not con-sidered. It is worth noting that different parts of a document are often associated with different labels. While understanding the semantics of each text in depth, it is necessary to capture these associations between the text and the label hierarchy. This has proven to be more effective in our work.

In this paper, we propose a new self-adaption semantic awareness network integrating text topic and label level information. The model first has a text encoder for feature extraction of input text. It utilizes Bi-GRU and CNN to jointly encode the local semantic features of the text. Meanwhile, the pre-trained LDA is used to encode the global topic features of the text. Secondly, the model also has a label encoder for feature extraction of label hierarchy information. We construct the hierarchy of labels as a label tree, where the labels are used as the node information in the tree, and the semantic similarity and dependency relationship (co-occurrence probability) between the labels are used as the edge information between nodes. Then it is encoded by GCN to get the features that contain the semantics of the label hierarchy. In order to aggregate the local semantics of the text, the global topic information and the label level semantics, we designed a self-adaption fusion strategy to extract appropriate information from these features as the final feature representation.

The main contributions of this paper are highlighted as follows:

- On the basis of the traditional text encoder, we add the global topic information of the text and the hierarchical information of the label, describe the text from different levels and effectively use the correlation between the labels.
- We design a new self-adaption fusion strategy, which adaptively extracts semantic information helpful for classification from three different levels of features as the final feature representation.
- On two widely-used benchmark datasets, the experimental results prove that the performance of our model on the six evaluation metrics outperforms the state-of-the-art baselines.

2   Related Work

Generally, the research work related to hierarchical multi-label classification can be divided into two aspects: global approaches and local approaches.

Global approaches aggregate all the labels of different levels together and use a single classifier for prediction to transform HMTC problem into a flat multi-label problem. Current research mainly focused on methods based on deep learning. Nam et al. [15] proposed a fully connected neural network to solve the multi-label text classification problem, Li et al. [12] proposed a joint learning method to solve the problem of fewer label samples in the dataset. Kurata et al. [9] and Baker et al. [2] used initialized neural networks to consider the correlation be-tween labels. There were some network structures for the purpose of obtaining better text features, such as TextCNN [7], TextRNN [13], TextRCNN [10], capsule network [1], LSAN [19]. Some deep learning architectures or mechanisms were also used in global models to utilize label hierarchy information, such as Reinforcement Learning [14], seq2seq [20], attention mechanism [22] and interaction mechanism [3].

Local approaches construct multiple hierarchical classifiers, each of which is responsible for predicting the corresponding label or the level of the corresponding label, and then traverse the hierarchy in a top-down manner. Prabhu et al. [16] used a balanced hierarchy of labels and established a joint label distribution probability model based on data point features and learning label levels. Shimura et al. [17] proposed the HFT-CNN model and used the fine-tuning technique to transfer the upper-layer label information to the lower-layer label learning. Peng et al. [5] designed a graph-cnn-based deep learning model that uses graph convolution operations to convolve word graphs, and uses the dependencies between labels to standardize the deep architecture. Wehrmann et al. [18] proposed HMCN model, which can simultaneously optimize local and global loss functions and punish hierarchical violations. Huang et al. [6] proposed HARNN to model the dependencies between different levels of the hierarchy in a top-down manner. Zhou et al. [23] used the hierarchical structure-aware global model to enhance text information with label structure features.

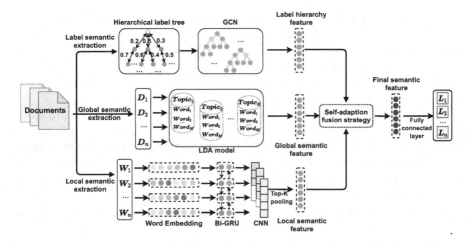

Fig. 2. The architecture of the proposed self-adaption semantic awareness network integrating text topic and label level information.

3   Proposed Method

Figure 2 shows the overall architecture of the model. It consists of three main parts: (1) The first part is to extract the local semantic information and global topic information of the text through the text encoder. (2) The second part is to extract the label hierarchy information through the label encoder. (3) The third part combines the attention mechanism and uses the self-adaption fusion strategy to obtain the final feature representation.

3.1   Text Encoder

For text feature extraction, we first use bidirectional GRU to extract low-level local semantic features of the text. The experimental effect of the GRU network is similar to that of the LSTM network, but it is easier to calculate and can improve training efficiency. $\overrightarrow{h_n}, \overleftarrow{h_n} \in \mathbb{R}^w$ denote the hidden states of the forward and reverse final steps respectively, and joint them together to obtain the global semantic feature of the text $H = \left[\overrightarrow{h_n}, \ \overleftarrow{h_n}\right] \in \mathbb{R}^{n \times 2w}$. n is the total number of words contained in the text.

Use H as the input of single-layer CNN to extract high-level local semantic features of the text. Specifically, we use three different filters with different window sizes to perform convolution operations on the text, and connect the output after top-k pooling operation to obtain a vector as the final local semantic feature $F_{local-semantic} \in \mathbb{R}^{n \times d}$, where n is the product of the number of convolution kernels and top-k, and d is the output dimension.

At the same time, we use the pre-trained LDA model from the corpus to extract the global topic features of the text, which has not been used in recent studies. The nature of hierarchical multi-label classification can be seen as a fine-grained division of text topics. By adding the topic in the document-word feature hierarchy and capturing the global high-level semantic structure of the text, a good representation of the text in the potential feature space of the topic can be realized. At the same time, the document feature vector obtained by the final text encoder can contain richer semantic information.

Specifically, for any text in the corpus, the corresponding topic probability distribution generated according to the pre-trained LDA model is $\theta_m = (z_{m,1}, z_{m,2}, \ldots, z_{m,n})$ is the i-th topic of the m-th document. The characteristics of each topic are expressed as $T_i = \frac{1}{M} \sum_{i=1}^{M} w_i$, where M is the number of topic words preset for the topic, w_i is the word vector. By setting a threshold, the K topics most likely to be contained in the current text are retrieved, and their probability distributions are weighted and summed. Finally, the global topic feature representation $F_{global-topic} = \sum_{i=1}^{K} z_{m,i} T_i$ of the document is obtained.

3.2   Label Encoder

The label hierarchy contains a wealth of prior knowledge, which is of great help to improve the final classification effect. In our model, the label hierarchical structure information and its semantic information are extracted by the label encoder, making it possible to learn different levels of label features in a single global model.

Specifically, a hierarchical label tree $T = (L, E)$, where $L = \{l_1, \ldots, l_i, \ldots, l_H\}$ denotes a collection of label nodes, and H is the total number of label nodes. $E = \{(l_i, l_j) \mid l_i, l_j \in L, l_j \in \text{Child}(l_i)\}$ denotes the edge relationship between the label nodes in the tree. For any edge relationship in E, its weight is expressed as

$$W_{l_i, l_j} = \alpha \cdot \frac{N_{l_i}}{N_{l_j}} + \beta \cdot \frac{\text{vector}(l_i) \cdot \text{vector}(l_j)}{|\text{vector}(l_i)| \cdot |\text{vector}(l_j)|}, \tag{1}$$

where N_{l_i}, N_{l_j} respectively represent the total number of the labels l_i and l_j appearing in the entire training corpus, and vector (l_i) and vector (l_j) represent corresponding word vectors. For the semantic similarity between labels and the proportion of their dependencies, we take $\alpha = \beta = 0.5$. At the same time, we scale and standardize the weights of the child nodes, so that the sum of the weights of the edge relations of each layer of the hierarchical label tree is 1. It is worth noting that the root node of the hierarchical label tree is a virtual node. For the edge relationship from the root node to its child nodes, we only calculate the label co-occurrence probability, not the semantic similarity relationship. At this time, $\alpha = 1, \beta = 0$.

After determining the structure of the label tree, we use GCN to perform feature extraction to obtain more fine-grained hierarchical information. Let $A \in \mathbb{R}^{m \times m}$ be the adjacency matrix, which is transformed from the label tree, and

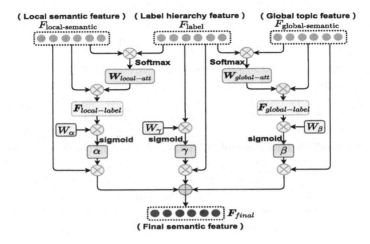

Fig. 3. The architecture of the self-adaption semantic fusion strategy.

m denotes the total number of labels. $X \in \mathbb{R}^{m \times d}$ is the feature matrix, and d denotes the dimension. The mode of propagation be-tween GCN model layers is

$$H^{(l+1)} = \text{ReLU}\left(\widetilde{D}^{-\frac{1}{2}}\widetilde{A}\widetilde{D}^{-\frac{1}{2}}H^{(l)}W^{(l)}\right), \tag{2}$$

where $\widetilde{A} = A + I$, I is the identity matrix. $\widetilde{D} \in \mathbb{R}^{m \times m}$ is the degree matrix of $\widetilde{A}$. H is the feature of each layer. For the input layer, H is X. Through the multi-layer GCN, the label feature matrix $F_{\text{label}} \in \mathbb{R}^{m \times d}$ containing more fine-grained hierarchical structure and semantic information is finally obtained.

3.3   Self-adaption Semantic Fusion Strategy

When predicting the label corresponding to a document, each word in the text plays a different role. In order to capture the potential relationship between labels and two text features, we add an attention mechanism, while fusing the three feature representations obtained by the text encoder and label encoder modules, and design a self-adaption semantic fusion strategy, as shown in Fig. 3. The attention mechanism [22] has been widely used in recent studies. We first obtain the attention weight $W_{\text{local-att}}$, $W_{\text{global-att}} \in \mathbb{R}^{n \times d}$ of the text feature to the label by separately calculating the matching score between the two text feature and each label, where n is the number of text features, and d is the feature dimension. Then we multiply the obtained attention weight with the text feature to obtain the $F_{\text{local-label}} \in \mathbb{R}^{m \times d}$ and $F_{\text{global-label}} \in \mathbb{R}^{m \times d}$, where m is the total number of labels, and d is the feature dimension. The specific calculation formula is

$$W_{\text{local-att}} = \text{softmax}\left(F_{\text{local-semantic}} \otimes F_{\text{label}}\right), \tag{3}$$

$$F_{\text{local-label}} = W_{\text{local-att}} \otimes F_{\text{label}}, \tag{4}$$

$$W_{\text{global-att}} = \text{softmax}\left(F_{\text{global-topic}} \otimes F_{\text{label}}\right), \tag{5}$$

$$F_{\text{global-label}} = W_{\text{global-att}} \otimes F_{\text{label}}, \tag{6}$$

$F_{\text{local-label}}$, $F_{\text{global-label}}$ and F_{label} feature representations related to label semantics, but their focus is different. $F_{\text{local-label}}$ focuses on the semantic association between the features of the document con-tent and the labels, $F_{\text{global-label}}$ focuses on the semantic association between the overall topic features of the document and the labels, and F_{label} is more inclined to the semantic information and label hierarchy information of the labels themselves. In order to make full use of the advantages of the three, we use the proposed strategy to adaptively extract appropriate information from these features. Specifically, we introduce three weight vectors $\alpha, \beta, \gamma \in \mathbb{R}^{1 \times m}$ to determine the importance of these features, and the calculation can be obtained through a fully connected layer. The calculation method is

$$\alpha = \text{sigmoid}\left(W_{\alpha} \cdot F_{\text{local-label}}\right), \tag{7}$$

$$\beta = \text{sigmoid}\left(W_{\beta} \cdot F_{\text{global-label}}\right), \tag{8}$$

$$\gamma = \text{sigmoid}\left(W_{y} \cdot F_{\text{label}}\right), \tag{9}$$

where $W_{\alpha}, W_{\beta}, W_{\gamma} \in \mathbb{R}^{1 \times d}$ are the parameter of the fully connected layer. $\alpha, \beta, \gamma \in \mathbb{R}^{1 \times m}$ respectively represent the importance of the three features in constructing the final feature vector and the degree of influence on the final prediction result, so we let $\alpha_i + \beta_i + \gamma_i = 1$. Finally, we can get the final feature $F_{\text{final}} \in \mathbb{R}^{1 \times d}$ used for label prediction. The calculation method is

$$F_{\text{final}} = \alpha \cdot F_{\text{local-label}} + \beta \cdot F_{\text{global-label}} + \gamma \cdot F_{\text{label}}. \tag{10}$$

3.4 Label Prediction

The final features are input into a fully connected layer for prediction. We use a binary cross-entropy loss function, and referring to the work of Gopal et al. [4], we add recursive regularization on the final fully connected layer. The final loss function we optimize is

$$L = -\sum_{i=1}^{N}\sum_{j=1}^{M}\left[y_{ij}\log\left(\hat{y}_{ij}\right) + (1 - y_{ij})\log\left(1 - \hat{y}_{ij}\right)\right] + \lambda \cdot \\ \sum_{l_i \in L}\sum_{l_j \in \text{child}(l_i)} \frac{1}{2}\left\|W_{l_i} - W_{l_j}\right\|^2, \tag{11}$$

where $\hat{y}_{ij} \in [0, 1]$ is the predicted probability of the j-th label of the i-th text, and $y_{ij} \in \{0, 1\}$ is its corresponding ground truth. $l_i, l_j \in L$, and label l_j is a sub-label of label l_i, W_{l_i} and W_{l_j} respectively represent its parameters in the last fully connected layer.

4   Experiments

4.1   Dataset Description

We selected two benchmark datasets with a predefined hierarchical structure for experiments: BlurbGenreCollection (BGC) [8] and Web-of-Science (WOS). Both datasets follow the strategy described in the RCV1 data set by Lewis et al. [11]. We add a virtual root node to convert its hierarchical structure into a hierarchical label tree.

BGC is a dataset composed of book advertisement description, which mainly includes book introduction (short advertisement text) and some book-related information. The WOS dataset is composed of abstracts published on Web of Science, which mainly includes abstracts, fields, and keywords of published papers. Table 1 further shows the important quantitative characteristics of these two datasets.

Table 1. Quantitative characteristics of both datasets.

	BGC	WOS
Number of texts	91895	46985
Average number of tokens (After removing the stop words)	77.98	108.03
Total number of labels	146	141
Hierarchical levels	4	2
Labels on level 1;2;3;4	7;46;77;16	7;134;–;–
Average number of labels	3.01	2.0
Train instances	73516	37516
Val instances	9189	4734
Test instances	9190	4735

4.2   Model Setting

For all datasets, we set the maximum length of sentences to 100. In all experiments, we set the maximum epoch to 100 and the batch-size to 32. For the LDA topic model, set the number of clustering topics $K = 7$(the number of top-level labels in label structure), and the number of topic words contained in each topic $M = 20$. For the entire model, we use the Adam optimization method to minimize the loss function of the training data, and set its learning rate $\alpha = 0.0001$. The penalty coefficient of recursive regularization is set to 1×10^{-6}. Set $threshold = 0.5$ in the final label prediction.

4.3   Evaluation Metrics and Baseline Models

We selected six evaluation metrics widely used in hierarchical multi-label classification to evaluate the performance of the model: Precision, Recall, Micro-F1, Macro-F1, One-Error and Hanming Loss.

To prove the effectiveness of our model, We compare it with the seven baselines: (1) TextRCNN [10]: The model structure is a two-way RNN connected with the pooling layer, which is the most classic classification model.(2) HAN [21]: The model architecture is divided into word level and sentence level, and each level includes an encoder and an attention model. (3) SGM [20]: The sequence generation model is constructed as a multi-label text classifier.(4) HAM [6]: This model uses a hierarchical attention strategy to capture the association between text and hierarchical structure, and integrates text and label hierarchy. (5) HiAGM [23]: An end-to-end hierarchical structure-aware global model, hierarchical-aware struc-ture encoder is introduced to model label dependency.

Table 2. Compare our model with six benchmark evaluation metrics on two datasets.

Dataset	Model	Precision	Recall	Micro-F1	Macro-F1	One-error	Hanming-loss
BGC	TextRCNN	77.36	66.34	71.43	45.61	5674	0.010932
	SGM	73.15	66.85	69.86	42.29	6142	0.012518
	HAN	72.71	63.13	67.58	43.83	6026	0.012476
	HAM	72.08	64.39	68.02	43.46	6068	0.012473
	HiAGM	78.92	73.31	76.01	54.84	5336	0.009545
	Our model	**80.34**	**74.99**	**77.48**	**56.08**	**5255**	**0.008998**
WOS	TextRCNN	84.51	80.09	82.24	73.25	1453	0.004906
	SGM	82.38	79.16	80.74	70.31	1503	0.005422
	HAN	83.71	76.06	79.70	70.81	1697	0.005495
	HAM	82.73	76.31	79.39	69.98	1683	0.005620
	HiAGM	87.35	83.65	85.46	79.36	1304	0.004322
	Our model	**88.13**	**85.41**	**86.75**	**81.15**	**1260**	**0.003825**

4.4   Results Comparison and Analysis

Table 2 compare the performance of our model with the baseline model. The effect of HiAGM is the state-of-the-art at present. The model we proposed makes up for the shortcomings of the HiAGM model in feature extraction, and obtains the text semantic features containing topic information and the hierarchical label structure features containing tag semantics. At the same time, we designed a new self-adaption fusion strategy, using the attention mechanism to determine the contribution of text features to all labels, and weighted them with the label level

Table 3. Result of the ablation test.

Dataset	Metrics	W	T+W	L+W	T+L+W
BGC	Precision	78.17	79.80	79.43	**80.34**
	Recall	**75.83**	75.03	75.06	75.21
	Micro-F1	76.98	77.34	77.18	**77.69**
	Macro-F1	55.88	56.43	56.26	**56.75**
	One-error	5289	5240	5255	**5214**
	Hanming-loss	0.009346	0.009071	0.009069	**0.008995**
WOS	Precision	87.14	87.84	87.75	**88.13**
	Recall	85.28	85.27	85.03	**85.42**
	Micro-F1	86.20	86.54	86.54	**86.75**
	Macro-F1	80.23	80.64	80.64	**81.15**
	One-error	1351	1256	1274	**1240**
	Hanming-loss	0.003947	0.003875	0.003862	**0.003825**

feature. Then we adaptively set the weight to get the final semantic representation of the text. On the BGC and WOS datasets, the performance of our model is always better than all the baselines. This result also confirms that the features fused by this strategy are helpful for hierarchical multi-label classification.

The model we proposed mainly includes three parts: a text encoder (denoted as T) that adds topic information, a label encoder (denoted as L) that integrates label hierarchy and semantic information, and a self-adaptive attention strategy that combines three features (denoted as W). We use ablation test to illustrate the influence of each part on the prediction result. It can be seen from the Table 3 that T+W and L+W get better experimental results than T and L respectively, which proves the effectiveness of the self-adaption fusion strategy we designed. Part T pays more attention to the feature extraction of the document itself. On the basis of traditional RNN and CNN, the topic features are added using the LDA model, but this part ignores the hierarchical structure information of the labels. Part L constructs a label tree and determines the edge relationship, and then we uses GCN to perform feature extraction on the tree structure, but some similar labels are still not easy to distinguish. the adaptive attention strategy we designed considers the advantages of both, so that the resulting features retain as many parts that are beneficial to classification as much as possible.

In order to verify the performance of our model for low-frequency labels, we divide the labels in the BGC dataset into three groups according to their frequency of occurrence: the first group is the label with a frequency greater than 1000 (denoted as group1), The label with frequency between 100 and 1000 is the second group (denoted as group2), and the label with frequency less than 100 is the third group (denoted as group3). Obviously, due to the lack of training samples, the labels in group 1 are much more difficult to predict than the other two groups. Table 4 shows the experimental results of TextRCNN, HAM,

HiAGM and our model on four evaluation metrics. Except that the precision fluctuates on group2 and group3, as the number of training samples corresponding to each label increases, the results of all methods are getting better and better, which is also in line with expectations. It is worth noting that our model can significantly improve the prediction performance of low-frequency labels. In particular, compared with the state-of-the-art methods, it improves the four metrics by 4.21%, 7.55%, 6.36% and 2.39% respectively. This result also proves Our model has made great progress in the feature extraction of sparse samples and the classification of corresponding low-frequency labels.

Table 4. Result of label group test on the BGC dataset.

Model	Number of samples	Number of labels	Precision	Recall	Micro-F1	Macro-F1
TextCRNN	>1000	58	77.36	66.34	71.43	45.61
	100–1000	73	77.93	58.05	66.54	43.91
	<100	15	71.43	48.56	57.82	10.26
HAM	>1000	58	72.08	64.39	68.02	43.46
	100–1000	73	73.78	56.98	64.30	42.91
	<100	15	74.07	50.36	59.96	11.09
HiAGM	>1000	58	78.36	73.32	76.22	54.41
	100–1000	73	79.12	66.16	72.47	53.48
	<100	15	71.56	54.32	61.76	13.58
Our model	>1000	58	**79.78**	**76.17**	**77.93**	**57.36**
	100–1000	73	**80.31**	**69.25**	**74.37**	**57.82**
	<100	15	**75.77**	**61.87**	**68.12**	**15.97**

5   Conclusion

This paper proposed a new self-adaption semantic awareness network integrating text topic and label level information for hierarchical multi-label text classification. Different from the previous research, we add global topic information when extracting text features, and use the semantic similarity and co-occurrence probability between labels to model the tag hierarchy. At the same time, we design a self-adaption semantic fusion strategy to make full use of the interaction between different levels of text features and label features to improve the final prediction performance. Through experiments on the two benchmark datasets of WOS and BGC, and compared with the state-of-the-art methods, the superiority of our proposed model is proved, especially in the prediction of low-frequency labels with sparse samples.

Acknowledgements. This work was supported by the National Key Research and Development Program of China (No. 2018YFB0704400). We thank all the anonymous reviewers for their valuable suggestions.

References

1. Aly, R., Remus, S., Biemann, C.: Hierarchical multi-label classification of text with capsule networks. In: Proceedings of the 57th Annual Meeting of the Association for Computational Linguistics: Student Research Workshop, pp. 323–330 (2019)
2. Baker, S., Korhonen, A.: Initializing neural networks for hierarchical multi-label text classification. BioNLP **2017**, 307–315 (2017)
3. Du, C., Chen, Z., Feng, F., Zhu, L., Gan, T., Nie, L.: Explicit interaction model towards text classification. Proc. AAAI Conf. Artif. Intell. **33**, 6359–6366 (2019)
4. Gopal, S., Yang, Y.: Recursive regularization for large-scale classification with hierarchical and graphical dependencies. In: Proceedings of the 19th ACM SIGKDD International Conference on Knowledge Discovery and Data Mining, pp. 257–265 (2013)
5. Hao, P., Li, J., Yu, H., Liu, Y., Qiang, Y.: Large-scale hierarchical text classification with recursively regularized deep graph-cnn. In: The 2018 World Wide Web Conference, pp. 1063–1072 (2018)
6. Huang, W., Chen, E., Liu, Q., Chen, Y., Wang, S.: Hierarchical multi-label text classification: An attention-based recurrent network approach. In: Proceedings of the 28th ACM International Conference on Information and Knowledge Management, pp. 1051–1060 (2019)
7. Kim, Y.: Convolutional neural networks for sentence classification. Eprint Arxiv (2014)
8. Kowsari, K., Brown, D.E., Heidarysafa, M., Meimandi, K.J., Barnes, L.E.: Hdltex: hierarchical deep learning for text classification, pp. 364–371 (2017)
9. Kurata, G., Xiang, B., Zhou, B.: Improved neural network-based multi-label classification with better initialization leveraging label co-occurrence. In: Proceedings of NAACL-HLT, pp. 521–526 (2016)
10. Lai, S., Xu, L., Liu, K., Zhao, J.: Recurrent convolutional neural networks for text classification. Proc. AAAI Conf. Artif. Intell. **29**, 2267–2273 (2015)
11. Lewis, D.D., Yang, Y., Rose, T.G., Li, F.: Rcv1: a new benchmark collection for text categorization research. J. Mach. Learn. Res. **5**, 361–397 (2004)
12. Li, L., Wang, H., Xu, S., Chang, B., Lei, S.: Multi-label text categorization with joint learning predictions-as-features method. In: Conference on Empirical Methods in Natural Language Processing, pp. 835–839 (2015)
13. Liu, P., Qiu, X., Huang, X.: Recurrent neural network for text classification with multi-task learning. In: Proceedings of the Twenty-Fifth International Joint Conference on Artificial Intelligence, pp. 2873–2879 (2016)
14. Mao, Y., Tian, J., Han, J., Ren, X.: Hierarchical text classification with reinforced label assignment. In: Proceedings of the 2019 Conference on Empirical Methods in Natural Language Processing, pp. 445–455 (2019)
15. Nam, J., Kim, J., Mencía, E., Gurevych, I., Fürnkranz, J.: Large-scale multi-label text classification - revisiting neural networks, pp. 437–452 (2014)
16. Prabhu, Y., Kag, A., Harsola, S., Agrawal, R., Varma, M.: Parabel: partitioned label trees for extreme classification with application to dynamic search advertising. In: the 2018 World Wide Web Conference, pp. 993–1002 (2018)

17. Shimura, K., Li, J., Fukumoto, F.: Hft-cnn: learning hierarchical category structure for multi-label short text categorization. In: Proceedings of the 2018 Conference on Empirical Methods in Natural Language Processing, pp. 811–816 (2018)
18. Wehrmann, J., Cerri, R., Barros, R.: Hierarchical multi-label classification networks. In: International Conference on Machine Learning, pp. 5075–5084. PMLR (2018)
19. Xiao, L., Huang, X., Chen, B., Jing, L.: Label-specific document representation for multi-label text classification. In: Proceedings of the 2019 Conference on Empirical Methods in Natural Language Processing, pp. 466–475 (2019)
20. Yang, P., Sun, X., Li, W., Ma, S., Wu, W., Wang, H.: Sgm: sequence generation model for multi-label classification. In: Proceedings of the 27th International Conference on Computational Linguistics, pp. 3915–3926 (2018)
21. Yang, Z., Yang, D., Dyer, C., He, X., Smola, A., Hovy, E.: Hierarchical attention networks for document classification. In: Proceedings of NAACL-HLT, pp. 1480–1489 (2016)
22. You, R., Zhang, Z., Wang, Z., Dai, S., Mamitsuka, H., Zhu, S.: Attentionxml: label tree-based attention-aware deep model for high-performance extreme multi-label text classification. Eprint Arxiv (2018)
23. Zhou, J., Ma, C., Long, D., Xu, G., Liu, G.: Hierarchy-aware global model for hierarchical text classification. In: Association for Computational Linguistics, pp. 1106–1117 (2020)

Sememes-Based Framework for Knowledge Graph Embedding with Comprehensive-Information

Qingyao Cui[✉], Yanquan Zhou, and Mingming Zheng

Beijing University of Posts and Telecommunications, Beijing 100876, China
{cuiqingyao,zhouyanquan,mingmingzheng}@bupt.edu.cn

Abstract. The goal of knowledge graph embedding is to represent both entities and relationships as low-dimensional, dense vectors that can be used to empower other machine learning models. While most approaches concentrate on modeling the structural information of the graph, part of the work also focuses on fusing entity descriptions, allowing entities to be fused with richer semantics. However, the complex entity text descriptions contain a lot of noise, which reduces the semantic purity. Therefore, in this paper, we propose a novel sememes-based framework for knowledge graph to streamline the semantic space of entities. More specifically, We replace entity descriptions with a finite set of semantics and encode the sememe labels of entities using a pre-trained Bert model, and finally jointly learning the symbolic triples and sememe labels. The experimental results show that our method outperforms other baselines on the task of link prediction and entity classification.

Keywords: Knowledge graph embedding · Link prediction · Sememes-based description

1 Introduction

Knowledge graphs (KG) store human knowledge in a structured way [2,5]. A typical KG usually represents as a symbolic triple (h, r, t), indicating the relation between two entities, which respective vector representations are denoted as $\mathbf{h}, \mathbf{r}, \mathbf{t}$.

In recent years, the development of translation-based approaches, inspired by the TransE model [3], has gained momentum, allowing the complex structure of relationships in a graph to be explored in depth through various complex transformations in entity and relationship vectors [8,10,13]. Other work has shifted the focus to the joint modeling of graph structure and text description of entities [13,15,16], but complex entity text descriptions may introduce a lot of noise and even cause serious shifts in entity semantics. As shown in Fig. 1, entity descriptions are peppered with a lot of redundant information, and even more so, only a few pieces of information represent the precise semantics of the entities.

© Springer Nature Switzerland AG 2021
H. Qiu et al. (Eds.): KSEM 2021, LNAI 12816, pp. 419–426, 2021.
https://doi.org/10.1007/978-3-030-82147-0_34

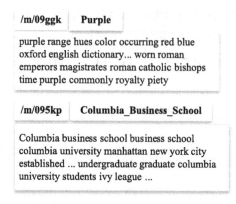

Fig. 1. Sample entity textual descriptions extracted from the FB15K dataset.

A sememe is an indivisible semantic unit for human languages defined by linguists [1,12]. The semantic meanings of concepts can be composed by a finite number of sememes. In this paper, inspired by the above idea, we try to describe all entities by a fixed set of sememes extracted from HowNet [5]. By observing on sememes, we manually divided into two groups, one representing words that be used to describe the external form of an entity, such as *FormValue, Performance-Value, AgeValue, Tasteless*, called the grammatical sememes, and the other be used to describe the abstract meaning of an entity, such as *Believe, Indifferent, Jealous*, called the pragmatical sememes, the details are shown in Table 1. The description of each entity is represented by a small number of grammatical and pragmatical sememes, respectively, and the resulting description of the entity is called the comprehensive-information [17,18].

To quickly obtain sememe labels for each entity, we use the SPWE model [9] for sememe prediction and a pre-trained Bert model [4,14] to encode the sememes. Finally, interact with the comprehensive-information of an entity and the triple structure information. We evaluated our model on the WN18 and FB15K datasets, the experimental results show that our method outperforms other baselines on the task of link prediction and entity classification. It is worth mentioning that our approach does not rely on entity text descriptions, and thus can be extended to arbitrary KG.

Table 1. Statistics of grammatical and pragmatic sememes.

Type	#Num
Grammatical sememes	1,120
Pragmatic sememes	835
Total	1,955

2 Formulation

Triplets are represented as (h, r, t), where h denotes a head entity, t denotes a tail entity and r denotes a relation. Their embeddings are denoted by $\mathbf{h}, \mathbf{r}, \mathbf{t} \in \mathbb{R}^d$, where the sememe embedding of the head and tail entities is denoted as $\mathbf{h_c}, \mathbf{t_c} \in \mathbb{R}^d$. We use Δ to represent golden triplets set, and use Δ' to denote negative triplets set. Entities set and relations set are denoted by E and R, respectively.

3 Sememe-Based Framework

Our model is depicted in Fig. 2. Its goal is to learn representations for the $\mathbf{h}, \mathbf{r}, \mathbf{t}$. We describe the model components in the paragraphs below.

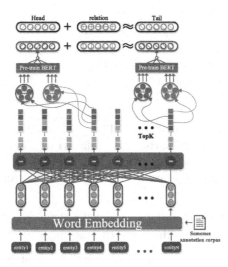

Fig. 2. Sememes-based framework for knowledge graph embedding architecture, where grammatical sememes (green) and pragmatic sememes (orange) co-represent entity's comprehensive-information. (Color figure online)

3.1 Sememe Prediction and Embedding

We utilize the SPWE model to predict semantic labels for the entities. The SPWE model is based on the assumption that similar words should have similar sememes, and the similarity of words is measured by cosine similarity. The score function $Q(s_j|e)$ of sememe s_j given a entity name e is defined as:

$$Q(s_j|e) \sim \sum_{e_i \in E} cos(\mathbf{e}, \mathbf{e_i}) \cdot \mathbf{M}_{ij} \cdot c^{r_i} \tag{1}$$

where $\mathbf{e}$ and $\mathbf{e_i}$ are pre-train word embeddings of entity names e and e_i. $\mathbf{M}_{ij} \in \{0, 1\}$ indicates the annotation of sememe s_j on entity name w_i, where $\mathbf{M}_{ij} = 1$

indicates the sememe $s_j \in S_{e_i}$ and other wise is not. r_i is the descend cosine word similarity rank between e and e_i, and $c \in (0,1)$ is a hyper-parameter. Based on the comprehensive-information theory, the set of sememes $S = G \cup P$, where $G = \{g1, g2, ..., g_n\}$, $P = \{p_1, p_2, ..., p_m\}$ are set of grammatical and pragmatic sememes, respectively. In order for the model to fairly weigh grammatical and pragmatic information, we select the top K grammatical and top K pragmatic sememes after obtaining the entity's sememe ranking sequence.

We then pass the grammatical and pragmatic sememes of the entities(a set of words describing the grammatical and pragmatic information of an entity) separately through the pre-trained Bert model:

$$\mathbf{e_g} = \frac{1}{K} \sum_{k=1}^{K} Bert(g_k) \tag{2}$$

$$\mathbf{e_p} = \frac{1}{K} \sum_{k=1}^{K} Bert(p_k) \tag{3}$$

The final sememes embedding of the entity is obtained by summing the grammatical and pragmatic embeddings:

$$\mathbf{e_c} = \mathbf{e_g} + \mathbf{e_p} \tag{4}$$

Based on the idea of the DKRL model [16], our model also defines the representation of an entity in two parts, one is the structure-based representation, another is the sememes-based (which can also be called the comprehensive-information representation of an entity), and the score function of the triple is defined as follow:

$$f_r(h,t) = w_1||\mathbf{h}+\mathbf{r}-\mathbf{t}|| + w_2||\mathbf{h}+\mathbf{r}-\mathbf{t_c}|| \\ + w_3||\mathbf{h_c}+\mathbf{r}-\mathbf{t}|| + w_4||\mathbf{h_c}+\mathbf{r}-\mathbf{t_c}|| \tag{5}$$

where $||\mathbf{h}+\mathbf{r}-\mathbf{t}||$ and $||\mathbf{h_c}+\mathbf{r}-\mathbf{t_c}||$ indicate that the structure-based and the sememes-based representation independently, while $||\mathbf{h}+\mathbf{r}-\mathbf{t_c}||$ and $||\mathbf{h_c}+\mathbf{r}-\mathbf{t}||$ reflect the interaction between the two parts. The overall scoring function is trade-offed by the $w1, w2, w3, w4$ hyper-parameters.

3.2   Objectives and Training

We define the following margin-based loss function as the training objective:

$$\mathcal{L} = \sum_{(h,r,t)\in\Delta} \sum_{(h',r',t')\in\Delta'} [f_{r'}(h',t') + \gamma - f_r(h,t)]_+ \tag{6}$$

where $[\cdot]_+ = max(\cdot,0)$ is the hinge loss, $\gamma > 0$ is a margin hyperparameter. We construct negative triplets set Δ' by randomly replacing the head, tail entities, and relations in a triplet, formally described as follows:

$$\Delta' = \{(h',r,t)|h' \in E\} \cup \{(h,r',t)|r' \in R\} \\ \cup \{(h,r,t')|t' \in E\} \tag{7}$$

We initialize the structure-based embedding via the Xavier method [6]. The learning process of our model is carried out using stochastic gradient descent (SGD). To avoid overfitting, we add the $L2$ regularization term to the model.

4   Experiments

4.1   Datasets and General Settings

In this paper, we evaluated our model on two benchmark datasets extracted from WordNet [11] and Freebase [2], where the FB15K dataset is identical to the one in DKRL [16], and we reproduced the TransE, TransH, TransR, and TransD models using OpenKE [7] since the version of FB15K differs from the version used in baselines. Please see Table 2 for more details.

Table 2. Statistics of data sets.

Date set	#Rel	#Ent	#Train	#Valid	#Test
WN18	18	40,943	141,442	5,000	5,000
FB15K	1,341	14,904	472,860	48,991	57,803

In addition, since the HowNet [5]'s sememes corpus is in Chinese and the dataset we want to experiment with is in English, we translated the entity names in the WN18 and FB15K datasets using Google Translate and manually adjusted a few of the translation results in order to make the SPWE model more accurate for the sememes prediction of entities. Finally, with the help of the SPWE model, we obtained the set of grammatical and pragmatic sememes corresponding to all the entities contained in the dataset.

4.2   Link Prediction

Evaluation Protocol. Link prediction aims to predict the missing h or t for a relation fact triple (h, r, t). Given a ternary group (h, r, t), we replace the head or tail entities with all entities, compute their scores by the scoring function, and rank them in descending order. We use two metrics for evaluation, Mean Rank, and the proportion of testing triple whose rank is not larger than 10 (as Hits@10). A good link predictor should achieve a lower mean rank or higher Hits@10. Referring to previous work, we perform two evaluation settings, "Raw" and "Filt", respectively. The difference between the two settings is whether or not the corrupted triple is ignored in the metrics calculation when it is present in the knowledge graph.

Implementation. As the datasets are the same, we directly reprint the experimental results of several baselines from the literature. We explore the optimal configuration of the model by performing experiments on the validation dataset

set. For WN18, learning rate $\alpha = 0.5$, number of sememe $K = 10$, $c = 0.8$, embedding dimension $d = 100$, margin $\gamma = 1.0$, $w_1 = 1, w_2 = w3 = 0.3, w4 = 0.1$. For FB15K, learning rate $\alpha = 0.5$, number of sememe $K = 10$, $c = 0.8$, embedding dimension $d = 150$, margin $\gamma = 2.0$, $w_1 = 1, w_2 = w_3 = 0.4, w_4 = 0.2$.

Table 3. Experimental results on link prediction, "unif" and "bern" indicate two different sampling strategies. The underlined results in the table are suboptimal.

Date set	WN18				FB15K			
Metric	Mean Rank		Hits@10		Mean Rank		Hits@10	
	Raw	Filt	Raw	Filt	Raw	Filt	Raw	Filt
TransE	263	251	75.4	89.2	210	119	48.5	66.1
TransH (unif)	318	303	75.4	86.7	173	44	52.1	78.7
TransH (bern)	401	388	73.0	82.3	165	71	53.4	77.1
TransR (unif)	232	219	78.3	91.7	275	128	45.0	75.1
TransR (bern)	238	225	79.8	92.0	188	75	51.3	<u>81.4</u>
TransD (unif)	242	229	79.2	92.5	177	<u>47</u>	51.8	78.6
TransD (bern)	224	212	79.6	92.2	163	68	54.0	78.2
DKRL (BOW)	–	–	–	–	200	113	44.3	57.6
DKRL (ALL)	–	–	–	–	181	91	49.6	67.4
SSP (Std.)	204	193	<u>81.3</u>	91.4	<u>154</u>	77	<u>57.1</u>	78.6
SSP (Joint)	<u>168</u>	<u>156</u>	81.2	<u>93.2</u>	163	82	**57.2**	79.0
Ours	**143**	**142**	**93.9**	**95.1**	**124**	**24**	54.5	**84.1**

Results. Evaluation results are reported in Table 3. Our model outperforms all baselines on almost all metrics. Comparing the translation-based model, the results show that fusing additional descriptive information from entities can enhance the performance of the knowledge graph embedding model. Comparing DKRL and SSP, the results show that the semantics of precisely depicted entities by its sememes can be stripped to some extent of the noise introduced in text-only descriptions.

4.3   Entity Classification

Evaluation Protocol. This task is essentially a multi-label classification, focusing on predicting entity types. We use embedding vectors of entities and relations as features. In the training phase, we use the one-vs-rest training strategy to train the logistic regression model to make multi-label predictions. Referring to previous work, we evaluate all models using the Mean Average Precision (MAP) metric. For more details, we recommend the reader to refer to [16]. In general, this is a multi-label classification task with 50 classes, which means that for each entity, the method should provide a set of types instead of a single type.

Implementation. As the datasets are the same, we directly reprint the experimental results of several baselines from the literature. We explore the optimal configuration of the model by performing experiments on the validation dataset set. For FB15K, learning rate $\alpha = 0.1$, number of sememe $K = 10$, $c = 0.8$, embedding dimension $d = 150$, margin $\gamma = 2.5$, $w_1 = 1, w_2 = w_3 = 0.6, w_4 = 0.1$.

Results. Evaluation results are reported in Table 4. Our model outperforms all baselines. The results show that the semantics of an entity can be accurately depicted by using a small number of sememes, and a better entity feature vector is obtained. Our model compresses the variable-length entity text description into a fixed $2K$ size set of grammatical and pragmatic sememes(comprehensive-information), which not only improves the coding efficiency of the model but also strips out a lot of noise.

Table 4. The MAP results of entity classification. Underlined results in the table are suboptimal.

Data set	FB15K
Metric	MAP
TransE	87.8
BOW	86.3
DKRL (BOW)	89.3
DKRL (ALL)	90.1
SSP (Std.)	93.2
SSP (Joint)	94.4
Ours	**95.2**

5 Conclusion

In this paper, we proposed a novel sememes-based framework for knowledge graph to streamline the semantic space of entities, which incorporates automatic semantics annotation techniques, compresses variable-length entity text descriptions into a fixed $2K$ size set of grammatical and pragmatic sememes(comprehensive-information), and makes the model less dependent on entity text descriptions. The experimental The results show that our method outperforms other baselines on the task of link prediction and entity classification.

References

1. Bloomfield, L.: A set of postulates for the science of language. Language **2**(3), 153–164 (1926)

2. Bollacker, K., Evans, C., Paritosh, P., Sturge, T., Taylor, J.: Freebase: a collaboratively created graph database for structuring human knowledge. In: Proceedings of the 2008 ACM SIGMOD International Conference on Management of Data, pp. 1247–1250 (2008)
3. Bordes, A., Usunier, N., Garcia-Duran, A., Weston, J., Yakhnenko, O.: Translating embeddings for modeling multi-relational data. In: Advances in Neural Information Processing Systems, pp. 2787–2795 (2013)
4. Devlin, J., Chang, M.W., Lee, K., Toutanova, K.: Bert: pre-training of deep bidirectional transformers for language understanding. arXiv preprint arXiv:1810.04805 (2018)
5. Dong, Z., Dong, Q.: HowNet-a hybrid language and knowledge resource. In: International Conference on Natural Language Processing and Knowledge Engineering, 2003. Proceedings. 2003, pp. 820–824. IEEE (2003)
6. Glorot, X., Bengio, Y.: Understanding the difficulty of training deep feedforward neural networks. In: Proceedings of the Thirteenth International Conference on Artificial Intelligence and Statistics, pp. 249–256 (2010)
7. Han, X., et al.: Openke: an open toolkit for knowledge embedding. In: Proceedings of EMNLP (2018)
8. Ji, G., He, S., Xu, L., Liu, K., Zhao, J.: Knowledge graph embedding via dynamic mapping matrix. In: Proceedings of the 53rd Annual Meeting of the Association for Computational Linguistics and the 7th International Joint Conference on Natural Language Processing (volume 1: Long papers), pp. 687–696 (2015)
9. Jin, H., et al.: Incorporating Chinese characters of words for lexical sememe prediction. arXiv preprint arXiv:1806.06349 (2018)
10. Lin, Y., Liu, Z., Sun, M., Liu, Y., Zhu, X.: Learning entity and relation embeddings for knowledge graph completion. In: Proceedings of AAAI, pp. 2181–2187 (2015)
11. Miller, G.A.: Wordnet: a lexical database for English. Commun. ACM **38**(11), 39–41 (1995)
12. Qin, Y., et al.: Improving sequence modeling ability of recurrent neural networks via sememes. IEEE/ACM Trans. Audio Speech Lang. Process. **28**, 2364–2373 (2020)
13. Wang, Z., Zhang, J., Feng, J., Chen, Z.: Knowledge graph embedding by translating on hyperplanes. In: AAAI, vol. 14, pp. 1112–1119. Citeseer (2014)
14. Xiao, H.: Bert-as-service. https://github.com/hanxiao/bert-as-service (2018)
15. Xiao, H., Huang, M., Meng, L., Zhu, X.: SSP: semantic space projection for knowledge graph embedding with text descriptions. In: Thirty-First AAAI Conference on Artificial Intelligence (2017)
16. Xie, R., Liu, Z., Jia, J., Luan, H., Sun, M.: Representation learning of knowledge graphs with entity descriptions. In: Thirtieth AAAI Conference on Artificial Intelligence (2016)
17. Yi-Xin, Z.: A study on information-knowledge-intelligence transformation. Acta Electronica Sinica **32**(4), 16 (2004)
18. Zhong, Y.: Mechanism-based artificial intelligence theory: a universal theory of artificial intelligence. CAAI Trans. Intell. Syst. **13**(1), 2–18 (2018)

Domain-Specific Sentence Encoder for Intention Recognition in Large-Scale Shopping Platforms

Chong Zhang[1], Zhiyuan Wang[2], Liuqing Yang[3], Xiao-Yang Liu[3(✉)], and Ling Jiang[1]

[1] XiaoduoAI Co., Ltd., Chengdu, China
{mon,jiangling}@xiaoduotech.com
[2] Huazhong University of Science and Technology, Wuhan, China
vinlee624@gmail.com
[3] Columbia University, New York, USA
{ly2335,xl2427}@columbia.edu

Abstract. Intelligent dialog robot is now a primary necessity in online shopping, since it can significantly improve the service quality of the online merchants with fewer customer service staffs. And the core functionality of such robots is to identify the customers' intention in order to provide better service. In this paper, we propose a domain-specific sentence encoder (DSSE) method for real-time online intent identification that hierarchically consists of a representation module and a classification module. We construct a large corpus using the dialog text from e-commerce platforms. We train the representation module of DSSE with the dialog corpus of all kinds of goods and then fine-tune the downstream multi-layer perceptron (MLP) classification module on the corpus of a specific kind of goods. Our model can be easily extended to new kinds of goods as it only needs a little training corpus to fine-tune the small MLP module on new goods chatting dialog text. In addition, our model has quick inference speed and relatively low resource requirement, as well as a higher intent identification accuracy score than BERT. Specifically, our model achieves 85.95% accuracy score and 81.62% F1 score. The inference time per-batch (size = 350) is 33 ms with CPU and only 5.8M parameters are loaded into the RAM.

Keywords: Intention recognition · Domain-specific · Sentence encoder · Deep learning · Large corpus · Online shopping

1 Introduction

Online shopping is very popular and important in nowadays commercial activities and it is crucial to recognize the customers' intentions through online chats. Many research works show the importance of customers' intentions on shopping platforms [17]. In online shopping platforms, customer service staffs are usually hired to chat with customers online, recognize customers' intentions and

© Springer Nature Switzerland AG 2021
H. Qiu et al. (Eds.): KSEM 2021, LNAI 12816, pp. 427–438, 2021.
https://doi.org/10.1007/978-3-030-82147-0_35

help them. However, hiring staffs usually takes up a large portion of business earnings, and the lack of service still occurs, especially when there is a sudden increase of dialog quantity like on "November 11" (An online shopping festival in China). Therefore, purely relying on the staffs to serve the customers is not a good solution on shopping platforms. Intelligent dialog robots are now used to understand the intentions of customers and respond to customers online. They can provide 24-h chatting service and process high-throughput chatting content in a cost-effective and efficient manner.

The core functionality of the online shopping robot is intention recognition. However, while humans can easily recognize the customers' intentions, it is usually hard for robots. The algorithms for robots not only need to maintain high accuracy for intention recognition and high speed for real-time needs, but also need to handle the challenge of low resource constraint.

The study of customer intention recognition has attracted lots of attention globally and researchers have proposed a variety of intention identification or recognition methods. [8,9]. Many recent works [5,10] try to encode the sentence with various approaches in order to obtain a good text classification result. The BERT/ALBERT models [5,10] utilize the transformer encoder [20] pretrained without supervision on huge corpus to achieve the state-of-the-art in many NLP classification tasks. However, it is hard to apply such models in low-resource and real-time situations such as the online dialog robot.

In this paper, we build a novel dataset of huge Chinese corpus labeled with proper intent from chat logs of online shopping platforms and propose a domain-specific sentence encoder (DSSE). With DSSE, our model is time- and memory-efficient as to be applied to real-time application efficiently.

Our major contributions are summarized as follows:

- We build a domain-specific intent dataset (DSID) with 245 domains and 16870 intentions. DSID consists of 80 million of labeled sentences and 200 million of unlabeled sentences.
- We build a domain-specific sentence encoder (DSSE) for intention recognition of dialog robots in the online shopping platform. The DSSE is small and quick, which is practical in real-time application.
- We evaluate our method in 3 major online shopping platforms and the results show that our model achieves state-of-the-art. Our proposed model achieves 85.95% accuracy score and 81.62% F1 score in testing dataset.

The remainder of the paper is organized as follows. In Sect. 2, we describe our dataset. In Sect. 3, we illustrate the network structure of DSSE model and the training procedure. In Sect. 4, we demonstrate the experimental evaluation results of DSSE in our datasets and comparisons of DSSE with other models. We analyze the threats to validity of our work in Sect. 5. The related works are shown in Sect. 6. We conclude the paper in Sect. 7.

2   Domain-Specific Intent Dataset

In this section, we introduce a new dataset constructed with data from top three Chinese online shopping platforms, i.e., Taobao (https://www.taobao.com), JD (https://www.jd.com), PDD (https://www.pinduoduo.com). We firstly describe the source data and then explain the detailed information of our dataset.

2.1   Source Data Description

There are many industries in online shopping platforms and each industry contains many categories of goods. According to our statistics, customers often show different intentions for different industries and they often share a proportion of common intentions for different categories in one industry. Table 1 shows the intentions distribution of some industries.

2.2   Details of the Dataset

Our dataset has been labeled and accumulated for several years which contains 80 million of labeled messages and 200 million of unlabeled messages. We remove duplicate messages and get 8,595,305 unique customer sentences that are labeled and they correspond to 16,870 intentions.

We define some notations here for convenience in later sections. Assume that there are I industries in DSID and there are J^i categories in the ith industry, $i = 1, 2, ..., I$. The jth category of the ith industry contains $m_{i,j}$ sentences and $n_{i,j}$ intentions, $j = 1, 2, ..., J^i$. The sentences and intentions are denoted as $D_{i,j} = \{(x_k, y_k)| 1 \leq k \leq m_{i,j}\}$ where x_k, y_k denote the sentence sent by customers and the intention of the sentence respectively. In our statistics, $I = 9$, $\sum_{i=1}^{I} J^i = 245$, $\sum_{i=1}^{I} \sum_{j=1}^{J^i} m_{i,j} = 8,595,305$ and $\sum_{i=1}^{I} \sum_{j=1}^{J^i} n_{i,j} = 16,870$.

We hire workers to label the sentences of customers with intentions previously defined by our goods expert. Sentences matching none of the intentions are labeled with a special mark. Table 2 shows some labeled results. We translate the messages and the intentions into English for the convenience of reading.

3   Intention Recognition Model with DSSE

3.1   Overview of the Proposed Model

The framework of the customer intention recognition model is illustrated in Fig. 1. The model consists of three major components: 1) Chinese text processor,

Table 1. Intentions distribution in some industries.

Industry	Samples	Categories	All intentions	Common intentions
Electrical	19,442,926	49	6,503	325
Clothing	6,545,090	15	2,020	172
Beauty makeup	4,303,256	8	1,409	268
Food	2,725,587	10	1,299	243

Table 2. Labeled messages with intent.

Message	Zhejiang Province XX City XX Street XX
Intent	A customer sent the address information
Message	Please give me a refund
Intent	Asking and reminding the issues about refund
Message	Is the price same as today tomorrow?
Intent	Will the price of the goods change?

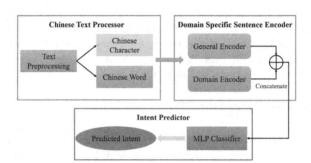

Fig. 1. Overview of our intention recognition method.

2) domain-specific sentence encoder, and 3) intent predictor. The Chinese text processor cleans and normalizes the message of customer and then transforms the message into Chinese characters and words. Domain-specific sentence encoder is the core functionality of the model that leverages a general encoder and a domain specific encoder to generate the vector representation of the message. Intent predictor is a multi-layer perceptron (MLP) neural network that outputs a softmax probability distribution over all the intents defined for a category. We shall describe each component in detail in the rest parts of the section.

3.2   Chinese Text Processor

The message sent by customers in online shopping platforms usually contains pictures, emotion flags, oral representation, shopping slang, etc. To build a model from natural language we make normalization for the messages and the rules are listed in Table 3. After text normalization, we leverage the jieba tools (https://github.com/fxsjy/jieba) that are designed for text segmentation for Chinese to segment the text into words. We add goods name and frequent description item phrase to the dictionary of jieba tools to prevent them from segmentation. We also cut the text into Chinese characters for each Chinese character contains rich information. The Chinese text processor outputs characters and words of a message text.

Moreover, we build two embedding matrices for word representation and character representation respectively, using the unlabeled sentences in DSID.

We leverage the skip n-gram approach proposed in [13] to train the embeddings. The Chinese word sequence and the Chinese character sequence in Fig. 1 are represented as a matrix of $seq \in R^{L \times d}$ (L and d represent the word/character length and the embedding dimension).

3.3 Domain-Specific Sentence Encoder

The domain-specific sentence encoder consists of a general sentence encoder and a domain sentence encoder that are of the same neural network structure. We adopt the network structure proposed in [22] that combines BLSTM-2DPooling and BLSTM-2DCNN to extract features by two-dimensional (2D) convolution and 2D max pooling operation for sequence modeling tasks. We feed the Chinese words sequence from Chinese text processor to the domain encoder and the Chinese characters sequence to the general encoder and each encoder outputs a feature vector. In the training phase, we feed the feature vector to a softmax output layer, and the output is used to compute the loss. In the inference phase, we concatenate the two feature vectors as the representation of the input message.

We leverage the cross entropy loss to train the network. All labeled sentences in DSID are used to train the general encoder. And labeled sentences from a specific domain are used to train the corresponding domain encoder. The training cross entropy loss (CE) of the general and domain encoders is formulated in Eq. 1 and 2, respectively. $emb(x_k)_c$ and $emb(x_k)_w$ represent the character sequence and word sequence of x_k output by the Chinese Text Processor. θ^g_{rep} and θ^g_{class} represent the parameters of the general encoder and the parameters of the softmax output layer for the general encoder, while θ^i_{rep} and θ^i_{class} have similar meanings for the domain encoder of the ith industry. f_{rep} and f_{class} represent the encoder network and softmax output network. D and D_i are the whole dataset containing all sentences from all industries and the dataset containing sentences from industry i. Finally, we train one general encoder and I domain encoders.

$$Loss(\theta^g_{rep}, \theta^g_{class}) = \sum_{x_k, y_k \in D} CE(y_k, f_{class}(f_{rep}(emb(x_k)_c; \theta^g_{rep}); \theta^g_{class})), \quad (1)$$

$$Loss(\theta^i_{rep}; \theta^i_{class}) = \sum_{x_k, y_k \in D_i} CE(y_k, f_{class}(f_{rep}(emb(x_k)_w; \theta^i_{rep}); \theta^i_{class})). \quad (2)$$

Table 3. Rules used for Chinese message text normalization.

Case	Normalization method
Pictures and emotion flags	Remove
Url links	Parse the goods or business order description from links
Traditional Chinese	Transform to simplified Chinese
Oral expression	Transform to formal expression

3.4   Intent Predictor

For a specific industry i, we feed the concatenated vector representation E_{rep} (refer to Eq. 3) of a sentence to the intent predictor.

$$E_{rep} = [f_{rep}(emb(x_k)_c; \theta^g_{rep}), f_{rep}(emb(x_k)_w; \theta^i_{rep})]. \tag{3}$$

The intent predictor is a multi-layer perceptron (MLP) with a softmax output layer. We use grid search methodology to find the best hyperparameters for building the MLP network structure. When training the intent predictor, we only use the sentences from a specific category and apply the cross entropy loss to optimize the parameters as shown in Eq. 4. $D_{i,j}$ represents the sentences in category j of industry i and $\theta^{i,j}_{mlp}$ is the parameters of MLP (f_{mlp}).

$$\text{Loss}(\theta^{i,j}_{mlp}) = \sum_{x_k, y_k \in D_{i,j}} \text{CE}(y_k, f_{mlp}(E_{rep}; \theta^{i,j}_{mlp})). \tag{4}$$

In DSID, there are about 500 intentions and 200,000 sentences in each category. Therefore, it is very efficient to train intent predictors in the downstream category dataset, which allows our model (Fig. 1) to be easily extended to new categories of goods. In total, we build $\sum_{i=1}^{I} J^i$ intent predictors.

4   Experiments and Discussion

In this section, we firstly describe the experimental design for model capacity test which introduces three research questions (**RQ**). Then we show the evaluation metrics and experimental setup. The experimental results of the research questions are discussed in the final three subsections.

4.1   Experimental Design

We conduct extensive experiments on DSID dataset to evaluate the effectiveness of the customer intention recognition model. Our evaluation focuses on the following research questions:

RQ1: How effective is the domain-specific sentence encoder? We test the accuracy score and F1 score of using general encoder only, domain encoder only and the proposed DSSE method. We also experiment feeding the encoder with different input features to find the proper input for the sentence encoder.

RQ2: How effective is the proposed customer intention recognition model? To evaluate the effectiveness of the proposed model, we compare it with BERT and the recently proposed state-of-the-art model, i.e. BERT-wwm, in terms of F1 score and accuracy score. The BERT-wwm model [4] is pretrained on Chinese wikipedia. We load the pretrained weights of BERT-wwm (https://github.com/ymcui/Chinese-BERT-wwm) and fine-tune the BERT-wwm on the category sentences.

RQ3: What is the performance of the proposed customer intention recognition model? In order to test whether our model meets the expected performance, we compare it with BERT and BERT-wwm in training resources, inferring resources, predicting speed and accuracy score.

4.2 Evaluation Metrics

Assume there are M intents for a specific category of goods. Our model will predict a label for each test sentence in the category and then we get a confusion matrix A, where A_{ij} represents the count of sentences whose intent is i^{th} intent and the model predicted intent is j^{th} intent, $i, j = 1, 2, ..., M$.

Accuracy score and F1 score are computed by Eq. 5 and 6 respectively. Higher accuracy and F1 scores refer to better model prediction.

$$\text{Accuracy} = \frac{\Sigma_i A_{ii}}{\Sigma_i \Sigma_j A_{ij}}. \tag{5}$$

$$F1 = \frac{2 * precision * recall}{precision + recall},$$

$$\text{where } precision = \frac{1}{M}\sum_{c=1}^{M}\frac{A_{cc}}{\Sigma_i A_{ic}}, \ recall = \frac{1}{M}\sum_{c=1}^{M}\frac{A_{cc}}{\Sigma_j A_{cj}}. \tag{6}$$

4.3 Experimental Setup

We select sentences of 6 categories from 3 major industries to evaluate the model. For a specific category in DSID, we shuffle and split the sentences into 2 parts: 90% as training dataset and 10% as validation dataset. For each category, we build a testing dataset using recently accumulated online dialog sentences that have not been included in the DSID for higher accuracy and reliability.

4.4 Experimental Results for RQ1

For this **RQ**, we firstly evaluate a single pretrained encoder (see Table 4). We feed the encoder with the Chinese character sequence or the word sequence. Both the domain encoder and the general encoder achieve higher accuracy and

Table 4. Evaluation of single encoder.

Sentence encoder	Input features	F1	Accuracy
Domain encoder	Character sequence	0.8004	0.8491
Domain encoder	Word sequence	0.7364	0.7951
General encoder	Character sequence	0.8088	0.8520
General encoder	Word sequence	0.7438	0.8042

Table 5. Evaluation of combination of the encoders.

	Sentence encoder	Input features	F1	Accuracy
(a)	Domain + domain encoders	Character + word sequence	0.8131	0.8584
(b)	General + general encoders	Character + word sequence	0.8185	0.8566
(c)	Domain + general encoders	Character + word sequence	0.8131	0.8584
(d)	Domain + general encoders	Word + character sequence	0.8162	0.8595

F1 scores using character sequence features. The domain encoder is trained with data from a specific industry that is only about 10% of that for training the general encoder, which accounts for its lower accuracy and F1 scores.

We then evaluate 4 combinations of the domain encoder and the general encoder with different input features (see Table 5). When we choose the (d) combination in Table 5, the sentence encoder achieves the highest accuracy score and high F1 score (0.8595 and 0.8162 respectively). For each industry, the sentences contain some domain-specific words. The domain encoder is unable to obtain the information of domain-specific words when using the characters as input features. Therefore, the accuracy and F1 scores of combination (a) and combination (c) are lower than that of combination (d).

The general encoder is trained with character sequence features across all industries, so using character features as input achieves higher F1 and accuracy scores than using the word sequence features. Because there are conflicts among the domain-specific words across different industries, feeding the general encoder with the word sequence features is not a good choice.

The experiment results in Table 4 and 5 demonstrate the effectiveness of the domain-specific sentence encoder.

Table 6. Evaluation of different intention recognition models.

Model	F1	Accuracy
BERT	0.7797	0.8455
BERT-wwm	0.7781	0.8486
Our model	0.8162	0.8595

4.5 Experimental Results for RQ2

We compare the proposed customer intention recognition model shown in Fig. 1 with BERT and BERT-wmm (see Table 6). Our model outperforms the BERT-wmm by 3.81% in F1 score and 1.09% in accuracy score. The BERT series of model is trained and optimized for open domain language processing, whereas our model is trained using the corpus from the online chatting message texts of customer. Therefore our model matches the probability distribution of the online shopping chatting application better. The experiment results show the superiority of our model over BERT and BERT-wmm in online shopping dialog.

4.6 Experimental Results for RQ3

Table 7. Evaluation of performance.

Model	Parameters	Train method	Training time	Predicting time	Accuracy
BERT	110M	Fine-tune	30 min/epoch	164 ms	0.8455
BERT-wmm	110M	Fine-tune	31 min/epoch	157 ms	0.8486
Our model	42M	Train MLP	0.3 min/epoch	33 ms	0.8595

We compare with BERT and BERT-wmm in several aspects to test the performance and application usefulness of our model (see Table 7). Our model size is less than 40% of that of BERT-wmm, and the downstream training MLP size (5.8M) is about 5% of that of BERT-wmm (110M). The small model size results in fast training speed with 0.3 min/epoch that is 100 times faster than BERT models. Using 12-core CPU with 2 GHz frequency for inference, our model only costs 33 ms to run a batch (size = 350) which is 5 times faster than BERT. Therefore, our model is both quicker and more accurate, making it practical and suitable for online shopping dialog robot.

5 Threats to Validity

Although our method achieves excellent results with a real online shopping dialog dataset DSID, there are still some works left to be improved in the future:

- Some recent research works focus on unknown intents detection in dialog system [6,12,18,21], where utterances hold intents that never appeared when training. According to our data, our model also faces unknown intents. We will explore methods to address the unknown intents detection problem.
- We need to design methods that can leverage the existing intent predictors for new categories goods instead of building new predictors.
- Sometimes it's hard to infer correct customers' intentions from a single sentence. Therefore, we will test whether contextual information is needed and build a contextual based intention recognition model.

6 Related Works

6.1 Human Intention Recognition Through Text

The earlier proposed deep learning method that utilizes Deep Belief Nets(DBNs) model [16] outperforms traditional algorithms like SVM. Deep Convex Network based models [19] build hierarchical neural networks with stacking method.

Microsoft Research proposed an RNN and LSTM based method [15] for utterance classification and demonstrated the superiority of automated feature extraction using RNN or LSTM model. MIT researchers [11] presented a model based on recurrent neural networks and convolutional neural networks that incorporates the preceding short texts.

Some works focus on analyzing the user intention [14] with more social media data using deep learning methods. Other works [2] analyze the use cases of speech recognition errors and build models to predict the user intention.

6.2   Sentence Encoder Models

Ahmad et al. proposed Shared-Private model [1] that consists of a private encoder and a shared encoder for robust text classification. They leveraged multi-task learning approach to train a general encoder and a task specific encoder jointly. Chen et al. [3] explored how to combine Chinese character embedding and word embedding to get the utterance representation. Jeremy et al. [7] proposed a novel language model (LM) fine-tuning method to transfer the knowledge learned from general domain to specific domain.

Zhou et al. [22] introduced two combined models BLSTM-2DPooling and BLSTM-2DCNN that extract features by two-dimensional (2D) convolution and 2D max pooling operation for sequence modeling tasks.

7   Conclusion

In this paper, we proposed a novel customer intention recognition model which consists of a Chinese text processor, a domain-specific sentence encoder (DSSE), and an intent predictor. We firstly built a domain-specific intent dataset (DSID) that contains 80 million labeled sentences and 200 million unlabeled sentences from online shopping platforms. The Chinese text processor cleans the customers' messages, leverages the Chinese character embedding matrix and Chinese word embedding matrix to produce distinct Chinese character sequence and word sequence for domain-specific sentence encoder. The DSSE leverages the general encoder trained with the whole dataset in DSID and the domain encoder trained with the data from a specific industry to represent the message of customer as a vector. The intent predictor is a multi-layer perception neural network with a softmax output, which takes the message representation vector as an input to predict its intent. Our model not only outperformed the current state-of-the-art Chinese text classification model, but also created a fast and memory-efficient online shopping dialog robot in real-time scenario.

References

1. Ahmad, W., Bai, X., Peng, N., Chang, K.W.: Learning robust, transferable sentence representations for text classification, Septermber 2018

2. Che, J., Chen, H., Zeng, J., Zhang, L.-J.: A Chinese text correction and intention identification method for speech interactive context. In: Liu, S., Tekinerdogan, B., Aoyama, M., Zhang, L.-J. (eds.) EDGE 2018. LNCS, vol. 10973, pp. 127–134. Springer, Cham (2018). https://doi.org/10.1007/978-3-319-94340-4_10

3. Chen, X., Xu, L., Liu, Z., Sun, M., Luan, H.: Joint learning of character and word embeddings. In: Yang, Q., Wooldridge, M.J. (eds.) Proceedings of the Twenty-Fourth International Joint Conference on Artificial Intelligence, IJCAI 2015, Buenos Aires, Argentina, 25–31 July 2015, pp. 1236–1242. AAAI Press (2015)

4. Cui, Y., Che, W., Liu, T., Qin, B., Wang, S., Hu, G.: Revisiting pre-trained models for chinese natural language processing. arXiv preprint arXiv:2004.13922 (2020)

5. Devlin, J., Chang, M., Lee, K., Toutanova, K.: BERT: pre-training of deep bidirectional transformers for language understanding. In: Burstein, J., Doran, C., Solorio, T. (eds.) Proceedings of the 2019 Conference of the North American Chapter of the Association for Computational Linguistics: Human Language Technologies, NAACL-HLT 2019, Minneapolis, MN, USA, 2–7 June 2019, Volume 1 (Long and Short Papers), pp. 4171–4186. Association for Computational Linguistics (2019)

6. Hendrycks, D., Gimpel, K.: A baseline for detecting misclassified and out-of-distribution examples in neural networks. In: 5th International Conference on Learning Representations, ICLR 2017, Toulon, France, 24–26 April 2017, Conference Track Proceedings. OpenReview.net (2017)

7. Howard, J., Ruder, S.: Universal language model fine-tuning for text classification. In: Gurevych, I., Miyao, Y. (eds.) Proceedings of the 56th Annual Meeting of the Association for Computational Linguistics, ACL 2018, Melbourne, Australia, 15–20 July 2018, Volume 1: Long Papers, pp. 328–339. Association for Computational Linguistics (2018)

8. Jiang, J., Wang, Z., Ying, H.: More information or less? Eidence from the biggest online shopping platform in china. In: Vogel, D., et al. (eds.) 24th Pacific Asia Conference on Information Systems, PACIS 2020, Dubai, UAE, 22–24 June 2020, p. 116 (2020)

9. Kai, X.: Study on feasibility and pattern about construction of university online shopping platform. In: The International Conference on E-Business and E-Government, ICEE 2010, 7–9 May 2010, Guangzhou, China, Proceedings, pp. 4577–4580. IEEE Computer Society (2010)

10. Lan, Z., Chen, M., Goodman, S., Gimpel, K., Sharma, P., Soricut, R.: ALBERT: A lite BERT for self-supervised learning of language representations. In: 8th International Conference on Learning Representations, ICLR 2020, Addis Ababa, Ethiopia, 26–30 April 2020. OpenReview.net (2020)

11. Lee, J.Y., Dernoncourt, F.: Sequential short-text classification with recurrent and convolutional neural networks. In: Knight, K., Nenkova, A., Rambow, O. (eds.) NAACL HLT 2016, The 2016 Conference of the North American Chapter of the Association for Computational Linguistics: Human Language Technologies, San Diego California, USA, 12–17 June 2016, pp. 515–520. The Association for Computational Linguistics (2016)

12. Lin, T., Xu, H.: Deep unknown intent detection with margin loss. In: Korhonen, A., Traum, D.R., Màrquez, L. (eds.) Proceedings of the 57th Conference of the Association for Computational Linguistics, ACL 2019, Florence, Italy, 28 July – 2 August 2019, Volume 1: Long Papers. pp. 5491–5496. Association for Computational Linguistics (2019)
13. Mikolov, T., Chen, K., Corrado, G., Dean, J.: Efficient estimation of word representations in vector space. In: Bengio, Y., LeCun, Y. (eds.) 1st International Conference on Learning Representations, ICLR 2013, Scottsdale, Arizona, USA, 2–4 May 2013, Workshop Track Proceedings (2013)
14. Mishael, Q., Ayesh, A., Yevseyeva, I.: Users intention based on Twitter features using text analytics. In: Yin, H., Camacho, D., Tino, P., Tallón-Ballesteros, A.J., Menezes, R., Allmendinger, R. (eds.) IDEAL 2019, Part I. LNCS, vol. 11871, pp. 121–128. Springer, Cham (2019). https://doi.org/10.1007/978-3-030-33607-3_14
15. Ravuri, S.V., Stolcke, A.: Recurrent neural network and LSTM models for lexical utterance classification. In: INTERSPEECH 2015, 16th Annual Conference of the International Speech Communication Association, Dresden, Germany, 6–10 September 2015, pp. 135–139. ISCA (2015)
16. Sarikaya, R., Hinton, G.E., Ramabhadran, B.: Deep belief nets for natural language call-routing. In: Proceedings of the IEEE International Conference on Acoustics, Speech, and Signal Processing, ICASSP 2011, 22–27 May 2011, Prague Congress Center, Prague, Czech Republic, pp. 5680–5683. IEEE (2011)
17. Shao, Z., Li, X., Guo, Y., Zhang, L.: Influence of service quality in sharing economy: understanding customers' continuance intention of bicycle sharing. Electron. Commer. Res. Appl. 40, 100944 (2020)
18. Shu, L., Xu, H., Liu, B.: DOC: deep open classification of text documents. In: Palmer, M., Hwa, R., Riedel, S. (eds.) Proceedings of the 2017 Conference on Empirical Methods in Natural Language Processing, EMNLP 2017, Copenhagen, Denmark, 9–11 September 2017, pp. 2911–2916. Association for Computational Linguistics (2017)
19. Tür, G., Deng, L., Hakkani-Tür, D., He, X.: Towards deeper understanding: deep convex networks for semantic utterance classification. In: 2012 IEEE International Conference on Acoustics, Speech and Signal Processing, ICASSP 2012, Kyoto, Japan, 25–30 March 2012. pp. 5045–5048. IEEE (2012)
20. Vaswani, A., et al.: Attention is all you need. In: Guyon, I., (eds.) 2017 Advances in Neural Information Processing Systems 30: Annual Conference on Neural Information Processing Systems, 4–9 December 2017, pp. 5998–6008. Long Beach, CA, USA (2017)
21. Yan, G., et al.: Unknown intent detection using Gaussian mixture model with an application to zero-shot intent classification. In: Jurafsky, D., Chai, J., Schluter, N., Tetreault, J.R. (eds.) Proceedings of the 58th Annual Meeting of the Association for Computational Linguistics, ACL 2020, Online, 5–10 July 2020, pp. 1050–1060. Association for Computational Linguistics (2020)
22. Zhou, P., Qi, Z., Zheng, S., Xu, J., Bao, H., Xu, B.: Text classification improved by integrating bidirectional LSTM with two-dimensional max pooling. In: Calzolari, N., Matsumoto, Y., Prasad, R. (eds.) COLING 2016, 26th International Conference on Computational Linguistics, Proceedings of the Conference: Technical Papers, 11–16 December 2016, Osaka, Japan, pp. 3485–3495. ACL (2016)

Chinese Event Detection Based on Event Ontology and Siamese Network

Chang Ni[1], Wei Liu[1(✉)], Weimin Li[1], Jinliang Wu[2], and Haiyang Ren[2]

[1] School of Computer Engineering and Science, Shanghai University,
Shanghai, China
liuw@shu.edu.cn
[2] The 54th Research Institute of China Electronics Technology Group,
Shijiazhuang, China

Abstract. Event detection (ED) aims to identify the events in raw text. Most existing methods for ED include two steps: locating triggers and classifying them into correct event types. However, such methods require a lot of labor costs to annotate triggers and face the problems of word-trigger mismatch and polysemy, especially in Chinese. To address these challenges, we propose a novel method for ED based on event ontology and Siamese network. First, event ontology is introduced as priori event-based knowledge base, which provides enormous different event types with event class specification. And then, textual specifications of event class elements (such as actions, person, places and objects) could be obtained from event ontology, thus event detection is transformed into the problem of judging which event class specifications are similar to the raw text to be detected through the Siamese network, which solves the problem of high cost of trigger annotation and word-trigger mismatch. Extensive experiments with comprehensive analyses illustrate the effectiveness of proposed method. The source code of this paper can be obtained from https://github.com/nicahead/event_detection.

Keywords: Event detection · Event ontology · Siamese recurrent network

1 Introduction

Event is the basic unit of human cognition, understanding and memory, which is a more dynamic and structured knowledge paradigm than concept. Extracting events from text is the key work to build event knowledge base, which consists of event detection and event element recognition. This paper focuses on the former and attempts to detect events in text in Chinese.

Supported by the National Key Research and Development Program of China (No. 2017YFE0117500), the National Natural Science Foundation of China (No. 61991410), the research project of the 54th Research Institute of China Electronics Technology Group (No. SKX192010019).

© Springer Nature Switzerland AG 2021
H. Qiu et al. (Eds.): KSEM 2021, LNAI 12816, pp. 439–451, 2021.
https://doi.org/10.1007/978-3-030-82147-0_36

Currently, the core task of most event detection methods is divided into event trigger detection and trigger classification. Event trigger refers to a word that can clearly indicate the occurrence of the event. Although this kind of method performs well, there are three problems. **(1)** During labeling training corpus, it is difficult for annotators to seek the triggers from the given sentences, which makes it difficult to complete the subsequent work. **(2)** Unlike event detection in English, there are not natural word delimiters in Chinese. Therefore, it is hard for model to detect event triggers because the result of word segmentation will lead to the mismatch between words and event triggers. Specifically, triggers can be part of a word or a combination of multiple words. As shown in Fig. 1(a), there are two characters "死" (died) and "伤" (injured) in one word "死伤" (died or injured) to trigger two different events *"Life.Death"* and *"Life.Injury"*, while "告上法庭" (sue), the trigger of *"Judiciary.Prosecution"* event, crosses three words. **(3)** There are also some polysemes in Chinese. As shown in Fig. 1(b), "离开" (leave) can trigger the event *"Organization.Quit"* with the meaning of leaving an organization. It can also trigger the event *"Life.Death"* with the meaning of death.

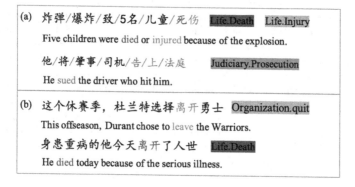

Fig. 1. Word-trigger mismatch (a) and polysemy (b) in Chinese event detection.

Obviously, due to the characteristics of Chinese language, there exist problems in event detection using triggers, such as semantic ambiguity and polysemy. To address these challenges, we propose a novel method for event detection based on event ontology and Siamese network without using event triggers.

Considering that there may be 0, 1 or n events in a sample, we model this multi-label classification as multiple binary classifications. Each binary classification contains two inputs: raw text to be detected and the specification of event class pre-defined in event ontology, which represents an event type through the elements of the event and contain more information than a single trigger. We will introduce the concept of it in detail in Sect. 3.

The Siamese network is a special network architecture, which contains two parts with the same structure and shared parameters. Previous works have proved its effectiveness in calculating the similarity of pair of input texts [14,15]. For the reason that the two inputs in our model have similar process, the structure of Siamese network is adopted to encode them. Besides, the attention mechanism is used to give more weight to the time, place, object, action and other words of the events contained in the text when the input is encoded. The element of action can indicate the occurrence of the event, and other element words can help the model to better understand the input text and solve the problem of word ambiguity in Chinese. Ultimately, our model judges whether the text to be detected is similar to the event class specification, and then determines whether the text contains an instance of the event class.

In summary, the contributions of this paper are as follows: (1) Unlike most of the previous works, we detect events from Chinese text without using triggers, which avoids the challenge of annotating triggers manually. (2) This paper proposes an effective deep learning model, which transforms the task of event detection into calculating the similarity of text pairs. (3) The event ontology is introduced as the priori knowledge, which makes use of semantic information of events and is more interpretable than the previous methods. (4) A series of comparative experiments show the effectiveness of proposed model.

2   Related Work

In recent years, event detection has attracted much attention in the natural language research community. Event detection methods usually include feature-based and representation-based methods.

The commonly used features in feature-based methods include: word features [20], sentence features [11] and textual features [3,4,7]. Such methods lack generalization and are prone to error propagation and data sparsity problems.

Representation-based methods solve the above problems through the end-to-end model without elaborately designed features. The dynamic multi-pool convolution neural network proposed by Chen et al. [1] dynamically retains the information of multiple events. Nguyen et al. [17] jointly predicted event triggers and parameters via sentence representations learned by RNN. Liu et al. [10] proposed a type-aware bias neural network with attention mechanisms to detect events without triggers. In addition, the graph convolution neural network is also proved to be effective in this task [16,19].

In the field of Chinese event detection, researchers are committed to solving the word-trigger mismatch problem. Ding et al. [2] introduced an external linguistic knowledge base to alleviate the problem of ambiguous triggers. Lin et al. [8] proposed the trigger nugget which is not restricted by the word boundaries for event classification. Xiangyu et al. [18] combined word information and language model representation into Chinese character representation.

Most existing event detection methods solved this task by recognizing and classifying event triggers, which requires a lot of manual annotation. Moreover, due to the characteristics of Chinese language, it is difficult to achieve the ideal effect in the event detection of Chinese text. This is also the motivation of this paper.

3   Prerequisites

In this paper, the event classes in the event ontology are used to describe the features of events semantically, and the event hierarchy model is used to organize the event types. Before introducing the method proposed by us, the concepts of event ontology should be interpreted.

Event ontology is a shared, formal and explicit specification of an event class system model that exists in real world objectively. Liu [12] defined the structure of event ontology as a 3-tuple: $EO := \{ECs, Rs, Rules\}$, where ECs is the set of event classes, R is the relationship between event classes, and $Rules$ is the rule sets.

The event class refers to a collection of events with common characteristics, which is formally defined as a 6-tuple:

$$e ::=_{def} (A, O, T, V, P, L) \tag{1}$$

The definition of event includes seven elements: A stands for action, O for object, T for time, V for environment, P for assertion, and L for linguistic expression. For example, an event "Plane crash" can be described with framework-based specification as Table 1.

Table 1. Specification of event class "plane crash".

Frame<Plane crash>	
Inheritance	Disaster
Action	Plane out of control; Plane crashed; Plane damage; Injured and died; Carry out rescue
Objects	Role 1: Aircraft Type; Role 2: Pilot; Role 3: Passenger; Role 4: Rescue Team; Role 5: Doctor
Place	Geographical Location
Time	Time class
Pre-status	Healthy (Passenger); Normal (Plane); Fly the plane (Pilot)
Post-status	Injured (Passenger); Damage (Plane); Rescue (Doctor)
Linguistic Expression	Action: Come down, Malfunction, Emergency rescue Object: Helicopter, Aircraft captain, Flight attendant

The relations between event classes include taxonomy relation(is-a relation) and non-taxonomy relations. The event hierarchy model consisting of taxonomy relation reflects the level of events. For instance, emergencies as the abstract events can be divided into natural disasters and accident disasters. The event hierarchy model can organize the event knowledge in the domain.

4   Methodology

In this paper, event detection is regarded as the task of calculating the similarity of text pairs. For the text to be detected, the model judges whether it is similar to an event class specification, and then determines whether the text contains an instance of the event type. By comparing with all event class specifications, events contained in the text are detected. The structure of the model is shown in Fig. 2:

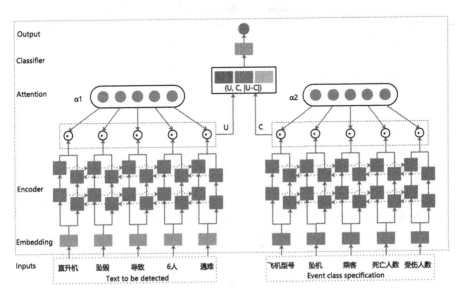

Fig. 2. Structure of event detection model proposed by us. The sequence of "直升机, 坠毁, 导致, 6 人, 遇难" (Helicopter crash killed 6 people) is the input text to be detected. And the sequence of "飞机型号 (aircraft type), 坠机 (crash), 乘客 (passenger), 死亡人数 (number of death), 受伤人数 (number of injured)" is the event class specification composed of event elements.

4.1   Inputs

The model consists of two parts of inputs: text to be detected and the specification of event class. The text is a sequence of Chinese characters. Since there are no natural word delimiters in Chinese, we process the text with the help of word segmentation tool to get the word sequence $S = \{w_1, w_2, \ldots, w_T\}$, where T is the maximum number of words in the text in this batch. The specification of event class is composed of the event elements. We believe that although the specification composed of these words do not strictly follow the grammatical rules, it is full of a strong semantics and can represent an event comprehensively. Therefore, we put the event elements sequence $D = \{e_1, e_2, \ldots, e_T\}$ as another input of the model.

4.2 Word Embedding

Pretrained word embedding has shown excellent performance in many natural language processing (NLP) projects. In this paper, we use the word vector in project [5], which is trained with corpus across various domains by the skip-gram [13] model in word2vec. After looking up the word embedding table $V \in \mathbb{R}^{d_w \times |V|}$, the input word sequence is transformed into the sequence of word embedding as $S' = \{w'_1, w'_2, \ldots, w'_T\}$, where $|V|$ is the vocabulary size, and $w'_i \in \mathbb{R}^{d_w}$ is the embedding of the ith word in the text with the embedding size d_w. Similarly, the sequence of elements D is also transformed into a word embedding sequence $D' = \{e'_1, e'_2, \ldots, e'_T\}$. In the process of training, the embeddings will be updated with the optimization of the model.

4.3 BiLSTM Encoder

In order to enable the awareness the contexts of the input text, we facilitate the exchange of information between the sequences of word embeddings S' or D' by an encoder layer.

Long short-term memory network (LSTM) is a variant of recurrent neural network (RNN), which can effectively solve the problem of gradient exploding or vanishing of simple RNN. A LSTM cell consists of a memory unit for storing the current state and three gates that control the updates of the input of the cell state and the output of LSTM block, respectively.

However, the ordinary LSTM can only take advantage of the information of the previous time. In order to better integrate contextual information, the embeddings will be encoded by Bi-LSTM in our model. As shown in Fig. 2, the model contains a forward LSTM $\overrightarrow{h_i}$ to capture the information of previous time, and a reverse LSTM $\overleftarrow{h_i}$ to capture the information after the forecast time. Then the two outputs of each moment will be connected to obtain the global context information.

$$h_i = \left[\overrightarrow{h_i} \bigoplus \overleftarrow{h_i} \right] \tag{2}$$

4.4 Attention

The importance of the words in the input text is different. For example, in the input of "8 月 31 日下午在挪威北部发生的民用直升机坠毁事故，已导致机上 6 人全部遇难" (The crash of a civilian helicopter in northern Norway on the afternoon of August 31 has killed all 6 people on board), "直升机" (helicopter) corresponds to the "aircraft type" in event class, and "坠机" (crash) best represents the *"Disaster.Plane-crash"* event (perhaps it is an implied event trigger). Therefore, we introduce the attention mechanism into our model to make these keywords receive more attention in the process of training and prediction.

The text to be detected, for instance, is transformed into $H = \{h_1, h_2, ..h_T\}$ after encoding. Firstly, the output h_t of each moment of Bi-LSTM is linearly transformed to get u_t.

$$u_t = tanh\left(W_w h_t + b_w\right) \tag{3}$$

We initialize the vector u_w randomly to represent the meaning of the text, and then multiply it with u_t to get the correlation between each word and the whole text. Then the attention score for the tth word in the input text can be obtained:

$$\alpha_t = \frac{exp\left(u_t^T u_w\right)}{\sum_{t=1}^{T} exp\left(u_t^T u_w\right)} \tag{4}$$

Finally, the representation of the text is obtained by the weighted summation of the output at each moment. In the process of training and prediction, more attention will be paid to h_t, which plays a more important role in expressing the meaning of the text, to extract more important information.

$$U = \sum_{t=1}^{T} \alpha_t \cdot h_t \tag{5}$$

4.5   Event Type Classifier

After the attention layer, the feature representation U and C of the two inputs can be obtained. Then we concatenate U, C, and $|U - C|$ as the feature vector f_c to describe the similarity between the two inputs, where $|U - C|$ is the element-wise difference of the two vectors. Then a fully-connected layer is applied to compute its scores assigned to 0 or 1:

$$O^c = W_c f_c + b_c \tag{6}$$

where $W_c \in \mathbb{R}^{m \times d}$ is the parameter matrix, $b_c \in \mathbb{R}^m$ is the bias.

After obtaining the scores for the feature vector, a softmax layer is applied to normalize the scores:

$$P\left(y_i | x; \theta\right) = \frac{exp\left(O_i^c\right)}{\sum_{j=1}^{2} exp\left(O_i^c\right)} \tag{7}$$

According to the probability distribution of the label, whether the text and event class specification are similar can be learned.

$$\hat{y} = argmax\left(P\left(y_i | x; \theta\right)\right) \tag{8}$$

Among above, $\hat{y}$ is the result of one binary classification. When we predict the events contained in a raw text, each event class will be combined with it to input into our model. The final result is composed of the event types whose binary classification result is 1 in all samples, where N is the number of predefined event types.

$$\hat{Y} = \{\hat{y}_i | \hat{y}_i = 1, i \in N\} \tag{9}$$

4.6   Bias Loss Function

Judging whether the input sentence is similar to all event classes leads to an extreme imbalance between positive and negative classes in the binary classification. Therefore, we introduce focal loss [9], which is widely used in object detection, to reduce the weight of negative samples in the process of training:

$$FL\left(P_t\right) = -\beta_t \left(1 - P_t\right)^\gamma log\left(P_t\right) \tag{10}$$

where $P_t \in [0, 1]$ is the estimated probability for the class with label $\hat{y} = 1$, and $-log\left(P_t\right)$ is standard cross-entropy loss function. On this basis, focal loss introduces a modulating factor $\gamma > 0$ to reduce the loss of samples which is easy to be classified. The weighting factor $\beta \in [0, 1]$ can balance the imbalance of the number of positive and negative samples.

5   Experiment

5.1   Experiment Settings

Dataset. Since the number of Chinese samples of ACE2005 and TAC-KBP datasets commonly used in previous work is very limited, we conduct experiments on DuEE [6], a open source event extraction dataset newly released by Baidu. As the largest Chinese event extraction dataset so far, it is composed of 19640 events, which can be further categorized into 9 event types and 65 event subtypes, and 13% of the samples contained multiple events. The goal of this experiment is to detect the event instances in the text and classify them into the corresponding event subtypes correctly.

Event Ontology. We construct an event hierarchy model including 9 major types of event classes and 65 fine-grained event classes according to the structure of event ontology and the dataset. It contains 340 event element words, which are applied for the experiment as event class specifications.

Evaluation Metrics. Following the previous work [1,10,16], we use Precision (P), Recall (R), F1-score (F_1) to evaluate the results, including in all comparative experiments:

- Precision(P): The proportion of correctly predicted event types to total predicted event types.
- Recall(R): The proportion of correctly predicted event types to total gold event types.
- F1-score(F_1): $(2 * P * R)/(P + R)$

Hyper Parameters. The dataset is divided into training set, verification set and test set at a ratio of 8:1:1, which is based on stratified sampling to ensure that the distribution of event types is consistent in each set. The model is trained for 30 epochs. For all experiments below, we use 300 as the dimension of word embeddings, 150 as the dimension of BiLSTM hidden layer. We set the number of hidden layers to 2 and the dropout rate between layers to 0.5. During the training, we set batch size to 400 and use Adam as the optimizer with a learning rate of 1e−3. We set the β_t in the loss function to 0.98 and γ to 2.

5.2 Overall Performances

In order to prove the effectiveness of the method, we compare it with four representative methods.

- ML Method [20]: feature-based machine learning method, event triggers are classified by logical regression.
- ENSEMBLE [11]: The joint model of RNN and CNN is used to encode and classify the input sequence generated by features.
- DMCNN [1]: The event trigger recognition is regarded as a sequence labeling problem based on the dynamic multi-pooling convolutional neural network.
- TBNNAM [10]: The latest approach of event detection, which is the first work to detect events without triggers in English.

Since the datasets used in these works are different from our paper, we process the corpus and follow the implementation described in their papers to obtain the performance on the DuEE dataset.

Table 2. Overall performance of different methods on the test set.

Model	Single-event			Multi-events			All-events		
	P(%)	R(%)	F_1(%)	P(%)	R(%)	F_1(%)	P(%)	R(%)	F_1(%)
ML Method	71.7	91.4	80.3	84.9	71.2	77.4	74.9	84.6	79.5
ENSEMBLE	80.9	89.2	84.9	93.6	**84.7**	**88.9**	84.6	87.7	86.1
DMCNN	90.6	91.5	91.1	95.2	79.0	86.3	91.9	87.4	89.6
TBNNAM	85.6	76.5	80.8	90.0	75.0	81.8	87.0	76.0	81.1
Our method	**92.6**	**96.3**	**94.4**	**95.8**	80.5	87.5	**93.5**	**91.1**	**92.3**

As Table 2 shows, our method achieves significant improvements over all baselines. Especially for samples that only contain one event, we have high precision and recall. Specifically, compared with the method based on machine learning, our method does not rely on elaborately designed features and complicated NLP tools. Although ENSEMBLE and DMCNN also perform well, the advantage of our model is that it saves the cost of annotating triggers. TBNNAM takes the annotated entity tags as the input feature, therefore, jieba[1] is applied for identifying entity tags in sentences to fit the model in this experiment. There is no denying that this difference will brings some effect on the experimental results, but it is worth noting that entity annotation takes a large amount of human

---

[1] https://github.com/fxsjy/jieba/.

effort, our method avoids this. More importantly, TBNNAM initializes the event type vector randomly for training, while our method defines the event class specifications, takes into account the participants, time, place, and other elements of the event, which brings richer semantics and stronger interpretability.

5.3   Ablation Study

This study aims to validate the impacts of feature extraction methods, attention mechanisms, and modes of feature combination. For this purpose, we design several groups of comparative experiments, and the experimental results are shown in Table 3.

Table 3. Experimental results of adjusting model structure.

Model	P(%)	R(%)	F_1(%)
LSTM	93.5	88.6	91.0
BiLSTM	**94.5**	88.7	**91.5**
CNN	86.0	**91.4**	88.6
No attention	**94.5**	88.7	91.5
With attention	93.5	**91.1**	**92.3**
(U,C)	93.4	89.3	91.3
(|U-C|)	**96.2**	80.8	87.8
(U,C,|U-C|)	93.5	**91.1**	**92.3**

- In the first group, different encoders are applied to extract the features from text. Since standard LSTM can only take advantage of the information of the previous time, it is slightly less effective than BiLSTM. Compared with RNN, which is good at capturing long-distance information, CNN is better at capturing local features. Missing some global information of text, it achieves worse performance in the text similarity learning.
- The second group verifies the importance of attention mechanism. As is shown in Fig. 3, in this sentence, "直升机" (helicopter) and "坠毁" (crash) are the most significant words for the event *"Disaster.Plane-crash"*, our model assigns it with a large attention score.
- In our model, after getting the feature vectors of the input text and the event class, we need to combine them. Different concatenation modes are compared in the third group. The best mode is $(U, C, |U - C|)$, which does not lose information about U and C, meanwhile, reflects their differences.

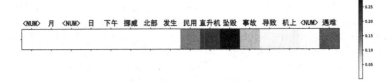

Fig. 3. Visualization of attention mechanism score.

Table 4. Experimental results of adjusting training strategy.

Model	P(%)	R(%)	F_1(%)
Cross entropy	89.3	**93.2**	91.2
Focal loss	**93.5**	91.1	**92.3**
Char-based	92.8	88.0	90.4
Word-based	**93.5**	**91.1**	**92.3**

In addition, we study the influence factors in the training process. As shown in Table 4, we illustrate the effectiveness of focal loss in the first group. Since the weight of positive samples is increased, the model tends to judge that the input text is similar to the event class specification. More positive samples are predicted correctly.

In the second group, we study the effect of the granularity of token on the experiment. In Chinese, characters, as well as word segmentations can be used as the token for training. The experimental result shows that the word-based method achieves better performance. The char-based method loses too much n-gram information and is difficult to fully express the semantics of the text.

6   Conclusions

This paper proposed a novel Chinese event detection method, which can address the problems of high cost of trigger labeling and word-trigger mismatch. The event ontology was introduced as priori knowledge which provides specifications of event classes of different domains. And then, event detection was transformed into the problem of judging which event class specifications are similar to the raw text to be detected through the Siamese network. Experiments showed that our method is effective in Chinese textual event detection, and future work will focus on reducing the dependence on event ontology.

References

1. Chen, Y., Xu, L., Liu, K.: Event extraction via dynamic multi-pooling convolutional neural networks. In: Proceedings of the 53rd Annual Meeting of the Association for Computational Linguistics and the 7th International Joint Conference on Natural Language Processing (vol. 1: Long Papers), pp. 167–176 (2015)

2. Ding, N., Li, Z., Liu, Z.: Event detection with trigger-aware lattice neural network. In: Proceedings of the 2019 Conference on Empirical Methods in Natural Language Processing and the 9th International Joint Conference on Natural Language Processing (EMNLP-IJCNLP), pp. 347–356 (2019)

3. Hong, Y., Zhang, J., Ma, B., Yao, J.: Using cross-entity inference to improve event extraction. In: Proceedings of the 49th Annual Meeting of the Association for Computational Linguistics: Human Language Technologies, pp. 1127–1136 (2011)

4. Ji, H., Grishman, R.: Refining event extraction through cross-document inference. In: Proceedings of ACL-08: Hlt, pp. 254–262 (2008)

5. Li, S., Zhao, Z., Hu, R., Li, W.: Analogical reasoning on Chinese morphological and semantic relations. arXiv preprint arXiv:1805.06504 (2018)

6. Li, X., et al.: DuEE: a large-scale dataset for Chinese event extraction in real-world scenarios. In: Zhu, X., Zhang, M., Hong, Yu., He, R. (eds.) NLPCC 2020. LNCS (LNAI), vol. 12431, pp. 534–545. Springer, Cham (2020). https://doi.org/10.1007/978-3-030-60457-8_44

7. Liao, S., Grishman, R.: Using document level cross-event inference to improve event extraction. In: Proceedings of the 48th Annual Meeting of the Association for Computational Linguistics, pp. 789–797 (2010)

8. Lin, H., Lu, Y., Han, X., Sun, L.: Nugget proposal networks for Chinese event detection. arXiv preprint arXiv:1805.00249 (2018)

9. Lin, T.Y., Goyal, P., Girshick, R., He, K.: Focal loss for dense object detection. In: Proceedings of the IEEE International Conference on Computer Vision, pp. 2980–2988 (2017)

10. Liu, S., Li, Y., Zhang, F., Yang, T.: Event detection without triggers. In: Proceedings of the 2019 Conference of the North American Chapter of the Association for Computational Linguistics: Human Language Technologies, vol. 1 (Long and Short Papers), pp. 735–744 (2019)

11. Liu, W., Yang, Z., Liu, Z.: Chinese event recognition via ensemble model. In: Cheng, L., Leung, A.C.S., Ozawa, S. (eds.) ICONIP 2018. LNCS, vol. 11305, pp. 255–264. Springer, Cham (2018). https://doi.org/10.1007/978-3-030-04221-9_23

12. Liu, Z.T., Huang, M., Zhou, W., Zhong, Z.: Research on event-oriented ontology model. Comput. Sci. **36**(11), 189–192 (2009)

13. Mikolov, T., Chen, K., Corrado, G.: Efficient estimation of word representations in vector space. arXiv preprint arXiv:1301.3781 (2013)

14. Mueller, J., Thyagarajan, A.: Siamese recurrent architectures for learning sentence similarity. In: Proceedings of the AAAI Conference on Artificial Intelligence, vol. 30 (2016)

15. Neculoiu, P., Versteegh, M., Rotaru, M.: Learning text similarity with Siamese recurrent networks. In: Proceedings of the 1st Workshop on Representation Learning for NLP, pp. 148–157 (2016)

16. Nguyen, T., Grishman, R.: Graph convolutional networks with argument-aware pooling for event detection. In: Proceedings of the AAAI Conference on Artificial Intelligence, vol. 32 (2018)

17. Nguyen, T.H., Cho, K., Grishman, R.: Joint event extraction via recurrent neural networks. In: Proceedings of the 2016 Conference of the North American Chapter of the Association for Computational Linguistics: Human Language Technologies, pp. 300–309 (2016)

18. Xiangyu, X., Tong, Z., Wei, Y., Jinglei, Z.: A hybrid character representation for chinese event detection. In: 2019 International Joint Conference on Neural Networks (IJCNN), pp. 1–8. IEEE (2019)

19. Yan, H., Jin, X., Meng, X.: Event detection with multi-order graph convolution and aggregated attention. In: Proceedings of the 2019 Conference on Empirical Methods in Natural Language Processing and the 9th International Joint Conference on Natural Language Processing (EMNLP-IJCNLP), pp. 5770–5774 (2019)
20. Zhao, Y., Qin, B., Che, W.X., Liu, T.: Research on Chinese event extraction. J. Chinese Inf. Process. **22**(1), 3–8 (2008)

Alzheimer's Disease Prediction Using EfficientNet and Fastai

Rahma Kadri[✉], Mohamed Tmar, and Bassem Bouaziz

Higher Institute of Computer Science and Multimedia University of Sfax Tunisia,
Sakiet Ezzit, Tunisia

Abstract. Deep Learning has shown promising results on the field of Alzheimer's computerized diagnosis based on the neuroimaging data. Alzheimer disease is an irreversible and progressive neurodegenerative disorder that destroys gradually the brain cells. This chronic disease affect the ability of the person to carry out daily tasks. It caused many problems such as cognitive deficits, problem with recognition, memory loss and difficulties with thinking. The major breakthrough in neuroscience today is the accurate early detection of the Alzheimer's disease based on various brain biomarkers. Magnetic resonance imaging (MRI) is a noninvasive brain modality widely used for brain diseases detection specifically Alzheimer disease. It visualize a discriminate feature of the neurodegeneration which is the progressive cerebral atrophy. Various studies based on deep learning models have been proposed for the task of Alzheimer's disease classification and prediction from brain MRI scans. However these models have been implemented from scratch. The training from scratch is tedious and time-consuming task. In this paper we conduct an analysis using Open Access Series of Imaging Studies (OASIS) dataset based on tuning different convolution neural networks. Further we propose a uni-modal Alzheimer method prediction using Efficientnet network. The Efficientnet network solve the main issues of the existing convolution neural network. Data preparation includes some preprocessing steps such as image resizing. We achieve 79% using VGG16, 92% using Resenet,93% using Densenet and we produce an accuracy of 96% using the Efficientnet model.

Keywords: Alzheimer's prediction · CNN · Transfer learning · Fast.ai · Efficientnet network

1 Introduction

The medical image analysis presents a powerful and unparalleled tool for the diseases diagnosis issued by a specialist. These images provide an efficient biomarkers for an accurate diagnosis and treatment of various neurodegenerative diseases. The early diagnosis of neurodegenerative disorders can slow the progression of these diseases and the degeneration process. Alzheimer's disease is a common neurological disorder that causes the death of brain cells. The early

© Springer Nature Switzerland AG 2021
H. Qiu et al. (Eds.): KSEM 2021, LNAI 12816, pp. 452–463, 2021.
https://doi.org/10.1007/978-3-030-82147-0_37

prediction of this disease has been a challenging task. Neuroimaging research focuses on the collection of different types of image modalities such as Magnetic Resonance Imaging(MRI) images, Functional magnetic resonance imaging(fMRI), Electroencephalography(EEG). These modalities present a powerful neuroimaging techniques for investigating the structure and the function of the human brain. Magnetic resonance imaging (MRI) is widely used for the neuropathology and for discovering the clinical mechanisms of Alzheimer's disease (AD). It reveal the brain atrophy and the characteristic cerebral changes. It enable to cover the patterns of brain damage that discriminate AD from other brain illnesses and brain abnormalities.

Machine learning techniques has unlocked unprecedented success and growing interest in neuroimaging research. Nevertheless, recent studies have proved that deep learning models are more accurate then the traditional machine learning techniques. The application of deep learning on healthcare problems such as brain disease prediction and detection has garnered significant interest.

Convolution neural network has been shown such outstanding performance on the AD detection. The success of convolution networks are typically reliance on the availability of large-scale datastes for model training. For this end researchers collect imaging data with large samples. The application of convolution neural networks face a serious challenges. The limited availability of labeled medical dataset. Further the data unbalance problem leads to the degradation of the network performance. After investigating the CNN models performance on the AD detection using the CNN models. We underline that the main issue of these networks how to choose correctly the key parameters such as the network depth, width and the resolution. In these networks these parameters are chosen arbitrary without an effective scale method. The Efficientnet network deal and solve this issue.

In this research study:

- We propose and evaluate the performance of different CNN models based on the transfer learning.
- We propose a multi class-AD detection based on the Efficientnet network using pytroch and fastai library.

This paper is organized as flows: Sect. 1 outlines the main recent contributions using deep learning for the Alzheimer's disease detection and prediction. Section 2 describes the proposed method and the Sect. 3 highlights the main outputs of each CNN model and the proposed newtork.

2   Related Work

Convolution neural network has garnered significant interest [5] applied CNN on T2-weighted brain magnetic resonance images for AD classification. They achieved a 90.47% accuracy. [14] combine 2D convolution neural network and ensemble learning. The CNN model involves eight layers. They identify patterns of MRI brain changes that characterize AD and MCIc. They address the problem of unbalance dataset by data augmentation techniques. They collect data from the ADNI dataset. Preprocessig steps include re-sliced the images into three 2D image sets, each of the sagittal, coronal, or transverse orientation. [3] also use 2D CNN composed by five convolutional layers. They collect data from OASIS dataset. These models are trained from scratch which is a tedious and time-consuming task. Various studies solve this problem by the transfer learning. [9] adopt a transfer learning based on deep convolutional neural network for an early diagnosis of Alzheimer's disease. They use the VGG16 as feature extractor pretrained on ImageNet dataset. [13] also adopt a pre-trained AlexNet model for AD classification. [10] accurately predict MCI-to-AD conversion with magnetic resonance imaging (MRI) data using a transfer learning. This method achieves an accuracy of 79.9%. [8] use only an MRI brain images for Alzheimer's disease classification. Here they achieve 95.73% as accuracy. [11] use the same modality MR imaging data the for automatic hippocampus segmentation and classification in Alzheimer's disease. They achieves an accuracy of 88.9% new deep. They propose a stack of CNN models for simultaneous hippocampal segmentation and disease classification using only an MRI data.

[1] use an structural MRI data for predicting the subset of MCI individuals that would progress to AD within three years (progressive MCI) and the subset of MCI individuals that do not progress to AD within this period (stable MCI). [7] distinguish between healthy people and the two types of MCI groups based on MRI results. The results showed the best overall classification between CN and LMCI groups in the sagittal view with an accuracy of 94.54%. In addition, 93.96% and 93.00% accuracy were reached for the pairs of EMCI/LMCI and CN/EMCI, respectively. [2] propose a method that combines the sMRI and MD imaging modalities for the classification of Alzheimer Disease. Here to meet the lack of data, they propose a method of a cross modal transfer learning. [12] compare the conventional machine learning and the transfer learning on the AD detection using MRI modality based on an ensemble of pretrained CNNs. They evaluated investigated the potential application of the transfer-learning approach using the ADNI dataset. They noticed that the transfer learning provide an accurate results over the tradional machine learning methods. They also proved that the deep-learning network trained from scratch provide a lower performance than the transfer learning methods. [4] also underline that the transfer learning provide a promising results. They compare different CNN models using the transfer learning on the ADNI dataset. According to their experiments, DenseNet showed better performance. Some studies focuses on the 3D CNN to overcome the infroramtion loss caused by the 2D CNN. For example [16] use a 3D VGG16 to avoid the information loss. They achieved 73.4% as classification accuracy on ADNI and 69.9% on OASIS dataset. [15] propose a three-way classification of AD-MCI-NC using cascaded three dimensional-convolutional neural network for AD classification They achieved a good accuracy 97.77%. However 3D CNN are slowly to train. [6] propose a 2d CNN for 3-class AD classification problem using T1-weighted MRI. The model is based on ResNet34 as feature extractor and then trained a classifier using 64×64 sized patches from coronal

2D MRI slices. They explores the MRI volumetric information, by using non-consecutive 2D slices as input channels of the CNN. They achieved an accuracy of 68%.

3   Materials and Methods

In this section, we explain the main components of our framework. We use different CNN models using pytroch and fast ai library. We opt fast AI library due to its flexibility. Further we adopt the EfficientNet network. The core idea behind this network is to scale the traditional convolution neural network to achieve a good accuracy. The main issue of the convolution neural network is model scaling. Model scaling is how to increase the model depth in size to obtain better prediction without degrading the training performance. The key challenge in the convolution neural network designing is the network depth and size. The EfficientNet model deal with this issue by uniformly scaling the depth network, the width and the resolution basing on a compound coefficient. As illustrated by the Fig. 1 the Efficientnet network is upon two strategies. The first strategy is an optimization baseline architecture that ensure a fast training. The second strategy is the scaling method that ensure a depth network without degrading the accuracy. The baseline architecture is relies on a 2D Depthwise convolution blocks. It is composed by a set of mobile inverted bottleneck convolution (MBConv). The main advantages of the EfficientNet model over the convolution neural networks is the method scaling with a set of fixed scaling coefficients. Whereas the convolution neural networks scales randomly these factors which decrease the accuracy. EfficientNet model achieve higher accuracy over the existing CNNs. We make use of the EfficientNet network because it provide a reliable compound scaling method that produce a good accuracy without degrading the network performance. Further this method enhance the ability of the model for prediction. In addition this method ensure a effective parameters reducing.

Fig. 1. Efficientnet architecture

3.1   Formalization

$x \in X$ is the input three-dimensional (3D) image.
$y \in Y$ is the output the classes non-demented, very mild dementia, mild dementia and moderate dementia, respectively

F : X → Y : the function which predicts a class y for an input image with minimum error rate.

3.2   Data Collection

In this study, we select data from OASIS dataset which is a well-known dataset. It is prepared by Dr. Randy Buckner from the Howard HughesMedical Institute (HHMI) at Harvard University, the Neuroinformatics ResearchGroup (NRG) at Washington University School of Medicine, and the BiomedicalInformatics Research Network (BIRN). This dataset encompasses 416 subjects aged 18 to 96. Each subject described by a set of attributes such as Clinical Dementia Rating (CDR), nondemented, very mild to mild Alzheimer's disease (AD), nondemented, and nondemented. The subjects were scanned all right-handed. This dataset includes tow types of subjects men (n = 62) and women (n = 88) (Fig. 2).

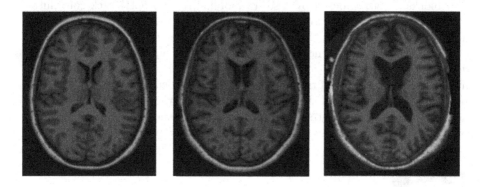

Fig. 2. Sample images from OASIS dataset

3.3   Image Pre-processing

The pre-processing of the images is an important factor to be considered before the feature extraction. Image pre-processing here includes image resizing. We resize all the input images to 224*224*3 in order to fit them with the different CNN models.

3.4   Training Strategy

Training strategy is based on fixing a set of parameters such as selection a training data, test data, batch size, number of epoches and the learning rate. In the proposed work, training data are form the OASIS dataset, we select 75% as the training dataset. We selected a batch size of 35 MRI images for training. Testing data is a 25% of the data was the testing dataset. We set the number of classes to 4 refers to the AD stages (Nondemented; very mild dementia; mild dementia and moderate dementia) We used a dropout technique rate of 0.5 to avoid the overfitting. We opt the cross-entropy as loss function. The dataset is unbalanced for this, we employed Stochastic Gradient Descent (SGD) as the optimizer. We set the learning rate parameter of 0.1 in the SGD optimizer.

3.5   Data Augmentation

Over-fitting problem and the imbalance dataset present a big challenge within the CNN models training. Data augmentation technique is used to mitigate these problems. It is a common method to enlarge the dataset. This process is the creation of synthetic data to increase the amount of training data. Data augmentation is based on the application of various transformations on the existing data to synthesize and create new data. Hence we adopt the six data augmentation techniques which includes image scaling, translation, random affine transformation ad depicted in the Fig. 3.

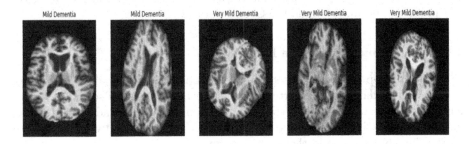

Fig. 3. Data augmentation

4   Results

In this section, we present the different network performances using OASIS dataset.

4.1   The Application of the VGG16

The VGG16 is a deeper network that ensure an effective feature extraction. The stacked layers with small kernel size increase the network depth. Hence it ensure a complex and representative feature extraction. We achieved an accuracy of 79%. Regarding the application of this network on the OASIS dataset. This network is very slow to train. It is a heavier model that require more training time. The application of the VGG 16 produce the vanishing gradient problem which degrades the network performance.

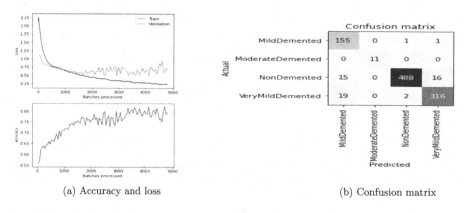

(a) Accuracy and loss   (b) Confusion matrix

Fig. 4. The application of the VGG16

Figure 4b illustrates the evaluation of the performance of the VGG16 on the OASIS dataset. This experiment demonstrate that VGG16 don't achieve a stable and promising performance on the OASIS datasest.

4.2   The Application of the Resent152

VGG16 and deep networks caused the problem of vanishing gradient. The skip connections or the identity shortcut connection between layers solve this problem. This connection skips the training from some layers and add them to the output. The core idea and the building blocks of the residual networks are based on the skip connection and the residual mapping.

We obtain 92% as an accuracy value as illustrated by the Fig. 5. Resent ensure a fast training and higher accuracy over the VGG16.

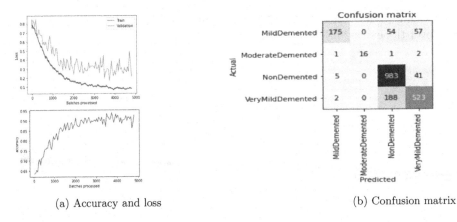

(a) Accuracy and loss   (b) Confusion matrix

Fig. 5. The application of the Resent152

4.3 AlexNet

Alexnet network is a deeper architecture that made up of eight layers. This network don't provide a good results. We achieve 0.63% as accuracy using Alexnet (Fig. 6).

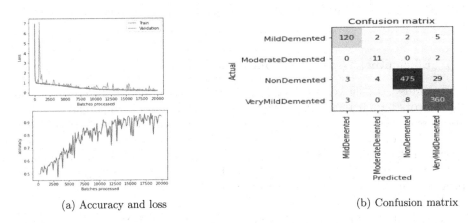

(a) Accuracy and loss   (b) Confusion matrix

Fig. 6. The application of AlexNet

This network showed the lowest accuracy over the CNN models.

4.4 Densenet

Densely Connected Convolutional Networks is a particular type of deep network that use specific connection between layers called dense connections. This network prove that the convolution neural network can be deeper without decreasing the training performance with the shorter connection. It requires fewer parameters over the exiting CNN networks.

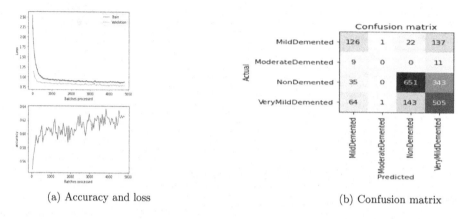

(a) Accuracy and loss   (b) Confusion matrix

Fig. 7. Densenet network application

The classification with DenseNets produce an accuracy of 92%. The main advantage of this network is that require a fewer parameters over the existing CNN models. Figure 7 illustrate the DenseNets performance on the OASIS dataset.

4.5 Efficientnet Network Application

The main issue of the convolution neural networks as illustrated by the results is the network parameters such as the depth, the width and the neurons numbers are chosen arbitrarily. The depth of the network is the total number of layers that composed network. The width is related to the number of neurons in each layer and the number of filters in a convolutions layer. The resolution refers to the height and width of the input image. Efficientnet as depicted in the Fig. 8 provide a higher accuracy (96%) over the CNN networks due to the scaling method.

The Table 1 compare the different performances of CNN models and the EfficientNet network Comparing to the studies in the literature during the last three years our method ensure an optimized training and optimal time complexity due to the optimization strategy of the EfficientNet network. Further the network require fewer parameters which reduce the time complexity. In addition Fastai is flexible framework that simplifies the training and make it faster.

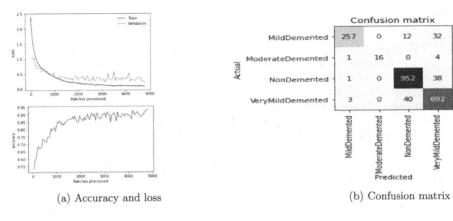

(a) Accuracy and loss   (b) Confusion matrix

Fig. 8. EfficientNet network application

Table 1. Comparative table between the different models

Network	Accuracy
VGG16	79%
ReseNet152	92%
AlexNet	63%
DenseNet	92%
EfficientNet	96%

5   Conclusion and Future Work

Deep Learning algorithm continue to provide a reliable results within the Alzheimer's disease detection and prediction. This disease is the most form of dementia. The early prediction of the AD disease prevent its progression. In this paper we proposed to evaluate different CNN models using transfer learning. The results shows that the densenet network achieve the better results over the vgg16, alexent and resenet networks. Further we proposed an Alzheimer prediction method based on the Efficientnet network. We proposed a model based the Efficientnet network to solve the main problems of the existing CNN models. The main limitation of the convolution neural networks is the degradation of the performance with deeper networks. EfficientNet model ensure a higher accuracy and better efficiency over the existing CNN models. It scaled the traditional CNN model with multiple dimensions. However Our proposed work is based only on the MRI modality. We propose as future work a multi-modality method based on the Alzheimer's Disease Neuroimaging Initiative (ADNI) dataset.

References

1. Abrol, A., Fu, Z., Du, Y., Calhoun, V.D.: Multimodal data fusion of deep learning and dynamic functional connectivity features to predict Alzheimer's disease progression. In: 2019 41st Annual International Conference of the IEEE Engineering in Medicine and Biology Society (EMBC), IEEE (July 2019). https://doi.org/10.1109/embc.2019.8856500

2. Aderghal, K., Khvostikov, A., Krylov, A., Benois-Pineau, J., Afdel, K., Catheline, G.: Classification of Alzheimer disease on imaging modalities with deep CNNs using cross-modal transfer learning. In: 2018 IEEE 31st International Symposium on Computer-Based Medical Systems (CBMS), IEEE (June 2018). https://doi.org/10.1109/cbms.2018.00067

3. Al-Khuzaie, F.E.K., Bayat, O., Duru, A.D.: Diagnosis of Alzheimer disease using 2d MRI slices by convolutional neural network. Appl. Bionics Biomech. **2021**, 1–9 (2021). https://doi.org/10.1155/2021/6690539

4. Ashraf, A., Naz, S., Shirazi, S.H., Razzak, I., Parsad, M.: Deep transfer learning for alzheimer neurological disorder detection. Multimedia Tools Appl. 1–26 (2021). https://doi.org/10.1007/s11042-020-10331-8

5. Basheera, S., Ram, M.S.S.: Convolution neural network–based alzheimer's disease classification using hybrid enhanced independent component analysis based segmented gray matter of t2 weighted magnetic resonance imaging with clinical valuation. Alzheimer's Dementia: Transl. Res. Clin. Interventions **5**(1), 974–986 (2019). https://doi.org/10.1016/j.trci.2019.10.001

6. de Carvalho Pereira, M.E., Fantini, I., Lotufo, R.A., Rittner, L.: An extended-2d CNN for multiclass alzheimer's disease diagnosis through structural MRI. In: Hahn, H.K., Mazurowski, M.A. (eds.) Medical Imaging 2020: Computer-Aided Diagnosis. SPIE (March 2020). https://doi.org/10.1117/12.2550753

7. Gorji, K.: A deep learning approach for diagnosis of mild cognitive impairment based on MRI images. Brain Sci. **9**(9), 217 (2019). https://doi.org/10.3390/brainsci9090217

8. Islam, J., Zhang, Y.: Early diagnosis of alzheimer's disease: a neuroimaging study with deep learning architectures. In: 2018 IEEE/CVF Conference on Computer Vision and Pattern Recognition Workshops (CVPRW), IEEE (June 2018). https://doi.org/10.1109/cvprw.2018.00247

9. Jain, R., Jain, N., Aggarwal, A., Hemanth, D.J.: Convolutional neural network based alzheimer's disease classification from magnetic resonance brain images. Cogn. Syst. Res. **57**, 147–159 (2019). https://doi.org/10.1016/j.cogsys.2018.12.015

10. Lin, W., et al.: Convolutional neural networks-based MRI image analysis for the alzheimer's disease prediction from mild cognitive impairment. Front. Neurosci. 12 (November 2018). https://doi.org/10.3389/fnins.2018.00777

11. Liu, M., et al.: A multi-model deep convolutional neural network for automatic hippocampus segmentation and classification in alzheimer's disease. NeuroImage **208**, (2020). https://doi.org/10.1016/j.neuroimage.2019.116459

12. Nanni, L., et al.: Comparison of transfer learning and conventional machine learning applied to structural brain MRI for the early diagnosis and prognosis of alzheimer's disease. Front. Neurology 11 (November 2020). https://doi.org/10.3389/fneur.2020.576194

13. Nawaz, H., Maqsood, M., Afzal, S., Aadil, F., Mehmood, I., Rho, S.: A deep feature-based real-time system for Alzheimer disease stage detection. Multimedia Tools Appl. 1–19 (2020). https://doi.org/10.1007/s11042-020-09087-y

14. Pan, D., Zeng, A., Jia, L., Huang, Y., Frizzell, T., Song, X.: Early detection of alzheimer's disease using magnetic resonance imaging: a novel approach combining convolutional neural networks and ensemble learning. Front. Neurosci. **14**, (May 2020). https://doi.org/10.3389/fnins.2020.00259
15. Raju, M., Gopi, V.P., Anitha, V.S., Wahid, K.A.: Multi-class diagnosis of alzheimer's disease using cascaded three dimensional-convolutional neural network. Phys. Eng. Sci. Med. 1–10 (2020). https://doi.org/10.1007/s13246-020-00924-w
16. Yagis, E., Citi, L., Diciotti, S., Marzi, C., Atnafu, S.W., Herrera, A.G.S.D.: 3d convolutional neural networks for diagnosis of alzheimer's disease via structural MRI. In: 2020 IEEE 33rd International Symposium on Computer-Based Medical Systems (CBMS), IEEE (July 2020). https://doi.org/10.1109/cbms49503.2020.00020

Interval Occlusion Calculus with Size Information

Juan Chen[1,2,3] (ID), Ang Gao[2], Haiyang Jia[1,2,3](✉) (ID), Yuanteng Xu[2], and Xianglu Zhou[1]

[1] College of Computer Science and Technology, Jilin University, Changchun 130012, China
Jiahy@jlu.edu.cn
[2] College of Software, Jilin University, Changchun 130012, China
[3] Key Laboratory of Symbolic Computation and Knowledge Engineering of Ministry of Education, Jilin University, Changchun 130012, China

Abstract. Spatial occlusion is an important way for human beings to build up the visual perceptions and the awareness of environments. Focusing on 2D disk-like objects, a new framework INterval and DUration (INDU) Occlusion Calculus is proposed. It includes 39 basic relations. This formalism extends Interval Occlusion Calculus with the relative size information. Also, it can be seen as an extension of INDU calculus with interval-based definitions of spatial occlusion. INDU Occlusion Calculus is closed under intersection, inverse and composition. And its running complexity results are presented. The partitions of the plane by the basic INDU occlusion relations are systematically discussed under different situations. These partitions decide the possible paths describing the continuous movements of the observers and the observed relations in the transition network. Several application scenarios observed by single or multiple viewpoints are discusses with examples.

Keywords: Qualitative Spatial Reasoning · Occlusion · Interval Occlusion Calculus · INDU calculus

1 Introductions

Spatial information is quite important in human daily life. Although quantitative approaches can provide the precise information, the numeric information is often unnecessary or unavailable. Qualitative approach dealing with spatial and temporal information known as Qualitative Spatial Reasoning (QSR) [1–4] is a promising way to handle the information at this level. It is a subfield of knowledge representation and reasoning in Artificial Intelligence, which concerns the qualitative formalism between spatial objects including topology, direction, size, motions and the integrations etc.

This paper concentrates on qualitative spatial occlusion relations, which arises when one object obscures the view of another. It is one of the visual perceptions we build up the awareness of environments. Occlusion calculi describe the binary relations between two objects, how their positions look from a viewpoint. Perhaps the first qualitative formalization of spatial occlusion is proposed in [5] which designed a set of axioms to

© Springer Nature Switzerland AG 2021
H. Qiu et al. (Eds.): KSEM 2021, LNAI 12816, pp. 464–473, 2021.
https://doi.org/10.1007/978-3-030-82147-0_38

constrain a point-based notion of occlusions. Considering the 2D convex regions, [6] proposes the Lines-of-Sight calculus that describes the relations between the projective images of the 3D bodies. Extending the images from convex regions to concave regions, [7] builds the Region Occlusion Calculus (ROC), which defines the occlusion and image parallax within a mereo-topological theory. [8] proposes a set of relations making explicit the distinctions of whether the observed objects are fragmented or not, and whether the occluder is a moving object or part of the background. [9] and [10] forward an Interval Occlusion Calculus (IOC) to describe the relative positions between the projective images of rigid convex regions and discuss the translation among the multiple viewpoints.

The above viewpoint-dependent QSR calculi concern only the topological relations between the projective images. However, size information is easy to observe and plays an important role. Building on IOC, INDU Occlusion Calculus is proposed to combine the size information. The paper is structured as follows. Section 2 describes the basic concepts in occlusion calculus. Section 3 presents the basic definitions of IOC. Section 4 gives the formal descriptions of INDU Occlusion Calculus and its computation complexity. Section 5 discusses the use of transition network in describing the continuous movement with one viewpoint and multiple viewpoints.

2   Basic Concepts

Let's consider two kinds of entities living in 2D Euclidean space: objects and observers which are rigid and convex. The objects can be identified by their centroids, and the observers as pairs $\sigma_i = (p_i, \overrightarrow{v}_i)$, where p_i is the position of the observer$_i$'s centroid and $\overrightarrow{v}_i$ is the unit vector representing the observer$_i$'s orientation.

The field of vision σ is a sector of the plane decided by the vision width of the devices, as shown in Fig. 1. An image of an object from a viewpoint σ is defined as the set of projected half-lines originating at σ, and contained in σ's field of view, that intersects the object [1]. Assume that function $image(A, \sigma) = a$ projects the real object A to its image a seen from the viewpoint σ. Images are intervals defined by the extreme points of observed objects projected on an observer's image plane i.e. the segments defined on arcs, curved intervals. Figure 1 shows a is overlapped by b and they are clockwise.

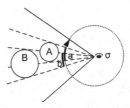

Fig. 1. See from the viewpoint σ, the images of A and B has IOC relations $a\ oi^+\ b : \sigma$

A layered image of a from the viewpoint σ is defined as a pair $a = (a', l_a)$ where l_a is the layer of a representing a linear ordering (the closer an object is to the observer, the greater is its associated l) of images observed from σ. Function $l(a) = l_a$ maps a layered image to its layer, $extent(a) = a'$ extracts the prime image of a, as Fig. 1 shows that a is overlapped and is in front of b from σ.

In this paper, we discuss the disk-like objects which identified by their centroids. Also, we suppose that the observer can get all the objects in its field of view, *i.e.* no object is partially perceived. So, all the images must be consecutive arcs distributed on a semi-circle. The size information is the pairwise relations between the length of image arcs.

3 Interval Occlusion Calculus

In 1983, Allen [11] proposed the Interval Algebra to solve the deduction problems of time intervals, and then it was introduced to the field of QSR. It includes 13 basic relations as shown in Table 1.

Table 1. The basic relations of interval algebra

Basic relation	Symbol	Inverse relation	Meaning	Basic relation	Symbol	Inverse relation	Meaning
Precedes	p	pi		During	d	di	
Meets	m	mi		Finishes	f	fi	
Overlaps	o	oi		Equal	e	e	
Starts	s	si					

The Interval Occlusion Calculus [9, 10] extends Allen's Interval Algebra and defines a set of 22 basic relations representing the possible occlusion relations between pairs of image arcs in a field of view less than 180°. Given two layered intervals a and b representing the observation of two distinct objects A and B from viewpoint σ, *i.e.* $image(A, \sigma) = a = (a', l_a)$ and $image(B, \sigma) = b = (b', l_b)$. The basic IOC relations can be defined as follows, where the original Allen's relations are assigned a superscript apostrophe. (For brevity, inverse relations are omitted).

- $a\,p\,b : \sigma$, read as "a precedes b from σ" iff $a'p'b'$ implies $l_a = l_b$
- $a\,m\,b : \sigma$, read as "a meets b from σ" iff $a'm'b'$ implies $l_a = l_b$
- $a\,o^+\,b : \sigma$, read as "a overlaps and is in front of b from σ" iff $a'o'b'$ and $l_a > l_b$
- $a\,o^-\,b : \sigma$, read as "a overlaps b and b is in front of a from σ" iff $a'o'b'$ and $l_a < l_b$
- $a\,s^+\,b : \sigma$, read as "a starts and is in front of b from σ" iff $a's'b'$ and $l_a > l_b$
- $a\,s^-\,b : \sigma$, read as "a starts b and b is in front of a from σ" iff $a's'b'$ and $l_a < l_b$
- $a\,d^+\,b : \sigma$, read as "a is during and is in front of b from σ" iff $a'd'b'$ and $l_a > l_b$
- $a\,d^-\,b : \sigma$, read as "a is during b and b is in front of a from σ" iff $a'd'b'$ and $l_a < l_b$
- $a\,f^+\,b : \sigma$, read as "a finishes and is in front of b from σ" iff $a'f'b'$ and $l_a > l_b$
- $a\,f^-\,b : \sigma$, read as "a finishes b and b is in front of a from σ" iff $a'f'b'$ and $l_a < l_b$
- $a\,c^+\,b : \sigma$, read as "a coincides with and is in front of b from σ" iff $a'eq'b'$ and $l_a > l_b$
- $a\,c^-\,b : \sigma$, read as "a coincides with b is in front of a from σ" iff $a'eq'b'$ and $l_a < l_b$

There is also a reflexive, symmetric and transitive relation a eq b : σ, read as "a equals b from σ" which only holds if $a'eq'b'$ and $l_a = l_b$. This relation may occur when two objects with same size are twisted together. As we only consider the rigid disk-like 2D objects, this relation cannot be realized. Note that the layer information only can be effectively used under the occlusion state. Figure 2 gives the plane partitions, *i.e.*, when A is smaller than B, how the positions of the viewpoint distributed *s.t.* A and B satisfies a certain basic IOC relation.

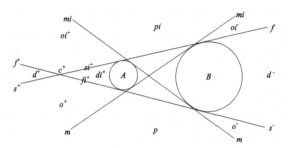

Fig. 2. The lines of sight between two objects A and B and the basic IOC relations.

4 INDU Occlusion Calculus

The INDU calculus [12, 13] extends the 13 basic Allen's interval relations with relative size information (also known as duration information) represented by $\{<,=,>\}$, resulting in 25 basic relations. For example, a $s_<$ b means that a starts b and a is shorter than b. So, it is natural to combines the IOC with the relative size information.

In IOC, 15 basic relations between any two image arcs implicitly represent the relations between their corresponding length. These include $\{s^+, s^-, d^+, d^-, f^+, f^-, c^+, c^-, eq\}$ and their inverse relations. The remaining relations, *i.e.* $\{o^+, o^-, p, m\}$ and their inverse relations, nothing is known about the length of the respective image arcs. Therefore, we need total 39 basic relations to model qualitative information about the image arcs and their lengths. They are $\{s_<^+, s_<^-, d_<^+, d_<^-, f_<^+, f_<^-, c_=^+, c_=^-, p_<, p_=, p_>, m_<, m_=, m_>, o_<^+, o_=^+, o_>^+, o_<^-, o_=^-, o_>^-, eq\}$ and their inverse relations. In another way the basic INDU occlusion relations are the combination of basic INDU relations with the layer function l mentioned in Sect. 2.

The composition of INDU occlusion relations, considering a single viewpoint is defined as follows, which is quite like the definitions in 9.

Definition 1. Composition of INDU occlusion relations. Let a basic relation in INDU occlusion calculus be either r_k, t_k, r_k^+, t_k^+, r_k^-, t_k^-, where $k \in \{<, =, >\}$ for a given viewpoint, and Let r'_k and t'_k denote the original INDU basic relation. Then, the composition in INDU occlusion calculus is defined by the following cases:

- $r_k^+ \circ t_k^+ = \left(r_k' \circ' t_k'\right)^+;$
- $r_k^- \circ t_k^- = \left(r_k' \circ' t_k'\right)^-;$
- $r_k^+ \circ t_k^-, r_k^- \circ t_k^+$ and $r_k \circ t_k = \{(r_k' \circ' t_k')^+ \cup (r_k' \circ' t_k')^- \cup \{eq\}\}$ if t_k' is the inverse of r_k';
- $r_k^+ \circ t_k^-, r_k^- \circ t_k^+$ and $r_k \circ t_k = \{(r_k' \circ' t_k')^+ \cup (r_k' \circ' t_k')^-\}$, otherwise.

where $\circ'$ refers to composition in INDU calculus, the symbol in the left of formula like $p_<^-$ is known as $p_<$.

Theorem 1. The INDU occlusion calculus is closed under the composition, but does not form a relation algebra.

Proof: For any basic INDU occlusion relation r_k^l is the cartesian product of basic IOC r^l with $\{<,=,>\}$, where IOC and PA (point algebra) are closed respectively [9], so the INDU occlusion is also closed.

In another aspect, the basic INDU occlusion relation r_k^l is the cartesian product of basic INDU r_k with layer information $\{+, -\}$. Since the weak composition table of INDU calculus does not define a relation algebra [13], the occlusion version does not form a relation algebra either.

Theorem 2. The consistency problem on a network of basic INDU occlusion relations is polynomial.

Proof: The basic INDU occlusion network can be divided into two orthogonal dimensions: the INDU network and the layer network. Ignoring the layer information, the INDU occlusion network can be reduced to the original INDU calculus. Therefore, the basic INDU network's consistency problem is polynomial [13].

Now consider the layer information. Relations such as $\{p, pi, m, mi\}$ result in the universal constraint for the layer. Other relations imply the basic relation of the point algebra. Therefore, the consistency can be solved in cubic time [14].

Theorem 3. The consistency problem on a network of a subset of basic INDU occlusion relations with the form $r_=^l$ can be decided in cubic time.

Proof: Similar as the proof of Theorem 2. The INDU networks consisted by the relation with the form $r_=$ can be decided in cubic time by $\Diamond$-closure method [13].

The partition of the plane by the basic INDU occlusion relations can gives direct correspondence between the changes of viewpoint positions and the basic relations, which is quite useful in many application scenarios (discussed in Sect. 5). Since the proposed calculus is closely related with relative size information, it is necessary to calculate where to place the viewpoint σ s.t. the image arcs are in the same length. We first construct a rectangular coordinate whose origin is the centroid of A, and the x-axis goes through the centroid of B. The question then is when $\angle\alpha = \angle\beta$, what does the track of σ look like (Fig. 3).

Let $m = R_A/R_B = |\sigma A|/|\sigma B|$ where R_A and R_B are the radiuses of object A and B, $k = x_B$, i.e. the distance between the two centroids. Then according to trigonometry, we have

$$x_\sigma^2 + y_\sigma^2 = |\sigma A|^2 = m^2 |\sigma B|^2 = m^2((k - x_\sigma)^2 + y_\sigma^2) \tag{1}$$

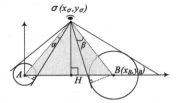

Fig. 3. The viewpoint σ and the angles corresponding to the two arbitrary objects.

After expanding,

$$x_\sigma^2 + \frac{2m^2k}{(1-m^2)}x_\sigma + y_\sigma^2 = \frac{m^2k^2}{1-m^2} \tag{2}$$

is satisfied, which is a circle formula as the following

$$(x_\sigma - \frac{m^2k}{m^2-1})^2 + y_\sigma^2 = (\frac{mk}{1-m^2})^2 \tag{3}$$

It means when $m \neq 1$, the track of the viewpoint *s.t.* the image arcs are in the same length is circular. Its center is $(m^2k/(m^2-1), 0)$ and the radius is $mk/(1-m^2)$. Obviously, the circle must go through the intersections of the internal and external tangent lines of A and B. Otherwise, A and B are in same size, the track degenerates to a vertical line, which is perpendicular to the parallel external tangent lines. And it goes through the intersection of the internal tangent lines of two objects, as shown in Fig. 4. If the viewpoint is on the left side of the vertical line, then the image arcs $a' > b'$. Otherwise, on the right side, $\angle\alpha < \angle\beta$, *i.e.* $a' < b'$.

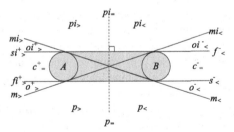

Fig. 4. The lines of sight between two objects A and B and the basic INDU occlusion relations when A is the same size as B.

When $m > 1$, A is greater than B, the track is around B. If the viewpoint is in the circle, then $a' < b'$. Otherwise, out of the circle, then $a' > b'$, as shown in Fig. 5.

Similarly, when $m < 1$, A is smaller than B, the track is around A. If the viewpoint is in the circle, then $a' > b'$. Otherwise, out of the circle, $a' < b'$, as shown in Fig. 6.

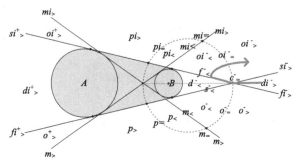

Fig. 5. The lines of sight between two objects A and B and the basic INDU occlusion relations when A is greater than B. The dashed circle is the track of viewpoints *s.t.* $a' = b'$.

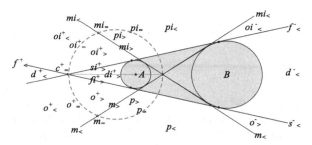

Fig. 6. The lines of sight between two objects A and B and the basic INDU occlusion relations when A is smaller than B. The dashed circle is the track of viewpoints *s.t.* $a' = b'$.

5   Discussions

Conceptual neighborhood [15] describes the connections between different relations, which can directly transform to another with continuous deforming. Figure 7 gives the transition network. When mapping the network to the partition of the plane shown in Fig. 4, Fig. 5, Fig. 6, it can be easily found that not all the paths in the network can be realized under the different cases. For example, when A and B are in same size, the possible paths are shown as the bold blue lines in Fig. 7. Only 18 relations can be realized. Another example is shown in Fig. 8.

The following application scenarios will be discussed from single viewpoint and multiple viewpoints respectively. Assume there is only one viewpoint, which can be known as one sensor or agent.

(1) If A, B are fixed, and the viewpoint moves around the convex hull of them (the convex region formed by their boundaries and external tangent lines, *e.g.* the gray part in Fig. 5); then according to the changing process of the relations, the relative size between A and B can be decided. When A is same size as B, Relation $c_=^-/c_=^+$ can appear for a long time. While A and B are not the same size, $c_=^-/c_=^+$ may flash or even not appear; since it can only appear at a special point.

(2) If A, B are fixed, and the relative size information is known; then the transition process implies the distance and moving direction of the viewpoint. For example,

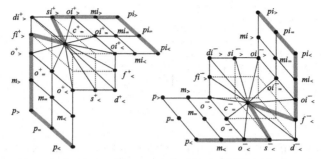

Fig. 7. The possible paths in the transition network of basic INDU occlusion relations when A is same as B. (Color figure online)

as the bold blue line with an arrow shown in Fig. 5 the changing process is $di^-_> \rightarrow c^-_= \rightarrow f^-_< \rightarrow oi^-_< \rightarrow oi^-_= \rightarrow oi^-_>$, it implies that the viewpoint first moves directly towards $B(di^-_> \rightarrow c^-_=)$, then slightly turns to the right of itself $(c^-_= \rightarrow f^-_<)$, next it moves towards the right $(f^-_< \rightarrow oi^-_<)$, finally it goes opposite to $B(oi^-_< \rightarrow oi^-_= \rightarrow oi^-_>)$ decided by the size changes.

(3) If the size of A and B is fixed, and the viewpoint doesn't move; then the relative moving direction of A and B can be deduced. As shown in Fig. 9, at beginning $A\,pi_>B$ is satisfied from the viewpoint σ. While A and B are moving toward each other mutually and attain the new position A' and B'. The occlusion relations must have a changing process $pi_> \rightarrow mi_> \rightarrow oi^+_>$.

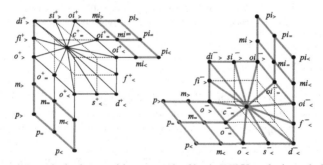

Fig. 8. The possible paths in the transition network of basic INDU occlusion relations when A is greater than B.

The above content does not consider the possible collaborations between multiple viewpoints [16]. For the applications of multiple viewpoints maybe as follows.

One application is the consistency checking of the reports from independent agents. An extreme example is that one agent reports $a\ oi^+_\pm\ b$ another is $a\ oi^-_\pm\ b$ simultaneously. Although there is no idea about the relative size of A and B, we can confirm one of the agents is lying. Since $oi^+_\pm$ and $oi^-_\pm$ cannot exist in one situation concurrently, as shown in Fig. 5 and Fig. 6.

472   J. Chen et al.

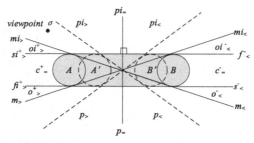

Fig. 9. The plane partition changes when A and B are moving toward each other. The viewpoint is σ. The solid line is the original and the dashed is the new.

Another application is reasoning about rough relative position between two agents. For example, if agent₁ and agent₂ report $a\ di^+_\geq b$ and $a\ mi_= b$ respectively, then it can deduce that agent₂ must be on the left side of agent₁ (assume that the agents cannot communicate with each other and agent₁ is facing object A), besides A is smaller than B, as shown in Fig. 6. If $a\ c^+_\equiv b$ and $a\ c^-_\equiv b$ got from two agents as shown in Fig. 4, then they are on the opposite sides of the convex hull of A and B and facing A and B respectively.

When agents can communicate with each other, one agent can deduce the relation between the observed objects through its own and another agent's observations by a translation table proposed in [9]. The fusion of distinct observation from multiply agents provides a way to check the wrong observation or faulty sensor. INDU occlusion calculus provides a more precise plane partition, so the translation table is more complex than IOC also includes some metric information such as m and k. It needs to find an automatic method to build up the table which is still under work. The equal circle (the dashed lines and circles in Fig. 4, 5 and 6) tells where the image arcs are in the same size, it provides a reference to describe the distance between the observer and objects.

6 Conclusions

This paper concentrates on combing the interval-based occlusion relations with relative size information obtained from observation and proposes a new formalism INDU occlusion calculus. Several application scenarios including single or multiple viewpoints are discussed with examples.

As in this work we are mostly interested in the occlusion relations between disk-like 2D objects. An issue for future work is to represent 3D objects where Rectangle Algebra [3, 4] can be used. And the rectangle relations will have a^+ and a^- versions with layer information. There is an area still without any discussion is inside the convex hull of the two objects. The observer may be surrounded by the object, so the field of vision is greater than 180°. The occlusions about concave objects are another working direction. In [9] the translation table plays an important role in the collaboration of multiple viewpoints but it only forwards the thought of building the table. Finding the automatic algorithm to calculate this table is the third direction.

Acknowledgements. This paper is supported by National Natural Science Foundation of China under Grant Nos. 61502198, 61472161, 61402195, 61103091 and the Science and Technology Development Plan of Jilin Province under Grant No. 20160520099JH.

References

1. Cohn, A.G., Hazarika, S.M.: Qualitative spatial representation and reasoning: an overview. Fund. Inform. **46**(1–2), 1–29 (2001)
2. Cohn, A.G.: Qualitative spatial representation and reasoning techniques. In: Brewka, G., Habel, C., Nebel, B. (eds.) KI 1997. LNCS, vol. 1303, pp. 1–30. Springer, Heidelberg (1997). https://doi.org/10.1007/3540634932_1
3. Cohn, A.G., Renz, J.: Qualitative spatial representation and reasoning. In: van Harmelen, F., Lifschitz, V., Porter, B. (eds.) Handbook of Knowledge Representation, pp. 551–596. Elsevier (2008)
4. Chen, J., Cohn, A.G., Liu, D., Wang, S., Ouyang, J., Yu, Q: A survey of qualitative spatial representations. Knowl. Eng. Rev. **30**(1), 106–136 (2015)
5. Petrov, A.P., Kuzmin, L.V.: Visual space geometry derived from occlusion axioms. J. Math. Imaging Vision **6**(1), 291–308 (1996)
6. Galton, A.: Lines of sight. In: AISB Workshop on Spatial and Spatio-temporal Reasoning, pp.1–15. Springer, Berlin (1994)
7. Randell, D., Witkowski, M., Shanahan, M.: From images to bodies: modelling and exploiting spatial occlusion and motion parallax. In: Proceedings of 17th International Joint Conferences on Artificial Intelligence, pp. 57–66. Morgan Kaufmann, Seattle (2001)
8. Guha, P., Mukerjee, A., Venkatesh, K.S.: OCS-14: you can get occluded in fourteen ways. In: Proceedings of 22nd International Joint Conference on Artificial Intelligence, pp. 1665–1670. AAAI Press, Barcelona (2011)
9. Santos, P.E., Ligozat, G., Safi-Samghabad, M.: An occlusion calculus based on an interval algebra. In: Proceedings of Brazilian Conference on Intelligent Systems, pp. 128–133. IEEE Computer Society, Natal (2015)
10. Ligozat, G., Santos, P.E.: Spatial occlusion within an interval algebra. In: AAAI Spring Symposium - Technical Report, pp.103–106. AAAI Press, California (2015)
11. Allen, J.: Maintaining knowledge about temporal intervals. Commun. ACM **26**(1), 832–843 (1983)
12. Pujari, A.K., Vijaya Kumari, G., Sattar, A.: INDu: an interval & duration network. In: Foo, N. (ed.) AI 1999. LNCS (LNAI), vol. 1747, pp. 291–303. Springer, Heidelberg (1999). https://doi.org/10.1007/3-540-46695-9_25
13. Balbiani, P., Condotta, J.-F., Ligozat, G.: On the consistency problem for the INDU calculus. J. Appl. Log. **4**(2), 119–140 (2006)
14. Ligozat, G.: Qualitative Spatial and Temporal Reasoning. Wiley (2013)
15. Freksa, C.: temporal reasoning based on semi-intervals. Artif. Intell. **54**(1), 199–227 (1992)
16. Kray, C.: The benefits of multi-agent systems in spatial reasoning. In: Proceedings of 14th International Florida Artificial Intelligence Research Society Conference, pp. 552–556. AAAI Press, Key West (2001)

Adaptive Entity Alignment for Cross-Lingual Knowledge Graph

Yuanming Zhang$^{(\boxtimes)}$, Tianyu Gao, Jiawei Lu, Zhenbo Cheng, and Gang Xiao$^{(\boxtimes)}$

College of Computer Science and Technology, Zhejiang University of Technology,
Hangzhou 310023, China
{zym,2111812095,viivan,czb,xg}@zjut.edu.cn

Abstract. Entity alignment is a key step in knowledge graph (KG) fusion, which aims to match the same entity from different KGs. Currently, embedding-based entity alignment is the mainstream. It embeds entities into low-dimensional vectors and transfers entities to the same vector space. However, the precision of entity alignment depends largely on the number of alignment seeds. Manually labelling alignment seeds is very expensive and inefficient. To address this problem, this paper proposes a novel adaptive entity alignment approach for cross-lingual KGs, namely AdaptiveEA. This approach adopts a new joint KG embedding network to accurately learn the embeddings of entities from both structural semantics and relational semantics. Then, it employs an adaptive entity alignment strategy to iteratively capture new aligned entity pairs that meet a dynamic alignment threshold. Then the new captured aligned entity pairs are utilized to expand alignment seeds to further guide the next embedding training. Experimental results on public datasets show that the proposed approach can achieve much better precision than the latest state-of-the-art models in a small number of labeled alignment seeds.

Keywords: Knowledge graph · Entity alignment · Adaptive alignment strategy · Graph attention network · KG embedding

1 Introduction

Recently, knowledge graph (KG) has been widely constructed and used in many fields of artificial intelligence, such as intelligent question answering, intelligent recommendation, intelligent reasoning, natural language processing and other knowledge-driven applications. Different KGs have complementary knowledge, and therefore integrating multiple KGs into a unified rich KG will provide more powerful support for applications. However, there are huge differences between cross-lingual KGs, such as diversified languages, diversified structures and diversified naming approaches. These differences bring great challenges to the integration of KGs. Entity alignment is a key step in KG fusion and its goal is to correlate entities that refer to the same object from two KGs.

Embedding-based entity alignment approaches, which determine the similarity between entities by comparing the distance of their embeddings, have received extensive attentions. The MTransE [1], IPTransE [2], JAPE [3] and BootEA [4] approaches embed

© Springer Nature Switzerland AG 2021
H. Qiu et al. (Eds.): KSEM 2021, LNAI 12816, pp. 474–487, 2021.
https://doi.org/10.1007/978-3-030-82147-0_39

entities via translation-based models and The GCN-Align [5], RDGCN [6] and AliNet [7] approaches embed entities via graph convolutional network (GCN) by aggregating structural information of entities. According to the embeddings, the entities from KGs are transferred to the same vector space based on alignment seeds.

However, current embedding-based entity alignment approaches greatly depend on the number of alignment seeds generally obtained by manually labelling according to our observations. A smaller number of pre-aligned entity pairs will generally result in lower alignment precision. For example, when the proportion of pre-aligned entity pairs is 10%, the alignment precision (Hits@1) of JAPE [3] and GCN-Align [5] is only about 22% on the DBP_{ZH-EN} dataset. As the proportion is improved to 40%, their alignment precision is about 50%. However, it will be costly and inefficient for large-scale KGs to increase manually labeled seeds. As a result, it will be of great significance to find a new entity alignment approach to achieve higher precision in the case of a small number of alignment seeds.

To this end, we propose a new adaptive entity alignment approach for cross-lingual KGs, namely AdaptiveEA. It adopts a new joint embedding network, which combines an improved graph attention network (GAT) with a translation-based model, to achieve accurate embeddings by simultaneously learning structural semantics and relational semantics of KG. In particular, it employs an adaptive entity alignment strategy, which can iteratively optimize an alignment threshold to capture further new aligned seeds in each training epoch. The new captured aligned seeds expand original alignment seeds and are used for the next epoch. The entity embedding procedure and entity alignment procedure are executed iteratively. Therefore, the entity embedding is more and more accurate and the number of alignment seeds becomes larger and larger. Our approach can achieve higher entity alignment precision with a small number of labeled alignment seeds.

Our main contributions include as follows:

- We propose a new joint embedding network by combing an improved graph attention network and a translation-based model. It can learn structural semantics and relational semantics to accurately embed entities.
- We propose an adaptive entity alignment strategy that can dynamically optimize alignment thresholds to capture further new aligned seeds in each training epoch. It can effectively expand original labeled alignment seeds.
- We evaluate the proposed approach on three public cross-lingual datasets and show that it can achieve much better precision than the latest state-of-the-art approaches in a small number of labeled alignment seeds.

The rest of this paper is organized as follows. Section 2 describe the related works on entity alignment. Section 3 givens an entity alignment framework and Sect. 4 presents the knowledge graph embedding network, and Sect. 5 shows the adaptive entity alignment strategy. Section 6 gives experimental results. Finally, Sect. 7 concludes this paper.

2 Related Work

Recently, embedding-based entity alignment has become a hot research topic in KG fusion. A key step of entity alignment is that the entities must be embedded into low-dimensional vectors. Generally, the main embedding models can be divided into three categories:

1) Translation-based Model: TransE [8] is a milestone in KG embedding model. It interprets relation r as a transformation from head entity h to tail entity t, i.e., $h + r = t$. Then, several improved models, such as TransH [9] and TransR [10], were proposed. These models extend TransE to model complex relations.

2) Semantic Matching Model: RESCAL [11] is a relational learning model based on factorization of a three-way tensor. It performs collective learning through latent components and provides an effective algorithm to calculate factorization. RotatE [12] interprets relation as rotation from source entity to target entity in complex vector space.

3) Deep Model: KBGAN [13] notes that the negative samples generated by randomly replacing the head and tail entities are easily distinguished from the positive triples, which is less helpful for training. Therefore, it introduces GANs [14] into KG embeddings. R-GCN [15] takes into account the types and directions of edges and distinguishes different neighbors through a relation-specific weight matrix.

Translation-based entity alignment approaches use TransE [8] to embed entities of KG. MTransE [1] uses TransE to learn the embeddings of two KGs and then transfers the KGs to the same vector space for alignment through alignment seeds. IPTransE [2] and BootEA [4] use iterative methods to extend training set in training process. Further BootEA uses an alignment editing method to reduce the accumulation of errors in alignment process. However, it is difficult to set a fixed threshold to apply in different stages of training, so that its performance is limited.

GCN-based entity alignment approaches adopt GCN [16] model to aggregate the feature of the entity's neighbors as its own embedding. GCN-Align [5] learns the entity embeddings through GCN and captures aligned entity pairs according to the embedding distance in the vector space. KECG [17] takes alignment loss function as training target of the cross-graph model, and trains the knowledge embedding model and the cross-graph model alternately and independently. RDGCN [6] introduces a dual relation graph to model complex relation. It fuses complex relation into entity embeddings through interactions of primal and dual graphs. However, the structures of most knowledge graphs are quite different, and heterogeneity becomes the bottleneck of most entity alignment methods. To handle this problem, MuGNN [18] enhances the isomorphism of KGs by complementing KGs with rules, and then embeds entities by multiple channels. AliNet [7] embeds entities by aggregating features of multi-hop neighborhoods to reduce the heterogeneity between KGs. However, it aggregates all one-hop neighbors of entities with the same weight. In fact, not all one-hop neighbors have a positive effect on the representation of the central entity. Therefore, completely aggregating one-hop neighbors will introduce much noises.

Some approaches also use additional semantics to learn entity embedding. JAPE [3] uses attribute types and AttrE [19] uses attribute values to improve the precision of entity alignment. RDGCN [6] incorporates entity name semantics into embedding, and MultiKE [20] uses entity name, attribute, and relation to jointly learn entity embedding and adopts three different strategies to combine multiple view-specific entity embeddings. Then the aligned entity pairs are captured with combined embeddings.

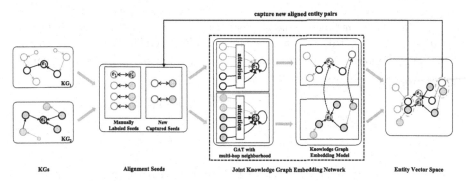

Fig. 1. Adaptive entity alignment framework

3 Entity Alignment Framework

To align entities from cross-lingual KGs in a small number of labeled alignment seeds, we propose an adaptive entity alignment framework, named AdaptiveEA, shown in Fig. 1. The left side shows two KGs to be aligned. A small number of alignment seeds are prepared by manually labeling. In each training epoch, AdaptiveEA uses an improved GAT to learn structural semantics, and then uses TransE to learn relational semantics. Alignment seeds are used to transfer entities from two KGs into the same vector space. After that, an adaptive alignment strategy is employed to capture entity pairs that meet an alignment threshold and meet the one-to-one alignment constraint from all unaligned entities. In each training epoch, the new captured aligned entities pairs are added to the alignment seeds to guide the next training epoch. When the training epoch is over, the captured aligned entity pairs will be discarded. Then the new aligned entity pairs will be recaptured once again, and are also added to alignment seeds for the next training.

4 Joint Knowledge Graph Embedding Network

The joint embedding network combines an improved GAT with TransE model to learn the structural semantics and relational semantics. The output of GAT is used as the input of the TransE in each training epoch. The improved GAT learns structural semantics of both direct neighbors and indirect neighbors and gives different attentions to direct neighbors as well as indirect neighbors to highlight critical neighbors.

The direct adjacency matrix and the indirect adjacency matrix are the inputs of GAT. Neighbors of entity i are aggregated in layer l, denoted as $h_i^{(l)}$:

$$h_i^{(l)} = \mu_1 \sigma_1 \left(\sum_{j \in N_{i,1} \cup \{i\}} \alpha_{ij}^{(l-1)} W_1^{(l)} h_j^{(l-1)} \right) + (1-\mu_1)\sigma_1 \left(\sum_{k \in N_{i,2} \cup \{i\}} \alpha_{ik}^{(l-1)} W_2^{(l)} h_k^{(l-1)} \right), \quad (1)$$

where $N_{i,1}$ is the set of direct neighbors of entity $i \in E$, and $N_{i,2}$ is the set of indirect neighbors of entity $i \in E$. $W_1^{(l)}, W_2^{(l)} \in \mathbb{R}^{d^{(l-1)} \times d^{(l)}}$ are respectively weight matrixes for direct neighbors and indirect neighbors in the layer l. σ_1 is an activation function, and μ_1 is a weight to balance the embeddings of direct neighbor aggregation and the embeddings of indirect neighbors aggregation. $\alpha_{ij}^{(l)}$ is attention weight between entity i and its neighbor j, and is calculated as follows:

$$\alpha_{ij}^{(l)} = softmax\left(e_{ij}^{(l)}\right) = \frac{\exp\left(e_{ij}^{(l)}\right)}{\sum_{k \in N_i \cup \{i\}} \exp\left(e_{ik}^{(l)}\right)}, \quad (2)$$

where $e_{ij}^{(l)}$ is attention coefficient that reflects the correlation between entities i and j. The activation function *softmax* is introduced to numerically transform attention coefficient $e_{ij}^{(l)}$. It can normalize the attention coefficient and map the coefficients into a probability distribution with the sum of all element weights being 1. It can also highlight the weight of important elements. $e_{ij}^{(l)}$ is computed as follows:

$$e_{ij}^l = sim\left(L_1^{(l)} h_i^{(l)}, L_2^{(l)} h_j^{(l)}\right), \quad (3)$$

where $sim(\cdot, \cdot)$ is a function to calculate similarity of entities by comparing the cosine similarity of embeddings of entities i and j after linear transformation by $L_1^{(l)}$ and $L_2^{(l)}$ respectively.

After learning structural semantics of entity, AdaptiveEA continues to learn relational semantics that are helpful to establish appropriate semantic relations between entities. Typically, we adopt the classic TransE model to embed the relations, and the variant of embedding loss function is defined as follows:

$$\mathcal{L}_{KE} = \sum_{t \in T^+} f(t) + \mu_2 \sum_{t' \in T^-} [\gamma_1 - f(t')]_+, \quad (4)$$

where T^+ denotes the set of positive triples, and T^- denotes the set of negative triples. T^- comes from T^+. For each positive triple $(h, r, t) \in T^+$, a negative triple is generated by replacing h or t with a negative head entity h' or a negative tail entity t' from the same KG, where h', t' are randomly sampled from the set of head entities $\mathcal{H}_i = \{h|(h,r,t) \in T_i\}$ and the set of tail entities $\mathcal{T}_i = \{t|(h,r,t) \in T_i\}$ respectively, $i \in \{1, 2\}$. $[\cdot]_+ = max(\cdot, 0)$, $\gamma_1 > 0$ is a margin hyper-parameter, and $\mu_2 > 0$ is a weight used to balance the losses of negative triples and positive triples. $f(t)$ is used to measure the deviation of a triplet $t = (h, r, t)$. This function is defined as follows:

$$f(t) = \|h + r - t\|_2, \quad (5)$$

where $\|\cdot\|_2$ denotes the L_2 vector norm.

AdaptiveEA minimizes the contrastive alignment loss to reduce the distance between aligned entity pairs and to increase the distance between nonaligned entity pairs. The embeddings of the two KG are transferred to the same vector space:

$$\mathcal{L}_{AL} = \sum_{(i,j)\in\mathcal{A}\cup\mathcal{Q}} \left\| \vec{v}(e_i) - \vec{v}(e_j) \right\|_2 + \mu_3 \sum_{(i',j')\in\mathcal{A}^-} \left[\gamma_2 - \left\| \vec{v}(e_{i'}) - \vec{v}(e_{j'}) \right\|_2 \right]_+,$$

(6)

where $\mathcal{A}$ is a set of manually labelled seeds, $\mathcal{Q}$ is a set of new captured seeds. $\mathcal{A}^-$ is a set of negative samples, which is generated by replacing e_i or e_j in $(e_i, e_j) \in A$ with an erroneous entity. There are two strategies to generate erroneous entities. One is the random sampling, and the other is the nearest neighbor sampling. Consider the one-to-one alignment constraint, the nearest neighbor sampling can better distinguish those entity pairs that are similar but not actually aligned. $\|\cdot_2\|$ denotes the L_2 norm of two vectors. γ_2 is a margin hyper-parameter, μ_3 is a weight, and $[\cdot]_+$ *is the* $\max(0, \cdot)$.

The optimization objective $\mathcal{L}$ of entity alignment is composed of alignment loss function and embedding loss function:

$$\mathcal{L} = \mathcal{L}_{AL} + \mu_4 \mathcal{L}_{KE},$$

(7)

where μ_4 is a weight to balance $\mathcal{L}_{AL}$ and $\mathcal{L}_{KE}$.

5 Adaptive Entity Alignment Strategy

To improve the precision of entity alignment for a small number of alignment seeds, we propose an adaptive entity alignment strategy. For each training epoch, it can dynamically capture new aligned entity pairs and then add these new captured entity pairs to alignment seeds to guide the next embedding training. When the training epoch is over, the captured entity pairs will be discarded, and new aligned entity pairs will be recaptured once again. This is necessary to reduce the accumulation of errors.

The impact of captured entity pairs on training mainly depends on two aspects: (1) Quality: In the captured entity pairs, the higher the proportion of truly aligned entity pairs, the higher the quality of the captured entity pairs. Higher quality of captured entity pairs will have fewer negative impact on training. (2) Quantity: The more the number of captured entity pairs, the greater the role of the captured entity pairs in the training.

To reduce the capture of nonaligned entity pairs and improve the quality of captured entity pairs, we capture entity pairs with high alignment probability via a high threshold at initial training epochs. As the training progresses, the distance of aligned entity pairs becomes closer, and the distance of nonaligned entity pairs becomes larger. During this process, the threshold will gradually decay to capture more aligned entity pairs and improve the quantity of captured entity pairs.

Actually, not all entities have their aligned entities in another KG. We define alignment probability to evaluate whether one entity is aligned with another entity. We denote the embeddings of entities as $\mathcal{V}^{(t)}$ in t_{th} training epoch. The alignment probability $\mathcal{P}_{e_i,e_j}^{V^{(t)}}$ that entity e_i is aligned with entity e_j is defined as follows:

$$\mathcal{P}_{e_i,e_j}^{V^{(t)}} = \sigma_2 \left(sim \left(\vec{v}_{e_j}^{(t)}, \vec{v}_{e_j}^{(t)} \right) \right),$$

(8)

where σ_2 is activation function, and $sim(\cdot, \cdot)$ is a similarity function to calculate the distance between entities, and $\vec{v}_e^{(t)} \in \mathcal{V}^{(t)}$.

Assume the entity $e \in U_i, i \in (1, 2)$ is an entity to be aligned, we collect all candidate entities from another KG whose alignment probabilities exceed the specific threshold, and a candidate set $S_e^{(t)}$ can be obtained:

$$S_e^{(t)} = \left\{ e' \in U_j | \mathcal{P}_{e,e'}^{V^{(t)}} > \theta(t), j \in (1, 2), j \neq i \right\}, \tag{9}$$

where $\theta(t)$ is a dynamic threshold function that gradually decays as the training goes on, and its range of value is $(0,1)$. $\theta(t)$ is defined as follows:

$$\theta(t) = \rho + \frac{\omega}{1 + \exp(\lambda t)}, \tag{10}$$

where ρ is an initial alignment threshold, $\omega < 0$ is a decay coefficient that determines the lower limit of the threshold, and λ is the rate of decay.

Consider the one-to-one constraint, in the tth training epoch, each entity $e_1 \in U_1$ is aligned with the entity $\hat{e}_1' \in S_{e_1}^{(t)}$ that has the highest alignment probability with e_i, and then a raw set $Q_1^{(t)}$ of possible aligned entities pairs for KG1 is obtained. In a similar way, each entity $e_2 \in U_2$ is aligned with the entity $\hat{e}_2' \in S_{e_2}^{(t)}$ that has highest alignment probability with e_2, and a raw set $Q_2^{(t)}$ of possible aligned entities pairs for KG2 is obtained. Then $Q_1^{(t)}$ and $Q_2^{(t)}$ are intersected to obtain the set of new captured aligned entity pairs $\mathcal{Q}^{(t)}$, defined as follows:

$$\mathcal{Q}^{(t)} = Q_1^{(t)} \cap Q_2^{(t)}, \tag{11}$$

$$Q_i^{(t)} = \left\{ \left(e_i, \hat{e}_i' \right) | \hat{e}_i' = argmax_{e_i'} \mathcal{P}_{e_i, e_i'}^{V^{(t)}}, e_i \in U_i, e_i' \in S_{e_i}^{(t)}, i \in \{1, 2\} \right\}, \tag{12}$$

Figure 2 describes the adaptive entity alignment process. The entity e_i and the entity e_j' come from two KGs respectively. The black dotted circle shows the alignment perception range of the center entity, and its radius is r. If two entities are located in each other's alignment perception range at the same time, they are possible entity pairs. The alignment perception range is negatively correlated with the threshold and will expand non-linearly as the training goes on.

Let's consider the entity e_2 in Fig. 2. Entity e_2' is the closest to e_2, and is also the only entity within the alignment perception range of e_2. That means that the e_2 tends to align with e_2'. However, the entities e_1 and e_2 are both within the alignment perception range of e_2', and e_1 is closer to e_2' than e_2, and e_2' tends to align with e_1. Similarly, e_1 also tends to align with e_2'. Therefore, e_2' and e_1 will be captured as new entity pairs, e_2' and e_2 will not be entity pairs. Let's continue to consider entity e_3'. Entity e_4 is closer to e_3' than e_3. However, e_4 and e_4' are manually labelled entity pairs, so they do not participate in the alignment process. Therefore, e_3' and e_3 will be captured as new entity pairs.

At the beginning of training, the alignment perception range is limited, and the number of entities perceived by the center entity is also limited. Only very similar entity

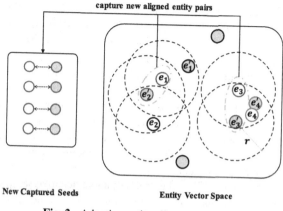

Fig. 2. Adaptive entity alignment process

pairs can perceive each other. At this time, a small number of high-quality entity pairs can be captured with a high threshold. As the training converges and the embedding accuracy is improved, the nonaligned entities are alienated from each other. Then the alignment perception range of the center entity gradually expands to capture more aligned entity pairs to increase the quantity of captured entity pairs. The time complexity of the adaptive entity alignment strategy is $O(n_1 n_2 d)$, where n_1, n_2 are the number of entities in the two KGs respectively and d is the dimension of embeddings.

6   Experiments

6.1   Environment Setting

Datasets. We evaluate AdaptiveEA on the currently a bit more popular cross-lingual dataset DBP15K. DBP15K has three large-scale cross-lingual datasets built from multi-lingual DBpedia, namely DBPZH-EN (Chinese to English), DBPJA-EN (Japanese to English) and DBPFR-EN (French to English). Each dataset has 15,000 reference entity alignments and about 400,000 triples. And the latest models [3, 4, 6, 7, 17] have been run on the DBP15K datasets, and the evaluation results are sufficient for references. Therefore, we choose these datasets to evaluate our model.

Comparative Models. We compare our AdaptiveEA with both the classic alignment models including MTransE [1], JAPE [3], IPTransE [2] and the latest models including BootEA [4],KECG [17], RDGCN [6], AliNet [7] to show the effectiveness. These models have been introduced in related work. MTransE [1], JAPE [3], IPTransE [2] and BootEA [4] are based on translation-based models, where IPTransE [2] and BootEA [4] employ an iterative approach, and JAPE [3] combines relation and attribute embeddings for entity alignment. RDGCN [6] and AliNet [7] are based on GNN, where RDGCN [6] employs entity name for embedding initialization. KECG [17] is a mixture of the two models.

Implementation Details. We search among the following value for hyper-parameters, i.e., the dimension of each layer in {100,200,300,400}, the learning rate in {0.1,0.01,0.001,0.0001}, the decay of learning rate in {0, 0.001, 0.01}, the initial value of ρ in {0.7, 0.9, 1.0}, the decay coefficient ω in {0.4, 0.6, 0.8}, the rate of decay λ in {−0.03, 0.05}, the margin γ_1 and γ_2 in {1.0, 1.5, ..., 3}, the number of negative samples in {1, 5, 10}, and the epoch to execute the adaptive alignment strategy in {0,10, ..., 70}. In the end, the extended GAT model includes an input layer and two hidden layers which can aggregate direct and indirect neighbors. We combine the results of three layers as the embeddings of the entities. The dimension of each layer is 300, and the dimension of the relations is 900. The activation function σ_1 and σ_2 are $tanh()$. The margin hyper-parameter γ_1 is 1.0 and γ_2 is 1.5. 10 negative samples are sampled from the near neighbors for each pre-aligned entity pair and a negative sample is sampled for each triple. The optimizer is Adam. The learning rate is 0.001, and the decay of learning rate is 0.01. After 40 training epochs, the adaptive alignment strategy will be executed at the end of each training epoch. The initial value of ρ is 0.9, the decay coefficient ω is −0.6, and the rate of decay λ is −0.05. The total training epochs are 400. The embedding vectors are initialized with the same method used in RDGCN [6]. The entity names are translated into English, and then their initial embeddings are word vectors extracted from glove.840B.300d[1]. The initialization of embeddings can be fully utilized by adaptive alignment strategy.

By convention, we report the Hits@1, Hits@10 and MRR (mean reciprocal rank) results to evaluate the entity alignment performance. Hits@k measures the percentage of correct alignment ranked at top k, and MRR is the average of the reciprocal ranks of results. Higher Hits@k and MRR scores indicate better performance. In addition, for a fair comparison with the baselines, we use a 30% proportion of labelled alignment seeds and the rest is for test.

6.2 Experimental Results

Table 1 shows the entity alignment results. We can see that AdaptiveEA outperforms the state-of-the-art baseline model for entity alignment by Hits@1, Hits@10 and MMR. For example, on DBP$_{ZH-EN}$, AdaptiveEA achieves a gain of 16.02% by Hits@1 compared with the best baseline. On DBP$_{JA-EN}$, it achieves a gain of 14.05% by Hits@1 compared with the best baseline, and on DBP$_{FR-EN}$, it achieves a gain of 7.5% by Hits@1 compared with the best baseline. These results have demonstrated that the superiority of AdaptiveEA.

In order to show that AdaptiveEA outperforms even with a small number of labelled alignment seeds, we evaluate the performance when the proportion of labelled alignment seeds is from 10% to 50% with step 10%. Figure 3 shows the experimental results of AdaptiveEA, RDGCN and BootEA with different proportions of labelled alignment seeds. It can be seen that the performances of all models are improved as the proportion increases. The obvious reason is that the more alignment seeds can provide more information to guide the alignment. However, it can be found that AdaptiveEA still has

---

[1] http://nlp.stanford.edu/projects/glove/.

Table 1. Results comparison on entity alignment

Methods	ZH-EN			JA-EN			FR-EN		
	Hits@1	Hits@10	MRR	Hits@1	Hits@10	MRR	Hits@1	Hits@10	MRR
MtransE(2016)	30.83	61.41	0.364	27.86	57.45	0.349	24.41	55.55	0.335
IPTransE(2017)	40.59	73.47	0.516	36.69	69.26	0.474	33.3	68.54	0.451
JAPE(2017)	41.18	74.46	0.49	36.25	68.5	0.476	32.39	66.68	0.43
BootEA(2018)	62.94	84.75	0.703	62.23	85.39	0.701	65.3	87.44	0.731
KECG(2019)	47.77	83.5	0.598	48.97	84.4	0.61	48.64	85.06	0.61
RDGCN(2019)	70.75	84.55	*	76.74	89.54	*	88.64	95.72	*
AliNet(2020)	53.9	82.6	0.628	54.9	83.1	64.5	55.2	85.2	0.657
AdaptiveEA	**86.77**	**94.11**	**0.908**	**90.79**	**96.314**	**0.933**	**96.14**	**98.83**	**0.973**

All results of baselines refer to their papers. "*" denotes the unreported metrics in their papers.

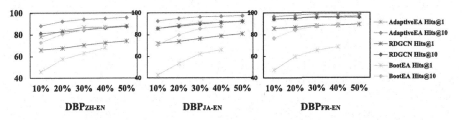

* Hits@k at 50% are not reported in BootEA.

Fig. 3. Hits@k on entity alignment w.r.t. proportion of alignment seeds.

better performance with a low proportion than other models. For example, when the proportion is 10%, the hits@1 of AdaptiveEA on DBP$_{\text{ZH-EN}}$ is 78.24%. AdaptiveEA achieves a gain of about 12% by Hits@1 compared with RDGCN, and achieves a gain of about 30% by Hits@1 compared with BootEA. These results further verify our approach is also effective in case of small number of labelled alignment seeds.

6.3 Analyses

Impact of Dynamic Threshold. We evaluate the impact of dynamic threshold on the performance of AdaptiveEA. Figure 4 shows the experimental results of dynamic threshold and fixed thresholds. We set the fixed thresholds {0.3, 0.5, 0.6, 0.7}. It can be found that the performance of dynamic threshold outperforms the performances of different fixed thresholds. For example, Hits@1 of dynamic threshold is 1.72%, 1.12% and 0.81% higher than the best control group on DBP$_{\text{ZH-EN}}$, DBP$_{\text{JA-EN}}$ and DBP$_{\text{FR-EN}}$ respectively. The experimental results verify the effectiveness of dynamic threshold.

To better analyze the effectiveness of dynamic threshold, we define an effective influence index (EII) to reflect the impact of the entity pairs captured by the fixed threshold and the dynamic threshold on training. As mentioned above, the impact of captured entity

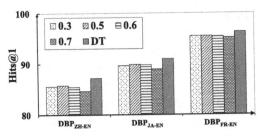

Fig. 4. Results comparison of fixed threshold {0.3,0.5,0.6,0.7} and dynamic threshold (DT)

pairs on training mainly depends on their quality and quantity. The quality reflects the quantitative relationship between the captured truly aligned entity pairs (*aligned*) and the captured nonaligned entity pairs (*nonaligned*). The quantity reflects the quantitative relationship between the all captured aligned entity pairs and the pre-aligned entity pairs (*pre*). We define the EII as follow:

$$EII = \frac{length(aligned) - length(nonaligned)}{length(pre)}, \qquad (13)$$

According to above definition, when the total number of captured entity pairs remains the same, a higher proportion of truly aligned entity pairs will lead to a higher EII. When the aligned/nonaligned ratio of captured entity pairs remains the same, more captured entity pairs will lead to a higher EII. EII is able to reflect the comprehensive situation of the captured entity pairs on quality and quantity.

Figure 5(a) shows the effective influence index (EII) of fixed threshold {0.3,0.7} and dynamic threshold (DT) in each training epoch (abscissa). We can find that the results of EII are consistent with the alignment performance in Fig. 4. And Fig. 5(b) shows the number of captured truly aligned entity pairs (aligned) and the number of all captured entity pairs (all) in each training epoch (abscissa). We can combine Fig. 5(a) and Fig. 5(b) for analysis. A high fixed threshold, such as 0.7, can capture high-quality aligned entity pairs, and the gap between *0.7 all* and *0.7 aligned* in Fig. 5(b) is small. However, high fixed threshold also causes the number of captured entity pairs is too insufficient to have a significant impact on training. Low fixed threshold, such as 0.3, can capture many entity pairs but also capture many nonaligned entity pairs, because embeddings of entities are not precise enough in the early training stage. As Fig. 5(b) shows, the line of *0.3 all* is at the top of the chart and the gap between *0.3 all* and *0.3 aligned* is the largest. Therefore, low-quality entity pairs cause the contaminated alignment seeds to have a negative impact on training.

However, dynamic threshold of adaptive entity alignment strategy changes in different training epochs. A high threshold in initial training epochs can reduce the introduction of nonaligned entity pairs. As a result, embedding of entities will be more accurate than those of low threshold. As the training goes on, the decayed threshold can capture more aligned entity pairs with high alignment probability. In the final stage of training, the number of all entity pairs captured by the dynamic threshold and the low fixed threshold is about the same, or even less in Fig. 5(b), but the number of truly aligned entity pairs

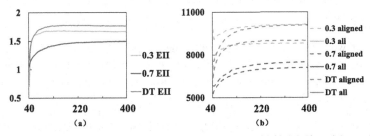

Fig. 5. (a) The effective influence index (EII) with fixed threshold {0.3,0.7} and dynamic threshold (DT) in training. (b) The number of captured truly aligned entity pairs (aligned) and the number of all captured entity pairs (all) with fixed threshold {0.3,0.7} and dynamic threshold (DT) in training.

captured by the dynamic threshold exceed those captured by the low fixed threshold. It can be seen that dynamic thresholds play an important role in entity alignment.

Impact of Neighborhood Expansion and Attention Mechanism. We also evaluate the impact of indirect neighbors and attention mechanism on performance of AdaptiveEA. We design three **variants**: AdaptiveEA-1 removes all indirect neighbors and the attention mechanism; AdaptiveEA-2 removes all indirect neighbors but retains the attention mechanism; and AdaptiveEA-3 removes the attention mechanism but retains all indirect neighbors.

We present the experimental results of AdaptiveEA and its three variants in Table 2. It can be found that AdaptiveEA outperforms the three variants. For example, the performance of AdaptiveEA is significantly better than that of AdaptiveEA-2. This demonstrates it is effective to aggregate indirect neighbors. In addition, we also observe that the performances of AdaptiveEA are different on the three datasets. For example, on DBP$_{ZH-EN}$, AdaptiveEA's Hits@1 is 2.62% higher than the best result of the control group. However, on DBP$_{FR-EN}$, AdaptiveEA achieves only 0.5% by Hits@1 compared with the best result of the control group. The reason is that the heterogeneity between Chinese KG and English KG is greater than that between French KG and English KG. Therefore, it can be concluded that the heterogeneity of KGs has a great negative impact on entity alignment. And the neighbor expansion and attention mechanism play a more important role in eliminating heterogeneity of KGs.

Table 2. Results comparison of four aggregation strategies

Methods	DBP$_{ZH-EN}$		DBP$_{JA-EN}$		DBP$_{FR-EN}$	
	Hits@1	Hits@10	Hits@1	Hits@10	Hits@1	Hits@10
AdaptiveEA-1	83.90	90.93	89.06	94.07	95.62	98.22
AdaptiveEA-2	83.94	91.51	89.02	94.13	95.27	98.02
AdaptiveEA-3	84.15	93.11	89.13	94.26	95.64	98.15
AdaptiveEA	**86.77**	**94.11**	**90.79**	**96.314**	**96.14**	**98.83**

7 Conclusions

In this paper, we proposed a novel entity alignment approach aiming at improving alignment precision with a small number of alignment seeds. This approach adopted a new joint KG embedding network by combining an improved GAT with a translation-based model to learn structural semantics and relational semantics. This network could accurately embed entities into low-dimensional vectors. Furthermore, an adaptive entity alignment strategy was presented to further capture new aligned seeds in each training epoch. This strategy could effectively expand manually labeled alignment seeds. Experimental results showed that our approach can achieve much better precision than the latest state-of-the-art approaches in a small number of labeled alignment seeds.

Acknowledgements. The work was supported by the National Natural Science Foundation of China (NO. 61976193), the Science and Technology Key Research Planning Project of Zhejiang Province (NO. 2021C03136), and the Natural Science Foundation of Zhejiang Province (No. LY19F020034).

References

1. Chen, M., Tian, Y., Yang, M., Zaniolo, C.: Multilingual knowledge graph embeddings for cross-lingual knowledge alignment. In: Proceedings of the 26th International Joint Conference on Artificial Intelligence, pp. 1511–1517 (2017)
2. Zhu, H., Xie, R., Liu, Z., Sun, M.: Iterative entity alignment via joint knowledge embeddings. In: Proceedings of the 26th International Joint Conference on Artificial Intelligence, pp. 4258–4264 (2017)
3. Sun, Z., Hu, W., Li, C.: Cross-lingual entity alignment via joint attribute-preserving embedding. In: d'Amato, C., et al. (eds.) ISWC 2017. LNCS, vol. 10587, pp. 628–644. Springer, Cham (2017). https://doi.org/10.1007/978-3-319-68288-4_37
4. Sun, Z., Hu, W., Zhang, Q., Qu, Y.: Bootstrapping entity alignment with knowledge graph embedding. In: Proceedings of the 27th International Joint Conference on Artificial Intelligence, pp. 4396–4402 (2018)
5. Wang, Z., Lv, Q., Lan, X., Zhang, Y.: Cross-lingual knowledge graph alignment via graph convolutional networks. In: Proceedings of the 2018 Conference on Empirical Methods in Natural Language Processing, pp. 349–357 (2018)
6. Wu, Y., Liu, X., Feng, Y., Wang, Z., Yan, R., Zhao, D.: Relation-aware entity alignment for heterogeneous knowledge graphs. In: Proceedings of the Twenty-Eighth International Joint Conference on Artificial Intelligence (2019)
7. Sun, Z., et al.: Knowledge graph alignment network with gated multi-hop neighborhood aggregation. In: Proceedings of the AAAI Conference on Artificial Intelligence, pp. 222–229 (2020)
8. Bordes, A., Usunier, N., Garcia-Duran, A., Weston, J., Yakhnenko, O.: Translating embeddings for modeling multi-relational data. In: Advances in Neural Information Processing Systems, pp. 2787–2795 (2013)
9. Wang, Z., Zhang, J., Feng, J., Chen, Z.: Knowledge graph embedding by translating on hyperplanes. In: Proceedings of the AAAI Conference on Artificial Intelligence, pp. 1112–1119 (2014)

10. Lin, Y., Liu, Z., Sun, M., Liu, Y., Zhu, X.: Learning entity and relation embeddings for knowledge graph completion. In: Proceedings of the AAAI Conference on artificial intelligence (2015)
11. Nickel, M., Tresp, V., Kriegel, H.-P.: A three-way model for collective learning on multi-relational data. In: Proceedings of the 28th International Conference on Machine Learning, pp. 809–816 (2011)
12. Sun, Z., Deng, Z.-H., Nie, J.-Y., Tang, J.: Rotate: knowledge graph embedding by relational rotation in complex space. In: Proceedings of the 7th International Conference on Learning Representations (2019)
13. Cai, L., Wang, W.Y.: KBGAN: adversarial learning for knowledge graph embeddings. In: Proceedings of the Conference of the North American Chapter of the Association for Computational Linguistics, pp. 1470–1480 (2018)
14. Goodfellow, I., et al.: Generative adversarial nets. In: Proceedings of the Advances in Neural Information Processing Systems, pp. 2672–2680 (2014)
15. Schlichtkrull, M., Kipf, T.N., Bloem, P., Van Den Berg, R., Titov, I., Welling, M.: Modeling relational data with graph convolutional networks. In: Proceedings of the European Semantic Web Conference, pp. 593–607 (2018)
16. Kipf, T.N., Welling, M.: Semi-supervised classification with graph convolutional networks. arXiv Preprint, arXiv:1609.02907 (2016)
17. Li, C., Cao, Y., Hou, L., Shi, J., Li, J., Chua, T.-S.: Semi-supervised entity alignment via joint knowledge embedding model and cross-graph model. In: Proceedings of the Conference on Empirical Methods in Natural Language Processing, pp. 2723–2732 (2019)
18. Cao, Y., Liu, Z., Li, C., Li, J., Chua, T.-S.: Multi-channel graph neural network for entity alignment. In: Proceedings of the 57th Annual Meeting of the Association for Computational Linguistics, pp. 1452–1461 (2019)
19. Trisedya, B.D., Qi, J., Zhang, R.: Entity alignment between knowledge graphs using attribute embeddings. In: Proceedings of the AAAI Conference on Artificial Intelligence, pp. 297–304 (2019)
20. Zhang, Q., Sun, Z., Hu, W., Chen, M., Guo, L., Qu, Y.: Multi-view knowledge graph embedding for entity alignment. In: Proceedings of the 28th International Joint Conference on Artificial Intelligence, pp. 5429–5435 (2019)

Similarity-Based Heterogeneous Graph Attention Network for Knowledge-Enhanced Recommendation

Fan Zhang, Rui Li, Ke Xu, and Hongguang Xu[(✉)]

Harbin Institute of Technology, Shenzhen, China
{19s152091,19s152089,18b95055}@stu.hit.edu.cn, xhg@hit.edu.cn

Abstract. The introduction of knowledge graphs (KG) has improved the accuracy and interpretability of recommendations. However, the performance of KG-based recommender system is still limited due to the lack of valid modeling of user/item similarity and effective constraints on user/item embeddings learning. In addition, common sampling and propagation methods for homogeneous graphs do not apply to KGs due to their heterogeneity. In this work, we propose *Similarity-based Heterogeneous Graph Attention Network* (SHGAT), which learns both the collaborative similarity and knowledge similarity of items by pre-training item embeddings with user-item interaction data and knowledge propagation in the KG. Meanwhile, users are represented by the items they have interacted with, thus establishing similarity between users and strengthening the learning of item embeddings. Besides, we design an importance sampling and aggregation method based on attention mechanism for heterogeneous graphs. We apply the proposed model on two real-world datasets, and the empirical results demonstrate that SHGAT significantly outperforms several compelling state-of-the-art baselines.

Keywords: Recommender systems · Knowledge graph · Similarity modeling · Heterogeneous graph attention network · Importance sampling

1 Introduction

Recommender system has become an indispensable part in many Internet applications to alleviate information overload. Traditional recommendation methods based on collaborative filtering (CF) learn user/item similarity from their co-occurrence matrix to infer users' preferences [6, 7, 10], and they have been widely used in the recommendation field due to simplicity and low cost. However, these methods usually suffer from sparsity and cold-start problems in default of side information. Recently, knowledge graph (KG) has been proved to be an effective side information to alleviate the above two problems [4, 13, 15, 16]. KG is a kind of heterogeneous graph, where entities act as nodes and relationships between entities act as edges. Items and their attributes can be mapped into the KG

© Springer Nature Switzerland AG 2021
H. Qiu et al. (Eds.): KSEM 2021, LNAI 12816, pp. 488–499, 2021.
https://doi.org/10.1007/978-3-030-82147-0_40

to understand the mutual relations between items [20]. Besides, various KGs have been proposed, such as Freebase [2], DBpedia [8] and YAGO [11], which makes it more convenient to build KGs for recommendation. The main challenge of KG-based recommendation is to learn efficient user/item embeddings from their interactions and KG's comprehensive auxiliary data [19]. However, most of the existing methods in this field lack sufficient discussion on user/item similarity modeling, which is the heart of collaborative filtering, and also the key to the performance of recommender system. In addition, many efforts have been devoted to applying graph neural networks (GNNs) to recommendation due to their superior performance in graph data learning. GNN is able to capture the high-order connectivity in graph data through iterative propagation, so as to integrate additional knowledge into user/item representation. For example, KGCN [15] uniformly samples a fixed size of neighbors for each entity as their receptive field, then utilizes user-specific relation-aware GNN to aggregate the information of entities in the neighborhood. KGAT [16] integrates users and items into one KG, and adopts the GAT mechanism [12] to fully exploit the relationship between entities. However, most of these models are more suitable for dealing with homogeneous graphs rather than heterogeneous graphs such as KGs. Therefore, more reasonable and effective model structures should be further investigated.

In this paper, we propose SHGAT for KG-based recommendation, with the aim to solve the above-mentioned shortcomings of existing methods. Our main contributions are summarized as follows:

- We adopt a two-stage item embedding learning method to capture both collaborative similarity and knowledge similarity of items. Meanwhile, users are represented by the items they have interacted with instead of random initialization, thereby spreading the item similarity to the user representations and making it easier to learn more effective item embeddings.
- We propose an importance sampling and aggregation strategy for heterogeneous graphs, in order to distinguish the differentiated interests of different users in a fine-grained way and aggregate significant neighbors of entities in a unified description space.
- We conduct extensive experiments on two public benchmarks, and the experimental results show that SHGAT significantly beats state-of-the-art methods in click-through rate prediction and top-K recommendation.

The remaining of this article is organized as follows: Sect. 2 formulates the KG-based recommendation problem. Section 3 presents the design of the SHGAT model. Section 4 demonstrates the experiments and discusses the results. Finally, Sect. 5 concludes this paper.

2   Problem Formulation

The KG-based recommendation problem is formulated as follows. In a typical recommendation scenario, we have a set of M users $\mathcal{U} = \{u_1, u_2, ..., u_M\}$ and a set of N items $\mathcal{V} = \{v_1, v_2, ..., v_N\}$. The user-item interaction matrix $\mathbf{Y} \in \mathbb{R}^{M \times N}$ is defined according to users' implicit feedback, where $y_{uv} = 1$ indicates that user u has interacted with item v, otherwise $y_{uv} = 0$. In addition, we also have a knowledge graph $\mathcal{G} = \{(h, r, t) | h, t \in \mathcal{E}, r \in \mathcal{R}\}$, where h, r, t denote the head, relation and tail in a knowledge triple, $\mathcal{E}$ and $\mathcal{R}$ are the sets of entities and relations in the KG, respectively. For example, the triple (*Titanic, film.film.director, James Cameron*) states the fact that the director of the film "Titanic" is James Cameron. Additional knowledge of an item can be obtained if it can be aligned with the corresponding entity in the KG through entity linking.

Given the user-item interaction matrix Y and knowledge graph $\mathcal{G}$, our goal is to learn a prediction function $\hat{y}_{uv} = \mathcal{F}(u, v | \Theta, \mathbf{Y}, \mathcal{G})$, where $\hat{y}_{uv}$ denotes the probability that user u will engage with item v, and Θ denotes the model parameters of function $\mathcal{F}$.

The notations we will use throughout the article are summarized in Table 1.

Table 1. Key notations used in this paper

Notations	Descriptions
$\mathcal{U} = \{u_1, u_2, ..., u_M\}$	Set of M users
$\mathcal{V} = \{v_1, v_2, ..., v_N\}$	Set of N items
u/v	Target user/item for CTR prediction
$\mathcal{S}_u$	Set of items interacted by user u
$\mathbf{e}_v$	Embedding of item v
$\mathbf{u}$	Representation of user u
$\mathbf{e}'$	Embedding of entity e
$\mathbf{W}_r$	Parameter matrix corresponding to relation r
$\mathcal{N}(\cdot)$	Set of neighbors in KG
π_e^u	Attention score of user u to entity e
$\mathcal{G}_{uv}^h$	The h-order KG subgraph of item v with respect to user u
$\mathbf{z}_{\mathcal{N}'(z)}^{(h)}$	The h-order neighbor representation of entity z
$\mathbf{z}^{(h)}$	The h-order knowledge representation of entity z
$\mathbf{v}^u = \mathbf{v}^{(H)}$	Overall knowledge representation of item v with respect to user u

3   Methodology

In this section, we introduce the SHGAT in detail. The workflow is shown in Fig. 1. The upper part models the similarity of items through Item2Vec and further spread it to user representations. The lower part calculates the user-specific attention scores for importance sampling and aggregation to obtain the knowledge representations of items. Finally, inner product is used to calculate the interaction probability between the user and the item.

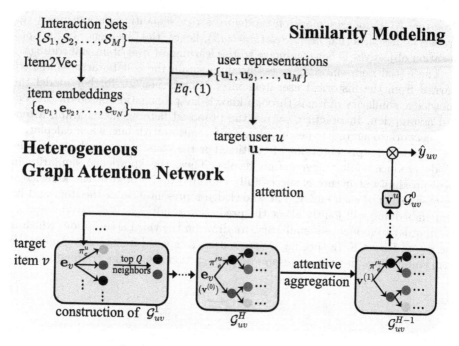

Fig. 1. The workflow of the proposed SHGAT

3.1 Similarity Modeling

Computing item similarities is the heart of Item-CF, and it is also a key building block in modern recommender systems [1]. Many studies focus on learning the low-dimensional embeddings of users and items simultaneously, but do not explicitly impose similarity constraints on these embeddings, which greatly limits the performance of recommender system. We model the user/item similarity based on three assumptions to get more effective user/item representation, namely: (1) Items preferred by the same user within a suitable time window are similar. (2) Items that share similar neighborhoods in the KG are similar. (3) Users with similar item preferences are similar.

Specifically, we denote the positive items that user u has interacted with as an interaction set: $\mathcal{S}_u = \{v|y_{uv} = 1\}$, and we can infer from the first assumption that similar items have similar interaction contexts whether they appear in the same interaction set or not, which is consistent with the idea in Word2Vec [9]. Word2Vec is a well-known algorithm to compute word vectors in Natural Language Processing, and Item2Vec [1] extends it to recommender system. Based on this, we take all the interaction sets $\{\mathcal{S}_1, \mathcal{S}_2, ..., \mathcal{S}_M\}$ as training data to use Item2Vec to get pre-trained item embeddings of dimension d: $\{\mathbf{e}_{v_1}, \mathbf{e}_{v_2}, ..., \mathbf{e}_{v_N}\}$, which will be further optimized with the training of SHGAT. In fact, some researches get entity embeddings through *knowledge graph embedding* (KGE), and then optimize them according to specific recommendation goals [16, 20].

However, KGE focuses more on modeling strict semantic relationships (e.g., TransE [3] assumes that *head+relation=tail*), hence, the divergence of the optimization objectives is not conducive to the learning of user/item embeddings.

The initial item embeddings essentially contain the collaborative similarity learned from the historical user-item interactions, then we further model the knowledge similarity of items through knowledge propagation based on the second assumption. In practice, we use the proposed heterogeneous graph attention network to aggregate neighborhood information with bias when calculating the knowledge representations of entities. For the same user, similar neighborhoods produce similar aggregation results. Thus, the knowledge similarity in local proximity structure is successfully captured and stored in the knowledge representation of each entity. The knowledge representation of the item and its own embedding will jointly affect the prediction result $\hat{y}_{uv}$.

In order to model user similarity, we draw on the third assumption, which is the key to User-CF. In specific, we treat users as special items by averaging the item embeddings in their corresponding interaction sets in the training phase:

$$\mathbf{u} = \frac{1}{|\mathcal{S}_u|} \sum_{v \in \mathcal{S}_u} \mathbf{e}_v. \tag{1}$$

Thus, users and items share the same representation space, user similarity can be obtained from items and can be maintained all the time. Moreover, because the user embedding matrix is discarded, the amount of model parameters can be reduced greatly, and the item embeddings can be optimized more sufficiently. Such a practice is simple and effective, especially for the recommendation scenarios with large number of users whose embeddings are difficult to learn.

3.2   Heterogeneous Graph Attention Network

To deal with large-scale graphs, existing works adopt sampling methods to construct subgraphs of KG. Most of them follow the sampling strategy proposed in GraphSage [5], i.e., uniformly sampling a fixed size of neighbors of an entity. This way of subgraph construction may cause problems such as ignoring important entities and introducing noise. For example, a user pours more attention into the director and the genre of a movie, but if the sampled subgraph does not contain these two entities except some unimportant ones, it becomes difficult for the model to infer this user's preference in the movie reasonably and accurately. Besides, as KG is a typical heterogeneous graph, most algorithms designed for homogeneous graphs cannot be directly applied to KG [17]. To address the above problems, we transform the entity embeddings into a unified description space, and design a user-specific attention calculation method to sample subgraphs and perform knowledge propagation.

Specifically, consider a candidate pair of user u and item v, we use $\mathcal{N}(v)$ to denote the set of entities directly connected to the target item v, and then perform the entity embedding transformation:

$$\mathbf{e} = \mathbf{W}_r \mathbf{e}', \tag{2}$$

where $\mathbf{e}' \in \mathbb{R}^d$ is the embedding of eneity $e \in \mathcal{N}(v)$, and $\mathbf{W}_r \in \mathbb{R}^{d \times d}$ is a learnable parameter matrix of the relation r between e and v. As a result, the related entitiy embeddings are projected to a unified description space. For example, the movie "Titanic" can be described as "directed by James Cameron", "released in 1997" and so on. In order to calculate the user's preference for this movie, we calculate u's attention to the above different knowledge descriptions by inner product and then normalize the result:

$$\pi_e^u = \text{SoftMax}(\mathbf{u}^\top \mathbf{e}). \tag{3}$$

Then we rank the entities according to the attention scores and keep the top Q most important entities as set $\mathcal{N}'(v)$, then renormalize their attention scores to $\pi_e'^u$, where Q is a configurable hyperparameter. Now we have completed the construction of the one-hop sub-graph of v, denoted as $\mathcal{G}_{uv}^1$. Then we replace v with each sampled entity and repeat the above operation until we obtain the H-hop sub-graph $\mathcal{G}_{uv}^H$, where H is also a hyperparameter indicating the maximum depth of item v's receptive field. However, the flexibility of attention scores makes the learning process prone to overfitting, so we follow the method proposed in [14] to perform label smoothness regularization to get better attention scores.

In order to obtain an overall knowledge-enhanced representation of item v, we iteratively aggregate the neighborhoods for entities in the subgraph. Specifically, for each entity z in sub-graph $\mathcal{G}_{uv}^{H-1}$, we calculate the linear combination of its neighborhood as:

$$\mathbf{z}_{\mathcal{N}'(z)}^{(0)} = \sum_{e \in \mathcal{N}'(z)} \pi_e'^u \mathbf{e}^{(0)}, \tag{4}$$

where $\mathbf{e}^{(0)} = \mathbf{e}$, then we update the representation of z by combining its own representation $\mathbf{z}^{(0)}$ and neighborhood representation:

$$\mathbf{z}^{(1)} = \sigma(\mathbf{z}_{\mathcal{N}'(z)}^{(0)} + \mathbf{z}^{(0)}), \tag{5}$$

where σ is the nonlinear activation function. Note that for the target item v, $\mathbf{z}^{(0)} = \mathbf{v}^{(0)}$ is its own embedding $\mathbf{e}_v$ without projection. The above process is repeated until the sub-graph is reduced to $\mathcal{G}_{uv}^0$, which only contains the target item v and its overall knowledge representation $\mathbf{v}^u = \mathbf{v}^{(H)}$. With $\mathbf{v}^u$ and the target user's representation $\mathbf{u}$, we use a prediction function $f : \mathbb{R}^d \times \mathbb{R}^d \to \mathbb{R}$ (i.e., inner product) to calculate the interaction probability between u and v:

$$\hat{y}_{uv} = \mathbf{u}^\top \mathbf{v}^u. \tag{6}$$

3.3   Model Training

To ensure effective model training, we sample the same number of negative samples as the positive samples for each user. Finally, we have the following loss function for SHGAT:

$$\mathcal{L} = \sum_{u,v} J(y_{uv}, \hat{y}_{uv}) + \lambda R(\mathcal{A}_{uv}) + \gamma \|\Theta\|_2^2, \tag{7}$$

where J is the cross-entropy loss function, $\mathcal{A}_{uv}$ is the attention scores in the user-specific sub-graph $\mathcal{G}_{uv}^H$, $R(\cdot)$ is the label smoothness regularization that can be seen as a constraint on the attention scores and the definition of $R(\cdot)$ can be found in [14], $\gamma \|\Theta\|_2^2$ is the L2-regularizer, λ and γ are balancing hyperparameters.

In order to explain the learning process of SHGAT more clearly, we summarize it into Algorithm 1.

Algorithm 1: Learning algorithm for SHGAT

Input: Interaction matrix Y, knowledge graph $\mathcal{G}$
Output: Prediction function $\mathcal{F}(u, v|\Theta, Y, \mathcal{G})$

1 Construct sample set from Y, and split it into training set, validation set and test set;
2 Get initial item embeddings $\{\mathbf{e}_{v_1}, \mathbf{e}_{v_2}, ..., \mathbf{e}_{v_N}\}$ through Word2Vec with training set;
3 Construct interaction sets $\{\mathcal{S}_1, \mathcal{S}_2, ..., \mathcal{S}_M\}$ from training set;
4 Initialize all parameters;
5 **while** *SHGAT not converge* **do**
6   **for** (u, v) *in training set* **do**
7   Calculate user representation **u** on Eq.(1);
8   **for** $h = 1, ..., H$ **do**
9   Do spatial transformation for related entities on Eq.(2);
10   Calculate attention score π_e^u for each entity on Eq.(3);
11   Filter the entities to get $\mathcal{G}_{uv}^h$;
12   **for** $h = H, ..., 1$ **do**
13   Attentively aggregate and update entity representation on Eq.(4)-(5);
14   Calculate predicted probability on Eq.(6);
15   Update parameters by gradient descent;
16 return $\mathcal{F}$;

---

4   Experiments

4.1   Datasets

We conduct our experiments against two realistic datasets, i.e., Movielens-20M and Last.FM. The codes and data are publicly available for reproducibility and further study.[1]

- **MovieLens-20M**[2] is a widely used dataset in movie recommendations, which contains nearly 20 million explicit ratings (ranging from 1 to 5) on the MovieLens website.

---

[1] https://github.com/GhostShipZ/SHGAT.
[2] https://grouplens.org/datasets/movielens/.

- **Last.FM**[3] is a music listening dataset collected from Last.fm online music systems and the tracks are viewed as the items.

We follow the procedures of [15] to process these two datasets, which are both linked to the sub-KGs extracted from the Microsoft KG Satori[4]. The basic statistics of the two datasets are presented in Table 2.

Table 2. Statistics and hyper-parameter settings (Q: neighbor sampling size, d: dimension of embeddings, H: depth of receptive field, λ: weight of label smoothness regularization, γ: weight of L2 regularization, η: learning rate.)

	MovieLens-20M	Last.FM
# users	138159	1872
# items	16954	3846
# interactions	13501622	42346
# entities	102569	9366
# relations	32	60
# KG triples	499474	15518
(Q, d, H, batch size)	(4, 128, 2, 8192)	(8, 16, 1, 256)
(λ, γ, η)	(0.1, 1×10^{-7}, 3×10^{-3})	(0.1, 1.5×10^{-4}, 2×10^{-3})

4.2 Baselines

- **BPRMF** [10] is a CF-based method that takes Matrix Factorization as the underlying predictor and minimizes the pairwise ranking loss for implicit feedback.
- **CKE** [20] combines CF with structural, textual, and visual knowledge for recommendation. We implement CKE as CF with a structural knowledge module in this paper.
- **RippleNet** [13] is a state-of-the-art model that propagates users' potential preferences in the KG for recommendation.
- **KGCN** [15] is another state-of-the-art model that aggregates neighborhood information with bias to learn the knowledge representations of items and users' personalized interests.
- **CKAN** [18] is also a state-of-the-art model that combines collaborative information with knowledge information together and learns user/item representations through a knowledge-aware attention mechanism.
- **SHGAT**$_{w/o\ c\_sim}$ is a variant of SHGAT that removes the collaborative similarity modeling of items, and item embeddings are initialized randomly.
- **SHGAT**$_{w/o\ u\_sim}$ is a variant of SHGAT that removes the user similarity modeling, and we assign a learnable embedding matrix for the users instead.

---

[3] https://grouplens.org/datasets/hetrec-2011/.
[4] https://searchengineland.com/library/bing/bing-satori.

– **SHGAT**$_{w/o\ hete}$ is another variant of SHGAT, it removes the importance sampling module and entity embedding transformation module, instead, we adopt the sampling and aggregation method proposed in KGCN.

4.3   Experimental Settings

In SHGAT, the activation function σ in Eq. (5) is set as *tanh* for the last aggregation and *ReLU* for the others. Other hyper-parameters are determined by optimizing $F1$ score on a validation set and the final settings of hyper-parameters are provided in Table 2. For the other baselines, we set the hyper-parameters according to their original papers. We split each dataset into training, validation and test set at a ratio of 6:2:2. Each experiment is repeated 3 times, and the average performance is reported. We evaluate these models in two experiment scenarios: (1) For click-through rate (CTR) prediction, we use the metrics *AUC* and $F1$ score. (2) For top-K recommendation, we use *Recall@K*. In terms of optimization, Adam algorithm is adpted to optimize all trainable parameters.

We use Skip-gram to pre-train item embeddings, where hierarchical softmax is enabled. The window size is set to 30 for both movie and music dataset. Since $|\mathcal{S}_u|$ and $|\mathcal{N}(e)|$ both have wide ranges, in order to ensure the effective use of video memory, we perform a non-replacement uniform sampling on them in advance, while retaining most of the information. The vacancies are padded with a special entity, which has no real impact. Specifically, for MovieLens-20M, the quantiles are set to 99 for interaction sets and 90 for entity neighbors, for Last.FM, the numbers are 99, 95. In addition, as the timestamps of user behavior are not available in the music dataset, we have to weaken the first assumption by removing the condition of time window.

4.4   Results

Table 3 summarizes the results of CTR prediction on the two datasets, and the results of top-K recommendation are presented in Fig. 2. The major findings from the experimental results are as follows:

Compared with these state-of-the-art baselines, SHGAT achieves strongly competitive performance on both two datasets, which proves the superiority of our purposed methods. Especially for the movie dataset, SHGAT outperforms other baselines by a large margin *w.r.t. AUC*, $F1$, and the excellent performance *w.r.t. Recall* shows that SHGAT can not only predict users' preferences for items well, but also with very high accuracy.

The KG-aware model CKE is inferior to the CF-based model BPRMF, which indicates that it is difficult for recommendation to directly benefit from the KGE task. The remaining models are all based on knowledge propagation in the KG, and their overall performance is better than that of CKE and BPRMF, which proves that knowledge propagation is an effective way to utilize KG to enhance recommendation.

The experimental results of the two ablation versions, SHGAT$_{w/o\ c\_sim}$ and SHGAT$_{w/o\ u\_sim}$, *w.r.t.* all three metrics in both datasets

Table 3. The results of AUC and $F1$ in CTR prediction.

Model	Last.FM		MovieLens-20M	
	AUC	$F1$	AUC	$F1$
BPRMF	0.752(−11.6%)	0.698(−9.7%)	0.962(−2.5%)	0.917(−3.2%)
CKE	0.745(−12.5%)	0.675(−12.7%)	0.931(−5.7%)	0.875(−7.6%)
RippleNet	0.777(−8.7%)	0.704(−8.9%)	0.976(−1.1%)	0.929(−1.9%)
KGCN	0.798(−6.2%)	0.715(−7.5%)	0.977(−1.0%)	0.931(−1.7%)
CKAN	0.845(−0.7%)	0.770(−0.4%)	0.972(−1.5%)	0.923(−2.5%)
SHGAT$_{w/o\ c\_sim}$	0.839(−1.4%)	0.765(−1.0%)	0.984(−0.3%)	0.940(−0.7%)
SHGAT$_{w/o\ u\_sim}$	0.819(−3.8%)	0.745(−3.6%)	0.978(−0.9%)	0.935(−1.3%)
SHGAT$_{w/o\ hete}$	0.847(−0.5%)	0.762(−1.4%)	0.987(0.0%)	0.947(0.0%)
SHGAT	**0.851**	**0.773**	**0.987**	**0.947**

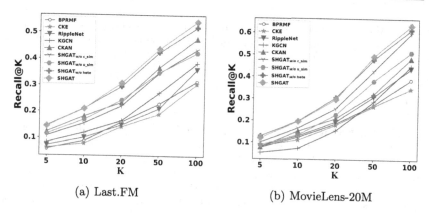

(a) Last.FM   (b) MovieLens-20M

Fig. 2. The results of $Recall@K$ in top-K recommendation.

prove the importance of similarity modeling for recommendation. What is more, we find out that fewer iterations are required for the model to achieve optimal performance if the similarity modeling is included. For example, in an experiment, the epochs corresponding to the best performance of the full SHGAT are 6, 13 for the movie and music datasets respectively, and the number is 12, 44 for SHGAT$_{w/o\ c\_sim}$ and 34, 31 for SHGAT$_{w/o\ u\_sim}$. It shows that similarity modeling makes it easier for the model to learn more effective item embeddings.

The comparison of full SHGAT and SHGAT$_{w/o\ hete}$ in CTR and top-K tasks shows that the adoption of importance sampling and heterogeneous aggregation can bring some benefits, but not as much as similarity modeling does. We believe that the following two reasons can explain this: (1) Due to the sparsity of the extracted sub-KGs of the two datasets, most of the entities have only a few neighbors. Thus, the filtering ability of importance sampling cannot be fully utilized. (2) The learned entity embeddings and attention scores are not effective enough due to the lack of explicit semantic constraints, which poses a challenge to the optimization of SHGAT.

5   Conclusions

In this paper, we propose SHGAT, a similarity-based heterogeneous graph attention network for knowledge-enhanced recommendation. Firstly, similarity modeling, a key component that has been rarely explored recently, is used to learn more effective user/item representations. Secondly, the heterogeneous graph attention network, which is composed of importance sampling and heterogeneous aggregation, is used to better distinguish users' personalized interests and propagate knowledge in a more reasonable way. Extensive experimental results demonstrate the superiority of SHGAT over the state-of-the-art baselines on two public benchmark datasets.

Acknowledgments. This work was supported by Pengcheng Laboratory under Project "The Verification Platform of Multi-tier Coverage Communication Network for Oceans (PCL2018KP002)".

References

1. Barkan, O., Koenigstein, N.: Item2vec: neural item embedding for collaborative filtering. In: 2016 IEEE 26th International Workshop on Machine Learning for Signal Processing (MLSP), pp. 1–6. IEEE (2016)
2. Bollacker, K., Evans, C., Paritosh, P., Sturge, T., Taylor, J.: Freebase: a collaboratively created graph database for structuring human knowledge. In: Proceedings of the 2008 ACM SIGMOD International Conference on Management of Data, pp. 1247–1250 (2008)
3. Bordes, A., Usunier, N., Garcia-Duran, A., Weston, J., Yakhnenko, O.: Translating embeddings for modeling multi-relational data. In: Neural Information Processing Systems (NIPS), pp. 1–9 (2013)
4. Guo, Q., et al.: A survey on knowledge graph-based recommender systems. IEEE Trans. Knowl. Data Eng. (2020). https://doi.org/10.1109/TKDE.2020.3028705
5. Hamilton, W.L., Ying, R., Leskovec, J.: Inductive representation learning on large graphs. arXiv preprint arXiv:1706.02216 (2017)
6. He, X., Liao, L., Zhang, H., Nie, L., Hu, X., Chua, T.S.: Neural collaborative filtering. In: Proceedings of the 26th International Conference on World Wide Web, pp. 173–182 (2017)
7. Koren, Y., Bell, R., Volinsky, C.: Matrix factorization techniques for recommender systems. Computer **42**(8), 30–37 (2009)
8. Lehmann, J., et al.: Dbpedia-a large-scale, multilingual knowledge base extracted from Wikipedia. Semant. Web **6**(2), 167–195 (2015)
9. Mikolov, T., Chen, K., Corrado, G., Dean, J.: Efficient estimation of word representations in vector space. arXiv preprint arXiv:1301.3781 (2013)
10. Rendle, S., Freudenthaler, C., Gantner, Z., Schmidt-Thieme, L.: Bpr: Bayesian personalized ranking from implicit feedback. arXiv preprint arXiv:1205.2618 (2012)

11. Suchanek, F.M., Kasneci, G., Weikum, G.: Yago: a core of semantic knowledge. In: Proceedings of the 16th international conference on World Wide Web, pp. 697–706 (2007)
12. Veličković, P., Cucurull, G., Casanova, A., Romero, A., Lio, P., Bengio, Y.: Graph attention networks. arXiv preprint arXiv:1710.10903 (2017)
13. Wang, H., et al.: Ripplenet: propagating user preferences on the knowledge graph for recommender systems. In: Proceedings of the 27th ACM International Conference on Information and Knowledge Management, pp. 417–426 (2018)
14. Wang, H., et al.: Knowledge-aware graph neural networks with label smoothness regularization for recommender systems. In: Proceedings of the 25th ACM SIGKDD International Conference on Knowledge Discovery & Data Mining, pp. 968–977 (2019)
15. Wang, H., Zhao, M., Xie, X., Li, W., Guo, M.: Knowledge graph convolutional networks for recommender systems. In: The world Wide Web Conference, pp. 3307–3313 (2019)
16. Wang, X., He, X., Cao, Y., Liu, M., Chua, T.S.: Kgat: knowledge graph attention network for recommendation. In: Proceedings of the 25th ACM SIGKDD International Conference on Knowledge Discovery & Data Mining, pp. 950–958 (2019)
17. Wang, X., Bo, D., Shi, C., Fan, S., Ye, Y., Yu, P.S.: A survey on heterogeneous graph embedding: Methods, techniques, applications and sources. arXiv preprint arXiv:2011.14867 (2020)
18. Wang, Z., Lin, G., Tan, H., Chen, Q., Liu, X.: Ckan: collaborative knowledge-aware attentive network for recommender systems. In: Proceedings of the 43rd International ACM SIGIR Conference on Research and Development in Information Retrieval, pp. 219–228 (2020)
19. Wu, S., Zhang, W., Sun, F., Cui, B.: Graph neural networks in recommender systems: A survey. arXiv preprint arXiv:2011.02260 (2020)
20. Zhang, F., Yuan, N.J., Lian, D., Xie, X., Ma, W.Y.: Collaborative knowledge base embedding for recommender systems. In: Proceedings of the 22nd ACM SIGKDD International Conference on Knowledge Discovery and Data Mining, pp. 353–362 (2016)

Accurate and Robust RGB-D Visual Odometry Based on Point and Line Features

Guojie Zhao[✉], Yupeng Zhang, Peichu Liu, Haoen Wu, and Mingyang Cui

College of Computer Science and Technology, Jilin University, Changchun 130000, Jilin, China

Abstract. Feature recognition is widely used in visual simultaneous localization and mapping and visual odometry system. The most popular feature is the point feature, which includes SIFT feature, SURF feature, ORB feature. But in low textured scenes, RGB-D simultaneous localization and mapping (SLAM) tend to fail due to lack of reliable point features. Line features are as rich as point features in a structured or a low textured environment. However, line feature always contains more texture information for the calculation of pose, making it more complex for a line feature to be extracted, described and parameterized. To overcome the problems. We proposed a robust VO system fusing both points and lines by linearizing points, which not only preserves the information provided by line features, but also speeds up the calculation process. The method in this paper is evaluated on the TUM public real-world RGB-D dataset. The experimental results demonstrate that the algorithm proposed in this paper is more accurate and robust than the pure feature point algorithm in consideration.

Keywords: Visual odmetry · Feature point · Feature line · Low-texture · RGB-D SLAM

1 Introduction

Simultaneous Localization and Mapping (SLAM) [3] is one of the key technologies in the mobile robots field, and Visual Odometry (VO) is also a significant part of SLAM. Visual SLAM is mainly divided into visual front-end and optimized back-end, and the front end is known as VO. According to the information of adjacent images, it (VO) can estimate the coarse camera motion and provide better information for the back-end initial value. According to whether the feather needs to be extracted or not, the implementation of VO is divided into the feature point feature-based method and the direct method without feature extraction. But in some scenes, these two methods are not particularly suitable [6, 7]: in the feature point feature-based method, feature point extraction takes a lot of time, and it is difficult to calculate the camera motion through a small number of feature points where features are missing due to the lack of texture, such as the walls with less texture, floors, and white sofas; while the non-convexity and sensitivity to light of the direct method only allow small motion and the Subtle lighting environment. There are great limitations in changing scenarios.

© Springer Nature Switzerland AG 2021
H. Qiu et al. (Eds.): KSEM 2021, LNAI 12816, pp. 500–510, 2021.
https://doi.org/10.1007/978-3-030-82147-0_41

At present, most of the SLAM systems only use point features for location and mapping, and few use line features due to the sophisticated transversion of extracting, matching and parameterizing the line features. However, as a structural feature, line feature contains structural information of the environment, it can acquire higher positioning accuracy especially in low texture scenes when utilized together with point feature. In this study, we build on the main ideas of ORB (Oriented Fast and Rotated Brief) and propose a Visual Odometry method combining point and line features with the following contributions:

- We set a threshold value for the number of feature points. When the number of feature points recognized by the ORB algorithm is less than the threshold, the line feature algorithm is enabled
- We proposed a method of "breaking" the line segments, breaking the line segments into feature points and forming a set of their own. In the process of line feature matching, we firstly determine the line mapping, and then match the set of feature points of the corresponding line.
- The breakup density of feature lines is based on the number of feature points in the whole image, which makes our algorithm run stably and efficiently in both muti-texture scenes and low-texture scenes.

In the rest of the paper, the related works on point feature and line feature are summarized in Sect. 2. The mathematical theory and system framework of the proposed system are given in Sect. 3. In Sect. 4, we run the algorithm on the TUM dataset and print out the results of point and line feature extraction. We also calculate the ATE.RMSE (m) value of the pure point feature algorithm and our algorithm, the mathematical analysis is carried out then. The conclusions are made in Sect. 5.

2   Related Work

2.1   Feature Point Based Method

Feature based method is also called indirect method [13], which runs stably and is insensitive to light and dynamic objects. It is a mature VO method at present. Through the feature matching (extract feature points of two adjacent frames and match descriptors), we can get the corresponding feature points in the two images. And using epipolar geometry, ICP, PNP and other methods, the camera motion can be estimated.

The early feature-based method of monocular SLAM is based on point features, using an extended Kalman filter for pose estimation. And PTAM (parallel tracking and mapping) system is the first system using nonlinear optimization, which is proposed by Klein [8] et al. laying a foundation for the prototype of monocular vision SLAM algorithm. It introduces keyframe mechanism. It realizes the parallelization of the tracking and composition process.

In history, many image features have been proposed, such as SIFT (scale invariant feature transform) [14], which fully considers the changes of illumination, scale, rotation in the process of image transformation, but the computational complexity is enormous. To speed up the calculation, it is acceptable to reduce the accuracy and robustness appropriately, so the ORB (Oriented FAST and Rotated BRIEF) [4] feature appears. It improved the problem that FAST detectors in SIFT are not directional, and used a very fast binary descriptor, which is a compromise between quality and performance. However, many feature matching algorithm still has the drawbacks of time-consuming, ignoring other features besides feature points. What's worse, in low-texture or weak-texture areas, these indirect methods cannot detect stable image features. Simultaneously, due to the weak gradient field distribution characteristics of low-texture regions, the descriptors generated by image features in these regions have low discrimination, which is prone to mismatch problems. For example, ORB performs well in scenes with rich textures, while in low-texture scenes including white walls, ceilings, corridors, etc., the algorithm cannot extract rich features to generate accurate descriptors, which results in a significant decrease in algorithm performance.

2.2 Feature Line Based Method

At present, there are many excellent line extraction algorithms, such as Hough line detection algorithm, EDlines line detection algorithm, LSD [11] fast line detection algorithm and Cannylines algorithm. The actual extraction results of these algorithms in low-texture scenes are relatively superior. Among them, the Cannylines algorithm has higher accuracy, and the LSD algorithm obtains sub-pixel precision detection results in a linear time, which is designed so that no parameter adjustment is required on any digital image. Furthermore, LSD is faster than Hough, but it is not satisfactory when dealing with intersection, partial blurring, line occlusion, etc.

At the same time, we can also discover that line features can provide more constraints than point features, and in scenes lack of texture, illumination change, line features are more robust than point features and pixel by pixel photometric information.

3 Our Method

3.1 System Overview

The input of the proposed system is the calibrated RGB and depth frames, and the output is the camera pose and 3D model. Feature points and feature lines are extracted in parallel. After the feature line is broken into points, it is merged with the original feature point set. Then we use the traditional feature point matching algorithm to map the point in two frames in adjacent time.

We use LSD as the line feature extractor, which can detect line segments with high accuracy and fast speed. Breaking the traditional way of matching, we break the lines up into key point set.

Neighbor algorithm, or k-nearest neighbor (KNN) classification algorithm is one of the simplest methods in data mining classification technology. The so-called k nearest neighbor means k nearest neighbors. It means that each sample can be represented by its nearest K neighbors. We use the KNN method to eliminate the matching points with large deviation to increase the accuracy of pose calculation (Fig. 1).

Fig. 1. System overview

We put the filtered matching points into the map and match the current frame with the map points. In comparing two frames, we only calculate the feature matching and motion relationship between the reference frame and the current frame, and set the current frame as a new reference frame after calculation. In VO using a map, each frame contributes some information to the map, such as adding new feature points or updating the position estimation of old feature points (Fig. 2).

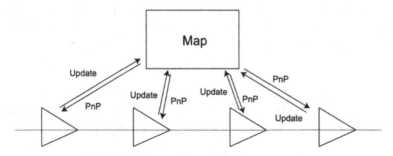

Fig. 2. Working principle of the VO using map

The advantage of this is that we can maintain a constantly updated map. As long as the map is correct, even if there is an error in a certain frame in the middle, it is possible to find the correct position of the subsequent frames.

3.2   Extraction and Matching of Points and Lines

We know that point-line feature matching is essential, and combining the two features precisely has a better effect. Feature points are some special points in the image. It is easier to identify the corners and edges than pixel blocks because they are more recognizable in different images. What we used in this experiment is the classic ORB feature. The extraction of ORB features can be divided into two steps, FAST corner extraction and BRIEF descriptor. In Fast corner extraction, we use Non-maximal suppression method to retain the maximum corner points, calculate the Harris [5] response value for the original FAST corner points. And ORB adds a description of scale and rotation to improve the weakness of FAST. The scale invariance is achieved by constructing an image pyramid and detecting corner points on each layer of the pyramid; the rotation of features is achieved by the gray-scale centroid method.

Through these methods, FAST corner points have scale and rotation, and the robustness is greatly improved. So in ORB, this improved FAST is called Oriented FAST.

After extracting the key points, we start to calculate the descriptor for each point. In ORB, BRIEF is a binary descriptor, its description vector is composed of many 0 and 1, where 0 and 1 encode the size relationship between two pixels near the key point. BRIEF uses random point selection for comparison, which is very fast, and it is also very convenient to store binary expressions, which is suitable for real-time image matching. In Feature matching, we use KNN matching [12] to avoid some errors produced by Brute-Force Matcher. Because we use RGB-D cameras in our experiments, so we use ICP. ICP (Iterative Closest Point) [10] is a method for solving 3D to 3D point pair motion. We can use nonlinear optimization to construct the iterative solution of the ordinary least squares problem, namely Bundle Adjustment.

There are n three-dimensional space points P and their projections p the objective world. We want to calculate the pose R, t of the camera, and its Lie algebra is expressed as ξ. s_i is the coefficient needed to convert to homogeneous coordinates. Suppose the coordinates of a certain spatial point are $P_i = [X_i, Y_i, Z_i]^T$, and its projected pixel coordinates are $u_i=[u_i, v_i]^T$. The relationship between pixel position and spatial point position is written in matrix form [9]:

$$s_i u_i = K exp(\xi^{\wedge}) P_i \tag{1}$$

Due to the unknown camera pose and the noise of the observation point, there is an error in this equation. Therefore, we sum the errors to construct a least squares problem and find the best camera pose through constant iteration [14]:

$$\xi^* = arg\,min\frac{1}{2} \sum_{i=1}^{n} \left\| u_i - exp(\xi^{\Lambda}) P_i \right\|_2^2 \tag{2}$$

Line features can provide more constraints than point features, but adding line features to the SLAM system faces parameterization and optimization. In our experiment, the LSD line detection algorithm [15] is used. The purpose of LSD is to detect local straight contours in an image. Contours are some special regions in an image. In these regions, the gray-scale of the image changes drastically from black to white or from white to black.

First, reduce the input image to 80% of the original size to weaken the aliasing effect. Second, the gradient calculation must be performed. Let I (x, y) be the gray value at the point (x, y) on the gray-scale image, then the gradient of the image can be calculated as follows:

$$g_x(x, y) = (i(x+1, y) + i(x+1, y+1) - i(x, y) - i(x, y+1))/2 \tag{3}$$

$$g_y(x, y) = (i(x, y+1) + i(x+1, y+1) - i(x, y) - i(x+1, y))/2 \tag{4}$$

The level-line angle needs to be calculated by the following formula:

$$\arctan(\frac{g_x(x, y)}{-g_y(x, y)}) \tag{5}$$

The gradient amplitude is:

$$G(x, y) = (g_x^2(x, y) + g_y^2(x, y))^{\frac{1}{2}} \tag{6}$$

Next, in order to start line segmentation detection from the pixel with the highest gradient magnitude, we need to sort the gradients. A small gradient amplitude represents a region where the gradient changes slowly. In this region, there will be many errors in the straight line detection segmentation, so the pixels with the gradient amplitude less than ρ(threshold we set) are not considered. In the region growth algorithm, unused pixels are selected from the previous sorting as seeds to generate a line support region. All unused pixels are detected recursively. Every time a new pixel is added, the angle of the area is continuously updated as:

$$\arctan \frac{\sum_j \sin(level - line - angle_j)}{\sum_j \cos(level - line - angle_j)} \tag{7}$$

At the same time, according to prior knowledge, we know that the straight-line division corresponds to this rectangle, that is, the divided line can be represented by a circumscribed rectangle, and the center of the rectangle can be represented as follows:

$$c_x = \frac{\sum_{j \in Region} G(j) \cdot x(j)}{\sum_{j \in Region} G(j)} \tag{8}$$

$$c_y = \frac{\sum_{j \in Region} G(j) \cdot y(j)}{\sum_{j \in Region} G(j)} \tag{9}$$

Finally, we count the main direction of the circumscribed rectangle of these lines support region. Use the a-contrario approach [16] method to determine whether the line support region is a straight line segment.

3.3 Observation Model of Line Feature

The length of a line segment in space may not be the same from different perspectives, therefore, the reprojection of the error cannot be compared from the length of the line segment observed in the two images.

However, the residuals of line observation in space can be measured by 3D-3D, that is, the line segments observed in two images are projected into 3D space, and the distance between two lines is compared in 3D space. At the same time, it can also be compared by 3D-2D, projecting the line in 3D space into 2D space, and measuring the distance between two line segments in 2D space.

In this paper, 3D-2D method is used to measure the line observation residual. Firstly, the line in the space is reprojected to the normalized camera coordinate system of current image to get I''. Two points C and D on the line γ are projected onto the image plane to form two points c and d respectively. The projection formula of obtaining the line segment I by projecting a straight line γ into the image plane in space is derived as follows:

$$c = KC, d = KD$$

$$\gamma = (n^T, v^T)^T$$

$$n = [C], D \tag{10}$$

$$I' = [c], d$$

$$I = K'n$$

where C and D are two points in the space, and C and D are two points in the image. γ is the space line, I' is the line segment in image plane, n is the normal vector of the line, v is the direction vector of the line, K' is the line internal parameter matrix, K is the point internal parameter matrix.

4 Analysis of Experimental Results and Evaluation of the Algorithm

We choose the TUM DATASET to test our algorithm. Dataset comes from TUM Department of Informatics of Technical University of Munich, each sequence of the TUM benchmark RGB-D dataset contains RGB images and depth images recorded with a Microsoft Kinect RGB-D camera in a variety of scenes and the accurate actual motion trajectory of the camera obtained by the motion capture system.

The algorithm is implemented on Ubuntu 16.04 LTS with 2 GHz four-core Intel Core i5 processor and 16 GB memory.

4.1 The Results of Feature Extraction

Firstly, the algorithm is compared with point feature VO and line feature VO on the TUM RGB-D dataset. We produce some images after feature extraction for comparison (Fig. 3).

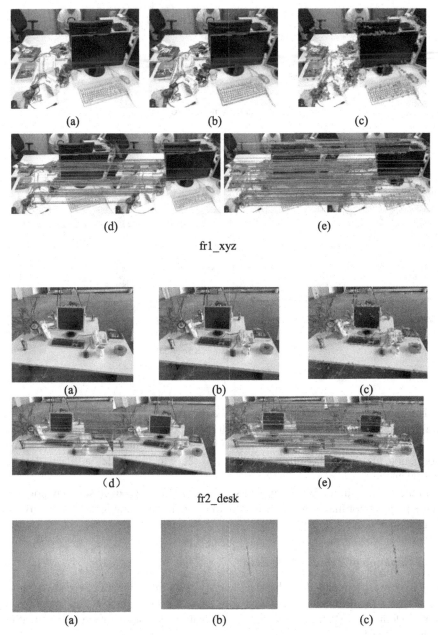

Fig. 3. The result of the three algorithms in the TUM dataset, (a) point features extracted from images. (b) line features extracted from images. (c) combination of point and line features. (d) pure point feature matching. (e) feature matching based on the combination of point and line features.

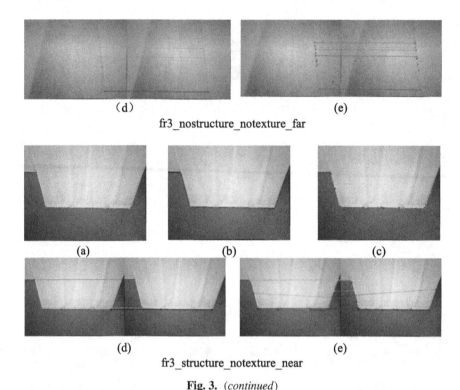

(d)   (e)

fr3_nostructure_notexture_far

(a)   (b)   (c)

(d)   (e)

fr3_structure_notexture_near

Fig. 3. (*continued*)

The experimental results show that only a few feature points can be recognized by pure feature points VO, which is not enough to support the calculation of the camera's pose transformation. Our method can extract line feature elements in the scene with less information, and break them into feature points set, which provides sufficient data for pose calculation.

In the scene with more feature points, our method may produce so many points in feature point vector that it may lead to a lot of errors in matching feature points. But in most cases, it works efficiently.

4.2 Evaluation of Relative Pose Error

Relative pose error mainly describes the accuracy of pose difference between two frames with a fixed time difference (compared with the real pose), which is equivalent to the error of odometer direct measurement. This evaluation technique is useful for estimating the drift (Table 1).

According to the comparison results given in the table, we can see that the algorithm in this paper produces less RPE.RMSE in most sequences than pure point feature VO which is due to our algorithm providing more feature points. In sequence freiburg1_ RPY (quick) and freiburg 1_ In XYZ, the proposed system delivers much worse results than pure feature VO, because in the face of continuous keyframes with large variation, we extract too many feature points, which will increase the drift amplitude and error.

Table 1. Comparison of ATE RMSE(m) on TUM RGB_D DATASET.

Algorithm\seq	VO based on feature points	Our method
freiburg1_rpy (quick)	0.056430745	0.991334741
freiburg1_floor	0.913374315	0.379414638
freiburg1_xyz	0.148905717	0.099764359
freiburg2_coke	0.844310693	0.554994991
freiburg2_xyz	0.06573862	0.047183847
reiburg3_nostructure_notexture_far	0.807717737	0.523411213
freiburg3_walking_rpy	0.344684709	0.278956582

5   Conclusion

This paper mainly builds the RGB-D visual odometer method based on feature points, and proposes a point line combination method to improve the feature information extraction ability of the visual odometer which provides more favorable information for pose calculation, and improve the robustness and accuracy of the visual odometer. The traditional line feature matching will greatly increase the calculation time of VO. We proposed a line segment method to transform line features into point features and participate in the matching calculation of point features. Experimental results suggest that our algorithm is very efficient in low texture scenes producing less error. The disadvantage is that when the lens moves fast, VO is easy to be lost. When there is no loop detection, these errors will lead to more and more drift.

References

1. Durrant-Whyte, H., Bailey, T.: Simultaneous localization and mapping: part I. IEEE Robot. Autom. Mag **13**(2), 99–110 (2006)
2. Lin, F., Liu, Y., Zhou, J., et al.: Optimization of visual odometry algorithm based on ORB feature. Laser Optoelectron. Prog. **56**(21), 180–187 (2019)
3. Tan, R., Zhu, M., Xu, Y.: Monocular SLAM feature point optimization based on ORB. In: 2019 International Conference on Big Data, Electronics and Communication Engineering, pp. 44–50 (2019)
4. Cai, L., Ye, Y., Gao, X., et al.: An improved visual SLAM based on affine transformation for ORB feature extraction. Optik **227**, 165421 (2021)
5. Bhowmik, M.K., Shil, S., Saha, P.: Feature points extraction of thermal face using Harris interest point detection. Procedia Technol. **10**(1), 24–730 (2013)
6. Lin, B., Wang, F., Sun, Y., et al.: Boundary points based scale invariant 3D point feature. J. Vis. Commun. Image Represent. **48**, 136–148 (2017)
7. Yongan, S., Kang, J.-G., Lee, L.-K., et al.: Line segment-based indoor mapping with salient line feature extraction. Adv. Robot. **26**(5–6), 437–460 (2012)
8. Zhang, Z., Liu, M., Diao, C., et al.: A survey of the simultaneous localization and mapping (SLAM) based on RGB-D camera. In: Proceedings of 2019 2nd International Conference on Mechanical, Electronic and Engineering Technology, pp. 48–58 (2019)

9. Li, L.: RGB-D visual odometry based on points and edges. Int. J. Comput. Eng. **5**(1), 212–220 (2020)

10. Liang, B., Wang, G.: Comparative analysis of position and pose estimation methods of RGB-D camera. In: Proceedings of the 2nd International Conference on Artificial Intelligence and Computer Science, pp. 1253–1259 (2020)

11. Liu, Y., Xie, Z., Liu, H.: LB-LSD: a length-based line segment detector for real-time applications. Pattern Recogn. Lett. **128**, 247–254 (2019)

12. Fanyang, M., Xia, L., Jihong, P.: A feature point matching based on spatial order constraints bilateral-neighbor vote. IEEE Trans. Image Process. **24**(11), 4160–4171 (2015)

13. Xiaoyun, L., Wang, H., Tang, S., et al.: DM-SLAM: monocular SLAM in dynamic environments. Appl. Sci. **10**(12), 1–16 (2020)

14. Han, B., Wu, W., Wang, Y., et al.: The semi-dense ICP algorithm based on the SIFT feature points neighborhood. In: Proceedings of the 2nd International Conference on Artificial Intelligence and Computer Science, pp. 396–401 (2020)

15. Grompone von, R.G., Jakubowicz, J., Morel, J.-M., et al.: LSD: a fast line segment detector with a false detection control. IEEE Trans. Pattern Anal. Mach. Intell. **32**(4), 722–732 (2010)

16. Patraucean, V., Gurdjos, P., Grompone von, G.R.: Joint a contrario ellipse and line detection. IEEE Trans. Pattern Anal. Mach. Intell. **39**(4), 788–802 (2017)

Sentence Extraction-Based Machine Reading Comprehension for Vietnamese

Phong Nguyen-Thuan Do[1,2], Nhat Duy Nguyen[1,2], Tin Van Huynh[1,2],
Kiet Van Nguyen[1,2(✉)], Anh Gia-Tuan Nguyen[1,2],
and Ngan Luu-Thuy Nguyen[1,2]

[1] University of Information Technology, Ho Chi Minh, Vietnam
{18520126,18520118}@gm.uit.edu.vn,
{tinhv,kietnv,anhngt,ngannlt}@uit.edu.vn
[2] Vietnam National University, Ho Chi Minh City, Vietnam

Abstract. The development of natural language processing (NLP) in general and machine reading comprehension in particular has attracted the great attention of the research community. In recent years, there are a few datasets for machine reading comprehension tasks in Vietnamese with large sizes, such as UIT-ViQuAD and UIT-ViNewsQA. However, the datasets are not diverse in answers to serve the research. In this paper, we introduce UIT-ViWikiQA, the first dataset for evaluating sentence extraction-based machine reading comprehension in the Vietnamese language. The UIT-ViWikiQA dataset is converted from the UIT-ViQuAD dataset, consisting of comprises 23.074 question-answers based on 5.109 passages of 174 Wikipedia Vietnamese articles. We propose a conversion algorithm to create the dataset for sentence extraction-based machine reading comprehension and three types of approaches for sentence extraction-based machine reading comprehension in Vietnamese. Our experiments show that the best machine model is XLM-R_{Large}, which achieves an exact match (EM) of 85.97% and an F1-score of 88.77% on our dataset. Besides, we analyze experimental results in terms of the question type in Vietnamese and the effect of context on the performance of the MRC models, thereby showing the challenges from the UIT-ViWikiQA dataset that we propose to the language processing community.

Keywords: Machine reading comprehension · Answer sentence extraction · Transformer

1 Introduction

NLP researchers have studied several works such as question answering, sentiment analysis, and part-of-speech. However, machine reading comprehension (MRC) is one of the critical tasks in NLP in recent years. MRC is an understanding natural language task that requires computers to understand a textual

© Springer Nature Switzerland AG 2021
H. Qiu et al. (Eds.): KSEM 2021, LNAI 12816, pp. 511–523, 2021.
https://doi.org/10.1007/978-3-030-82147-0_42

context and then answer questions based on it. MRC is widely used in many applications, such as search engines, intelligent agents, and chatbots.

In the experiments, datasets and models are important in solving the MRC task. For the models, various significant neural network-based approaches have been proposed and made a significant advancement in this research field, such as QANet [27] and BERT [7]. To evaluate these methods, we need different datasets; thus, creating a dataset is vital for computing on MRC models. In recent years, researchers have developed many MRC datasets in other languages such as English [19,25], Chinese [5], French [8], Russian [9], Korean [13], and Italian [4].

Table 1. An example of question-context-answer triples extracted from UIT-ViWikiQA.

Context:**Paris nằm ở điểm gặp nhau của các hành trình thương mại đường bộ và đường sông, và là trung tâm của một vùng nông nghiệp giàu có.** Vào thế kỷ 10, Paris đã là một trong những thành phố chính của Pháp cùng các cung điện hoàng gia, các tu viện và nhà thờ. Từ thế kỷ 12, Paris trở thành một trong những trung tâm của châu Âu về giáo dục và nghệ thuật.Thế kỷ 14, Paris là thành phố quan trọng bậc nhất của Cơ Đốc giáo và trong các thế kỷ 16, 17, đây là nơi diễn ra Cách mạng Pháp cùng nhiều sự kiện lịch sử quan trọng của Pháp và châu Âu. Đến thế kỷ 19 và 20, thành phố trở thành một trong những trung tâm văn hóa của thế giới, thủ đô của nghệ thuật và giải trí. (*Paris is at the meeting point of road and river trade routes and is at the heart of a rich agricultural region. In the 10th century, Paris was one of the main cities of France with royal palaces, monasteries, and churches. From the 12th century, Paris became one of Europe's centers for education and the arts. In the 14th century, Paris was the most important city of Christianity. In the 16th and 17th centuries, this was the place where the French Revolution took place and many important historical events of France and Europe. By the 19th and 20th centuries, the city had become one of the world's cultural centers, the capital of art and entertainment.*)
Question 1: Vị trí địa lý của Paris có gì đặc biệt? (*What's so special about Paris's geographical location?*)
Answer: Paris nằm ở điểm gặp nhau của các hành trình thương mại đường bộ và đường sông, và là trung tâm của một vùng nông nghiệp giàu có. (*Paris is at the meeting point of road and river trade routes and is at the heart of a rich agricultural region.*)

Vietnamese datasets in the MRC task are still really limited over the years. Examples of MRC resources available for Vietnamese language are span-extraction MRC datasets: UIT-ViQuAD [17] and UIT-ViNewsQA [22], and a multiple-choice dataset: ViMMRC [21]. Because Vietnamese is a language with insufficient resources for MRC task, we introduce UIT-ViWikiQA, a new dataset for sentence extraction-based MRC for the Vietnamese. Sentence extraction helps readers understand and know more information related to the question than the shorter span. Besides, a new dataset is our vital contribution to assess different MRC models in a low-resource language like Vietnamese. Table 1 shows an example for Vietnamese sentence extraction-based MRC.

In this paper, we have three primary contributions described as follows.

- We build UIT-ViWikiQA, the first dataset for evaluating sentence extraction-based machine reading comprehension for the Vietnamese language, extracted from the UIT-ViQuAD dataset based on our conversion algorithm. Our dataset comprises 23.074 questions on Wikipedia Vietnamese articles. Our dataset is available for research purposes at our website[1].
- We analyze the dataset in terms of the question words for each question type (What, When, Who, Why, Where, How, How many, and Others) in

---

[1] https://sites.google.com/uit.edu.vn/kietnv/datasets.

Vietnamese, thereby providing insights into the dataset that may facilitate future methods.

- We propose three types of approaches for the sentence extraction-based MRC for Vietnamese: ranking-based approaches, classification-based approaches, and MRC-based approaches. For each approach, we experiment on different models and compare the experimental results together. In addition, we analyze the dependence of the MRC model on the context.

2 Related Work

The ranking-based approach is inspired by calculating the similarity between two sentences with several previously published algorithms. For example, the word count algorithm is used for the WikiQA dataset [25]. The BM25 (Best Matching) algorithm is a ranking function used by search engines to rank text according to the relevance of a given query. BM25 is used for text similarity calculation or information retrieval in many previous studies [12,20].

The second approach is the classification-based approach. We use the classification model to find out the sentence containing the answer to the question. The model we use is the maLSTM model [14]. maLSTM is a version of the LSTM model whose input is two sentences, and the output is one of two labels (answerable and unanswerable). maLSTM solved the task of the similarity of two sentences [10]. In addition, we also use the BiGRU model [1], which has good performance in classification tasks [6,26].

Vietnamese MRC has several datasets to evaluate reading comprehension models, such as the multiple-choice question-answer-passage triple dataset (ViMMRC [21]) and the span-extraction datasets such as UIT-ViQuAD [17] for Wikipedia-based texts and UIT-ViNewsQA [22] for health-domain news texts. For the MRC models, the first one we use in this paper is the QANet model [27], which has been applied in previous reading comprehension studies in Vietnamese [17,22]. Next, we use the BERT model and its variants (e.g., XLM-Roberta) proposed by Devlin et al. [7], and Comeau et al. [3]. These models are also used for the previous question answering and MRC tasks in Vietnamese [17,22], Chinese [5,11], and English [7,18]. We also use a variant of BERT called PhoBERT as a monolingual pre-trained language model [16] for Vietnamese.

3 The ViWikiQA Dataset

We describe the UIT-ViWikiQA dataset and the process of creating it from the UIT-ViQuAD dataset (proposed by Nguyen et al. [17]), as well as several analyses on our dataset.

3.1 Task Definition

The main task in this paper is **sentence extraction-based machine reading comprehension** for Vietnamese. This is a task that requires the computer to find the sentence in a context that contains the answer to a specific question. The input to the task includes question Q and the context S $= (S_1, S_2...S_n)$ containing the answer. The output of the task is a sentence S_i in the context, the condition that this sentence S_i includes the answer to the question Q in the input. The examples we show are in Table 1, where the input consists of **Question** and **Context**, the output is **Answer**, the sentence is colored in the **Context**.

3.2 Dataset Conversion

We create the UIT-ViWikiQA dataset based on the UIT-ViQuAD dataset. Answers and their answer start are updated by Algorithm 1.

Algorithm 1. Converting the UIT-ViQuAD dataset into the UIT-ViWikiQA dataset.

Input: The context **C** and the answer start of answer **AS**
Output: Returning the sentence **ST** that contains the answer and its start **SS** .

```
 1: procedure CONVERTING THE DATASET
 2:     Sentences ← Segmenting the context C into the list of sentences;
 3:     Start ← 0;
 4:     End ← -1;
 5:     for S in Sentences do
 6:         Start ← End + 1;
 7:         End ← Start + len(S);
 8:         if Start ≤ AS < End then
 9:             break;
10:         end if
11:     end for
12:     ST ← i;
13:     SS ← C.find(ST); //SS is starting position of sentence ST in context C.
14:     return ST, SS
15: end procedure
```

In the UIT-ViQuAD dataset, a sample includes context, question, answer, answer start, and id. Based on **Algorithm 1**, we change the answer and the answer start using context and answer start **(AS)** of UIT-ViQuAD. Next, we use a sentence segmentation tool to segment the context **(C)** into the list of sentences $S = (S_1, S_2, S_3, ...S_n)$, then $S_i \in S$ is an answer of the question in UIT-ViWikiQA such that: $Start(S_i) \leq$ **AS** $< End(S_i)$, where $Start(S_i)$ and $End(S_i)$ are the starting and ending positions of the S_i in context.

3.3 Dataset Analysis

Similar to UIT-ViQuAD, UIT-ViWikiQA comprises 23,074 questions based on 5,109 passages collected from 174 articles. We split our dataset into three sets:

Table 2. Overview of the UIT-ViWikiQA dataset.

	All	Training set	Development set	Test set
Articles	174	138 (79.32%)	18 (10,34%)	18 (10,34%)
Passages	5,109	4,101 (80.27%)	515 (10.08%)	493 (9.65%)
Questions	23,074	18,579 (80.52%)	2,285 (9.90%)	2,210 (9.58%)

training (Train), development (Dev), and Test. Table 2 shows statistics on the number of articles, passages, and questions in each set.

Based on UIT-ViQuAD proposed by Nguyen et al. [17], we divide the questions of the UIT-ViWikiQA dataset into seven categories: What, When, Who, Why, Where, How, How many[2], and Others. The Vietnamese question types were done manually and inherited from the UIT-ViQuAD dataset.

Figure 1 shows the distributions of question types on the Dev and Test sets of our dataset. What questions account for the largest proportion, with 49.06% on the Dev set and 54.48% on the Test set of our dataset. The type of questions with the lowest proportion is the Others with 0.83% on the Dev set and 1.13% on the Test set. The remaining types of questions account for a fairly similar proportion from 4% to 10% in both Dev and Test sets.

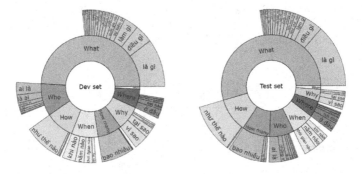

Fig. 1. Distribution of the question types on the Dev and Test sets of UIT-ViWikiQA.

In Vietnamese, the question words to ask for each type of question are varied, as shown in Fig. 1. The What question has the most range of question words. Figure 1 only shows the words to question with a large frequency of occurrence (approximately 0.7% or more). For example, in What questions, question words such as "là gì", "cái gì", "**điều gì**" or "làm gì" all mean "what" where "là gì" has the highest rate with 20.69% in the dev set and 24.42% in the test set. Similar to What questions, the phenomenon of varied words to question also occurs in the Who, When, Why, and Where question types. Specifically, for the Vietnamese

---

[2] Questions are related to quantities, numbers, and ratios.

When question type, the question words to pose such as "khi nào", "năm nào" or "thời gian nào" has the same meaning as the question word "When". However, the How question type and the How many question type, the question words are mostly the same. The question word "như thế nào" accounts for 87.79% of the How questions in the Dev set and 95.02% in the Test set. In the UIT-ViWikiQA dataset, it is difficult for the models to not only in deductive questions such as Why and How but also in the variety of question words in each question type.

4   Approaches

In this section, we propose three different approaches to sentence extraction-based MRC for Vietnamese.

4.1   Ranking-Based Approaches

The ranking approach is inspired by calculating the similarity of two sentences. From the context, we choose a sentence that has the greatest similarity with the question, which means that the selected sentence contains the answer to the question. For example, given a question Q and $S = (S_1, S_2, S_3, ..., S_n)$ are sentences in a context containing the answer to question Q. The sentence ranking task is that S_i is assigned a value $rank(S_i)$ for each sentence, which is the similarity between question Q and sentence S_i. For each pair of sentences S_i and S_j if $rank(S_i) > rank(S_j)$, the answer to question Q is more likely to be in question S_i than in question S_j and vice versa.

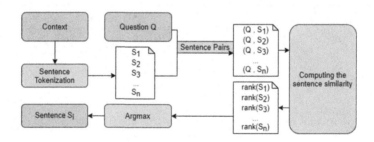

Fig. 2. The overview architecture of the sentence ranking-based approach.

Figure 2 describes the process of solving the sentence extraction problem following the sentence ranking approach. Input includes context and question Q; after tokenizing sentences for context, we obtain a set of sentences $S = (S_1, S_2, S_3, .., S_n)$. Then, for each sentence $S_i \in S$ is paired with Q, each (Q, S_i) is calculated a value representing the similarity between S_i and Q. The result is S_i, under the condition that S_i is the one with the greatest similarity to the question Q among the sentences in the set S.

4.2   Classification-Based Approaches

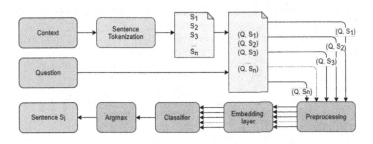

Fig. 3. The overview architecture of the text classification-based approach.

In the second approach, we apply the classification model to solve the task of sentence extraction-based MRC. For example, give a question Q and $S = (S_1, S_2, S_3, ..S_n)$ are sentences in a context that houses the answer for question Q, then we pair each $S_i \in S$ with question Q into n pairs of sentences (Q, S_i). We conduct preprocessing n pairs of sentences to match the model. For each pair (Q, S_i), we use the binary classification model with two labels, 0 and 1. If the label of the sentence pair (Q, S_i) is 1, it means that S_i is the sentence containing the answer to question Q, and if the question pair (Q, S_i) is labeled 0, that means sentence S_i is unanswerable for the question Q.

Figure 3 depicts the process of solving the sentence extraction problem based on a classification approach. Similar to Sect. 4.1, input includes question Q and a context contains the answer to question Q. Next, separate the sentences for the context and obtain a set of sentences $S = (S_1, S_2, S_3, ..S_n)$, each sentence $S_i \in S$ are combined with Q and get n sentence pairs (Q, S_i). N sentence pairs (Q, S_i) are preprocessed by algorithms suitable for the model type. Then we use the trained word embedding models to encode text into vectors of numbers. The binary classification model takes the newly coded vectors as input to define the label for each data sample. The argmax function ensures that the context has only one sentence labeled 1. The output receives a sentence S_i that contains the answer to the question Q.

4.3   Machine Reading Comprehension-Based Approaches

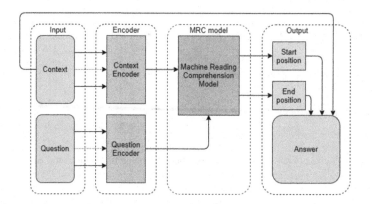

Fig. 4. The overview architecture of the MRC-based approach.

We define the input and output for the task of reading comprehension. Given a question Q and a context $S = (S_1, S_2, S_3, ..S_n)$ consisting n sentences. The goal of the model is to identify a sentence $S_i \in S$ that answers question Q.

Figure 4 depicts the architecture of our approach. The model consists of four components: input, encoder, machine reading comprehension model, and output. Inputs include a question Q, and a context S provides the answer to question Q. Next, the encoder converts the context and question into vectors of numbers with a format that matches the type of MRC model in the next step. The machine reading comprehension model takes the vectors of numbers as input and processes it to give the start and end position of the answer in the context S. With the start and end positions of the answers we just found from the model, we combine them with context to find the sentence $S_i \in S$ for answers question Q in the input.

5   Experiments and Result Analysis

5.1   Experimental Settings

For the sentence ranking approach, we use the underthesea toolkit[3] to separate the context into individual sentences. Based on Vietnamese language characteristics, we utilize Python Vietnamese Toolkit[4] to segment words. We implement the word count algorithm and the BM25 algorithm to evaluate. For BM25, we use Rank-BM25: a two-line search engine[5] to aid in computation.

---

[3] https://pypi.org/project/underthesea/.
[4] https://pypi.org/project/pyvi/.
[5] https://pypi.org/project/rank-bm25/.

For all models of sentence extraction-based machine reading comprehension using the text classification-based approach, we use a single NVIDIA Tesla K80 via Google Colaboratory to train them. Based on the word structure of the Vietnamese language, we use VnCoreNLP[6], published by Vu et al. [23], to separate words. We use the pre-trained word embedding PhoW2V introduced by Nguyen et al. [15] for maLSTM and BiGRU. We set batch size = 64 and epochs = 20 for both two models.

In the MRC-based approach, we train models in a single NVIDIA Tesla K80 via Google Colaboratory. We employ PhoW2V [15] word embedding as the pre-trained Vietnamese word embedding for the QANet [27] model to evaluate our dataset, and we set epochs = 20 and batch-size = 32. We use the baseline configuration provided by HuggingFace[7] to fine-tune a multilingual pre-trained model mBERT [7], the pre-trained cross-lingual models XLM-R [3], and the pre-trained language models for Vietnamese PhoBERT [16]. We set epochs = 2, learning rate = $2e^{-5}$, a maximum string length of 384, and maximum query length of 128 for all three models. For the characteristics of the PhoBERT$_{Base}$ model, we follow its default parameters except for the maximum string length which is set to 256 and use VnCoreNLP to segment the word for data before training with PhoBERT.

5.2   Evaluation Metrics

To evaluate performances of MRC models, we use two evaluation metrics following UIT-ViQuAD [17] and SQuAD [19], including Exact Match and F1-score. Considering a predicted answer sentence and a human-annotated answer sentence, if the two sentences are exactly the same, EM is set to 1, EM is set to 0 otherwise. F1-score measures the overlap tokens between the predicted answer and the human-annotated answer.

5.3   Experimental Results

Table 3 shows the performance of models on the Dev and Test sets. The models in the classification-based approach achieve the lowest performance, and the highest performance belongs to the models of the MRC-based approach. The best model (XLM-R$_{Large}$) reaches 88.77% (in F1-score) and 85.87% (in EM) on the Test set. The performance of the best model in the ranking-based approach (BM25) with 10.54% in F1-score and 12.70% in EM. When compared to the best model of classification-based approach (BiGRU), the XLM-R$_{Large}$ model outperforms with 26.21% (in F1-score) and 30.71% (in EM).

---

[6] https://github.com/vncorenlp/VnCoreNLP.

[7] https://huggingface.co/.

Table 3. Machine performances (EM and F1-score) on the Dev and Test sets.

Approach	Model	Dev		Test	
		EM	F1-score	EM	F1-score
Ranking	Word count	68.14	73.69	67.47	73.21
	BM25	74.05	78.86	73.17	78.23
Classification	maLSTM	30.28	42.04	33.85	45.60
	BiGRU	52.12	60.60	54.30	62.68
Machine reading comprehension	QANet	74.79	80.70	74.84	81.20
	mBERT	86.35	89.16	84.74	88.57
	PhoBERT	83.33	85.13	79.91	81.93
	XLM-R$_{Base}$	83.14	87.04	82.97	87.10
	XLM-R$_{Large}$	**91.79**	**93.95**	**85.87**	**88.77**

5.4   Result Analysis

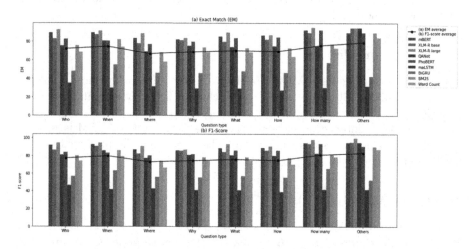

Fig. 5. Performance of the models on each question type in UIT-ViWikiQA. The line graphs are the average performance of the models for each question type.

We measure the performance of each model for each question type using F1-score and EM on the Dev set of our dataset, and the results are shown in Fig. 5. In general, most models of the MRC-based approach outperform the rest in all question types. The second are models of the ranking-based approach, and the last is the classification-based approach models. Among them, the BERT models and their variants have the best performance. In particular, the XLM-R$_{Large}$ model has the highest F1-score and EM in all question types. The models score lower for the questions such as Where, Why, What, and How. We found that the amount of data, the variety of question words, and the difficulty of the questions affected the performance of the models. In particular, Where questions have a low quantity and a wide variety of words to pose questions (see Fig. 1), all models have a lower F1-score and EM in this question type. The What question has many data samples (49.06%), but it has a very high diversity of words to ask. It makes it difficult for the models to predict answers. Why and How are difficult questions that require the computer to understand context and questions, which achieve low F1-score and EM scores. The question types where the question word to pose is not diverse have yielded high scores for models such as How many type questions. The analysis of experimental results is based on question types to evaluate the difficulty of questions for Vietnamese sentence extraction-based MRC on our data set, helping researchers have more ideas for the research in future.

Table 4. Performance of MRC models on UIT-ViWikiQA and its shuffle version.

Model	Original version				Shuffle version			
	Dev		Test		Dev		Test	
	EM	F1-score	EM	F1-score	EM	F1-score	EM	F1-score
QANet	74.79	80.70	74.84	81.20	73.85	80.19	73.84 (−1.00)	80.48 (−0.72)
PhoBERT	83.33	85.13	79.91	81.93	81.88	84.34	78.09 (−1.82)	80.74 (−1.19)
mBERT	86.35	89.16	84.74	88.57	83.80	87.67	83.56 (−1.18)	87.93 (−0.64)
XLM-R$_{Base}$	83.14	87.04	82.97	88.57	81.82	86.13	81.34 (−1.63)	85.43 (−3.14)
XLM-R$_{Large}$	**91.79**	**93.95**	**85.87**	**88.77**	**90.30**	**92.91**	**84.25 (−0.79)**	**87.98 (−1.62)**

Of the three approaches we propose in Sect. 4, the approach based on MRC has context attached to the input. We conduct experiments to demonstrate the dependence of the models of the MRC-based approach to the context, and Table 4 shows the result. We create another version of the UIT-ViWikiQA dataset by shuffling sentences in its context. The performance of all models decreased in the version with the shuffle context. All models have an average decrease of 1.45% in EM and an average decrease of 1.00% in F1-score on the Test set, which proves that context influences the performances of the models. The XLM-R$_{Large}$ model has the highest performance in both EM and F1-score in both versions of our dataset.

6   Conclusion and Future Work

In this paper, we introduced UIT-ViWikiQA, a new sentence-extraction dataset for evaluating Vietnamese MRC. This dataset comprises 23.074 question-answers based on 5.109 passages of 174 Vietnamese articles from Wikipedia. According to our experimental results when extracting the sentence, the XLM-R$_{Large}$ model achieved the highest performances on the Test set with 85.87% of EM and 88.77% of F1-score. On the contrary, when shuffling sentences to change context, the MRC models obtained an average decrease of 1.45% in EM and an average decrease of 1.00% in F1-score on the Test set, proving that context influences the performances of the models. Our result analysis explored the challenging questions to be addressed in further studies: Where, Why, What, and How.

In future, we propose several directions: (1) increasing the quantity of complex questions can boost the performance of models; (2) addressing the challenging questions using knowledge base [24] is to enhance the performance of this task; (3) researchers will exploit the challenging task of multilingual sentence extraction-based MRC; (4) extracting evidence sentences can help improve span-extraction reading comprehension on the multiple MRC datasets which are SQuAD [19], UIT-ViQuAD [17], FQuAD [8], SberQuAD [9], KorQuAD [13], SQuAD-IT [4], and CMRC [5]; (5) sentence answer-extraction question answering can be developed inspired by this study and DrQA [2].

References

1. Cao, Y., Li, T., Jia, Z., et al.: BGRU: New method of Chinese text sentiment analysis. J. Front. Comput. Sci. Technol. **13**(6), 973–981 (2019)
2. Chen, D., Fisch, A., Weston, J., Bordes, A.: Reading wikipedia to answer open-domain questions. In: Proceedings of the 55th Annual Meeting of the Association for Computational Linguistics (Volume 1: Long Papers), pp. 1870–1879 (2017)
3. Conneau, A., et al.: Unsupervised cross-lingual representation learning at scale. arXiv preprint arXiv:1911.02116 (2019)
4. Croce, D., Zelenanska, A., Basili, R.: Neural learning for question answering in Italian. In: Ghidini, C., Magnini, B., Passerini, A., Traverso, P. (eds.) AI*IA 2018 - Advances in Artificial Intelligence, pp. 389–402. Springer, Cham (2018)
5. Cui, Y., et al.: A span-extraction dataset for Chinese machine reading comprehension. In: Proceedings of the 2019 Conference on Empirical Methods in Natural Language Processing and the 9th International Joint Conference on Natural Language Processing (EMNLP-IJCNLP), pp. 5886–5891 (2019)
6. Dai, J., Chen, C.: Text classification system of academic papers based on hybrid Bert-BiGRU model. In: 2020 12th International Conference on Intelligent Human-Machine Systems and Cybernetics (IHMSC), vol. 2, pp. 40–44. IEEE (2020)
7. Devlin, J., Chang, M.W., Lee, K., Toutanova, K.: Bert: pre-training of deep bidirectional transformers for language understanding (2019)
8. d'Hoffschmidt, M., Belblidia, W., Brendlé, T., Heinrich, Q., Vidal, M.: FQuAD: French question answering dataset (2020)
9. Efimov, P., Chertok, A., Boytsov, L., Braslavski, P.: SberQuAD – Russian reading comprehension dataset: description and analysis. In: Arampatzis, A., et al. (eds.) CLEF 2020. LNCS, vol. 12260, pp. 3–15. Springer, Cham (2020). https://doi.org/10.1007/978-3-030-58219-7_1
10. Imtiaz, Z., Umer, M., Ahmad, M., Ullah, S., Choi, G., Mehmood, A.: Duplicate questions pair detection using siamese malstm. IEEE Access **8**, 21932–21942 (2020)
11. Jing, Y., Xiong, D., Zhen, Y.: Bipar: a bilingual parallel dataset for multilingual and cross-lingual reading comprehension on novels (2019)
12. Karpukhin, V., et al.: Dense passage retrieval for open-domain question answering. arXiv preprint arXiv:2004.04906 (2020)
13. Lim, S., Kim, M., Lee, J.: Korquad1.0: Korean QA dataset for machine reading comprehension. arXiv preprint arXiv:1909.07005 (2019)

14. Mueller, J., Thyagarajan, A.: Siamese recurrent architectures for learning sentence similarity. In: Proceedings of the AAAI Conference on Artificial Intelligence, vol. 30 (2016)
15. Nguyen, A.T., Dao, M.H., Nguyen, D.Q.: A pilot study of text-to-SQL semantic parsing for Vietnamese. Find. Assoc. Comput. Linguist. EMNLP **2020**, 4079–4085 (2020)
16. Nguyen, D.Q., Nguyen, A.T.: PhoBERT: pre-trained language models for Vietnamese. Find. Assoc. Comput. Linguist. EMNLP **2020**, 1037–1042 (2020)
17. Nguyen, K., Nguyen, V., Nguyen, A., Nguyen, N.: A Vietnamese dataset for evaluating machine reading comprehension. In: Proceedings of the 28th International Conference on Computational Linguistics, pp. 2595–2605 (2020)
18. Qu, C., Yang, L., Qiu, M., Croft, W.B., Zhang, Y., Iyyer, M.: Bert with history answer embedding for conversational question answering. In: Proceedings of the 42nd International ACM SIGIR Conference on Research and Development in Information Retrieval, pp. 1133–1136 (2019)
19. Rajpurkar, P., Zhang, J., Lopyrev, K., Liang, P.: Squad: 100,000+ questions for machine comprehension of text. In: Proceedings of the 2016 Conference on Empirical Methods in Natural Language Processing, pp. 2383–2392 (2016)
20. Sarrouti, M., El Alaoui, S.O.: A passage retrieval method based on probabilistic information retrieval model and UMLS concepts in biomedical question answering. J. Biomed. Inform. **68**, 96–103 (2017)
21. Van Nguyen, K., Tran, K.V., Luu, S.T., Nguyen, A.G.T., Nguyen, N.L.T.: Enhancing lexical-based approach with external knowledge for Vietnamese multiple-choice machine reading comprehension. IEEE Access **8**, 201404–201417 (2020)
22. Van Nguyen, K., Van Huynh, T., Nguyen, D.V., Nguyen, A.G.T., Nguyen, N.L.T.: New Vietnamese corpus for machine reading comprehension of health news articles. arXiv preprint arXiv:2006.11138 (2020)
23. Vu, T., Nguyen, D.Q., Nguyen, D.Q., Dras, M., Johnson, M.: VnCoreNLP: a Vietnamese natural language processing toolkit. arXiv preprint arXiv:1801.01331 (2018)
24. Yang, A., et al.: Enhancing pre-trained language representations with rich knowledge for machine reading comprehension. In: Proceedings of the 57th Annual Meeting of the Association for Computational Linguistics, pp. 2346–2357 (2019)
25. Yang, Y., Yih, W.T., Meek, C.: Wikiqa: a challenge dataset for open-domain question answering. In: Proceedings of the 2015 Conference on Empirical Methods in Natural Language Processing, pp. 2013–2018 (2015)
26. Yin, X., Liu, C., Fang, X.: Sentiment analysis based on BiGRU information enhancement. In: Journal of Physics: Conference Series, vol. 1748, p. 032054. IOP Publishing (2021)
27. Yu, A.W., et al.: Qanet: combining local convolution with global self-attention for reading comprehension. In: International Conference on Learning Representations (2018)

Analyzing and Recommending Development Order Based on Design Class Diagram

Wenhan Wu[1], Yongxin Zhao[1(✉)], Chao Peng[1(✉)], Yongjian Li[2], and Qin Li[1]

[1] Shanghai Key Laboratory of Trustworthy Computing,
East China Normal University, Shanghai, China
{yxzhao,cpeng}@sei.ecnu.edu.cn
[2] State Key Laboratory of Computer Science, Institute of Software,
Chinese Academy of Sciences, Beijing, China

Abstract. In the system design process, it is an important issue to consider the order of class development. Different orders of class development may have great impact on the cost, efficiency and fault tolerance of the project. Because of that, it is an essential issue to consider which class should be developed before the others. In this paper, we present an approach to recommend a reasonable development order of classes with minimum development cost based on design class diagram and genetic algorithm. It helps the designer to improve their development strategy and to prevent mistakes resulted from improper development order of classes. We also provide a phase tree to help developers visualize and analyze the details of each development phase. At last, we implement a tool and illustrate that the proposed approach is sound and effective with two case studies.

Keywords: Development order · Project management · Development cost · Genetic algorithm · System analyst · Design class diagram

1 Introduction

With the increasing complexity and integration of products, object-oriented development becomes a mainstream development method. Not only the development cost of traditional Internet applications, like Facebook, Twitter or Instagram, is increasing, but also the new technologies, such as artificial intelligence and Internet of things (IoT) [1–3], are moving towards scale, modularization and industrialization, which also increase the cost. The hardware of a battery management system is designed with both IoT as battery control and software codes as management strategy. Furthermore, a collaborative filtering recommendation algorithm is applied to improve the system with users' habits [4]. These complex software structures make the complexity of software become an important problem in the field of software engineering. High complexity of software increases the potential risks and defects of software system. If all classes in these software

© Springer Nature Switzerland AG 2021
H. Qiu et al. (Eds.): KSEM 2021, LNAI 12816, pp. 524–537, 2021.
https://doi.org/10.1007/978-3-030-82147-0_43

systems are developed without a proper order, the probability of failures can be very high, which makes it more difficult to improve the quality of software and ensure its correctness.

There are many organizations trying to improve the development methodology, which generate many concepts to optimize the developing process. It seems that there is no risk in the project arranged in this way. But when we design each phase, there might be a lot of doubts on development orders again [5]. Based on this consideration, we aim to propose a practical approach to optimize the development order and reduce the complexity of software based on design class diagram, which is a recommendation on fine-grained development order.

Many related works focus on software structures. Sinha et al. proposed a formula for complexity calculation on software structure [6]; Cao et al. proposed a complexity decreasing scheme based on software structure [7]. But, these methods are trying to decrease software complexity, but not directly for the development process of the structure.

In this paper, we will focus on the classes in the software module of the system and aim to seek a reasonable development order to develop the software with fewer risks and failures. Our recommendation approach optimizes the development order from the design class diagram, which is exported from the requirement document. Besides, we analyze each development phase and implement a tool for project managers to use our recommended methods for optimization. The main contributions of our work are summarized as follow:

- **Hierarchical development order structure.** We propose a hierarchical structure to express the development order, which is named as phase tree. This structure not only shows the sequence among different development stages, but also shows the development cost of each class and relationship of each class in each stage, so as to help designers to further analyze.
- **Recommendation tool.** We also implement a tool for S/W developers to use our recommended methods for optimization, and the optimized development order is visually displayed to project managers for analysis, where a project manager can find how it reduces the cost and risk of developing.

The remaining of the paper is organized as follows. Section 2 introduces the recommendation approach on development order of classes. Section 3 implements the tool for developers to use this recommendation. Besides, we present two cases to show the usage of our approach. Section 4 concludes our work and presents the future work.

2   The Recommendation Approach of Development Order

In this section, we present a recommendation approach of development order based on the design class to optimize the developing process and decrease its cost. As is shown in Fig. 1, software can be developed with a less development cost in this approach. Next, we give the explanation to each of the five steps.

2.1 Requirement Export

The system analyst extracts the design class diagram as a XMI file from requirement document. In this subsection, we explain details of requirement export, which is a premise of the recommendation and an input in the next part. From the view of project management, software developing life cycle (SDLC) includes four major stages [8]: perception, elaboration, construction and transition. Each stage contains several iterations, through which the software can be evolved incrementally in developing. After each iteration, a working software is produced as the output, which may be tagged as a subset of the full version number. Usually, an iteration consists of the following steps: iteration planning, requirements analyzing, designing, implementing and testing. These steps account for different proportion according to the position of iteration in SDLC.

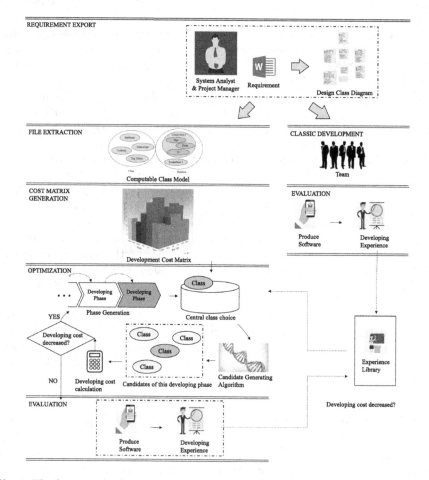

Fig. 1. The framework of our recommendation approach of development order of classes

In each iteration, software needs to be analyzed in details at the requirement analyzing step, and then enter the design stage. Therefore, system analysts need to finish the transformation from requirement analysis to the designing stage at this part. After this transformation, the product should be implementable to a working software. Products after transformation, that is, products to show the implementability of the software, are usually represented in the form of design class diagram. It is one of the reasons why the recommendation approach choose the design class diagram as the start point.

In conclusion, system analyst transforms from the requirement to design class diagram, which is also a major step in SDLC.

2.2   File Extraction

In this subsection, we extract design class diagram into a computable class model, which increases the scalability of this input of this recommendation.

As mentioned above, the design class diagram is the input to this recommendation approach. However, the presentation format and file type of the design class diagram are not standard. There are many languages that can be used to express design class diagrams. For example, SysML and UML are two different languages.

Therefore, the recommendation approach first needs to analyze and normalize various models and retaining only the necessary elements, that is, the parts needed in the development order optimization, which helps the recommendation better identify and develop. For this reason, we introduces the computable class model. In the future, file parsing can be adapted to various file types and the recommendation approach can still be used as long as the output is a computable class model, thus enhancing the scalability of this recommendation approach.

Figure 2 shows the structure of the computable class model, which is an abstraction of the design class diagram. It includes all classes and their relationships that need to be designed in this iteration, which is generated directly from a UML diagram. Other contents are used as a supplement to the design class diagram, and the core should be limited to this.

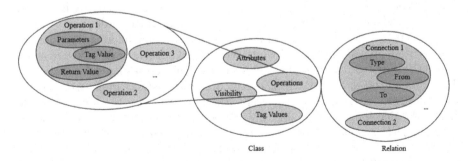

Fig. 2. Composition of computable class model

In conclusion, input files are normalized as a computable class model in this part, which is the foundation of cost matrix generation. This step is an abstraction of design class diagram. It filters the unimportant factors, and expresses the design class diagram models with different file formats in a unified way.

2.3 Cost Matrix Generation

In this subsection, we calculate the development cost of each class and relation, which is represented as a cost matrix. Based on that, we introduce an approach to compute the development cost by re-organizing the computable class diagram into a hierarchical structure of classes, which indicates the development order of classes.

The development cost of implementing the class is generated mainly focusing on the attributes and methods of class. Different attributes and methods are given different weights. The more the number of attributes and methods, the more difficult the class is implemented, where the potential risk of the class in the working software is higher [9,10]. The analysis of relationship are based on different types in UML, which is extracted in the previous section. After setting weights for each attribute and method, a cost matrix is generated for further section. Usually, cost matrix is symmetric, since the difficulty to develop the relation from one class to another should be the same as developing the relation from another class to this.

2.4 Optimization

Based on the development cost matrix, we optimize the development order of classes to reduce the development cost using generating algorithm. In this subsection, we optimize the cost matrix to find the minimum cost to develop a working software. The simplest way is to enumerate each possible development order and calculate its development cost. However, it leads to a huge time cost, where the complexity has increased beyond the exponential level. Therefore, based on the situation to optimize the developing process, we adopt a more efficient algorithm to optimize the method of optimizing the development order. Before that, we should define the development cost of a sequence, which is an important indicator to evaluate the cost of the development order.

Development cost is calculated from cost matrix. For different development process, development cost is different. With Sinha's research on software structure [11], we notice that the development cost can be estimated by evaluating the energy of the cost matrix. The energy of software structure matrix evaluate the complexity of a software effectively. The more complex the software is, the higher the development cost and the human and material resources it needs. Therefore, we can refer to this evaluator as the approximate evaluation method, and its formula is as formula (1), which is also referred effectively as architecture complexity in [12].

$$Development\ Cost = \sum_{i=0}^{len-1} mat[i][i] + \sum_{i=0}^{len-1}\sum_{j=0}^{len-1} mat[i][j] * \frac{sing(mat)}{len} \quad (1)$$

where mat is the development cost matrix described (Row and column labels start from 0), len is the number of column (the number of column and row are equal since it's a square matrix). Singular function $sing()$ is used to calculate the summation of the singular values of the development cost matrix.

Hence, the algorithm is divided into four parts, as follows. Each recursion of this algorithm generates a developing phase, which will end if the development cost is not decreased. In this situation, we conclude that the development cost has been optimized to the best situation.

Central Class Choice. In general, the class with highest development cost in a software should be developed first. This is because its development cost leads to the increase of the loss caused by its mistakes. If the class with highest development cost in a software can not be developed as scheduled, then the software can not work even if other classes have been developed. Therefore, in early stage of project development, the development team should do their best to study the development of class with highest development cost, and take it as priority, which is the reason why we name it as *central* class.

Therefore, central class is chosen by calculating the total connection relationship with other classes. A class which has the most connections with other classes (i.e. the summation of all connection complexities with other classes) is chosen as central class. Since the connection summation of this class is highest, this class will be developed first as the central class in this phase, so as to continue to the next part.

Candidate Generating Algorithm. After selecting a central class as the core of this developing phase, all the other classes radiated by the class are found to be taken consideration into generating a development phase for developers to develop in this part. Genetic algorithm is used to select the class developing with the core class together, which is expressed as follows:

- Encoding. All the classes which are connected with the central class are the candidates of classes that should be implemented in the same phase. In this step, all possible results of the classes implemented in this phase is encoded as a binary string (excluded the central class itself). Classes connected with the central class are tagged as 1, otherwise 0.
- Adaption Function. After encoding, an adaption function is used to judge whether the result is an optimal result for this phase. The aim of this step is

to generate the candidates with minimum development cost, so the adaption function is the inversion of the development cost of the new developing matrix. Formula to calculate the development cost is written in (1).

- Choice and variation. After calculating the adaption function of each value, candidates are chosen randomly in the restriction of probability. The larger the value calculated from adaption function is, the more possible the choice is chosen. In fact, probability of a choice $P(choice)$ which is chosen as the result in this part is calculated as follow:

$$P(choice) = \frac{f(choice)}{\sum_{i \in all\ choices} f(i)} \tag{2}$$

where f is the adaption function. After choosing from candidates, variation is used as the genetic algorithm described. Variation used in this recommendation is two point crossover [13], which can increase the variation of choices and avoid falling into local optimal solution.

- Termination. After the choice and adaption, new candidates are generated from the choices chosen in this phase, and a new recursion will open until one of the following rules is matched, where the optimal solution is found at this time.
  1. The number of phases is already satisfied to the upper bound of phases.
  2. The classes in last phase is less than the threshold, where classes can be developed together without necessity to iterate again.

Candidates of this Developing Phase. Now, we have calculated the candidate classes developed with the central class. In order to give project manager a better feedback, we calculate the development cost among all selected classes and form a new development cost matrix. This matrix is intuitively seen by users to facilitate them to make corresponding development decisions. At the same time, it also helps the project manager to evaluate the cost reduction effect of this method.

Development Cost Calculation. This step calculates the development cost of this developing phase and observes whether the cost of this phase has decreased. If the cost has decreased, the algorithm continues to execute so as to find out if there is a lower cost development order. If there is no decreasing, it indicates that the optimal solution has been reached. The task of this part is finished, where the optimized development order is generated.

2.5   Evaluation

Algorithm 1: generateCostMatrix

---

   input : node: Phase node to generate the cost matrix

   input : um: The cost matrix before optimization provided by the parent node, which includes all the leaf nodes in the node

   output: om: The cost matrix of the phase node

   if *node is empty* **then**

      | om := um ;

      | return om;

   end

   Initialize a map named classCost;

   for *all the nodes r of all nodes in node* **do**

      | subnodes := findAllLeafNodes(r);

      | submatrix := extract data related to subnodes;

      | submatrix := *generateCostMatrix*(r, *submatrix*);

      | subMatrixCost := calculate the cost of submatrix;

      | record the pair $(r, subMatrixCost)$ in the classCost

   end

   Initialize om as a matrix with nodes.size() * nodes.size() elements;

   for *all elements om[i][j] in om* **do**

      | **if** $i==j$ **then**

      | | om[i][j] := get the cost of this node i

      | **else**

      | | om[i][j] := the summary of the submatrix of this node

      | **end**

   end

   return om;

After the complexity of each phase is given, analysis of the results is carried out at this stage, such as the decreasing rate. Besides, we also extract the experience from this development process to experience library, which can facilitate to develop other software. Experience, such as the base classes should be always developed before their extended classes, can also be obtained from classic development methods, which is shown in the right part in Fig. 1.

Both the development order and the development cost matrix of each phase are presented to the user. In order to facilitate the visualization, evaluation and analysis of each developing phase, we need to calculate development cost of each stage based on development order and original cost matrix. To calculate these matrices more efficiently, we propose the concept of phase tree, which is composed with phase nodes. Phase node is an abstraction of each developing phase in the development order, including the name of this phase, the tasks (that is, the names of each class) in this phase and the cost matrix between them. All phase nodes are connected as a phase tree.

Now we give the algorithm of generating the cost matrix of phase node. The algorithm is divided into two stages. In the first stage, the algorithm calculates the development cost of each sub node; in the second stage, the algorithm generates the connection cost of these sub phases. The generating algorithm is a recursive process. That is, the first stage of the algorithm may need to call the algorithm itself again, and after executing the two stages, the algorithm returns to second stage of the algorithm. The pseudo code of the complete algorithm process refers to Algorithm 1.

3   Implementation and Case Study

In this section, we implement a tool ReDO[1] to recommend the development order of classes according to our proposed approach. Besides, two examples are introduced to demonstrate the effectiveness of our recommendation approach (Fig. 3).

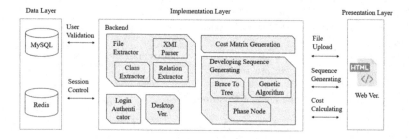

Fig. 3. The architecture of ReDO

3.1   Spring Messaging Module

As a tool for developers and analysts, this subsection introduces the developing suggestions in the mainstream developing platform Spring, in which the messaging passing [14] of Spring is taken as analysis. The message passing module in Spring plays an important role in the Spring framework, which is widely used in the project based on Spring. Therefore, it is very important to ensure the stability of message passing module, which is based on the appropriate development order.

---

[1] For the server part, you can visit https://github.com/Ivyee17/ReDO-server; for the client part, you can visit https://github.com/Ivyee17/ReDO-website.

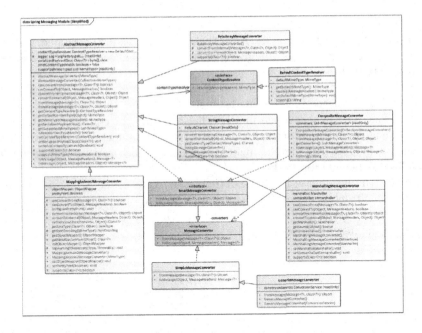

Fig. 4. The design class diagram of spring messaging

The design class diagram of the spring messaging module is depicted in Fig. 4. Here, only the classes in the *messaging* and *messaging.converter* package in the messaging module are taken into consideration. Even so, there are still many classes which need to be analyzed in the design class diagram.

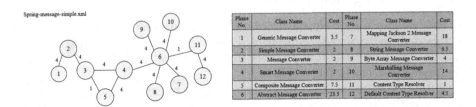

Fig. 5. Development cost matrix of spring messaging

We transform the class diagram into a computable class module to show the development cost matrix of its software structure, as shown in Fig. 5, and provide a development order based on this design class diagram.

It is divided into four phases, as shown in Fig. 6. The first phase C2 includes three classes which are needed to be developed. Since *AbstractMessageConverter* is the most expensive class, we should design and develop this class first. If a development team tries to modify the information in *AbstractMessageConverter*, it will inevitably result in the modification of all other information. Similarly, the interface *SmartMessageConverter* implemented by it needs to be implemented in this phase. Next, we implement *ContentTypeResolver*, which is a simple implementation of the other two classes. After these three classes are developed, the core components of a message system have been developed. The second phase is simply the abstraction of the first level.

In the CCC2 phase, a large number of message converters are created. Since the details of interface is given in the first two phases, the implementation of this part can even be developed in a parallel way, and the coupling relationship has been significantly reduced in this layer. All components of this layer have become an independent development component, which can be transferred to specialized personnel for work.

Finally, the last phase is the *GeneticMessageConverter*, which is a simple extension of *SimpleMessageConverter*. At the same time, this component does not involve the development of other components, so this part can be implemented in the last development phase.

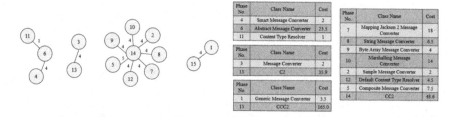

Fig. 6. Phase C2, CC2, CCC2 of spring messaging

3.2 File Parsing Module in ReDO

At last, we give the development order of the file parsing module in this tool. In this tool, we've already implemented the extraction from XMI file to class module, but there are still many other file formats that is useful to develop the file parsing part used in this tool.

In this diagram, the XML file parser is only recorded as a whole class called *XMIHandler* for simplicity.

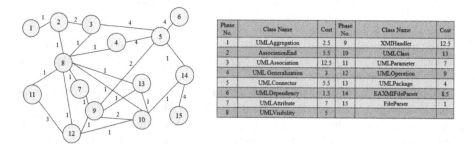

Phase No.	Class Name	Cost	Phase No.	Class Name	Cost
1	UMLAggregation	2.5	9	XMIHandler	12.5
2	AssociationEnd	5.5	10	UMLClass	13
3	UMLAssociation	12.5	11	UMLParameter	7
4	UML Generalization	3	12	UMLOperation	9
5	UMLConnector	5.5	13	UMLPackage	4
6	UMLDependency	1.5	14	EAXMIFileParser	8.5
7	UMLAttribute	7	15	FileParser	1
8	UMLVisibility	5			

Fig. 7. Development cost matrix of file parsing module

The structure complexity matrix of the original matrix is shown in Fig. 7. Different from the previous example, although the coupling relationship in this example is small in value, the number of entries in the association relationship is more than that in the previous example, which is unfavorable for the development process. Besides, it is a great challenge for analysts to analyze the development process by hand, since it's error-prone, which will lead to the failure and repetition of the development process caused by the failure of the development order. Therefore, we use this tool to help developers analyze and decouple this part.

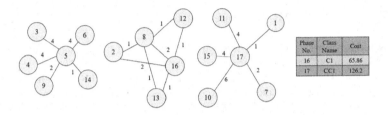

Fig. 8. Phase C1, CC1, CCC1 of file parsing module

As shown in Fig. 8, the development order is composed with three phases, the cost of each class is the same as in Fig. 7. First phase is the implementation of file parsing class *XMIHandler*, the implementation of file parser *EAXMIFileParser*, the definition of connection component *UMLConnector* and the implementation of all connections. After the phase, the standard of file parsing has been determined, and the parsing of the connections in the file has been basically completed.

The second phase is a connection between the first and third phase. First of all, this layer implements the detail of *AssociationEnd* in the connection part, which makes the analysis of the connection part more complete. Secondly, this phase implements the basic parsing elements of UML class, such as the visibility of classes, the package of classes and the operations in classes. The implementation of these three classes will directly affect whether the parsing of UML class can be completed.

Finally, the implementation of UML class and its related components is implemented in the last phase. The complexity of the system is reduced by about 14% after reconstruction (from 211.77 to 182.01, calculated recursively through formula (1)). It can also be seen from the figure that the complexity in each phase is not complex except the second phase. The other two layers are very simple connection, which effectively reduces the difficulty and risk of development, and clarifies the development relationship among them.

4 Conclusion and Future Work

This paper investigated a way of development order recommendation, which is divided into five parts: requirement export, file extraction, cost matrix generation, optimization and evaluation. A tool ReDO has been implemented based on our proposed approach, which can be widely used by developers and designers to analyze and generate the development order of the project in the design stage of the SDLC, so as to reduce the risk of failure due to the improper development order. Among them, the introduction of phase tree can help developers and users better understand and analyze the optimized development order. In the future, more ways in reducing development cost can be introduced, and files will support more forms such as SysML to ensure that the tool can be used more widely.

Acknowledgements. This work was partially supported by the Scientific and Technological Innovation 2030 Major Projects under Grant 2018AAA0100902, the Shanghai Science and Technology Commission under Grant No.20511100200 and OneSmart Education Group. Also, we sincerely acknowledge AI Project of Shanghai Science and Technology Committee (STCSM 20DZ1100300) and the foundation of Shenzhen Institute of Artificial Intelligence and Robotics for Society in support.

References

1. Gai, K., Qiu, M.: Reinforcement learning-based content-centric services in mobile sensing. IEEE Network **32**(4), 34–39 (2018)
2. Gai, K., Qiu, M.: Optimal resource allocation using reinforcement learning for IoT content-centric services. Appl. Soft Comput. **70**, 12–21 (2018)
3. Gai, K., Qiu, M., Zhao, H., Sun, X.: Resource management in sustainable cyber-physical systems using heterogeneous cloud computing. IEEE Trans. Sustain. Comput. **3**(2), 60–72 (2017)
4. Faika, T., Kim, T., et al.: A blockchain-based Internet of Things (IoT) network for security-enhanced wireless battery management systems. In: IEEE Industry Applications Society Annual Meeting, vol. 2019, pp. 1–6. Baltimore (2019)
5. Kikuno, T.: Why do software projects fail? Reasons and a solution using a Bayesian classifier to predict potential risk. In: 11th IEEE Pacific Rim International Symposium on Dependable Computing, Changsha, Hunan, China, p. 4 (2005)
6. Sinha, K., de Weck, O.L.: A network-based structural complexity metric for engineered complex systems. In: IEEE International Systems Conference, USA (2013)
7. Cao, S., Zhao, Y., Shi, L.: Software complexity reduction by automated refactoring schema. In: International Symposium on Theoretical Aspects of Software Engineering, Guilin, China (2019)
8. Aksit, M., Marcelloni, F., Tekinerdogan, B.: Developing object-oriented framworks using domain models. ACM Comput. Surv. **32**(1), 11 (2000)
9. Tsunoda, T., Washizaki, H., Fukazawa, Y., Inoue, S., Hanai, Y., Kanazawa, M.: Developer experience considering work difficulty in software development. Int. J. Networked Distrib. Comput. **6**(2), 53–62 (2018)
10. Jiang, R.: An information-entropy-based risk measurement method of software development project. J. Inf. Sci. Eng. **30**(5), 1279–1301 (2014)

11. Gutman, I., Soldatovic, T., Vidovic, D.: The energy of a graph and its size dependence. A Monte Carlo approach. Chemical Phys. Lett. **297**, 428–432 (1998)
12. Rebentisch, E., Schuh, G., et al.: Measurement of organizational complexity in product development projects. In: 2016 Portland International Conference on Management of Engineering and Technology (PICMET), pp. 2445–2459 (2016)
13. Sarafis, I., Trinder, P., Zalzala, A.: Mining comprehensible clustering rules with an evolutionary algorithm. In: Cantú-Paz, E., et al. (eds.) GECCO 2003. LNCS, vol. 2724, pp. 2301–2312. Springer, Heidelberg (2003). https://doi.org/10.1007/3-540-45110-2_123
14. Gutierrez, F.: Spring Boot Messaging, Messaging APIs for Enterprise and Integration Solutions. Apress, Berkeley (2017). https://doi.org/10.1007/978-1-4842-1224-0

HCapsNet: A Text Classification Model Based on Hierarchical Capsule Network

Ying Li[1], Ming Ye[2(✉)], and Qian Hu[2]

[1] Department of Computer and Information Science, Southwest University, Chong Qing, China
[2] Department of Artificial Intelligence, Southwest University, Chong Qing, China
zmxym@swu.edu.cn

Abstract. In text classification tasks, RNNs are usually used to establish global relationships. However, RNNs have the problems that the semantic information coding of key words is not prominent and cannot be calculated in parallel. In addition, hierarchical information of text is usually ignored during feature extraction. Aiming at the above problems, a text classification model based on hierarchical capsule network (HCapsNet) is proposed. In order to capture the hierarchical features, text is divided into granularities and constantly aggregate according to the characteristics of the data. A parallel LSTM network fused with self-attention is utilized to complete the encoding of multiple natural sentences. Then, we construct sentence features into sentence capsules to extract richer semantic information. The spatial relationship between sentence capsule as part and chapter capsule as whole is established by dynamic routing algorithm. Our experiments show that HCapsNet gives better results compared with the state-of-the-art methods on six public data sets.

Keywords: Text classification · Capsule network · Hierarchical aggregation · Parallel computing · Multi-granularity features

1 Introduction

The intelligent society converts human activities into data, data has become an important new strategic resource [1, 2]. In the face of massive text data, how to efficiently extract valuable information from data is currently a problem to be solved in Natural Language Processing (NLP). Text classification is an important branch of NLP, its purpose is to extract text features based on text information, establish a relationship model between text features and categories, and use the learned relationship model to automatically classify text samples of unknown categories [3].

With scholars' research on text classification tasks, deep learning have gradually become the mainstream. Convolution neural network CNN uses convolution detectors to encode text features [4, 5], but a fixed-size convolution kernel only extract local features. The recurrent neural network RNN uses the recurrent structure to model the entire text sequence [6] and extract global semantic features. However, the calculation of the recurrent neural network structure at each moment depends on the information

H. Qiu et al. (Eds.): KSEM 2021, LNAI 12816, pp. 538–549, 2021.
https://doi.org/10.1007/978-3-030-82147-0_44

of the previous moment, so a single loop structure cannot achieve parallel calculation [7]. The sequential structure of RNN also leads to its inability to extract skip interval features, and there is a problem of imbalance in semantic information [8]. With the research and innovation of neural network structure, more new network structures are applied to text classification tasks. Capsule network (CapsNet) uses vector neurons as nodes for storing feature information [9]. Compared with CNN, capsules can store richer text semantic features [10]. However, the quality of the capsule is highly dependent on the previous feature extraction work. Traditional capsule networks usually use a single-layer convolution to extract feature [11], so that the capsules only contain local features. Therefore, optimizing the quality and quantity of capsules in text classification tasks is a problem to be solved.

In view of the loss of hierarchical information during feature extraction, and the poor quality of capsules extracted by single-layer convolution, a text classification model based on hierarchical capsule network is proposed. The main works of this paper are as follows:

- In order to extract the hierarchical information of the text, we divide the text into a hierarchical structure and aggregate it layer by layer according to the characteristics of data.
- At sentence feature level, a parallel LSTM network fused with self-attention is proposed to complete multiple natural sentence encodings. Self-attention mechanism is used to enhance the expression ability of important words. A parallel LSTM structure is used to realize the encoding of multiple sentences and speed up the calculation of the model.
- We construct sentence features into sentence capsules, and through vector-structured capsules to extract richer text semantic features.
- We utilize dynamic routing algorithm to establish the spatial relationship between sentence capsule and chapter capsule to realize hierarchical aggregation.

The remainder of this paper is organized as follows: Some concepts are explained and related work is introduced in Sect. 2. Section 3 introduces overall framework of HCapsNet and calculation methods of each layer. Section 4 shows experimental design and results. Section 5 concludes whole paper.

2 Related Work

Text classification is the core and basic problem in NLP. At present, it has achieved rich research results in many fields. There are a number of related works discussed from different perspectives in this section.

Multi-granularity theory granulates knowledge. The different granularities reflect the subsets of different granularities [12, 13]. Ge et al. [14] tries to combine global topic granularity features [15] with local features to achieve the purpose of enriching the meaning of features. However, considering that the text is a string composed of characters and punctuation marks. As a whole, characters form words, words form phrases, and then form the structure of sentences and paragraphs. Therefore, some works represent text features from the perspective of hierarchical granularity. Yang et al. [16] proposed a hierarchical attention network (HAN), which aggregates features from the aspects of word and sentence granularity.

Recurrent neural network (RNN) can effectively process contextual data and extract global features, but it is prone to the problems of gradient disappearance and explosion when processing long-sequence text [17]. Long Short-term Memory network LSTM is a kind of recurrent network based on gated structure [18], LSTM realizes the filtering and screening of information through the gate structure and improves the memory ability of the model. Nie et al. [19] Stacks three layers of bidirectional LSTM through the idea of residual network. Zhou et al. [20] propose C-LSTM, which extracts fixed local phrase features through CNN, and then encodes global features of text through LSTM. These methods have achieved good experimental results, but LSTM cannot highlight the importance of key words.

Attention mechanism can focus on the key features of the text and has a positive effect on feature extraction [21]. Zhan et al. [22] proposes knowledge attention method that fuses external semantic and structural knowledge to calculate attention efficiently. Tang et al. [23] utilize one-dimension convolution with dense connections to extract attention signals from text sequences and the attention signals are combined with GRU network.

Capsule Network (CapsNet). A capsule [10, 11] is a group of neurons that represent different attributes of a specific type of entity. Unlike Max-Pooling, which chooses to retain the salient information, CapsNet routes capsules in lower layer to the most similar parent capsule [24]. Zhao et al. [25] introduced CapsNet to the text classification field for the first time, and proposed a four-layer structure model: N-gram convolution layer, capsule layer, convolution capsule layer, and fully connected capsule layer. Authors found that the capsule network is beneficial to extract rich text features. Kim et al. [26] uses a similar architecture, the difference is that they use gated linear units to generate feature maps to increase the global features of the capsule. Capsule-B [25] extracts text feature through a parallel multi-scale convolution capsule network, and Gong et al. [27] uses a dynamic routing method to aggregate features. Deng et al. [28] uses a cross-layer connected gated recurrent unit to strengthen the transfer between the features of each layer, and further uses the capsule network to obtain rich spatial position information. Capsule storage high-level abstract features, its quality depends on the previous feature extraction work. Past work often used convolution operations or LSTM, GRU to extract shallow features, and then used capsule networks to extract deep features. Most of past works directly model the entire text sequence, ignoring the hierarchical granularity information of text.

3   Model

Based on the above research, we propose a new model for processing text classification, which is named HCapsNet. HCapsNet consists of five parts and is shown in Fig. 1. First, we divide text into sentence and word structure according to the hierarchical division rules, see Sect. 3.1 for details. Then, all words in sentence are represented as corresponding word embedding. Furthermore, a parallel LSTM network fused with self-attention is used to complete the encoding of multiple natural sentences. Next, sentence feature is used as the input of the sentence capsule, and the aggregation of the sentence capsule to the chapter capsule is realized through the dynamic routing algorithm. Finally, classification prediction is realized by the classifier.

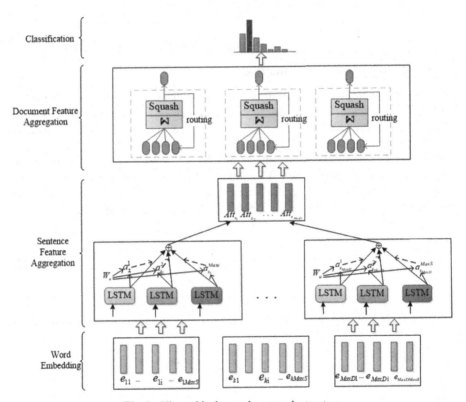

Fig. 1. Hierarchical capsule network structure.

3.1 Hierarchical Division

For a document D, firstly divide the sentences by regular expressions based on the sentence separator, such as [?, ., !]. Furthermore, we segment the sentence to get the word granularity. For English text, the space character is a natural separator between words. For Chinese text, there is no obvious gap between words, we use the word segmentation tool Jieba to achieve word segmentation.

An input sample D will get the text structure $D' \in \mathbb{R}^{MaxD \times MaxS}$ after completing the hierarchical granularity division, w_{ij} represents the index value of the j-th word in i-th sentence. MaxD represents the maximum length of the sentence contained in the text sample D. MaxS represents the maximum length of the words contained in sentence s_i.

$$D' = [s_1, s_2, ..., s_{MaxD}] = \begin{bmatrix} [w_{11} & w_{12} & \cdots & w_{1MaxS}] \\ [w_{21} & w_{22} & & w_{2MaxS}] \\ [\vdots & & \ddots & \vdots \\ [w_{MaxD1} & w_{MaxD2} & \cdots & w_{MaxDMaxS}] \end{bmatrix} \tag{1}$$

3.2 Word Embedding Representation

Words are the smallest granularity processed in HCapsNet. In order to improve the quality of text representation, we use Word2Vec to generate word embedding for each word. Word2Vec uses a neural network model to map a word from a high-dimensional space to a fixed-size low-dimensional space, and each dimension contains the potential characteristics of word. The word embedding table $E^w \in \mathbb{R}^{|V| \times d_w}$ is obtained through the pre-training Word2Vec model, $|V|$ is the vocabulary size for words and d_w is the dimensional of word embedding. The index value w_{ij} of each word is used to find the corresponding word embedding $e_{ij} \in \mathbb{R}^{d_w}$, and MaxS words in the sentence s_i are mapped as embeddings matrix $E^{s_i} \in \mathbb{R}^{MaxS \times d_w}$.

$$e_{ij} = E^w(w_{ij}) \tag{2}$$

$$E^{s_i} = [e_{i1}, e_{i2}, ..., e_{iMaxS}] \tag{3}$$

Furthermore, by splicing the MaxD sentences together in order, the word embedding matrix $E^{D'} \in \mathbb{R}^{MaxD \times MaxS \times d_w}$ is obtained.

$$E^{D'} = [E^{s_1}, E^{s_2}, ..., E^{s_{MaxD}}] \tag{4}$$

3.3 Parallel LSTM Sequence Coding Based on Self-attention

The overall semantics of a sentence will be affected by the interaction of its constituent words. Therefore, when the word features are aggregated into sentence features, RNN is used to encode the global dependencies of all words in a sentence. From the perspective of a sentence, its length is short and the semantic information is not rich. In order to make up for this shortcoming, this section uses LSTM, which has complex gating structure but superior memory ability, to implement sentence encoding.

$$\begin{bmatrix} i_{s_i}^t \\ o_{s_i}^t \\ f_{s_i}^t \\ \tilde{C}_{s_i}^t \end{bmatrix} = \begin{bmatrix} \sigma \\ \sigma \\ \sigma \\ \tanh \end{bmatrix} (W^t \begin{bmatrix} x_{s_i}^t \\ h_{s_i}^t \end{bmatrix} + b^t) \tag{5}$$

$$C_{s_i}^t = f_{s_i}^t \times C_{s_i}^{t-1} + i_{s_i}^t \times \tilde{C}_{s_i}^t \tag{6}$$

$$h_{s_i}^t = o_{s_i}^t \times \tanh(C_{s_i}^t) \tag{7}$$

Among them, W^t and b^t respectively represent the weight matrix and bias, σ and tanh are the activation functions, where σ represents the sigmoid function. $x_{s_i}^t$ represents the t-th word embedding in sentence s_i.

In order to enhance the expression ability of important words and optimize the problem of LSTM semantic imbalance, we construct a LSTM based on self-attention (SA-LSTM) to encode sentence sequences. An external weight W^u is introduced to represent contextual semantics, which used to score the importance of the hidden state. Next, we use softmax to assign weights to each hidden state and normalize it. Finally, we accumulate the attention score of each hidden state to get the weighted feature of a sentence, calculation method is as follows.

$$score_{s_i}^t = \tanh(W^u h_{s_i}^t) \tag{8}$$

$$a_{s_i}^t = \frac{exp(score_{s_i}^t)}{\sum_{j=1}^{MaxS} exp(score_{s_i}^j)} \tag{9}$$

$$Att_{s_i} = \sum_{j=1}^{MaxS} a_{s_i}^j h_{s_i}^j \tag{10}$$

Input of the sequence coding layer is $E^{D'}$, which is composed with MasD sentences. SA-LSTM can only encode one sentence into a sentence feature Att_{s_i}. In order to improve the coding efficiency of model, we construct a parallel LSTM structure based on self-attention (PSA-LSTM). HCapsNet builds MasD SA-LSTM structures, and then inputs each sentence into its own computing network to achieve parallel computing. Finally, output result Att_{s_i} of each SAD-LSTM is spliced to form the final output result.

3.4 Dynamic Routing Aggregation

In text information, not all substructures are positively related to task, and there is a lot of redundant information, which affect classification effect. We use the capsule network to adjust the importance of features from the perspective of similarity between features and tasks, hierarchical aggregation is shown in Fig. 2.

Sentence feature Att_{s_i} is input data of dynamic routing aggregation layer, because dynamic routing uses capsule as basic processing unit, the scalar neuron in each sentence feature is need to stretch into a vector, and then converted to sentence capsule u_i by the compression function. The input of text data containing MaxD sentences in the dynamic routing aggregation layer are $SentCaps = [u_1, u_2, \ldots, u_{MaxD}]$.

$$u_i' = reshape(Att_{s_i}) \tag{11}$$

$$u_i = squash(u_i') = \frac{\|u_i'\|^2}{1 + \|u_i'\|^2} \frac{u_i'}{\|u_i'\|} \tag{12}$$

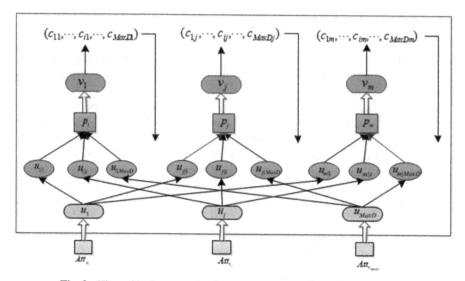

Fig. 2. Hierarchical aggregation from sentence capsule to chapter capsule.

Furthermore, hierarchical feature aggregation is realized through dynamic routing, and the partial and overall relationship between sentences and chapter is constructed. First, the transformation matrix W_{ij} is used to generate the prediction vector $\hat{u}_{j|i}$ from sentence capsule to each chapter capsule. Chapter capsule is the weighted sum of all the prediction vectors, calculation method is as follows.

$$\hat{u}_{j|i} = W_{ij}u_i \tag{13}$$

$$p_j = \sum_i c_{ij}\hat{u}_{j|i} \tag{14}$$

$$v_j = squash(p_j) \tag{15}$$

c_{ij} is the coupling coefficient, its value changes dynamically and determined during the iterative dynamic routing process. For each capsule, dynamic routing is used to increase or decrease the connection strength to express the features that exist in text. Without loss of specific spatial information, it can detect whether there are similar features in sentences in different positions of the text.

$$c_{ij} = soft\max(b_{ij}) \tag{16}$$

$$b_{ij} \leftarrow b_{ij} + v_j\hat{u}_{j|i} \tag{17}$$

After completing the hierarchical clustering through dynamic routing, for the classification task of m categories, a matrix of $E^o \in \mathbb{R}^{m \times (1 \times \text{OutCaps\_dim})}$ will be output. Finally, in order to complete the classification task, a fully connected layer is built for the HCapsNet, and classification prediction is realized through the softmax classifier.

4   Experiment and Result Analysis

4.1   Experiment Setting

- **Evaluation Metrics and Datasets.** In order to verify the effectiveness of the HCap-sNet model, we apply accuracy as our evaluation metrics in the experiments. To verify the effectiveness of our proposal, experiments are conducted on six public datasets, the detailed information of the data set is shown in Table 1.

Table 1. Data set.

Data set	Training set	Test set	Categories	Classification task
SUBJ	5952	500	2	Subjective classification
SST1	6900	1800	5	Subjective classification
SogouCS	16838	1600	8	News topic
THUCNews	45000	9000	8	News topic
ChnSentiCorp	8000	2000	2	Hotel reviews
Movie Review	2000	400	2	Movie review

- **Implementation Details.** In order to facilitate the reproduction of the experimental results, the operating environment and related parameters of the model are described as follows: The experiments are implemented on the Windows 10, using Python 3.6 and TensorFlow 14.0 as the programming language and network construction framework. Adam is used as the model's optimizer, and mini-Batch is used to implement batch training. We tuned the hyper-parameters of our model by grid searching using three-validation on the training set, and the optimal hyper-parameters are shown underlined. We selected the LSTM hidden size $h_{s_i} \in \{100, \underline{150}, 200, 250\}$, word embedding size $d^w \in \{100, \underline{150}, 200, 250\}$, MaxS $\in \{5, 10, \underline{15}, 20, 25\}$, Iter $\in \{1, 2, \underline{3}, 4, 5\}$, the dropout rate is set to 0.5. Since other hyper-parameters have little effect on the over-all results, we set them empirically.

4.2   Analysis of Comparative Experiment Results

We compare HCapsNet with multiple state-of-the-art methods, and conduct experiments on six public data sets.

- **LSTM:** LSTM applies a LSTM layer on the top of pre-trained Word2Vec for text classification, which is the basic part of HCapsNet.
- **CNN-Multichannel:** CNN-Multichannel [4] uses multi-channel convolution to propose local features of different scales. In our experiment, the scale of the convolution kernel is selected as 3, 4, 5
- **C-LSTM:** C-LSTM [20] is a word-level neural model for text classification. It composes a CNN layer and a LSTM layer for the feature extraction.

- **CapsNet-A:** CapsNet-A [25] constructs a four-layer structure model: N-gram convolutional layer, capsule layer, convolutional capsule layer, and fully connected capsule layer.
- **CapsNet-B:** CapsNet-B [25] extracts text feature representation through a parallel multi-scale convolutional capsule network.
- **CBiGRU_CapsNet:** CBiGRU_CapsNet [28] uses a cross-layer connected gated recurrent unit to strengthen features, and further uses the capsule network to obtain rich spatial position information in the deep high-level semantic representation.

Table 2. Experimental results of classification accuracy (%).

Data set	SST1	ChnSentiCorp	SUBJ	Movie review	SogouCS	THUCNews
LSTM	45.84	87.94	92.54	78.46	94.43	94.91
CNN-Multichannel	46.01	89.61	90.71	80.22	91.34	93.68
C-LSTM	48.72	90.10	92.14	81.34	96.51	96.62
CapsNet-A	46.84	89.77	90.63	80.73	95.24	96.29
CapsNet-B	48.60	91.01	92.55	82.04	97.38	97.86
CBiGRU_CapsNet	48.11	90.04	92.49	81.59	96.47	95.24
HCapsNet	48.23	91.53	93.17	82.60	97.64	98.13

It can be seen from the experimental results in Table 2 that the classification effect of the hybrid neural network model is generally better than that of the single model. Compared with the LSTM, HCapsNet has improved accuracy by 2.39%, 3.59%, 0.63%, 4.14%, 3.21%, 3.22% on the six data sets. The reason for the analysis is that the semantic information extracted by the single model is not comprehensive and the feature utilization rate is not high. CNN and CapsNet are closely related and different in the way of neuron construction and feature aggregation. In the experimental results, it can be seen that the accuracy of CapsNet on the six data sets is generally higher than that of CNN-Multichannel. On the THUCNews, CapsNet-A is up to 4.45% higher than CNN-Multichannel. It shows that the vector structure neurons of the capsule can enrich the sentence features, allowing the model to dig deep semantic information from the horizontal. The analysis of HCapsNet and the variant model based on the capsule network is as follows: performance of the HCapsNet model on the five data sets is better than that of the three-way parallel capsule network CapsNet-B. On the SUBJ data set, accuracy of HCapsNet is 0.62% higher than that of CapsNet-B. The performance of the HCapsNet model on the six data sets is all better than CBiGRU_CapsNet. It shows that the HCapsNet model has a better processing effect on shallow semantics, and the LSTM integrated with the attention mechanism can effectively capture key semantic information and global timing dependencies, and improve the quality of capsules.

On the whole, HCapsNet has achieved better classification results than the baseline model on six data sets. This is mainly due to three points: (1) In the stage of shallow semantic extraction, the parallel LSTM network fused with self-attention is used to encode sentences, which improves the expression ability of important words and accelerates the calculation speed of the model. (2) We give full play to the advantages of the capsule network in processing the part-whole relationship, establish the aggregation of the part of the sentence capsule and the whole of the chapter capsule, and dig out more hidden semantic features. (3) Using the vector structure neurons of the capsule to enrich sentence features can fully allow the model to dig out deep semantic information from the horizontal. Further, we will analyze calculation efficiency of HCapsNet.

4.3 Calculation Efficiency Verification

In order to further explore the advantages of the HCapsNet model in terms of computational efficiency, we select several different types of baseline models and compare the time and cost consumed by various methods in the calculation. Taking the sogouCS data set as an example, models are drawn to test the same data. The comparison chart of the time consumed at the time is shown in Fig. 3.

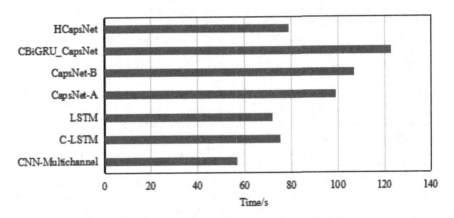

Fig. 3. Run time of the benchmark on the test set.

We find that the HCapsNet model has better time performance than the same type of capsule network-based hybrid model (CapsNet-dynamic-routing, CapsNet-B, CBiGRU_CapsNet), which is mainly due to the parallel LSTM encodes sentences and lets sentence features as capsules. It is worth noting that the time cost of HCapsNet in computing the test set is higher than that of CNN-Multichannel. This is mainly due to the time-consuming process of capsule structure and dynamic routing iteration. However, from the results in Table 2, it can be seen that the classification of the hybrid model based on the capsule network accuracy rate is generally higher than that of CNN-Multichannel. This is because the hybrid model based on the capsule network enriches semantic information at the cost of time, in exchange for better accuracy performance.

5 Conclusion

This paper proposed a text classification model based on hierarchical capsule network. First, the text granularity division rules are explained, which lays the foundation for the aggregation of features from a hierarchical perspective. Aiming at the problem of unbalanced semantic features extracted by recurrent network and incapable of parallel calculation, a parallel LSTM network fused with self-attention is constructed in the sentence feature encoding stage, the MaxD LSTM network encodes MaxD sentences at the same time to speed up the calculation of the model. With the help of the capsule structure, semantic features are enriched from a horizontal perspective, the hierarchical aggregation from sentence capsule to chapter capsule is realized through dynamic routing. Comparing and verifying with 6 baseline algorithms on six public data sets, results show that the HCapsNet proposed in this paper performs better. The next step is to optimize the model and reduce model training time through distributed computing.

References

1. Lu, Z., Gai, K., Duan, Q., Xu, Y.: Machine learning empowered content delivery: status challenges and opportunities. IEEE Netw. **34**, 228–234 (2020)
2. Dai, W., Qiu, L., Wu, A., Qiu, M.: Cloud infrastructure resource allocation for big data applications. IEEE Trans. Big Data **4**, 313–324 (2016)
3. Li, Q., et al.: A survey on text classification: from shallow to deep learning. ACM Comput. 4–41 (2020)
4. Kim, Y.: Convolutional neural networks for sentence classification. In: Proceeding of the 2015 Conference on Empirical Methods in Natural Language Processing, pp. 1746–1751 (2014)
5. Johnson, R., Zhang, T.: Deep pyramid convolutional neural networks for text categorization. In: Meeting of the Association for Computational Linguistics, pp. 562–570 (2017)
6. Dai, J., Chen, C.: A backdoor attack against LSTM-based text classification systems. IEEE Access **7**, 138872–138878 (2019)
7. Chowdhury, S., Rahman, M., Ali, S.: A RNN based parallel deep learning framework for detecting sentiment polarity from Twitter derived textual data. In: 11th International Conference on Electrical and Computer Engineering (2020)
8. Lin, J.C.-W., Shao, Y., Djenouri, Y., Yun, U.: ASRNN: A recurrent neural network with an attention model for sequence labeling. Knowl.-Based Syst. **212**, 106548–106556 (2020)
9. Katarya, R., Arora, Y.: Study on text classification using capsule networks. In: 2019 5th International Conference on Advanced Computing & Communication Systems (2019)
10. Chen, B., Xu, Z., Wang, X., Long, X., Zhang, W.: Capsule network-based text sentiment classification. IFAC-PapersOnLine **53**, 698–703 (2020)
11. Sabour, S., Frosst, N.: Dynamic routing between capsules. In: Conference and Workshop on Neural Information Processing Systems (NIPS), pp. 3856–3866 (2017)
12. Bing, L., Pan, W., Lu, J.: Multi-granularity dynamic analysis of complex software networks. In: IEEE International Symposium on Circuits & Systems (2011)
13. Pavlinek, M., Podgorelec, V.: Text classification method based on self-training and LDA topic models. Expert Syst. Appl. **80**, 83–93 (2017)
14. Ge, J., Lin, S., Fang, Y.: A text classification algorithm based on topic model and convolutional neural network. J. Phys. Conf. Ser. 32–36 (2021)
15. Zeng, J., Li, J., Song, Y.: Topic memory networks for shorttext classification. In: Proceedings of Empirical Methods in Natural Language Processing, Brussels, Belgium, EMNLP, pp. 3120–3131 (2018)

16. Yang, Z., Yang, D., Dyer, C.: Hierarchical attention networks for document classification. In: Annual Meeting of the Association for Computational Linguistics, pp. 1480–1489 (2016)

17. Tong, G., Li, Y., Gao, H., Chen, H., Wang, H., Yang, X.: MA-CRNN: a multi-scale attention CRNN for Chinese text line recognition in natural scenes. Int. J. Document Anal. Recogn. (IJDAR) **23**(2), 103–114 (2019). https://doi.org/10.1007/s10032-019-00348-7

18. Klaren, B., Ek, G., Harmanny, R., Cifola, L.: Multi-target human gait classification using LSTM recurrent neural networks applied to micro-doppler. In: European Radar Conference, pp. 167–170 (2017)

19. Nie, Y., Bansal, M.: Shortcut-stacked sentence encoders for multi-domain inference. In: Proceedings of Empirical Methods in Natural Language Processing (EMNLP), pp. 41–45 (2017)

20. Zhou, C., Sun, C., Liu, Z.: A C-LSTM neural network for text classification. Comput. Sci. **1**, 39–44 (2015)

21. Cao, Y., Ma, S., Pan, H.: FDTA: fully convolutional scene text detection with text attention. IEEE Access **8**, 155441–155449 (2020)

22. Zhan, Z., Hou, Z., Yang, Q.: Knowledge attention sandwich neural network for text classification. Neurocomputing **406**, 1–11 (2020)

23. Tang, X., Chen, Y., Dai, Y.: A multi-scale convolutional attention based GRU network for text classification. In: 2019 Chinese Automation Congress (2020)

24. Min, Y., Wei, Z., Lei, C.: Investigating the transferring capability of capsule networks for text classification . Neural Netw. **118**, 247–261 (2019)

25. Zhao, W., Ye, J., Yang, M.: Investigating capsule networks with dynamic routing for text classification. In: Proceedings of Empirical Methods in Natural Language Processing (EMNLP), pp. 3110–3119 (2018)

26. Kim, J., Jang, S.: Text classification using capsules. Neurocomputing. **376**, 214–221 (2020)

27. Gong, J., Qiu, X., Wang, S.: Information aggregation via dynamic routing for sequence encoding. In: Annual Meeting of the Association for Computational Linguistics, pp. 2742–2752 (2018)

28. Deng, X., Yin, S., Deng, H.: A short text classification model based on cross-layer connected gated recurrent unit capsule network. In: Big Data, pp. 1–17 (2020)

Sentence Matching with Deep Self-attention and Co-attention Features

Zhipeng Wang and Danfeng Yan[✉]

State Key Laboratory of Networking and Switching Technology,
Beijing University of Posts and Telecommunications, Beijing, China
{wangzhipeng,yandf}@bupt.edu.cn

Abstract. Sentence matching refers to extracting the semantic relation between two sentences which is widely applied in many natural language processing tasks such as natural language inference, paraphrase identification and question answering. Many previous methods apply a siamese network to capture semantic features and calculate cosine similarity to represent sentences relation. However, they could be effective for overall rough sentence semantic but not sufficient for word-level matching information. In this paper, we proposed a novel neural network based on attention mechanism which focuses on learning richer interactive features of two sentences. There are two complementary components in our model: semantic encoder and interactive encoder. Interactive encoder compares sentences semantic features which are encoded by semantic encoder. In addition, semantic encoder considers the output of interactive encoder as supplementary matching features. Experiments on three benchmark datasets proved that self-attention network and cross-attention network can efficiently learn the semantic and interactive features of sentences, and achieved state-of-the-art results.

Keywords: Sentence matching · Natural language processing · Neural network · Attention mechanism

1 Introduction

Sentence matching requires a model to identify the semantic relation between two sentences which has a wide range of practical applications such as natural language inference, paraphrase identification and so on. In natural language inference (also known as recognizing textual entailment) task [1], it is utilized to predict the reasoning relationship (entailment, contradiction, neutral) given premise and hypothesis sentences. In paraphrase identification task [2], sentence matching needs to judge whether two sentences have the same meaning or not.

Supported by National Key Research and Development Program of China under Grant 2018YFC0831502 and State Grid Shandong Electric Power Company Science and Technology Project Funding (2020A-074).

H. Qiu et al. (Eds.): KSEM 2021, LNAI 12816, pp. 550–561, 2021.
https://doi.org/10.1007/978-3-030-82147-0_45

Recently, deep neural networks make progress in the field of natural language processing and become the most popular methods for sentence matching. There are two mainstream framework [3] in deep neural networks: sentences-encoding-based method and features-interaction-based method. The first method [4] is that encodes each sentence to a fixed-length vector and uses the vectors to predict the relation. Another method [5] makes an improvement base on the first method and captures the interactive features while encoding the sentence. Semantic gap [6] between the two sentences is a puzzle for determining the semantic relation without the interactive features.

Inspired by multi-head attention mechanism [7], we proposed a model DAMM (Deep Attention Matching Model) for sentence matching task constituted only by attention mechanism network, while many previous and powerful models [8–10] almost consist of deep CNN (Convolutional Neural Network) or LSTM (Long Short Term Memory) network. Attention mechanism network could extract the word order information, although CNN had achieved a huge success in compute vision field and was widely utilized in natural language processing field recently. Compared to LSTM network, attention mechanism network has a stronger ability for long distance dependence because LSTM network has the multi-step multiply operation which may cause gradient vanishing. Base on the analysis, our model could have a more better result than the previous CNN-based or LSTM-based sentence matching models.

In DAMM, multi-head self-attention network is firstly employed for deep sentence semantic features. Then, multi-head cross-attention network is utilized for sentences interactive features with sentence semantic features as input. We designed a alignment layer to integrate semantic and interactive features by using feed-forward network, resnet [11] and layer-norm [12]. Furthermore, to achieve a better performance, our model applyed a stacked framework.

In the remaining of this paper, we will first introduce the related work of sentence matching, the design of DAMM model in detail. Then, we will analysis the experiments on SNLI, SciTail and Quora Question Pairs (Quora). Experimental results show our model achieve the state-of-the-art performance. Finally, we will draw a conclusion of our work.

In summary, our contributions are as follows:

- We only used attention mechanism in the encoder of the sentence matching model and achieve the state-of-the-art performance.
- Compared with previous features-interaction-based model, our model proposed multi-head cross-attention mechanism to capture more powerful interactive features.

2   Related Work

Big data analysis has attracted a lot of research work, including computer vision, natural language processing and cloud computing [13–15]. Early work of sentence matching in natural language processing mainly focus on conventional methods and small datasets, which works only on specific tasks [16]. Recently, many human annotated sentence pairs high quality datasets opened which make a big progress for sentence matching tasks, including SNLI [1], Quora Questions Pairs [2] and so on.

The development of deep learning algorithm makes natural language processing task to have more flexible and complex solving methods. As described in Sect. 1, sentences-encoding-based methods and features-interaction-based methods both are effective to sentence matching. Sentences-encoding-based methods encode each sequence individually into a vector and then calculate cosine similarity or build a neural network classifier upon the two vectors. DSSM(Deep Structured Semantic Model) [4] based on feed-forward neural networks is more automated and has a good performance compared to human-features-based methods. R-DSSM [17] and C-DSSM [10] apply recurrent networks and convolutional networks as their sequence encoder respectively which have a more powerful encoder than DSSM. More recently, features-interaction-based methods consider that the interactive features could make a difference to the prediction. ESIM [5] uses bidirectional LSTMs as encoders and employs a attention mechanism as interactive features collector. BiMPM [2] interacts two sentences vectors from multi-perspective matching operation. DIIN [3] utilizes a deep convolutional network to extract interactive information.

3   Model Description

In this section, we will introduce DAMM which is composed of the following major components: embedding layer, self-encoder, cross-encoder, alignment layer, pooling layer and prediction layer. Figure 1 shows the overall architecture of our model.

The input of model are two sentences as $A = (A_1, A_2, ..., A_I)$ with the length I and $B = (B_1, B_2, ..., B_J)$ with the length J where A_i is the ith word of sentence A and B_j is the jth word of sentence B. The sentence matching's goal is to give a label y to represent the relationship between sentence A and sentence B.

In DAMM, two sentences are firstly embedded by the embedding layer into a matrix. And then, N same-structured blocks encode the matrix where each block has a self-encoder, a cross-encoder and an alignment layer. The output of last block is fed into a self-encoder again to integrate the features and a pooling layer to get the final vector representation of the whole sentence. Finally, DAMM uses the two final vector representation as input and makes a prediction.

3.1   Embedding Layer

The goal of embedding layer is to represent each token of the sentence to a d-dimensional vector by using a pre-trained vector such as GloVe [18] and Word2Vec [19]. In our model, we use GloVe vector (840B Glove) to get the vector for sentence A and sentence B and the vector is fixed during training. Now, we have sentence A representation $E_a \in R^{l_a * d}$ and sentence B representation $E_b \in R^{l_b * d}$, where l_a refers to the max sequence length of sentence A, l_b

refers to the max sequence length of sentence B and d refers to the dimension of word embedding.

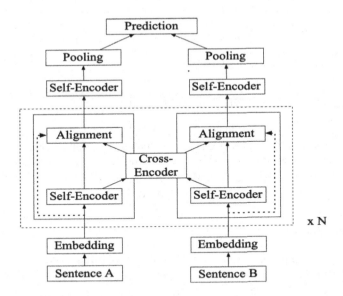

Fig. 1. Architecture of Deep Attention Matching Model (DAMM). Dashed frame including Self-Encoder, Cross-Encoder and Alignment could be repeated N times. Self-Encoder and Cross-Encoder respectively extract single sentence semantic information and interactive features between two sentences.

3.2 Self-encoder

The sentence A representation E_a and the sentence B representation E_b are fed into the Self-Encoder which is composed of a multi-head self-attention layer and a feed-forward layer to capture the richer semantic features of each sentence themselves.

Firstly, the multi-head self-attention network consists of query matrix Q_i, key matrix K_i and value matrix V_i. Each matrix respectively uses a linear transformation on the output of embedding layer representations E_a and E_b. Then, the scaled dot-product attention is employed to compute the self-attention output. Finally, we concatenate the multi-head self-attention outputs and feed the concatenate vector into a two layer feed-forward network with *gelu* activative function. This process can be described by the following formulas and the formulas for H_b are similar and omitted here:

$$Q_i^s = A_i S_i^q \tag{1}$$

$$K_i^s = A_i S_i^k \tag{2}$$

$$V_i^s = A_i S_i^v \tag{3}$$

$$Att_i^s = softmax(\frac{Q_i^s(K_i^s)^T}{\sqrt{d_q}})V_i^s \tag{4}$$

$$M_a = [Att_1^s; ...; Att_h^s] \tag{5}$$

$$H_a = gelu(M_a W_1^s)W_2^s \tag{6}$$

where h is number of the head of the multi-head self-attention network, i is an integer from 1 to h, d_q refers to the dimension of self-attention, $A_i \in R^{d_q * d_q}$ refers to hidden states, the projections are parameter matrices $S_i^q \in R^{d_q * d_q}$, $S_i^k \in R^{d_q * d_q}$, $S_i^v \in R^{d_q * d_q}$, $W_1^s \in R^{d * d'}$, $W_2^s \in R^{d' * d}$ where d' refers to intermediate hidden size, $[...; ...]$denotes the concatenation operation.

3.3 Cross-Encoder

In a sentence matching task, sentences interactive features could be important as same as the sentences semantic features generating by Self-Encoder above. Our model employs a Cross-Encoder to extract the sentences interactive features. The Cross-Encoder is the similar with the Self-Encoder but the key and value matrix are different. We calculate the interactive features from sentence A to sentence B as following, we omitted the another direction here:

$$Q_i^c = A_i C_i^q \tag{7}$$

$$K_i^c = B_i C_i^k \tag{8}$$

$$V_i^c = B_i C_i^v \tag{9}$$

$$CrossAtt_i^c = softmax(\frac{Q_i^c(K_i^c)^T}{\sqrt{d_q}})V_i^c \tag{10}$$

$$M_{b2a} = [CrossAtt_1^c; ...; CrossAtt_h^c] \tag{11}$$

$$H_{b2a} = gelu(M_{b2a}W_1^c)W_2^c \tag{12}$$

where H_{b2a} denotes the interactive features from sentence A semantic features H_a to sentence B semantic features H_b, other parameters are similar with Self-Encoder.

3.4   Alignment Layer

After the Self-Encoder and Cross-Encoder, we have two features matrices H_a and H_{b2a} which respectively represents the sentence A semantic matrix and interactive matrix between two sentences. The two features both are significant components for a sentence matching task. We make an alignment for stacking operation and apply residual connection to avoid overfitting as following:

$$C_a = [H_a; H_{b2a}]W_a \qquad (13)$$

$$O_a = H_a + E_a \qquad (14)$$

where the projections are parameter matrices $W_a \in R^{2d*d}$.

3.5   Pooling Layer

The pooling layer's goal is to converts the matrices O_a and O_b to fixed-length vectors v_a and v_b which will be fed into prediction layer to classify. As we all know, both average and max pooling are useful strategies for sentence matching. Hence, we combine the max pooling strategy and mean pooling strategy in our model. Our experiments show that this leads to significantly better results. Formulations for v_b are similar and omitted here. This process is described by the following formulas:

$$v_a^{max} = \max_{i=1}^{l_a} O_{a,i} \qquad (15)$$

$$v_a^{mean} = \sum_{i=1}^{l_a} \frac{O_{a,i}}{l_a} \qquad (16)$$

$$v_a = [v_a^{max}; v_a^{mean}] \qquad (17)$$

3.6   Prediction Layer

In our model, v_a and v_b are the sentence A and sentence B feature vectors from the output of the pooling layer. The prediction layer is to aggregate the vectors v_a and v_b in a proper way, and then predicts the label by using a feed-forward neural network.

Firstly, similarity and difference between two sentences are meaningful features for a symmetric task [20]. Hence, we aggregates v_a and v_b in various ways as follows:

$$v = [v_a; v_b; v_a - v_b; v_a * v_b] \qquad (18)$$

where $-$, $*$ are the element-wise subtraction and element-wise product.

Then, with the aggregated features v, we employ a two-layer feed-forward neural network for classification task and *gelu* activative function is adopted after the first layer. Finally, we use multi-class cross-entropy loss function with Label Smooth Regularization (LSR) [21] to train our model.

$$\hat{y} = softmax(gelu(vW_1^o)W_2^o) \tag{19}$$

$$y = \hat{y}(1 - \epsilon) + \frac{\epsilon}{C} \tag{20}$$

$$Loss = -\sum_{j=1}^{C} y_j log(\hat{y_j}) + \lambda \sum_{\theta \in \Theta} \theta^2 \tag{21}$$

where feature vector is $v \in R^{1*d}$, the projections are parameters $W_o^1 \in R^{d*d'}$, $W_o^2 \in R^{d'*C}$ and C is the number of label classes, y is the ground truth, hyperparameter ϵ denotes the degree of smooth of LSR, θ denotes the parameters of DAMM.

4   Experiments

We conduct experiments on three sentence matching benchmark datasets: SNLI, Scitail, Quora Question Pairs (Quora).

SNLI (The Stanford Natural Language Inference corpus) is a popular benchmark dataset for natural language inference. It focuses on three basic relationships between a premise and a hypothesis: entailment(the premise entails the hypothesis), contradiction(the premise and the hypothesis contradict), neutral(the premise and the hypothesis are not related).

SciTail is a textual entailment dataset from science question answering. The premises and hypothesis in SciTail are different from existing entailment datasets. The hypothesis is generated from science questions and the corresponding answer candidates, and the premises are retrieved from a large corpus. The generated way of SciTail make it more challenging.

Quora Question Pairs is a dataset for paraphrase identification provided by Quora. This task is a binary classification task which need to determine whether one question is a paraphrase of another.

4.1   Implementation Details

In our experiments, word embedding vectors are initialized with 300d GloVe vectors pre-trained from the 840B Common Crawl corpus. Embeddings of out of the vocabulary of GloVe is initialized to zeros. All embeddings are fixed during the training. All other parameters are initialized with a normal distribution where *mean* is 0.0 and *standard deviation* is 0.02. Dropout with a keep probability of 0.8 is applied after the word embedding layer and every fully-connected layer. We also apply attention dropout with a keep probability of 0.8 after the attention operation of Self-Encoder and Cross-Encoder. The hidden size is 300 in all experiments. Activative functions in all feed-forward networks are *gelu* function. After the residual connections and two-layer feed-forward networks, we use LayerNorm with a norm epsilon of $1e - 12$ to accelerate training model. Adam optimizer with weight decay of 0.01 is employed in our model. Learning rate is tuned from 0.00001 to 0.0005 and an exponentially decaying learning rate with a linear warmup is applied for learning rate.

Table 1. Classification accuracy (%) on SNLI test set.

Model	Acc. (%)
BiMPM [2]	86.9
ESIM [5]	88.0
DIIN [3]	88.0
DRCN [9]	88.9
RE2 [22]	**88.9**
DAMM (ours)	88.8
BiMPM (ensemble)	88.8
DIIN (ensemble)	88.9
DRCN (ensemble)	**90.1**
RE2 (ensemble)	89.9
DAMM (ensemble)	**90.1**

4.2 Results on SNLI and SciTail

We evalutated our model on the natural language inference task over SNLI and SciTail datasets. Results on SNLI and SciTail are listed in Tables 1 and 2. Our method obtains a performance which achieves state-of-the-art results. For SNLI dataset, our method get a accuracy score 88.8% in single model and 90.1% by ensemble in test dataset which obtains a state-of-the-art performance. We employ 8 different randomly initialized models with same hyper-parameters for our ensemble approach. For SciTail dataset, we obtain a result nearly the most highest performance. SciTail dataset is a more difficult and challenging task for natural language inference, because it has only 27k samples while SNLI has 570k samples.

4.3 Results on Quora Question Pairs

The results on Quora Qustion Pairs are shown in Table 3. Most methods such as BiMPM and DIIN, apply attention method for features alignment after bidirectional long short-term memory or convolutional neural network encoder. However, DAMM abandons complex encoder methods and uses a stacked structure based on simple attention mechanism. The performance of our model is on par with the state-of-the-art on this dataset.

Table 2. Classification accuracy (%) on Scitail test set.

Model	Acc. (%)
ESIM [5]	70.6
DecompAtt [8]	72.3
DGEM [26]	77.3
HCRN [23]	80.0
CAFE [24]	83.3
RE2 [22]	**86.0**
DAMM (ours)	85.7

Table 3. Classification accuracy (%) on Quora test set.

Model	Acc. (%)
BiMPM [2]	88.2
DIIN [3]	89.1
MwAN [10]	89.1
CSRAN [25]	89.2
RE2 [22]	89.2
DAMM (ours)	**89.4**

4.4   Analysis

Ablation Study. We conducted an ablation study of our model for 7 ablation baselines: (1) replaced fix-embedding with trainable-embedding in embedding layer, (2) removed Cross-Encoder in every block, (3) replaced Self-Encoder with LSTM network in every block, (4) removed Cross-Encoder and replaced Self-Encoder with LSTM network in every block, (5) removed residual connections in alignment layer (Equation 14), (6) removed the last Self-Encoder before pooling layer, (7) removed difference and similarity features between two sentences ($v_a - v_b$ and $v_a * v_b$ in Equation 18). Ablation study is conducted on the test set of SNLI and alation experiments results are shown in Table 4.

We compared the difference of fix embedding and trainable embedding in embedding layer in ablation experiment (1). The result shows that fix embedding is more effective, and we think trainable embedding may be easier to overfit than fix embedding. In (2), we verified the effectiveness of interactive features which is captured by Cross-Encoder. Without Cross-Encoder, DAMM becomes a siamese network and its performance decreases significantly. In (3), we replaced Self-Encoder with LSTM network. It means that different encoding ways have a marked impact of the model. The result shows that attention mechanism works well for sentence matching task. The result of experiment (4) could be a supplement to experiments (2–3). The result of ablation experiment (5) demonstrate that residual connection is a key component of alignment layer. With the residual connection, DAMM has more powerful capability to aggregate semantic features and interactive features. In (6), we applied Self-Encoder to integrate semantic and interactive features rather than the features are fed into pooling layer. The result shows the last Self-Encoder before pooling layer is necessary. The result of experiment (7) show that difference and similarity features are important for sentence matching task.

Table 4. Ablation study on the SNLI test set.

Model	Acc. (%)
DAMM	88.8
(1) − Fix. + Tr.	88.4
(2) − Cross.	86.3
(3) − Self. + LSTM	85.5
(4) − Self. + LSTM − Cross.	84.7
(5) − RES	87.6
(6) − Last Self.	87.2
(7) − Symmetry	88.3

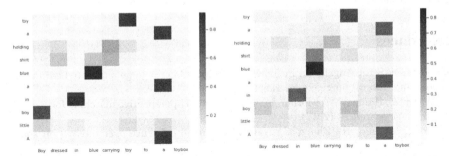

(a) Attention weight results in the first block (b) Attention weight results in the last block

Fig. 2. A case study of the natural language inference task. The premise is "A little boy in a blue shirt holding a toy", and the hypothesis is "Boy dressed in blue carrying toy to a toybox".

Case Study. In this section, we used a premise *"A little boy in a blue shirt holding a toy"* and a hypothesis *"Boy dressed in blue carrying toy to a toybox"* from SNLI test set as a case study. As show in Fig. 2, we visualized the attention weights in the first and last Cross-Encoder between the premise and hypothesis. There are multi-head cross-attention in Cross-Encoder, and multi head could obtain more information from different perspectives. Because each head in Cross-Encoder has its own attention weights, our attention weights in visualization are calculated by concatenating all head attention weights and the relation between words is represented by consine similarity.

From Fig. 2(a), we can see that the word **"blue"** of hypothesis is highly related to the phrase **"blue shirt"** of premise. In the first block of DAMM, our model mainly pays attention to the word-level interaction. But as in Fig. 2(b), the attention weights between the word **"blue"** of hypothesis and the phrase **"A little boy"** were increased obviously, which proves our model is able to take into consideration of the whole sentence-level semantic and the interaction between the premise and hypothesis.

5   Conclusions and Future Work

In this paper, we proposed a novel attention-based network for semantic matching. We aligned the semantic features and interactive features which both were captured from attention mechanism. The alignment features have sufficient context information towards the two sentences. Our model achieveed the state-of-the-art performance on most of the datasets of highly challenging natural language tasks.

For future work, we will explore how to introduce external knowledge to improve performance.

References

1. Bowman, S.R., Angeli, G., Potts, C., Manning, C.D.: A large annotated corpus for learning natural language inference (2015)
2. Wang, Z., Hamza, W., Florian, R.: Bilateral multi-perspective matching for natural language sentences (2017)
3. Gong, Y., Luo, H., Zhang, J.: Natural language inference over interaction space (2017)
4. Huang, P.-S., et al.: Learning deep structured semantic models for web search using clickthrough data. In: Proceedings of the 22nd ACM International Conference on Information & Knowledge Management, pp. 2333–2338 (2013)
5. Chen, Q., Zhu, X., Ling, Z., Wei, S., Jiang, H., Inkpen, D.: Enhanced lstm for natural language inference (2016)
6. Liu, P., Qiu, X., Chen, J., Huang, X.-J.: Deep fusion lstms for text semantic matching. In: Proceedings of the 54th Annual Meeting of the Association for Computational Linguistics (Volume 1: Long Papers), pp. 1034–1043 (2016)
7. Vaswani, A., et al.: Attention is all you need. In: Advances in Neural Information Processing Systems, pp. 5998–6008 (2017)
8. Parikh, A.P., Täckström, O., Das, D., Uszkoreit, J.: A decomposable attention model for natural language inference (2016)
9. Kim, S., Kang, I., Kwak, N.: Semantic sentence matching with densely-connected recurrent and co-attentive information. In: Proceedings of the AAAI Conference on Artificial Intelligence, pp. 6586–6593 (2019)

10. Tan, C., Wei, F., Wang, W., Lv, W., Zhou, M.: Multiway attention networks for modeling sentence pairs. In: IJCAI, pp. 4411–4417 (2018)
11. He, K., Zhang, X., Ren, S., Sun, J.: Deep residual learning for image recognition. In: Proceedings of the IEEE Conference on Computer Vision and Pattern Recognition, pp. 770–778 (2016)
12. Ba, J.L., Kiros, J.R., Hinton, G.E.: Layer normalization (2016)
13. Gai, K., Qiu, M.: Reinforcement learning-based content-centric services in mobile sensing. IEEE Network 32(4), 34–39 (2018)
14. Dai, W., Qiu, L., Wu, A., Qiu, M.: Cloud infrastructure resource allocation for big data applications. IEEE Trans. Big Data 4(3), 313–324 (2016)
15. Gai, K., Qiu, M., Zhao, H., Sun, X.: Resource management in sustainable cyber-physical systems using heterogeneous cloud computing. IEEE Trans. Sustainable Comput. 3(2), 60–72 (2017)
16. Romano, L., Kouylekov, M., Szpektor, I., Dagan, I., Lavelli, A.: Investigating a generic paraphrase-based approach for relation extraction. In: 11th Conference of the European Chapter of the Association for Computational Linguistics (2006)
17. Conneau, A., Kiela, D., Schwenk, H., Barrault, L., Bordes, A.: Supervised learning of universal sentence representations from natural language inference data (2017)
18. Pennington, J., Socher, R., Manning, C.D.: Glove: global vectors for word representation. In: Proceedings of the 2014 Conference on Empirical Methods in Natural Language Processing (EMNLP), pp. 1532–1543. 2014
19. Mikolov, T., Sutskever, I., Chen, K., Corrado, G.S., Dean, J.: Distributed representations of words and phrases and their compositionality. In: Advances in Neural Information Processing Systems, pp. 3111–3119 (2013)
20. Wang, S., Jiang, J.: A compare-aggregate model for matching text sequence. arXiv preprint arXiv:1611.01747 2016
21. Szegedy, C., Vanhoucke, V., Ioffe, S., Shlens, J., Wojna, Z.: Rethinking the inception architecture for computer vision. In: Proceedings of the IEEE Conference on Computer Vision and Pattern Recognition, pp. 2818–2826 (2016)
22. Yang, R., Zhang, J., Gao, X., Ji, F., Chen, H.: Simple and effective text matching with richer alignment features (2019)
23. Tay, Y., Luu, A.T., Hui, S.C.: Hermitian co-attention networks for text matching in asymmetrical domains. In: IJCAI, pp. 4425–4431 (2018)
24. Tay, Y., Tuan, L.A., Hui, S.C.: Compare, compress and propagate: Enhancing neural architectures with alignment factorization for natural language inference (2017)
25. Tay, Y., Tuan, L.A., Hui, S.C.: Co-stack residual affinity networks with multi-level attention refinement for matching text sequences (2018)
26. Khot, T., Sabharwal, A., Clark, P.: SciTaiL: a textual entailment dataset from science question answering. In: AAAI, pp. 41–42 (2018)

Not Only the Contextual Semantic Information: A Deep Fusion Sentimental Analysis Model Towards Extremely Short Comments

Liping Hua[1], Qinhui Chen[1], Zelin Huang[1], Hui Zhao[1,2(✉)], and Gang Zhao[3]

[1] Software Engineering Institute, East China Normal University, Shanghai, China
hzhao@sei.ecnu.edu.cn
[2] Shanghai Key Laboratory of Trustworthy Computing, Shanghai, China
[3] Microsoft, Beijing, China
gang.zhao@microsoft.com

Abstract. Extremely short comments (ESC) often contain rich information to convey users' emotions towards content. However, conducting sentiment analysis on ESC is challenging due to the limited contextual semantic information and colloquial expressions. Traditional methods mainly focus on contextual text features. In this work, we propose a novel model, named Chinese Phonetic-Attentive Deep Fusion Network (CPADFN) that attentively fuse the Chinese phonetic alphabet features of the ESC, meta-information about the ESC along with the contextual text features. First, the multi-head self-attention mechanism is utilized to obtain the phonetic alphabet representation and the sentence representation separately. Also, a fully-connected layer is used on the embeddings of the meta-information about the ESC to obtain the meta-information representation. Then, the local activation unit is employed to attentively fuse these feature representations. Bi-LSTM is applied to address the sequence dependency across these fused features separately. Third, a fully-connected layer with *softmax* function is applied to predict emotional labels. We conduct experiments on a self-crawled ESC dataset DanmuCorpus, and two public Chinese short text datasets, MovieReview and WeiboCorpus. The experimental results demonstrate that CPADFN achieves better performances.

Keywords: Extremely short comments · Deep Fusion · Chinese phonetic alphabet · Sentiment classification · Multi-head self-attention

1 Introduction

With the rapid development of video sharing websites and live streaming platforms, such as Bilibili [1], Douyu [2], and Niconico [3], the audience can write their comments synchronized with the video, and the comment named *Danmu* will appear in the real-time image. Unlike the traditional review which usually

© Springer Nature Switzerland AG 2021
H. Qiu et al. (Eds.): KSEM 2021, LNAI 12816, pp. 562–576, 2021.
https://doi.org/10.1007/978-3-030-82147-0_46

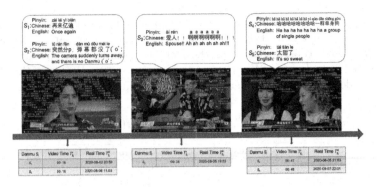

Fig. 1. Illustration of *Danmu*s associating with three sequential frames in a video clip.

includes a numerical rating attached to a textual comment and often reflects viewers' holistic understandings, *Danmu*s are usually extremely short. Individual *Danmu*s commonly contain even less than 15 words. They often expresses viewers' instantaneous emotions. As Fig. 1 shows, the middle row is an individual *Danmu* S_i, whose English translation is at the bottom. In top is the phonetic transcription of S_i, called Pinyin, which is the Romanization of the Chinese characters based on their pronunciation. S_i is associated with two timestamps, i.e., the video time $T_{S_i}^V$ and the real time $T_{S_i}^N$. Sentiment analysis on extremely short comments(ESC) could provide valuable insights for content providers, who can promote the effectiveness of many services, such as video popularity prediction, opinion mining, and online advertising. However, performing sentiment analysis on ESC is challenging due to the issues of the extremely short length and abundant colloquial expressions that accompany the ESC.

Colloquial expressions in ESC bring two major problems: abundant noise and Chinese word segmentation error. The usage of phonemic loans and partial tone words is very common in ESC, such as '再来亿次 (Once again)' and '魂淡 (bastard)'. These colloquial words are informal, short, fast-evolving, but frequently used in ESC that contribute to a high overall noisiness. Additionally, the Chinese word segmentation error is generally caused by new expressions or typos. Take the trans-pronunciation word '刚爸爹 (がんばって, (Come on)' as an example. If the word segmentation is performed on the *Danmu* '刚爸爹, 你可以成功! (Come on, you can make it!)', then the result is '刚/爸/爹/, /你/可以/成功/!' in which '刚', '爸', '爹' are single-character words. The performance of Chinese sentiment analysis task suffers from Chinese word segmentation error [19]. Furthermore, the effectiveness of many traditional sentiment analysis methods is inevitably compromised when directly applied to the noisy and informal ESC.

Phonetic features are of great value to the representation [21,22] and sentiment analysis [15] of Chinese in natural language processing. Each symbol of Chinese character can be phonetically transcribed into Latin alphabets, called Pinyin, consisting of an initial (optional), a final, and the tone. There are five tones in Chinese that help clarify meanings, including 4 main tones and 1 neutral tone, as illustrate in Table 1. Numbers or accent marks are often used to denote the tone. Table 2 illustrates the Pinyin examples corresponding to the ESC selected from *Danmu*, Weibo posts and movie reviews. We argue that Pinyin could provide complementary semantic cues to their textual form in ESC.

Table 1. Illustration of five tones in the word 'ma'

Intonation	Chinese Character	Pinyin	Meaning
First tone	妈	ma1/mā	mother
Second tone	麻	ma2/má	hemp
Third tone	马	ma3/mǎ	horse
Fourth tone	骂	ma4/mà	scold
Neutral tone	吗	ma0/ma	Is that right

Table 2. Examples of Pinyin that provide complementary semantic cues to the ESC.

ESC	Pinyin	Meaning	Sentiment Polarity
魂淡:(	['hu2n', 'da4n']	混蛋:((Bastard)	Negative
蜜汁感动	['mi4', 'zhi1', 'ga3n', 'do4ng']	迷之感动 (Inexplicable affection)	Positive
刚爸爹!!	['ga1ng','ba1','die1']	がんばって!! (Come on)	Positive

In general, ESC are ambiguous and lack sufficient contextual semantic information due to their short length. To address the issue, some researchers put emphasis on a group of constituent ESC from a video clip [6,11]. Although these methods empirically improve the classification performance, they ignore the emotional independence of individual ESC. For example, as Fig. 1 shows, *Danmu* S_1 presents the 'positive' sentiment towards the contestants in the show. In the same frame, *Danmu* S_2 presents the 'negative' sentiment to the screen. It's observed that one video frame typically involves a mixture of various emotions.

Previous researchers seldom conduct sentiment analysis on individual ESC. Existing works on the short text classification are mainly based on feature expansion [4,12,16]. A growing number of approaches leverage the external knowledge to alleviate the data sparsity problem [4,16]. Although these methods have shown considerable improvement, they heavily rely on the scale and quality of the external data. Also, they are domain-specific. The reference data may be inconsistent with the current domain or languages, leading to the expanded feature less discriminative.

In this work, we emphasize the challenges of extremely short length and colloquial expressions towards individual ESC. We fuse the Chinese phonetic alphabet feature of the ESC along with the contextual text features. A novel model, named Chinese Phonetic-Attentive Deep Fusion Network (CPADFN) is proposed. It is worth noting that CPADFN does not rely on any external resources.

First, the multi-head self-attention mechanism is utilized to obtain the Pinyin and the sentence representation separately. For *Danmus*, a fully-connected layer is used on the embeddings of the meta-information about *Danmu*/video frame to obtain the meta-information representation. Then, the local activation unit is employed to fuse these feature representations. Bi-LSTM is applied to address the sequence dependency across these fused features separately. Finally, a fully-connected layer with *softmax* function is applied to predict emotional labels. We evaluate the proposed model on three Chinese short text datasets, including a self-crawled *Danmu* dataset collected from the Bilibili website, a public movie reviews dataset, and a public social media posts dataset from Weibo. Weibo posts share many similarities with the ESC in social and textual styles. The results demonstrate the effectiveness of the proposed CPADFN model for the problem.

2 Related Work

In this section, we discuss some most related research works of phonetics for Chinese representation and sentiment analysis on extremely short comments (ESC).

A limited number of works spend efforts in taking advantage of phonetic information for Chinese representation. Some researchers represents Chinese at Pinyin level, thus taking Chinese as a western language [21,22]. However, a pure phonetic representation is arguably further away from semantics. Peng et al. [15] integrated pronunciation information to Chinese representation, and designed a reinforcement learning based framework to learn the correct intonation of each pinyin. Nevertheless, they simply concatenated textual and phonetic representation together, without considering the mutual influence between them. In this paper, we augment the ESC representation with additional phonetic cues. We focus on the dynamic fusion of textual and phonetic representation.

Conducting sentiment analysis on the ESC is considered a very challenging task due to their shortness and sparsity. Existing works mainly focus on the overall sentiment of a group of ESC [6,11,20]. The emotional independence of individual ESC is overlooked. Some approaches leverage external knowledge to enhance the information of extremely short texts. Bollegala et al. [4] used the available web content to enhance existing words and entities information. Phan et al. [16] expanded short document features using hidden topics learned from a large-scale reference data collection, including Wikipedia (30M words) and MEDLINE (18M words). Shen et al. [17] used an ensemble of search engines to obtain auxiliary contexts for web-query classification. Although these feature expansion methods have shown considerable improvement, they heavily rely on the scale and quality of external resources. Additionally, the expanded features may be less discriminative if the reference data is inconsistent with the current domain or languages. In our work, we emphasize enriching the information of ESC by collectively incorporating contextual text features, Chinese phonetic alphabet features and meta-information about the ESC.

3   Proposed Chinese Phonetic-Attentive Deep Fusion Network

Take individual *Danmus* as an example. Given a set of *Danmu* collections $Doc = \{D_1, ...D_d, ..., D_P\}$, D_d comes from V_d in videos $V = \{V_1, ..., V_d..., V_P\}$. For individual *Danmu* $S_i = \{c_1, ..., c_e, ...c_n\}$ in D_d with n characters, $c_i^{(p)}$ denotes the phonetics and intonation of each character c_e in S_i. With Pinyin converter, S_i is translated into the pinyin-character sequence $S_i^p = [c_1^{(p)}, c_2^{(p)}, ..., c_n^{(p)}]$. With embedding, the Chinese phonetic alphabet embeddings are represented by $\mathbf{P} = [p_1, p_2, ..., p_n]$. We use the same word segmentation strategy as that of ERNIE [18]. S_i is split into word sequence $S_i^w = [b_1, ..., b_f, ...b_m]$. The sentence embeddings are represented by $\mathbf{W} = [w_1, ..., w_f, ..., w_m]$, where $\mathbf{w}_f$ denotes the corresponding word embeddings of each word b_f in S_i^w. $\mathbf{W}$ is initialized by ERNIE pre-training model, and fine-tuned during the training process. S_i is associated with a vector about meta-information $\mathbf{E}_i = [\mathbf{E}^{V_i}; \mathbf{E}^{D_i}]$, which is composed of two sub-vectors: Video-Meta embeddings $\mathbf{E}^{V_i}$ and *Danmu*-Meta embeddings $\mathbf{E}^{D_i}$. The task is to predict the sentiment polarity $Y_i^j \in \{0, 1\}$ of S_i in video V_j, where 0 and 1 denote 'Positive' and 'Negative' sentiments respectively.

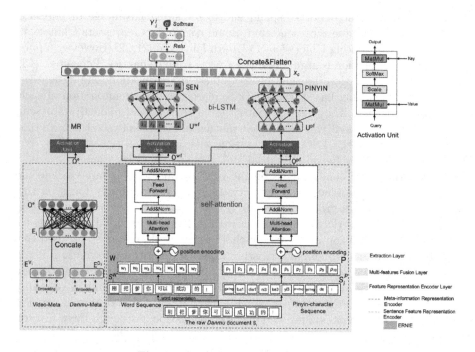

Fig. 2. The architecture of CPADFN

The architecture of CPADFN is demonstrated in Fig. 2. The proposed model contains three modules: a feature representation encoder layer, a multi-features fusion layer, and an extraction layer. First, the multi-head self-attention mechanism is utilized to obtain the phonetic alphabet representation $\mathbf{O}^{pf}$ and the sentence representation $\mathbf{O}^{wf}$ separately. Also, a fully-connected layer is used on the meta-information embeddings $\mathbf{E}_i$ to obtain the high-dimensional meta-information representation $\mathbf{O}^e$. Then, the local activation unit is employed to attentively fuse these three feature representations to obtain the fused sentence representation $\mathbf{U}^{wf} = \{I_1, I_2, ..., I_k\}$, the fused phonetic alphabet representation $\mathbf{U}^{pf} = \{I_1^{(p)}, I_2^{(p)}, ..., I_k^{(p)}\}$ and the fused meta-information representation $\mathbf{MR}$. Bi-LSTM is applied to mix I and $I^{(p)}$ with contextual information as hidden states H and $H^{(p)}$, respectively. We concatenate these three representations, generating a final *Danmu* representation $\mathbf{x}_c$. Finally, $\mathbf{x}_c$ is fed into a fully-connected layer with *softmax* function to obtain the sentiment polarity.

3.1 Feature Representation Encoder Layer

In this section, we introduce the meta-information representation encoder and sentence feature representation encoder in CPADFN. We train a wide linear model to memorize correlations between meta-information features, and train two deep neural network models to generalize better contextual text features and Chinese phonetic alphabet features.

Meta-Information Representation Encoder. To memorize feature interactions through a wide set of low-dimensional sparse meta-information embeddings $\mathbf{E}_i$, a fully-connected layer with the *RELU* activation function is applied to generate the high-dimensional interacted meta-information representation $\mathbf{O}^e$.

$$\mathbf{O}^e = F(\mathbf{E}_i) \tag{1}$$

where $F(\cdot)$ is a fully-connected layer, $\mathbf{E}_i$ is the meta-information embeddings.

Sentence Feature Representation Encoder. We apply the multi-head self-attention mechanism in CPADFN. The multi-head self-attention mechanism is the most important part of Google's network structure named 'Transformer'. It is an attention mechanism relating to position information to generate the sequence's representation. Compared with the one-head attention mechanism, multi-head self-attention allows jointly modeling the information in different representation subspaces at different positions. It has been successfully applied in many tasks, like sentiment analysis [8] and machine translation [9].

In CPADFN, multi-head self-attention mechanism are employed to generate sentence representation $\mathbf{O}^{wf}$ and Pinyin-character representation $\mathbf{O}^{pf}$. The input is a matrix of n query vectors $\mathbf{Q} = [Q_1; Q_2; ...; Q_h; ...; Q_H]$ where $\mathbf{Q}_h \epsilon \mathbb{R}^{n \times d_{model}}$ is the h_{th} head of $\mathbf{Q}$. The number of parallel heads is H. The output of $head_h$ is calculated as follows:

$$head_h = Attention(Q_h W^Q, Q_h W^K, Q_h W^V)$$
$$= Softmax(\frac{Q_h W^Q W^{K^T} Q_h^T}{\sqrt{d_{model}}})Q_h W^V \tag{2}$$

where W^Q, W^K, W^V are linear parameter weight matrices to be learned. The vectors of H heads are concatenated together and then fed into a feed-forward network to obtain the sentence feature representation $\mathbf{O}^f$.

$$\mathbf{O}^f = FFN(Concat(head_1, ..., head_H)W^o) \tag{3}$$

where $FFN(\cdot)$ is a feed-forward network layer and W^o is the linear weight matrix.

To make use of position information, multi-head self-attention mechanism applies positional encoding to the input embeddings. In CPADFN, we parameterize position embedding $\mathbf{PE}_i^w \epsilon R^{d_{model}}$, $i = 1, ..., m$. Given sentence embeddings $\mathbf{W} = [w_1, w_2, ..., w_m]$ as input, the position embedding $\mathbf{PE}_i^w$ is simply added to $\mathbf{W}$. The word-position union embedding $\mathbf{W}^{wpos}$ is updated as follows:

$$\mathbf{W}^{wpos} = \mathbf{W} + \mathbf{PE}_i^w \tag{4}$$

Then $\mathbf{W}^{wpos}$ is feed as queries matrix $\mathbf{Q}$ to the multi-head attention component. Finally, a feed-forward layer is applied to generate the word representation $\mathbf{O}^{wf} = \{O_1^{wf}, O_2^{wf}, ..., O_m^{wf}\}$.

In the same light, we parameterize Pinyin's position embedding $\mathbf{PE}_i^p \in R^{d_{model}}$, $i = 1, ..., n$. Given Pinyin-character Representation $\mathbf{P} = [p_1, p_2, ..., p_n]$ as input, the position embedding $\mathbf{PE}_i^p$ is simply added to $\mathbf{P}$. The Pinyin-position union embedding $\mathbf{P}^{ppos}$ is updated as follows:

$$\mathbf{P}^{ppos} = \mathbf{P} + \mathbf{PE}_i^p \tag{5}$$

Also, $\mathbf{P}^{ppos}$ is feed as queries matrix $\mathbf{Q}$ to the multi-head attention component. At last, a feed-forward layer is applied to generate the Pinyin-character representation $\mathbf{O}^{pf} = \{O_1^{pf}, O_2^{pf}, ..., O_n^{pf}\}$.

3.2 Multi-features Fusion Layer

Multiple unique features of the ESC can reveal users' sending behaviors, thus reflect their potential emotional tendency and intensity [13], i.e., meta-information features, contextual text features, and Chinese phonetic alphabet features. The weights of these features need to be reallocated. Attention mechanism has been proved effective as a weight allocation mechanism [14].

In CPADFN, three activation units are applied to dynamically fuse these features. The activated sentence representation $\mathbf{U}^{wf}$ is calculated as follows:

$$head^w = Attention(Q^{wf}W^Q, Q^{wf}W^K, Q^{wf}W^V)$$
$$= Softmax(\frac{Q^{wf}W^Q W^{K^T} Q^{wf^T}}{\sqrt{d_{model}}})Q^{wf}W^V \tag{6}$$

$$\mathbf{U}^{wf} = FFN(head^w W^O) \tag{7}$$

where W^Q, W^K, W^V, W^O are the parameter matrices to be learned. In the same way, the activated Pinyin-character representation $\mathbf{U}^{pf}$ is calculated as follows:

$$head^p = Attention(Q^{wf}W^Q, Q^{pf}W^K, Q^{pf}W^V)$$

$$= Softmax(\frac{Q^{wf}W^Q W^{K^T} Q^{pf^T}}{\sqrt{d_{model}}})Q^{pf}W^V \tag{8}$$

$$\mathbf{U}^{pf} = FFN(head^p W^O) \tag{9}$$

Also, the activated meta-information representation $\mathbf{MR}$ is obtained:

$$head^e = Attention(Q^{wf}W^Q, Q^{ef}W^K, Q^{ef}W^V)$$

$$= Softmax(\frac{Q^{wf}W^Q W^{K^T} Q^{ef^T}}{\sqrt{d_{model}}})Q^{ef}W^V \tag{10}$$

$$\mathbf{MR} = FFN(head^e W^O) \tag{11}$$

Bi-LSTM is excellent at capturing sequential relations and naturally applied to capture contextual semantic information: $H_i = \overleftrightarrow{LSTMs}(H_{i(+,-)1}, I_i)$, for $i = 1, 2, ..., N$, where I_i and H_i are context-independent and sequential context-aware word representations, respectively.

Thus, we feed the activated sentence representation $\mathbf{U}^{wf}$ and the activated Pinyin-character representation $\mathbf{U}^{pf}$ into Bi-LSTM to obtain the context-aware sentence representation $\mathbf{SEN} = \{H_1, H_2, ..., H_k\}$ and the context-aware Pinyin-character representation $\mathbf{PINYIN} = \{H_1^{(p)}, H_2^{(p)}, ..., H_k^{(p)}\}$ respectively.

3.3   Extraction Layer

After feature fusion, we obtain the higher-dimensional meta-information representations $\mathbf{MR}$, the context-aware sentence representations $\mathbf{SEN}$, and the context-aware Pinyin-character representations $\mathbf{PINYIN}$. However, these feature vectors have different sizes. A flexible approach is to flatten and concatenate them:

$$\mathbf{x}_c = \mathbf{MR} \oplus \mathbf{SEN} \oplus \mathbf{PINYIN} \tag{12}$$

where $\mathbf{x}_c$ is the final *Danmu* representation, $\oplus$ denotes for the concatenation operation, c represents the length of the fused feature representation.

Thus, $\mathbf{x}_c$ is classified using a fully-connected network:

$$Y_i^j = Softmax(\mathbf{x}_c)$$

$$= Softmax(W_{smax}\mathbf{x}_c + b_{smax}) \tag{13}$$

where W_{smax} and b_{smax} are trainable parameters.

To reduce the impact of sample imbalance, we adopt the weighted cross-entropy loss function for all training samples:

$$L = -\sum_i \frac{1}{w_i} y_i \log p_i \tag{14}$$

where y_i and p_i are the one-hot true-value and the predicted probability respectively, and w_i is the proportion of i_{th} sample in the dataset.

4 Experiments

Extensive experiments were conducted in two steps. First, we compare the cross-domain validation performance of CPADFN with the baselines. Second, we conduct ablation tests to validate the contribution of Chinese phonetic alphabet features, meta-information features, and the Activation Units.

Datasets. To demonstrate the generalization of CPADFN, we evaluate it on three Chinese short text datasets. The basic statistics are shown in Table 3.

Table 3. Basic statistics of datasets.

DanmuCorpus								
#docs	#pos	#neg					$\#D_{avg}$	#label
347281	244914	102367					8.054	2
MovieReview_2								
#docs	#pos	#neg					$\#D_{avg}$	#label
590359	300000	290359					34.341	2
MovieReview_5								
#docs	#1	#2	#3	#4	#5		$\#D_{avg}$	#label
750000	150000	150000	150000	150000	150000		34.077	5
WeiboCorpus								
#docs	#hp	#sd	#dg	#lk	#fe	#sp	#ag	$\#D_{avg}$	#label
39661	9959	14052	4876	4540	661	1011	4562	46.617	7

DanmuCorpus is a self-crawled *Danmu* dataset collected from the Bilibili website, which contains 347281 *Danmu*s of 83 videos spanning from 2017 to 2020. Each individual *Danmu* consists of four features, including Video-Meta, *Danmu*-Meta, Word Sequence, and Pinyin-character Sequence, as is illustrated in Table 4. Classification involves detecting positive/negative *Danmu*s.

MovieReview[1] is a public movie reviews dataset from the Douban website, which contains 2,120,000 reviews of 28 movies. It is made up of numerical ratings (scores ranging from 1 to 5, all integer) and textual comments. To speed up the training process and tackle the class imbalance problem, we adopt the under-sampling technique. We use the same label processing method as references [5]. The sample data consists of 590359 and 750000 reviews selected randomly. We evaluate the model on both 2-class and 5-class classification tasks.

WeiboCorpus[2] is a public social media posts dataset from Sina Weibo. Weibo posts share many similarities with the ESC in social and textual styles. There are 7 emotion classes, i.e., hp (happy), sd (sad), dg (disgust), lk (like), fe (fear), sp (surprise), and ag (anger).

---

[1] https://www.kaggle.com/utmhikari/doubanmovieshortcomments/.
[2] https://github.com/MingleiLI/emotion_corpus_weibo/.

Table 4. An example of the considered features in *Danmu* '刚把爹，你可以成功的! (Come on, you can make it!)'.

Features Groups	Features	Explanation	Examples
Video-Meta	Video time	T^V, the unit is in seconds	'40.41600'
	Frequency	$d_{fre} = \frac{n}{t_{(T^V-3, T^V+3)}}$, n is the number of *Danmus* in the time interval $t_{(T^V-3, T^V+3)}$	'35'
Danmu-Meta	Font color	*font_color*, decimal representation of the HTML color value	'16777215'
	Font size	*font_size*, $font\_size \in \{12, 16, 18, 25, 36, 45, 64\}$	'25'
	Mode	*display_mode*, $1 \sim 3$: scrolling, 4: bottom, 5: top, 6: reverse, 7: precise positioning, 8: advanced	'1'
	Real time	T^N, publication date (unix time) of the *Danmu*	'1513662857'
Word Sequence.	The sequential words	$S_i^W = [b_1, ..., b_i, ..., b_m]$	{'刚','把','爹','你', '可以','成功','的','! '}
Pinyin-character Sequence.	The sequential corresponding Pinyin characters	$S_i^P = [c_1^{(p)}, ..., c_i^{(p)}, ..., c_n^{(p)}]$	{'ga1ng','ba3','die1', 'ni3','ke3','yi3','che2ng', 'go1ng','de1','!'}

For all datasets, we remove empty documents, duplicates, and meaningless data. Text-based emoticons are a kind of facial expression using punctuation marks, numbers, and letters. Thus, some standard stopwords, such as ' : ', ' (', and ') ', are remained. For these experiments, all datasets are partitioned randomly into two splits, where 75% is the training set and 25% is the test set.

Experimental Setup. In CPADFN, we use the pre-trained ERNIE model[3] for fine-tuning. It's acknowledged that ERNIE has achieved state-of-the-art performance on the Chinese sentiment analysis task via knowledge masking strategies. Pre-trained model's embedding includes general and position information of words, thus prior knowledge is used to fill the gap of contextual information in individual ESC. ERNIE is not for Pinyin. Thus, we first construct a combined Pinyin corpus called PinyinCorpus, including Pinyin-character sequences converted from DanmuCorpus, MovieReview, and WeiboCorpus. Then, we perform *word2vec*[4] on PinyinCorpus to train Pinyin-character embeddings. Existing works [5,23] have proved that performing unsupervised pre-training of word

---

[3] https://ernie-github.cdn.bcebos.com/model-ernie1.0.1.tar.gz.
[4] https://code.google.com/archive/p/word2vec/.

embeddings can improve model performance. *Word2vec* can capture the semantic representation of Pinyin-character in a vector, thus prior knowledge is generated.

For phonetic experiments, we employ *pyPinyin*, an open-source Python module, to convert Chinese characters to Pinyin with tones. Video-Meta/*Danmu-Meta* values are scaled to range [0, 1] to make them comparable. *Danmus* are zero-padded to the length of 50. For WeiboCorpus and MovieReview, the documents are zero-padded to the length of 128. To alleviate overfitting, the dropout is used on the output of the multi-head attention component(d_{att}), the meta-information embedding(d_{meta}), the sentence embeddings(d_{sen}) and the Chinese phonetic alphabet embeddings(d_{pin}). We set $d_{meta} = 0.1$ for DanmuCorpus, and set $d_{att} = 0.1$, $d_{sen} = 0.2$, $d_{pin} = 0.2$ for all three datasets. The maximal epoch is set to 10. All the models are implemented with PaddlePaddle1.8.0[5] with configuration as 16G VRAM, 32G RAM, and NVIDIA Tesla V100 GPUs.

Comparison Methods. We compare CPADFN with the following baselines. All of these models adopt a fully-connected layer (FC) with *softmax* function to perform label prediction.

- ERNIE [18]-FC is the transformer-based model that constructs word representations by summing the corresponding token, segment, and position embeddings. It captures the contextual information through attention mechanism.

- ERNIE-TextCNN [10]-FC uses ERNIE Fine-tuning and the convolutional neural network to end-to-end learn sentence-level features.

- ERNIE-LSTM [7]-FC uses ERNIE Fine-tuning and the long short-term memory network model for the sentiment classification. The LSTM model uses a single-layer LSTM with 512 dimensions.

- ERNIE-StaBiLSTM [24]-FC uses ERNIE Fine-tuning and the stacked bidirectional recurrent network model for the sentiment classification. It uses a gating mechanism that controls the memoizing process with 3 hidden bidirectional LSTM layers.

- ERNIE-AttBiLSTM [25]-FC uses ERNIE Fine-tuning and the bi-directional LSTM with the attention mechanism for the sentiment classification.

Experimental Results. For evaluation, Accuracy (Acc), Macro-F1 (F1), Precision (P), and Recall (R) are used as metrics in our experiments. Every experiment is repeated 3 times. The mean result is shown in Table 5.

-Comparisons with RNN-based Models. As shown in Table 5, CPADFN achieves satisfactory performance compared with above RNN-based models (i.e., ERNIE-LSTM-FC, ERNIE-StaBiLSTM-FC and ERNIE-AttBiLSTM-FC) over all datasets. This well verifies the effectiveness of CPADFN on sentiment analysis of the ESC. Overall, extracting text features using RNNs mostly fail to perform well in this case, since the long-term dependency is not absolutely necessary in the short text sentiment analysis task.

---

[5] https://github.com/PaddlePaddle/Paddle/.

Table 5. Experimental results on DanmuCorpus, WeiboCorpus and MovieReview

Models	DanmuCorpus (2-class)				WeiboCorpus (7-class)			
	Acc(%)	F1(%)	P(%)	R(%)	Acc(%)	F1(%)	P(%)	R(%)
ERNIE-FC(T.*)	92.99	91.68	90.45	93.27	72.47	61.40	70.68	62.81
ERNIE-TextCNN-FC(T)	93.84	92.59	91.73	93.60	69.32	54.65	63.49	54.99
ERNIE-LSTM-FC(T)	93.29	92.02	90.81	93.59	69.46	44.34	61.03	47.11
ERNIE-StaBiLSTM-FC(T)	93.77	92.49	91.65	93.48	69.88	50.96	67.66	52.02
ERNIE-AttBiLSTM-FC(T)	93.48	92.68	91.69	93.87	71.75	58.32	**70.80**	58.52
CPADFN(T)	93.96	92.74	91.82	93.83	72.87	61.46	65.85	64.91
CPADFN(T+P.*)	94.95	93.78	93.79	93.77	**73.90**	**62.11**	65.87	**65.21**
CPADFN(T+P+MR.*)	**95.34**	**94.18**	**94.09**	**94.23**	-	-	-	-
Models	MovieReview_2 (2-class)				MovieReview_5 (5-class)			
	Acc(%)	F1(%)	P(%)	R(%)	Acc(%)	F1(%)	P(%)	R(%)
ERNIE-FC(T)	78.55	78.61	78.53	78.53	40.03	40.27	41.62	40.03
ERNIE-TextCNN-FC(T)	78.79	78.75	78.96	78.76	42.69	43.60	47.81	42.69
ERNIE-LSTM-FC(T)	78.33	78.31	78.37	78.31	42.85	43.66	47.62	42.85
ERNIE-StaBiLSTM-FC(T)	78.99	78.97	79.05	78.97	42.63	43.43	47.16	42.63
ERNIE-AttBiLSTM-FC(T)	79.06	78.99	79.37	79.02	43.01	43.66	**48.52**	43.01
CPADFN(T)	79.34	79.54	79.29	79.31	43.79	44.37	48.22	43.79
CPADFN(T+P)	**79.96**	**80.18**	**79.91**	**79.93**	44.15	**44.76**	46.78	**44.15**
CPADFN(T+P+MR)	-	-	-	-	-	-	-	-

* Best Accuracy, Macro-F1, Precision and Recall is marked with bold font.
* T, P, MR represent textual, Chinese phonetic alphabet and meta-information features respectively. + means the fusion operation. FC means 'fully-connected layer'.

-Comparisons with CNN-Based Model. Over all datasets, CPADFN outperforms ERNIE-TextCNN-FC. Specifically, on WeiboCorpus, CPADFN(T+P) increases Accuracy by 4.58%, Macro-F1 by 7.46%, Precision by 2.38% and Recall by 10.22%.

-Comparisons with Transformer-Based Model. ERNIE-FC also performs inferior to CPADFN over all datasets. Transformer works based on the self-attention mechanism. Thus, Transformer is heavily dependent on contextual information, while word overlap is little or non-existent in this case. This well demonstrates that enriching the knowledge of ESC by incorporating Pinyin-character features and meta-information are helpful in improving sentiment analysis performance.

Ablation Study. We consider the following variant models to conduct ablation experiments:

- CPADFN (without PY.*), which removes the Pinyin-character features.
- CPADFN (without AU.*), which removes the Activation Units.
- CPADFN (without MR.*), which removes the *Danmu*/Video frame meta-information. For public datasets, there is no meta-information features about the documents. Thus, MR is not considered in MovieReview and WeiboCorpus.

The comparison results are shown in Fig. 3. In addition to the above changes, other experimental settings are the same as that of CPADFN. We can find that:

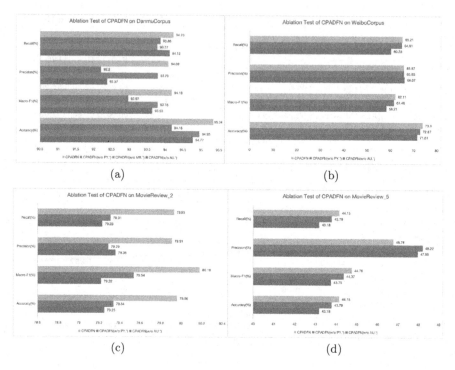

Fig. 3. Ablation Tests of CPADFN on (a) DanmuCorpus (2-class) (b) WeiboCorpus (7-class) (c) MovieReview_2 (2-class) (d) MovieReview_5 (5-class) * **w/o** means without. * **MR** refers to the *Danmu*/Video frame meta-information. * **PY** refers to the Pinyin-character features. * **AU** refers to the Activation Units.

- Pinyin-character features are beneficial to enrich the knowledge of ESC and encode the emotion into CPADFN. Regarding the model without Pinyin-character features, its performance drops significantly over all datasets (For DanmuCorpus, drops Precision by 1.89%, drops Macro-F1 by 1.21%, drops Accuracy by 1.16%, and slightly decreases Recall by 0.37%). The phonetics and intonation features are available to provide complementary semantic cues to Chinese.

- Activation Units play a crucial role in reallocating the weights of the various features. The degradation of performance is substantial over all datasets (For DanmuCorpus, drops Precision by 1.72%, drops Accuracy by 0.57%, drops Macro-F1 by 0.55%, and slightly drops Recall by 0.11%). The result verifies that the activation units can enhance multi-features fusion performances.

- Adding Meta-information can achieve better improvements. CPADFN outperforms the best result on DanmuCorpus, denoting that the extended *Danmu*-Meta/Video-Meta features are helpful for further improvement.

5   Conclusion

In this paper, we studied on sentiment analysis of individual ESC. We believe that Chinese phonetic alphabet feature can enhance the sentiment analysis of the ESC. To enrich the information of the ESC and encode emotion into the sparse word embeddings, we proposed the Chinese Phonetic-Attentive Deep Fusion Network (CPADFN). Ablation experiment shows that Pinyin-character features are beneficial to enrich the knowledge of the ESC and provide complementary semantic cues to Chinese, and the extended *Danmu*-Meta/Video-Meta features are helpful for further improvement. The experiment results on three different datasets show that the CPADFN can explicitly improve the performance of the ESC classification over baseline methods. CPADFN can be applied in the scenarios when content providers are interested in the sentiment on individual ESC for fine-grained content analysis. In future work, we plan to integrate more ESC characteristics into CPADFN, such as the emoji and word splitting phenomenon in hieroglyphs.

Acknowledgment. This work is supported by the National Key Research and Development Program (2019YFB2102600) and the MOE Project of Key Research in Philosophy and Social Science (Grant No. 19JZD023).

References

1. Bilibili homepage. https://www.bilibili.com/. Accessed 4 Jan 2021
2. Douyu homepage. https://www.douyu.com/. Accessed 4 Jan 2021
3. Niconico homepage. https://www.nicovideo.jp/. Accessed 4 Jan 2021
4. Bollegala, D., Matsuo, Y., Ishizuka, M.: Measuring semantic similarity between words using web search engines. In: WWW, pp. 757–766 (2007)
5. Dos Santos, C., Gatti, M.: Deep convolutional neural networks for sentiment analysis of short texts. In: COLING, pp. 69–78 (2014)
6. He, M., Ge, Y., Wu, L., Chen, E., Tan, C.: Predicting the popularity of danmu-enabled videos: a multi-factor view. In: DASFAA, pp. 351–366 (2016)
7. Hochreiter, S., Schmidhuber, J.: Long short-term memory. Neural Computation, pp. 1735–1780 (1997)
8. Huang, Z., Zhao, H., Peng, F., Chen, Q., Zhao, G.: Aspect category sentiment analysis with self-attention fusion networks. In: DASFAA (2020)
9. Iida, S., Kimura, R., Cui, H., Hung, P.H., Utsuro, T., Nagata, M.: Attention over heads: a multi-hop attention for neural machine translation. In: ACL, pp. 217–222. ACL (2019)
10. Kim, Y.: Convolutional neural networks for sentence classification. In: EMNLP, pp. 1746–1751 (2014)
11. Li, C., Wang, J., Wang, H., Zhao, M., Li, W., Deng, X.: Visual-texual emotion analysis with deep coupled video and danmu neural networks. IEEE Transactions on Multimedia, pp. 1634–1646 (2019)
12. Li, X., Yang, B.: A pseudo label based dataless naive Bayes algorithm for text classification with seed words. In: COLING, pp. 1908–1917 (2018)
13. Lwowski, B., Rad, P., Choo, K.R.: Geospatial event detection by grouping emotion contagion in social media. IEEE Trans. Big Data pp. 159–170 (2020)

14. Mikolov, T., Chen, K., Corrado, G., Dean, J.: Efficient estimation of word representations in vector space. In: ICLR (2013)
15. Peng, H., Ma, Y., Poria, S., Li, Y., Cambria, E.: Phonetic-enriched text representation for chinese sentiment analysis with reinforcement learning. ArXiv abs/1901.07880 (2019)
16. Phan, X.H., Nguyen, L.M., Horiguchi, S.: Learning to classify short and sparse text & web with hidden topics from large-scale data collections. In: WWW pp. 91–100 (2008)
17. Shen, D., et al.: Query enrichment for web-query classification. TOIS, pp. 320–352 (2006)
18. Sun, Y., Wang, S., Li, Y., Feng, S., Wu, H.: Ernie: Enhanced representation through knowledge integration. CoRR (2019)
19. Tian, Y., Song, Y., Xia, F., Zhang, T., Wang, Y.: Improving Chinese word segmentation with wordhood memory networks. In: ACL, pp. 8274–8285 (2020)
20. Wu, B., Zhong, E., Tan, B., Horner, A., Yang, Q.: Crowdsourced time-sync video tagging using temporal and personalized topic modeling. In: SIGKDD, pp. 721–730 (2014)
21. Zhang, X., LeCun, Y.: Text understanding from scratch. ArXiv abs/1502.01710 (2015)
22. Zhang, Y., et al.: Learning Chinese word embeddings from stroke, structure and pinyin of characters. CIKM (2019)
23. Zheng, X., Chen, H., Xu, T.: Deep learning for Chinese word segmentation and POS tagging. In: EMNLP, pp. 647–657. ACL (2013)
24. Zhou, J., Xu, W.: End-to-end learning of semantic role labeling using recurrent neural networks. In: ACL, pp. 1127–1137 (2015)
25. Zhou, P., et al.: Attention-based bidirectional long short-term memory networks for relation classification. In: ACL, p. 207 (2016)

A Label Noise Robust Cross-Modal Hashing Approach

Runmin Wang[✉] ⓘ, Yuanlin Yang ⓘ, and Guangyang Han

College of Computer and Information Sciences, Southwest University,
Chongqing, China
{rmwang,ylyang,gyhan}@email.swu.edu.cn

Abstract. Cross-modal hashing has attracted more and more research interest for its high speed and low storage cost in solving cross-modal approximate nearest neighbor search problem. With the rapid growth of social networks, a large amount of information is generated every day, which inevitably contains some noisy information. However, most existing cross-modal hashing methods do not take label noise into consideration and simply assume that all training data are completely reliable. Therefore, these methods will be affected by label noise and reduce the effectiveness on the real-world data. In this paper, we propose a novel end-to-end cross-modal hashing method called label noise robust cross-modal hashing (LNRCMH) to solve the cross-modal hashing problem on data with label noise. LNRCMH first calculates the local outlier factor (LOF) for each instance to evaluate the probability that the instance is corrupted by the label noise. Then LNRCMH assigns lower weights to the instances with high probabilities to be corrupted. Finally, LNRCMH uses different neural networks to learn features for instances from different modalities and transforms them into binary hash codes. Our experimental results on multi-modal benchmark datasets demonstrate that LNRCMH performs significantly better than other related and comparable methods with noisy label annotations. Our approach also achieves competitive results in noise-free situations.

Keywords: Cross-modal hashing · Approximate nearest neighbor search · Deep learning · Label noise

1 Introduction

With the rapid expansion of Internet and an ever-increasing range of social networks available, there are more and more data sources. Tremendous amounts of information is generated every day, making it harder to find the information we care about. Thus, the approximate nearest neighbor (ANN) search becomes more and more important. Hashing is a kind of dimension reduction method that maps arbitrary data into binary codes. To handle the ANN search problem, we can first transfer data into binary hash codes while preserving the semantic similarity. Then we can use hash codes for efficient retrieval. Because of its high

© Springer Nature Switzerland AG 2021
H. Qiu et al. (Eds.): KSEM 2021, LNAI 12816, pp. 577–589, 2021.
https://doi.org/10.1007/978-3-030-82147-0_47

retrieval speed and low extra storage cost, hashing has been proved to be a better method to solve ANN search problem [6,16].

On the other hand, with the development of multimedia technology, the representation of information shows the characteristics of multi-modal, *i.e.*, data can be expressed in different forms/modalities (*e.g.* text, image, video, audio, etc.). We prefer to be able to search information among different modalities, for example, we may want to find an image with similar semantics to our query text, and vice versa. However, the traditional single-modal hashing methods only focus on data from a single modal which can not be applied on multi-modal data. Thus, cross-modal hashing methods have been proposed and become more and more important.

Cross-modal hashing (CMH) methods can be broadly divided into two categories: unsupervised cross-modal hashing methods and supervised cross-modal hashing methods. Generally, supervised cross-modal hashing methods can achieve better performance than unsupervised ones because class labels contain rich semantic information which is relatively easy to use. But most existing supervised cross-modal hash do not take label noise into consideration and simply assume that all the labels of training data are reliable. In fact, in the real-world applications, many labeled data are not very reliable, for example, the labeled date obtained from crowdsourcing. Since the main aim of supervised cross-modal hashing methods is to preserve the similarity information contained in class labels, label noise can greatly affect the effectiveness of supervised cross-modal hashing methods. On the other hand, it will take a lot of manpower and material cost for experts to label or manually identify noise samples. Therefore, we need a label noise robust method.

Thus, in this paper, we take label noise into consideration and propose a novel label noise robust cross-modal hashing method called LNRCMH. The main contribution of this paper are listed as follows:

- We focus on cross-modal hashing data with label noise, which is a practical and important but largely overlooked topic in supervised single/multi-modal hashing.
- We propose a novel weighting method to reduce the affect of label noise on cross-modal hashing. We first calculate the outlier degree of each sample and then measure probability of each instance to be corrupted by the label noise. Finally, in the training procedure, we assign lower weights to the instances more likely to be corrupted by label noise to reduce the effect of label noise.
- Our experiments on benchmark datasets show that LNRCMH outperforms other related and recent competing cross-modal hashing methods in cross-modal data retrieval with noise labels, and performs comparatively well with 'noise-free' data.

The rest of this paper is organized as follows. We briefly introduce the related and representative works in Sect. 2. Section 3 elaborates on the proposed method. Experimental results and analysis are provided in Sect. 4. The conclusions are given in Sect. 5.

2   Related Works

In recent years, cross-modal hashing methods have been widely studied for their fast query speed on multi-modal data. CMH methods can be roughly divided into two categories: unsupervised and supervised.

Unsupervised CMH methods adopt a similar idea to canonical correlation analysis (CCA) [7], which finds a common Hamming space to maximize the correlation among different modalities. Collective matrix factorization hashing (CMFH) [5] aims to find a common latent semantic subspace for different modalities via matrix factorization and then converts features in the latent subspace into hash codes.

In recent years, deep neural networks have emerged as a dominant machine learning tool for a wide variety of domains. Several unsupervised deep CMH methods have been proposed recently. Deep joint-semantic reconstructing hashing (DJSRH) [14] constructs a novel joint-semantic affinity matrix and then reconstructs the affinity matrix to generate the binary hashing code. Generally, unsupervised CMH methods focus only on the correlation among different modalities, but they typically ignore the rich semantic information embedded in class labels.

Supervised CMH methods can leverage semantic information and often achieve a better performance than their unsupervised counterparts. To name a few, cross-modality similarity sensitive hashing (CMSSH) [2] regards every bit of hash code as a classification task and learns the whole hash code bits one by one. Multi-modal latent binary embedding (MLBE) [20] establishes a probabilistic graphical model and treats the binary latent factors as hash codes. Semantic correlation maximization (SCM) [19] optimizes the hashing functions by maximizing the correlation between two modalities with respect to the semantic similarity obtained from the labels. Interestingly, SCM degenerates to CCA if the semantic similarity matrix is equal to an identity matrix I_n, just like CVH under the unsupervised setting. ASCSH [13] decomposes the hash mapping matrices into a consistent and a modality-specific matrix to sufficiently exploit the intrinsic correlation between different modalities, and then uses a novel discrete asymmetric framework to explore the supervised information and solves the binary constraint problem without any relaxation. Deep supervised CMH methods have also spurred much research interest in recent years. Deep cross-modal hashing (DCMH) [10] uses features learned by convolutional neural networks rather than hand-crafted features. DCMH also integrates both a feature learning procedure and hash code learning procedure into the same deep learning framework. Pairwise relationship guided deep hashing (PRDH) [18] uses both a pairwise intra-modal and inter-modal similarity obtained from semantic labels to learn the hash code.

Generally speaking, unsupervised CMH methods neglect class labels that contain much semantic information. In contrast, most supervised CMH methods completely trust the collected class labels. They all ignore the fact that the obtained labels maybe corrupted by noise. To apply CMH in a more practical setting, we take label noise into consideration and propose LNRCMH, which explicitly models the label noises of training data for effective CMH on data with noisy labels.

3   Proposed Method

3.1   Notations and Problem Definition

In this paper, we use boldface uppercase letters (like $\mathbf{F}$) and boldface lowercase letters (like $\mathbf{v}$, $\mathbf{f}$) to represent matrices and vectors respectively. The same letters represent the same matrix and its row (column) vector without special instructions. For example, s_{ij} represents the element in the i-th row and j-th column of matrix $\mathbf{S}$, $\mathbf{F}_{*j}$ represents the j-th column of $\mathbf{F}$, and $\mathbf{F}_{i*}$ represents the i-th row of $\mathbf{F}$. $\mathbf{F}^T$ is the transpose of $\mathbf{F}$. We use $\| \cdot \|_F$ to denote the Frobenius norm of a matrix, and $sgn(\cdot)$ is the signum function.

Although our method can be easily adopted to more than two modalities, for convenience, we will only discuss the case of two modalities (image and text).

Assuming that $\mathcal{O} = \{\mathbf{o}_i\}_{i=1}^n$ is the training set, each instance $\mathbf{o}_i = \{\mathbf{x}_i^{(1)}, \mathbf{x}_i^{(2)}\}$ contains two modalities, we use $\mathbf{X}^{(1)} = \{x_i^{(1)}\}_{i=1}^n$ to denote the image modal and $\mathbf{X}^{(2)} = \{x_i^{(2)}\}_{i=1}^n$ to denote the text modal. $\mathbf{L} \in \{0,1\}^{l \times n}$ is the label matrix, where the i-th column $\mathbf{l}_i$ is the label vector of $\mathbf{o}_i$. $l_{ij} = 1$ means the i-th instance belongs to the j-th category and $l_{ij} = 0$ means the i-th instance does not belong to the j-th category. We can then derive the similarity matrix $\mathbf{S}$ from the label matrix $\mathbf{L}$. Generally, we consider $\mathbf{x}_i^{(1)}$ and $\mathbf{x}_j^{(2)}$ to be similar if $\mathbf{x}_i^{(1)}$ and $\mathbf{x}_j^{(2)}$ share at least one class label and then we let $s_{ij} = 1$. If $\mathbf{x}_i^{(1)}$ and $\mathbf{x}_j^{(2)}$ do not share any class label, we consider them to be dissimilar and let $s_{ij} = 0$.

Then the goal of CMH is to find a hash function for each modal while preserving the similarity in similarity matrix $\mathbf{S}$. We use $H^{(1)}(\mathbf{x}) \in \{+1, -1\}^c$ and $H^{(2)}(\mathbf{x}) \in \{+1, -1\}^c$ to denote these two hash functions. And we use $b_i^{(1)} = H^{(1)}(\mathbf{x}_i^{(1)})$ and $b_j^{(2)} = H^{(2)}(\mathbf{x}_j^{(2)})$ to denote learned hash codes for different modalities. If $s_{ij} = 1$, the Hamming distance between $\mathbf{b}_i^{(1)}$ and $\mathbf{b}_j^{(2)}$ should be small, and vice versa.

The whole architecture of our method is shown in Fig. 1. LNRCMH contains two main modules: the noise detection module and hash code learning module. We first evaluate the probability of each instance being corrupted by the label noise, then we assign different weights for instances in the training procedure. Then we use different neural networks to learn features for different modalities. Finally, we transfer features into binary hash codes and get our hash codes (as well as hash functions).

3.2   Feature Learning

Due to the powerful representation learning ability of neural networks, we introduce two neural networks to learn the features of different modalities. For images, we use a fine-tuned CNN-F [3], which is originally a convolutional neural network

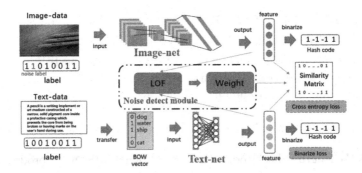

Fig. 1. The whole architecture of LNRCMH. LNRCMH first learns deep feature of different modalities. Then it calculates LOF for each instance and assigns different weights for instances in training procedure to alleviate the affect of noisy labels.

with eight layers for image classification. The first five layers are convolutional layers and the last three layers are fully-connected layers. We take the output of the last layer before softmax as the deep features. For text modality, we first represent the texts into bag-of-words (BOW) vectors. Then we use a neural network to learn text feature. The learned features are denoted by $\mathbf{F}^{(1)} \in \mathbb{R}^{d \times n}$ and $\mathbf{F}^{(2)} \in \mathbb{R}^{d \times n}$ for image and text, respectively. The parameters of image-net and text-net are denoted as θ_1 and θ_2.

Here we must emphasize that, in this paper, we focus on the whole architecture of label noise robust hashing and the noise detection mechanism rather than the design of neural networks, we just use a convolutional neural network for its good performance in feature learning. Therefore, other feature learning models can also be used here as an alternative. For example, we may use ResNet [8] for image modal or transformer [15] for text modal.

3.3 Hash Code Learning

The principle of cross-modal hashing is to preserve the proximity of data. In other words, if image $\mathbf{x}_i^{(1)}$ and text $\mathbf{x}_j^{(2)}$ are semantically similar ($s_{ij} = 1$), the hash codes we learned $\mathbf{b}_i^{(1)}$ and $\mathbf{b}_j^{(2)}$ should be similar. Thus, given the similarity matrix $\mathbf{S}$, we want to learn the hash codes $\mathbf{B}^{(1)}$ and $\mathbf{B}^{(2)}$ with the highest probability. Then we use logarithm maximum a posteriori estimation and Bayes formula as follows:

$$
\begin{aligned}
\log p(\mathbf{B}^{(1)}, \mathbf{B}^{(2)} | \mathbf{S}) &\propto \log p(\mathbf{S} | \mathbf{B}^{(1)}, \mathbf{B}^{(2)}) p(\mathbf{B}^{(1)}) p(\mathbf{B}^{(2)}) \\
&= \sum_{i,j} \log p(s_{ij} | \mathbf{b}_i^{(1)}, \mathbf{b}_j^{(2)}) p(\mathbf{b}_i^{(1)}) p(\mathbf{b}_j^{(2)})
\end{aligned}
\tag{1}
$$

where $p(s_{ij} | \mathbf{b}_i^{(1)}, \mathbf{b}_j^{(2)})$ is the likelihood function we should define, $p(\mathbf{b}_i^{(1)})$ and $p(\mathbf{b}_j^{(2)})$ are prior probabilities that we do not care about.

Because $\mathbf{b}_i^{(1)} \in \{-1, +1\}^c$ and $\mathbf{b}_j^{(2)} \in \{-1, +1\}^c$ are binary codes, we can use Hamming distance to evaluate the similarity between $\mathbf{b}_i^{(1)}$ and $b_j^{(2)}$. The smaller the Hamming distance between $\mathbf{b}_i^{(1)}$ and $\mathbf{b}_j^{(2)}$, the more similar $\mathbf{b}_i^{(1)}$ and $\mathbf{b}_j^{(2)}$ are. But the Hamming distance is not differentiable. Therefore we use a property of binary codes and transfer Hamming distance into inner product:

$$dist_H(\mathbf{b}_i^{(1)}, \mathbf{b}_j^{(2)}) = \frac{1}{2}(c - \langle \mathbf{b}_i^{(1)}, \mathbf{b}_j^{(2)} \rangle) \qquad (2)$$

where c is the length of hash codes, $\langle \mathbf{b}_i^{(1)}, \mathbf{b}_j^{(2)} \rangle$ denotes the inner product of $\mathbf{b}_i^{(1)}$ and $\mathbf{b}_j^{(2)}$. From Eq. (2), we know that $dist_H(\mathbf{b}_i^{(1)}, \mathbf{b}_j^{(2)})$ is negatively correlated with there inner product. Here we use ϕ_{ij} to denote the inner product of $\mathbf{b}_i^{(1)}$ and $\mathbf{b}_j^{(2)}$. Thus, we can define our likelihood function as follows:

$$p(s_{ij}|\mathbf{b}_i^{(1)}, \mathbf{b}_j^{(2)}) = \begin{cases} \sigma(\phi_{ij}) & s_{ij} = 1 \\ 1 - \sigma(\phi_{ij}) & s_{ij} = 0 \end{cases} \qquad (3)$$
$$= \sigma(\phi_{ij})^{s_{ij}}(1 - \sigma(\phi_{ij}))^{1-s_{ij}}$$

Then let $\mathbf{F}^{(1)} = H^{(1)}(\mathbf{x}^{(1)}; \theta_1) \in \mathbb{R}^c$ and $\mathbf{F}^{(2)} = H^{(2)}(\mathbf{x}^{(2)}; \theta_2) \in \mathbb{R}^c$ denote the learned features of image and text modality, while θ_1 and θ_2 are the parameters of image-net and text-net, respectively. We can define our loss function as follows:

$$\min_{\mathbf{B}, \theta_1, \theta_2} \mathcal{J} = -\sum_{i,j=1}^{n} (s_{ij}\Phi_{ij} - log(1 + e^{\Phi_{ij}})) + \alpha(||\mathbf{B} - \mathbf{F}^{(1)}||_F^2 + ||\mathbf{B} - \mathbf{F}^{(2)}||_F^2)$$
$$+ \beta(||\mathbf{F}^{(1)}\mathbf{1}||_F^2 + ||\mathbf{F}^{(2)}\mathbf{1}||_F^2)$$
$$s.t. \quad \mathbf{B} \in \{+1, -1\}^{c \times n}$$

$$(4)$$

where $\mathbf{F}^{(1)} \in \mathbb{R}^{c \times n}$ with $\mathbf{F}_{*i}^{(1)} = H^{(1)}(\mathbf{x}_i^{(1)}; \theta_1)$, $\mathbf{F}^{(2)} \in \mathbb{R}^{c \times n}$ with $\mathbf{F}_{*j}^{(2)} = H^{(2)}(\mathbf{x}_j^{(2)}; \theta_2)$ are outputs (features) of image-net and text-net, respectively. $\Phi_{ij} = \frac{1}{2} \langle \mathbf{F}_{*i}^{(1)}, \mathbf{F}_{*j}^{(2)} \rangle$ denotes the inner product. $\mathbf{B}_{*i}$ is the unified binary hash code for sample $\mathbf{o}_i$. $\mathbf{1}$ is a vector with all elements being 1. α, β are hyper-parameters. The first term of the loss function $-\sum_{i,j=1}^{n}(s_{ij}\Phi_{ij} - log(1 + e^{\Phi_{ij}}))$ is the negative log-likelihood of the cross-modal similarities, as defined in Eq. (3). Here we relax the binary constraints and regard the features as hash codes. We will binarize these features later. Minimizing this term can make the features we learn preserve the similarity in $\mathbf{S}$. More intuitively, by minimizing $-\sum_{i,j=1}^{n}(s_{ij}\Phi_{ij} - log(1 + e^{\Phi_{ij}}))$, we make two instances with shared label ($s_{ij} = 1$) having a large inner product, which implies a small Hamming distance in the hash code. The second term $\alpha(||\mathbf{B} - \mathbf{F}^{(1)}||_F^2 + ||\mathbf{B} - \mathbf{F}^{(2)}||_F^2)$ is the binariza-tion loss. By minimizing this term, we can force $\mathbf{B}$ as close as possible to both $\mathbf{F}^{(1)}$ and $\mathbf{F}^{(2)}$ and get the unified hash code. The third term $\beta(||\mathbf{F}^{(1)}\mathbf{1}||_F^2 + ||\mathbf{F}^{(2)}\mathbf{1}||_F^2)$ is to balance the hash code on all training instances. More intuitively, by min-imizing this term, we can make the number of -1 and $+1$ in hash codes as balanced as possible, which helps to generate a lager coding space.

From the loss function we can see that, the effectiveness of LNRCMH depends heavily on the similarity matrix derived by class label. Therefore, label noise significantly compromises the performance of cross-modal hashing. Other supervised single/cross-modal hashing methods also suffer from this issue [2,10,12,17,20]. In the following section we will propose a noise detection module and alleviate the effects of label noise.

3.4 Noise Detection Module

In general, we use re-weighting to alleviate the effects of label noise. In training procedure, we assign small weights to instances with high probabilities to be corrupted and large weights to credible ones. In supervised machine learning, well-learned features can make samples belong to same category show certain aggregation. As we can see in Fig. 2(a), instances with label noise tend to be outliers. Therefore, inspired by [1], we propose a noise detection module based on Local Outlier Factor (LOF).

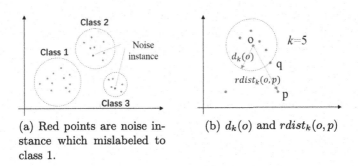

(a) Red points are noise instance which mislabeled to class 1.

(b) $d_k(o)$ and $rdist_k(o, p)$

Fig. 2. Noise detection module.

Then we will briefly introduce LOF. For data point p, LOF is defined as follow:

$$LOF_{Pts}(p) = \frac{\sum_{o \in N_{Pts}(p)} \frac{Ird_{Pts}(o)}{Ird_{Pts}(p)}}{|N_{Pts}(p)|} \quad (5)$$

where Pts is a parameter specifying a minimum number of objects. $N_{Pts}(p)$ is the set of Pts nearest neighbors of p. More precisely, data point q belongs to $N_{Pts}(p)$ if $d(q,p) < d_{Pts}(p)$. Where $d(q,p)$ is the distance between p and q. $d_k(p)$ denotes the distance between p and its k-th nearest neighbor. $Ird_{Pts}(p)$ is the local reachability density of p. It is used to describe the density of neighboring points near p and it is defined as follows:

$$Ird_{Pts}(p) = 1 / \frac{\sum_{o \in N_{Pts}(p)} rdist_{Pts}(p, o)}{|N_{Pts}(p)|} \quad (6)$$

where $rdist_{Pts}(p,o)$ is the reach distance from p to o and $rdist_{Pts}(p,o) = max\{d_{Pts}(p), d(p,o)\}$. In general, LOF measures the ratio of the data points density around a target point to the density around its neighbors. If a point p has a very low density around it while its neighbors have a very high density around them, then p is a outlier and $LOF(p)$ will be relatively large.

Given the definition of LOF, we then calculate the weight of each training instance. In cross-modal retrieval problems, there are many instances with more than one label. Therefore, for each instance p, we should calculate a LOF value in every category that instance p belongs to and get a mean LOF value to measure outlier degree. Thus, we have:

$$meanLOF(p) = \frac{\sum_{1_i=1} LOF^i(p)}{|1|} \tag{7}$$

where $LOF^i(p)$ only consider samples in the i-th category.

Then we use ω_p to denote the normalized reciprocal of LOF values

$$\omega_p = \frac{max_i(meanLOF(i)) - min_j(meanLOF(j))}{meanLOF(p)} \tag{8}$$

For loss function 4 we can see, in the training procedure, training samples are trained in pairs, thus we should assign a weight for each training pair. Here we use geometrical mean to calculate the weight ω_{ij} of each pair:

$$\omega_{ij} = \sqrt{\omega_i \omega_j} \tag{9}$$

Finally, the weighted loss function becomes as follows:

$$\min_{\mathbf{B}, \theta_1, \theta_2} \mathcal{J} = - \sum_{i,j=1}^{n} \omega_{ij}(s_{ij}\Phi_{ij} - log(1 + e^{\Phi_{ij}})) + \alpha(||\mathbf{B} - \mathbf{F}^{(1)}||_F^2 + ||\mathbf{B} - \mathbf{F}^{(2)}||_F^2)$$

$$+ \beta(||\mathbf{F}^{(1)}\mathbf{1}||_F^2 + ||\mathbf{F}^{(2)}\mathbf{1}||_F^2)$$

$$s.t. \quad \mathbf{B} \in \{+1, -1\}^{c \times n} \tag{10}$$

Note that, we use the learned feature to calculate the weight ω_{ij} and update it every 10 epoch. This is a tradeoff between efficiency and effectiveness that we make, as we'll see in the ablation study.

3.5   Optimization

There are three parameters (θ_1, θ_2 and $\mathbf{B}$) in Eq. (10), therefore we use an alternating strategy to learn these parameters. In other words, we update one while fixing the others. For θ_1 and θ_2, we first calculate the derivative of the corresponding network output and then update θ_1 and θ_2 using chain rule and back propagation. Since space is limited, we give all the updating formulas (or derivatives for back propagation) without derivation:

$$\frac{\partial \mathcal{J}}{\partial \mathbf{F}_{*i}^{(1)}} = \frac{1}{2} \sum_{j=1}^{n} \omega_{ij}(\sigma(\Phi_{ij})\mathbf{F}_{*j}^{(2)} - a_{ij}\mathbf{F}_{*j}^{(2)}) + 2\alpha(\mathbf{F}_{*i}^{(1)} - \mathbf{B}_{*i}) + 2\beta \mathbf{F}^{(1)}\mathbf{1} \tag{11}$$

$$\frac{\partial \mathcal{J}}{\partial \mathbf{F}_{*i}^{(2)}} = \frac{1}{2} \sum_{j=1}^{n} \omega_{ij}(\sigma(\varPhi_{ij})\mathbf{F}_{*j}^{(1)} - a_{ij}\mathbf{F}_{*j}^{(1)}) + 2\alpha(\mathbf{F}_{*i}^{(2)} - \mathbf{B}_{*i}) + 2\beta\mathbf{F}^{(2)}\mathbf{1} \quad (12)$$

$$\mathbf{B} = sign(\mathbf{F}^{(1)} + \mathbf{F}^{(2)}) \quad (13)$$

4 Experiments

4.1 Experimental Setup

We conduct experiments on two benchmark datasets: *Flickr-25K* [9] and *NUS-WIDE* [4].

The *MirFlickr-25K* dataset contains 25,000 images collected from the Flickr website. Each instance contains an image from Flickr and its corresponding textual tags and is annotated with at least one label from a total of 24 different semantic labels. Textual tags of each instance are converted into a 1386-dimensional BOW vector and regarded as text modal. For methods based on hand-crafted features, each image is converted to a 512-dimensional GIST vector.

The *NUS-WIDE* dataset contains 269,648 images and the associated textual tags are collected from the Flickr website. Each instance is annotated with one or more labels from 81 concept labels. Just like instances in *MirFlickr-25K*, we take textual tags as the text modality and convert them into a series of 1000-dimensional BOW vectors. We use 186,577 instances that belong to the most frequent ten concepts. For hand-crafted features based methods, each image is converted into a 500-dimensional bag-of-visual-words (BOVW) vector.

These datasets are manually labeled; thus, the original labels are 'noise-free'. We manually inject random noise into these datasets for our noise-robust experiments. We set different noise level and use noise rate r to indicate noise level. In this paper, noise rate r means $r \times 100\%$ labels in the one-hot coding label vector are randomly shifted from 0 to 1. In our experiments, we use two settings with $r = 0.2$ (low noise level) and $r = 0.4$ (high noise level).

For comparison methods, we choose several relevant and representative CMH methods, including: DCMH [10], SCM [19], SePH [11], CMFH [5] and SDCH [17]. SCM and SePH are traditional supervised CMH methods, DCMH and SDCH are deep CMH methods. CMFH is an unsupervised CMH method which will not be affected by label noise. For all these comparison methods, we use the parameters recommended in the corresponding paper. For LNRCMH, we set $\alpha = \beta = 1$ and $Pts = 30$.

To quantitatively study the performance, we choose the widely used evaluation metric, mean average precision (mAP), to quantify the performance of hashing retrieval methods [2,19].

4.2 Experimental Results

The detailed experimental results are listed in Table 1 and 2. In these tables, "I to T" means the query instance is an image and we search for relevant text instances and "T to I" means the query instance is a text. r means the noise level and $r = 0$ means the "noise-free" scenario. From Table 1 and 2 we have following observations:

(i) Under "noise-free" settings, LNRCMH is slightly weaker than SDCH, but can basically achieve state-of-the-art performance. This is because under "noise-free" settings LNRCMH reduces the weight of the correct sample to some extent. But this is innocuous because we almost never use a noise-robust method on noise-free data. (ii) Under "noise-free" settings, the advantages of LNRCMH begin to emerge, and as the noise level increases, the advantages of our method become more obvious. This is because our noise detection module can mitigate the impact of noise on the whole model. (iii) The performance of CMFH does not vary with the noise level, because CMFH is an unsupervised method and do not take

Table 1. Results(mAP) on MirFlickr-25K under different noise rates r.

	Noise rate r	0				0.2				0.4			
	Hash bits c	16bit	32bit	64bit	128bit	16bit	32bit	64bit	128bit	16bit	32bit	64bit	128bit
I to T	SCM-seq	0.628	0.635	0.632	0.621	0.607	0.609	0.612	0.620	0.577	0.578	0.581	0.588
	SCM-orth	0.580	0.581	0.590	0.587	0.561	0.565	0.568	0.572	0.545	0.546	0.554	0.557
	SePH	0.657	0.660	0.667	0.662	0.596	0.602	0.608	0.607	0.510	0.514	0.522	0.527
	CMFH	0.610	0.612	0.624	0.625	0.608	0.617	0.627	0.626	0.607	0.615	0.620	0.623
	DCMH	0.741	0.746	0.754	0.749	0.711	0.715	0.719	0.714	0.660	0.679	0.682	0.685
	SDCH	**0.771**	**0.780**	**0.781**	**0.779**	0.725	0.730	0.733	0.731	0.665	0.670	0.672	0.671
	LNRCMH	0.752	0.745	0.745	0.753	**0.729**	**0.732**	**0.737**	**0.734**	**0.687**	**0.690**	**0.697**	**0.698**
T to I	SCM-seq	0.619	0.630	0.635	0.640	0.608	0.610	0.621	0.617	0.570	0.574	0.577	0.564
	SCM-orth	0.590	0.598	0.610	0.602	0.588	0.580	0.598	0.597	0.565	0.554	0.567	0.569
	SePH	0.648	0.652	0.655	0.658	0.627	0.633	0.638	0.635	0.533	0.534	0.541	0.539
	CMFH	0.625	0.629	0.637	0.640	0.621	0.629	0.636	0.644	0.628	0.632	0.635	0.640
	DCMH	0.782	0.790	0.794	0.779	0.758	0.767	0.762	0.768	0.721	0.732	0.735	0.737
	SDCH	**0.806**	**0.812**	**0.817**	**0.810**	0.765	0.772	0.774	0.778	0.730	0.736	0.741	0.739
	LNRCMH	0.782	0.785	0.787	0.793	**0.771**	**0.775**	**0.779**	**0.783**	**0.742**	**0.745**	**0.752**	**0.750**

Table 2. Results(mAP) on NUS-WIDE under different noise rates r.

	Noise rate r	0				0.2				0.4			
	Hash bits c	16bit	32bit	64bit	128bit	16bit	32bit	64bit	128bit	16bit	32bit	64bit	128bit
I to T	SCM-seq	0.452	0.463	0.467	0.462	0.412	0.426	0.428	0.431	0.392	0.404	0.407	0.409
	SCM-orth	0.431	0.440	0.447	0.451	0.403	0.407	0.415	0.412	0.382	0.384	0.391	0.390
	SePH	0.487	0.492	0.497	0.503	0.435	0.447	0.448	0.452	0.419	0.426	0.428	0.430
	CMFH	0.449	0.457	0.468	0.467	0.452	0.455	0.460	0.468	0.447	0.460	0.466	0.465
	DCMH	0.624	0.630	0.641	0.645	0.589	0.592	0.598	0.594	0.554	0.559	0.561	0.564
	SDCH	**0.645**	**0.658**	**0.662**	**0.664**	0.606	0.608	0.611	0.620	0.545	0.550	0.558	0.563
	LNRCMH	0.623	0.631	0.638	0.637	**0.611**	**0.617**	**0.627**	**0.632**	**0.567**	**0.578**	**0.579**	**0.585**
T to I	SCM-seq	0.495	0.502	0.498	0.497	0.467	0.471	0.475	0.478	0.426	0.428	0.431	0.435
	SCM-orth	0.481	0.492	0.495	0.489	0.452	0.458	0.461	0.462	0.413	0.415	0.421	0.428
	SePH	0.514	0.526	0.529	0.532	0.476	0.487	0.489	0.488	0.447	0.451	0.463	0.465
	CMFH	0.477	0.479	0.484	0.481	0.469	0.480	0.485	0.487	0.472	0.479	0.483	0.485
	DCMH	0.653	0.664	0.665	0.668	0.621	0.638	0.642	0.643	0.601	0.612	0.619	0.617
	SDCH	**0.672**	**0.684**	**0.687**	**0.689**	0.632	0.635	0.647	0.646	0.612	0.619	0.626	0.629
	LNRCMH	0.654	0.663	0.669	0.671	**0.643**	**0.647**	**0.651**	**0.650**	**0.631**	**0.633**	**0.631**	**0.642**

advantage of class label. But LNRCMH can always achieve better performance than CMFH so as most supervised methods. This is because supervised methods can take advantage of class labels, which contains rich semantic information.

4.3 Parameter Analysis

There are three different hyper-parameters in our method: α and β are trade-off parameters, and Pts is the parameter in calculating LOF. We conduct a series of experiments on *Flickr* dataset to test parameter sensitivity and the results are shown in Fig. 3. We can observe that, when $0.01 < \alpha < 10$, our method is not very sensitive to parameter α, but when $\alpha > 10$, mAP drops sharply. Similar results were found for parameter β. Thus, we choose $\alpha = \beta = 1$ in our experiments. As for Pts, we can find when $Pts = 30$, mAP gets the maximum. Pts is too large or too small will affect the effectiveness of the method.

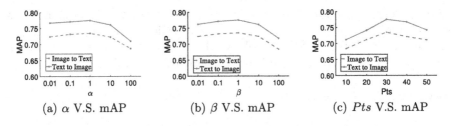

(a) α V.S. mAP   (b) β V.S. mAP   (c) *Pts* V.S. mAP

Fig. 3. Parameter analysis on *Flickr* with $r = 0.2$.

4.4 Ablation Study

In this section, we conduct a series of experiments on *Flickr* dataset to evaluation the effectiveness of different module of LNRCMH. We use three variations of LNRCMH: (i) "LNRCMH-n": remove the noise detection module. (ii) "LNRCMH-e": update weight ω_{ij} every epoch. (iii) "LNRCMH-f": fix weight ω_{ij} and never update it.

The detailed results are listed in Table 3. We can observe that while the noise detection module slightly reduces the effect in the case of noise-free, it greatly improves the effect in the case of noise. This shows the effectiveness of our noise detection module. We can also observe that updating weights more frequently don't improve the results much. So we make a tradeoff and choose to update the weights every 10 epoch.

Table 3. Results(mAP) on MirFlickr-25K under different noise rates r.

	Noise rate r	0			0.2			0.4		
	Hash bits c	16bit	32bit	64bit	16bit	32bit	64bit	16bit	32bit	64bit
I to T	LNRCMH	0.752	0.745	0.745	0.729	0.732	**0.737**	0.687	0.690	**0.697**
	LNRCMH-n	**0.754**	**0.751**	**0.749**	0.710	0.712	0.723	0.667	0.664	0.670
	LNRCMH-e	0.741	0.740	0.743	**0.731**	**0.733**	0.734	**0.688**	**0.691**	0.695
	LNRCMH-f	0.745	**0.751**	0.744	0.715	0.720	0.725	0.671	0.673	0.679
T to I	LNRCMH	0.780	0.778	0.781	0.771	**0.775**	**0.779**	0.742	0.745	0.752
	LNRCMH-n	**0.783**	**0.779**	**0.785**	0.752	0.761	0.762	0.721	0.723	0.730
	LNRCMH-e	0.772	0.778	0.784	**0.775**	0.773	0.778	**0.747**	**0.751**	**0.753**
	LNRCMH-f	0.782	0.785	0.787	0.755	0.763	0.770	0.725	0.730	0.735

5   Conclusion

Real-world data often contains label noise while label noise significantly compromises the effectiveness of supervised machine learning methods. Thus, in this paper, we proposed a novel end-to-end label noise robust CMH method. It can alleviate the effect of label noise in cross-modal retrieval problem. Experiments on different datasets showed that LNRCMH achieves a better performance in noise scenarios than other state-of-the-art methods.

References

1. Breunig, M.M., Kriegel, H.P., Ng, R.T., Sander, J.: Lof: identifying density-based local outliers. In: ACM SIGMOD International Conference on Management of Data, pp. 93–104 (2000)
2. Bronstein, M.M., Bronstein, A.M., Michel, F., Paragios, N.: Data fusion through cross-modality metric learning using similarity-sensitive hashing. In: IEEE Conference on Computer Vision and Pattern Recognition, pp. 3594–3601 (2010)
3. Chatfield, K., Simonyan, K., Vedaldi, A., Zisserman, A.: Return of the devil in the details: delving deep into convolutional nets. In: British Machine Vision Conference, pp. 1–12 (2014)
4. Chua, T., Tang, J., Hong, R., Li, H., Luo, Z., Zheng, Y.: Nus-wide: a real-world web image database from national university of Singapore. In: International Conference on Image and Video Retrieval, p. 48 (2009)
5. Ding, G., Guo, Y., Zhou, J.: Collective matrix factorization hashing for multimodal data. In: CVPR, pp. 2075–2082 (2014)
6. Gai, K., Qiu, M.: Reinforcement learning-based content-centric services in mobile sensing. IEEE Network, pp. 34–39 (2018)
7. Hardoon, D.R., Szedmak, S., Shawe-Taylor, J.: Canonical correlation analysis: an overview with application to learning methods. Neural Comput. **16**(12), 2639–2664 (2004)
8. He, K., Zhang, X., Ren, S., Sun, J.: Deep residual learning for image recognition. In: CVPR, pp. 770–778 (2016)
9. Huiskes, M.J., Lew, M.S.: The mir flickr retrieval evaluation. In: ACM International Conference on Multimedia Information Retrieval, pp. 39–43 (2008)
10. Jiang, Q., Li, W.: Deep cross-modal hashing. In: IEEE Conference on Computer Vision and Pattern Recognition, pp. 3232–3240 (2017)

11. Lin, Z., Ding, G., Hu, M., Wang, J.: Semantics-preserving hashing for cross-view retrieval. In: IEEE Conference on Computer Vision and Pattern Recognition, pp. 3864–3872 (2015)
12. Liu, X., Yu, G., Domeniconi, C., Wang, J., Ren, Y., Guo, M.: Ranking-based deep cross-modal hashing. AAAI, pp. 4400–4407 (2019)
13. Meng, M., Wang, H., Yu, J., Chen, H., Wu, J.: Asymmetric supervised consistent and specific hashing for cross-modal retrieval. TIP **30**, 986–1000 (2020)
14. Su, S., Zhong, Z., Zhang, C.: Deep joint-semantics reconstructing hashing for large-scale unsupervised cross-modal retrieval, pp. 3027–3035 (2019)
15. Vaswani, A., et al.: Attention is all you need. arXiv preprint arXiv:1706.03762 (2017)
16. Wang, J., Zhang, T., Sebe, N., Shen, H.T., et al.: A survey on learning to hash. IEEE TPAMI **40**(4), 769–790 (2017)
17. Yan, C., Bai, X., Wang, S., Zhou, J., Hancock, E.R.: Cross-modal hashing with semantic deep embedding. Neurocomputing **337**, 58–66 (2019)
18. Yang, E., Deng, C., Liu, W., Liu, X., Tao, D., Gao, X.: Pairwise relationship guided deep hashing for cross-modal retrieval. In: AAAI Conference on Artificial Intelligence, pp. 1618–1625 (2017)
19. Zhang, D., Li, W.: Large-scale supervised multimodal hashing with semantic correlation maximization. In: AAAI Conference on Artificial Intelligence, pp. 2177–2183 (2014)
20. Zhen, Y., Yeung, D.Y.: A probabilistic model for multimodal hash function learning. In: ACM SIGKDD International Conference on Knowledge Discovery and Data Mining, pp. 940–948 (2012)

Acoustic Modeling for Indoor Spaces Using Ray-Tracing Method

Andreea Bianca Lixandru[1], Sebastian Gorobievschi[2],
and Alexandra Baicoianu[1(✉)]

[1] Faculty of Mathematics and Informatics, Transilvania University of Brasov,
Brasov, Romania
andreea.lixandru@student.unitbv.ro, a.baicoianu@unitbv.ro
[2] Siemens Industry Software, Brasov, Romania
sebastian.gorobievschi@siemens.com

Abstract. This paper focuses on the matter of sound propagation in various indoor spaces by means of the Ray-Tracing method. Nowadays, this is an issue that is often encountered both in the academic environment and in real-life situations, being present in fields such as acoustic engineering. This research study provides an acoustic model meant to support engineers in the proper construction, by careful consideration of the acoustics in various indoor spaces such as amphitheaters, concert halls, churches, mosques, factories and many more. Moreover, this recommended model for efficiency comes as a long awaited development for people to be able to listen to sounds produced at a higher quality level. A number of different experiments have been carried out to determine suitable parameters such as the most suitable construction material for the walls of the room, the maximum sound frequency, the dimensions of the room and other factors equally important.

Keywords: Acoustic model · Sound indoor spaces · Ray-Tracing · Sound convolution · Microphone · Fast Fourier Transform · Inverse Fast Fourier Transform

1 Introduction and Background of the Study

This article is the result of our common wish to assist people who have mild hearing problems or those who work in factories and other similar spaces, characterized by a high level of industrial noise that can harm ear health over time, but also for engineers who want to create and build rooms by means of this acoustic model. The human ear is sensitive to air vibrations with frequencies 20 Hz and 20 kHz, and with age this range narrows. The way we perceive sound differs from one space to another, and this happens due to the different size and shape of the rooms, as well as to the various materials used for different surfaces within the room.

When discussing about acoustics in various spaces, a very important aspect to keep in mind is that we should position the audio sources and microphones

© Springer Nature Switzerland AG 2021
H. Qiu et al. (Eds.): KSEM 2021, LNAI 12816, pp. 590–599, 2021.
https://doi.org/10.1007/978-3-030-82147-0_48

should be positioned in such manner as to obtain the best possible sound quality and to reduce as much as possible the echo and reverberation effect.

Inside a room, sound waves hit different surfaces that can absorb or reflect sound. It is very important for engineers who design acoustic models to choose the right materials so as to ensure optimal results. For example, factories and halls have many metal surfaces that favor the echo effect, this phenomenon can be verified by engineers who design the models to ensure that the room meets all standards, and the health of the people working in those spaces is not compromised.

In his study [3], David Oliva Elorza provides an acoustic model using Ray-Tracing method and proves his findings by demonstrating how the acoustics of amphitheatres works. The differences between his model and our model is that we will use a different technique to distribute rays evenly in the room, with different selection criteria, with the benefit that our design is an almost real-time model.

Aside from what Christoffer A. Weitze proposes in his article, we have created an acoustic model that can be used in a much more generic way [8]. If the start point was an acoustic model intended only for Mosques and Byzantine Churches distinguished by their spherical and cylindrical shapes, our model is broader and more non-specific.

In the next section the three main stages necessary in the realization of the acoustic model will be exposed: geometrical calculation, physical calculation and post-processing data. Bear in mind that these steps are sequential, so the output of a step is the input for the next step. This study will present the acoustic model we designed using the Ray-tracing method [3], three of the spaces for which we tested this algorithm and the results obtained in the comparison section. The last part contains a section which discusses the open problems, while also concludes the paper.

2   Acoustic Model

Acoustics is part of the field of physics and deals with the study of mechanical waves in gases, liquids, solids, being present in all aspects of today's society, the most obvious field being that of industry for noise control. This branch also includes the study of sounds, vibrations, ultrasound and infrasound.

An acoustic model will involve, in the most generic way, the simulation of the paths that the sound travels from source to destination. Most often, these models propose to solve Helmoltz-Kirchoff integral [4] using various approaches of calculation, such as: numerical solutions to the wave equations, high frequency approximations to the wave equation and perceptually base statistical models. The model we created is part of the second category.

The acoustic model will consist of three stages. The first stage includes the geometric calculations, the second stage focuses on physical calculations based on the results obtained in the previous step, while the third stage deals with the post-processing of data obtained from the physical model.

Throughout this process it is very important to note that the stages are closely related and interdependent. So, the geometric calculation stage is particularly important because the way the rays are distributed in the room and the way the rays are selected dictates the model's performance and its optimality.

Post-processing algorithms are used to suppress noise or any artefact created in the first two phases (geometric and physical), and focuses on eliminating distortion and echo. Equalization and filtering are popular post-processing techniques to ensure reverberation and noise control. For the proposed acoustic model, the convolution of sound was used, with all these key aspects being further presented in detail in the next pages.

2.1 Geometrical Approach

For geometric calculation we will consider as input data the room surfaces, the audio source and the microphones placed in the room. With their help we will be able to evenly distribute rays in the room using the Fibonacci sphere algorithm and we will keep only those rays we need with using a duplicate rays reduction algorithm.

This algorithm is based on a spiral movement on the surface of the sphere incrementally with the golden angle, which is related to the golden ratio. Two quantities, a and b, are in the golden ratio if: $\dfrac{a}{b} = \dfrac{a+b}{a} = \varphi$, where $a > b$, and this ratio is approximately equal to $\varphi = \dfrac{1+\sqrt{5}}{2}$. The golden angle, ϑ, is defined according to the golden ratio as follows: $\vartheta = 2\pi(2 - \varphi)$.

Now that we have established the starting points for each ray we can create the rays taking into account several parameters such as the maximum possible length of a ray or the maximum number of reflections. To generate the rays it is possible to use Physics class from Unity [1] or other similar tools.

After determining which are the rays that reach the microphone we can reduce the similar ones. Two rays are duplicated if the following conditions are true:

1. the two rays must have the same number of collision points;
2. the absolute difference between the lengths of the two rays must not exceed a threshold chosen; the threshold we used for the proposed algorithm was $\epsilon = 10^{-2}$;

If we kept all the rays, then we would increase the complexity of the algorithm without bringing value to the results.

Algorithm 1 presents how the reduction of duplicates was performed after having considered only those rays that reach the microphones. Until this stage, we have established how the rays will be distributed in the room, what the geometry of the room will be and we kept only the information of interest, namely those rays that reach the microphones in the room, but without duplicates. The time complexity for this step is linear, because we need to go through all the rays.

Algorithm 1. Remove duplicates

1: **procedure** *remove_duplicates(rays)*
2:     *index* = 0
3:     **while** *index < no(rays)* **do**
4:         **if** *ray$_{index}$* and *ray$_{index+1}$* are direct rays **then**
5:             remove *ray$_{index}$* from *rays*
6:         **else if** |distance(*ray$_{index}$*) - distance(*ray$_{index+1}$*)| < ϵ
7:                 **and** *no(ray$_{index}$.collisionPoints) = no(ray$_{index+1}$.collisionPoints)*
      then
8:             **if** P1 = true **then**
9:                 remove *ray$_{index}$* from *rays*
10:                *index* ← *index* + 1
11:            **end if**
12:        **else** *index* ← *index* + 1
13:        **end if**
14:     **end while**
15: **end procedure**

2.2 Physical Calculations

We have reached the middle stage of the application, which proposes the calculation of several elements in order to simulate the physics of a room. In the previous step, we completed the geometry of an indoor space, and further we needed to calculate the intensities, pressures, distances, times and frequency response functions.

The Inverse Square Law, which states that a specified physical size is inversely proportional to the square of the distance from the source of that physical size, was used to compute the intensities for each ray. In the case of our algorithm, when a ray passes through this room, it hits different materials that have an absorption variable factor α based on the material of the surface. In order to take into account the absorption phenomenon, we have included this factor in the formula of intensity:

$$\frac{I_n}{I_{n+1}} = \frac{d_{n+1}}{d_n}(1 - \alpha_k)^2 \qquad (1)$$

where d_n represents the distance from the source to n^{th} point and α_k represents the coefficient of absorption for the kth material.

In order to compute the pressures, we will use the intensities calculated in the previous step, taking into account the density of the air and the speed of sound through the air. We will consider that the density of air, ρ_{air}, has the value $1.2041\frac{kg}{m^3}$, and the speed of sound through the air, c_{air}, is $343.21\frac{m}{s}$ and the temperature is $20\,^\circ C$ [2].

For each frequency in the interval we will compute the phase and the magnitude:

$$\begin{cases} t = \dfrac{c_{air}}{fr} \\ w = \dfrac{2\pi}{t} \\ \theta = \arctan \dfrac{-\sin w \cdot d}{\cos w \cdot d} \end{cases} \quad (2)$$

where fr is the frequency, θ is the phase we want and d is the length of the ray. Thus, for each frequency we get a complex number of magnitude, w, and phase, θ. To make the transformations from intensity to pressure and to calculate the intensities, magnitude and phase for each frequency, a linear time complexity has been maintained.

2.3 Post-processing Data

We have reached the last stage where we will apply post-processing operations in order to be able to listen to the sound on the microphones placed in the rooms. So, in this phase we will apply an algorithm for sound convolution.

The convolution of the sound is achieved on the basis of the impulse response function. The answer consists of a list of real values that are transformed into a discrete signal. Convolution involves a system that receives a signal as input and transforms it to get an output signal. In the case of this model, the input signal is a function of impulse response and sound in the time domain, and the output is represented by the sound on a specific microphone. These operations are accomplished with the help of Fast Fourier Transform and Inverse Fast Fourier Transform [5].

Sound convolution, time-to-frequency transformations (and the other way around) were performed using NWaves library [7] which is a .NET library for 1D signal processing focused specifically on audio processing. The main features we used in our experiments are from Operations and RealFft classes, particularity:

- *DiscreteSignal Operation.Convolve(DiscreteSignal signal, DiscreteSignal kernel)*
- *void RealFft.Inverse(float[] re, float[] im, float[] output)*.

The sound convolution takes as input the impulse response function and the sound from the user provided audio source. Two frequency domain signals that must be multiplied are obtained. The result achieved is in the frequency domain, and in order to calculate the output we have to go back in the time domain by means of the Inverse Fast Fourier Transform (see Fig. 1). The procedure is significantly more computationally efficient when using the Fast Fourier Transformation (FFT) and it takes $n \log_2 n$ operations.

3 Comparing Rooms and Results

In order to validate the results obtained using our acoustic model, an application using $C\#$ programming language was implemented. We created an interactive way to allow us to visualize and compare the results obtained by our model

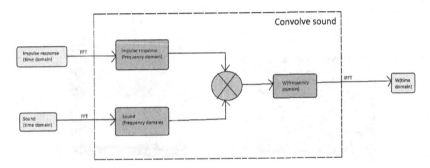

Fig. 1. Stages for convolving sound

using Unity platform to manage and develop an acoustic simulation software by means of a game engine.

In our experiments we used following rooms:

1. Rectangular room with dimensions: 3 m width, 5 m height, 3 m high
2. Rectangular room with dimensions: 30 m width, 30 m height, 15 m high
3. Spherical room with radius of 5 m

These experiments take into account several essential parameters such as: the number of rays that will be distributed in the room, the number of reflections that a maximum radius can reach, the maximum length that a radius can have and the frequency step. We will also use the same configuration for all rooms and the same song will be heard in the spaces.

We will consider the following configuration for all rooms:

- 100 000 uniform rays distributed in the rectangular rooms and 5 000 in the spherical room
- 10 maximum reflections
- 200 m maximum length of a ray
- 8192 the frequency resolution

We placed 3 microphones in rectangular rooms, where the distance between audio source and first microphone is 2.85, between audio source and second microphone is 2.37 m and between audio source and third microphone is 13.1 m.

After setting the configuration for each room we obtained the following results. In the small room, 709 rays reached the first microphone, 759 rays reached the second microphone and no ray reached the third microphone. For this case, the third microphone was outside the room so no ray could reach it. For the big room, 86 rays reached the first microphone, 91 rays reached the second microphone, whiled 80 rays reached the third microphone.

We can notice how for the same number of distributed rays, a very different result for rooms of various sizes was obtained. In Fig. 2 we highlighted the microphones with white dots, while the source is placed at the center of the room, on the floor.

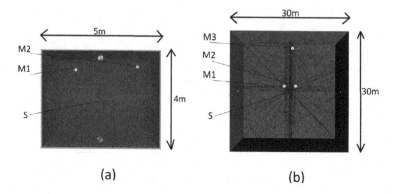

Fig. 2. All rays in small room (a) and big room (b)

The spherical room has 7 microphones placed in circle at equal distances around the audio source. We tried to see what happens to the rays when we place an obstacle in the shape of a sphere between 5th microphone and 6th microphone (see Fig. 3). For this model we considered the same configuration as the one for rectangular rooms, with the difference that in the spherical room we considered the number of rays equal to 5000. Following the calculations performed, we noticed that 442 rays reached the microphones in the case shown in Fig. 2 (a) and 378 in the case shown in Fig. 2 (b). Moreover, we learnt that if we have an obstacle in the room the rays are more scattered and that certain parts are not so dense, because due to the obstacle new propagation paths are created. We can discern that a ray follows one of these patterns: the ray can hit the obstacle, it can not hit it at all or it can pass above or below the inside object. Considering all of this, the rays can have very different ways of reaching the microphone, the longer the path, the later the sound will reach it (see Fig. 4).

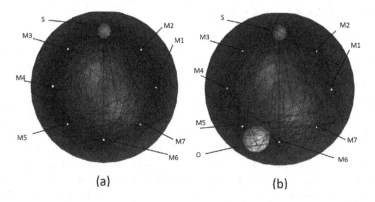

Fig. 3. (a) Spherical room without obstacle, (b) Spherical room with obstacle

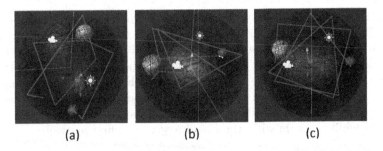

(a)   (b)   (c)

Fig. 4. Different scenarios for rays: (a) Ray passing over obstacle, (b) Ray not hitting the obstacle, (c) Ray hitting multiple times the obstacle

If the number of rays is not too small compared to the size of the room, it will not be possible to propagate the sound very well, because there is a possibility that no ray or too few will reach the microphones. So, the larger the size of the room, the greater the number of rays that will be distributed in the room, with the same happening for the number of reflections and for the maximum possible length of a ray. We can observe there is impulse response for the third microphone in the big room. Normally, we should have seen a strictly decreasing graph. However, this is not the case because of the occurring echo phenomenon. Those increment segments are due to the echo effect, see Fig. 5. Based on the scenarios presented above, it can be concluded that in the case of rectangular areas, it is more difficult for rays to reach the corners of the room, while in the case of spherical rooms, it is more difficult for the rays to reach the center of the sphere.

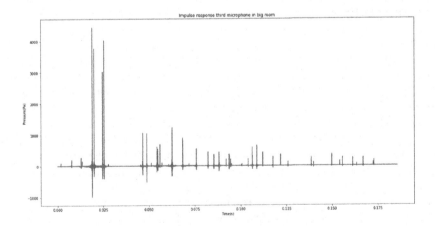

Fig. 5. Impulse response for third microphone in big room

The results obtained in these rooms are impressive, since even in the small room one can differentiate between the sound on the first microphone and the one on the second microphone. Moreover, the sound obtained using our model for the third microphone is varies significantly from the other microphones in the room. In addition to what we can hear, the sound rays can be viewed through the impulse responses already calculated by us in the previous steps. All this can be studied in Fig. 6, where the red plot represents the sound on first microphone, the green plot is the sound on second microphone and the blue plot is the sound on third microphone. The microphone that the sound reaches the last is the third one, while to begin with, the sound reaches the first microphone.

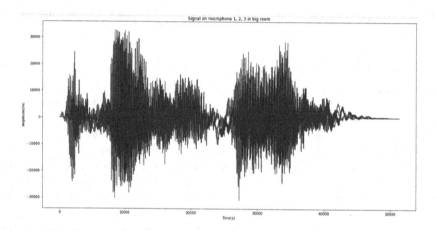

Fig. 6. Signals obtained in the big room for each microphone (Color figure online)

4   Conclusions

This research study provides an acoustic model that supports engineers in the optimal construction by taking into consideration the acoustics of the indoor spaces such as amphitheaters, concert halls, churches, mosques, factories and more. This analysis comes to support of acoustic engineers who design acoustic models, while also offering an efficient solution for reducing work associated risks for those who work in areas that endanger ear health.

This study requires that the steps be performed sequentially because the output of one step is the input of the next step. Geometric calculation is especially important because it often dictates the efficiency of the algorithm. As the time complexity was presented at each step we could observe that the geometric calculation and physical calculation has the linear complexity and the post-processing computation takes $n \log_2 n$ operations. Certainly, there are improvements that could be made to the physical computation stage.

The acoustic model proposed by us is an efficient tool that can be adapted and used in the context of any indoor space design, in order to help create a room with optimal parameters to provide people with the comfort they seek. As any other acoustic model, it is subject to improvements such as the approach of other geometric calculation techniques. A possible solution could be to start by creating the rays from the microphones to the source. Another solution could be to keep the distribution of the rays with the observation that when a ray meets a surface, it breaks into several other rays. More than improving the simulation mode of the room geometry, it can improve the overall calculation mode of the application, so all calculations could be moved to the GPU.

References

1. Unity documentation (2020). https://docs.unity3d.com/ScriptReference/Physics. Raycast.html
2. Berlin, U.: Conversion: Sound pressure to sound intensity and vice versa (formulas)
3. Elorza, D.: Room Acoustics Modeling Using the Raytracing Method: Implementation and Evaluation (2005). https://books.google.ro/books?id=vgiJmwEACAAJ
4. Hargreaves, J.A., Lam, Y.W.: An energy interpretation of the Kirchhoff-Helmholtz boundary integral equation and its application to sound field synthesis. Acta Acust. United Acust. **100**(5), 912–920 (2014)
5. Haynal, S., Haynal, H.: Generating and searching families of FFT algorithms. J. Satisf. Boolean Model. Comput. **7**(4), 145–187 (2011)
6. Jeong, C.H., Ih, J.G., Rindel, J.H.: Consideration of wall reflection and diffraction in the room acoustic prediction using the phased beam tracing method (2007)
7. Sharii, T.: Nwaves documentation (2019). https://github.com/ar1st0crat/NWaves
8. Weitze, C.A., Christensen, C.L., Rindel, J.H.: Computer simulation of the acoustics of mosques and byzantine churches. ACUSTICA **86**, 943–956 (2000)

Learning Path Recommendation for MOOC Platforms Based on a Knowledge Graph

Hui Chen[1], Chuantao Yin[2]($\boxtimes$), Xin Fan[2], Lei Qiao[2], Wenge Rong[1], and Xiong Zhang[1]

[1] Computer Science and Engineering School, Beihang University, Beijing, China
{chenhui,w.rong,xiongz}@buaa.edu.cn
[2] Sino-French Engineer School, Beihang University, Beijing, China
chuantao.yin@buaa.edu.cn, rachel.fan.xin@centralepekin.cn

Abstract. With the development of Internet technologies and the increasing demand for knowledge, increasingly more people choose online learning platforms as a way to acquire knowledge. However, the rapid growth in the types and number of courses makes it difficult for people to make choices, which leads to a series of problems, such as unsystematic learning processes and a low learning efficiency. Based on the current course situation of MOOC (massive open online courses) platforms, this paper proposes a new automated construction method for course knowledge graphs. A course knowledge graph is constructed by annotating the pre-knowledge of each course and calculating the similarity between courses, and it is displayed using the Neo4j graph database platform. After completion of the course knowledge graph, the knowledge graph of the courses is used to study learning path recommendation algorithms, including rule-based and machine learning based algorithms, and to perform a comparative analysis using the higher education formation program of a university.

Keywords: Smart learning · MOOC · Knowledge graph · Learning path recommendation · Machine learning

1 Introduction

Nowadays, MOOCs (massive open online courses) have been hot topics in the field of education. Moocs ease learning tasks and enable users to learn at their own pace and comfort [1], but they face a few challenges. On one hand, the unstructured learning resources have brought unprecedented problems of cognitive overload to learners. On the other hand, the course recommendation model ignores the semantic relation between the actual content of the course and the keywords.

Supported by the National Natural Science Foundation of China (No. 61977003).

H. Qiu et al. (Eds.): KSEM 2021, LNAI 12816, pp. 600–611, 2021.
https://doi.org/10.1007/978-3-030-82147-0_49

The course knowledge graph can solve the first problem. The knowledge graph is a graph-based data structure, composed of nodes and edges, where nodes refer to entities and edges refer to relations between entities. It integrates scattered courses with knowledge points, and fully reflects the relation between courses and knowledge points [2]. To solve the second problem, the learning path recommendation can select a suitable learning path to the learner according to the learner's information.

We propose a learning path recommendation for MOOC platforms based on the course knowledge graph. It can provide learners with personalized learning programs and with greater autonomy by flexibly arranging teaching methods.

The main contributions of this paper are as follows: proposition of an improved course text vector calculation method based on TF-IDF by using the course information of MOOC; establishment of course knowledge graph according to the course model, which includes courses nodes, knowledge points nodes, and their relations; visualization of course knowledge graph with Neo4j graph database platform; classification of courses in the course knowledge graph by using machine learning classification algorithms; and course recommendation based on the knowledge graph and student information.

2 Related Studies

The course knowledge graph construction process includes the definition of the course knowledge graph model, entity recognition, and relation extraction.

2.1 Course Knowledge Graph Model

Yongyou Zhong et al. [3] proposed a method for constructing the ontology of course knowledge points. The relation of course knowledge points includes inheritance relation, integral part relation, instance relation, dependency relation and parallel relation.

Pingyi Zhou et al. [4] proposed a method for automatically constructing a course knowledge graph based on a semantic relation model. The method is mainly composed of three parts: the extraction of the semantic entities, the expression of the course semantics and topic semantics, and the construction of the course dependencies.

2.2 Entity Recognition

Entity recognition [5] automatically discovers the named entities from Internet texts. The main methods include rule-based methods, statistical machine learning-based methods, and deep learning-based methods.

Rau et al. [6] proposed for the first time a method of combining manually written rules with heuristic ideas, which realized the automatic extraction of named entities of company name type from the text.

In recent years, many works have proposed the use of neural networks to automatically capture effective features from text, and then complete named entity recognition.

2.3 Relation Extraction

Relation extraction [7] automatically extracts the relations between the entities from the Internet text. The main methods include template-based and machine learning-based methods.

For the first time, Kambhatla et al. [8] used a feature vector-based method to integrate entity context information, syntactic analysis trees, dependency relations and other features, and combine vocabulary, syntax and semantic features with the maximum entropy model to classify relations.

Hasegawa et al. [9] first proposed the use of unsupervised methods for relation extraction. They first obtained named entity recognition and its context information, then clustered similar named entity pairs, and finally selected core vocabulary to label various semantic relations.

2.4 Learning Path Recommendation

Learning path design is the main activity of learning design, which is usually a very complex task for learners. The learning recommendation system can help learners find suitable learning objects and establish effective learning paths in the learning process. Durand earlier proposed a graph-based learning path recommendation method [10].

Lumy Joseph et al. [11] believe that in an online learning environment, the system ignores the student's personal information and provides predefined learning content for everyone, which will affect the student's learning process.

Zhu et al. [12] proposed a learning path recommendation based on knowledge graph. They first divided the learning scenario into four different models, and then adjusted the variables and weights according to the scenario's preference for learning paths. Finally, the knowledge graph is used as the basis of the recommendation algorithm, and the learning path is recommended, and a good recommendation effect is achieved.

3   Construction of Course Knowledge Graph

First, this paper collected data from the Chinse MOOCs. Then, this paper proposed a method for constructing the MOOC course knowledge graph. Based on the course knowledge graph, this paper recommended the learning path for the learner. The process is shown in Fig. 1.

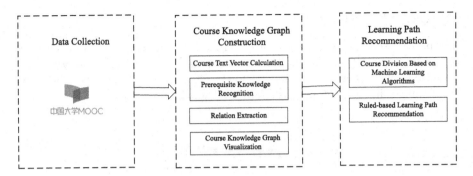

Fig. 1. The research process.

3.1   Course Knowledge Graph Model

This paper used the course text from a Chinese MOOC, took the courses and knowledge points as nodes, took the similarity and prerequisite relations as edges. The attributes and relations of the course nodes and the knowledge point nodes are shown in Fig. 2.

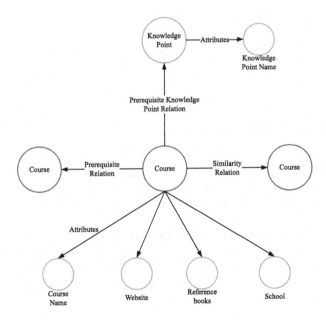

Fig. 2. The diagram of course knowledge graph model.

3.2 Data Collection

This paper used the Selenium tool [13] to obtain information from all 1808 courses from the MOOC, including the course name, website, summary, school, reference books, agenda, preliminary knowledge, and course category. The number of courses in each category is shown in Table 1.

Table 1. Number of courses in each category

Course category	Number of courses
Computer	203
Management	259
Psychology	20
Language	53
History	142
Design	101
Engineering	420
Science	310
Biology	220
Philosophy	20
Law	60
Total	**1808**

3.3 Course Text Vectorization

The main methods of constructing course text vectors are: TF-IDF algorithm and Word2Vect algorithm. Word2Vec is a commonly used method, which mainly includes Continuous Bag-of-Words Model (CBOW) and Skip-gram. This type of method mainly completes the prediction and classification task by training a neural network.

In this paper, we choose the Skip-gram model to train the word vector, and then construct the text vector based on the word vector. As shown in Eq. 1, we add the word vectors of all words in the text and take the average value as the vector of the text s_i, where $e_{i,j}$ is the word vector of the jth word in the text d_i, and l_i is the number of words.

$$s_i = \frac{1}{l_i} \sum_{j=1}^{l_i} e_{i,j} \qquad (1)$$

Due to the serious unevenness of the number of courses in different categories, this paper proposes to use LDA (Linear Discriminant Analysis) [14] to reduce the dimensionality of the course text vector. Based on supervised learning, LDA projects the data to the low-dimensional feature space while minimizing the variance of data belonging to the same category, and maximizing the variance of data belonging to different categories. Therefore, we can use LDA to obtain dense course text vectors that incorporate course category information.

We take two categories of data as examples to illustrate the principle of the LDA algorithm. Given a dataset $X = \{x_1, ..., x_m\}$, where x_i represents the n-dimensional feature vector of the i sample, $Y = \{y_1, ..., y_m\}$ represents the category label corresponding to each sample, and $y_i \in \{0, 1\}$ is the binary label of the ith sample. X_i, N_i are the set of samples in the i class and the number of samples in the i class, and μ_i and Σ_i are the mean value and feature of the feature vector of the i class samples. The calculation process is shown in Eqs. 2 and 3.

$$\mu_i = \frac{1}{N_i} \sum_{x \in X_i} x \tag{2}$$

$$\Sigma_i = \sum_{x \in X_i} (x - \mu_i)(x - \mu_i)^T \tag{3}$$

w is the project vector, and the projections of the mean vector of class 0 and class 1 are respectively $w^T \mu_0$ and $w^T \mu_1$, LDA maximizes $\left\| w^T \mu_0 - w^T \mu_1 \right\|_2^2$ to make the distance between classes as large as possible, and at the same time minimizes $w^T \Sigma_0 w + w^T \Sigma_1 w$ to make the distance between the features in same category as close as possible. Therefore, the optimization goals of LDA are:

$$\arg\max_{w} J(w) = \frac{\left\| w^T \mu_0 - w^T \mu_1 \right\|_2^2}{w^T \Sigma_0 w + w^T \Sigma_1 w} = \frac{w^T (\mu_0 - \mu_1)(\mu_0 - \mu_1) w}{w^T (\Sigma_0 + \Sigma_1) w} \tag{4}$$

Then, we calculated the silhouette coefficient [15] of TF-IDF algorithm, Word2Vect algorithm and the related algorithms that add LDA. The value of the silhouette coefficient is between -1 and 1. The closer to 1, the better the cohesion and separation.

3.4   Relation Extraction

For a course, the paper first established the prerequisite relations according to the preliminary knowledge tag of the courses. If there is a course that matches the preliminary knowledge tag, a prerequisite relation between courses will be established; if there is no matching course, a prerequisite relation between the course and preliminary knowledge points will be established. In addition, we directly add the course series to the prerequisite relations, such as analysis 1, analysis 2, etc. Finally, the similarity relations between courses were calculated based on the cosine similarity.

4   Learning Path Recommendation Based on a Course Knowledge Graph

Based on the course knowledge graph, this paper combines students' learning information, such as information about the courses they already studied, to recommend personalized and complete learning paths for students.

4.1   Division of Course Levels Based on Machine Learning Algorithms

This paper considers the process of recommending courses in the initial state as a multi-classification problem of assigning courses to four levels.

The division is divided into two steps. The first thing to do is to create the prior set. We assign certain courses to four different levels according to certain rules to establish the prior set. The rules are as follows.

- All courses without prerequisite courses are listed as the first level.
- If a course has a prerequisite course in the $k-1$ level, it is listed as the k level.

In the second step, we use a machine learning classification algorithm to complete the multi-classification of the courses that cannot be assigned according to the rules. The class labels of the divided courses are used as the training set to train the classifier, and the trained classifier is used to classify the courses without class labels.

4.2   Rule-Based Learning Path Recommendation

After students have completed a certain number of courses, we will formulate the rules based on the knowledge graph and students' MOOC information to complete the learning path recommendation. We can define the degree of recommendation of a course as Eq. 5, where n_{pass} indicates the number of prerequisite courses passed of the course, n_{total} means the total number of prerequisite courses, $avg\left(\frac{note_{obtain}}{note_{pass}}\right)$ means the average value of the ratio of the score obtained of the prerequisite course and the passing score of the prerequisite course, $n_{similar}$ represents the number of failed courses whose cosine similarity with the course is greater than 0.2, $n_{total\_non\_pass}$ indicates the total number of failed courses, and $avg(\frac{note_{similar}}{note_{pass}})$ represents the average of the score obtained and passing score of similar failed courses. Finally, this paper uses the Min-Max Normalization method [16] to calculate the recommendation degree, and recommends a list of courses sorted by recommendation degree to learners.

$$r = (\frac{n_{pass}}{n_{total}}) * avg(\frac{note_{otain}}{note_{pass}}) + (\frac{n_{similar}}{n_{total\_non\_pass}}) * avg(\frac{note_{similar}}{note_{pass}}) \qquad (5)$$

5   Results and Discussions

5.1   Knowledge Graph Construction Results

Course Text Vector Construction. This paper used the text of the course name, summary, and agenda to calculate the course text vectors. The Silhouette coefficients of the text vectors constructed by TF-IDF algorithm, Skip-gram algorithm, TF-IDF+LDA algorithm and Skip-gram+LDA algorithm are 0.0117, 0.0370, 0.1445, and 0.2454 respectively. Therefore, this article chooses the Skip-gram+LDA algorithm.

Course Knowledge Graph Construction and Visualization. In the course similarity relation construction, we calculated the similarity between courses. Through statistics, we found that the similarity between courses is widely distributed, and the similarity between courses over 90% is less than 0.05. For one course, this article chooses the course with a similarity of more than 0.2 as its similar course.

5.2   Results of Course Division Based on Machine Learning

This paper compares the results of classification based on KNN [17] and logistic regression on the basis of the course vector constructed by the Skip-gram+LDA algorithm. When using the KNN algorithm for multi-classification, we will use 60% of the courses in the dataset to train the classifier and 40% of the courses as the test set, and set the coefficient $k = 5$. When using the logistic regression, we select one level as a positive example and the other three levels as negative examples to complete multi-classification. The result is shown in Table 2. This paper selected logistic regression for multi-classification.

Table 2. The results of KNN classifier and logistic regression on Skip-gram+LDA.

Level		Precision	Recall	F1
First level	KNN	0.77	0.78	0.78
	Logistic regression	0.91	0.53	0.67
Second level	KNN	0.23	0.21	0.22
	Logistic regression	0.20	0.38	0.26
Third level	KNN	0.25	0.19	0.21
	Logistic regression	0.19	0.53	0.28
Fourth level	KNN	0.36	0.41	0.38
	Logistic regression	0.34	0.68	0.45

The learning path recommendation results based on the Logistic Regression are shown in Fig. 3. The recommended learning path is shown in the form of a graph. The connections between the courses indicate the prerequisite relations.

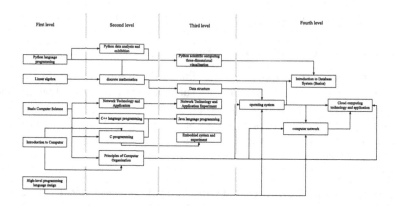

Fig. 3. Logistic regression-based learning path recommendation results.

5.3   Rule-Based Learning Path Recommendation Results

In order to verify the effectiveness of the learning path recommendation algorithm based on the course knowledge graph proposed in this paper, this paper uses two hypothetical student cases to simulate the results of the recommendation.

For student A, it is assumed that he has taken two courses at the beginning, and his scores are 78 points for Basic Computer Science and 89 points for data structure, of which 60 is a passing score. The recommended list is shown in the Table 3:

Table 3. Results of learning path recommendation for student A.

Course	Scores for course recommendation for student A
Principles of Computer organization	0.20
C programming	0.20
C++ language programming	1.00
Network technology and application	1.00
Introduction to database system (Basics)	0.00
Operating system	0.00

Later, it is assumed that student A has passed two more courses. The current academic scores are 78 points for Basic Computer Science, 89 points for data structure, 63 points for computer organization principles, and 93 points for high-level language programming. The list of recommended courses is shown in the Table 4:

Table 4. Results of learning path recommendation for Student A.

Course	Scores for course recommendation for student A
Principles of Computer organization	0.35
C programming	0.35
C++ language programming	1.00
Network Technology and Application	1.00
Introduction to Database System (Basics)	0.12
Operating system	0.88
Computer network	0.45
Cloud computing technology and application	0.00

When the student's learning information changes, the recommendation result also changes. It realizes the student's personalized course path recommendation, and also confirms the effectiveness of the recommendation degree for the student's course recommendation.

For student B, the scores are as follows: 56 points for Python programming, 66 points for discrete mathematics, 56 points for C programming, and 53 points for operating systems. There are 3 failed courses. The list of recommended courses is shown in the Table 5:

Table 5. Results of learning path recommendation for Student B.

Course	Scores for course recommendation for student B
Python data analysis and exhibition	0.79
Data structure	1.00
Java language programming	0.22
Introduction to Database System (Basics)	0.64
Computer network	0.00
Cloud computing technology and application	0.00

Later, student B passed the 2 failed courses and got 65 points for Python language programming, 79 points for discrete mathematics, 70 points for C programming, and 59 points for operating system. The list of recommended courses is shown in the Table 6:

From the table, when students have failed courses, such as student B's Python language programming, C programming, operating system, etc., the algorithm

Table 6. Results of learning path recommendation for student B.

Course	Scores for course recommendation for student B
Python data analysis and exhibition	0.76
Data structure	1.00
Embedded system and experiment	0.85
Java language programming	0.25
Introduction to database system (Basics)	0.61
Computer network	0.00
Cloud computing technology and application	0.00

will no longer recommend subsequent courses of these courses, but recommend similar courses of the failed courses. When failed course is passed, the algorithm can normally recommend subsequent courses. This verifies the effectiveness of the recommendation algorithm in recommending similar courses and subsequent courses.

6 Conclusion

With the rapid development of Internet technology, increasingly more people choose online platforms for learning. To solve the problem of the explosion in the number of course resources on an online learning platform, this paper combined the relevant machine learning algorithms and used the course information on a Chinese MOOC platform to analyze and model the courses. Then, this paper constructed a course knowledge graph based on the MOOCs. The course knowledge graph better shows the relations between the courses on the MOOC website. Then, this paper completed the learning path recommendation based on the constructed course knowledge graph. This paper provided an application basis for online learning platforms and had important practical significance.

In the future, we will try to include multiple data sources, such as the Baidu Encyclopedia, open source databases, etc. We will also compare the recommended results with other modern course recommendation method.

References

1. Nabizadeh, A.H., Gonçalves, D., Gama, S., et al.: Adaptive learning path recommender approach using auxiliary learning objects. Comput. Educ. **147**, 103777 (2020)
2. Morsi, R., Ibrahim, W., Williams, F.: Concept maps: development and validation of engineering curricula. In: 2007 37th Annual Frontiers in Education Conference-Global Engineering: Knowledge Without Borders, Opportunities Without Passports. IEEE (2007). T3H-18-T3H-23

3. Yongyou, Z.: Ontology-based curriculum knowledge point modeling of major of information management and information system. Inf. Res. **8**, Article no. 28 (2013)
4. Zhou, P., Liu, J., Yang, X., et al.: Automatically constructing course dependence graph based on association semantic link model. Personal Ubiquit. Comput. **20**(5), 731–742 (2016)
5. Bikel, D.M., Schwartz, R., Weischedel, R.M.: An algorithm that learns what's in a name. Mach. Learn. **34**(1), 211–231 (1999)
6. Rau, L.F.: Extracting company names from text. In: Proceedings of the Seventh IEEE Conference on Artificial Intelligence Application. IEEE Computer Society (1991). 29, 30, 31, 32–29, 30, 31, 32
7. Zelenko, D., Aone, C., Richardella, A.: Kernel methods for relation extraction. J. Mach. Learn. Res. **3**(2003), 1083–1106 (2003)
8. Kambhatla, N.: Combining lexical, syntactic, and semantic features with maximum entropy models for information extraction. In: Proceedings of the ACL Interactive Poster and Demonstration Sessions, pp. 178–181 (2004)
9. Hasegawa, T., Sekine, S., Grishman, R.: Discovering relations among named entities from large corpora. In: Proceedings of the 42nd Annual Meeting of the Association for Computational Linguistics (ACL-2004), pp. 415–422 (2004)
10. Durand, G., Belacel, N., LaPlante, F.: Graph theory based model for learning path recommendation. Inf. Sci. **251**, 10–21 (2013)
11. Joseph, L., Abraham, S.: Instructional design for learning path identification in an e-learning environment using Felder-Silverman learning styles model. In: 2017 International Conference on Networks and Advances in Computational Technologies (NetACT), pp. 215–220. IEEE (2017)
12. Zhu, H., Tian, F., Wu, K., et al.: A multi-constraint learning path recommendation algorithm based on knowledge map. Knowl. Based Syst. **143**, 102–114 (2018)
13. De Medio, C., Gasparetti, F., Limongelli, C., et al.: Automatic extraction and sequencing of Wikipedia Pages for smart course building. In: 2017 21st International Conference Information Visualisation (IV), pp. 378–383. IEEE (2017)
14. Blei, D.M., Ng, A.Y., Jordan, M.I.: Latent Dirichlet allocation. J. Mach. Learn. Res. **3**, 993–1022 (2003)
15. Thalamuthu, A., Mukhopadhyay, I., Zheng, X., et al.: Evaluation and comparison of gene clustering methods in microarray analysis. Bioinformatics **22**(19), 2405–2412 (2006)
16. Panda, S.K., Bhoi, S.K., Singh, M.: A collaborative filtering recommendation algorithm based on normalization approach. J. Ambient Intell. Humanized Comput. **3**, 1–23 (2020)
17. Fresco, R., Pederiva, A.: An approach to the process maps based on semantic web methodologies. In: Meersman, R., Tari, Z. (eds.) OTM 2003. LNCS, vol. 2889, pp. 98–108. Springer, Heidelberg (2003). https://doi.org/10.1007/978-3-540-39962-9_22

Spy the Lie: Fraudulent Jobs Detection in Recruitment Domain using Knowledge Graphs

Nidhi Goyal[1][(✉)], Niharika Sachdeva[2], and Ponnurangam Kumaraguru[3]

[1] Indraprastha Institute of Information Technology, New Delhi, India
nidhig@iiitd.ac.in
[2] InfoEdge India Limited, Noida, India
niharika.sachdeva@infoedge.com
[3] International Institute of Information Technology, Hyderabad, India
pk.guru@iiit.ac.in

Abstract. Fraudulent jobs are an emerging threat over online recruitment platforms such as LinkedIn, Glassdoor. Fraudulent job postings affect the platform's trustworthiness and have a negative impact on user experience. Therefore, these platforms need to detect and remove these fraudulent jobs. Generally, fraudulent job postings contain untenable facts about domain-specific entities such as mismatch in skills, industries, offered compensation, etc. However, existing approaches focus on studying writing styles, linguistics, and context-based features, and ignore the relationships among domain-specific entities. To bridge this gap, we propose an approach based on the Knowledge Graph (KG) of domain-specific entities to detect fraudulent jobs. In this paper, we present a multi-tier novel end-to-end framework called FRaudulent Jobs Detection (FRJD) Engine, which considers a) fact validation module using KGs, b) contextual module using deep neural networks c) meta-data module to capture the semantics of job postings. We conduct our experiments using a fact validation dataset containing 4 million facts extracted from job postings. Extensive evaluation shows that FRJD yields a 0.96 F1-score on the curated dataset of 157,880 job postings. Finally, we provide insights on the performance of different fact-checking algorithms on recruitment domain datasets.

Keywords: Recruitment domain · Fraudulent jobs · Knowledge graphs

1 Introduction

Online recruitment platforms such as Glassdoor, Indeed, LinkedIn are of paramount importance for employers and candidates to connect, recruit, and

P. Kumaraguru—Major part of this work was done while Ponnurangam Kumaraguru was a faculty at IIIT-Delhi.

H. Qiu et al. (Eds.): KSEM 2021, LNAI 12816, pp. 612–623, 2021.
https://doi.org/10.1007/978-3-030-82147-0_50

find jobs. These platforms attract millions of job seekers per month. Unfortunately, candidates often come across fraudulent jobs offering more wages, flexible working hours, and appealing career growth opportunities. Federal Trade Commission (FTC) registered 101,917 fraud complaints[1] from job seekers over the period of 2014 to 2019. The proliferation of fraudulent jobs not only hamper candidate's experience [37] but also act as a repressing factor[2] in an enterprise's reputation. Therefore, it is desirable to detect and take off these fraudulent jobs. Fraudulent jobs[3] are dishonest, money seeking, intentionally and verifiably false that mislead job seekers.

Data Entry Clerks Position	Data Entry Clerk
We have several openings available in this area earning $1000.00-$2500.00 per week. We are seeking only honest, self-motivated people with a desire to work in the home typing and data entry field, from the comfort of their own homes.The preferred applicants should be at least 18 years old with Internet access. No experience is needed. However the following skills are desirable: Basic computer and typing skills, ability to spell and print neatly, ability to follow directions. Earn as much as you can from the comfort of your home typing and doing data entry. You do NOT need any special skills to get started.	Responsibilities include, but are not limited to: Review and process confidential and extremely time-sensitive applications. Identify objective data and enter (""key what you see"") at a high level of productivity and accuracy. Perform data entry task from a paper and/or document image. Utilize system functions to perform data look-up and validation. High volume sorting, analyzing, indexing, of insurance, legal and financial documents. Maintain high degree of quality control and validation of the completed work Identify, classify, and sort documents electronically.

Fig. 1. Examples of job postings a) fraudulent job on the left and b) legitimate at the right. These job postings are taken from publicly available dataset.

Existing approaches mainly focus on supervised machine learning (e.g., ANN, bagging ensemble methods, and random forests) based on handcrafted feature engineering to detect fraudulent jobs [1]. However, these methods are unable to perform and scale well for larger datasets. Thereafter, NLP researchers also proposed linguistic, string-based [39], writing styles [32], textual, and contextual features [22] of job postings. These methods ignore the factual information among domain-specific entities present in job postings, which are important to capture relationships [35]. Figure 1 shows that the [left] job is fraudulent, which mentions implausible facts such as { *'offering very high weekly salary- $1000 − $2500'*, *'No experience required'*, *'Earn as much as you can'*} for *Data Entry Clerks* position. In contrast, the [right] job is legitimate that covers genuine facts related to role and responsibilities such as { *'Review and process confidential time-sensitive applications'*, *'Identify, classify, and sort documents'*} for same position.

To address these issues, we construct a fact-validation dataset consisting of 4 million facts of job postings from a popular recruitment platform. We utilize the fact validation dataset and employ automatic fact-checking algorithms [5] to find missing facts and validating the triples present in job postings using the triple

---

[1] https://www.aarp.org/money/scams-fraud/info-2020/ftc-job-scams.html.

[2] https://hrdailyadvisor.blr.com/2015/01/19/what-is-recruitment-fraud-is-your-company-at-risk/.

[3] https://www.consumer.ftc.gov/articles/0243-job-scams.

classification task. Towards this end, we propose a multi-tier novel unified framework to leverage the fact-checking module, the contextual module using deep neural network-based approaches, and a unique meta-data knowledge module to accomplish fraudulent job detection tasks. We demonstrate the efficacy of our proposed approach on an annotated (proprietary & public) dataset of 157,880 job postings and validate them on open-source datasets, thus demonstrating our solution's generalizability. We summarize the contributions as follows:

- We propose a multi-tier novel unified framework called FRJD, which employs a fact-checking module using knowledge graph representations, the contextual module using deep neural networks, and considers unique meta-data properties of job postings to accomplish fraudulent jobs detection task.
- We study the fact validation dataset that consists of 4 million facts in form of entities and relationships and utilize it for the triple classification task.
- Extensive experiments on real-world recruitment domain datasets demonstrate the promising performance of FRJD compared to state-of-the-art models.

The organization of the rest of the paper as follows. Section 2 reviews the related literature of fraudulent content detection in the recruitment domain as well as in general. Thereafter, In Sect. 3, we formulate our problem. Our proposed framework FRJD is described in Sect. 4. Section 5 demonstrates the experimental setup along with datasets, experimental settings, and comparison with different approaches. Section 6 demonstrates our evaluation results. Section 7 describes ablation study. We conclude this work and provide future work in Sect. 8.

2   Related Works

This section describes the related literature of fraud detection in domain-specific scenarios and in general.

Content-Based Approaches. Research explores the textual content using TF-IDF [7], stylometric [31], and RNN (recurrent neural networks) [6,21]. Some approaches [20] exploits the graph-based techniques for fake content detection while others [8,13] use contextual embedding models such as ELMO and BERT [34] to learn language-based features.

Fact Checking Using Knowledge Graphs. Existing research [30] suggests knowledge graph-based techniques for fact checking in the news domain. Knowledge graph representation methods [14,41] are used to predict the plausibility of the facts using external KGs (DBpedia [18], Freebase [4]).

Most of the fact-checking methods also rely on experts, such as journalists or scientists, to assess the content and the crowd's wisdom [17]. Another set of approaches finds streams in knowledge graphs to support fact checking [36]. Some works [15] leverage unstructured and structured sources [40] for automatic fact-checking.

Despite the popularity of knowledge graph-based approaches, these are still underexplored in the recruitment domain, and there is limited information available in external knowledge bases [4,18] for domain-specific scenarios. Additionally, expert-based methods are expensive as they need the hiring of experts, and also are limited in number and unable to treat all the content being produced.

Domain-Specific Scenarios. Recent research [1,39] focuses on content-based approaches that use handcrafted features such as empirical ruleset (binary, categorical, string-based) and Bag-of-words to identify fraudulent jobs in the recruitment domain. Works [22,29] conducted the research using behavioral activity or binary features as context. Kim et al. [16] propose hierarchical clustering deep neural network to detect fraud in the work processes of job placement automatically. We compare the most relevant studies with our work in Table 1.

Our research uniquely inclined towards using a hybrid approach consisting of the knowledge graph, contextual, and meta-data features at the same time requiring no job seeker responses and providing different insights on fact-checking algorithms.

Table 1. Different kind of features used in related literature.

	Content	Knowledge	Context
Vidros et al. [39]	✔		
Mahbub et al. [22]			✔
Nindyati et al. [29]			✔
Alghadmi et al. [1]	✔		
This work (FRJD)	✔	✔	✔

3   Problem Formulation

Let $\mathcal{J} = \{ \mathcal{J}_1, \mathcal{J}_2, ..., \mathcal{J}_N \}$ be the set of job postings and $\mathcal{Y} = \{ y_1, y_2, ..., y_n \}$ be corresponding labels such that $y_i \in \{0, 1\}$. For every $\mathcal{J}_i$, we extracted a set of triples T^i where $T^i = \{t_1^i, t_2^i, t_3^i, ..., t_k^i\}$ and $k > 0$; using *OpenIE*. A triple t_j^i $\in T^i$ is of the form (subject (s), predicate (p), object(o)) where $(s, o) \in \mathcal{E}$ and $p \in \mathcal{P}$. We further define $m^i \in \mathcal{M}$ and $c^i \in \mathcal{C}$ as meta features and contextual features extracted from $\mathcal{J}_i$ (See Sect. 4).

Given a job posting $\mathcal{J}_i$ and its corresponding extracted set of triples T^i, contextual vector c^i, and meta vector representation m^i. Our objective is to learn function φ where $\varphi \colon \mathcal{F} \ (\mathcal{KG}_{false}^A \ (T)^i, \mathcal{KG}_{true}^A \ (T)^i, c^i, m^i)$ where $\mathcal{KG}_{true}^A \ (T)^i$ is the scoring function, we learn from triple $t^i \in T^i | y_i = 0$ of legitimate job postings and $\mathcal{KG}_{false}^A \ (T)^i$ from triple $t^i \in T^i | y_i = 1$ of fraudulent job postings. Here $\mathcal{KG}^A$ $\in \{ TransE, TransR, TransH, TransD, DistMult, ComplEx, HolE, RotatE \}$ which are popular fact-checking algorithms from existing knowledge graph literature.

4   FRaudulent Jobs Detection Engine

This section describes our multi-tier novel framework- FRaudulent Job Detection Engine (FRJD) using knowledge graphs and deep neural networks. Figure 2 depicts the overall architecture for the detection of fraudulent job postings. This framework consists of three components a) *Fact-checking module*, b) *Contextual embedding generation*, c) *Meta-features generation*.

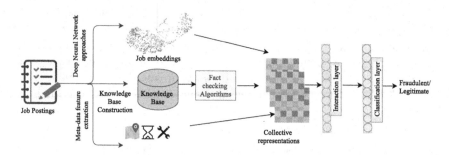

Fig. 2. An overview of our proposed framework- FRaudulent Jobs Detection Engine (FRJD).

Fact-Checking Module. This module identifies fraudulent job postings using fact-checking algorithms separately trained on legitimate and fraudulent jobs. We construct two domain-specific knowledge graphs ($\mathcal{KG}_{false}$, $\mathcal{KG}_{true}$) using triples extracted from legitimate ($T^i|y_i = 0$) and fraudulent ($T^i|y_i = 1$) jobs postings respectively. We pre-process the job postings and apply *OpenIE5* [24] to get triples[4] in the form of (s, p, o) as an output. We follow the similar methodology [11] to construct domain-specific knowledge graph. Thereafter, we obtain the low-dimensional knowledge graph representation for each entity and relation using various fact-checking algorithms [5,14,19,28,38]. Our objective is to obtain a separate score from both the knowledge graphs i.e. ($\mathcal{KG}_{true}$, $\mathcal{KG}_{false}$) for each triple t^i using scoring function $\mathcal{G}_p(s^i, o^i)$ introduced in [41]. We also provide the comparative analysis of these algorithms (see Table 3).

$$G_p(s^i, o^i) = \left\| (s - w_p^\top sw_p) + d_p - (o - w_p^\top ow_p) \right\|_2^2 \qquad (1)$$

Furthermore, we obtain b^i_{true} and b^i_{false} $\forall\, T^i$ of a job posting $\mathcal{J}_i$ from $\mathcal{KG}_{true}$ and $\mathcal{KG}_{false}$ respectively.

$$b^i = \sum_{\gamma=1}^{k} (G_p(s^i_\gamma, o^i_\gamma))/k \qquad (2)$$

---

[4] Triples and facts are used interchangeably.

where $\gamma \in |T^i|$. Finally, we fuse both b^i to obtain a representation vector f^i.

$$f^i = b^i_{true} \bigoplus b^i_{false} \tag{3}$$

Contextual Embedding Generation. We employ a pre-trained deep neural network i.e., sentence BERT [33] to generate contextual features for all job postings. S-BERT uses siamese networks to capture meaningful semantic representations of the sentences. It adds a pooling operation on top of BERT, which is computationally efficient. Research works suggest that for real-time applications light weight model should be preferred [9,10,25]. Hence, we use distilled version of S-BERT which requires fewer parameters, less space and time complexity while retaining 97% performance of BERT. Finally, we obtain s-dimensional ($s = 768$) vector representation for each job posting $\mathcal{J}_i$ in the space $\in \mathcal{R}^\omega$ such that c^i

$$c^i = SBERT(\mathcal{J}_i) \tag{4}$$

Meta-features Generation. In this module, we describe the meta-features of a job posting $\mathcal{J}_i$. We identify the domain-specific entities such as skills, companies, salary, locations, experience, and educational degree using state-of-the-art Named Entity Recognizer (NER) techniques [23] and rule-based heuristics. We consider the meta-information such as the number of skills mentioned, job length, educational degree, job location, telecommuting, and employment type. We perform normalization of these features to maintain the general distribution of the data. After extracting these features, we obtain a fused representation m^i such that $m^i = [m^i_1, m^i_2, m^i_3, m^i_4, \ldots, m^i_k]$ where k is the number of meta-features extracted from job posting $\mathcal{J}_i$.

Finally, we concatenate together the factual, contextual, and meta representations to form $\mathcal{F}$ and pass them through the fully connected neural network layers.

$$\mathcal{F} = \{f^i \oplus c^i \oplus m^i\} \tag{5}$$

We use the Rectified Linear Units [26] as the non-linearity for faster training and drop out layers to avoid overfitting. We apply the sigmoid ($\sigma(.)$) layer and binary cross-entropy loss to classify the job postings into the legitimate and fraudulent. We use *ADAM* as an optimizer [2] to handle sparse gradients.

5   Experimental Setup

In this section, we describe the dataset, experimental settings, and approaches that are used for comparison.

5.1   Dataset Description

Proprietary Dataset. We use the real-world job posting dataset from one of the largest online recruitment platforms in India. We curated a balanced dataset by sampling 70K Legitimate and 70K Fraudulent job postings from the legacy database annotated by domain-experts. We obtain 4 million triples from these job postings using OpenIE5 [24]. OpenIE results in noisy triples, therefore we improve the quality of these triples using Named Entity Recognizer (NER) to extract the important entities such as companies, institutes, skills, locations, qualifications, and designations to construct knowledge graph.

Public Dataset. The dataset of Employment Scam Aegean Dataset (EMSCAD)[5] contains 17,014 legitimate and 866 fraudulent jobs. For all experiments, we apply class balancing techniques by penalizing the class (legitimate) having more samples [39]. Table 2 reports the statistics of our dataset.

5.2 Experimental Settings

We use OpenKE [12] toolkit implementation to obtain knowledge graph representations. Given a set of triples (s, p, o) where entity pairs are (s, o) and p is the relation between them. We use these knowledge representations to map each entity to a v-dimensional vector and relation to a w-dimensional vector in the embedding space where v and w are hyperparameters. We use the best hyperparameter settings to train all fact checking algorithms such as *TransH*, *TransE*, *TransR*, *TransD*, *DistMult*, *ComplEx*, *HolE* [5,28,38,41]. To train FRJD, we use stratified sampling to split the train/test datasets into 70:30 and learning rate as 0.001.

Table 2. Statistics of fraudulent and legitimate jobs on proprietary dataset.

Statistic	Count
# of fraudulent jobs	70K
# of legitimate jobs	70K
Avg. words per fraudulent job	70
Avg. words per legitimate job	231
Avg. skills per legitimate job	12
Avg. skills per fraudulent job	9
# of entities	37.5K
# of relations	4.5K
# of triples	4M

Table 3. Results of triple classification task on proprietary dataset.

Model	MRR Raw	MRR Filter	Hits @ 1	Hits @ 3	Hits @ 10
TransH	**0.52**	**0.69**	**0.63**	**0.73**	**0.82**
TransD	0.50	0.67	0.62	0.69	0.80
TransR	0.20	0.60	0.55	0.64	0.73
TransE	0.51	0.60	0.56	0.62	0.68
HolE	0.22	0.48	0.34	0.49	0.71
ComplEx	0.29	0.34	0.25	0.35	0.52
DisMult	0.30	0.40	0.30	0.40	0.50
RotatE	0.28	0.41	0.39	0.40	0.43

5.3 Competing Methods

We compare our method against several baselines for classification of fraudulent job postings.

- **Random Forest Classifier.** The approach [39] consists of ruleset-based binary classifier which consists of three categories: linguistic, contextual, and

---

5 http://emscad.samos.aegean.gr/.

metadata. We report the results of model trained on the empirical ruleset against the complete imbalanced dataset of 17,880 job postings in public dataset (reported in published work). On other dataset, we use the same rulesets to report the results.

- **Logistic Regression.** Logistic regression is a statistical model that is popular for classification as well as regression tasks. We model the textual features using count-vectorizer and perform classification using LR.
- **Support Vector Machines.** SVM is a supervised machine-learning algorithm that is widely used for binary classification tasks. We use a spacy tokenizer to clean the text and utilize the textual features present in job postings to train SVM.

6 Evaluation Results

In this section, we evaluate and provide insights on various fact checking algorithms on our datasets. Table 3 reports the results on triple classification task using OpenKE [12]. We report the raw and filtered *MRR* (*Mean Reciprocal Rank*) and Hits@ (1, 3, 10) for all the models. Hits metrics are filtered (removal of the triples from test list which appeared while evaluation in the dataset). *TransH* and *TransD* achieve significant performances on these metrics, i.e., filtered *MRR* (0.69 and 0.67) and on hits@10 (0.82 and 0.80). Table 3 shows that *TransH* [41] outperforms *TransE* [5] on our dataset. According to [41] it better utilizes the one-to-many and many-to-many properties of the relation. Similarly, other algorithms such as *RotatE* are unable to perform well due to large number of many-to-many relations in our knowledge graph. We utilize *TransH* as fact checking algorithm in our fact-checking module in FRJD. We report the Precision (P), Recall (R) and F1-score (F1) of FRJD on proprietary and public datasets in Table 4. Our results show the efficacy of FRJD approach as compared to baseline methods. Therefore, it is noted that fact-checking contributes in our framework and help in identification of facts missed by content-based approaches. Our contextual module using S-BERT shows 0.88 shows transformer models better capture the context in comparison to traditional approaches such as SVM and random forests which fail to perform well for fraudulent class. We further, demonstrate that incorporating the contextual, factual, and meta features together provide an average performance of 0.96.

7 Ablation Study

In this section, we study the effect of each component in detail. Table 4 shows the performance of all of the components of our proposed framework, FRJD. We use contextual features (M1), factual (M2), metadata features (M3) separately as sub-models 'M1', 'M2', and 'M3' in Table 4. The ablation study reveals that component M1 captures context with a precision of 0.88 for fraudulent job postings. Furthermore, the component M2 gives a Precision of 0.84 for fraudulent job postings but yields Precision of 0.65 for legitimate job postings. The possible

Table 4. Performance of different models on proprietary and public datasets where M1, M2, M3 are contextual, factual, and meta features.

Dataset	Approaches	Metrics					
		Fraudulent			Legitimate		
		P	R	F1	P	R	F1
Proprietary dataset	LR	0.71	0.64	0.67	0.94	0.31	0.74
	SVM	0.95	0.53	0.68	0.83	0.15	0.25
	RF	0.84	0.75	0.79	0.96	0.48	0.64
	FRJD (M1)	0.88	0.52	0.65	0.92	0.25	0.39
	FRJD (M2)	0.84	0.82	0.83	0.65	0.49	0.55
	FRJD (M3)	0.49	0.79	0.61	0.21	0.32	0.25
	FRJD (M1+M2+M3)	0.98	0.99	0.98	0.97	0.96	0.96
Public dataset	LR	0.90	0.90	0.90	0.86	0.60	0.70
	SVM	0.57	0.83	0.67	0.98	0.97	0.97
	RF	0.28	0.75	0.41	0.98	0.90	0.94
	FRJD (M1)	0.60	0.80	0.69	0.40	0.20	0.27
	FRJD (M2)	0.94	0.90	0.92	0.90	0.73	0.80
	FRJD (M3)	0.91	0.61	0.73	0.81	0.22	0.34
	FRJD (M1+M2+M3)	**0.98**	**0.98**	**0.98**	**0.98**	**0.98**	**0.98**

reason could be the similar facts present in both the knowledge graphs. Finally, we test the M3 component, which reveals that the meta-features such as number of skills, qualifications, job length are rudimentary. Additionally, we also verified the significant reasons to mark these job postings as fraudulent include seek money, use of legitimate employer names, advertise paid training-based courses, share multiple accounts for promotion, etc. We identified some facts where the model fails to distinguish between true and false facts. These facts are demanding visa fees, that were common to both legitimate and fraudulent job postings for some job titles.

8   Conclusion and Future Work

We proposed a multi-tier novel end-to-end framework called FRaudulent Jobs Detection (FRJD), which jointly considers a) fact validation module using knowledge graphs, b) contextual module using deep neural networks c) meta-data inclusion to capture the semantics of job postings. We conducted our study on a fact validation dataset containing 4 million facts extracted from job postings. We compared and performed an extensive evaluation of 157,880 job postings. Finally, we provided various insights on fact-checking algorithms for our dataset. We believe that our framework is generalizable to other datasets in the recruitment domain. We intend to study the time complexity of FRJD and compare it with other approaches. In future, we plan to apply and test our approach for hierarchy-based [3], neural network-based [27], and path-based [36] fact-checking algorithms. We wish to compare different algorithms for learning heterogeneous documents such as CVs to build an integrated framework and explore user features in future studies.

Acknowledgements. We would like to acknowledge the support from SERB, InfoEdge India Limited, and FICCI. We are grateful to PreCog Research Group and Dr. Siddartha Asthana for critically reviewing the manuscript and stimulating discussions.

References

1. Alghamdi, B., Alharby, F.: An intelligent model for online recruitment fraud detection. J. Inf. Secur. **10**(3), 155–176 (2019)
2. Bello, I., Zoph, B., Vasudevan, V., Le, Q.V.: Neural optimizer search with reinforcement learning. arXiv preprint arXiv:1709.07417 (2017)
3. Bianchi, F., Rossiello, G., Costabello, L., Palmonari, M., Minervini, P.: Knowledge graph embeddings and explainable AI. arXiv preprint arXiv:2004.14843 (2020)
4. Bollacker, K., Evans, C., Paritosh, P., Sturge, T., Taylor, J.: Freebase: a collaboratively created graph database for structuring human knowledge. In: Proceedings of the 2008 ACM SIGMOD International Conference on Management of Data. ACM (2008)
5. Bordes, A., Usunier, N., Garcia-Duran, A., Weston, J., Yakhnenko, O.: Translating embeddings for modeling multi-relational data. In: Advances in Neural Information Processing Systems, pp. 2787–2795 (2013)
6. Bourgonje, P., Schneider, J.M., Rehm, G.: From clickbait to fake news detection: an approach based on detecting the stance of headlines to articles. In: Proceedings of the 2017 EMNLP Workshop: Natural Language Processing meets Journalism, pp. 84–89 (2017)
7. Chen, L.C., Hsu, C.L., Lo, N.W., Yeh, K.H., Lin, P.H.: Fraud analysis and detection for real-time messaging communications on social networks. IEICE Trans. Inf. Syst. **100**(10), 2267–2274 (2017)
8. Cruz, J.C.B., Tan, J.A., Cheng, C.: Localization of fake news detection via multitask transfer learning. arXiv preprint arXiv:1910.09295 (2019)
9. Gai, K., Qiu, M.: Reinforcement learning-based content-centric services in mobile sensing. IEEE Netw. **32**(4), 34–39 (2018)
10. Gai, K., Qiu, M., Zhao, H., Sun, X.: Resource management in sustainable cyber-physical systems using heterogeneous cloud computing. IEEE Trans. Sustainable Comput. **3**(2), 60–72 (2017)
11. Goyal, N., Sachdeva, N., Choudhary, V., Kar, R., Kumaraguru, P., Rajput, N.: Con2kg-a large-scale domain-specific knowledge graph. In: Proceedings of the 30th ACM Conference on Hypertext and Social Media, pp. 287–288. HT 2019, ACM, New York (2019)
12. Han, X., et al.: Openke: an open toolkit for knowledge embedding. In: Proceedings of the 2018 Conference on Empirical Methods in Natural Language Processing: System Demonstrations, pp. 139–144 (2018)
13. Huang, G.K.W., Lee, J.C.: Hyperpartisan news and articles detection using Bert and Elmo. In: 2019 International Conference on Computer and Drone Applications (IConDA), pp. 29–32. IEEE (2019)

14. Ji, G., He, S., Xu, L., Liu, K., Zhao, J.: Knowledge graph embedding via dynamic mapping matrix. In: Proceedings of the 53rd Annual Meeting of the Association for Computational Linguistics and the 7th International Joint Conference on Natural Language Processing, vol. 1, Long Papers, pp. 687–696 (2015)

15. Khandelwal, S., Kumar, D.: Computational fact validation from knowledge graph using structured and unstructured information. In: Proceedings of the 7th ACM IKDD CoDS and 25th COMAD, pp. 204–208. CoDS COMAD 2020. ACM, New York (2020)

16. Kim, J., Kim, H.-J., Kim, H.: Fraud detection for job placement using hierarchical clusters-based deep neural networks. Appl. Intell. **49**(8), 2842–2861 (2019). https://doi.org/10.1007/s10489-019-01419-2

17. Kim, J., Tabibian, B., Oh, A., Schölkopf, B., Gomez-Rodriguez, M.: Leveraging the crowd to detect and reduce the spread of fake news and misinformation. In: Proceedings of the Eleventh ACM International Conference on Web Search and Data Mining, pp. 324–332 (2018)

18. Lehmann, J., et al.: DBpedia-a large-scale, multilingual knowledge base extracted from wikipedia. Semantic Web (2015)

19. Lin, Y., Liu, Z., Sun, M., Liu, Y., Zhu, X.: Learning entity and relation embeddings for knowledge graph completion. In: Twenty-Ninth AAAI Conference on Artificial Intelligence (2015)

20. Lu, Y.J., Li, C.T.: GCAN: Graph-aware co-attention networks for explainable fake news detection on social media. arXiv preprint arXiv:2004.11648 (2020)

21. Ma, J., et al.: Detecting rumors from microblogs with recurrent neural networks. In: Proceedings of the Twenty-Fifth International Joint Conference on Artificial Intelligence, pp. 3818–3824, IJCAI 2016. AAAI Press (2016)

22. Mahbub, S., Pardede, E.: Using contextual features for online recruitment fraud detection. In: International Conference on Information Systems Development, August 2018

23. Manning, C.D., Surdeanu, M., Bauer, J., Finkel, J.R., Bethard, S., McClosky, D.: The Stanford CoreNLP natural language processing toolkit. In: Proceedings of 52nd Annual Meeting of the Association for Computational Linguistics: System Demonstrations, pp. 55–60 (2014)

24. Mausam, M.: Open information extraction systems and downstream applications. In: Proceedings of the Twenty-Fifth International Joint Conference on Artificial Intelligence, pp. 4074–4077 (2016)

25. Mozafari, J., Fatemi, A., Moradi, P.: A method for answer selection using DistilBERT and important words. In: 2020 6th International Conference on Web Research (ICWR), pp. 72–76. IEEE (2020)

26. Nair, V., Hinton, G.E.: Rectified linear units improve restricted Boltzmann machines. In: ICML (2010)

27. Nguyen, D.Q., Nguyen, D.Q., Nguyen, T.D., Phung, D.: A convolutional neural network-based model for knowledge base completion and its application to search personalization. Semantic Web **10**(5), 947–960 (2019)

28. Nickel, M., Rosasco, L., Poggio, T.A., et al.: Holographic embeddings of knowledge graphs. In: AAAI (2016)

29. Nindyati, O., Nugraha, I.G.B.B.: Detecting scam in online job vacancy using behavioral features extraction. In: 2019 International Conference on ICT for Smart Society (ICISS), vol. 7, pp. 1–4. IEEE (2019)

30. Pan, J.Z., Pavlova, S., Li, C., Li, N., Li, Y., Liu, J.: Content based fake news detection using knowledge graphs. In: Vrandečić, D., et al. (eds.) ISWC 2018. LNCS, vol. 11136, pp. 669–683. Springer, Cham (2018). https://doi.org/10.1007/978-3-030-00671-6_39

31. Potthast, M., Kiesel, J., Reinartz, K., Bevendorff, J., Stein, B.: A stylometric inquiry into hyperpartisan and fake news. arXiv preprint arXiv:1702.05638 (2017)

32. Niharika Reddy, M., Mamatha, T., Balaram, A.: Analysis of e-recruitment systems and detecting e-recruitment fraud. In: Kumar, A., Mozar, S. (eds.) ICCCE 2018. LNEE, vol. 500, pp. 411–417. Springer, Singapore (2019). https://doi.org/10.1007/978-981-13-0212-1_43

33. Reimers, N., Gurevych, I.: Sentence-BERT: sentence embeddings using Siamese BERT-networks. In: Proceedings of the 2019 Conference on Empirical Methods in Natural Language Processing and the 9th International Joint Conference on Natural Language Processing (EMNLP-IJCNLP). Association for Computational Linguistics, Hong Kong, November 2019

34. Sanh, V., Debut, L., Chaumond, J., Wolf, T.: Distilbert, a distilled version of bert: smaller, faster, cheaper and lighter. arXiv preprint arXiv:1910.01108 (2019)

35. Shaar, S., Babulkov, N., Da San Martino, G., Nakov, P.: That is a known lie: Detecting previously fact-checked claims. In: Proceedings of the 58th Annual Meeting of the Association for Computational Linguistics, pp. 3607–3618. Association for Computational Linguistics, July 2020

36. Shiralkar, P., Flammini, A., Menczer, F., Ciampaglia, G.L.: Finding streams in knowledge graphs to support fact checking. In: 2017 IEEE International Conference on Data Mining (ICDM), pp. 859–864. IEEE (2017)

37. Thakkar, D., Kumar, N., Sambasivan, N.: Towards an AI-powered future that works for vocational workers. In: Proceedings of the 2020 CHI Conference on Human Factors in Computing Systems, pp. 1–13 (2020)

38. Trouillon, T., Welbl, J., Riedel, S., Gaussier, É., Bouchard, G.: Complex embeddings for simple link prediction. In: International Conference on Machine Learning (2016)

39. Vidros, S., Kolias, C., Kambourakis, G., Akoglu, L.: Automatic detection of online recruitment frauds: characteristics, methods, and a public dataset. Future Internet 9(1), 6 (2017)

40. Vrandečić, D., Krötzsch, M.: Wikidata: a free collaborative knowledgebase. Commun. ACM 57(10), 78–85 (2014)

41. Wang, Z., Zhang, J., Feng, J., Chen, Z.: Knowledge graph embedding by translating on hyperplanes. In: AAAI (2014)

Performance Evaluation of Multi-class Sentiment Classification Using Deep Neural Network Models Optimised for Binary Classification

Fiachra Merwick[1], Yaxin Bi[2($\boxtimes$)], and Peter Nicholl[2]

[1] Trading Department, Power NI, Belfast, Northern Ireland, UK
[2] School of Computing, Faculty of Computing, Engineering and the Built Environment,
Ulster University, Belfast, UK
{y.bi,p.nicholl}@ulster.ac.uk

Abstract. This paper presents a comparative study on the performance of binary- and multi-class Deep Neural Network classification models that have been trained with the optimized hyperparameters. Four sequential models are developed using Tensorflow and Keras to perform sentiment classification of product reviews posted on Amazon, IMDb, Twitter and Yelp. Preprocessing is carried out to cleanse text reviews and to extract informative features. 5-fold cross evaluation results demonstrate that the final multiclass model perform with an accuracy of 74.7% and 72.4%, whereas the binary model achieves of 80.0% and 69.5% indicating better performance. The conclusion of this study is that an optimized binary model architecture can be used to train multiclass classification models and save significant amounts of computing time.

Keywords: Sentiment analysis · Deep neural networks · Word embedding

1 Introduction

Sentiment classification, which aims to predict the attitude of users based on their reviews, has become a major field of research over the past decade due to the rapid increase in information being produced by social networks and user-based review websites [1]. Applications of sentiment analysis include customer feedback, product research and reputation monitoring [2]. Also, it has been noted that "opinionated postings in social media have helped reshape businesses, and sway public sentiments and emotions, which have profoundly impacted on our social and political systems" [3].

Historically, the main approaches to sentiment analysis have been lexicon-based methods, machine learning methods, both supervised and unsupervised and hybrid approaches. More recently, deep learning methods have proven to be highly effective, however they typically require large amounts of data and compute time to train the models [4].

Given the fact that deep learning methods often require such high computing time, the significant aspect of the research carried out in this work aims at evaluating the

H. Qiu et al. (Eds.): KSEM 2021, LNAI 12816, pp. 624–635, 2021.
https://doi.org/10.1007/978-3-030-82147-0_51

performance of a model architecture optimised for binary classification on multiclass data, effectively making the additional optimisation of the multiclass model redundant. The results of the evaluation procedure show that the multiclass models trained using the optimised binary architecture and hyperparameters performed very well in comparison to the binary model accuracy results.

The remainder of this paper is organised in the following manner: Sect. 2 details a non-exhaustive process in which sentiment of online reviews may be classified, Sect. 3 provides a descriptive overview of the data used in this paper, Sect. 4 documents the data pre-processing methods used in this study, Sect. 5 details the model development for both the binary and multiclass classification models, Sect. 6 outlines the model evaluation procedure and presents the results of the models, Sect. 7 discusses the results and summary of the study.

2 Sentiment Classification Process Review

Online reviews typically contain the attitude, opinion, and satisfaction level of customers of products and often are accompanied by a rating system. The reviews typically include adjectives which are a primary feature for learning sentiment. In addition to the valuable information, there are also a lot of unnecessary characters and words used in online reviews and thus, data pre-processing is a requirement to generate a clean dataset that can more readily be learned by a neural network algorithm. Artificial Neural networks require numeric data as inputs; therefore, features from text inputs such as letters, words and word sequences, known as n-grams, must be represented by using a method of encoding.

However, prior to representing the features, they must first be selected. Feature selection is a process of down selecting the most important aspects of the raw data and eliminating noisy features, which is considered to be a feature that is represented in the training set that increases classification error in the test set and subsequent unseen data [5]. Removing common words that add no contextual value to the text is a typical first step for feature selection, as the remainder of the text should have a higher probability of representing the target outcome more appropriately. This also makes it easier for an algorithm to generalise as there is reduced complexity in the input. N-grams are a core feature in this study and both unigram and bigrams were analysed during the model development. Unigram representation for an arbitrary four word sentence would take the form ["I", "own", "a", "dog"], whereas the bigram representation would be ["I own", "own a", "a dog"]. This is especially important in sentiment classification as the unigram representation of ["like"] could be considered positive but if the context, captured with a bigram, is ["don't like"] then the unigram may misclassify the sentiment.

In [6], the author states that "feature learning is the most important first step, with large subsequent impact on the performance of the model". Therefore, improving the initial representation vector so that relationships between words can be learned is an important aspect of natural language processing and can be achieved by using an embedding layer. Word embeddings are trained dense vectors, rather than purely hard-coded vectors, such as the output from one hot encoding, that "map semantically similar words on the embedding space". The embedding layer can either be trained using the input text that is being used to train a neural network, or a pretrained library can be imported and used in the model [7]. The embedding layer will be trained using the input data for the purpose of this study.

Sentiment classification aims at deducing the attitude of a user based on a sentence or document level analysis and is considered a subset of text categorisation. Specifically, sentiment analysis typically tries to deduce the opinion of the author of the text as being either positive, negative or neutral. By contrast, in text categorisation, many more categories can be considered for the labelled target outcome, such as document topic, document language, urgency of author, spam detection etc. [8].

The current main approach to sentiment classification is to: (1) collate text data which can be labelled with a sentiment, (2) clean the data and perform feature selection and representation, (3) generate an appropriate model for training on the data, (4) split the data into training and testing subsets, (5) fit the model to the training set and (6) evaluate the model and improve the performance, where possible. There are myriad ways of representing the text and no definitive best method. Currently, a "trial and error" approach is required to optimise both the text representation and the model architecture to best fit the text being classified.

3   Data Description

Four datasets are used in this study, with a matrix of user reviews and sentiment or star ratings from Amazon, IMDb [9] Twitter [10] and Yelp [11]. The Amazon, IMDb and Twitter datasets already had the target sentiment classified correctly; however, the Yelp reviews used a 5-point star rating which needed to be manipulated to convert it to sentiment.

3.1   Star Rating

The star rating used by Yelp is a 5-star category, with one star generally meaning dissatisfaction and typically a corresponding poor review, and five stars meaning highly satisfied and an accompanying good review. The distribution of star ratings for the dataset used in this study is shown in Fig. 1. The star ratings are skewed towards the higher ratings and this imbalance is addressed prior to the implementation of the model by extracting a balanced set of Positive, Neutral and Negative sentiments.

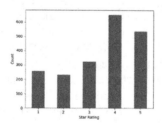

Fig. 1. Frequency of star rating occurrence in the Yelp dataset

3.2 Review Text

The content of the reviews is as per typical online reviews and contains numerous characteristics that are not required for analysis. These include stop words, capitalisation, punctuation, numbers, and symbols etc. After pre-processing the data, which is described in Sect. 4, the words were visualised using the WordCloud library, as shown in Fig. 2. This image is useful for deducing that there is an imbalance towards positive words, given that the words "good" and "great" are the most prominent adjectives, which correlates with the imbalance in star ratings, strengthening the argument for attempting to remove any class imbalance.

Fig. 2. WordCloud of processed text

4 Data Preprocessing

The main aspects of data pre-processing for this task are: (1) convert the star rating to appropriate sentiment categories for the Yelp dataset, (2) reduce the review text data to alphabetic words with high probability of commonality, (3) perform feature extraction and (4) split the dataset appropriately for training and testing.

4.1 Conversion of Star Rating Multiclass Labels

It was necessary to create a column of labelled target sentiment, based on the star ratings provided in the raw data, which could then be encoded by the model as the target value. The criteria for converting the star ratings are shown in Table 1 and aims at minimising the class imbalance, based on the dispersion of ratings, shown in Fig. 1.

Table 1. Criteria for sentiment classification from star rating

Classification model	Sentiment		
	Positive	Negative	Neutral
Multiclass classification	>3	<3	3

The outcome of this conversion is shown in Fig. 3, where the imbalance for the multiclass model is heavily skewed towards positive ratings. To combat this, down sampling of the larger subsets was performed to produce an equal subset of each sentiment.

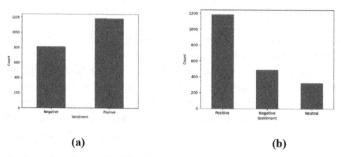

(a)   **(b)**

Fig. 3. Distribution of sentiment classification for the (a) Binary Classification Model and the (b) Multiclass Classification Model

4.2 Data Cleansing

Data cleansing is imperative to ensure the inputs to the model do not contain irrelevant pieces of information, and to try and introduce consistency in the content of the reviews, where often there are slight differences in words that have the same meaning. The process of the data cleansing is relatively straightforward and consisted of 6 main steps: (1) converting all capital letters to lowercase, (2) tokenising the text in each row so that each distinct bit of string may be analysed, (3) removing any token that is not alphabetic, (4) removing stop words, (5) lemmatizing all words that can be converted to their lemma and (6) stemming any remaining words that can be reduced. This results in a clean set of alphabetic words, with an increase in commonality across reviews due to the lemmatizing and stemming process which should boost the performance of the model.

Text vectorization is the "initial step towards making the text documents machine-readable" [12] and using the Tensorflow Keras TextVectorization function the text is vectorized for two main purposes: (1) to encode each reviews set of strings as a vector of numbers and (2) to determine the sequence length of strings to be encoded as a single number. The total number of unique strings in the review text was calculated and entered as the vocabulary size parameter in the TextVectorization function, as opposed to choosing an arbitrary number which may inflate the model. Representation of n-grams can also be captured using this function. In the case of this study, the n-gram parameter was analysed for both unigram and bigram feature representations which are extracted and encoded as inputs to the model. The output mode was chosen as integer as the remaining options were too computationally expensive and would have required more than 10% of the systems available memory.

An additional component of feature extraction used in this model, which is not technically a pre-processing step, is the use of the embedding layer. This layer allows the model to learn relationships between words and is a key component in this study to achieve good results in generalising on positive and negative sentiment. This layer is discussed further in Sect. 5.

5   Model Development

The neural network is developed within the Python environment using the Tensorflow Keras sequential model. The model development consisted of multiple steps, including: (1) determining initial model architecture with appropriate activation functions, (2) compiling the model with appropriate loss functions and evaluation metrics, and (3) fitting the model and recording the result of each epoch for subsequent evaluation. The detail of the binary classification model described below, is applicable to the multiclass classification model also, except for a few minor changes.

5.1   Model Architecture

The graphs in Fig. 4 show the model architecture for both the binary and multiclass classification models, after testing and evaluation was carried out, as per the methods described in Sect. 6. The embedding layer consisted of an input dimension equal to the vocabulary size, the sequence length which is equal to the length of the input vector and the output dimension which was set at 20. A flattening layer is then used to transform the embedding space into an input vector for the dense layer. The dense hidden layer used the ReLU activation function as it is considered a good activation function to try initially [13] and the dense output layer, used the sigmoid activation function, which is an effective choice for binary classification problems [14]. As the initial model very quickly fitted the training data, it was deemed appropriate not to increase the embedding layer output dimension or the number of neurons in the dense layer. This also applied to the activation functions used as they were clearly appropriate for the task. Dropout layers were introduced and L_2 regularization introduced to the hidden layer to reduce the rate at which the model fit the training data and for better performance on the test data.

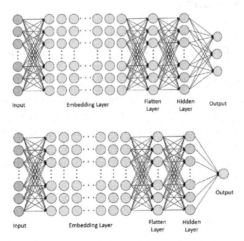

Fig. 4. Graph representation of the multiclass model and binary model architecture

Hyperparameters Considered

As there are both categorical and continuous hyperparameters that can be set for the model, an infinite number of variables could theoretically be considered. Therefore, in the interest of time, a test matrix of hyperparameters considered to be most relevant was created and is shown in Table 2 in Sect. 6. The methodology employed is described in that section also.

Optimiser and Loss Function Selection

The optimizer chosen for this model was Adam, as it combines the advantages of the adaptive gradient algorithm (AdaGrad) and root mean square propagation (RMSProp), and it employs an adaptive learning rate and performs well on problems with sparse gradients and noisy problems [15]. The loss function used for this model was binary cross entropy as the output of the model is a single binary result and this has been the primary loss function used in this scenario for decades [16]. As the initial model quickly fitted the training data, the optimizer and loss function were deemed appropriate, and no further change was made to them.

Model Regularization

The initial model was overfitting on the training data, which was evident from the graph of test loss vs training loss per epoch. Based on [17], L_2 regularization was deemed appropriate for introducing weight decay into the model in this study and was applied to the dense layer.

Additionally, two dropout layers were added to the model, which effectively remove inputs to the dense hidden layer and dense output layer at a constant rate. This is a proven technique for enhancing the effectiveness of artificial neural networks as it reduces overfitting [18].

6   Testing and Evaluation

Once the initial binary models were developed and running successfully, two hyperparameters were tested with the aim of improving the model performance: Batch size and Epochs.

The tested parameters and methods of evaluation are detailed below, as well as the results of the evaluation process. Note that the models were initialised with a seeded value and the train test split was also provided with a random state variable, to ensure that the same initial weights were assigned to the neural network and the same training data and testing data was being analysed, otherwise the testing process would not be consistent. The multiclass models were then trained using the optimised binary model architectures for performance evaluation.

6.1   Hyperparamaters Assessed

Rather than completing a full suite of testing of the test variables, which would involve running the model >1000 times, a trial-and-error based approach was adopted for the majority of the variables and as improvements to the binary model were observed, those variables were maintained, and the next variable was evaluated. The variables and their corresponding values that were tested out are provided in Table 2, with the chosen variables used in all models highlighted in grey. A complete test matrix of epoch and batch size was completed, and results are provided in Sect. 6.3

Table 2. Hyperparameters considered for model improvement

Variable name	Value considered		
	Trial variable 1	Trial variable 2	Trial variable 3
Ngram	1	**2**	
Regularisation	0.01	**0.001**	
Dropout (embedding layer)	0.30	0.50	**0.80**
Dropout (dense layer)	0.30	0.50	**0.80**
Learning rate	0.01	**0.001**	0.0001

6.2 Evaluation Methods

The methods for evaluating the models included a visual comparison of historical plots of model loss and model accuracy, final model accuracy and visual evaluation of a Confusion Matrix. After these metrics were analysed, 5-fold cross validation was performed on the models that produced the best results to ensure the initial train and test split was not influencing the result to a major degree.

6.3 Testing Results

Binary Classification Model
The accuracy results for each epoch & batch size of the binary models are presented in Table 3 and Table 4.

Table 3. Results of epoch and batch variable testing on model accuracy – Amazon dataset

Number of epochs	Batch size		
	1%	2%	3%
50	76.8%	76.4%	76.8%
100	78.0%	80.0%	81.6%
200	79.6%	80.4%	80.4%
400	78.0%	79.2%	79.6%
800	77.2%	78.8%	78.4%

Table 4. Results of epoch and batch variable testing on model accuracy – IMDb dataset

Number of epochs	Batch size		
	1%	2%	3%
50	65.8%	66.8%	46.0%
100	69.0%	67.4%	62.0%
200	46.0%	71.7%	65.8%
400	70.6%	69.5%	72.7%
800	67.4%	73.3%	72.2%

Based on these initial results, a batch size of 2–3% of dataset size and > 100 epochs result in the best performing models, however the difference between the results is small. Therefore, further investigation was performed on these variables. Initially, the model loss and model accuracy at each epoch was plotted to visually evaluate the performance of each model and the confusion matrix was plotted to provide more context. It was clear that in both cases, training the model beyond 100 epochs resulted in severe overfitting of the model and it was prudent to set that level as a cutoff. The plots are presented in Figs. 5 and 6.

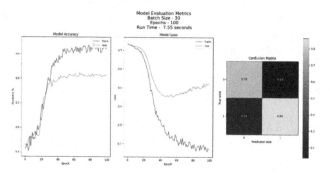

Fig. 5. Model accuracy, loss and the confusion matrix for the Amazon binary dataset

Subsequently, k-fold cross validation which split the data into 5 folders, was used to evaluate these two models. The mean accuracy is presented in Table 5. It is clear from the IMDb value that the initial accuracy of 62% from Table 4 was low due to the initial split; thus, this strengthens the argument for the 3% batch and 100 epoch hyperparameters.

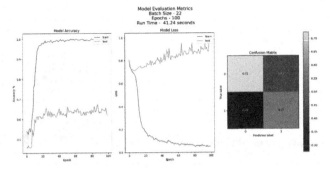

Fig. 6. Model accuracy, loss and the confusion matrix for the IMDb binary dataset

Table 5. Mean accuracy from 5-fold cross validation of binary models

Dataset	Mean accuracy
Amazon	80.0%
IMDb	69.5%

Multiclass Classification Model

The model architecture and optimized hyperparameters were used to train the two multi-class classification models, with the loss, accuracy and confusion matrix results presented in Figs. 7 and 8.

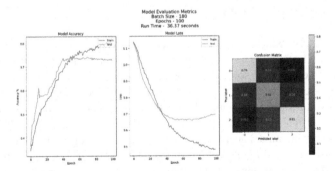

Fig. 7. Model accuracy, loss and the confusion matrix for the Twitter multiclass dataset

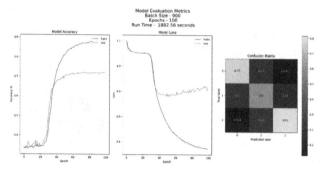

Fig. 8. Model accuracy, loss and the confusion matrix for the Yelp multiclass dataset

Subsequently, 5-fold cross validation was used to evaluate these two datasets. The mean accuracy is presented in Table 6.

Table 6. Mean accuracy from 5-fold cross validation of multiclass models

Dataset	Mean accuracy
Twitter	74.7%
Yelp	72.4%

7 Discussion and Summary

The Amazon dataset binary model generalised quite well on the test data, given accuracies of up to 81.6% were recorded on the initial validation stage. Interrogating the confusion matrices showed some discrepancy in the sentiment classification, with an 86% true positive classification versus a 78% true negative classification for the final model chosen. Interrogating the model loss in Fig. 5, it appears that the 100-epoch model has begun to overfit slightly on the training set as the curve for the test set has begun to increase, however the model accuracy improves over the 50-epoch model.

The IMDb dataset did not perform well in comparison to the Amazon dataset, with much higher discrepancies in the confusion matrix, and a much lower mean accuracy. The poor performance may be attributable to the nature of the reviews in conjunction with the small dataset size (1000 rows).

The multiclass models both performed very well based on the binary models optimised hyperparameters and it appears from Figs. 7 and 8 that the models were just at the point of beginning to overfit. This would naturally have been a cut-off point during a model optimisation sequence, thus validating the binary model hyperparameters as a suitable alternative to going through that process.

In this paper we investigated the suitability of optimised binary classification model architecture for training multiclass classification models. The results of this study clearly indicate that the model architecture of a binary classification model is sufficiently transferable to a multiclass classification model, without further optimisation being performed. This has the main benefit of saving time in the hyperparameter tuning process of large multiclass classification models.

References

1. Wangz, C.-J., Tsaiy, M.-F., Liuy, T., Changzy, C.-T.: Financial sentiment analysis for risk prediction. In: International Joint Conference on National Language Process, pp. 802–808, 14–18 October (2013)
2. Liu, S.: Sentiment analysis of Yelp reviews: a comparison of techniques and models. arXiv: 2004.13851v1
3. Lei Zhang, L., Wang, S., Liu, B.: Deep learning for sentiment analysis: a survey. WIREs Data Min. Knowl. Discov. **8**, e1253 (2018)
4. Iglesias, C.A., Sánchez-Rada, J.F.: Social context in sentiment analysis: formal definition, overview of current trends and framework for comparison. Inf. Fusion **52**, 344–356 (2019)
5. Stanford: Feature selection. https://nlp.stanford.edu/IR-book/html/htmledition/feature-select ion-1.html. Accessed Feb 2021
6. Vu, T.: Feature representation in mining and language processing (2017)
7. Janakiev, N.: Practical text classification with Python and Keras, Real Python. https://realpy thon.com/python-keras-text-classification/. Accessed Feb 2021
8. Monkey Learn: Text classification, Monkey Learn. https://monkeylearn.com/text-classific ation/. Accessed Feb 2021
9. Kotzias, D., Smyth, P., Denil, M., de Freitas, N..: From group to individual labels using deep features. In: Proceedings of the 21th ACM SIGKDD International Conference on Knowledge Discovery and Data Mining (KDD 2015), New York (2015)
10. Kaggle: Twitter US airline sentiment | Kaggle. https://www.kaggle.com/crowdflower/twitter-airline-sentiment. Accessed Apr 2021
11. Yelp: Download Yelp Dataset. https://www.yelp.com/dataset/download. Accessed Feb 2021
12. Shashi, M., Kumari Singh, A.: Vectorization of text documents for identifying unifiable news articles. Int. J. Adv. Comput. Sci. Appl. **10**(7), 305–310 (2019)
13. Brownlee, J.: A gentle introduction to the rectified linear unit (ReLU), Machine Learning Mastery. https://machinelearningmastery.com/rectified-linear-activation-function-for-deep-learning-neural-networks/. Accessed Feb 2021
14. Pratiwi, H., et al.: Sigmoid activation function in selecting the best model of artificial neural networks, J. Phys. Conf. Ser. **1471**(1), 2020
15. Brownlee, J.: Machine learning mastery | gentle introduction to the Adam optimization algorithm for deep learning. https://machinelearningmastery.com/adam-optimization-algorithm-for-deep-learning. Accessed Feb 2021
16. Richard, M.D., Lippmann, R.P.: Neural network classifiers estimate Bayesian a posteriori probabilities. Neural Comput. **3**(4), 461–483 (1991)
17. Brownlee, J.: How to use weight decay to reduce overfitting of neural network in Keras. Machine Learning Mastery (2018). https://machinelearningmastery.com/how-to-reduce-ove rfitting-in-deep-learning-with-weight-regularization/. Accessed Feb 2021
18. Srivastava, N., Hinton, G., Krizhevsky, A., Sutskever, I., Salakhutdinov, R.: Dropout: a simple way to prevent neural networks from overfitting. J. Mach. Learn. Res. **15**(1), 1929–1958 (2014)

Discovering Stable Ride-Sharing Groups for Commuting Private Car Using Spatio-Temporal Semantic Similarity

Yuhui Ye, Linjiang Zheng$^{(\boxtimes)}$, Yiling Chen, and Longquan Liao

Chongqing University, Chongqing 400044, China
`zlj_cqu@cqu.edu.cn`

Abstract. The commuting behavior of private cars is the main cause of traffic congestion in the morning and evening rush hours. The discovery of stable ride-sharing groups for commuting private car is a necessary work to solve the morning and evening peak traffic congestion, and the discovery of ride-sharing groups is to match similar travelers. But different from the traditional ride sharing service based on passenger request, commuting private car users expect a long-term stable ride sharing service. This paper proposed a commuting private car ride-sharing groups discovery model based on spatio-temporal semantic similarity. The model considers the similarity of commuting time and space, and adds the user feature of commuting workplace's semantics to provide stable sharing matching for commuters of similar occupations, and adds the semantic of commuting place to provide stable ride-sharing matching for commuters with similar occupations. Commuting workplace's semantics refers to the functional area type of commuting workplace, which can reflect the nature of commuters' work. The main research content includes two parts: functional area identification and ride-sharing groups' discovery. In the process of functional area recognition, based on POI and road network data, multi classification support vector machine is used to identify urban functional areas. In the process of ride-sharing groups' discovery, based on the travel data of commuter private cars, DBSCAN clustering algorithm with spatio-temporal semantic distance measurement is used to complete ride-sharing group discovery.

Keywords: Electronic registration identification · Ride-sharing group discovery · Urban functional area identification

1 Introduction

In recent years, with the rapid progress of social urbanization, the size of urban population and the number of urban motor vehicles are growing rapidly. Private cars have become one of the main modes of transportation for urban residents [1], and urban road construction cannot maintain the same growth rate. Therefore, the popularity of private cars leads to the deterioration of urban traffic environment to a certain extent, increases the difficulty of traffic management, and brings problems such as traffic congestion,

© Springer Nature Switzerland AG 2021
H. Qiu et al. (Eds.): KSEM 2021, LNAI 12816, pp. 636–646, 2021.
https://doi.org/10.1007/978-3-030-82147-0_52

exhaust pollution, parking difficulty, non renewable energy consumption, and long rush hour journey to and from work [2, 3]. It is necessary to find the experience of commuting private car ride-sharing group to solve the morning and evening peak traffic congestion.

In the past, the research on carpooling mainly comes from taxi data and public transport data, while private car data is rarely involved at home and abroad because of its high difficulty in obtaining privacy. Electronic registration identification of the motor vehicle (ERI) is a new technology that uses radio frequency identification (RFID) signal to collect information of motor vehicles [4], which provides a new driving force for the research of commuting private car sharing.

Based on ERI data of commuting private cars, this paper studies the commuting private car ride-sharing group. Carpooling group discovery is to match similar travelers. Although this process has been applied in carpooling based on taxi data and public transport data, there are still some challenges to be overcome when it is applied to commuting private car groups, as follows:

1) Research shows that only a small number of commuting residents choose to use sharing software such as Uberpool and DiDi carpool in the morning and evening rush hours [5]. The fundamental reason is that commuting private car users expect a long-term and stable sharing service. On the premise of ensuring that the travel time and space are similar, if the characteristics of each user can be considered, such as the gender, age and occupation of the user, the possibility of stable ride sharing of commuter private cars can be improved.

2) The existing model of ride-sharing group discovery mainly comes from taxi data and public transport data, which is based on passenger request and then matches the single trip. For example, Santi Paolo et al. [6] Proposed a method framework of taxi ride sharing, which takes the increased travel time after ride sharing as the evaluation index of passengers' discomfort. Wen et al. [7] extracted the conventional path from the historical trajectory data of residents, and proposed a co ride recommendation scheme for residents with similar conventional paths. Hong et al. [8] designed a shared travel matching method for commuter private cars based on trajectory clustering using the traffic data obtained by Chicago Urban Planning Bureau, but the amount of data is small, and 80% of them are simulated by using user balance rules. The commuter private car needs to first extract the features of all its commute trips, mine the commuter representative trips, and then discover the ride-sharing group according to the commuter representative trips.

In order to solve these problems, this paper first proposed a ride-sharing group discovery model based on spatio-temporal semantic similarity clustering of commuting private car trips. The specific contributions are as follows:

1) The model aims at the shortcomings of existing ride-sharing passengers who find that they do not consider the characteristics of ride-sharing passengers. The paper obtains the user feature of commuter travel work place semantics by using the urban functional area identification model based on multi classification support vector machine. The working place semantics refers to the functional area type of commuter travel work place, which can reflect the commuter's occupation to a certain extent.

2) The model aims at the characteristics of common group discovery of commuter private cars different from that of common passenger group discovery based on passenger request. Firstly, the travel representative travel is extracted, then the travel representative travel is taken as input, and the spatial and temporal semantic distance measurement function is defined, and the model of common passenger group discovery is realized.

3) Evaluation. The method is verified by using ERI data of Chongqing for one week. The experimental results show that the semantic distance added to the model is reasonable.

The second section introduces the functional area identification model. The third section introduces the ride-sharing group discovery model. The fourth section gives the relevant experimental results and analysis. Finally, the conclusion is drawn in fifth section.

2 Functional Area Recognition Model

2.1 Problem Description

In order to identify the urban functional areas, the first step is to select the research area, establish the corresponding traffic grid, complete the statistics of POI data and map the road network data to the grid; Then the traffic area is divided and the POI data of traffic area is counted; The recognition model of urban functional areas is designed and the recognition results is obtained (Fig. 1).

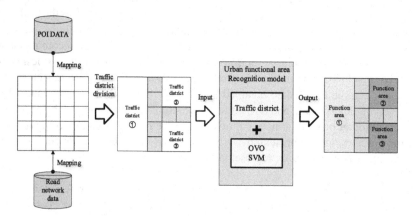

Fig. 1. Framework of urban functional area identification

2.2 Traffic District Division

Using Baidu map API road network data, the road network data in the rectangular research area of Chongqing inner ring is mapped to the corresponding grid and marked as road network grid. Then all grids are traversed and the area surrounded by road network grid and rectangular boundary is recorded as traffic area.

The longitude and latitude of the rectangular study area are about 106.327–106.727° east longitude and 29.36–29.76° north latitude. In order to eliminate most of the main road network in the main urban area and obtain the traffic district, the length and width of the grid is set as 20 * 20 to make it close to the width of the main road, and Chongqing is divided into 2000 * 2000 grids.

After obtaining the traffic grid mapped with road network data, the traffic area can be divided by traversing the traffic grid satisfying *status* = 0 with depth first search DFS.

2.3 Discovery of Urban Functional Areas

Urban functional area identification refers to the identification of social functional attributes of urban units through certain model methods. Common social functional attributes include housing, industry, commerce, education, culture, medical treatment and transportation [9]. Internet based POI data has the advantages of wide access, low difficulty and fast update iteration. The original POI has 16 categories and 181 subcategories, which are reclassified, and the POI categories *{P1, P2, P3, P4, P5, P6, P7}* that we want to make statistics are selected, corresponding to business, office, transportation facilities, medical services, education and training, tourist attractions and residential. We select six categories *{func1, func2, func3, func4, func5, func6}* from all the functional areas in the urban and rural planning map to use as classification labels. The six categories are residential, commercial office, education, medical, transportation and tourism.

In the final divided traffic districts, 170 suitable traffic districts are selected as samples. The statistical quantity of various types of POI in the districts is the characteristics of each sample, and the corresponding categories of the districts in the urban and rural planning land are used as the label of supervised learning.

Then data preprocessing is carried out. Because the area of each traffic area is different, first we divide the statistical quantity of various types of POI in each area by the area of traffic area, and then we process the data dimensionless. Because the statistical quantity of all kinds of POI basically conforms to the normal distribution, and the amount of data is large, we use Z-score standardization to dimensionless process the sample characteristics. Finally, we randomly divide the sample data into training set and test set with the ratio of 3:1.

3 Ride-Sharing Group Discovery Model

3.1 Problem Description

This section puts forward the definitions of commuting itinerary and commuting representative itinerary, and then formally describes the problem of commuting private car sharing group discovery.

Definition 1 Peak hour trip (*PT*): given the trip OD_i^e of motor vehicle electronic identification, where e is the commuting private car, and the departure time and arrival time of od are within the range of morning and evening peak, we define the morning peak period as [06:00–10:00], and the evening peak period as [16:00–20:00], which can be described by formula (4.1)

$$OD_i^e \bullet R_1 \bullet t \geq 06:00 \cap OD_i^e \bullet R_n \bullet t \geq 10:00$$
$$\cup \qquad\qquad (1)$$
$$OD_i^e \bullet R_1 \bullet t \geq 16:00 \cap OD_i^e \bullet R_n \bullet t \geq 20:00$$

Travel OD_i^e meeting the above conditions is defined as the morning and evening rush hour travel PT_i^e of commuter private cars.

Definition 2 Group of Trips for Commuting (GTC): given a set of morning and evening rush hour trips set $PTset = \{PT_1^e, PT_2^e, ..., PT_n^e\}$, the Pt with similar time and space between the departure and destination is divided into a group, which is defined as GTC. A commuting private car CPC can have multiple GTC.

Definition 3 Representative Trips for Commuting (RTC): given a GTC, we use the most frequent OD, earliest departure time and latest arrival time in GTC to describe it, and define the generalized trip as RTC. A commuting private car CPC can have more than one commuting representative trip RTC.

Definition 4 Commuter's Private Car's ride-sharing group (CPCCG): given two commuting private car's CPC, if one of their RTCs has spatio-temporal semantic similarity, the two CPC belong to the same ride-sharing group, and all the commuting private car sets with similar RTCs are defined as CPCCG. The relationship between CPC and CPCCG is many to many.

Then, in order to find the commuting private car sharing group, the commuting trip group GTC should be extracted according to the temporal and spatial similarity of Pt, and then the commuting representative trip RTC should be extracted from the GTC; The space-time semantic distance function between RTCs is defined, and the semantic distance between RTCs is defined by the recognition result $Func_{Ri}$ of urban functional area which represents the working place of commuting, so as to complete the discovery of commuting private car group CPCCG (Fig. 2).

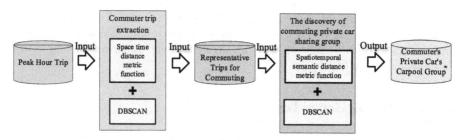

Fig. 2. Framework of find CPCCG

3.2   Commuter Trip Extraction

Since commuter private cars have more than one trip a week, in order to obtain valuable trip information and complete the work of finding the shared group, it is necessary to extract its features and find its representative trip. By defining the space-time distance function between trips, the clustering between trips is completed to obtain the representative trips. In this section, we design the space-time distance measurement function between trips, and propose a trip clustering method based on joint space-time attributes, which uses DBSCAN clustering algorithm.

Since we use a six tuple $OD = \{TID, EID, OID, DID, Otime, Dtime\}$ to describe a trip, we need to use the time and space attributes of O and D to calculate the similarity between trips, that is, the distance function. The space-time distance function proposed by us mainly includes space distance and time distance. The spatial distance mainly includes vertical Euclidean distance and parallel distance between the departure and destination; The time distance is expressed by the sum of the difference between the start time and the arrival time of the two segments. Next, we will explain the space distance and time distance in combination with Fig. 3, where L_i and L_j represent two trips respectively.

Vertical Euclidean distance: if two OD line segments are parallel, the vertical Euclidean distance remains unchanged, but the probability of occurrence is very low. Firstly, we need to calculate the vertical Euclidean distance from the shorter line segment to the longer line segment by comparing the length between two OD line segments:

$$d_\perp = \frac{l_{\perp 1}^2 + l_{\perp 2}^2}{l_{\perp 1} + l_{\perp 2}} \tag{2}$$

Among them,

$$\begin{cases} l_{\perp 1} = \sqrt{\left\| \overrightarrow{P_cP_a} \right\|^2 - (\frac{\overrightarrow{P_cP_a} \cdot \overrightarrow{P_cP_d}}{\left\| \overrightarrow{P_cP_d} \right\|})^2} \\ l_{\perp 2} = \sqrt{\left\| \overrightarrow{P_dP_b} \right\|^2 - (\frac{\overrightarrow{P_dP_b} \cdot \overrightarrow{P_dP_c}}{\left\| \overrightarrow{P_dP_c} \right\|})^2} \end{cases} \tag{3}$$

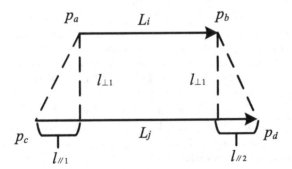

Fig. 3. Space distance diagram

Parallel distance: in Fig. 3, $l_{\|1}$ and $l_{\|2}$ together constitute the parallel distance. We take the larger of $l_{\|1}$ and $l_{\|2}$ as the parallel distance:

$$d_\| = \max(l_{\|1}, l_{\|2}) \tag{4}$$

Among them,

$$\begin{cases} l_{\|1} = \dfrac{\overrightarrow{P_cP_a} \cdot \overrightarrow{P_cP_d}}{\left\| \overrightarrow{P_cP_d} \right\|} \\ l_{\|2} = \dfrac{\overrightarrow{P_dP_b} \cdot \overrightarrow{P_dP_c}}{\left\| \overrightarrow{P_dP_c} \right\|} \end{cases} \tag{5}$$

Time distance: time distance is used to measure whether the departure time and arrival time of two trips are similar. The calculation formula is:

$$d_t = \left| t_s^{L_i} - t_s^{L_j} \right| + \left| t_e^{L_i} - t_e^{L_j} \right| \tag{6}$$

Min max normalization is used to unify several distance measures, which is convenient for the weighted summation. The normalization formula of min max is as follows:

$$x' = \frac{x - \min}{\max - \min} \tag{7}$$

The weighted Minkowski distance formula is used to construct the spatio-temporal semantic distance function, where $d_{\perp'}$, $d_{\|'}$ and $d_{t'}$ are the vertical Euclidean distance, parallel distance and time distance normalized by min max, respectively. The weighted summation formula is defined as follows:

$$dist(L_i, L_j) = (w_1 \cdot d_{\perp'}^2 + w_2 \cdot d_{\|'}^2 + w_3 \cdot d_{t'}^2)^{\frac{1}{2}} \tag{8}$$

We input all the itinerary sets of a commuter private car in the morning and evening rush hours of a week. Finally, for each commuter private car, we will get one or two clusters. Due to the small amount of data, our MinPts is set to 3, which means that a cluster commuter journey C_i in the result contains at least 3 itineraries, that is, there are at least three similar itineraries in the morning and evening rush hours of a week, it can be regarded as the *GTC* of the commuter group.

These commuter itinerary clusters have similar temporal and spatial characteristics. Next, we need to extract them as commuter representative itinerary. Extract the origin O and destination D of commuting representative trip *RTC*. For a commuting trip *PT* of a commuting private car in a cluster, the O and D representing the trip are selected by similar voting counting method, that is, $RTC_O = max(count(PT_O))$, $RTC_D = max(count(PT_D))$.

Then we extract the departure time and arrival time of the *RTC*. For the PT of a commuting private car in a cluster, we select the earliest departure time of all the travel segments as the departure time of the commuting representative journey, and the latest arrival time of all the travel segments as the arrival time of the commuting representative journey, namely $RTC_{Otime} = min(PT_{Otime})$, $RTC_{Dtime} = min(PT_{Dtime})$.

3.3 The Discovery of Shared Population

Considering that commuter private car users need a long-term stable ride sharing service, we need to consider the characteristics of each user, such as occupation, travel purpose, family members, gender, etc. Therefore, we have made some modifications to the previous travel distance measurement function by adding the commuter's commuting workplace semantics, which can reflect the nature of commuters' work to a certain extent. In this section, the object of clustering is *RTC*, and the semantic measure of commuting workplace comes from the result $Func_{Ri}$ of urban functional area recognition. DBSCAN is also used for clustering.

Semantic distance: first of all, the semantics of the itinerary workplace is encoded by one hot. For the commuting trip in the morning peak, the workplace of the itinerary is the destination D, on the contrary, the destination o in the evening peak. The coding rule is to take the first four areas closest to the electronic identification collection point of the travel workplace, and set the attribute of the functional area category to 1. Sem_i is used to represent the semantic vector of commuting trip RTC_i, and then Jaccard coefficient is used to calculate the vector distance between Sem_{Li} and Sem_{Lj} of two trips. In the table, the distance between them is 3/4. The formula is as follows:

$$\begin{cases} d_{sem} = 1 - \left|\frac{D_{Li} \cap D_{Lj}}{D_{Li} \cup D_{Lj}}\right| & morning \ peak \\ d_{sem} = 1 - \left|\frac{O_{Li} \cap O_{Lj}}{O_{Li} \cup O_{Lj}}\right| & evening \ peak \end{cases} \tag{9}$$

The weighted Minkowski distance formula is used to construct the spatio-temporal semantic distance function, where, and are the normalized vertical Euclidean distance, parallel distance and time distance. The weighted summation formula is defined as follows:

$$dist(L_i, L_j) = (w_1 \cdot d_{\perp'}^2 + w_2 \cdot d_{\parallel'}^2 + w_3 \cdot d_{t'}^2 + w_4 \cdot d_{sem}^2)^{\frac{1}{2}} \tag{10}$$

4 Experiment Analysis

4.1 Datasets

This paper uses ERI data of Chongqing in 2016 (February 29, 2016 to March 6, 2016) to study the group discovery of commuting private cars, including 888739 data of 220341 commuting private cars.

The road network data and POI data used in this paper are all from Baidu map API, and the scope is within the research scope of the main urban area of Chongqing (106.327–106.727° east longitude, 29.36–29.76° north latitude). Among them, the amount of POI data is 202716, and the original data contains a total of 16 categories and 181 subcategories.

4.2 Functional Area Identification Results

Due to the small amount of data in the training set of the test set, our parameter selection strategy adopts the violent search method in the optional interval, in which the optional interval of the penalty factor C is $\{2^\lambda | \lambda \in [-5, 15]\}$, Gaussian kernel parameter σ The optional interval of is $\{2^\lambda | \lambda \in [-15, 3]\}$.

In order to get a reliable and stable model and make full use of samples, we use 50% cross validation in the experiment. The total sample data set D is divided into five mutually exclusive subsets with similar size, $D = D_1 \cup D_2 ... \cup D_5, D_i \cap D_j = \emptyset (i \neq j)$. Each time, any subset is selected as the test set, and the rest as the training set. Finally, we choose the best super parameter, where the penalty factor $C = 1024$, Gaussian kernel parameter $\sigma = 2$。

In order to comprehensively analyze the performance of the functional area recognition model of ovo SVMs, this paper also constructs the common multi classification model random forest, and compares the macro average macro, micro average and weight average with the same samples under the same experimental conditions. For this study, we expect to achieve high precision, the correct traffic district function recognition ability is stronger. It can be seen from Table 1 that ovo SVMs have stronger recognition ability and higher stability for traffic district functions, while the recognition ability of random forest is not good.

Table 1. Prediction effect evaluation of different classification models

Algorithm						
Evaluating indicator	OVO SVMs			Random forest		
	Micro avg.	Macro avg.	Weighted avg.	Micro avg.	Macro avg.	Weighted avg.
Precision	92%	94%	94%	84%	94%	87%
Recall	92%	90%	92%	84%	80%	84%
F1-score	92%	91%	92%	84%	83%	83%

4.3 The Results of Finding Ride-Sharing Groups

Firstly, we search the parameters in the small-scale reference model. The evaluation indexes of various parameter combinations are v-measure, ARI, AMI and contour coefficient of external indexes from left to right. As shown in Fig. 4, we first select the minimum travel amount MinPts. Previously, we have said in the parameter selection strategy that MinPts must be greater than or equal to 3, so the selection range is from 3 to 7. It can be seen from the figure that when MinPts $= 3$, the effect of various evaluation indexes is the best.

As shown in Fig. 5, after we have determined the minimum travel amount MinPts, we then calculate the neighborhood radius ε Made a choice, we chose ε It is shown in Fig. 6 that when the search is carried out in steps of 0.01, the range of the search is 0.3 to 0.45 $\varepsilon = 0.37$, so our final choice of two super parameters is 0{$\varepsilon = 0.37$, MinPts $= 3$}.

In this experiment, the RTC of 297113 commuting representative trips is used as the clustering input, and the commuting private car sharing group discovery algorithm is used to cluster them. A total of 2562 groups are found, and the total number of passengers

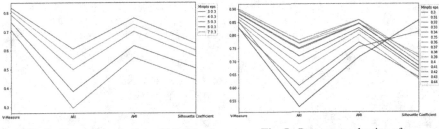

Fig. 4. Parameter selection of MinPts   **Fig. 5.** Parameter selection of ε

can be shared is 72468. The results of clustering using only spatio-temporal clustering are taken as the control group, as shown in Table 2. We can see that only using the spatial-temporal distance for clustering results, the number of communities is only 1778, which is less than the final result, and the number of CO multipliers is 81060, which is slightly more than the final result. The reason may be that with the increase of semantic measure, the constraints become more and more, the original cluster is further subdivided, and the number of other segments in the neighborhood radius of some segments is less than the minimum number of MinPts, so these segments are identified as noise points.

Table 2. Results of community discovery based on different distance function clustering

	Number of ride-sharing groups	Number of people in the largest group	Total number of riders
Space time distance	1778	366	81060
Spatio-temporal semantic distance	2562	316	72468

4.4 Group Travel Mode of Carpooling

In order to analyze the flow transfer of commuting private car sharing groups in the city, we extract the five groups with the largest number of members in the morning and evening peak, visualize their travel O and D in the form of white lines, and analyze them combined with the functional areas. (a) shows the five major flow transfers before the morning peak, (c) is the five major flow transfers before the evening peak, (b) and (d) is the analysis of the morning and evening flow transfers combined with the spatial distribution map of the functional area. The white line in the figure represents the flow transfer. The scattered end is the origin o, and the centralized end is the destination D.

As can be seen from figure (a) (c), the flow transfers of the first five groups in the morning and evening have a certain degree of overlap, for example, the flow transfers from Beihuan interchange to Jiangbei Airport, and the flow transfers from tea garden area to Nanping area. Combined with (b) (d), it can be seen that these areas have both residential functional areas and commercial office functional areas, and there are more people using private cars for commuting (Fig. 6).

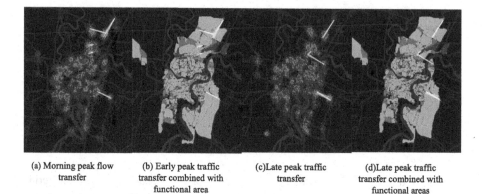

(a) Morning peak flow transfer   (b) Early peak traffic transfer combined with functional area   (c)Late peak traffic transfer   (d)Late peak traffic transfer combined with functional areas

Fig. 6. Flow transfer of morning and evening peak of ride-sharing groups

5   Conclusion

Based on Chongqing motor vehicle electronic identification data and POI data, this paper proposed a commuter private car discovery model based on spatio-temporal semantic similarity clustering. Although the research of this paper has made some achievements, due to the influence of time and other constraints, some deficiencies and errors are inevitable in the completion process, which need to be further improved. 1) User information is added into the model, but only the commuting workplace semantics of private car users is considered. If we can get the information of gender, age, number of commuters, we will have the opportunity to provide more long-term and stable commuting services for private cars. 2) After the functional area is identified, for some small cells with the same type of functional area, regional fusion can be carried out.

References

1. Diao, M., Kong, H., Zhao, J.: Impacts of transportation network companies on urban mobility. Nature Sustain. **4**(6), 494–500 (2021). https://doi.org/10.1038/s41893-020-00678-z
2. González, M., Hidalgo, César. A., Barabási, A.-L.: Understanding individual human mobility patterns. Nature **453**(7196), 779–782 (2008). https://doi.org/10.1038/nature06958
3. Çolak, S., Lima, A., González, M.: Understanding congested travel in urban areas. Nature Commun. **7**(1), 10793 (2016). https://doi.org/10.1038/ncomms10793
4. Want, R.: An introduction to RFID technology. IEEE Pervasive Comput. **5**(1), 25–33 (2006)
5. Savelsbergh, E.A., et al.: Optimization for dynamic ride-sharing: a review. **15**(3), 13–15 (2002)
6. Santi, P., Resta, G., Szell, M., et al.: Quantifying the benefits of vehicle pooling with shareability networks. Proc. Natl. Acad. Sci. U.S.A. **111**(37), 13290–13294 (2014)
7. He, W., Hwang, K., Li, D.: Intelligent carpool routing for urban ridesharing by mining GPS trajectories. IEEE Trans. Intell. Transp. Syst. **15**(5), 2286–2296 (2014)
8. Hong, Z., Chen, Y., Mahmassani, H.S., et al.: Commuter ride-sharing using topology-based vehicle trajectory clustering: methodology, application and impact evaluation. Transp. Res. Part C Emerg. Technol. **85**, 573–590 (2017)
9. Wang, Z., et al.: Identifying urban functional areas and their dynamic changes in Beijing: using multiyear transit smart card data. J. Urban Plan. Dev. **147**(2), 04021002 (2021). https://doi.org/10.1061/(ASCE)UP.1943-5444.0000662

SA2SL: From Aspect-Based Sentiment Analysis to Social Listening System for Business Intelligence

Luong Luc Phan[1,2], Phuc Huynh Pham[1,2], Kim Thi-Thanh Nguyen[1,2],
Sieu Khai Huynh[1,2], Tham Thi Nguyen[1,2], Luan Thanh Nguyen[1,2],
Tin Van Huynh[1,2], and Kiet Van Nguyen[1,2(⊠)]

[1] University of Information Technology, Ho Chi Minh City, Vietnam
{18521073,18521260,18520963,18520348,18521384,
17520721}@gm.uit.edu.vn
[2] Vietnam National University, Ho Chi Minh City, Vietnam
{tinhv,kietnv}@uit.edu.vn

Abstract. In this paper, we present a process of building a social listening system based on aspect-based sentiment analysis in Vietnamese, from creating a dataset to building a real application. Firstly, we create UIT-ViSFD, a **V**ietnamese **S**martphone **F**eedback **D**ataset, as a new benchmark dataset built based on a strict annotation scheme for evaluating aspect-based sentiment analysis, consisting of 11,122 human-annotated comments for mobile e-commerce, which is freely available for research purposes. We also present a proposed approach based on the Bi-LSTM architecture with the fastText word embeddings for the Vietnamese aspect-based sentiment task. Our experiments show that our approach achieves the best performances (in F1-score) of 84.48% for the aspect task and 63.06% for the sentiment task, which performs several conventional machine learning and deep learning systems. Lastly, we build SA2SL, a social listening system based on the best performance model on our dataset, which will inspire more social listening systems in the future.

Keywords: Sentiment analysis · Aspect-based sentiment analysis ·
Social listening · Bi-LSTM · Business intelligence

1 Introduction

Sentiment Analysis (SA) is a significant task and widely applied in many fields such as education, commerce, and marketing. However, a regular SA system may not seem sufficient for business organizations and customers. Simple SA systems consisting of three classes: positive, negative, and neutral, have apparent weaknesses that make them difficult to apply in reality. While enterprises expect an accurate system, the SA systems cannot accurately predict if the sentence does not explicitly express a clear sentiment or an opinion. Aspect-Based Sentiment

© Springer Nature Switzerland AG 2021
H. Qiu et al. (Eds.): KSEM 2021, LNAI 12816, pp. 647–658, 2021.
https://doi.org/10.1007/978-3-030-82147-0_53

Analysis (ABSA), an extended research form of SA, has the ability to identify sentiments of specific aspects, features, or entities extracted from user comments or feedback.

According to Statista Research Department[1], in 2017, the number of smartphone users in Vietnam was estimated to reach approximately 28.77 million. This indicates that around 31% of the population used a smartphone at this time, with this share predicted to rise to 40% by 2021. In Vietnam, smartphones are used for more than just making and receiving phone calls; they are also used for work, communication, entertainment, and shopping. The phone is chosen differently depending on the needs and purposes of the user. Seeing the potential of the ABSA task on the smartphone data domain in the Vietnamese, we build UIT-ViSFD, a **Vi**etnamese **S**martphone **F**eedback **D**ataset for evaluating ABSA. To ensure the data is plentiful and accurate, we collect feedback from a popular e-commerce website in Vietnam.

High-quality and large-scale datasets are essential in natural language processing for low-resource languages like Vietnamese. Hence, we aim to build a dataset and implement an approach using machine learning techniques for a social listening system. The task is described as follows: the input of the task is a textual comment related to smartphones that customers generate on social media, outputs are aspects of smartphones and their sentiments are mentioned in the textual comment. Several examples are presented in Table 1.

In this paper, we have three main contributions summarized below.

- We present UIT-ViFSD, a new benchmark Vietnamese dataset for evaluating ABSA in mobile e-commerce, consisting of 11,122 human-annotated comments with two tasks: aspect detection and sentiment classification. Our dataset is freely available for research purposes.
- We propose an approach using the Bi-LSTM for the Vietnamese ABSA, achieving the best F1-score performances: 84.48% for the aspect detection and 63.06% for the sentiment detection, which performs other systems based on conventional machine learning (Naive Bayes, SVM, and Random Forest) and other deep learning models (LSTM and CNN).
- We propose SA2SL, a new social listening system based on ABSA for Vietnamese mobile e-commerce texts, which is the basis for making purchase decisions for users and the evidence for managers to improve their products and services.

2   Related Work

SA is a vibrant field to create many studies and their applications in various fields such as economics, politics, and education. In particular, there are a variety of datasets and methods built in different languages and domains. For English,

---

[1] https://www.statista.com/forecasts/1145936/smartphone-users-in-vietnam# statisticContainer.

datasets are available for electric fields [2]; books, equipment kitchen, and electronic products [20]. Besides, a range of competitions in SemEval 2014 Task 4 [19], SemEval 2015 Task 12 [18], and SemEval 2016 Task 5 [17] attracted significant attention.

Although Vietnam has nearly 100 million people, Vietnamese is a low-resource language. The research works in the field of SA in Vietnamese such as student feedback detection [27], hate speech detection [26], emotion analysis [10], constructive and toxic detection [15], and complaint classification [16]. However, these tasks are relatively not as complicated as the ABSA task. The first ABSA shared-task in Vietnamese was organized by the Vietnamese Language and Speech Processing (VLSP) community in 2018 [14]. Nguyen et al. [14] created datasets for studying two tasks: aspect detection and sentiment classification in the hotel and restaurant. Nguyen et al. [13] proposed the dataset on the same domains as restaurant and hotel.

We aim to create a high-quality dataset about smartphones to evaluate the ABSA task in Vietnamese. The smartphone is a top-rated commercial product that is still thriving today. The amount of feedback data from users about the smartphone is enormous and has great potential for exploitation. Therefore, we review several studies related to this domain. The competition SemEval 2016: Task 5[2] introduced a couple of datasets in Chinese and English. Singh et al. [25] presented a dataset with many aspects: camera, OS, battery, processor, screen, size, cost, storage aspect, and two sentiments labels: positive, negative for three types of phones: iPhone 6, Moto G3, and Blackberry. Yiran et al. [28] built a dataset with aspects such as display, battery, camera, and three sentiment labels: positive, negative, and neutral. In Vietnamese, Mai et al. [12] proposed a small dataset including 2,098 annotated comments about smartphones at the sentence level, not enough to evaluate current SOTA models. As a result, our dataset is more complex and extensive than the previous Vietnamese dataset [12]. Inspired from previous studies [7,29], we also propose an approach using Bi-LSTM for Vietnamese aspect-based sentiment analysis. From the best performance of this approach and the study [6], we present a new system based on aspect-based sentiment analysis for business intelligence.

3   Dataset Creation

The creation process of our dataset comprises five different phases. First, we collect comments from a well-known e-commerce website for smartphones in Vietnam (see Sect. 3.1). Secondly, we build annotation guidelines for annotators to determine aspects and their sentiments and how to annotate data correctly (see Sect. 3.2). Annotators are trained with the guidelines and annotate data for two tasks in the two following steps: aspect detection and aspect polarity classification (see Sect. 3.3). The inter-annotator agreement (IAA) of annotators in the training process is ensured that it reaches over 80% before performing data annotation independently. Finally, we provide an in-depth analysis of the dataset

---

[2] https://alt.qcri.org/semeval2016/task5/.

that helps AI programmers or experts choose models and features suitable for this dataset (see Sect. 3.4).

3.1 Data Preparation

We crawl textual feedback from customers on a large e-commerce website in Vietnam. To ensure diverse and valued data, we collect feedback from the top ten popular smartphone brands used in Vietnam. There are various long comments, rambling reviews, and contradictory reviews, which are ambiguous to understand to determine the correct label of them. Therefore, the comments that are longer than 250 tokens (makes up a very small rate) are removed. We also delete comments that contain too many misspellings in them, which are not easy to understand and annotate correctly.

3.2 Annotation Guidelines

Data annotation is performed by five annotators who follow annotation guidelines and a strict annotating process to ensure data quality. Annotators determine aspects of each comment and then annotate their sentiment polarity labels: positive (Pos), neutral (Neu), and negative (Neg). Table 1 summarizes all aspects (10 aspects) and sentiment polarities (3 sentiment polarities) in the guidelines, including illustrative examples. For some comments that do not relate to any aspect or do not evaluate the product, we annotate an OTHERS label for these cases which do not express the sentiment.

Table 1. The annotation guidelines for labeling the aspects and their sentiment.

Aspect	Mean	User comments	Sentiment
SCREEN	User comments express screen quality, size, colors, and display technology.	màn hình đẹp (a nice screen)	Pos
CAMERA	The comments mention the quality of a camera, vibration, delay, focus, and image colors.	điện thoại chụp hình mờ (the phone took blur picture)	Neg
FEATURES	The users refer to features, fingerprint sensor, wifi connection, touch and face detection of the phone.	nhận diện khuôn mặt chậm (the face detection is slow)	Neg
BATTERY	The comment describes battery capacity and battery quality.	pin trâu (long battery life)	Pos
PERFOMANCE	The reviews describe ramming capacity, processor chip, performance using, and smoothness of the phone.	cấu hình có thể chấp nhận được (acceptable configuration)	Neu
STORAGE	The comment mention storage capacity, the ability to expand capacity through memory cards.	bộ nhớ lớn (large storage)	Pos
DESIGN	The reviews refer to the style, design, and shell.	điện thoại thiết kế thô (rough design phone)	Neg
PRICE	The comments present the specific price of the phone.	giá cả ở mức trung bình (the price is at average)	Neu
GENERAL	The reviews of customers generally comment about the phone.	mọi thứ đều ok (everything is ok)	Pos
SER&ACC[7]	The comments mention sales service, warranty, and review of accessories of the phone.	nhân viên tư vấn nhiệt tình (shop assistants advice enthusiastic)	Pos

[7] SER&ACC is short for SERVICE and ACCESSORIES.

3.3 Annotation Process

Annotators spend six training rounds to obtain a high inter-annotator agreement, and the strict guidelines are complete. In the first round, after building the first guidelines, our annotators annotate 200 comments together to understand the principles of data annotation. For the five remaining rounds, each round, we randomly take a set of 200 comments and individually annotate these 200 comments. For disagreement cases, we decide the final label by discussing and having a poll among annotators. These causes of disagreement are discussed and corrected in the guidelines; we also add cases that the guidelines have not covered after thorough discussion. The six training rounds resulted in a high inter-annotator agreement of the team and sufficiently completed full guidelines to achieve the dataset. The inter-annotator agreement is estimated by Cohen's Kappa coefficient [2]. The formula is described as follows.

$$k = \frac{Pr(a) - Pr(e)}{1 - Pr(e)} \tag{1}$$

where k is the annotator agreement, $Pr(a)$ is the relative observed agreement among raters, and $Pr(e)$ the hypothetical probability of chance agreement. To ensure the dataset quality, we calculate inter-annotator agreements of pairs of team members that annotate both the aspect annotation task and the sentiment annotation task. Until the inter-annotator agreement of all labels reaching over 80% and completing the annotation guidelines, annotators have labeled the comments independently. During this annotating phase, in case of encountering difficult feedback, we discuss together the correct annotation and then revise the guidelines to obtains more high-quality guidelines. Figure 1 shows the inter-annotator agreements on two tasks during training phases.

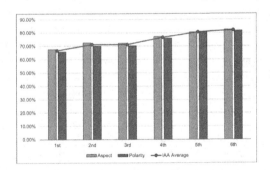

Fig. 1. Inter-annotator agreements of six different annotation training rounds.

3.4 Dataset Statistics

Our dataset consists of 11,122 comments, including five columns: index (row number), comment (comments), n_star (customer star ratings), date_time (comment time), and label (label of a comment). We randomly divide the dataset into three sets: the training (Train), development (Dev), and test (Test) sets in the 7:1:2 ratio.

Table 2. Overview statistics of Train/Dev/Test sets of our dataset.

	Train	Dev	Test
Number of comments	7,786	1,112	2,224
Number of tokens	283,460	39,023	80,787
Number of aspects	23,597	3,371	6,742
Average number of aspects per sentence	3.3	3.2	3.3
Average length per sentence	36.4	35.1	36.3

Table 2 presents overview statistics of our dataset. The splitting ratio corresponds to the number of words and labels in the Train, Dev, and Test sets. Each comment has three aspect labels and is approximately 36 tokens on average.

Table 3. The distribution of aspects and their sentiments of our dataset.

Aspect	Train			Dev			Test			Total
	Pos	Neu	Neg	Pos	Neu	Neg	Pos	Neu	Neg	
BATTERY	2,027	349	1,228	303	51	150	554	92	368	5,122
CAMERA	1,231	288	627	172	36	88	346	71	171	3,030
DESIGN	999	77	302	135	12	40	274	28	96	1,963
FEATURES	785	198	1,659	115	33	233	200	52	459	3,734
GENERAL	3,627	290	949	528	34	127	1,004	83	294	6,936
PERFORMANCE	2,253	391	1,496	327	45	210	602	116	454	5,894
PRICE	609	391	316	72	144	36	162	328	79	2,882
SCREEN	514	56	379	62	12	47	136	17	116	1,339
SER&ACC	1,401	107	487	199	13	78	199	27	167	2,678
STORAGE	59	107	21	11	1	2	18	3	6	132
Total	13,505	2,903	7,464	1,924	381	1,011	3,495	817	2,210	

Table 3 describes the distribution of aspects and their sentiment in the Train, Dev, and Test sets of our dataset. Through our analysis, the dataset has an uneven distribution on both the aspect and sentiment labels. While some aspect labels have many data points, another has a negligible number (the General aspect has 6,936 data points compared to the Storage with 132 annotated comments). In addition, we notice a significant difference between the three sentiment polarities. Positive accounts for the most significant number of 56.13% of the total number of labels followed the negative polarity with 31.70%, whereas the neutral polarity only accounts for 12.17%. Our dataset is imbalanced and includes diverse comments on different smartphone products on social media, which is challenging to evaluate ML algorithms on social media texts.

4   Our Approach

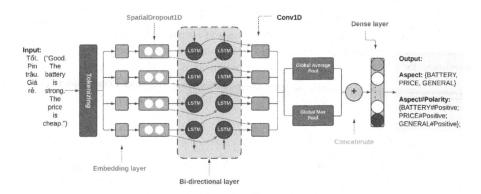

Fig. 2. An overview of our Vietnamese ABSA system using Bi-LSTM.

Inspired by Bi-LSTM for text classification [29], we propose an approach using the Bi-LSTM model for Vietnamese ABSA. The overview architecture is depicted in Fig. 2. This architecture consists of a tokenizer, embedding layer, SpatialDropout1D layer, Bi-LSTM layer, convolutional layer, two pooling layers, and a dense layer. First, the comment goes through a tokenizer, which converts each token in the comment to an integer value based on the vocabulary index. Then, they are processed through an embedding layer to convert into representative vectors. The architecture uses the fastText embeddings [3] as input token representations. FastText has good token representations, and it encodes for rare tokens that do not appear during training and is a good selection for Vietnamese social media texts [11]. To minimize overfitting, we utilize Spatial-Dropout1D to lower the parameters after each train. We employ a Bi-LSTM layer to extract abstract features, which is made up of two LSTMs with their outputs stacked together. The comment is read forward by one LSTM and backward by the other. We concatenate the hidden states of each LSTM after they have processed their respective final token. The Bi-LSTM uses two separate LSTM units, one for forward and one for backward. A convolutional layer is used to convert a multi-dimensional matrix from Bi-LSTM to a 1-dimensional matrix. The pooling layer consists of two parallel layers: the global average pool and the global max pool. The function of the pooling layer is conducted to reduce the spatial size of the representation. The idea is to choose the highest element and the average element of the feature map to extract the most salient features from the convolutional layer. Finally, the labels of the two sub-tasks for the ABSA task is obtained after normalizing in the dense layer.

5   Experiments

5.1   Baseline Systems

We compare the proposed approach with the following baselines. For traditional machine learning, we experiment with a system based on Naive Bayes [21], Support Vector Machine (SVM) [1], and Random Forest [4], which are popular methods for text classification. For deep neural networks, we implement systems based on Convolutional Neural Networks (CNN) [8] and Long Short-Term Memory (LSTM) [23], which achieved SOTA results in different NLP tasks.

5.2   Experimental Results

There are two phases to measure the ABSA systems: aspect detection and sentiment prediction. We use the precision, recall, and F1-score (macro average) to measure the performance of models. We do not detect sentiments of OTHERS aspect because they cannot show their sentiments, so we give it the NaN value.

Table 4 presents overall results on aspect-based and sentiment-based tasks on machine learning systems. According to our results, we can see that deep learning models have significantly better performance than traditional machine learning models. In particular, Bi-LSTM achieves the best F1-scores of 84.48% and 63.06% for the aspect detection and sentiment prediction, whereas SVM shows the lowest performances. Besides, the sentiment detection task makes it difficult for the first models when the F1-score are low (below 70%). There is a considerable discrepancy between deep learning and machine learning models. In particular, the deep learning model (Bi-LSTM) obtains the best F1-score of 84.48%, whereas the best machine learning model (Naive Bayes) only gains 64.65% in F1-score.

Table 4. Performances (%) of different ABSA systems.

System	Aspect detection			Sentiment detection		
	Precision	Recall	F1-score	Precision	Recall	F1-score
Naive Bayes	72.18	59.53	64.65	49.07	30.43	37.56
SVM	36.45	51.34	42.63	16.09	23.35	19.69
Random Forest	45.72	50.15	47.83	17.11	24.56	20.17
CNN	77.25	63.49	69.70	33.34	22.92	27.16
LSTM	82.61	78.05	80.27	56.51	48.39	52.13
Our Approach	87.55	83.22	**84.48**	65.82	60.53	**63.06**

The results of the Bi-LSTM on the aspects and sentiment classification are shown in Table 5. As mentioned above, the sentiment detection performance of the Bi-LSTM is lower than that of the aspect detection results (F1-score of

84.48% for the aspect detection task and that of 63.06% for the sentiment detection task). In the aspect detection task, the Bi-LSTM system also achieves relatively high and positive results (F1-score for all aspects is 60% higher, and many aspects have F1-score below 80%). On the contrary, the system performance on the sentiment-aspect detection task is relatively low (F1-score for all aspects is below 75% and the aspect with the highest F1-score is Camera with 74.69%). In terms of aspects detection, the highest is the Battery with 95.00% F1-score. As for the sentiment detection, the Storage aspect polarity is only 30.10% F1-score. The Storage label result explains the lack of quantity uniformity in the labels (the Storage aspect only covers 1.19% of the dataset). These results are pretty interesting to explore further models on this dataset. In general, the Bi-LSTM system outperforms other algorithms when it comes to detecting aspects and their sentiments. However, their ability to extract sentiment features for each aspect is limited in all machine learning models, which will be exploited in future work.

Table 5. Performances (%) of our approach in terms of different aspects.

Aspect	Aspect detection			Sentiment detection		
	Precision	Recall	F1-score	Precision	Recall	F1-score
Screen	89.41	85.22	87.26	64.22	60.50	62.30
Camera	85.35	85.00	85.17	76.22	73.23	**74.69**
Features	89.01	88.29	88.64	70.10	60.20	64.77
Battery	95.00	94.21	**94.60**	73.33	72.14	72.73
Performance	89.22	88.33	88.77	68.44	65.15	66.75
Storage	84.11	70.12	76.48	32.32	28.18	30.10
Design	89.30	86.46	87.85	72.35	70.71	71.41
Price	90.28	90.12	90.19	72.13	70.71	71.41
General	82.28	81.17	81.72	67.18	64.34	65.72
Ser&Acc	88.19	86.16	87.16	62.23	56.50	59.22
Others	61.34	60.31	60.82	NaN	NaN	NaN
Macro Avg	85.77	83.22	**84.48**	65.82	60.53	**63.06**

6 SA2SL: Social Listening System Using ABSA

Inspired by the best performance results and the investigation [6], we propose SA2SL, a social listening system architecture based on Vietnamese ABSA for analyzing what customers discuss about products on social media. Figure 3 depicts a social listening system for smartphones that uses aspect-based sentiment analysis. This application assists customers and business companies in automatically categorizing comments and determining consumer perspectives.

The application assists shoppers in selecting a phone that meets their specific requirements. Moreover, manufacturers can focus on the needs, expectations of the customers and propose suitable improvement options to improve product quality in future. Aspect sentiment analysis is crucial because it can assist businesses in automatically sorting and analyzing consumer data, automating procedures such as customer service activities, and gaining valuable insights.

Firstly, the user selects the name of the phone, and the application collects all comments on that phone. Secondly, we do the pre-processing of the comments, and then we feed them into word embedding, and they become vectors. Next, the vectors are then analyzed using two models: aspect detection and sentiment detection (aspect#sentiment). The input is a list of comments, and the output is aspects and their sentiments. The final analyses are visualized as follows: (1) Depending on which aspect they are interested in, the consumer or business company recognizes the analysis of user feedback regarding the sentiment polarity in the first chart. To clearly understand an aspect, the user of the system can select one of ten aspects, and then the system detail displays the distribution of its sentiment polarities. (2) The second chart describes the proportion (%) of the predicted aspects and summarizes their sentiments of all comments.

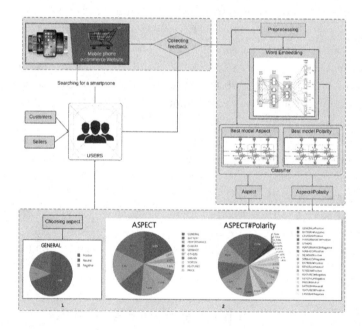

Fig. 3. Social listening architecture using ABSA for smartphone products.

7   Conclusion and Future Work

We have three main contributions, which are (1) creating UIT-ViSFD, a benchmark dataset of smartphone feedback for the ABSA task, (2) proposing the approach for this task, and (3) building a social listening system based on the primary technology of ABSA. We experimented with two different types of models: traditional machine learning and deep learning on our dataset to compare with our approach. Our approach outperformed the others, achieving F1-scores of 84.48% and 63.06% for aspect detection and sentiment detection, respectively. Although the aspect detection results were positive, the sentiment detection results were relatively low, which is challenging for further machine learning-based systems. Finally, we presented a novel social listening system based on ABSA for the low-resource language like Vietnamese.

NLP experts can develop a new span detection dataset using our ABSA dataset. Besides, we conduct experiments based on powerful aspect-based systems using BERTology models [22], transfer learning approaches [24], and reinforcement learning [9]. We utilize the relationship between the rank of input data and the performance of a random weight neural network [5] to enhance the overall performance of the task. Lastly, we recommend that a social listening system should be integrated with different social media tasks [10, 15, 16] into the social listening system, which benefits social business intelligence.

References

1. Al-Smadi, M., Qawasmeh, O., Al-Ayyoub, M., Jararweh, Y., Gupta, B.: Deep recurrent neural network vs. support vector machine for aspect-based sentiment analysis of Arabic hotels' reviews. J. Comput. Sci. **27**, 386–393 (2018)
2. Bhowmick, P.K., Basu, A., Mitra, P.: An agreement measure for determining inter-annotator reliability of human judgements on affective text. In: COLING 2008 (2008)
3. Bojanowski, P., Grave, E., Joulin, A., Mikolov, T.: Enriching word vectors with subword information. Trans. Assoc. Comput. Linguist. **5**, 135–146 (2017)
4. Breiman, L.: Random forests. Mach. Learn. **45**(1), 5–32 (2001)
5. Cao, W., Hu, L., Gao, J., Wang, X., Ming, Z.: A study on the relationship between the rank of input data and the performance of random weight neural network. Neural Comput. Appl. **32**(16), 12685–12696 (2020). https://doi.org/10.1007/s00521-020-04719-8
6. Chaturvedi, S., Mishra, V., Mishra, N.: Sentiment analysis using machine learning for business intelligence. In: 2017 IEEE International Conference on Power, Control, Signals and Instrumentation Engineering (ICPCSI), pp. 2162–2166. IEEE (2017)
7. Do, H.T.T., Huynh, H.D., Van Nguyen, K., Nguyen, N.L.T., Nguyen, A.G.T.: Hate speech detection on vietnamese social media text using the bidirectional-LSTM model. arXiv preprint arXiv:1911.03648 (2019)
8. Dos Santos, C., Gatti de Bayser, M.: Deep convolutional neural networks for sentiment analysis of short texts (2014)
9. Gai, K., Qiu, M.: Reinforcement learning-based content-centric services in mobile sensing. IEEE Network **32**(4), 34–39 (2018)
10. Ho, V.A., et al.: Emotion recognition for Vietnamese social media text. In: Nguyen, L.-M., Phan, X.-H., Hasida, K., Tojo, S. (eds.) PACLING 2019. CCIS, vol. 1215, pp. 319–333. Springer, Singapore (2020). https://doi.org/10.1007/978-981-15-6168-9_27

11. Huynh, H.D., Do, H.T.T., Van Nguyen, K., Nguyen, N.L.T.: A simple and efficient ensemble classifier combining multiple neural network models on social media datasets in vietnamese. arXiv preprint arXiv:2009.13060 (2020)
12. Mai, L., Le, B.: Aspect-based sentiment analysis of Vietnamese texts with deep learning. In: Nguyen, N.T., Hoang, D.H., Hong, T.-P., Pham, H., Trawiński, B. (eds.) ACIIDS 2018. LNCS (LNAI), vol. 10751, pp. 149–158. Springer, Cham (2018). https://doi.org/10.1007/978-3-319-75417-8_14
13. Nguyen, H., Nguyen, T., Dang, T., Nguyen, N.: A corpus for aspect-based sentiment analysis in Vietnamese, pp. 1–5 (2019)
14. Nguyen, H., et al.: VLSP shared task: sentiment analysis. J. Comput. Sci. Cybern. **34**, 295–310 (2019)
15. Nguyen, L.T., Van Nguyen, K., Nguyen, N.L.T.: Constructive and toxic speech detection for open-domain social media comments in vietnamese. arXiv preprint arXiv:2103.10069 (2021)
16. Nguyen, N.T.H., Phan, P.H.D., Nguyen, L.T., Van Nguyen, K., Nguyen, N.L.T.: Vietnamese open-domain complaint detection in e-commerce websites. arXiv preprint arXiv:2104.11969 (2021)
17. Pontiki, M., et al.: Semeval-2016 task 5: aspect based sentiment analysis. In: International Workshop on Semantic Evaluation, pp. 19–30 (2016)
18. Pontiki, M., Galanis, D., Papageorgiou, H., Manandhar, S., Androutsopoulos, I.: Semeval-2015 task 12: aspect based sentiment analysis. Proc. SemEval **2015**, 486–495 (2015)
19. Pontiki, M., et al.: SemEval-2014 task 4: Aspect based sentiment analysis. In: Proceedings of SemEval 2014, pp. 27–35. Association for Computational Linguistics, Dublin, Ireland (2014)
20. Popescu, A.M., Etzioni, O.: Extracting product features and opinions from reviews. In: Kao A., Poteet S.R. (eds.) Natural language processing and text mining, pp. 9–28. Springer, London (2007) https://doi.org/10.1007/978-1-84628-754-1_2
21. Rish, I.: An empirical study of the naïve bayes classifier. In: IJCAI 2001 Work Empirical Methods in Artificial Intelligence, vol. 3 (2001)
22. Rogers, A., Kovaleva, O., Rumshisky, A.: A primer in bertology: What we know about how bert works. Trans. Assoc. Comput. Linguis. **8**, 842–866 (2020)
23. Ruder, S., Ghaffari, P., Breslin, J.: A hierarchical model of reviews for aspect-based sentiment analysis. In: EMNLP (2016)
24. Ruder, S., Peters, M.E., Swayamdipta, S., Wolf, T.: Transfer learning in natural language processing, pp. 15–18 (2019)
25. Singh, S.M., Mishra, N.: Aspect based opinion mining for mobile phones. In: 2016 2nd International Conference on Next Generation Computing Technologies (NGCT), pp. 540–546 (2016)
26. Van Huynh, T., Nguyen, V.D., Van Nguyen, K., Nguyen, N.L.T., Nguyen, A.G.T.: Hate speech detection on vietnamese social media text using the Bi-GRU-LSTM-CNN model. arXiv preprint arXiv:1911.03644 (2019)
27. Van Nguyen, K., Nguyen, V.D., Nguyen, P.X., Truong, T.T., Nguyen, N.L.T.: UIT-VSFC: Vietnamese students' feedback corpus for sentiment analysis. In: KSE 2018, pp. 19–24. IEEE (2018)
28. Yiran, Y., Srivastava, S.: Aspect-based sentiment analysis on mobile phone reviews with lda. In: Proceedings of the 2019 4th International Conference on Machine Learning Technologies, pp. 101–105 (2019)
29. Zhou, P., Qi, Z., Zheng, S., Xu, J., Bao, H., Xu, B.: Text classification improved by integrating bidirectional lstm with two-dimensional max pooling. Proc. COLING **2016**, 3485–3495 (2016)

Author Index

Printed in the United States
by Baker & Taylor Publisher Services